T0402461

Police Intelligence

Police Intelligence: Totality of Circumstances is an essential resource and is designed for any individual who may encounter the field of criminal justice, whether the person is a police chief who oversees the department's standard operating procedures, a police officer who enforces the law, a civilian who is expected to follow the law, a lawyer who may challenge an action in court, or a judge who will interpret the law. This book, in part, applies math and logic to laws and policies to objectively assess them. Laws and policies are written as English logical statements. English logical statements can be converted into mathematical logical statements, which can be objectively assessed via Boolean algebra. Specifically, truth tables, Venn diagrams, flowcharts, logic gates, and logic circuits can all be used to assess laws, policies, and proper police actions. For example, mathematically *it is not a glass, blue, marble* means almost the exact opposite of *it is not glass, not blue, and not marble*. In addition, one must consider existential and universal quantifiers, conditional statements, and subsets to correctly interpret laws and policies. Thus, it is important for individuals to understand how to mathematically assess English logical statements (e.g., the law) because if they do not, opponents in court may do it for them.

This book is important because collecting and understanding information and effectively communicating are vital skills in law enforcement. It discusses different reference points for assessing good behavior, different lenses of truth, limitations of information, and assumptions. Furthermore, it examines a variety of ways to collect and assess information, which include interrogation techniques, interviewing techniques, an interrogatory and a deposition, ciphering and deciphering messages, body language, handwriting analysis, job interview questions, and crime scene search patterns.

The chapters present a methodological reasoning process that is sorely lacking among police agencies—and one that is essential for developing critical thinking skills and carrying out orders within legal confines. **Police Intelligence: Totality of Circumstances** is an indispensable resource for helping students and officers to collect and assess information. Whether it is verbal or nonverbal information, ciphered messages, or using different bases for numeric communication, individuals in criminal justice should learn to think outside the box to collect and understand available information.

Police Intelligence
Totality of Circumstances

$$(\exists x)P(x) \neq (\forall x)P(x)$$

$$P \Rightarrow Q \neq Q \Rightarrow P$$

$$\sim(A \cap B \cap C) \neq \sim A \cap \sim B \cap \sim C$$

Wayne L. Davis, Paul J. Leslie, and Ashley B. Davis

Illustrated by Dawn Larder
www.theglimmertwinarthouse.com

CRC Press
Taylor & Francis Group
Boca Raton London New York

CRC Press is an imprint of the
Taylor & Francis Group, an **informa** business

Cover image: Dawn Larder, www.theglimmertwinarthouse.com

First edition published 2023
by CRC Press
6000 Broken Sound Parkway NW, Suite 300, Boca Raton, FL 33487-2742

and by CRC Press
4 Park Square, Milton Park, Abingdon, Oxon, OX14 4RN

CRC Press is an imprint of Taylor & Francis Group, LLC

© 2023 Wayne L. Davis, Paul J. Leslie, and Ashley B. Davis

Reasonable efforts have been made to publish reliable data and information, but the author and publisher cannot assume responsibility for the validity of all materials or the consequences of their use. The authors and publishers have attempted to trace the copyright holders of all material reproduced in this publication and apologize to copyright holders if permission to publish in this form has not been obtained. If any copyright material has not been acknowledged please write and let us know so we may rectify in any future reprint.

Except as permitted under U.S. Copyright Law, no part of this book may be reprinted, reproduced, transmitted, or utilized in any form by any electronic, mechanical, or other means, now known or hereafter invented, including photocopying, microfilming, and recording, or in any information storage or retrieval system, without written permission from the publishers.

For permission to photocopy or use material electronically from this work, access www.copyright.com or contact the Copyright Clearance Center, Inc. (CCC), 222 Rosewood Drive, Danvers, MA 01923, 978-750-8400. For works that are not available on CCC please contact mpkbookspermissions@tandf.co.uk

Trademark notice: Product or corporate names may be trademarks or registered trademarks and are used only for identification and explanation without intent to infringe.

ISBN: 978-1-032-18094-6 (hbk)
ISBN: 978-1-032-18093-9 (pbk)
ISBN: 978-1-003-25283-2 (ebk)

DOI: 10.4324/9781003252832

Typeset in Minion
by Newgen Publishing UK

Contents

Preface vii
About the Authors ix

1. U.S. Constitutional Law — 1
2. Grammar, Math, Theories, and Persuasion — 29
3. Intelligences, Reasoning, and Flowcharting — 61
4. The Law, Truth Tables, and Venn Diagrams — 85
5. The Law, Logic Gates, and Logic Circuits — 123
6. Probable Cause Affidavit, Information, Evidence, and Search Warrant — 151
7. Code Communication — 187
8. Meaning of Truth — 221
9. Interrogatory and Deposition — 249
10. Interviewing and Identifying Suspects — 275
11. Body Language — 305
12. Interrogation Techniques — 331
13. Individuals with Disabilities — 357
14. Science and Truth — 371
15. Media, Cybercrime, Technology, and Special Situations — 391
16. Qualitative Information — 417
17. Résumé, Job Interview, and Oral Presentations — 433
18. Crime Scene Investigations — 459

Glossary 481
Index 487

Preface

This book provides an overview of effectively collecting, assessing, and communicating police intelligence (i.e., information). First, it provides some highlights of U.S. Constitutional law and presents various criminal theories, then it discusses the importance of grammar and math (Boolean algebra, quantifiers, and conditional statements) in law enforcement. It is important for officers to understand these concepts so they may be able to effectively articulate their actions in court. Second, this book applies flowcharts, truth tables, Venn diagrams, logic gates, and logic circuits to create and objectively assess laws and policies. A law, which is written as an English logical statement, can be converted into a mathematical logical statement to determine its truth values based on the values of the input variables, which are the elements of the law. In other words, truth values can be used to determine whether police officers and/or residents acted lawfully. Third, the book discusses ciphers and the meaning of truth. Ciphered information may be important in a prison environment, and different reference points are used to assess information, truth, and good behaviors. Fourth, it provides examples of questions that may be asked in an interrogatory and deposition. The defense lawyer may ask certain questions to discredit the officer or to undermine the officer's report. Police officers should ask themselves about the purpose of each question that is being asked. Fifth, the book discusses interviews, body language, interrogation techniques, and handwriting analysis. Different strategies are available to trick or motivate someone to provide the information sought. Sixth, it discusses the media, special situations, such as hostage situations, methods to collect and assess qualitative information, and questions likely to be asked at a law enforcement job interview. Knowing what kind of questions may be asked during a law enforcement interview and knowing how to respond may be useful to a job applicant. Some questions and expected responses are provided. In addition, a table is provided that can be used to practice impromptu responses. Finally, the book discusses crime scene search patterns and information that should be collected at a crime scene. Examples of a crime scene entry log sheet and a photographic log sheet are provided.

About the Authors

WAYNE L. DAVIS, PH.D.

Wayne L. Davis holds a bachelor's degree in electrical engineering, a master's degree in business administration, and a doctoral degree in criminal justice. In addition, Dr. Davis has earned a helicopter pilot license, an advanced open water scuba diver certification, a technician plus amateur radio license (N8ZFG), and a basic emergency medical technician certificate from the state of Michigan.

Dr. Davis worked as a product design engineer at the Ford Motor Company. In addition, he has graduated from city, state, and federal law enforcement academies and has over 20 years of law enforcement experience with city, state, and federal law enforcement agencies. Dr. Davis has earned the U.S. Customs & Border Protection Commissioner's Award and the U.S. Customs & Border Protection Scholastic Award, and was a field training officer with the Indiana State Police. He has three U.S. patents and over 20 academic research publications.

PAUL J. LESLIE, ED.D.

Paul J. Leslie is a psychotherapist, researcher, international trainer, and author in Aiken, South Carolina. Paul has a doctorate in Counseling Psychology and is a licensed professional counselor in the states of Georgia and South Carolina. Paul's work primarily focuses on the applications of strategic and resource-directed approaches to psychotherapy. He is presently the coordinator of the psychology program at Aiken Technical College in South Carolina.

ASHLEY B. DAVIS, M.A.

Ashley B. Davis has a M.A. in French and a bachelor's degree in French and Japanese from Michigan State University. She is currently working in Japan as a coordinator of international relations for Otsu City and as a consultant for MICE affairs.

$$(\exists x)P(x) \neq (\forall x)P(x)$$

$$P \Rightarrow Q \neq Q \Rightarrow P$$

$$\sim (A \cap B \cap C) \neq \sim A \cap \sim B \cap \sim C$$

Why are grammar and math important in law enforcement? They are important because they allow for an objective interpretation of the law and other statements. Officers cannot effectively enforce the law if they do not understand the law. To determine the legality of actions, it is important to understand the above equations. The first equation states that an existential quantifier does not equal a universal quantifier. In other words, just because a statement is true at least once does not necessarily mean it is true every time. For example, suppose I have two coins that equal 30 cents and *one* of them is not a nickel. This does not mean *all* the coins are not nickels (answer: 30 cents = one quarter and one nickel; the quarter is the one coin that is not a nickel). If I say I like soda pop, my answer is truthful if I like one type of soda pop. It is not required that I like all types of soda pop. In short, an existential quantifier makes a statement true if the statement is true at least one time. On the other hand, a universal quantifier makes a statement false if the statement is false at least one time. It is important not to interchange an existential quantifier with a universal quantifier. The second equation states that the converse of a conditional statement is not necessarily true. I cannot simply switch the variables in a statement and assume the statement is still true. Suppose the following statement is true: If I am to enter the United States, then I must possess a passport. I cannot assume that if I possess a passport, then I must be able to enter the United States. Finally, the third equation stresses the importance of grammar and math in the interpretation of a sentence. For example, "it is not a glass, blue, marble" has almost the exact opposite meaning as "it is not glass, not blue, and not marble." These differences can be confirmed via truth tables, Venn diagrams, logic gates, and logic circuits. Which one does the law say and which one is in the police report? It is important to know that Boolean algebra has different rules than those in elementary algebra.

CHAPTER 1

U.S. Constitutional Law

LEARNING OBJECTIVES

Explain when the Miranda warning is required.

Differentiate between reasonable suspicion and probable cause.

Differentiate between detention and arrest.

Differentiate between stop and frisk.

Explain the exclusionary rule.

Explain some exceptions to the exclusionary rule.

Explain when the exclusionary rule does not apply.

INTRODUCTION

This chapter will provide an overview of the 4th, 5th, 6th, and 14th Amendments as they apply to law enforcement. U.S. Constitutional law is designed to control the behavior of police officers. It is important for all residents to understand the legal authority of police officers because there is always that chance that individuals may encounter the police. A person who does not comply with the legal orders of a police officer may be arrested for disobeying or resisting the officer. Furthermore, police officers are not required to play guessing games, and they are allowed to make decisions based on the available information. Because the top priority for police officers is safety—including their own safety—they may be able to violate a person's rights. Furthermore, although U.S. Constitutional law is designed to protect a person's privacy against the government, it only provides the minimal amount of protection. Indeed, there are exceptions to the law and times when the law does not apply.

U.S. CONSTITUTIONAL LAW

What is the difference between U.S. Constitutional law and criminal law? U.S. Constitutional law involves laws that are designed to protect civilians against the government. In other words, U.S. Constitutional law controls the behavior of law enforcement officers when they interact with civilians. Criminal law, on the other hand, involves laws that are designed to control the behavior of all persons. State law books will provide laws that the general public are expected to obey.

This chapter provides an overview of U.S. Constitutional law (the 4th, 5th, 6th, and 14th Amendments) as it applies to law enforcement investigations. It is expected that the reader has already studied U.S. Constitutional law for law enforcement and knows the difference, for example, between detaining a person and arresting a person. Because this book deals with the collecting and assessing of information by law enforcement officers, U.S. Constitutional law is important because it provides legal guidelines for police actions. This chapter provides a summary of select U.S. Constitutional laws and decisions made by the U.S. Supreme Court that are relevant to police investigations. When the word "Court" is capitalized in this chapter, it is referring to the U.S. Supreme Court.

The U.S. Constitution only provides civilians with the minimal amount of protection against the government (del Carmen & Hemmens, 2017). The U.S. Constitution does not protect civilians against other civilians. In addition, the Court has clearly distinguished federal jurisdiction from state jurisdiction. For example, the Court has upheld a homeowner's conviction after the police trespassed onto his private property, which clearly violated a state law, in order to collect evidence to make the arrest. Because trespassing was not a federal violation, it was treated separately from the homeowner's arrest. In other words, the state law of trespassing was irrelevant in federal court. Because the police found the evidence in open field, the homeowner had no right to privacy in that area of his own property under U.S. Constitutional law. Thus, the homeowner was convicted. As far as the trespassing incident, a complaint could have been filed against the officers with the local police.

There are several situations that address mistakes made by police officers during the collection of evidence (del Carmen & Hemmens, 2017). If the police violate someone's rights during evidence collection, does that mean the evidence must be dismissed in court? The answer is no. There are several exceptions that will allow mistakes by police officers to be overlooked by the Court. Some of these exceptions include good faith (e.g., the police searched the wrong home by honest mistake), purged taint (e.g., the police let the suspect go to dissipate the mistake—the investigation will start anew), inevitable discovery (e.g., the police would have found the evidence anyway, independent of the mistake), and the use of an independent source to confirm the information. In addition, the exclusionary rule, which would prevent illegally obtained evidence from being admitted into court, does not apply to parole revocation hearings, noncriminal proceedings, sentencing, grand jury investigations, and searches by private persons who are not agents of the police. However, the state can always give the suspect more rights that tighten the control over police officers.

The Court will consider the needs of the state versus the needs of the defendant when allowing evidence into court (del Carmen & Hemmens, 2017). For example, the police were in hot pursuit of a man who committed a crime with a gun, but the man threw the gun away before he was captured by the police. The police asked him about the gun's location without reading the man the Miranda warning. The police knew the man was under arrest before they asked him about the gun. The man told the police the gun's location, and the police subsequently found the gun, which was used against the man in court. The Court stated that an abandoned gun in public presented a risk to the public's safety, and this risk was more important than the cost of violating the suspect's right to remain silent. Thus, the Court allowed the statement and gun to be admitted in court.

When a police officer has probable cause to search a location, and when exigent circumstances exist, the police officer may legally search the location without a search warrant (del Carmen & Hemmens, 2017). Under these conditions, a warrantless entry into a home or vehicle is justified. Of course, the police officer must be able to articulate the situation in a police report and in court.

The police must be able to articulate a certain level of confidence that a crime is occurring or has occurred for specific actions to be taken (del Carmen & Hemmens, 2017). With reasonable suspicion (about a 30% confidence level that a crime is occurring or has occurred), the police may stop and detain a person, which is a seizure. The person is not free to leave, and the officer can investigate the incident. As always, the police can only hold someone long enough to do the job. In addition, the officers must use the least amount of force necessary and the least intrusive methods available to do their jobs. Police officers can never use excessive force. Police officers must use the appropriate amount of force according to their use-of-force continuum, which includes deadly force.

Because vehicle stops are not very intrusive, the police only need reasonable suspicion to make a traffic stop investigation (Ryan, 2018). Furthermore, a pretextual stop, which is a stop used as a pretext to search a vehicle, does not violate the 4th Amendment (del Carmen & Hemmens, 2017). If the police could legally have stopped the vehicle for a traffic violation, then the actual intent of the stop is irrelevant. The Court ruled that the personal, or subjective, motives of an officer are not a factor.

Unprovoked flight provides reasonable suspicion for the police to stop a car or person (del Carmen & Hemmens, 2017). If safety is an issue, then the police may also frisk the car or person for weapons. During the Terry Stop, for example, the suspect mumbled when asked to self-identify, which allowed the police to immediately frisk the suspect for weapons. The Court ruled that the burden to dispel a safety risk is on the suspect. Because the suspect failed to do so when he mumbled, this allowed the police to conduct a frisk.

To make an arrest, which is also a seizure, and to obtain a warrant, the police need probable cause, which is a 51% confidence level that a crime is occurring or has occurred (del Carmen & Hemmens, 2017). The police are not required to be correct. They are only required to be 51% confident that they are correct.

The police are not always required to read an arrestee the Miranda warning (del Carmen & Hemmens, 2017). Two conditions must exist before the Miranda warning is required: (1) the person must be under arrest; and (2) the police must question the arrestee about the crime for which the person is being charged. In other words, an arrestee does not have the right to a lawyer during typical booking procedures. The Miranda warning only protects individuals against testimonial information that self-incriminates and does not apply to evidence that simply identifies the arrestee and/or places the arrestee at the scene of the crime. In addition, the Court has allowed a confession to be used in court when the arrestee confessed to an undercover officer in a neighboring jail cell because the arrestee did not perceive that they were being questioned by the police.

A volunteered statement, which occurs when a person provides a statement freely without being interrogated, is different than a voluntary statement, which is when a suspect provides a statement without coercion and of their own free will (del Carmen & Hemmens, 2017). The police are not required to provide the Miranda warning for volunteered statements. However, if the police interrogate a suspect, they will be required to provide the Miranda warning before collecting voluntary statements. A volunteered statement will always be a *voluntary* statement, but a voluntary statement will not necessarily be a *volunteered* statement.

A police decision should be based on a totality of circumstances, which means the police officer should consider all available evidence, if given the time, before making a decision. The officer should be open-minded and willing to consider all points of view. If only partial information is considered, then the final decision may be less than optimal.

The proper actions of a police officer will be judged based on how other officers with the same training and experience would have acted in the same situation (del Carmen & Hemmens, 2017). In other words, two officers may experience the same event, but their available legal actions may differ. For example, if two officers smell the same odor, one may recognize it as an illegal substance and one may not. The officer who recognizes the odor as an illegal drug will have probable cause to search, but the other officer who does not recognize the odor as an illegal drug will not have probable cause to search.

Americans like their privacy, and the Fourth Amendment is about protecting privacy (del Carmen & Hemmens, 2017). The general standard is based on whether the general public would recognize a person's expectation of privacy in a certain situation. For example, the general public would not recognize that a person speaking in public expects privacy. However, the general public would recognize that a person speaking in a closed phone booth expects privacy. Likewise, if a police officer is in a location where the officer can legally be, such as flying a helicopter at a legal altitude, then the police have the right to look around. This is called plain view. If a police officer can legally be on the roadway, for example, and if the police officer sees something illegal through the window of a home, then the police officer may be able take legal action. The general public would not recognize a window as providing privacy because windows are transparent. However, looking through the walls of a home would be problematic because the general public would recognize walls, which are not transparent, as barriers that provide privacy.

For property searches, the Court has recognized the right to privacy inside curtilage, but not in open field (del Carmen & Hemmens, 2017). Curtilage is the location where a person engages in daily intimate activities linked to the sanctity of their home. Open field is the area outside of curtilage. Even if items are in your own yard, if the items are not inside curtilage, then the 4th Amendment right to privacy does not apply. Evidence can be collected by law enforcement without a search warrant in open field because 4th Amendment protections do not apply to items in open field.

The use of a dog by police to sniff the air around a vehicle during a traffic stop does not violate the driver's 4th Amendment right to privacy (del Carmen & Hemmens, 2017). The Court has ruled that dog sniffs are not searches and do not violate the driver's privacy, as long as the dog sniffs are in public (versus bringing the dog onto someone's front porch). However, police officers can only detain someone long enough to do their job. Thus, if it only takes a police officer five minutes to write a speeding ticket, then detaining a speeder for 20 minutes while waiting for a dog to arrive at the scene may be problematic. However, to buy more time for a dog to arrive at a scene, an officer may run computer checks sequentially instead of simultaneously. For example, an officer may run and confirm the driver's identification before checking the passenger's identification. When the computer checks for all occupants have been completed, then the officer may run a computer check on the vehicle.

Police officers make decisions based on the available information. For example, if police officers believe that someone has the authority to let them search a home, then the officers may legally search the home (del Carmen & Hemmens, 2017). It does not matter whether the person actually had the authority to let the police officers search the home. However, the police officers must attempt to corroborate the information to justify their actions.

Police officers are charged with investigating crimes, which include collecting and assessing information. They are trained and expected to control the scene and to promote safety, which includes their own safety. A person who fails to comply with the legal orders of a police officer may create an unsafe situation, which may result in a criminal charge.

However, federal law is not always clear and may be inconsistent across the country. Because the U.S. Supreme Court hears only about 1–2% of all cases appealed to it, this means that the U.S. circuit courts are the final word for most cases (del Carmen & Hemmens, 2017). There are 13 different federal judicial circuit courts in the United States. When there is a circuit split, which occurs when two or more circuit courts provide conflicting rulings on the same legal issue, federal laws may not necessarily be consistent from state to state. Furthermore, if a state contains multiple federal district courts, federal district court rulings can be divergent and conflicting within the state until a higher court makes a ruling.

Below is a summary of select U.S. Constitutional laws (del Carmen & Hemmens, 2017).

U.S. CONSTITUTIONAL LAW OVERVIEW

- *4th Amendment:* People and their homes, papers, and belongings are protected from being searched or taken without good reason, and probable cause is required to search a place for specific people or items.
- *5th Amendment:* No persons can be tried twice for the same crime in the same jurisdiction or be forced to say things that may be used against them in court. Each person has the right to remain silent. In addition, a grand jury is required to try a person for a crime that is punishable by death.
- *6th Amendment:* An arrestee has the right to a speedy trial with a fair jury. Accused persons will be told what crimes they have been charged with, they have the right to face their accusers and witnesses, and they have the right to a lawyer.
- *14th Amendment:* States shall not deprive any person of life, liberty, or property without due process of law. This means that the 4th Amendment now applies to all law enforcement, not just federal law enforcement.

CERTAINTY LEVELS

- No information (not sufficient in any legal proceedings)   **LOWEST**
- Suspicion (starts criminal investigation)
- Reasonable suspicion (detain; stop & frisk by police)
- Preponderance of the evidence (needed to win civil case)*
- Probable cause (warrant; indictment; arrest)*
- Clear & convincing evidence (needed to overturn warrant in court)
- Guilt beyond a reasonable doubt (conviction of defendant in court)
- Absolute certainty (not required)   **HIGHEST**

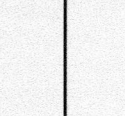

* Levels are equal

Scale: No information = 0%; Suspicion = 20%; Reasonable suspicion = 30%; Probable cause = Preponderance of the evidence = 51%; Clear & convincing evidence = 75%; Beyond a reasonable doubt = 95%; Absolute certainty = 100%

TOTALITY OF CIRCUMSTANCES FOR ASSESSING PROPER POLICE BEHAVIOR

- Reviewing courts must look at the totality of circumstances.
- Each factor, in and of itself, may not indicate a crime.
- Together, the factors may indicate a crime.
- Officers are allowed to draw upon personal experience and specialized training.
- Probable cause and reasonable suspicion are fluid and cannot be defined with precision.

INTERVIEW AND INTERROGATION

- Interview = general questioning; questioning a person who may know something about a crime, but there is no probable cause to believe that the person committed the crime (no Miranda warning required).
- Interrogation = formal and adversarial; person is believed to have committed a crime; questioning a person about a specific crime when there is probable cause that the person is directly or indirectly involved in that specific crime (Miranda warning is required).

Factor	Difference between interview and interrogation	
	Interview	Interrogation
Purpose	Obtain information	To test information
Relationship between interrogator and suspect	Cooperative	Adversarial or hostile
Level of certainty	Less than probable cause of guilt	Probable cause of guilt
Planning	Moderate	Extensive
Environment	Private or semi-private	Private
Person under arrest	No	Yes
Miranda warning given	No	Yes

CONFESSION VS. ADMISSION

- **Confession** = information supporting the elements of a crime given by a person involved in committing the crime; suspect says they committed the act.
- **Admission** = the suspect admits to something related to an act but does not claim that they committed the act; contains some information concerning the elements of a crime but falls short of a full confession.
- **Adoptive admission** = After being provided incriminating evidence, a person does not deny allegations made against them when given the opportunity.

SUSPECT'S CONFESSION

- May be obtained orally or in writing.
- Needs to be corroborated by other evidence.
- Permission from parent/guardian needs to be obtained before questioning a juvenile.

5TH AMENDMENT

5th Amendment – No person shall be compelled in any criminal case to be a witness against himself, and he shall not be deprived of life, liberty, or property without due process of law.

MIRANDA WARNING

Miranda v. Arizona (1966): law enforcement officers must give suspects the following warnings whenever there is a custodial interrogation: (1) You have the right to remain silent; (2) Anything you say can be used against you in a court of law; (3) You have the right to the presence of an attorney; (4) If you cannot afford a lawyer, one will be appointed to you prior to questioning; and (5) You may terminate the interview at any time. A person subjected to custodial interrogation must be given the Miranda warning regardless of the nature or severity of the offense.

Exception: The roadside questioning of a motorist detained pursuant to a routine traffic stop does to constitute a custodial interrogation, so there is no need to give the Miranda warning.

MIRANDA WARNING REQUIREMENT
- When suspect is in custody (not free to leave).
- Before being interrogated (questioned about the crime that is being charged).

THREE TESTS FOR MIRANDA
Three questions are posed to determine whether the Miranda warning was given properly.

1. Was the Miranda warning given by police?
2. If given, did the suspect provide a waiver?
3. If there was a waiver, was it given intelligently and voluntarily?

WAIVER OF RIGHT TO REMAIN SILENT
- **Intelligently** – suspect knows what they are doing and is sufficiently competent to waive right.
- **Voluntarily** – not the result of any threat, force, or coercion; waiver is made of own free will. Court ruled that statements are not admissible in court if coercion is exerted by the *police* and not by someone else (e.g., God).
- Signed waiver is not required.

RIGHT TO REMAIN SILENT INVOKED
Once the suspect has invoked the right to remain silent, the suspect cannot be questioned again for the same offense unless they initiate further communication, exchanges, or conversations with police.

SUSPECT'S RIGHT TO COUNSEL
- Right to counsel falls under the 6th Amendment.
- Suspect is entitled to a lawyer during interrogation so that the right against self-incrimination is protected.
- Even if the Miranda warning is properly given, the evidence is not admissible if the right to counsel under the 6th Amendment is violated.

PROLONGED INTERRUPTION AFTER MIRANDA WARNING WAS GIVEN
The Court hinted that after a police officer reads a suspect the Miranda warning and then takes a *prolonged* break, the Miranda warning should be read again to the suspect before re-questioning the suspect.

How long is prolonged?
Although the time has not been clearly established by the Court, several hours may be considered prolonged.

MIRANDA RIGHT VIOLATION—INVALID CONFESSIONS
- Confessions are invalid if the police use coercion or brutality.
- Confessions are invalid if deception is used as a means of psychological pressure.
- Confessions are invalid if the suspect does not have complete freedom of mind.

WHEN THE MIRANDA WARNING IS NOT REQUIRED
- When police officers ask no questions (no information sought; nothing to waive).
- During general on-the-scene questioning (no intent to arrest a specific person).
- When police ask routine identification questions (not testimonial self-incrimination).
- When police question individuals who are not suspects of a crime (no intent to arrest).
- When there is a threat to public safety (immediate danger to public, such as when a gun has been thrown away by a suspect).
- When the statement is unsolicited (statement is volunteered).
- In stop-and-frisk situations (no custodial interrogation involved).
- During lineups, showups, or photographic identifications (not testimonial self-incrimination).
- Before statements are made to private persons (private persons are not the government).
- Before statements are made to the grand jury (not a custodial interrogation).
- When an undercover officer poses as an inmate and asks questions (lacks the perception of a police-dominated environment).

SUSPICION
- Suspicion alone is never sufficient for an arrest.
- Mere suspicion may develop into probable cause.
- Once probable cause is developed, any and all evidence may be used in court.
- Courts recognize that affidavits are often prepared hastily and in the midst of criminal investigations; therefore, they are to be interpreted with common sense over technical manners.

REASONABLE SUSPICION
- Quantum of knowledge that is sufficient to induce an ordinarily prudent and cautious person under similar circumstances to believe criminal activity is at hand. It must be based on articulable facts, which, taken together with rational inferences from those facts, reasonably warrant intrusion.
- Suspicion < Reasonable Suspicion < Probable Cause.

PROBABLE CAUSE
- Probable cause = enough factual information to make the average reasonable person with the same training and experience to believe that the suspect has committed a crime.
- Practical definition = 51% confident (i.e., 51% certain).
- Must use totality of the circumstances.

FACTORS USED TO ESTABLISH PROBABLE CAUSE

- Police officer training
- Education
- Knowledge of culture
- Unique life experiences
- Knowledge of community
- Prior criminal record of suspect
- Suspect flees when officer arrives
- Highly suspicious conduct displayed by the suspect
- Admission or confession by suspect
- Presence of incriminating evidence
- Unusual hour
- Resemblance of a suspect to the perpetrator
- Failure to answer questions satisfactorily

ESTABLISHING PROBABLE CAUSE

- Officer may use any trustworthy information to establish probable cause, even if the evidence is not admissible in court (e.g., hearsay and prior criminal record).
- Evidence may include tips from citizens, police radio bulletins, reports from victims, anonymous tips, tips from informants, etc.
- Judge may consider any evidence, regardless of the source.
- Probable cause is based on totality of circumstances.
- More information means better probable cause.
- Officer's own knowledge of particular facts and circumstances.
- Information given by a reliable third person.
- Information + corroboration.
- Probable cause is not based on hard certainty, but on probabilities and confidence levels.

PROBABLE CAUSE: AFTER-THE-FACT

- Probable cause must exist at the time when it was required for the police action.
- Probable cause determined after-the-fact does not make the act legal (evidence found in such cases will not be allowed in court).
- What is not included in an affidavit cannot later be used to establish probable cause.

PROBABLE CAUSE: WITHOUT A WARRANT

- If an officer acts without a warrant, then the officer will need to establish probable cause by oral testimony in court during the trial.
- In some jurisdictions, the judge may require a written affidavit in addition to oral testimony.

4TH AMENDMENT

- Right of individuals to be secure in their persons, houses, papers and effects against unreasonable searches and seizures and no warrant shall be issued but upon probable cause, supported by oath or affirmation, that particularly describes the place to be searched, and the persons or things to be seized.
- For an arrest, it must be determined whether a seizure has occurred.
- If no seizure, then 4th Amendment does not apply.
- If seizure, then must determine what kind of seizure.
- Not all contact with the police is considered a seizure under the 4th Amendment.
- Whether a seizure exists will depend upon the level of intrusiveness.

WHO HAS AUTHORITY TO GIVE POLICE CONSENT TO SEARCH?

(Intent of police is to seize evidence)

- A spouse can give consent to search the home; however, if the co-occupant is present and denies consent, then no search is allowed.
- If a former girlfriend or boyfriend has apparent authority over the residence, then the person can give consent.
- Roommates can give consent, but only for their own areas and common areas.
- A landlord has no authority to give consent to search a renter's apartment.
- An apartment manager can give consent but only for common areas.
- The driver of a vehicle can give consent to search the entire vehicle, even if the driver is not the owner of the vehicle.
- College administrators, according to most lower courts, have no authority to give consent to search a dormitory, but this issue has not been settled by the Court.
- High school administrators can request police to search a student's locker if there is reasonable suspicion.

- Any evidence obtained by the government in violation of the 4th Amendment guarantee against unreasonable search and seizure is not admissible in a criminal prosecution to prove guilt.
- The Court has stated that the exclusionary rule is a judicially created remedy to safeguard 4th Amendment rights.
- Therefore, not every violation (e.g., 5th and 6th Amendment violations) comes under the exclusionary rule.
- Evidence collected from other U.S. Constitutional violations is also excludable, but under other exclusionary rules.
- For example, the self-incrimination clause (5th Amendment) contains its own exclusionary rule.

PURPOSE OF THE EXCLUSIONARY RULE

- To deter police misconduct.
- *Assumption:* If illegally obtained evidence is not allowed in court, then police misconduct will be minimized.
- Applies to state and federal cases.

DUE PROCESS
- Evidence obtained in violation of the constitutional right to due process is inadmissible under the 5th and 14th Amendments.
- Due process violations can lead to civil liability under federal law.

ERRONEOUSLY ADMITTED EVIDENCE
- Erroneously admitted evidence during trial will be overturned on appeal unless the prosecutor can show that the error was harmless.

INVOKING EXCLUSIONARY RULE
- May be invoked at about any stage of the criminal justice proceeding.
- May be invoked while serving time after conviction.

WRIT OF HABEAS CORPUS: INVOKING THE EXCLUSIONARY RULE
- Seeks release from confinement due to violation of U.S. Constitutional rights before and/or during trial.
- The defendant may find new evidence that police misconduct took place after the defendant has been convicted of a crime and the time to appeal has passed.
- Evidence was not made available to the suspect during trial.
- Although a prisoner may file a writ of habeas corpus, federal law limits what prisoners can do. A writ of habeas corpus is not a substitute for an appeal and is seldom successful.

EXCEPTIONS TO THE EXCLUSIONARY RULE: FOUR CATEGORIES
- Good faith
- Inevitable discovery
- Purged taint
- Independent source

Some states may not allow for exceptions in order to provide more protection to suspects.

GOOD FAITH
Evidence is admissible if the error or mistake was not committed by police or, if committed by the police, it was honest and reasonable (i.e., based on good faith).

Below are examples of good faith mistakes.

- When the error is committed by a judge.
- When the error is committed by a court employee.

- When police believed the information was true and accurate.
- When police believed the person had the authority to give entry.
- When the police action was based on a law that was later declared unconstitutional.

ERROR BY JUDGE

If the error is made by a judge: The Court ruled that evidence is admissible in court because the judge, and not the police, erred. Therefore, the exclusionary rule does not apply because it is designed to control the conduct of police, not judges.

ERROR BY COURT EMPLOYEE

The Court ruled that evidence was admissible in court because a court employee, and not the police, had erred. The exclusionary rule is designed to control the conduct of police, not court employees. Therefore, the exclusionary rule does not apply if there is no evidence that the court employee tried to ignore or subvert the 4th Amendment.

WHEN POLICE ERRED ACCIDENTALLY

- Constitutionality of police conduct is based on the information that was available to the officer at the time of the action.
- Evidence obtained as a result of a mistake is admissible as long as the officer thought that their actions were legal and correct.
- Legality of police action will be based on the information the officers disclosed or had a duty to discover and disclose to the judge.
- Police must act within scope of search warrant—for example, the police cannot search a desk drawer for a 60-inch TV.

POLICE BELIEVED THEY HAD AUTHORITY TO ENTER

- If police have probable cause to believe a person has control over property and authority to give consent, then any evidence discovered on the property is admissible in court.
- *Example:* A woman has a key to an apartment. She states that she lives there with her boyfriend, and that she has furniture and clothes there. She lets the police into the apartment and the police find drugs. The drugs are admissible in court if the police believed the woman, even if the woman lied to police.

LAW LATER DECLARED UNCONSTITUTIONAL

- If the mistake is with the law and not the police, evidence is admissible.
- *Example:* Police legally search a car and collect evidence, but the law changes later in a way that would have made the search illegal. Evidence is admissible in court because the act was legal at the time the evidence was collected.

INEVITABLE DISCOVERY
- States that evidence is admissible if the police can prove they would inevitably have discovered it anyway by lawful means, regardless of their illegal action.
- Not *could* have led to discovery but *would* have led to discovery.

PURGED TAINTED
- The defendant's subsequent voluntary act dissipates the taint of the initial illegality.
- There is a break in the causal connection after the taint.
- The defendant uses free will after the break and self-incriminates.
- Whether the taint has been purged is decided on a case-by-case basis.
- *Example:* An initial confession was illegal and the suspect was released. If the suspect returns to sign a confession, then the second confession will be admissible.

INDEPENDENT SOURCE
- Holds that evidence obtained is admissible if the police can prove it was obtained from an independent source not connected with the illegal search or seizure.
- *Example:* Police conduct an illegal search of a home and find a girl. The girl claims she has been raped by the suspect. Her parents had filed a missing person report the day before. An informant saw the girl at the location. The girl's statement is not related to the illegal search.

WHEN EXCLUSIONARY RULE DOES NOT APPLY
- Police violate the knock and announce rule.
- Searches done by private persons.
- Grand jury investigations.
- Sentencing.
- Arrest based on probable cause that violates state law.
- Violations of agency rules.
- Noncriminal proceedings.
- Parole revocation hearings.

GRAND JURY
- A person cannot refuse to answer questions from a grand jury on the grounds that the evidence was illegally obtained.
- This would unduly interfere with grand jury's investigative function.

ILLEGALLY OBTAINED EVIDENCE—DURING SENTENCING
- May be admissible if state law does not prohibit it.
- Evidence may be reliable even if illegally obtained.
- The judge should consider all evidence at sentencing.

CONSENSUAL ENCOUNTER WITH POLICE CAR
- Police may pull alongside someone and ask questions.
- Police should not block a person's car so the person cannot leave.
- The person must be free to leave.
- Police may shine a spotlight in car.
- The Court has stated that person in car has no legal authority to submit to police when illuminated by white light.
- Once red and blue lights are illuminated, the person is required to submit to the police; the officer is using legal authority to detain the person.

SEIZURE
- A person has been seized if, under the totality of the circumstances, a reasonable person would not have felt free to leave. This applies to seizures of persons in general, such as stop and frisk, not just in arrest cases.
- The police have communicated that the person was not at liberty to ignore the police and go about their business.

SEIZURE
- When does a stop constitute a seizure under the 4th Amendment and require reasonable suspicion?
- When is a stop not a seizure under the 4th Amendment?
- A person is seized under the 4th Amendment if, *in view of all of the circumstances* surrounding the incident, a *reasonable person* would have believed that they were *not free to leave*.

FACTORS THAT INVOLVE SEIZURE: NOT FREE TO LEAVE
The Court gave examples indicating when a person is not free to leave.
- Threatening presence of police.
- Officer displays weapon.
- Touching of person by officer.
- Use of language or tone of voice by officer compelling a suspect's compliance.
- Absence of such evidence amounts to less than a seizure.

SEIZURE TEST
- The Court ruled that a seizure has occurred if a reasonable person, considering the totality of the circumstances, would conclude that the police had in some way restrained a person's liberty so they were not free to leave.
- The Court ruled that there is no single, clear, hard-and-fast rule applicable to all investigatory pursuits.

DEGREE OF INTRUSION
- What degree of intrusion is permissible?
- The least intrusive and most reasonably available method to verify or dispel the officer's suspicion.
- The greater the degree of police control, the greater the likelihood the Court will impose the probable cause standard.

REASONABLE PERSON
- Who decides the definition of a reasonable person?
- The jury or the judge who tries the case.
- The standard is subjective and may vary.

ARTICULATION FOR SEIZURE
- Must be able to articulate facts in report and in court.
- For reasonable suspicion to be valid, there is a 2-prong test.
- Criminal activity may be taking place.
- The person detained is somehow connected to possible criminal activity.

POLICE OFFICER'S AUTHORITY TO DETAIN
- Temporary stopping of a person by exerting police authority (e.g., verbal direction).
- The person is not free to leave; the person has been detained; the person has been seized.
- Less than arrest but more than consensual encounter.
- Need reasonable suspicion = 30% confidence level of criminal activity.
- Hunch < reasonable suspicion < probable cause < beyond reasonable doubt.

DETENTION MAY EXIST IF
- Person is restrained.
- Officer gives a specific order that the person feels obligated to obey.
- Actions or questions indicate the person is the suspect of a crime.

FIELD DETENTION—FINGERPRINTING
The Court ruled that field detention, for purposes of fingerprinting a suspect, does not require probable cause as long as:
- There is reasonable suspicion that the suspect committed a crime.
- There is reasonable belief that the fingerprinting will either negate or establish the suspect's guilt.
- The procedure is promptly executed.

EXAMPLES NOT CONSIDERED SEIZURES
- Police asking questions of people on the street to gather general information.
- Police asking a driver to get out of the car after a stop.
- Police boarding a bus and asking questions that a person is free to refuse to answer.
- Police riding alongside a person to see where the person is going.
- Police asking witnesses questions about a crime.

STOP AND FRISK
- *Stop and frisk:* police practices that allow an officer to stop a person in a public place and ask questions to determine whether that person has committed a crime or about to commit a crime and to frisk the person for weapons.
- Two separate acts, not one continuous act.
- *Stop:* the brief detention of a person when the police officer has reasonable suspicion, in light of their experience, that criminal activity has taken place or is about to take place.
- *Frisk:* the pat-down of a person's outer clothing after a stop to see whether the person has a weapon, which the officer can seize. If the officer does not fear for their personal safety, then a frisk is not allowed.
- Both stop and frisk only require reasonable suspicion to be valid because they are less intrusive than an arrest or search.
- Stop and frisk are intrusions upon a person's freedom.
- During this scenario, no arrest can be made.
- If probable cause is developed, then this may lead to an arrest.
- Several states have passed laws that allow the practice.
- Other state courts and some federal courts have upheld such practices.

TERRY V. OHIO
- *Terry v. Ohio* (1968) is the leading case on stop and frisk.
- *Terry v. Ohio* sets guidelines that officers must follow for stop and frisk.

The Stop
- A **stop** has only one purpose: to determine whether criminal activity has taken place or is about to take place.
- An investigatory stop does not constitute an arrest.
- The officer must identify that they are a police officer.
- The officer must make reasonable inquiries.
- The officer may question the suspect about their identification and conduct, may contact others to verify story and identification, can check for outstanding warrants, can check nearby buildings to determine whether a crime occurred, and can bring a witness to the suspect for a showup.
- Stops based on race alone are not valid.
- Lower courts disagree on whether race can be taken as one factor in determining reasonable suspicion for a stop.
- Persons stopped by the police cannot be forced to answer questions, but they may be forced to identify themselves as authorized by state law.

The Frisk

- A **frisk** has only one purpose: officer safety.
- A frisk should not automatically follow a stop.
- A frisk is valid only if there is reasonable suspicion that a threat to officer safety exists.
- If stop requirements are satisfied, the officer may conduct a limited search (i.e., pat-down) of the outer clothing in an attempt to discover dangerous weapons.
- Initially limited to pat-down of outer clothing.
- A frisk that goes beyond a mere pat-down for weapons is illegal.
- The officer may seize the object if it feels like a weapon.
- The officer may not seize the object if does not feel like weapon; if seized, it cannot be admitted in court.
- If an arrest is made, then a body search may be conducted.
- When actions by police exceed the bounds permitted by reasonable suspicion, the seizure becomes an arrest and must be supported by probable cause.

FRISK

Can an officer frisk a person after a stop without asking questions?

- Reasonable inquiries are required before a frisk.
- In some instances, a frisk may be justified without the officer asking questions if the officer believes safety is a concern.
- *Exception:* if state law requires the officer to make reasonable inquiries before a frisk.
- Does a frisk include things carried? The Court has not directly addressed this issue. If belongings are easily accessible, then search may be justified.
- The burden of proof is on police to demonstrate an extended frisk was necessary for officer safety.
- A frisk cannot be used to fish for evidence.
- Contraband must be immediately apparent to the officer to be seized (plain touch).

PLAIN TOUCH DOCTRINE

- If an officer touches or feels something that is immediately recognized as something needing to be seized, the object can be seized as long as such knowledge amounts to probable cause.
- If the officer has to manipulate the object to determine what it is, then the evidence may be inadmissible in court.

CONSENT TO FRISK

- Is consent to frisk based on submission to police authority valid?
- If the officer does not fear for their safety, then consent is required.
- Validity depends on how consent was obtained.
- Consent to authority may not necessarily be voluntary.
- Burden of proof that consent was involuntary lies with person who gave consent.

SUMMARY

Stop

1. Observe.
2. Approach and identify.
3. Ask questions.

Frisk

1. Conduct a pat-down of the outer clothing.
2. If a weapon is felt, confiscate it and arrest the suspect (optional).
3. Conduct a full-body search after the arrest (optional).

STOP AND FRISK VS. ARREST

	Stop and frisk	Arrest
Degree of certainty	Reasonable suspicion	Probable cause
Extent of intrusion	Pat-down for weapons	Full body search
Purpose	Stop: prevent crime Frisk: safety	To take person into custody for committing a crime
Warrant	Not needed	Required, unless exception
Duration	No longer than necessary	Until legally released
Force allowed	Stop: none	Reasonable

STOP: MOTOR VEHICLES

- Motorists are subject to stop and frisk under the same circumstances as pedestrians.
- Motorists may be stopped if there is reasonable suspicion of unlawful activity.
- After the vehicle is stopped, the officer may order the driver out of the vehicle, even if the officer has no reasonable suspicion that the driver poses a threat to the officer.

STOP: UNPROVOKED FLIGHT

- Does unprovoked flight constitute reasonable suspicion?
- Yes, reasonable suspicion may exist to justify a stop.
- Headlong flight—wherever it occurs—is an act of evasion: it is not necessarily indicative of wrongdoing, but it is certainly suggestive of such.
- Reasonable suspicion is based on commonsense judgments and inferences about human behavior.
- Flight may be innocent, but the stop afterwards does not violate the 4th Amendment.
- Because of the Court's language, lower courts may render conflicting decisions about whether unprovoked flight alone generates reasonable suspicion.

STOPS BASED ON HEARSAY
- Are stops based on hearsay information valid?
- Yes, information from a known informant carries sufficient indicia of reliability to justify the forcible stop of a suspect.

STOPS BASED ON ANONYMOUS TIPS
- An anonymous tip, corroborated by independent police work, may provide reasonable suspicion to make an investigatory stop *if it carries sufficient indicia of reliability.*
- Should provide predictive information that allows police to test the informant's knowledge or credibility.
- Reasonable suspicion depends on the quality and quantity of the information, and both factors are considered in the totality of the circumstances.

STOPS BASED ON FLYER FROM ANOTHER POLICE JURISDICTION
- Is information based on a flyer from another jurisdiction enough for a stop?
- Yes, the Court decided that the police may stop a suspect on the basis of reasonable suspicion that the person is wanted for investigation in another jurisdiction; must articulate that the suspect is the wanted person.
- A Terry-type stop is permissible.

STOP OF PAROLEES
- Are stops of parolees without suspicion valid?
- Yes, because a parolee does not have an expectation of privacy that society would recognize as legitimate.
- Parolees are still in the legal custody of the Department of Corrections until the conclusion of their sentence.
- Parolees provide consent to a suspicion-less search at just about any time.

STOP: FORCED TO ANSWER QUESTIONS
- Can stopped suspects be forced to answer questions?
- No; however, the failure to answer questions may give the officer reasonable suspicion to frisk the suspect because it may fail to dispel suspicions of danger. It may also lead to probable cause if other circumstances are present.

STOP: FORCED TO SELF-IDENTIFY
- Can a stopped person be forced to identify who they are?
- Yes, but only under certain circumstances.
- Balance the intrusion on the individual's rights against the promotion of legitimate governmental interests.
- For example, where an officer identifies a person who may have committed a crime or when circumstances lead a reasonable person to believe that public safety requires such identification.

DURATION OF STOP
- May only last as long as necessary to achieve its purpose.
- Officers cannot detain a person for as much time as they deem convenient.
- The Court ruled that a 90-minute delay to get K-9 exceeded permissible limits for an investigatory stop.
- The Court ruled that isolating a suspect at an airport was more intrusive than necessary to carry out a limited investigation permitted under stop and frisk.
- The Court ruled that detaining a person for longer than necessary to write a ticket was unreasonable (the officer ran warrant checks based on a hunch).
- In one case, the Court ruled that detaining a person for 20 minutes was reasonable, considering the particulars of the case.
- Reasonableness must take into account the length of time for the stop and the needs of law enforcement.
- Determined on a case-by-case basis.

STATIONHOUSE DETENTION
- A form of detention—usually at a police facility—that is short of arrest but greater than on-the-street detention of stop and frisk. It is used by many departments for obtaining fingerprints or photographs, ordering police lineups, administering polygraph tests, or securing other identification or non-testimonial evidence.

STATIONHOUSE DETENTION
- Stops, frisks, and stationhouse detention fall under the 4th Amendment.
- They are not subject to the same limitations as arrests and searches.
- Stops, frisks, and stationhouse detention follow different rules than arrests and searches.
- For legal purposes, even though less intrusive than an arrest, a stationhouse detention should be considered equivalent to an arrest.

STATIONHOUSE DETENTION—FINGERPRINTING
- Can stationhouse detention be used to obtain fingerprints?
- The Court ruled that reasonable suspicion alone does not permit police to detain a suspect at the police station to obtain fingerprints.
- The suspect may consent to stationhouse detention.
- Consent may be challenged because the police station is intimidating.
- Police must tell the suspect that they are not under arrest.
- Police must tell the suspect that they are free to leave at any time.
- Police must tell the suspect that fingerprinting is voluntary.
- Police should get the suspect's signature on a waiver form.
- Police should have a witness sign the waiver form.
- The Court implied that detention for fingerprinting might be permissible even without probable cause to arrest; narrowly circumscribed procedures are required.
- Must have objective basis for suspecting person of crime.
- Must have legitimate investigatory purpose for detention (such as fingerprinting).
- Must not be an inconvenient time for the suspect.
- Must have adequate evidence to justify detention.

STATIONHOUSE DETENTION—INTERROGATION
- The Court ruled that probable cause is required for stationhouse detention involving interrogation, even if no arrest is made.
- The suspect is not questioned on the street but is transported to the police station.
- Thus, an arrest has been made.
- Probable cause is needed at this point, and any statements made afterwards will be inadmissible in court.

AIRPORT STOPS
- Are airport stops and searches valid?
- Yes, as long as terrorism is a threat, courts will likely allow practices that do not grossly violate constitutional rights.
- Even if racial profiling is employed, legal challenges to this type of profiling may prove difficult because of serious and valid security concerns.
- The 9th U.S. Circuit Court ruled that airport security may conduct a random check of a traveler's carry-on bag, even if it has passed through x-ray without suspicion.
- Airport searches are a form of administrative search with lower 4th Amendment protection.
- Airport searches are easily justified as a special needs search rather than as law enforcement activity.
- The Court has ruled that special needs searches have lower 4th Amendment protection.

U.S. BORDER: DETENTION OF FOREIGN NATIONALS
- For the purpose of questioning, immigration officers may detain persons against their will if the officers reasonably believe that the persons are undocumented foreign nationals.
- The searched person does not have to enter the United States (may be at the border).
- Any person found in the border area, including employees and visitors, is subject to search based on reasonable suspicion.
- Search is not limited to actual point of entry; it may be conducted at the functional equivalent of the border (e.g., an international airport in Kansas).

BORDER SEARCHES
- Full 4th Amendment protections do not apply at the border, particularly at the point of entry.
- Border searches at the point of entry do not come under the 4th Amendment, but searches inside the border do.
- Searches made at the border are based on the longstanding right of a nation to protect itself by stopping and examining persons and property entering the country.
- Searches may be conducted by immigration and border agents without probable cause, reasonable suspicion, or suspicion.
- No amount of certainty is required in border searches, whether the person is a U.S. citizen or not.

- There is a compelling state interest involved in stopping illegal immigration and the flow of prohibited goods into the country.
- Rules for border stops and searches are governed by immigration laws and policies, subject to minimum rights required by the Bill of Rights.
- Since 9/11, border policies have been tightened. These rights may be challenged in court, but they should prevail if they do not violate the minimum rights required.
- No suspicion is needed to disassemble a fuel tank of a motor vehicle at the border.
- Vehicles may be stopped at fixed checkpoints and their occupants questioned, even without reasonable suspicion that the vehicle contains undocumented foreign nationals (because the stops are not arbitrary). Moreover, no warrant is needed to set up a checkpoint for immigration purposes.
- For vehicle searches away from the border, a warrant or probable cause is required (roving agents cannot profile occupants to make a stop, but they can detain and question occupants of a car as long as they have reasonable suspicion).

BORDER SUMMARY

- Foreigners who attempt to enter the United States do not have full 4th Amendment protection at the border.
- They can be stopped and searched without reasonable suspicion.
- Their vehicles and belongings can be extensively searched without probable cause.
- Once foreigners are legally inside the United States, they are entitled to constitutional protection.
- Advanced technologies are being used in border searches to detect illegal entries and contraband.

DETENTION OF ALIMENTARY CANAL SMUGGLERS

- Reasonable suspicion is sufficient for an immigration officer to detain a foreign traveler who is suspected of swallowing contraband. Immigration officers detained a person for 27 hours before the drugs were discovered in the alimentary canal. The Court ruled that the action was reasonable because of the hard-to-detect nature of the crime and because it was at the border.

FACTORY SURVEYS OF FOREIGN NATIONALS

- Immigration officers may visit factories and ask employees questions to determine whether they are undocumented foreign nationals.
- Does not constitute a seizure under the 4th Amendment so the officer does not have to show an objective basis for suspecting the worker of being an undocumented foreign national before conducting the survey.

ARREST → SEIZURE

- If an arrest occurs, then it is a seizure.
- Every arrest is a seizure, but not every seizure is an arrest.*
- There are different types of seizures.
- Arrest is one type of seizure.
- Arrest requires an intentional acquisition of physical control and only applies when there is governmental termination of freedom of movement through means intentionally applied.

* A conditional statement is not logically equivalent to its converse.

MERE WORDS

- Mere words alone do not constitute an arrest.
- Saying "You are under arrest" is not sufficient.
- An actual or constructive seizure must be present for an arrest to take place.

ARREST

- The taking of a person into custody against the person's will for the purpose of criminal prosecution or interrogation.
- Occurs only when there is a governmental termination of freedom of movement through means intentionally applied.
- Arrest deprives a person of liberty by legal authority.
- There must be some kind of restraint.
- It does not matter what state law calls it, if person is taken into custody against their will for the purpose of criminal prosecution or interrogation, then it is an arrest under the 4th Amendment.
- Totality of circumstances is the standard.
- Test of reasonableness = reasonable person.
- Not free to leave.

ARREST

- Needs probable cause.
- Taking a person into custody in a manner authorized by law.
- Physically restraining or touching the person.
- The person is required to submit to authority.
- If arrest, then will handcuff.*
- May use reasonable force to overcome resistance.

* A conditional statement is not logically equivalent to its converse.

LENGTH OF DETENTION AND ARREST

- How long can a suspect be detained and how intrusive must the investigation be before a stop becomes an arrest, which requires probable cause?
- It depends upon the reasonableness of the detention and the level of intrusion.
- The detention must not be longer than that required by the circumstances, and it must take place by the least intrusive means to verify or dispel the officer's suspicions.

MOTOR VEHICLES: ARREST OF PASSENGERS

- Can police arrest passengers if they have probable cause to arrest the driver?
- Yes, if occupants have knowledge of and exercise control over the crime scene (e.g., drugs in the passenger compartment of a car).
- A motor vehicle is a relatively small area and not a public environment.
- Guilt by association is not a good defense.
- Police must decide whether the crime was committed solely or jointly—this may be decided on case-by-case basis in court.

DISPOSITION OF PRISONERS AFTER ARREST

- After a person is arrested, does the person have a U.S. Constitutional right to make a phone call?
- The Supreme Court has not addressed this issue.
- It is safe to say that there is no constitutional right to a phone call; however, state law may allow a phone call.
- The point in time when a call is actually permitted varies by jurisdiction (e.g., before or after booking procedures).
- However, an arrestee is constitutionally entitled to call an attorney prior to an interrogation.

BOOKING AFTER ARREST

- Involves making an entry in the police arrest book indicating the suspect's name, time of arrest, and offense with which the person has been charged.
- The suspect may be fingerprinted or photographed for serious offenses.
- If it is a minor offense, the suspect may be released on stationhouse bail, which involves posting cash and promising to appear in court for a hearing at a specific date.
- If the offense is serious, the arrestee will be held in a temporary holding facility (jail) until bail, as set by the magistrate, is posted.
- In the process of booking, an inventory of the arrestee's personal property may be conducted without a warrant.
- However, such an inventory cannot be used as a fishing expedition to find evidence.
- For example, if a non-evidentiary letter is found in a purse, the letter will be inventoried but may not be read by police.

JURY TRIAL

- Jury members cannot consciously be restricted to a particular group; jurors should be representative of all different persons within the community.
- Federal court jury verdicts must be unanimous.
- In state court jury verdicts, unanimity is not always required. Less-than-unanimous verdicts are not unconstitutional.
- In state courts, whether a jury needs to be unanimous depends on the state and the type of trial.
- A six-member jury is not unconstitutional, except for death penalty cases.
- Verdicts of six-member juries must be unanimous.
- The Court ruled that five-member juries are unconstitutional.
- The Court prohibits a guilty verdict by a less-than-six majority.
- Jury nullification means that the jury's ruling contradicts the evidence, which is permitted.
- Only a few states allow the defense attorney to inform the jury about jury nullification.
- Jurors are not subject to subsequent legal inquiry to explain their decision.
- A jury trial is not required for a criminal case unless the maximum potential punishment exceeds six months' imprisonment.

PLEA BARGAIN

- In exchange for a guilty plea, the prosecutor will make a deal with the client to reduce the seriousness of the charges, to drop other charges, or to reduce the sentence imposed.
- The prosecutor's promise must be fulfilled; otherwise, the plea can be enforced or withdrawn.
- The prosecutor is not required to disclose everything that the prosecutor has for the plea agreement to be valid.
- If the defendant wants to see everything that the prosecutor has, then the defendant must go to court.
- The plea bargain agreement is not valid until it is accepted by the judge.

DISPOSITION OF CASE

- The final outcome of the case.

KEYWORDS

Detention
Exclusionary rule
Miranda warning
Probable cause
Reasonable suspicion

CHAPTER PROBLEMS

U.S. Constitutional Law

Circle correct choice

1. Indicate the correct order of certainty from lowest to highest
   1 = beyond a reasonable doubt; 2 = hunch; 3 = clear and convincing evidence; 4 = reasonable suspicion; 5 = probable cause
   - a 2-4-3-1-5
   - b 2-5-4-3-1
   - c 4-2-5-3-1
   - d 2-4-5-3-1

2. Waivers that are obtained before interrogations must be
   - a In writing
   - b In writing and signed
   - c Given orally
   - d Given voluntarily

3. What level of certainty is required to obtain an arrest warrant?
   - a Hunch
   - b Reasonable suspicion
   - c Probable cause
   - d Clear and convincing evidence

4. All of the following are tests used to determine whether the Miranda warning was properly given by police, except:
   - a Was the Miranda warning provided by police?
   - b Did the suspect provide a waiver?
   - c Was the waiver signed?
   - d Was the waiver given intelligently and voluntarily?

5. Right to counsel falls under the
   - a 4th Amendment
   - b 5th Amendment
   - c 6th Amendment
   - d 8th Amendment

6. Exceptions to the exclusionary rule include all of the following, except:
   - a Double jeopardy
   - b Inevitable discovery
   - c Good faith
   - d Purged taint

7. Searches and seizures not fully protected by the 4th Amendment include the following, except:
   - a Plain view
   - b Open fields
   - c Border searches
   - d Use of deadly force

8   The 4th Amendment involves
    a   Right to privacy
    b   Right to lawyer
    c   Prisoner rights
    d   Right to remain silent
9   The Miranda warning includes the following, except:
    a   Right to remain silent
    b   Right to presence of an attorney
    c   May terminate interview at any time
    d   The right to a phone call during booking procedures
10 Select the following that is most likely to be considered outside of curtilage:
    a   Houses
    b   Apartments
    c   Fenced wooded area on own property with "no trespassing" signs
    d   Hotel room
11 Probable cause is always required for the following, except:
    a   Search without a warrant
    b   Search with a warrant
    c   Arrest with a warrant
    d   All of the above require probable cause
12 If the following conditions exist, then a warrant is required
    a   Time
    b   Witnesses are present
    c   Probable cause
    d   a and c
    e   a, b, and c
13 Persons who do not deny allegations made against them have made:
    a   An admission
    b   An adoptive admission
    c   A confession
    d   A declaration
14 The following are examples from the Court that may give the perception that a person is in custody, except:
    a   Officer forcing a person to identify who they are
    b   Officer displaying weapon
    c   Touching of person by officer
    d   Tone of officer's voice
15 The exclusionary rule applies to
    a   Searches by private citizens
    b   Noncriminal proceedings
    c   Parole revocation hearings
    d   Searches by private citizens who are encouraged by police

16 What level of certainty is required to stop a person?
   a Hunch
   b Reasonable suspicion
   c Probable cause
   d Clear and convincing evidence

17 Each of the following is used by police to establish probable cause, except:
   a Tips from citizens
   b Reports from victims
   c Police radio bulletins
   d Habeas corpus

18 Which of the following is not part of a stop?
   a Approach and identify
   b Ask questions
   c Conduct pat-down
   d Observe

19 What level of certainty is required to frisk a person?
   a Hunch
   b Reasonable suspicion
   c Probable cause
   d Clear and convincing evidence

20 Which type of roadblock is unconstitutional?
   a For general law enforcement purposes
   b To control drunk drivers
   c To check for driver's licenses
   d To control flow of undocumented foreign nationals

True or false (circle best answer)

21 T F DNA test results cannot be disputed in court because they are scientifically based.
22 T F Probable cause must exist for a traffic stop.
23 T F Inevitable discovery states that evidence is admissible in court if the police could have found the evidence anyway.
24 T F Police may stop a person who engages in unprovoked flight.
25 T F According to the Department of Justice, for showups the witnesses should discuss the facts and come to a group consensus in identifying the correct suspect.

REFERENCES

Del Carmen, R.V., & Hemmens, C. (2017). *Criminal procedures: Laws & practice* (10th ed.). Boston, MA: Wadsworth.

Ryan, K. (2018). Reasonable suspicion and the investigative traffic stop. The Texas Municipal Police Association. https://tmpa.org/tmpa/tmpa-news/Articles/Reasonable_Suspicion_and_the_Investigative_Traffic_Stop.aspx?WebsiteKey=6d64a7a3-39ad-4f74-b699-fe7ecb77724a.

Chapter 2

Grammar, Math, Theories, and Persuasion

LEARNING OBJECTIVES

Explain the importance of grammar in law enforcement.

Explain the importance of Boolean algebra in law enforcement.

Explain the difference between correlation and causation.

Explain the difference between descriptive statistics and inferential statistics.

Explain the difference between a quantitative study and a qualitative study.

Describe various criminal theories and their limitations.

Describe how persuasion theories can be used in court.

INTRODUCTION

This chapter is not designed to teach all the details involving English, math, or logic. Its purpose is to show their importance in law enforcement. If some of the material does not make sense, then this should lead students to seek out these courses in college to better understand the material. Laws, which are written as English logical statements, can be converted into mathematical logical statements to determine their truth values. Indeed, the legality of the actions of police officers and residents may be assessed objectively using grammar, punctuation, and Boolean algebra. In addition, individuals should understand subsets, conditional statements, and the difference between existential quantifiers and universal quantifiers because they can all affect the interpretation of the law. Furthermore, to avoid making bad decisions, it is essential for individuals to understand the difference between descriptive statistics and inferential statistics, and to understand the assumptions and limitations of information. Failure to consider grammar, punctuation, math, assumptions, and limitations may result in less-than-optimal decisions.

MISPLACED AND DANGLING MODIFIERS

Grammar is important in police reports because an officer's credibility is linked to their written reports. If police officers make mistakes in their reports, the officers should expect defense attorneys to ask them whether they have performed their jobs to the best of their ability. On one hand, if the officers claim that they have done their best work, then mistakes in their reports will make them appear incompetent or dishonest. On the other hand, if the officers claim that they have not done their best work, then mistakes in their reports will make them appear lazy and uncaring. Thus, police officers need to use proper grammar when writing police reports.

Misplaced and dangling modifiers can be problematic if they exist in a police report. Although mistakes in grammar may make police officers look incompetent, lazy, or dishonest in court, some mistakes in grammar may significantly alter the meaning of a police report and/or make the report incomprehensible. A modifier, for example, changes, clarifies, qualifies, or limits a particular word in a sentence to make its meaning more specific. A misplaced modifier is a modifier that is located too far away from the word that it is supposed to modify, and it is applied to the wrong word, which may change the meaning of the sentence. A dangling modifier exists when the intended subject is missing from the sentence altogether, which may make the report incomprehensible. Indeed, because a misplaced modifier incorrectly modifies the wrong word, and because a dangling modifier has no referent in the sentence, misplaced and dangling modifiers may alter the meaning of the sentence.

Adjectives and adverbs should be placed as closely as possible to the words that they are supposed to modify, and active voice should be employed (American Psychological Association, 2010). This may help to eliminate any unintended meanings. In court, the police officers should expect defense attorneys to ask them whether they write true and accurate reports. If the officers state that their reports are true and accurate, then the defense attorney may argue that the reports should be accepted at face value, especially if misplaced modifiers change the meanings of sentences in the reports to mean what the defense attorneys want them to mean. However, if the officers state that their reports are not true and accurate, then the reports will have little value, the officers' credibility will be ruined, and the officers could be criminally charged for filing false police reports.

Consider the following examples.

> **SUPPOSE A MAN AND HIS WIFE ARE AT SCHOOL AND HE TELLS HER THAT HE LOVES HER.**
>
> *Incorrect statement:* He told his wife that he loves her at the school.
>
> *Correct statement:* While at the school, he told his wife that he loves her.

The incorrect statement does not indicate that he loves his wife, but it does indicate that he loves his wife's presence at the school. This would be appropriate, for example, if his wife worked at a school and he did not want her to quit her job and to leave the school.

> **SUPPOSE A PERSON'S CAR RAN OUT OF GAS.**
>
> *Incorrect statement:* Running out of gas, she walked to the gas station.
>
> *Correct statement:* She walked to the gas station because her car ran out of gas.

The incorrect sentence indicates that she, rather than her car, ran out of gas (the word "car" is missing from the sentence). This may imply that she was jogging, became tired, and started to walk.

> **SUPPOSE A DRIVER ON A TRIP SAW A DEAD DEER.**
>
> *Incorrect statement:* I saw a dead deer driving on the highway.
>
> *Correct statement:* While driving on the highway, I saw a dead deer.

The incorrect sentence indicates that a dead deer was driving. This does not make sense.

Consider the following two statements. Is there a difference between statement 1 and statement 2?

> **SUPPOSE A BET WAS MADE BASED ON STATEMENT 1.**
> *Statement 1:* I can knock down the wall with my bare hands.
> *Statement 2:* I can knock the wall down with my bare hands.

Statement 1 indicates that a person can knock on the wall from top to bottom. In this case, the word "down" is linked to knocking. Statement 2 indicates that the wall will tumble down. In this case, the word "down" is linked to the wall.

> **SUPPOSE A POLICE OFFICER IS ASKING A WITNESS ABOUT A CAR CRASH.**
> *Valueless witness statement:* I did not see the driver look before he pulled out into traffic.
> *Valued witness statement:* I saw the driver not look before he pulled out into traffic.

The valueless witness statement indicates what was not seen (not witnessed). This statement would be true if the witness were at home sleeping. The valued witness statement indicates what was seen (witnessed). Because the police officer wants to record what was witnessed, the valued witness statement is the correct statement.

> **SUPPOSE A PERSON WANTS TO PAINT TWO SWING SETS.**
> *Incorrect statement:* When the kids left the swing sets, I painted them.
> *Correct statement:* I painted the swing sets after the kids left.
>
> In the introductory clause for the incorrect statement, the kids are the nouns or actors being discussed. Because the introductory clause provides background information for the main part of the sentence, the kids were the nouns painted, not the swing sets.

CONDITIONAL STATEMENTS

Conditional statement = If A, then B

Converse of the conditional statement = If B, then A

The converse of a conditional statement is not necessarily true. The truth table for a conditional statement is listed below (Smith et al., 2006). Proposition A is the antecedent and B is the consequent. The truth table (Table 2.1) indicates that the conditional statement is true if, and only if, A is false or B is true.

Table 2.1 Conditional statement A → B

If A, then B

A	B	A → B
T	T	T
F	T	T
T	F	F
F	F	T

Suppose a father states to his child that if she behaves, then he will give her candy, which is a conditional statement. There are two variables (behaves and give candy), each with a binary option (yes or no) for a total of four possibilities. Let us look at the four possibilities and their associated truth values. For the father to be truthful, which conditions allow for the giving of candy to the child (Table 2.2)?

Table 2.2 Assessing a conditional statement

Let **A = Child behaves; B = Father gives the child candy**

A	B	A → B
A = False (The child misbehaves)	B = True (Father gives child candy)	Father is truthful (T) because his promise did not address the child's misbehavior.
A = False (The child misbehaves)	B = False (Father does not give child candy)	Father is truthful (T) because his promise did not address the child's misbehavior.
A = True (The child behaves)	B = True (Father gives child candy)	Father is truthful (T) because he honored his promise.
A = True (The child behaves)	B = False (Father does not give child candy)	Father is not truthful (F) because he did not honor his promise.

The only promise that the father makes is that he will act in a certain way if his daughter behaves. However, the father never addressed what he would do if his daughter misbehaved. Thus, if the daughter misbehaves, the father's actions will be truthful whether or not he gives his daughter candy. The only time that a promise would be broken is if the child behaved and no candy was provided to the child. Because understanding truthful statements is essential for law enforcers, understanding conditional statements is important.

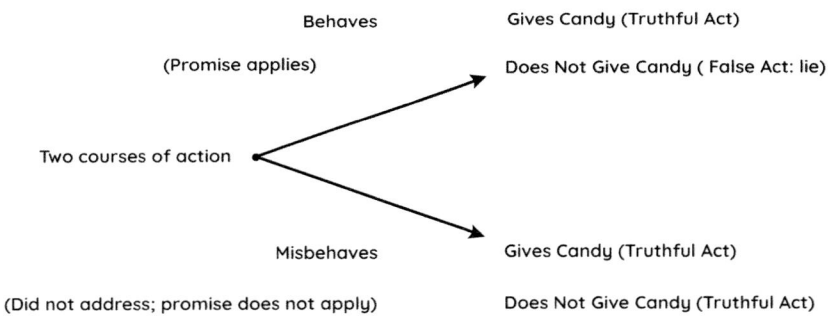

```
                    Behaves              Gives Candy (Truthful Act)
                (Promise applies)
                                         Does Not Give Candy (False Act: lie)

Two courses of action

                    Misbehaves           Gives Candy (Truthful Act)
        (Did not address; promise does not apply)
                                         Does Not Give Candy (Truthful Act)
```

Figure 2.1 Interpretation of conditional statement

Following are conditional statements along with converse statements. (The converse of a conditional statement is not necessarily true.)

If the person was aggressive, then the person was arrested.
If the person was arrested, then the person was aggressive.

If you interrogated the suspect, then you Mirandized the suspect.
If you Mirandized the suspect, then you interrogated the suspect.

If you arrested a person, then you seized the person.
If you seized the person, then you arrested the person.

If you are a student, then you must pay to eat at the cafeteria.
If you must pay to eat at the cafeteria, then you are a student.

Let us examine two of the conditional statements in more detail.

Following are two examples to demonstrate that the converse of a conditional statement is not necessarily true.

Conditional Statement 1: If you are arrested, then you have been seized. However, if you are seized does not necessarily mean that you have been arrested (you may have simply been detained).

Conditional Statement 2: If I am a student, then I must pay to eat at the school's cafeteria. However, if I must pay to eat at the school's cafeteria does not necessarily mean that I am a student (faculty must also pay to eat at the school's cafeteria).

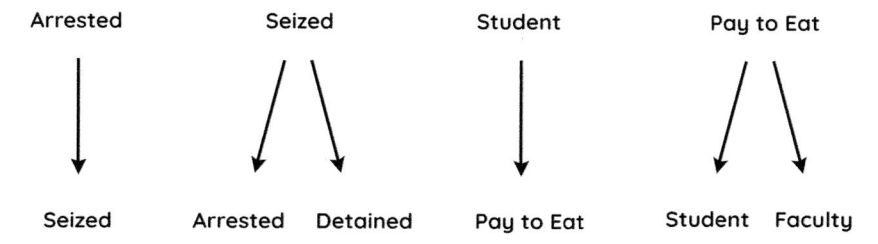

```
Arrested          Seized           Student          Pay to Eat
   |              /    \              |             /       \
   ↓             ↓      ↓             ↓            ↓         ↓
 Seized      Arrested  Detained    Pay to Eat   Student   Faculty
```

Conditional statements apply to the law. For example, a U.S. visa is an entry document issued by the U.S. government that allows a non-citizen to seek entry into the United States (LexisNexis, 2005). A non-American passport is issued by the person's native country and is a travel document that is used for identification and proof of citizenship.

Suppose federal law states that if a foreigner does not have a passport, then the foreigner cannot enter the United States. Thus, if the foreigner has properly entered the United States, then the foreigner must have had a passport (this is a true statement). However, it is not necessarily true that if the foreigner has a passport, then the foreigner will be allowed to enter the United States. The law states that not having a passport will prevent the person's entry into the United States, but the law does not address what will happen if the person does have a passport. Indeed, there are many reasons why a foreigner with a passport may be denied entry into the United States. Thus, understanding the converse of conditional statements is important in law enforcement.

Table 2.3 Interpretation of passport law

	Passport law: Cannot enter the United States without a passport	
	Have passport	Consequence
Foreign passport	Yes	May or may not be able to enter the United States
	No	May not enter the United States

SUBSETS

A set is a group of objects that follow a rule or that have something in common (Tan, 2015). A subset is a set that belongs to a larger set. Suppose a friend states to you on January 1 that you may borrow his car any day of the year, whenever you want. Then suppose you borrow the car on July 7 and get pulled over by the police. The police officer decides to charge you with driving another person's car without permission. The police officer asks you, "Did you have permission to drive the car specifically on July 7?" The police officer wants a *yes* or *no* answer. The correct answer is yes, because July 7 is a part of the year. In other words, the year includes July 7 and you had permission to drive the car on every day of the year.

Suppose John has $20. True or false, John has $10. The answer is true because $10 is a subset of $20. If John has $20, then John has $10.

Suppose John has $20. True or false, John has exactly $10. The answer is false because $20 is not exactly $10. For two numbers to be equal, they must be the same in quantity or value.

QUANTIFIERS

$(\exists x)P(x) \neq (\forall x)P(x)$

The above equation is very important. It states that an existential quantifier $[(\exists x)P(x)]$ is not the same as a universal quantifier $[(\forall x)P(x)]$. For an open sentence that uses an existential quantifier, the sentence is true if the truth set is nonempty (Smith et al., 2006). This means that an existential quantifier is true if the condition is true at least one time. However, for an open sentence that uses a universal quantifier, the sentence is true only if the truth set is the entire universe. This means that a universal quantifier is true only if the condition is always true.

Police officers need to understand the difference between an existential quantifier and a universal quantifier because quantifiers are present in everyday law enforcement. It is important for a police officer not to change the meaning of a statement by changing an existential-quantifier statement into a universal-quantifier statement and vice versa. For example, if a suspect states that he likes beer, this statement is true if the suspect likes at least one type of beer. Thus, for the suspect to be lying, an officer will have to prove that the suspect dislikes all types of beer. However, if the suspect states that he likes all beer, then the officer only needs to show that the suspect dislikes one type of beer for the suspect to be considered untruthful.

Suppose the signs on a roadway indicate that speed is controlled via RADAR. Then suppose you receive a speeding ticket, but the officer used a Visual Average Speed Computer And Recorder (VASCAR) to clock your speed. Your argument is that the ticket is invalid because the officer used VASCAR and the signs indicate that RADAR will be used. *What will you have to do in court to show that the signs are not truthful and what does the officer have to do to show that the signs are truthful?*

The signs are truthful if at least one officer in the area uses radar. In other words, if the situation exists, then the signs are truthful. Thus, the officer only has to show that one officer in the area uses radar. You, on the other hand, will have to show that every officer in the area does not use radar. In short, if no one uses radar, then the signs are not truthful. However, even if the radar signs are false, the radar signs do not necessarily exclude or prohibit the use of other types of speed control devices. For radar to be the only device permitted, the signs would need to say "Speed controlled by RADAR ONLY."

Let us look at a common riddle. Suppose the following information is true: I have three coins, which total 25 cents. However, one of them is not a nickel. What are the three coins? The correct answer to the riddle is two dimes and a nickel. Two of the coins are not nickels, which satisfies the requirement that one of the coins is not a nickel.

This riddle is determining whether you know the difference between an existential quantifier and a universal quantifier. The placement of the modifier is also important. Examine the three statements below, involving three coins, which are either nickels or dimes, and consider what they could mean.

Table 2.4 Using quantifiers to solve three-coin riddle

Statement	Possible coins using nickels and dimes
One of them is not a nickel.	1 dime and 2 nickels; 2 dimes and 1 nickel; 3 dimes
All of them are not nickels.	3 dimes
Not one of them is a nickel.	3 dimes

You can see how math and English are important in law enforcement. In the previous example, notice that the negation of an existential statement is logically equivalent to a universal statement (Not one is = All are not). In addition, the placement of the modifier changes an existential quantifier into a universal quantifier and vice versa (One is not ≠ Not one is).

NOT TRUE DOES NOT NECESSARILY MEAN FALSE

Although the law is based on yes-or-no decisions, people's responses may not always be restricted by yes-or-no answers. A binary variable (i.e., a dichotomous variable) is a categorical variable with two possible values. A trichotomous variable is a categorical variable with three possible values. When dealing with binary variables, not false equals true. Indeed, if there are only two options, if it is not false, then it must be true. Likewise, if it is not true, then it must be false. However, when dealing with variables that have three possible responses (positive, neutral, and negative), not false is not the same thing as true. In other words, not negative does not necessarily mean positive (i.e., it may be neutral).

For example, if a basketball team has played 10 games and is undefeated, what is the team's record? It is unknown because the team may have tied any number of the 10 games. If by some chance the team had tied all 10 games, a defense attorney may claim that the team had never lost, while the prosecutor may claim that the team had never won. Both statements are true, yet they seem to be contradictory. However, the two statements do not necessarily conflict with one another. This is how statistics can be misleading. Should consumers buy the same shoes used by the team? Either decision may be argued and supported with statistical data.

Police officers need to detect diversionary flares (i.e., red herrings) that are intended to lead the officer off track. The way to do this is to get the sought-after answers to their questions via active voice questions and answers. However, this may be problematic if the officer believes they are asking a binary variable question and the suspect provides a trichotomous variable response. For example, if an individual answers questions via double negatives or through misplaced modifiers, this may be a clue that the suspect is trying to deceive the officer without lying (i.e., deceive the officer in a truthful manner). If the suspect tells the truth, but the officer misunderstands the information and takes improper legal action, the officer may be sued. Thus, the officer must clarify the answers by asking direct questions that elicit active voice responses. For example, suppose an athlete played 10 games and the officer wants to know how many games the athlete won. See the questioning below. The officer should not stop questioning the athlete until they hear the specific words relating to *the number of games won*. It should be pointed out that in Table 2.5, *I have won ≠ I have not lost*.

Police officer: How many games did you play?
Athlete: I have played 10 games.
Police officer: How many games did you win?
Athlete: I am undefeated.
Police officer: That is not what I asked. How many games did you win?
Athlete: I have never lost.
Police officer: That is not what I asked. How many games did you win?
Athlete: I have won five games.
Police officer: Then, if you are undefeated, are you saying that your record is five wins, zero losses, and five ties?
Athlete: Yes.

Table 2.5 Interpretation of sport statement

	What the statement means		
	Won (+)	Tied (neutral)	Lost (−)
Suspect statement			
I have won.	X		
I have not lost.	X	X	
I have lost.			X
I have not won.		X	X

Another way to think about a trichotomous variable is by thinking of food. If a woman says she likes mustard, she will actively pursue it and request it on her food. If she does not like mustard, she may eat it if it is on the food, but she will not actively seek it. She will likely not want to pay for it because she does not desire it. If she dislikes mustard, she will actively resist eating it. If she hates the taste of mustard, she may decide not to eat any food with mustard on it because it may make her sick. It should be pointed out that in Table 2.6, *I do not like ≠ I dislike*.

Table 2.6 Interpretation of food statement using a trichotomous variable

	What the statement means		
	Like (+)	Neutral (0)	Negative (−)
	Person desires it and wants it on food; person will pay for it.	Person can take it or leave it; person will not go out of way to seek it and will not pay for it.	Person does not want it and will not eat the food if mustard is on it; may make the person sick.
Suspect statement			
I like mustard.	X		
I do not like mustard.		X	X
I dislike mustard.			X

ENTRAPMENT EXAMPLE

Entrapment occurs when a person is encouraged or tricked into committing a crime in order to secure the person's prosecution in court. A police officer will decide whether a situation such as entrapment occurred based on a binary decision. Either the person was encouraged, or they were not encouraged, to commit a crime. However, some people may argue that the failure to stop a person from committing a crime is entrapment. They would be arguing that a person must be discouraged from committing the crime. Their argument would be flawed because the law does not discuss the act of discouraging individuals from committing crimes.

Suppose the police hide in the dark and observe traffic laws. If you were charged with a traffic violation and argued entrapment in court, you would need to demonstrate that you were actively encouraged to commit the violation. Not discouraging someone from committing a violation is not the same as encouraging someone to commit the violation. Think about it: if not stopping a crime is entrapment, then all home invaders could argue that they were entrapped by the homeowners (i.e., the victims), who enticed them to commit the crime because the targets were easy.

Table 2.7 Assessing Entrapment

	What the statement means		
	Positive (+)	Neutral (0)	Negative (−)
	Person was encouraged to commit a crime in order to secure the person's prosecution in court.	Person was neither encouraged to commit a crime nor discouraged from committing a crime.	Person was discouraged from committing a crime.
Entrapment			
Police officer's argument (valid argument)	Entrapment	Not entrapment	Not entrapment
Violator's argument (flawed argument)	Entrapment	Entrapment	Not entrapment

NOT CLOUDY ALL DAY ≠ SUNNY ALL DAY

For another example, suppose you state that the sky was not cloudy all day. Not cloudy all day does not mean sunny all day. All day means 100% of the time. Therefore, not cloudy all day means that it was not cloudy 100% of the time. In other words, it could have been cloudy 0% to 99% of the time, which is a huge range. If you were writing a police report and it was important that the sky was sunny during the crime, stating that the sky was not cloudy all day may undermine your argument. See Table 2.8.

Table 2.8 Interpretation of weather statement

	Interpretation of statement		
Statement	Cloud-free all day (0% cloudy)	Cloudy 1% to 99% of the day	Cloudy all day (100% cloudy)
Not cloudy all day	X	X	
Sunny all day	X		

WITNESS STATEMENT FOR VEHICLE CRASH

Now suppose a police officer arrives at a crash scene. A car that was parked near a curb pulled out into traffic and was struck by another car headed in the same direction. If the police officer asks a witness to the crash what she saw, and if she states that she did not see the driver in the parked car look before he pulled out into traffic, the statement is basically valueless. See the following table.

Table 2.9 Interpretation of witness statement

	Interpretation of witness Statement		
Witness statement	I witnessed the driver not look. (valuable statement)	I saw nothing. (valueless statement)	I witnessed the driver look. (valuable statement)
I did not see the driver in the parked car look before they pulled out into traffic.		X	
I saw the driver in the parked car not look before they pulled out into traffic.	X		
I saw the driver in the parked car look before they pulled out into traffic.			X

Now, let us consider the valueless statement. Notice the first four words in the statement: "I did not see." This is problematic because the police officer wants to know what the witness *did* see. Indeed, the valueless witness statement never claimed that the driver of the parked car did not look before pulling out into traffic. The witness statement would be true even if the witness was not looking in the right direction at the time of the crash. It would be wrong to assume that the witness was looking in the right direction. To argue in court that the witness saw the driver of the parked car not look would be changing the truth value of the witness statement. In short, a police officer needs to be careful about modifiers and quantifiers in a witness statement. Get responses that provide direct and positive answers.

VALIDITY OF QUESTION

There is a difference between validity and reliability. Valid means true and accurate; reliable means consistent. However, it is possible to be consistently wrong. Hence, if something is reliable, that does not necessarily mean it is valid. However, if it is valid, then it is reliable.

Practical Application

Police officers must not assume that all individuals define words in the same way. For example, consider the following statements.

Unclear: Where were you during dinner?

Clear: Where were you during supper?

The first sentence that mentions dinner is problematic because dinner is not time dependent. Although supper is the last meal of the day, dinner is typically the largest meal of the day. Thus, for some people, dinner may not be the same as supper. In other words, if you were to question a suspect about their alibi during dinnertime, you may be thinking about 5:00 pm and the individual may be speaking about noon. If this happens, the question will not be valid. Therefore, seek precise times of day that do not have different meanings to different individuals.

CORRELATION ≠ CAUSATION

Correlation does not mean causation (Leedy & Ormrod, 2005). Just because two events are highly correlated, it does not necessarily mean that one event causes the other. A correlation is a statistical measure that expresses the extent to which two variables are linearly related. Because the two variables change together at a constant rate, predictions can be determined. Correlational studies are attractive because they are time and cost effective; they do not require a true experimental design. In addition, they can determine which variables should be examined further via a causal design. However, a limitation of a correlational study is that it cannot determine cause-and-effect relationships. A causal study, on the other hand, can determine cause-and-effect relationships with the use of a true experimental design. A true experimental design will help to eliminate spurious relationships, which are created by extraneous variables.

Practical Application

If you believe the sky gets dark at night because the sun is on the other side of the Earth, then you have made a flawed assumption (Verma, 2005). The flawed assumption is that the sun is the only light in the sky and that the lack of sunlight causes darkness. Getting dark at night and the sun being on the other side of the Earth are correlated, but it is not a causal relationship. There is another reason why it gets dark at night. Thus, an investigation based on wrong assumptions may produce poor results. Therefore, to reduce the possibility of error based on flawed assumptions, investigators should always seek valid information by asking properly worded questions.

QUANTITATIVE STUDIES VS. QUALITATIVE STUDIES

Quantitative investigations are scientific, objective, and effective at describing phenomena in terms of magnitude (Balian, 1988). Quantitative investigations use numeric values and statistics to identify patterns, to objectively quantify relationships between variables, and to make predictions. In addition, because larger sample sizes are used, data can be generalized to larger populations. However, numeric values are ineffective for describing the subjective interpretations of human emotions (Wakefield, 1995). Because individuals have unique lived experiences and their realities are based on their own perceptions, a single objective truth is unattainable; indeed, there are multiple realities when dealing with perceptions. Thus, quantitative investigations are ineffective for the reconstruction of meanings. In short, quantitative studies ask *how* variables are related but not *why* they are related. For example, a quantitative research question may ask, "Is there a relationship between ice cream sales and the murder rate?" By the way, there is a positive correlational relationship.

When investigating a topic that cannot be quantitatively predicted, such as human nature, qualitative investigations are most effective. Indeed, qualitative investigations are preferred for describing and interpreting experiences in context-specific settings because each person's reality is construed in their own mind; qualitative research attempts to reveal the meanings that participants have given to various phenomena (Adams, 1999; Ponterotto, 2005). This kind of information cannot be attained through quantitative analysis and requires probing the participants for greater detail through in-depth interviews using open-ended questions. However, qualitative studies cannot make numeric predictions. In short, qualitative studies ask *why* variables are related but not *how* they are related. For example, a qualitative research question may ask, "Why do you feel that ice cream sales are related to the murder rate?"

FALSIFICATION

Theories are an organized body of principles and concepts intended to explain specific phenomena (Leedy & Ormrod, 2005). A police officer can test a theory to determine whether it is a viable explanation of a phenomenon by developing and statistically verifying a conjecture concerning the relationship between the variables. However, because human knowledge is limited, hypotheses cannot actually be proved true (Shields, 2007). For example, we will never know for sure if any of the many extraneous variables have affected a particular relationship between known variables (there may be spurious relationships). However, extraneous variables do not affect the lack of relationships between variables. Therefore, during academic research it is more conservative to say there is no relationship between the independent and dependent variables and then attempt to show that the lack of relationship is false. This same idea is applied in the courtroom. Defendants are presumed innocent, and the prosecutor then attempts to show that the lack of relationship between the defendant and criminal act is false. This is called falsification. Instead of proving that a defendant is truly guilty of a crime, a prosecutor attempts to show, with a certain confidence level, that the defendant is not innocent of the crime. If there is a 95% confidence level that a defendant is not innocent, for example, then jurors may find the defendant guilty. In other words, if hypotheses are not proved false, then they are accepted as true at a certain confidence level. This implies that there is an acceptable level of wrongful conviction. Thus, innocent persons may sometimes be wrongfully convicted. Notice that this argument is not influenced by the penalty of the conviction, such as the death penalty. In other words, it is expected that innocent persons will sometimes be convicted and will be put to death. However, because a person must be judged guilty beyond a reasonable doubt and not innocent beyond a reasonable doubt, the American court system strives to keep the level of wrongful convictions to a minimum (see Figure 2.2).

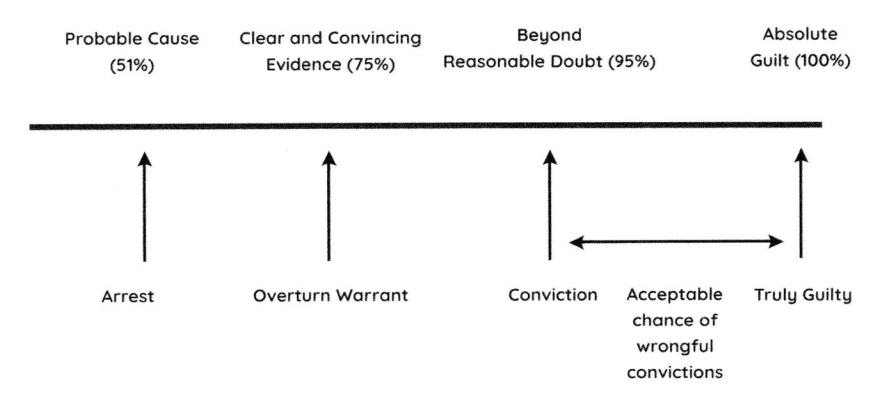

```
Probable Cause      Clear and Convincing      Beyond                      Absolute
    (51%)             Evidence (75%)       Reasonable Doubt (95%)       Guilt (100%)
```

```
   ↑                      ↑                      ↑           ↔        ↑
 Arrest             Overturn Warrant         Conviction   Acceptable   Truly Guilty
                                                           chance of
                                                           wrongful
                                                          convictions
```

Figure 2.2 Acceptable chance of wrongful conviction (not to scale)

Court rulings are similar to academic research studies in the sense that two types of errors can be made: Type I and Type II. A Type I error is believing that there is a relationship between the independent and dependent variables when there is no relationship. A Type II error is believing that there is no relationship between the variables when there actually is a relationship. In the courtroom, a Type I error is to convict an innocent person, while a Type II error is to set a guilty person free. A juror can ensure that one type of error is never made, but this will require either (1) always setting defendants free, or (2) always convicting defendants. On the one hand, if one juror wants to ensure that they never make the mistake of letting a guilty person go free, then that juror must always vote guilty. Their reasoning may be that the police do not arrest innocent persons. With this reasoning, there is no need for a trial because everyone arrested will be convicted by this type of juror. On the other hand, if another juror wants to ensure that they will never make the mistake of sending an innocent person to jail, then that juror must always vote not guilty. With this reasoning, there is no need for a trial because everyone arrested will be set free by this type of juror. Thus, in both cases there is no need for a trial. However, there are trials in the United States, which means that there is compromise and the chance of making mistakes. In the U.S. courts, as in academic research, making a Type II error is a mistake, but making a Type I error is a more serious mistake.

Negotiations are required among jury members. If a mistake is made, then the question is whether U.S. jurors want to err on the side of convicting innocent individuals or to err on the side of setting guilty individuals free. By design, the U.S. legal system is set up to err on the side of letting guilty persons go free. A conviction is based on guilt beyond reasonable doubt; an acquittal is not based on innocence beyond reasonable doubt.

ASSUMPTIONS

An assumption is something believed to be true without proof. Most decisions depend on assumptions, and we will never know whether all the assumptions are 100% accurate. Although we may be confident about a decision, we cannot know with absolute certainty that the decision is correct. However, understanding the assumptions that were relied upon in making a decision is important because the assumptions may change, which may impact an objective decision. In law enforcement, if the assumptions change, then police officers must be willing to modify their position.

Magic shows are successful because they challenge the audience's assumptions. The audience is led to believe that something is true when it is not true (Stoddard, 1954). The next time that you watch a magic trick, try to determine what assumptions you are making. For example, the magic box in Figure 2.3 indicates that the box should be over 5 inches deep. However, the ruler on the right that is placed inside the box seems to disappear. Both rulers are exactly the same, and both rulers are true and accurate.

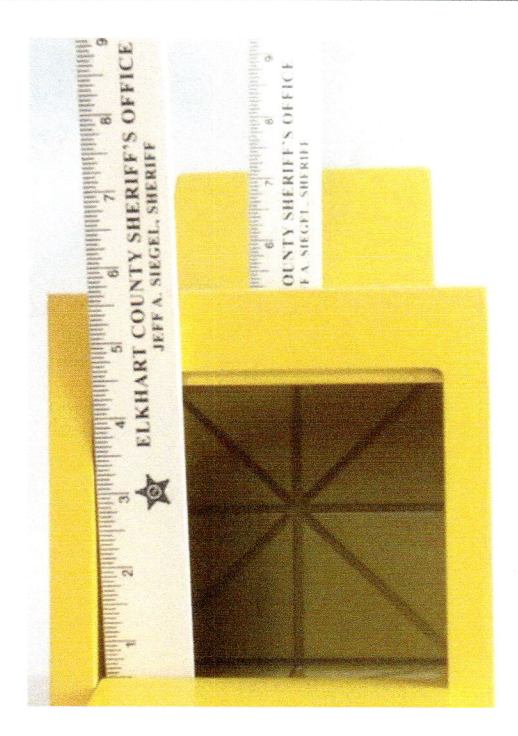

Figure 2.3 Magic box

Table 2.10 Magic Definitions (Evans & Keable-Elliot, 1989)

Deception Technique	Example
Illusion	Intellectually misleading the viewer via imagery
Sleight of hand	Skilled movements of the hand to mislead the viewer
Misdirection	Hides information
Distraction	Draws attention away from the information

Criminals may try to use misdirection and distraction to conceal information. Misdirection hides information while distractions draw attention away from information (Evans & Keable-Elliot, 1989). Distractions only work a few times before the information-seeker becomes aware of what is happening. Misdirection, on the other hand, is more effective because it exploits flawed assumptions made by the information seeker. Until the flawed assumptions are corrected, the information-seeker will continue to be fooled.

Table 2.11 Misdirection (Evans & Keable-Elliot, 1989)

Misdirection technique	Example
Fool the eyes	People believe what they think they have seen; perform a move realistically and people will believe it.
Attract attention	Draw attention to one hand while the other hand goes unnoticed; this can be extremely dangerous to a police officer in the field.
Psychological moment	Strike when a break is expected in the action because this is the time when the viewer is least attentive.
Cover-up	If something cannot be hidden, such as an incriminating noise, cover it up with a louder unrelated noise.
Repetition	If actions are continually repeated, the viewer will come to expect them and will fail to notice anything out of the ordinary.
Time lapse	People have a short memory and, if a lot of things are happening, people will forget to focus on something that may initially have caught their attention.

CONSEQUENCE OF WRONG ASSUMPTIONS

Let us return to the positive relationship between ice-cream sales and the murder rate. If the government tried to eliminate the murder rate by outlawing ice cream sales, the law would probably fail because of a flawed assumption. The law would fail because it would have been assumed that there was a causal relationship between the variables, but it is actually only a correlational relationship. Because heat impacts both ice cream sales and the murder rate, the elimination of ice cream sales would not solve the murder rate problem.

Assumptions are important because a law that is based on the wrong assumptions may be ineffective. For example, Megan's Law, which is the sex offender community notification process, relies on the assumptions of the labeling and deterrence theories. Authorities rely on labeling and deterrence in order to get sex predators to *rationally* decide not to commit additional sex crimes due to the high cost associated with committing the crime. First, people learn to identify other individuals by the way they are labeled (Vold et al., 2002). Thus, the labeling theory indicates that sex offenders will easily be recognized by local community members if sex offenders are publicly labeled and if their crimes are advertised. In regard to Megan's Law, it is assumed that all sex offenders are alike, and consequently they are all labeled as a homogenous group of sex predators (Corrigan, 2006). However, different types of sex offenders are motivated by different reasons, so a single program designed to modify their various behaviors will not work. Second, Megan's Law relies on the idea that most sex offenders are strangers to their victims and that offenders are mentally disturbed predators who attack without warning or reason. In other words, mentally disturbed predators are expected to make rational decisions (i.e., rationally decide that the cost of crime is too high). In fact, most sex crimes against children are committed by friends or family members and not by strangers. Thus, community notification efforts are ineffective because they are not in alignment with the problem. Because the research findings do not support the argument that community notification deters stigmatized sex offenders from committing repeat sex offenses, then perhaps programs that rely on theories that support the argument that sex offenders are mentally disturbed need to be investigated (Langevin et al., 2004; Zevitz, 2006). In other words, limited resources may be better spent on programs that address mental illness instead of labeling and rational choice. As stated earlier, the solution to the problem must be in alignment with the theory used to explain the crime.

WHY THEORY IS IMPORTANT

Theories help explain problems and provide possible solutions to the problems. However, all theories rely on assumptions and have limitations, which may impact the effectiveness of decisions based on those theories. An assumption is something believed to be true without proof, and a limitation is a restriction of the theory's application. Understanding criminal theories is important because police officers need to make best-practice decisions to solve current problems. Applying the wrong theory to solve the problem at hand will be less than optimal. As stated earlier, this is why Megan's Law is proving to be less than effective. According to research on Megan's Law, the deterrence theory and labeling theory are being used to solve a biological-based problem (Corrigan, 2006). Thus, the proposed solution is not in alignment with the theories used to explain the problem and, consequently, Megan's Law is not working effectively.

Theories also control the types of questions that should be asked in surveys during academic research. Data-collecting surveys need to ask questions that are in alignment with the theory used to describe the problem. Otherwise, the survey itself may not be valid. For example, if the biological theory is used to explain a problem, it does not make sense to ask questions about social learning experiences. For the instrument to be effective, it must collect biological-related information that is relevant to the study.

In short, every criminal theory has a limitation and there is always an exception to the rule when trying to explain human behavior. Law enforcers must understand the various limitations of information so that they can anticipate problems before and after they have made their best-practice decisions. Understanding information will help prevent police officers from being deceived. To minimize risk and vulnerability, the law enforcer must understand information. See Table 2.12 for various criminal theories and their limitations.

Table 2.12 Various criminal theories and their limitations (Akers & Seller, 2009; Fay, 1987; Sower, & Gist, 1994; Sower et al., 1957; Turvey & Petherick, 2009)

Theory	Description	Limitations
Rational choice theory/ deterrence theory	People freely choose their behaviors. Individuals evaluate the benefits versus costs ratio for each potential course of action. If the benefits are greater than the costs, then the decision to perform that act is favorable. Rational choice emphasizes the benefits and deterrence theory emphasizes the costs. Deterrence theory relies on three factors: celerity, severity, and certainty of punishment.	Overemphasizes importance of individual choice; social factors, such as poverty, are dismissed; does not adequately consider emotions; target hardening causes displacement of crime; deterrence factors may promote crime if all three factors (certain, severe, and swift punishment) are not effectively implemented simultaneously.
Routine activities theory	Crime occurs when three elements converge: motivated offenders, attractive targets, and the absence of capable guardians.	Level of motivation is not well defined; because attractive targets and the absence of capable guardians are emphasized more than the motivated offender, identifying and measuring the motivation of offenders is avoided.
Neoclassical theory	Being tough on crime and retribution will curtail future crime.	Does not explain why crime decreases in areas without tough-on-crime policies; crime rate reductions may be due to demographic changes in the population.
Biological theory	First, human beings are biological creatures who are born with certain hardware, such as a brain that controls thought and behavioral development. Because the brain uses a complex chemical-electrical process during the processing of information, any impairment in this process may interfere with the effective operation of the brain. Body shape, diet, hormones, environmental pollution, and chemical factors cause crime.	Denies role of free will; not everyone who is exposed to the same chemicals will behave in the same way. Why is there no specific diet to cure crime? Increased exposure to pollution and chemicals has not increased the crime rate; cannot explain crime in different parts of the country.
Age-graded theory	There is a positive relationship between social capital and pro-social behaviors; positive relations are developed over time and lead to pro-social behaviors and reduced crime.	Positive relationships are subjective; some positive relations may provide greater opportunity to commit crime; does not explain why social capital does not prevent everyone from committing crime.
Sociobiology theory	Behaviors are embedded in the process of natural selection and human survival; crime is the result of territorial struggles.	Fails to consider culture, social learning, and personal experiences; equates humans to animals.
Psychoanalytic perspective theory	Crime is the result of poorly developed superegos.	Lacks scientific support; elements of theory were not applied to a wide context for society as a whole.
Modeling theory	Individuals learn behaviors by observing others who are in the vicinity; individuals are rewarded for aggressive behaviors.	Lacks comprehensive explanatory power.
Behavior theory	The surrounding environment impacts behavior.	Dismisses cognition in human behavior; punishments may not deter martyrs; some groups believe punishments are status-enhancing.

(continued)

Table 2.12 Cont.

Theory	Description	Limitations
Self-control theory	Individuals have low self-esteem and seek immediate gratification; individuals have little patience and are frustrated easily, which lead to conflict.	Dismisses external factors during different stages of life; oversimplifies the causes of crime.
Ecological theory	Crime is associated with urban transition zones; crime is higher in low-income zones near city.	Too much credence to spatial location; does not explain crime outside of socially disorganized areas; correlation does not mean causation.
Strain theory	Crime is the result of frustration due to blocked opportunities, which prevent success.	The United States provides opportunities for all Americans to financially succeed; delinquent juveniles do not report being more stressed than law-abiding juveniles; claims that wealth is the single most important goal in life; does not adequately explain the lack of crime for women, who may be stressed as a result of continual discrimination.
Cultural conflict theory	Those individuals in power pass laws to protect their own interests.	Can be tautological and may lack explanatory power; may be racist because minorities (who have little power) are labeled as criminals.
Differential association theory	Criminal behaviors are learned through communications with intimate others; definitions favorable to crime exceed definitions unfavorable to crime; frequency, duration, intensity, and importance impact the learning of behavior.	Does not sufficiently explain crime; does not consider free choice; does not explain why those surrounded by crime do not commit crime; only accounts for the communication of criminal values, not the emergence of criminal values.
Social learning theory	Behaviors are reinforced over time according to the intensity, duration, and frequency of social learning experiences.	Deviant and conforming behaviors are simultaneously learned and modified through the same cognitive and behavioral mechanisms.
Containment theory	Crime results when internal (e.g., positive self-esteem) and external (e.g., social groups) control mechanisms fail to protect the individual, like an illness in which only some people who are exposed to social pressures commit crime.	May be feelings of the moment that have been conditioned through individual thought mechanisms.
Social bond theory	Weak bonds between an individual and the social group result in crime; crime is reduced if a person has a strong bond with society, has strong attachments, is committed, and is involved.	Individuals commit crime even when they know that it is wrong; social bonds do not appear strong enough to negate criminal behavior.
Social control theory	Delinquent behavior occurs when social constraints on antisocial behaviors are weakened; control ratio predicts criminal behavior; control ratio = amount of control personally experienced versus amount of control exercised over others; too much and too little self-control are equally dangerous.	Assumes that all individuals are automatically deviant unless socialized through control mechanisms; dismisses learned behavior and human motivations.

Table 2.12 Cont.

Theory	Description	Limitations
Labeling theory	If individuals are arrested, they may be labeled. This may result in a negative stigma being attached to them. This may consequently disrupt their personal relationships and may block their future legitimate economic opportunities, which may lead to more crime.	Does not explain the origin of crime; does not explain secret deviants.
Broken window theory	Broken windows, graffiti, litter, abandoned vehicles, homeless persons, and public drinking indicate disorder and a lack of caring. If people do not care about what happens in their neighborhood, then this attracts crime.	May be an artifact of police decision-making practices; may bear little objective relationship to the actual degree of crime in area; police may focus more efforts in poor areas, and this may mislead media. For example, if the department patrols a certain area with more officers, police will make more arrests in that area. Do more arrests mean safer streets or a more dangerous area?
Life course theory	Human lives are embedded in social relationships across the lifespan; the impact of various experiences depends on when they occur in life; each person makes choices, which impact their life-course; a life-course is shaped by historic times and places.	Many important life course determinants are experienced during childhood; this means adults may not be accountable for their crimes; individuals may select components of their life course and may influence their own trajectories.
Interactional theory	Crime is the result of a weakened bond between an individual and society combined with the learning of anti-social behaviors that are rewarded.	Does not fully appreciate childhood maltreatment as an important factor, which leads to crime.
Social conflict theory	People in power pass laws to protect their own interests. There is a struggle for power and laws are passed that penalize the disadvantaged.	Over-stresses social change and dismisses other well-developed theories of crime; fails to recognize that most people believe crime should be controlled.
Normative sponsorship theory	Indicates that people who have a convergence of interest may cooperate with one another in order to satisfy their needs.	Community members will only work together as long as the goals are within the normal limits of established standards.
Dual taxonomic theory	There are two types of offenders: life course persistent offenders (e.g., due to family dysfunction, poverty, neurophysiological deficits, and failure in school) and adolescence-limited offenders (e.g., due to structural disadvantages).	Most antisocial children do not become criminals; family and psychological dysfunction are not shown to be directly correlated to parent control or individual trajectories.
Postmodern criminology	Skeptical of science and scientific method; crime is an integral part of society.	Challenges other theories of crime prevention and control, but fails to offer feasible alternatives.
Convict criminology	Prisons are too big, hold too many people, and do not reduce crime; to control crime upon release from prison, prisons should focus more on treatment and less on security; based on the lived experiences of convicted felons and ex-inmates.	Most of the authors of the theory are white males, but not all are ex-convicts; authors are biased with agendas; non-convict feminists have been adding to the field, moving the theory from its roots.
Victim precipitation	Victim unconsciously exhibits behaviors or characteristics that instigate or encourage the attacker; explains multiple victimizations.	Relevant only to violent crime or to particular forms of unlawful violence; assumes that victims and offenders interact prior to crime occurring.

(continued)

Table 2.12 Cont.

Theory	Description	Limitations
Critical social theory	Practical social science that encourages individuals to become socially and politically active in order to change and improve their current social conditions; endorses the enlightenment, empowerment, and emancipation of the people. People are enlightened when they obtain empirical knowledge about their states of oppression and their potential capacity to improve their situations; people are empowered when they are galvanized to engage in a socially transformation action; people are emancipated when they know who they are, what they genuinely want, and when they have collective autonomy and power to determine the nature and course of their collective existence freely and rationally.	Must raise the people's awareness of their current oppression; must demonstrate the possibility of a qualitatively different future; must hold community members responsible for actively getting involved and creating their own liberation.
Situational crime prevention/ Crime prevention through environmental design	SCP is a crime-prevention strategy that attempts to eliminate or reduce the opportunities to commit specific crimes in specific locations by making crime riskier to attempt and more difficult to accomplish. Instead of relying upon law enforcers, the SCP strategy depends on public and private organizations. Furthermore, SCP does not focus on the persons committing the crimes nor the underlying causes of crime, such as unjust social and economic conditions, but instead focuses on the settings for crime.	Only protects a limited geographical area; crime may be displaced.
Developmental pathways	Anti-social behaviors are age-dependent; as children age, they develop verbal coping skills, which help them manage conflict.	Fails to explain free choice in human development.
Delinquent development theory	Persistence in crime is influenced by many risk factors, such as broken homes, low family income, and harsh discipline. Desistance in crime has four factors: deceleration, specialization, de-escalation, and reaching a ceiling (plateau).	Aging causing desistance is meaningless because the theory fails to explain why desistance occurs.
Peacemaking criminology	Crime can be managed, not by stopping crime, but by making peace; citizens and social control agencies need to work together through education, social policies, human rights, and community involvement.	Is utopian and fails to recognize the realities of law enforcement and crime control limitations.
Feminist criminology	Men have dominated the field of criminal justice and have developed theories and written laws for the explanation and control of crime based on their own limited perspectives.	Inadequately accounts for crimes committed by females. Currently, there is no single well-developed theory that explains female crime.

POLICE OFFICERS ARE COMMUNICATORS

Police officers need to be effective and efficient communicators. In law enforcement, police officers strive to be consistent writers rather than creative writers. Officers should write in active voice and clearly make their point in a concise manner. Remember, the goal of a police report is to accurately document and communicate the events that actually happened. This requires that police officers clearly communicate with the jurors. In addition, police officers must understand that jurors have emotions, and these emotions may come into play in the courtroom. Therefore, a police officer must not alienate the jurors by writing in terms that are unclear or that create a gradient between the jurors and the officer. In short, jurors may not be familiar with law enforcement jargon, and they may be negatively impacted by artificial or unnatural language.

Compare the following sentences:

Natural: I was notified by dispatch that there was a crash on US 20.

Unnatural: This unit was notified by dispatch that there was a 10-50 on US 20.

Natural: When I arrived at the scene, I parked my police car on the shoulder of the road.

Unnatural: When this unit went 10-23, this unit parked his commission on the berm.

Natural: I watched the home for an hour.

Unnatural: This unit engaged in visual surveillance of the residence for one hour.

Should a police report be written in first person or third person? It depends on the target audience. For a U.S. Customs and Border Protection officer, for example, writing a report in third person is valuable because it is directed to other officers who may read the report years later in different parts of the world. Reports written in third person provide objectivity, and they clearly identify the officers involved, which is important if there are a great many officers with the agency. However, writing a police report in third person may appear artificial and unnatural to jurors. Reports written in first person may be more personal to the jurors when the report is explained in court. After all, law enforcement is about relationships. A report written in first person allows an officer to take ownership of the report. In short, a police report written in third person is written for the police department while a police report written in first person is written for the jury.

Police report writing is not creative writing in the sense that all police reports should have a consistent format that should be followed. Do not use creative writing to deviate from the standard format. Prosecutors collect reports from many different police departments, such as city police, county police, state police, conservation officers, and excise police. Thus, prosecutors need to be able to evaluate reports quickly and easily. In other words, information needs to be straightforward and presented in a consistent manner. Many different police forms within a department may contain the same information, and consistency from form to form is important.

The state law book is a very valuable tool when enforcing state laws. It provides the elements of a crime, which are needed when an officer completes affidavits and charging forms. Although laws may contain multiple headings and subheadings, not all sections of the law need to be violated for the law to be enforced. It depends on the words "and" and "or" within the law. The word "and" means that all items must be satisfied. The word "or" means that only one of the items needs to be satisfied. For example, consider the fictious law below.

> Whoever borrows a book, newspaper, *and* magazine from any city library, college library, *or* museum shall return the book within 15 days after given written notice.

In this case, the word *and* means that all three items (i.e., book, newspaper, and magazine) must have been borrowed at the same time. If only a book was borrowed, then this law would not apply. In the same law, the word *or* means that only one of the locations (i.e., city library, college library, or museum) is necessary for the law to be enforced.

If Jane Doe simultaneously borrowed a book, a newspaper, a magazine, a movie, and a manuscript from a museum and failed to return them when required, the officer only needs to list the relevant parts of the law in the paperwork. The movie and manuscript are not part of the law and are irrelevant. The city library and college library do not need to be mentioned because they are irrelevant due to the "or" disjunction. For example, the elements of the law on the probable cause affidavit and charging form can be described as below.

> Jane Doe borrowed a book, newspaper, and magazine from the museum and failed to return the book within 15 days after given written notice.

Only relevant sections of the law should be recorded on the probable cause affidavit (i.e., sworn statement) and information (i.e., charging form). For example, the law involving driving while intoxicated may have a section A for the first offense and a section B for the second offense. If an officer is filing a charge for the first offense, then section B becomes irrelevant and should not be included on the probable cause affidavit and information.

As mentioned earlier, if an officer changes the wording of a statement (i.e., the law), this may change its meaning. Thus, a police officer should use the language of the law when enforcing it. In addition, when looking at the elements of the law, you will notice that a word is never used to define itself. For example, the crime of arson is not a person who engages in arson. In addition, arson is not setting fire to a building. If this were the case, firemen should be arrested during their training exercises. Therefore, the crime of arson must be looked up in the law book, which will provide the correct elements of the crime.

Let us apply this idea to the driving while intoxicated per se law. Suppose the law states that it is illegal for a person to drive a motor vehicle in this state with a blood-alcohol concentration of 0.08% or more. For the elements of the law, the prosecutor will expect to see something like the statement below.

> Jane Doe drove a motor vehicle in this state with a blood-alcohol concentration of 0.08% or more.

Notice that the elements of the crime as described above do not mention unsafe lane movement, excessive speed, bloodshot eyes, slurred speech, the walk and turn test results, the one leg stand test results, or any other clues that the driver may have exhibited during the investigation. The law is dictated by the state law book. If you were to add, for example, the traffic violations and field sobriety test results to the elements of the law, then you would be changing the law, which you do not have the authority to do. You would mention the traffic violations and field sobriety test results in other parts of the paperwork, but not as elements of the law.

HEARSAY INFORMATION

Police officers must report information accurately. Police officers must not change hearsay information into first-hand information. For example, if John told Mary that he was late for work because his car had broken down, and if Mary told the supervisor that John was late because his car had broken down, then Mary has changed the value of the information. Mary is testifying that John's car broke down. If John had lied to Mary and he was late because he had overslept, it is irrelevant as far as Mary's testimony is concerned. Mary should be held accountable for her statement. Mary stated that John's car broke down, which is a false statement. Mary should have stated that John told her that his car had broken down, which would be a true statement.

DESCRIPTIVE STATISTICS ≠ INFERENTIAL STATISTICS

It is very important to know the difference between descriptive statistics and inferential statistics. A person who does not know the difference can easily be fooled. Descriptive statistics, such as the mode, mean, median, range, variance, and standard deviation, describe the data set; they are used to provide various diagrams, such as scatter plots, boxplots, and histograms so trends and patterns can easily be recognized and parametric assumptions can be verified. For example, descriptive statistics provide information such as the skewness and kurtosis of the data, which will help determine whether there is sampling normality (Leedy & Ormrod, 2005). Notice that descriptive statistics do not provide p-values, do not assess relationships, and do not make predictions. Inferential statistics, on the other hand, do provide p-values to assess relationships, and inferential statistics are used to make predictions (i.e., inferences). The smaller the p-value, the stronger the evidence that the null hypothesis, which states that there is no relationship between the independent variable and the dependent variable, should be rejected. Using inferential statistics, data from samples can be generalized to a population.

In the social sciences, a p-value of less than 0.05 is typically considered statistically significant. When the p-value is less than 0.05, the null hypothesis will be rejected. In other words, when the p-value is less than 0.05, a researcher will state that a relationship exists between the independent variable and the dependent variable. However, because there is always the chance of error, a researcher should not say that a p-value less than 0.05 proves a relationship exists.

It is the writer's responsibility to provide enough information to convince the reader that the writer's claim is valid. If, for example, a student is truly using an inferential statistic, and if the student makes a statement about the relationship between two variables, then the student should be able to provide the name of the inferential statistic that was used to assess the relationship, along with the resulting p-value. If the student cannot do this, a problem exists, and the student's claim will be less than credible. In fact, you can expect that the reader will want to know information about: (1) the study's purpose, which should include the variables of interest; (2) the sample; (3) the method used to collect data; (4) the inferential statistic used to assess the data, along with its justification; (5) the findings, along with the p-value; and (6) the study's limitations.

EXAMPLE OF MISUSING DESCRIPTIVE STATISTICS

Using descriptive statistics, individuals can create a moral panic to justify their own agenda. The following is a short example to illustrate the point.

Answer the following question. Assuming that the populations of the two cities are the same, which city is safer at the end of 2020?

	Crime in 2019	Crime in 2020
City A:	100,000	200,000
City B:	100,000	100,000

Answer: There is insufficient information to answer the question.

City A is safer if more of the criminals have been arrested (the streets are safer because the criminals are in jail).

City B is safer if the number of crimes in City A has doubled.

City A = City B if the difference is based solely on a change in the paperwork. For example, suppose the chief of police has asked the board for more money. The chief warns the board that if more money is not provided, the crime rate will increase significantly. However, suppose the board denies the request for more money. The chief will then give the order for the officers to file two charges per event. For example, if someone gets into a fight, the officers will charge the offender with battery and disorderly conduct. Because the number of crimes is measured by the number of charges filed, the chief can effectively control the crime rate at will. In this case, the crime rate doubled over night. Once the board provides the requested money, the chief will then order the officers to file only one charge per event. Thus, the police chief can cut the crime rate by 50% overnight.

The problem with the example is that you cannot use descriptive statistics to assess the relationship between variables (e.g., the relationship between money and the crime rate). When assessing the relationship between variables, descriptive statistics are necessary but insufficient. Descriptive statistics will indicate which type of inferential statistic should be used. There are two types of inferential statistics: parametric and nonparametric.

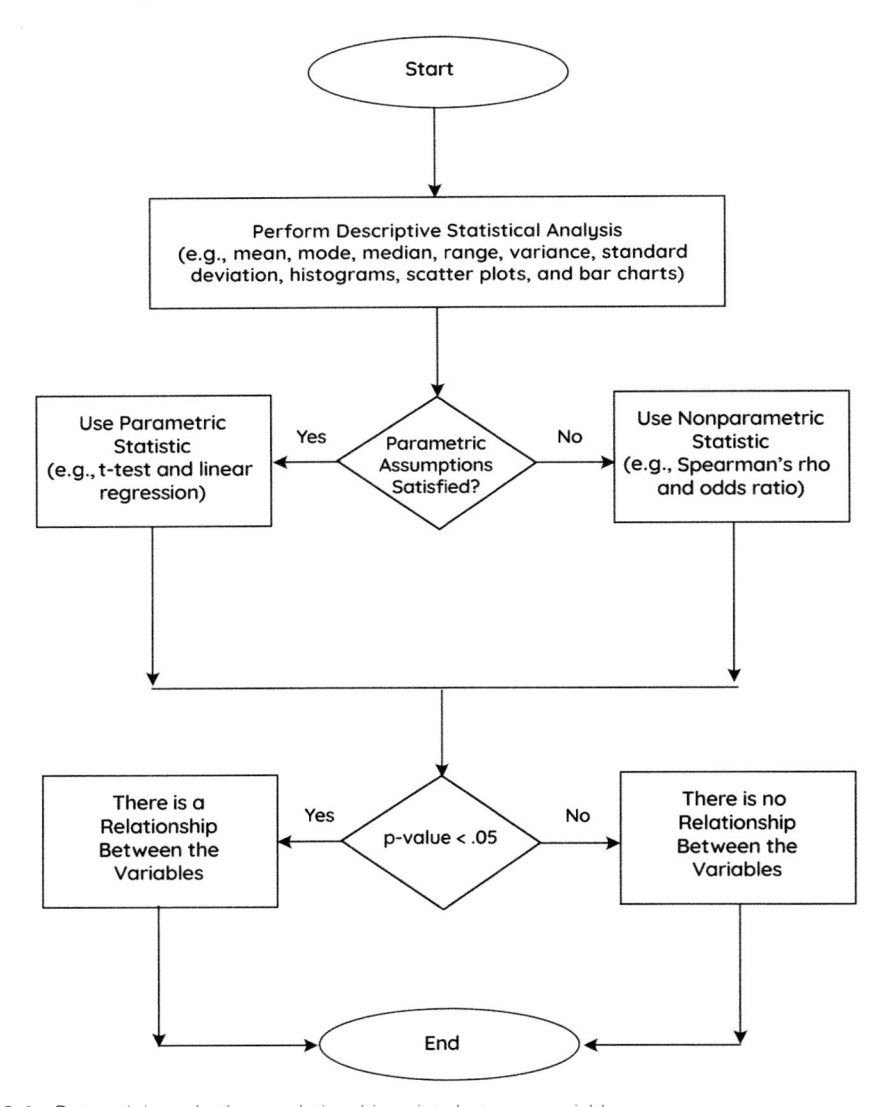

Figure 2.4 Determining whether a relationship exists between variables

Parametric statistics are based on assumptions about the distribution of the population from which the sample was taken, while this does not apply to nonparametric statistics. Thus, parametric statistics should be used whenever the parametric assumptions have been satisfied because they are more powerful and provide more detailed information than do nonparametric statistics (Norusis, 2008). Either way, it is necessary to use inferential statistics (parametric or nonparametric) to determine relationships between variables. There is no other way (see Figure 2.4).

Look at the following two graphs. Suppose someone said that there is a positive linear relationship between the number of crimes and the number of guns. As the number of guns go up, so do the number of crimes. Thus, a politician may argue that to reduce the number of crimes, we must reduce the number of guns. Is this a valid argument based solely on the data in the graphs?

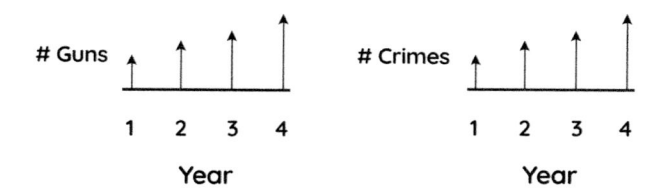

```
# Guns                          # Crimes
      ↑  ↑  ↑                         ↑  ↑  ↑
  1   2  3  4                     1   2  3  4
       Year                            Year
```

No, it is not a valid argument. It if were a simple linear regression, then the politician should be able to provide the linear equation that will make the prediction. Given the number of guns, the politician should be able to predict the number of crimes. Think of it this way, there are many different lines of prediction that could be selected to assess the relationship between the independent and dependent variables. However, the line-of-best-fit is the correct line to use because it will have the minimum amount of error. If the politician does not have the line-of-best-fit, then the politician is using emotions to make arguments, not intelligence. Thus, you can see that if the voters do not understand the difference between descriptive and inferential statistics, they can easily be misled.

HISTORY OF COMMUNICATION AND PERSUASION THEORIES

Communication theory as it relates to persuasion theory started around the fifth century BCE (Schiappa, 1991). During this time, Protagoras (490–421 BCE), a philosophical thinker in Athens, became the pioneer of the study of language; he invented a new way of thinking and speaking. Protagoras, the father of debate and a promoter of democracy, organized dialogue and invented the lecture between teachers and students. Each side presented an argument in an informal discussion group and then had to defend it. About the same time, in 466 BCE, the Sicilian government was overthrown. That government subsequently changed from tyranny to democracy. As a result, there was a high demand for people to be able to speak their minds in assemblies and to be able to testify for themselves in court. There were few lawyers at that time. Meeting this demand, Corax and Tisias, two Sicilians, developed the argument from probability. Thus, persuasive arguments had begun.

In 1776, the American Revolution took place. During this era, the U.S. Constitution was written, which affords each person charged with a crime the right to a trial by jury. As in the United Kingdom and several other countries, trials are based on an adversarial model, where debate is expected (Resnick & Knoll, 2007). Thus, the founding fathers have promoted communication theory and persuasive arguments within the courtroom. Indeed, persuasion has always been a part of the U.S. legal system.

MODES OF PERSUASION

Police departments, which have a history of corruption, need to persuade the public to trust them (Carter, 2002). In trying to convince individuals to change their opinions, there are three different modes of persuasion: ethos, pathos, and logos (Honeycutt, 2004). *Ethos* is based on credibility, which is the attitude or perception that the audience member has of the speaker—in other words, it is based on the speaker's reputation. *Pathos*, on the other hand, is based on emotional appeals. Referencing emotions in the heat of the moment, pathos is very effective and is commonly used, especially by salespeople. Indeed, a common technique used by salespeople is to make emotional appeals to potential customers and then to close the deal before the customers have time to cool down and reason things out. Finally, *logos*, which maintains personal beliefs for the longest, is based on critical thinking and reasoning. Although police officers may need to use all three modes of persuasion when they perform their duties, officers also need to understand when suspects are employing the techniques on them.

COMMUNICATION AND PERSUASION

To effectively serve the public, a police officer must be a credible witness in the courtroom during a jury trial. Part of the job of police officers is to arrest criminals, to complete the proper paperwork, and then to testify in the courtroom. If police officers make arrests, complete the paperwork, but fail to effectively testify in the courtroom, then those police officers have failed to do their jobs and have failed to adequately protect the public. Because police officers are public servants and are expected to protect society, it is vital that police officers learn how to effectively present their arguments in the courtroom and how to persuade jurors.

Democracy and truth rely upon open debate within the courtroom. However, jurors select their own truths based on their perceptions of the credibility of the information they receive. One way by which this credibility is determined is through the jurors' assessment of the way police officers communicate, both verbally and nonverbally. Thus, police officers must communicate well, be credible, and learn to persuade effectively.

COMMUNICATION THEORY

U.S. democratic principles rely upon truth being discovered via open debate within the courtroom (Bank, 2001). Hence, communication theory is very important in law enforcement, especially within the courtroom. How police officers communicate within the courtroom will influence the jurors' decisions. The basic assumptions of communication theory indicate that jurors will perceive information that will affect their attitudes, allowing them to make decisions that could be significant (Tucker et al., 1999). For example, based on the information they receive and perceive, the jurors may set a killer loose; on the other hand, they may convict an innocent person. Thus, police officers, who are the messengers of information, must use persuasion to affect the attitudes and opinions of the jurors in order to arrive at an appropriate verdict.

While most police officers receive very little training in courtroom testimony, the jurors believe otherwise (Smith & Hilderbrand, n.d.). Indeed, the jurors already have a misconception about how police officers should testify. Thus, police officers must learn how to communicate effectively in the courtroom so their testimonies will be credible. In short, credibility is directly related to persuasiveness.

Verbal Persuasion

A police officer's verbal communication in the courtroom will impact the officer's credibility as a witness. Verbal communication can be either written or spoken. If it is written, then it takes the form of police reports. If it is verbal, then it takes the form of oral testimony. Indeed, both types of verbal communication will impact the officer's credibility as a witness. In all cases, any courtroom testimony that is less than truthful is illegal and unacceptable. This being said, it is assumed that the police officers have made justifiable arrests in which they are testifying.

A police officer's written report will impact the officer's credibility as a witness. First, a police report must have good content, and the officer must be familiar with its content (Speaking Successfully, 2006). Because it is not uncommon for trials to take place years after the event, the police officer should review the report immediately prior to the court date. In other words, a police officer should never go onto the stand without knowing what is in their report. If the officer is unprepared, it will not take long for the jurors to find the officer less than credible. Furthermore, the police report must contain all pertinent information; if it is not written down in the report, then it cannot be used in court (Stewart, 2007). In other words, there is no pulling a rabbit out of a magic hat.

The report must be objective, complete, accurate, clear, and relevant. The report must be organized and structured (Navarro, 2004). To keep the jurors' attention and to help them understand the flow of events, the report must be presented like one complete television show (do not keep changing channels, which may frustrate the jurors). Furthermore, if there are grammatical mistakes within the report, the jurors may view the officer as incompetent. Jurors may perceive that the police officer is unprofessional, uncaring, and/or a fool. If the officer is judged to be unprofessional or uncaring, then the jurors may perceive that the report is incomplete and less than accurate (if it is not important to the police officer to do a good job, then it is not important to the juror to convict). If the jurors perceive the officer as a fool, then they may feel that they will be bigger fools if they follow a fool. In both cases, weaknesses in a police officer's written report will be exposed and this may impact the police officer's credibility as a witness (Lewis, 2001).

A police officer's oral testimony will impact the officer's credibility as a witness. Although testifying on the stand can be intimidating and cause anxiety, the police officer must be professional and objective (Klimon, 1985). When testifying, it is more important to make a lasting impression than to present a perfect testimony (Maxey & O'Connor, 2007). If the officer makes a mistake or cannot remember a particular event, then the officer must admit it; the officer must not weave a web of deceit (Lewis, 2001). First, lawyers set traps and look for contradictions. Indeed, lawyers are experts at finding deceit. Furthermore, once a police officer has been discovered to be untruthful, jurors will lose confidence in the officer, which may impact the jurors' final verdict.

When police officers are testifying, they should never start a sentence with, "To be honest ..." or "To tell the truth ..." because this will lead the jurors to believe that the rest of the testimony is untruthful. If an officer makes a mistake during a testimony, then the officer should admit it as soon as it is realized (Lewis, 2001; Navarro, 2004; Reynolds, 1990; Stewart, 2007). Jurors understand that not everyone is perfect and that mistakes will be made. If the police officer admits to a mistake right away, then the jurors may perceive the officer as an honest person who will correct a mistake instead of trying to cover it up. In addition, when testifying, the officers need to use plain language. If police officers use slang or police lingo, the jurors may become confused or they may feel that the officers are trying to insult them by making them feel dumb. For example, suppose an officer said, "District 21, 21-43, 10-23, 7 south, signal 6, 10-0." Although this message is quite clear to an Indiana state police officer on the toll road, the message is meaningless to the average civilian or juror (the message is notifying the South Bend Indiana state police post that the trooper has arrived on I-80 at mile post 125 eastbound in Lagrange County, is in the service area, is requesting immediate backup, and that someone has been killed).

Testifying in the courtroom is an art and the police officer is a performer (Navarro, 2004). A good way to think about this is to consider the courtroom as an amusement park and the jurors as customers who love thrills. If the police officer rehearses and memorizes the testimony, the jurors will perceive the testimony as a boring and lame merry-go-round (Boccaccini, 2002). Also, if an officer continually pauses during the testimony, jurors will perceive this as a frustrating Ferris wheel, which keeps stopping every few seconds to let passengers on (Navarro, 2004). However, by speaking moderately fast with variations in pitch and volume, the jurors will perceive this as a rollercoaster, something interesting and exciting. Moreover, the officers must project their voices with confidence, like a big-screen television. This will eliminate any perception of doubt in their voices (Defoe, 2007). In short, just as in written communications, weaknesses in a police officer's oral testimony will be exposed. Thus, police officers must practice testifying so that they are perceived as credible witnesses.

Nonverbal Persuasion

In addition to communicating verbally, police officers communicate in many nonverbal ways (Carter, 2002). Similar to verbal communication, nonverbal communication in the courtroom will impact the police officer's credibility as a witness. First, a police officer's appearance sets the stage for the perception of their credibility as a witness. Because jurors make judgments on the outward appearances of police officers, the officers must dress appropriately and professionally (Navarro, 2004; Stewart, 2007). The jurors may make the analogy that a dirty yard equals a dirty house. In other words, if the officers do not even care enough to take care of themselves, then they probably also do not care about their work. Second, a police officer's body language impacts their credibility as a witness. Indeed, police officers must have postures that show interest (Boccaccini, 2002; Lambert, 2008; Navarro, 2004). For instance, if a boy is interested in a girl and is about to kiss her, he will lean toward her and focus his eyes upon her. This is an example of a person showing interest, and it is obvious when it is observed. On the other hand, negative body language, such as fidgeting, crossing the arms, looking at one's watch, and looking at the ceiling, gives the impression that the officer has more important things to do than to be in court (Navarro, 2004; Tower, 2011). Thus, if the officers are perceived as being disinterested, the jurors will perceive the officers as less than sincere.

IMPLEMENTING COMMUNICATION THEORIES WITHIN THE COURTROOM

There are several landmark theories that involve communication theory and interpersonal persuasion (Reardon, 1981). These include: (1) balance theory; (2) attribution theory; (3) congruity principle theory; (4) cognitive dissonance theory; (5) learning theory; (6) functional theory; (7) inoculation theory; and (7) counter-attitudinal advocacy theory. These theories may be applied in the courtroom by the prosecutor to manipulate the jurors' attitudes toward the defendant.

Because, according to *balance theory*, people like consistency and resist change, they must be motivated to change their attitudes (Reardon, 1981). In this case, a prosecutor can achieve persuasion by distancing the criminal from the jurors. For example, if a person was being tried for public intoxication, the jurors may be strongly resistant to convicting the defendant. The jurors may feel that they have personally consumed too much alcohol at one time or another, and that this could be one of them on the stand. However, to overcome this perception, the prosecutor must differentiate the criminal from the jurors. First, by drawing a target with concentric circles around it, the prosecutor could start at the outer most ring and state that this level represents the subject's bloodshot eyes. Second, the prosecutor could move to the next circle inward, which represents a person with bloodshot eyes and slurred speech. Third, the prosecutor could move to the next circle inward, which represents bloodshot eyes, slurred speech, and staggering. Fourth, the prosecutor could move to the next circle inward, which represents all of the previous symptoms plus the subject urinating upon the roadway. This process will continue until the center of the target is reached. In this way, the jurors can clearly distance themselves from the defendant and this may help persuade them to change their attitudes (see Figure 2.5)

Using Totality of Circumstances to Change Jurors' Attitude

- Staggered
- Urinated on Roadway
- Slurred Speech
- Alco-sensor Test
- Bloodshot Eyes
- Nystagmus

Intoxicated - Beyond a Reasonable Doubt

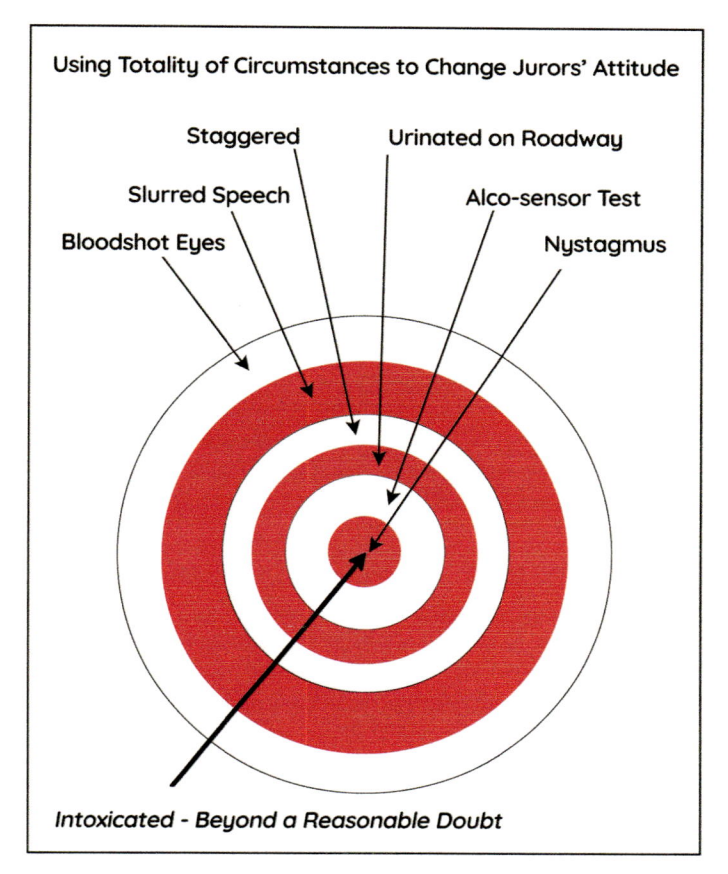

Figure 2.5 Using totality of circumstances to persuade jurors (balance theory)

Attribution theory states that people seek reasons to justify someone else's behavior; they try to find a motive when a person commits a crime (Reardon, 1981). If a person commits a benevolent act but it is perceived by someone else to be a criminal act, then the motive may be the determining factor for whether a crime has been committed. Because the jurors do not want to convict an innocent person of a crime, and because they do not want themselves to be wrongly convicted of a crime, they desire to find reasons for the actions. Thus, with no motive for committing a crime, the jurors will be less likely to convict a person. As part of the criminal investigation, it is the police officer's job to determine a motive. Once the motive is determined, it will be included as part of the written case report. It is then up to the police officer to explain the motive, in simple language, to the jurors so they will understand it.

Congruity principle theory states that jurors will try to align two or more incompatible concepts (Reardon, 1981). The prosecutor and police officer can take advantage of this by aligning the criminal activity to a negative concept held by the jurors. For example, if the local county is dry and the jurors disapprove of alcoholic beverages, then a person who is being tried for possession of marijuana can be associated with being an alcoholic. In this case, the prosecutor can say that marijuana, like alcohol, causes intoxication and leads to car crashes, which kill innocent people. Furthermore, marijuana is an addictive habit, just like alcohol.

Cognitive dissonance theory states that people behave in ways that reduce dissonance between two cognitive elements (Reardon, 1981). In this case, the prosecutor can suggest that if the defendant is set free, then one of the jurors may be the defendant's next victim. This stressful perception will persuade the jurors to convict the accused; they will associate the defendant's freedom to negative feelings. Furthermore, by persuading the jurors that justice and democracy demand fair payment for the defendant's actions, and that jail is the perfect place for the accused, the jurors will appropriately align the two cognitive elements.

Learning theory describes how people are conditioned to respond in particular ways (Reardon, 1981). The county prosecutor is an elected official and knows the local community issues. By associating the particular crime with something that the jurors, who are local community members, find upsetting, the prosecutor can direct their anger toward the accused. For example, if the jurors are upset about paying higher taxes, the prosecutor can illustrate how the accused could not care less about their money problems, as is evidenced by the commission of the criminal act, and how the accused is now mocking them by using their tax dollars to get away with it.

According to *functional theory*, people refuse to humble themselves and tend to perform only those actions that they find favorable (Reardon, 1981). In this case, the prosecutor can use the jurors' pride against them by linking the conviction of the accused with the jurors' intelligence. This can be achieved by indicating to the jurors that they are too smart to be fooled by a common criminal (who was not too smart to get caught). By stating that the jurors are community pillars, upon whom the local residents are relying to protect them, the jurors may find it beneficial to convict the accused.

Inoculation theory states that the best persuasion supports one side of an argument while at the same time refuting the other side of the argument (Reardon, 1981). In this case, the prosecutor can argue that in order to reduce crime, the accused needs to be locked up. On the other hand, if the jurors fail to convict, their safety will be at risk. Thus, the jurors can reduce crime and promote safety at the same time. In order to reinforce this argument and to make it as persuasive as possible, all submitted evidence related to the crime should be emphasized, including victim statements, witness statements, photographs, and laboratory reports (Tucker et al., 1999).

Finally, *counter-attitudinal advocacy theory* states that people will best construe their own beliefs and behaviors when rewards are not associated with their activities (Reardon, 1981). In this case, the prosecutor can remind the jurors that by serving on the jury, they are serving their community. Convicting the perpetrator is not for personal gain, but rather is their patriotic duty as U.S. citizens. Democracy and freedom depend upon law and order, for without law and order there can be no democracy.

In short, truth in the courtroom relies upon persuasion. Jurors determine their own truths based on the information they receive (Peterson, 1954). By using multiple persuasion theories, and by simultaneously employing as many of them as possible, prosecutors can align information in ways that will be well received by the jurors.

Table 2.13 Persuasion theories (Reardon, 1981)

Persuasion theory	Persuasion of jurors
Balance theory	Jurors like consistency and they resist change; jurors must be motivated to change their attitudes.
Attribution theory	Jurors seek reasons to justify someone else's behavior; jurors try to find a motive when a person commits a crime.
Congruity principle theory	Jurors will try to align two or more incompatible concepts.
Cognitive dissonance theory	Jurors will behave in ways that reduce dissonance between two cognitive elements.
Learning theory	Jurors are conditioned to respond in particular ways.
Functional theory	Jurors refuse to humble themselves and tend to perform only those actions that they find favorable.
Inoculation theory	Jurors will need to be persuaded by supporting one side of an argument and at the same time refuting the other side of the argument.
Counter-attitudinal advocacy theory	Jurors will best construe their own beliefs and behaviors when rewards are not associated with their activities.

KEYWORDS

Causational relationship
Conditional statement
Correlational relationship
Existential quantifier
Falsification
Modifier
Qualitative study
Quantitative study
Universal quantifier
Subset
Theory

CHAPTER PROBLEMS

1. Explain how misplaced modifiers can change the meaning of a sentence. Provide five examples of sentences written with misplaced modifiers along with their corresponding properly written sentences. Explain what each sentence means.
2. Describe what conditional statements and the converse of conditional statements mean. Provide five examples of conditional statements along with their converses. Explain the difference in meaning between each set of sentences.
3. Discuss the following statement:

    "If the road signs state that vehicle speed is radar controlled, then if you receive a speeding ticket, the officer must have used radar to determine your speed."

4. If a sports team has played 10 games and is undefeated, what is the team's record?
5. Discuss why it is important to understand the limitations of a theory.
6. Discuss the difference between a correlational relationship and a causational relationship.
7. Discuss the difference between a quantitative academic research study and a qualitative academic research study. Provide an example of each.
8. Discuss the difference between descriptive statistics and inferential statistics. Provide an example of each.
9. Describe the difference between ethos, pathos, and logos.
10. Describe how nonverbal persuasion applies to police officers in court. Provide five examples of bad nonverbal behavior that a police officer may exhibit in court.

REFERENCES

Adams, W. (1999). The interpretation of self and world: Empirical research, existential phenomenology, and transpersonal psychology. *Journal of Phenomenological Psychology, 30*(2), 39–65.

Akers, R., & Sellers, C. (2009). *Criminological theories: Introduction, evaluation, and application* (5th ed.). New York: Oxford University Press.

American Psychological Association. (2010). *Publication manual of the American Psychological Association* (6th ed.). Washington, DC: APA.

Balian, E.S. (1988). *How to design, analyze, and write doctoral or master's research* (2nd ed.). New York: University Press of America.

Bank, S. (2001). From mental health professional to expert witness: Testifying in court. *New Directions for Mental Health Services, 91*, 57–66.

Boccaccini, M. (2002). What do we really know about witness preparation? *Behavioral Sciences and the Law, 20*(1/2), 161–189.

Carter, D. (2002). *Issues in police–community relations: Taken from the police and the community* (7th ed.). Boston, MA: Pearson.

Corrigan, R. (2006). Making meaning of Megan's Law. *Law & Social Inquiry, 31*(2), 267–312.

Defoe, T. (2007). The truth is, you gave a lousy talk. *Chronicle of Higher Education, 54*(17), C1–C4.

Evans, C., & Keable-Elliott, I. (1989). *The Usborne complete book of magic*. Tulsa, OK: Usborne.

Fay, B. (1987). *Critical social science*. Ithaca, NY: Cornell University Press.

Honeycutt, L. (Ed.). (2004). *Aristotle's rhetoric*. http://rhetoric.eserver.org/aristotle/index.html

Klimon, E. (1985). "Do you swear to tell the truth?" *Nursing Economics, 3*(2), 98–102.

Lambert, D. (2008). *Body language 101: The ultimate guide to knowing when people are lying, how they are feeling, what they are thinking, and more*. New York: Skyhorse.

Langevin, R., Curnoe, S., Federoff, P., Bennett, R., Langevin, M., & Peever, C., et al. (2004). Lifetime sex offender recidivism: A 25-year follow-up study. *Canadian Journal of Criminology and Criminal Justice, 46*(5), 531–552.

Leedy, P., & Ormrod, J. (2005). *Practical research: Planning and design* (8th ed.). Upper Saddle River, NJ: Pearson Merrill Prentice Hall.

Lewis, D. (2001). *The police officer in the courtroom*. Springfield, IL: Charles C Thomas.

LexisNexis (2005). *Immigration law handbook*. Longwood, FL: Gould.

Maxey, C., & O'Connor, K. (2007). Dealing with blunders. *T+D, 61*(3), 78–79.

Navarro, J. (2004). Testifying in the theater of the courtroom. *FBI Law Enforcement Bulletin, 73*(9), 26–30.

Norusis, M.J. (2008). *SPSS 16.0 guide to data analysis*. Upper Saddle River, NJ: Prentice Hall.

Peterson, R. (1954). I swear to tell. *Saturday Evening Post, 227*(10), 88.

Ponterotto, J. (2005). Qualitative research in counseling psychology: A primer on research paradigms and philosophy of science. *Journal of Counseling, 52*(2), 126–136.

Reardon, K. (1981). *Persuasion: Theory and context*. Beverly Hills, CA: Sage.

Resnick, P. & Knoll, J. (2007). Being an effective psychiatric expert witness. *Psychiatric Times, 24*(6). www.psychiatrictimes.com/view/being-effective-psychiatric-expert-witness

Reynolds, D. (1990). *The truth, the whole truth and nothing but …* Springfield, IL: Charles C Thomas.

Schiappa, E. (1991). *Protagoras and logos*. Columbia, SC: University of South Carolina Press.

Shields, L. (2007). Falsification. *Pediatric Nursing, 19*(7), 37.

Smith, R., & Hilderbrand, D. (n.d.). *Courtroom testimony techniques: Success instead of survival*. www.ronsmithandassociates.com

Smith, S., Eggen, M., St. Andre, R. (2006). *A transition to advanced mathematics* (6th ed.). Belmont, CA: Thomson Brooks/Cole.

Sower, C., & Gist, G.T. (1994). *Formula for change: Using the urban experiment station methods and the normative sponsorship theory*. East Lansing, MI: Michigan State University Press.

Sower, C., Holland, J., Tiedke, K., & Freeman, W. (1957). *Community involvement: The webs of formal and informal ties that make for action*. Glencoe, IL: The Free Press.

Speaking Successfully (2006). *Techniques: Connecting Educations & Careers, 81*(8), 10–11.

Stewart, S. (2007). Effective courtroom performance by Indiana law enforcement. *Clark County Prosecuting Attorney for Police Officers*. www.clarkprosecutor.org/html/police/police2.htm

Stoddard, E. (1954). *The first book of magic*. New York: Franklin Watts.

Tan, S.T. (2015). *Finite mathematics: For the managerial, life, and social sciences*. Stamford, CT: Cengage.

Tower, W. (2009). Courtroom demeanor. *Kidjacked*. http://kidjacked.com/defense/courtroom_demeanor.asp

Tucker, J., Donovan, D., & Marlatt, G. (Eds.) (1999). *Changing additive behavior: Bridging clinical and public health strategies*. New York: Guilford Press.

Turvey, B.E., & Petherick, W. (2009). *Forensic victimology: Examining violent crime victims in investigative and legal contexts.* Burlington, MA: Academic Press.

Verma, S. (2005). *The little book of scientific principles, theories, & things.* New York: Sterling.

Vold, G., Bernard, T., & Snipes, J. (2002). *Theoretical criminology* (5th ed.). New York: Oxford University Press.

Wakefield, W. (1995). When an irresistible epistemology meets an immovable ontology. *Social Work Research, 19*(1), 9–11.

Zevitz, R.G. (2006). Sex offender community notification: Its role in recidivism and offender reintegration. *Criminal Justice Studies, 19*(2), 193–208.

CHAPTER 3

Intelligences, Reasoning, and Flowcharting

LEARNING OBJECTIVES

Understand how to apply multiple intelligences.
Make binary decisions.
Create procedures via flowcharts.
Follow directions via flowcharts.

INTRODUCTION

This chapter will discuss multiple intelligences, elements of reasoning, intellectual standards, totality of circumstances, and flowcharts. Critical thinking is the open-minded process of assessing all available evidence simultaneously and cumulatively to make best-practice decisions. This is an important statement because defense attorneys will attempt to undermine the reports of police officers by isolating and considering one fact at a time, independent of other facts. In addition, flowcharts—which are based on logic and reasoning—can be used to graphically represent the process of making best-practice decisions. Thus, an important objective for this chapter is to understand how to use flowcharts. Flowcharts utilize binary data to make decisions that control behaviors. Flowcharts can be used to describe laws, policies, or activities, and will provide consistent actions for a large number of individuals. If, when working through a flowchart, a person can behave in a manner that is unexpected, then the flowchart is not valid. Indeed, various data can be placed into flowcharts to test for desired outcomes.

MULTIPLE INTELLIGENCES

Howard Gardner, who is well known worldwide for his theory of multiple intelligences, argues that people learn through nine different intellectual capacities (Lunenburg & Lunenburg, 2014). These distinct intelligences are: (1) linguistic; (2) logical-mathematical; (3) bodily-kinesthetic; (4) musical; (5) spatial; (6) intrapersonal; (7) interpersonal; (8) natural; and (9) existential. This essentially means that different people learn best in different ways. Thus, some individuals may learn best via hands-on exercises, while other individuals may learn best via logical-mathematical reasoning. Police departments can utilize these multiple intelligences to communicate effectively with the public and to train police employees in the most productive way.

Linguistic learners learn best through language (Ryan & Cooper, 2007). Thus, police departments can utilize computers to teach concepts through writing and editing. For example, police departments can teach local residents to express abstract concepts by using poems and word processing documents.

Logical-mathematical learners learn best through tangible and inquiry-based projects (Ryan & Cooper, 2007). Police departments can use computer games to teach critical thinking skills and drill-and-practice programs to teach essential knowledge. In addition, database programs can be used to illustrate quantitative information.

Bodily-kinesthetic learners learn best through movement (Ryan & Cooper, 2007). Computers are effective tools for bodily-kinesthetic learners because, when using a computer, individuals must actively use the keyboard, joystick, mouse, disk burner, and other devices. In addition, police departments can use presentation software to simulate real-life scenarios. In these cases, the local residents and police officers can interact with the computer, make important decisions, and act out their choices.

Musical learners learn best by listening and by creating rhythms and patterns (Ryan & Cooper, 2007). Computers are effective tools for musical learners because many computer programs are readily available that play music. Furthermore, individuals can develop critical thinking skills by breaking down and rebuilding melodies.

Visual spatial learners learn best through visual experiences (Ryan & Cooper, 2007). Computers are effective tools for spatial learners because residents can learn through graphic programs, such as computer-aided designs and paint programs. These programs allow local residents to visualize concepts. Furthermore, local residents can express themselves with the use of presentation software.

Intrapersonal learners are self-motivated and learn best through meta-cognitive processes (Ryan & Cooper, 2007). Because individuals have different learning abilities, computers allow residents to learn at their own pace. Furthermore, computers can provide individuals with additional instruction and training in areas where they need help. Because intrapersonal learners are not sure how to share their ideas beyond their own community, residents can be encouraged to use blogs, which will allow them to express themselves in an ordered manner and to a larger community.

Interpersonal learners learn best through interactions with other people (Ryan & Cooper, 2007). For these individuals, computers encourage cooperative learning by allowing individuals to work together. For example, an interpersonal learner can use online survey tools to generate data for one another. This will enhance the creative and communication skills of the individuals.

Naturalist intelligence is the ability to understand living things and things of nature, such as soil (Lunenburg & Lunenburg, 2014). Individuals with naturalist intelligence may conduct academic research on environmental pollution and animal habitats and publish their results on the topics, which may be valuable to the Department of Natural Resources. However, some academics consider naturalistic intelligence more of an interest than a learning style.

Existential intelligence is the ability to look at the big picture about life and death and other aspects of the world (Lunenburg & Lunenburg, 2014). Individuals with existential intelligence may attempt to solve difficult problems that require deep thought. Existential intelligence, for example, will allow a person to explain to other individuals the value of a new police-community program and what makes the new program different. However, some academics have not fully accepted existential intelligence in the classroom.

Table 3.1 Multiple intelligences ("How are you," n.d.; Lunenburg & Lunenburg, 2014)

Type of intelligence	Individual learns via	Examples of application	Careers
Linguistic	Words that express meaning	Reading, writing, playing word games, and telling stories	Translator; magazine editor; poet; English instructor; author; attorney
Logical-mathematical	Applying reason and detecting suitable patterns to arrive at a solution	Creating truth tables and ciphering and decipher codes	Mathematician; banker; computer programmer; accountant
Bodily-kinesthetic	Hands-on exercises coordinating the mind with the body	Practicing firearm malfunction drills over and over	Professional athlete; coach; trainer; welder
Musical	Sounds, tones, pitch, rhythms, and timbre; singing, whistling, humming, and listening	Reciting poetry aloud and tapping a tambourine to accentuate the rhythm of the words	Band teacher; singer; musician; repair and sell instruments
Visual spatial	Designing, drawing, and visualizing	Visualizing and designing a flowchart; painting a picture; sculpting	Artist; photographer; astronomer; landscape architect; advertiser
Intrapersonal	Understanding your own thoughts and feelings	Creating journals, portfolios, and self-reflection papers; working alone	Real estate agent; entrepreneur; artist
Interpersonal	Working with others; understanding the feelings and needs of others	Working on group projects; brainstorming; connecting assignments to other cultures	Guidance counselor; healthcare provider; qualitative researcher
Naturalist	Understanding nature	Growing plants; caring for animals	Zookeeper; botanist; geologist; farmer; park ranger
Existential	Looking at the big picture about life and death and other aspects of the world	Explaining why people live and die	Philosopher; pastor; psychologist

Howard Gardner argues that intelligence is not the same as logic, reason, or knowledge (Brualdi, 1998). He maintains that intelligence is defined as the ability to solve problems or to make products that are valued by society. One way that intelligence was measured, the psychometric approach, was to use standardized tests to measure performance. As a way to indicate intellectual abilities, interrelationships among performances on intelligence tests were determined. This eventually led to classifications of intelligence, which were labeled secondary mental abilities. Within the secondary mental abilities are crystallized intelligence and fluid intelligence (Cavanaugh & Blanchard-Fields, 2006).

Crystallized intelligence is knowledge accumulated through formal education and general life experiences (Cavanaugh & Blanchard-Fields, 2006). Crystallized intelligence is primarily language-based accumulated knowledge in a particular culture, which provides a bank of knowledge to organize and solve familiar problems (Bell et al., 2002). Due to accumulated knowledge in a particular culture, a person with crystallized intelligence can effectively communicate, judge, and understand cultural conventions. Jobs that utilize crystallized intelligence involve writing, music, drama, accounting, and practicing law. Crystallized intelligence is learned and continues to increase until very late in life (Stoner, 1982).

Fluid intelligence is basically innate and independent of acquired knowledge and experience (Stoner, 1982). Fluid intelligence involves forming and recognizing concepts, recognizing relationships among patterns, and being adaptive and flexible, which means using deductive and inductive reasoning to solve novel problems. Occupations that utilize fluid intelligence include mathematicians and scientists (Bell et al., 2002). Fluid intelligence increases until neural maturation, and then it progressively declines through adulthood along with the neurophysiology status of the individual (Cavanaugh & Blanchard-Fields, 2006; Stoner, 1982).

As it relates to police officers, intelligence involves applying reasoning and intellectual standards to answer questions and solve problems. Reasoning is the action of thinking about something in a logical and sensible manner. Intellectual standards provide a means of checking the quality of reasoning. Intelligence also refers to information: better and more comprehensive information (i.e., intelligence) will help officers make better decisions. Furthermore, having clear and logical problem-solving procedures (e.g., flowcharts) in place will help to minimize errors.

Table 3.2 Elements of reasoning (Paul & Elder, 2009)

	Element of reasoning	Description
1	Purpose	The reason needs to be clear and justifiable.
2	Question	The subject or topic under investigation needs to be clearly expressed; the question must be unbiased and must address the complexity of the matter.
3	Information	The data must be valid, must address the complexity of the issue, and must be supported by credible references.
4	Concepts	The notions may need to be clarified; the concepts need to be justifiable.
5	Assumptions	The investigator needs to consider assumptions and limitations of the data; human intelligence is limited.
6	Inferences	Correlation does not equal causation; hypotheses cannot be proved true (need to demonstrate falsification); use deductive and inductive reasoning to make decisions based on confidence levels.
7	Point of view	Different cultures, lenses of truth, ethical systems, and department orientations may influence perceptions and interpretations of data.
8	Implications	The investigator needs to consider the consequences of an investigation; public safety is essential; actions that are punitive in nature are inappropriate.

Table 3.3 Intellectual standards (Paul & Elder, 2009)

#	Intellectual standard	Description
1	Clarity	A statement needs to be clear so it can be determined to be accurate and relevant; elaborate; provide examples.
2	Accuracy	A statement needs to be valid; a reliable statement may not necessarily be valid; seek confirmation.
3	Precision	Continuous data are more detailed than categorical data; be more exact.
4	Relevance	Statements need to be related to the subject of investigation; do not target diversionary flares (red herrings); contribute toward solution.
5	Depth	A statement should be more than superficial and should address the most significant factors and complex issues under investigation; use open-ended questions; consider multiple and interacting variables.
6	Breadth	All perspectives should be considered; multiple realities may exist; multiple truths may exist; consider various lenses of truth.
7	Logic	Multiple statements should support one another; deductive and inductive reasoning should be applied to confirm the data.
8	Completeness	Totality of circumstances will enhance the credibility of the evidence; all evidence should be evaluated simultaneously and cumulatively.
9	Significance	The statements need to keep focused on the most important problems; the central ideas need to be addressed.
10	Fairness	The evidence should be unadulterated; the evidence should be evaluated objectively and reported without bias.

CRITICAL THINKING AND POLICE ACTION

Critical thinking is the open-minded process of collecting, analyzing, and evaluating information in order to make best-practice decisions. For police officers, critical thinking is the process needed to establish probable cause. By applying intellectual standards to the elements of reasoning, police officers should be able to effectively articulate their actions in court based on totality of circumstances (Paul & Elder, 2009).

Intellectual Standards

↓ (applied to)

Elements of Reasoning

↓ (to develop)

Police Action (based on totality of circumstances)

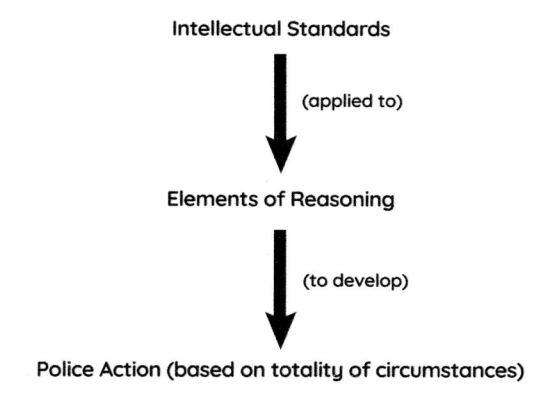

Figure 3.1 Determining proper police action

REASONING

In criminal justice, it is crucial to practice and enhance the skill of reasoning. If officers operate on flawed assumptions, it could hamper their ability to successfully perform their law enforcement duties. If police officers act on inaccurate assumptions, it could lead to wrongful arrests and wrongful releases.

Deductive reasoning involves drawing conclusions from statements that are accepted as true (Smith et al., 2006). A person employing deductive reasoning will start with a general principle and will apply the information to a specific case. In other words, deductive reasoning arrives at a specific conclusion based on generalizations. Applying this method, individuals may be eliminated as suspects because they do not fall within the initial general principle. Following is an example of deductive reasoning.

All shoplifters are arrested.

You were arrested.

Therefore, you are a shoplifter.

If the first premise is not true in and of itself, then the following conclusion will not hold. In this case, shoplifters are not the only violators who are arrested.

Inductive reasoning involves an individual making observations and then developing a generality based on those observations (Smith et al., 2006). In other words, the observer detects patterns and then makes predictions based on those patterns. However, if the observations are proved false just once, then the conclusions will be flawed. For example, if I have only seen pink flamingos every day for my entire life, I may come to predict that all flamingos will be pink. If I happen to see one white flamingo the next day, then my prediction has failed. Below is an example of inductive reasoning. Predict the next response.

•   • •   • • •   _____
‾   ‾‾   ‾‾‾

TOTALITY OF CIRCUMSTANCES

Police officers should consider a totality of circumstances—which is all available evidence—to make best-practice decisions. Decisions based on partial information make be less than optimal. Because police departments have limited resources, they may try to focus their efforts on the greatest risks.

It is easy to see how inductive reasoning can be used to reduce future criminal activity. Indeed, law enforcers have used inductive reasoning, as a part of the totality of the circumstances, to profile possible terrorists. For example, a traveler who comes from a geographical area that has been linked to terrorism, a traveler who has been caught in the past with a modified shipping manifest, the frequency with which the traveler crosses the U.S. border, the number of foreign entry stamps that are posted in the traveler's passport, the foreign countries that have been visited by the traveler, a consignor who has been linked to terrorism, and a consignee who has been linked to terrorism are all factors that may be used cumulatively to determine whether a traveler should be inspected.

Now, let us examine how the totality of circumstances can be applied in a court case that involves a driving while intoxicated charge. Suppose the driver of a vehicle had bloodshot eyes and slurred speech, exhibited poor driving behaviors, failed the field sobriety tests, failed the alco-sensor test, and admitted that they had consumed alcoholic beverages shortly before driving the vehicle. The defense attorney will attempt to get the jury to assess each factor individually because each factor, in and of itself, is not enough to show guilt beyond a reasonable doubt. For example, the defense attorney will ask the police officer in court whether a person who admits that they had been drinking is intoxicated. The police officer's answer will be "no." The defense attorney will then ask the police officer whether a person is intoxicated because they have bloodshot eyes. The police officer's answer will be "no." The defense attorney will then ask the police officer whether a person is intoxicated because they have slurred speech. The police officer's answer will be "no." The defense attorney will then ask the police officer whether a person is intoxicated because they were speeding. The police officer's answer will be "no." The defense attorney will then ask the police officer whether a person is intoxicated because they failed the one leg stand test. The police officer's answer will be "no." In the end, the police officer will have admitted that every piece of evidence that the driver provided does not indicate that the driver was intoxicated.

As previously discussed in the section on balance theory (Chapter 2), the prosecutor knows that the jury may be more likely to convict a defendant if the prosecutor can distinguish the defendant from the jurors in a meaningful way. In other words, the jurors may be afraid to convict the defendant for having bloodshot eyes because they themselves may sometimes have bloodshot eyes. Therefore, they may not convict a defendant unless the prosecutor can show that the suspect is different from them in a meaningful way.

To accomplish this task, the prosecutor will address the situation by considering the totality of the circumstances (i.e., by linking all of the clues together). Instead of considering each score in isolation, the cumulative score will be used. For example, if each clue adds 16% toward guilt, then confessing to drinking alcoholic beverages, having bloodshot eyes, having slurred speech, speeding at a high rate, failing field sobriety tests, and failing the alco-sensor test will all add up to a 96% confidence level toward guilt. This may be enough to separate the defendant from the jurors in a meaningful way and for the jury to find the driver guilty beyond a reasonable doubt.

TOTALITY OF CIRCUMSTANCES: POLICE OFFICER PERFORMANCE REVIEW

This section is important because, as stated earlier, the use of descriptive statistics (e.g., quotas) can be misleading. Remember, the use of an inferential statistic is required to determine the relationship between an independent variable and a dependent variable. When quotas are used to assess police officer performance, only descriptive statistics are being utilized. This may be important if the department wants to know where an officer falls on the bell curve for quotas. However, quotas are insufficient for answering academic research questions to reduce crime or to promote public satisfaction.

Traffic and arrest quotas are not used to solve social problems; they are used to account for an officer's time, like an assembly line worker. For a certain number of hours worked, the officer is expected to produce a certain level of output in the form of traffic tickets and criminal arrests. If the police department does not use some sort of inferential statistic to investigate the relationship between variables, then it will be difficult to make numeric predictions and to make things better. In other words, without inferential statistical analysis, a police department would be guessing about how variables are numerically related. A competent police department would never say, for example, that there is a relationship between handgun ownership and the number of crimes without the inferential statistical analysis to support such a claim.

Effective feedback for program enhancement should include the results from inferential statistical analysis. As they say in the field of electrical engineering, any system without feedback is unstable. Using quotas without inferential statistical analysis fails to provide the feedback that is necessary to effectively improve programs.

If a police department relies solely on ticket quotas and arrest quotas to assess officer performance, then this would a sign of laziness or incompetence. Police management may simply find it easier to gain public support by providing the public with numbers that they can understand. It is also possible that police management may not know the difference between descriptive and inferential statistics.

Using quotas is problematic. Using quotas to gauge police performance will only promote egoism, which is self-serving. When quotas are used, more arrests will result in a better performance review. Thus, police officers will be motivated to make more arrests. However, if the department's police officers were most effective and prevented all crime, then there would be zero arrests. Although zero arrests are optimal, zero arrests will result in a bad performance review.

Instead of using quotas to assess police officer performance, a police department can use a totality of circumstances and a rating scale to assess its employees. To better serve the public by using crime-preventative techniques, police administration must be willing to change its paradigm and implement a new method for assessing police officer performance (Whisenand, 2011). Police officer performance reviews must reflect activities related to serving the public. Therefore, qualities such as problem-solving, teamwork, initiative, judgment, commitment, and work quality must be assessed. See Table 3.4 for an example of a police officer performance review form, which assesses a variety of factors.

Table 3.4 Police officer public service performance review (Whisenand, 2011)

	1	3	5
Customer service (problem-solving)			
Participates in crime preventative programs (e.g., Neighborhood watch meetings)			
Positive community image			
Responsive to community requests			
Uses available community and government resources			
Follows up on services provided to residents			

(continued)

Table 3.4 Cont.

	1	3	5
Teamwork			
Displays behaviors that gain respect/trust from fellow officers			
Assists other officers			
Adequately resolves conflict			
Helps eliminate bias within the department			
Shares information that promotes police-community efforts			
Communications			
Radio			
Reports			
Courtroom			
Listens to citizens			
Ability to adjust to audience			
Initiative			
Identifies and addresses community concerns			
Requires minimal supervision			
Serves as a role model			
Strives to improve performance			
Follows up on work details on own initiative			
Productivity meets the expectations that were agreed upon			
Judgment			
Aware of consequences of work-related decisions			
Ability to make best-practice decisions with available information			
Sensitive to the needs of the community			
Use of discretion			
Willing to take reasonable risks			
Work quality			
Knows law			
Applies law			
Effectively uses available equipment			
Completed work product (e.g., reports, collecting evidence)			
Personal appearance			
Uniform			
Police Car			
Driving			

Table 3.4 Cont.

	1	3	5
Commitment			
Pride in department			
Loyalty to department			
Helps eliminate conflict in the community			
OVERALL SCORE			
REMARKS TO IMPROVE PERFORMANCE:			
INCREASE IN SALARY BASED ON PERFORMANCE SCORE:			
IF SCORE ≥ 50% THEN INCREASE IN SALARY = [% SCORE] X [.07] CURRENT SALARY			
IF SCORE < 50% THEN DECREASE IN SALARY = [% SCORE] X [.07] CURRENT SALARY			

REGULATIONS, PROCEDURES, AND LAWS

Regulations, procedures, and various laws exist that are designed to control police officer behaviors. Even the local prosecutor and court will have rules and procedures for police officers to follow. Failure to comply with these rules, procedures, and laws may result in lawsuits, injuries, or death. Regulations, procedures, and various laws can be represented via flowcharts.

FLOWCHARTS

A police commander must control the actions of the officers within the department. Standard operating procedures dictate what police officers shall do in the field. These guidelines help to ensure that all officers across the department will behave in the same manner when handling specific details. Being consistent and following the same set of rules will promote public confidence in the police. In addition, the procedures that officers follow during their investigations will be scrutinized in court, and failure to follow the proper procedures will be a disservice to the public. In short, law enforcement is very serious about following the rules. An officer who fails to follow proper procedures may experience serious negative consequences.

Flowcharts are used to analyze, design, document, and manage proper police procedures. Flowcharts are algorithms that provide instructions designed to perform specific tasks. They allow officers to make *yes* or *no* decisions by asking one question at a time. Only one comparison can be made at each decision point. If the flowchart does not completely control all possible actions as expected, based on the available information, then the flowchart is flawed. In other words, if officers follow the flowchart, make decisions based on the available information, and do something unexpected, then—as in academic research—the procedure would be deemed invalid. Having invalid procedures may be difficult to defend in the courtroom. Having invalid procedures may lead to bad decisions and to lawsuits.

A flowchart must control all possible actions based on the available information. Although there may be multiple entries into the various boxes in a flowchart, only one flowline will be allowed to leave each box, except for a decision box. A decision box is different because it requires a choice: it is based on a binary decision. Thus, there will always be two flowlines exiting a decision box. The output is either yes or no and the appropriate path will be followed. For a decision box, only one question can be asked at a time and only one decision can be made at a time.

Before we begin discussing flowcharts, three points need to be made. First, improperly designed flowcharts may lead to infinite loops. If this happens, the user of the flowchart will be stuck in an endless cycle that is inescapable. In this happens, an output may be continually repeated. If the numbers 7 and 8 are continually printed, for example, then the output may be displayed as the numbers below.

7, 8, 7, 8, 7, 8, 7, 8, $\overline{7, 8}$ or as   7, 8, 7, 8, 7, 8, 7, 8, (7, 8) …

It is the student's responsibility to clearly indicate the output.

With that being said, what is the difference between the following two printed outputs?

0   and   0, 0, 0, 0 …

The two printed responses are not the same. The first response indicates that the flowchart will print the number 0 only once. The second response indicates that the number 0 will be printed indefinitely. The second response is stuck in an endless loop. If an endless loop was not the purpose, then this will indicate that a mistake exists in the flowchart.

Second, in a flowchart, if the first step states that A = 1, then this will set A to a value of 1. If the second step states A = A + 1, this means to take the current value of A, which is one, add 1 to it, and make the result, which is 2, the new value of A at that location and time. In computer terms, the statement A = A + 1 will go to a memory location, grab A, add 1 to it, then place it back into the same memory location. In short, it updates the value of A.

Finally, never assume that you know the values of the initial data. If you do not set the initial values, then they can be anything. For example, if your first statement is A = A + 1, then the output will be unknown. Because we do not know the current value of A, adding 1 to it will not better define the result. In this case, the correct output will be unknown. Unknown is not the same as 0, and 0 is not the same as repeating zeros.

Output: <u>Unknown</u>

Important note: Unknown ≠ 0 ≠ 0,0,0…

FLOWCHARTING: FOLLOWING DIRECTIONS

The following are some definitions of flowchart symbols.

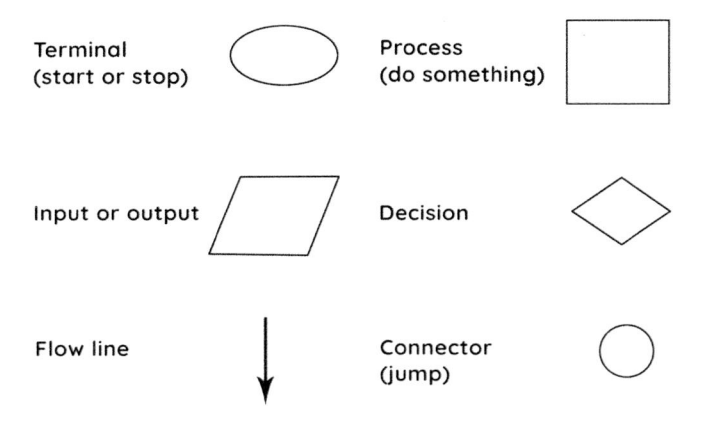

Terminal (start or stop) — ellipse

Process (do something) — rectangle

Input or output — parallelogram

Decision — diamond

Flow line — arrow

Connector (jump) — circle

The terminal symbol indicates the starting point and ending point of the algorithm ("Flow Chart," 2002). The process symbol is used to represent arithmetic functions and data movement instructions. The input/output symbol is used to denote any function of an input/output device. For example, data may be collected from a disk (input) or delivered to a printer (output). The decision symbol is used to indicate a point where a decision is made and there are two consequences. Flow lines simply provide the path of travel for the flow of operation. The on-page connector allows a point to jump elsewhere. This is useful if the flow lines become congested and start to crisscross in a particular area.

Below are two examples of flowcharts. Describe the numbers that are printed in each of the algorithms below. Work through the flowcharts and see whether you can come up with the answers provided. Notice that changing the print box's location changed the output.

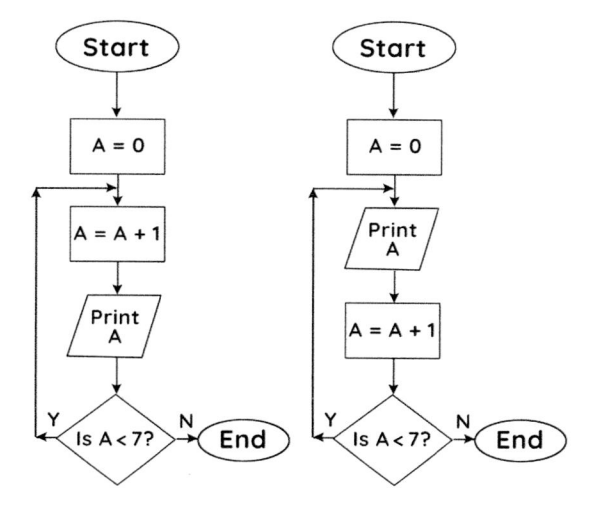

Output: 1,2,3,4,5,6,7   Output: 0,1,2,3,4,5,6

Below are two examples of flowcharts. Work through the flowcharts and see if you can come up with the answers provided. Notice that both outputs started as unknown, but the two outputs are not the same.

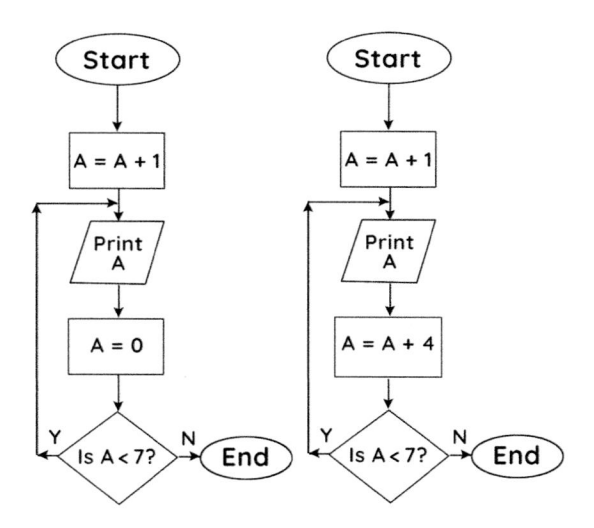

Output: Unknown,0,0,0,$\bar{0}$ Output: Unknown

Below are two examples of flowcharts. Work through the flowcharts and see if you can come up with the answers provided.

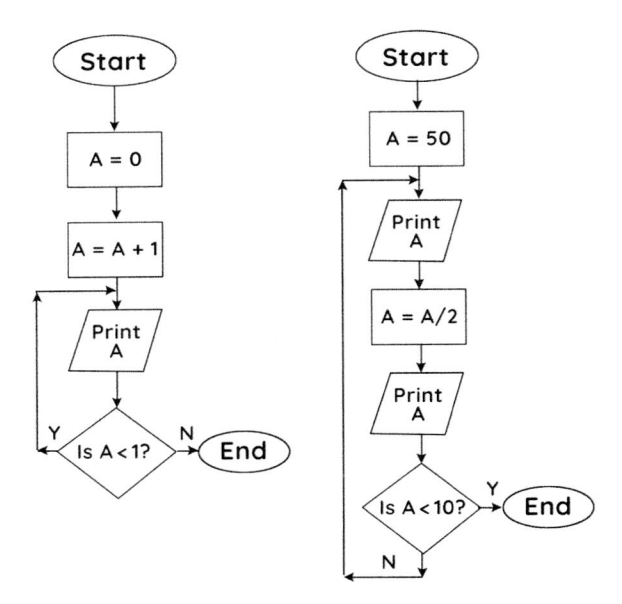

Output: 1   Output: 50,25,25,12.5,12.5,6.25

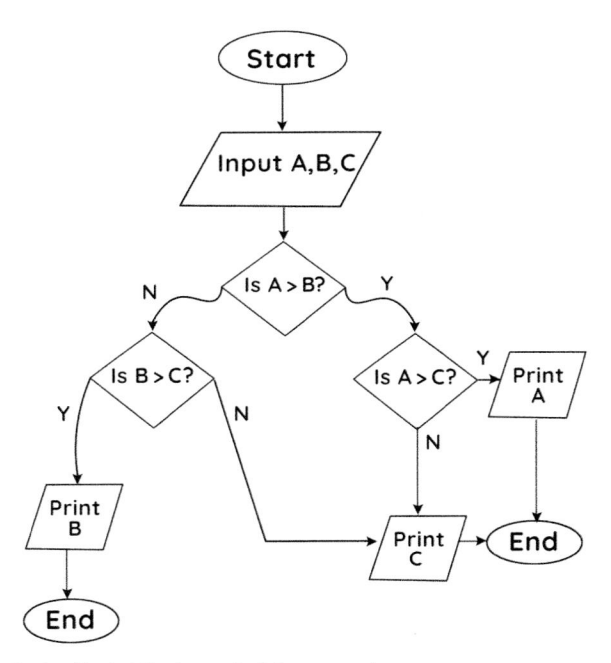

Figure 3.2 Algorithm that will print the largest of three numbers

For the algorithm that will print the largest of three numbers, you can test the algorithm to confirm the results. Given the various combinations of the three input values, work through the flowchart and determine which number will be printed. Notice that each letter will be printed an equal number of times.

A	B	C	Letter printed	Number printed
1	2	3	C	3

A	B	C	Letter printed	Number printed
1	3	2	B	3
2	1	3	C	3
3	1	2	A	3
2	3	1	B	3
3	2	1	A	3

DRIVING UNDER THE INFLUENCE (DUI) INVESTIGATION

The procedures for a Driving Under the Influence (DUI) investigation are described over the next several pages. The police will stop every fifth car for four hours. The officers stopping the vehicles are on the Initial Contact Team (ICT). The officers conducting the Field Sobriety Tests and the DataMaster tests, when required, are on the FST Team (FSTT).

Definitions: V = V+ 1 means to take the current value of V, add 1 to it, then make the result the new value of V. BAC = Breath Alcohol Concentration. Alco-sensor test = unofficial breath-alcohol concentration test collected from a handheld device. DataMaster test = official breath-alcohol concentration test collected from a certified machine.

Rules

Initial Contact Team (ICT)

1. The project will run for four hours. The ICT will monitor traffic, will stop every fifth vehicle, and will administer an alco-sensor test to the driver.
2. If the alco-sensor test at initial contact is less than 0.05% BAC, then the driver will be released.
3. If the alco-sensor test at initial contact is at least 0.05% BAC, then the driver will be passed off to the Field Sobriety Test Team, who will continue the investigation via field sobriety tests (FSTs). The ICT will return to traffic.

Field Sobriety Test Team (FSTT)

4. If the alco-sensor test at initial contact is at least .05% BAC but less than .08% BAC, and if the driver passes the FSTs, then the FSTT will release the driver.
5. If the alco-senor test at initial contact is at least .05% BAC but less than .08% BAC, and if the driver fails the FSTs, then the driver will be given a DataMaster test.
6. If the alco-sensor test at initial contact is at least 0.08% BAC, then the driver will automatically be given a DataMaster test after the FSTs.
7. If the DataMaster test is less than .05% BAC, then the FSTT will release the driver.
8. If the DataMaster test is at least .05% BAC but less than .08% BAC, and if the driver passes the FSTs, then the FSTT will release the driver.
9. If the DataMaster test is at least .05% BAC but less than .08% BAC, and if the driver fails the FSTs, then the FSTT will charge the driver with public intoxication.
10. If the DataMaster test is at least .08% BAC, then the FSTT will charge the driver with DUI misdemeanor for the driver's first offense and DUI felony for the driver's second offense.

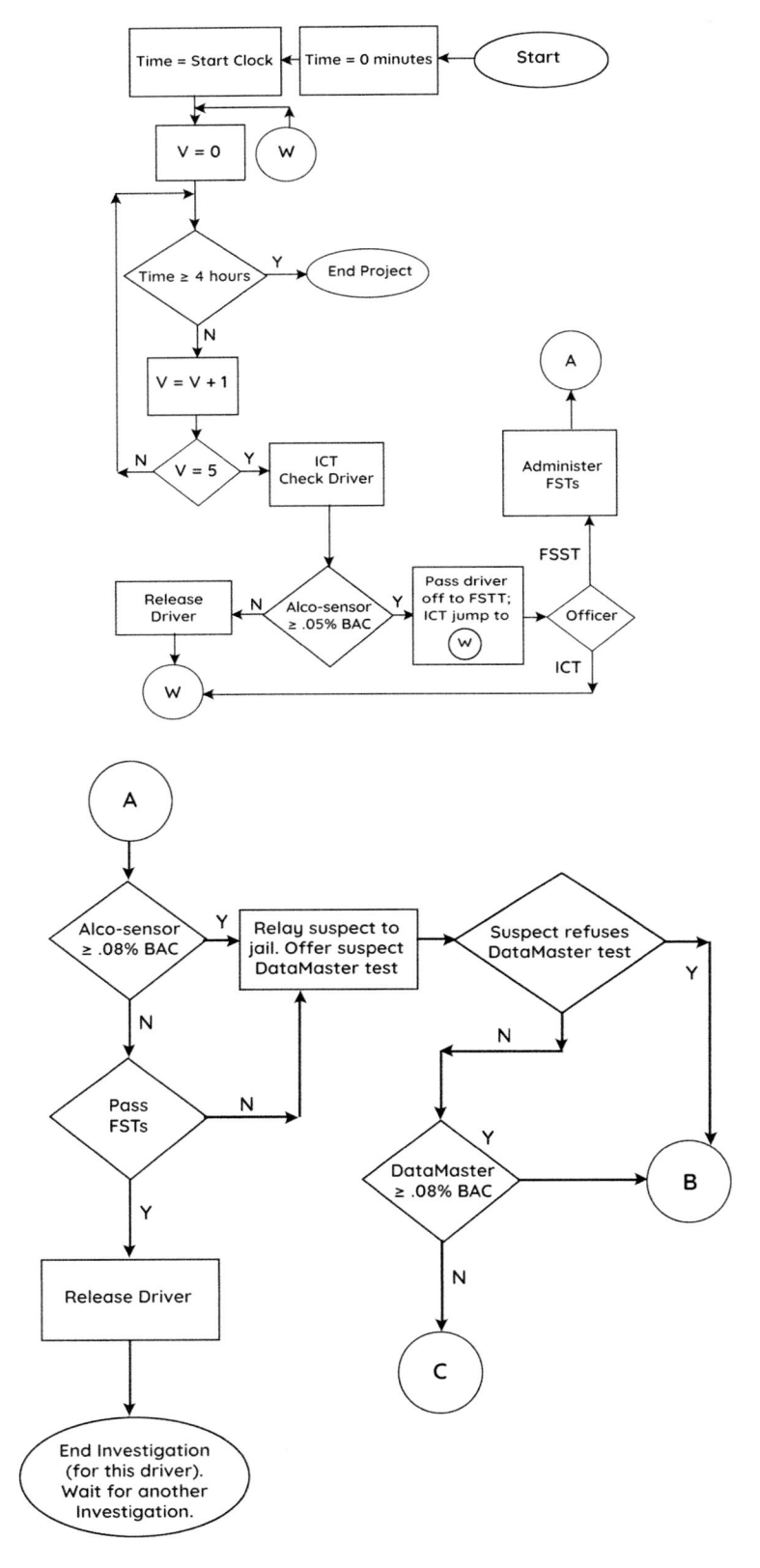

Figure 3.3 Driving under the influence (DUI) investigation

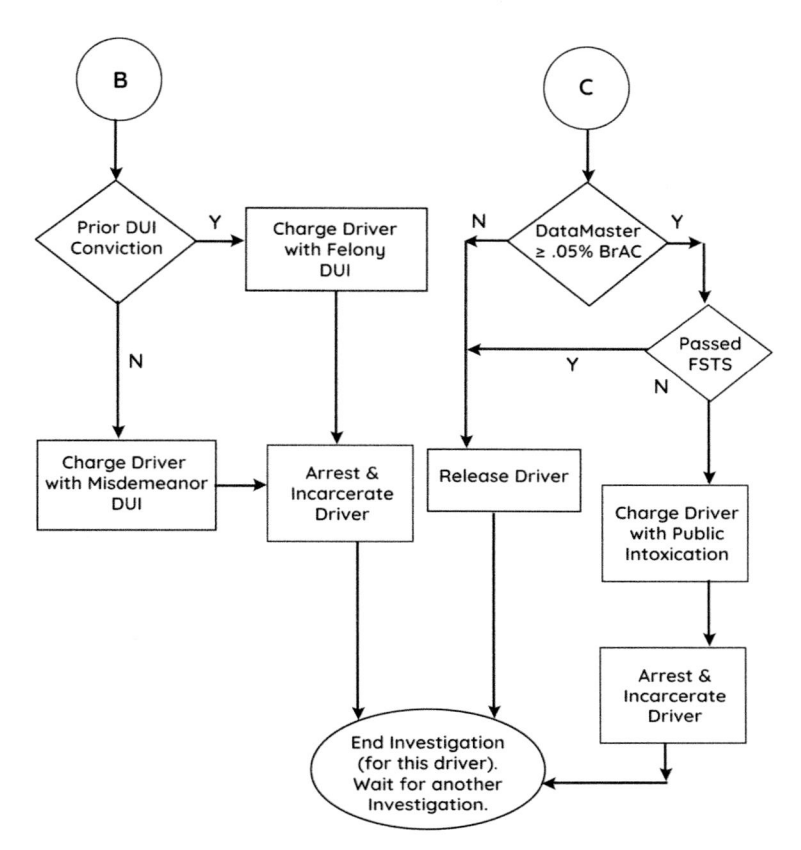

Figure 3.3 (continued)

Below is a flowchart that explains the stop and frisk procedure. For the following flowchart, probable cause means it is more likely than not that a crime has occurred (51% confident for practical purposes).

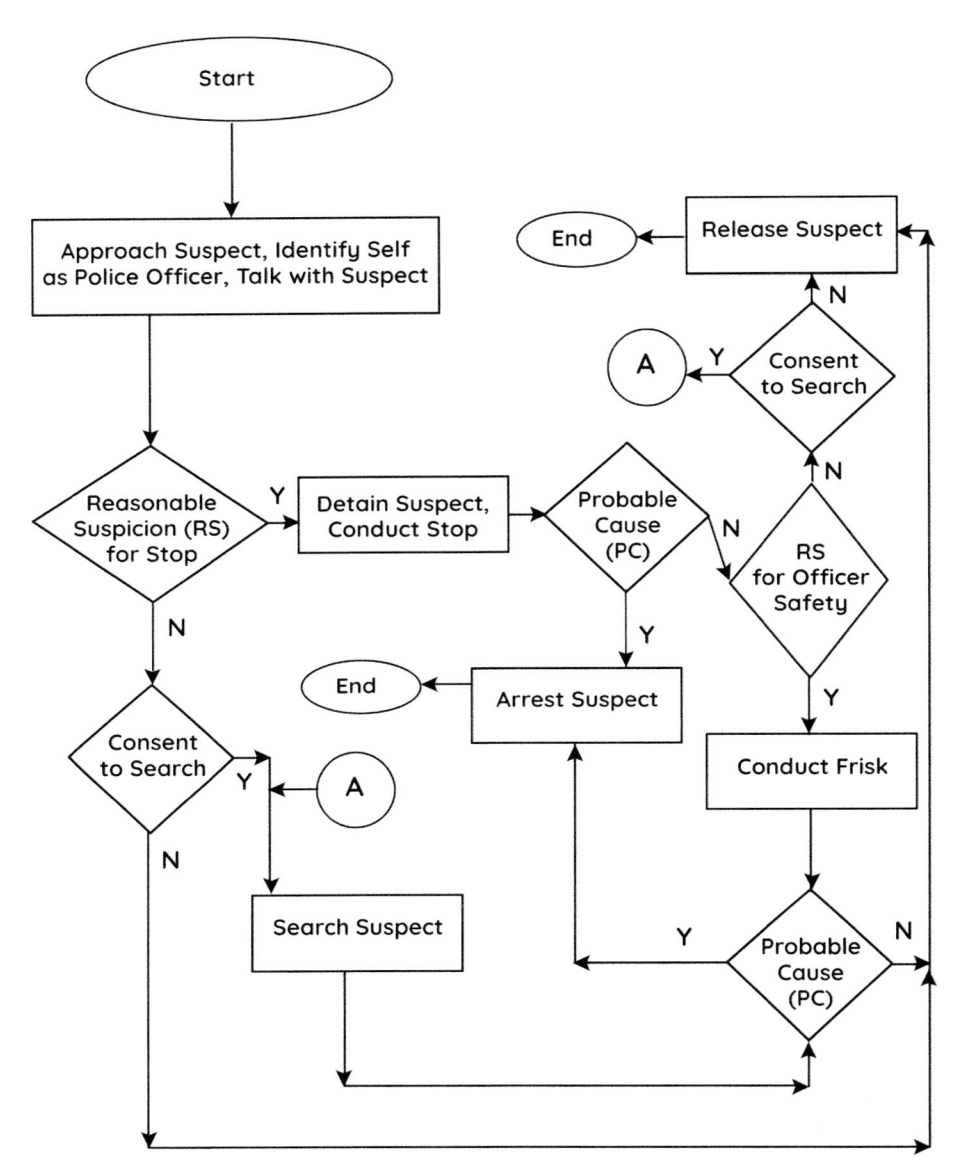

Figure 3.4 Stop and frisk flowchart

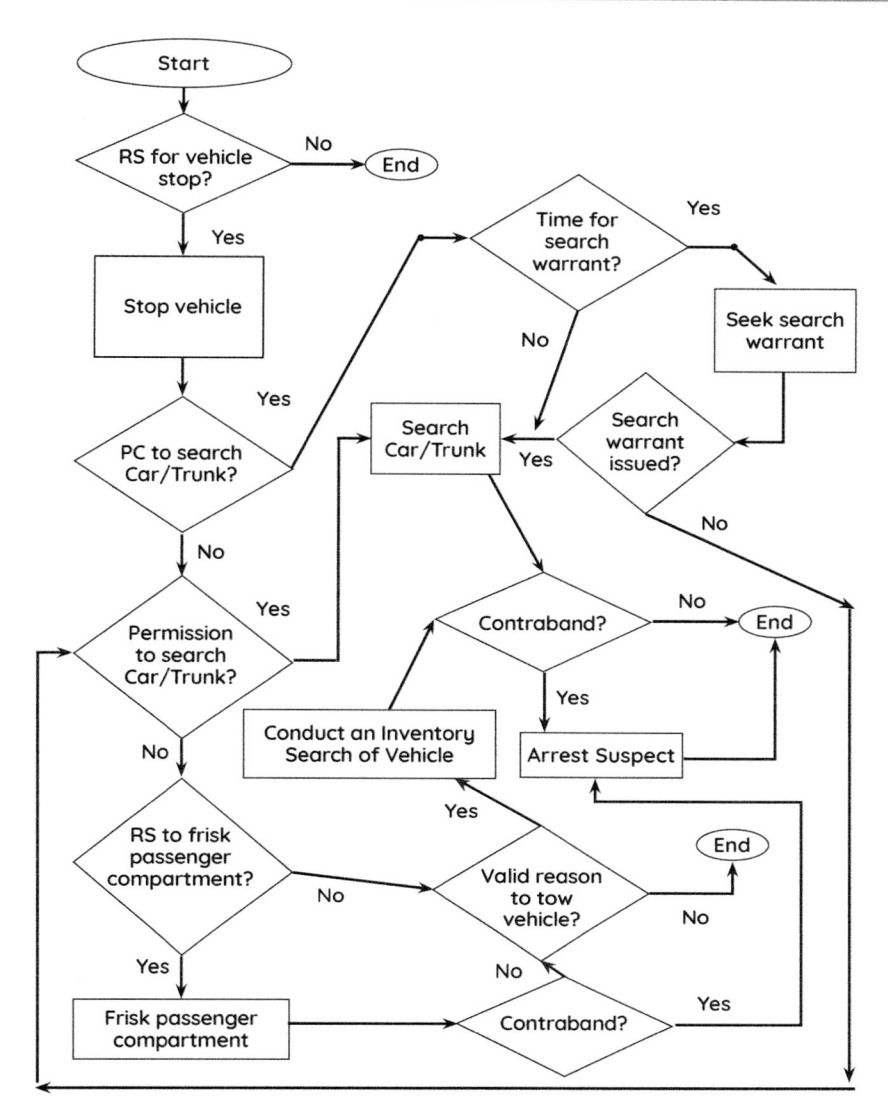

Figure 3.5 Vehicle search

Law – Sexual Violation Law Between a Man and a Woman

Draw a flowchart for the law below.

Law = Sexual Violation Law Between a Man and a Woman

1. It is a crime of seduction for a male who is at least 16 years of age to use deception and promise of marriage and to engage in carnal intercourse with a female.
2. Furthermore, it is a crime for a person who is at least 16 years of age to have habitual carnal intercourse with the opposite sex or to live with the opposite sex and to have carnal intercourse. If both, male and female, are unmarried (i.e., if both are single), it is a crime of fornication. If not both are unmarried, (i.e., if at least one of them is married to a third party), then it is a crime of adultery.

See the following flowchart of the law for the solution. The flowchart will apply to each person individually. Notice that the flowchart only applies to individuals who are at least 16 years of age. There are other laws that may apply if one of the persons is under 16 years of age, but that would involve other flowcharts. Many times, a single act may fall under multiple laws. In other words, just because other laws may apply does not negate the law of interest.

You need to be careful in your mathematical interpretation of the law. The adultery/fornication law considers both sexual partners simultaneously. Let unmarried = single. Both persons unmarried means both persons are single (the fornication flow line). Both persons not unmarried means both persons are not single, which means at least one of the persons is married to a third party (the adultery flow line). In addition, if both persons are married, then at least one of the persons is married. In the adultery flow line, both persons would be charged with engaging in adultery if at least one of the individuals is married to a third party.

Let us look closer at the modifier for the adultery flow line in the following flowchart. Focus on the **no** flow line for the *both unmarried* decision box, which means *not both are unmarried*. Does the word **not** apply to both or to being unmarried? Using percentages, does it mean **not** 100% are unmarried (i.e., **not** 100% are single) or does it mean 100% are **not** unmarried (i.e., 100% are **not** single)?

Not 100% are single means at least one person is married (existential quantifier).

100% are not single means everyone is married (universal quantifier).

Because the word *no* in the adultery flow line is outside the decision box, it will apply to the entire phrase: not (both are unmarried). It cannot simply be inserted into the middle of the phrase. In short, not (both are unmarried) means not 100% are single, which means at least one person is married to a third party.

Correct interpretation: not (both are unmarried). Incorrect interpretation: Both are not unmarried.

Solution: Law – Sexual Violation Law Between a Man and a Woman

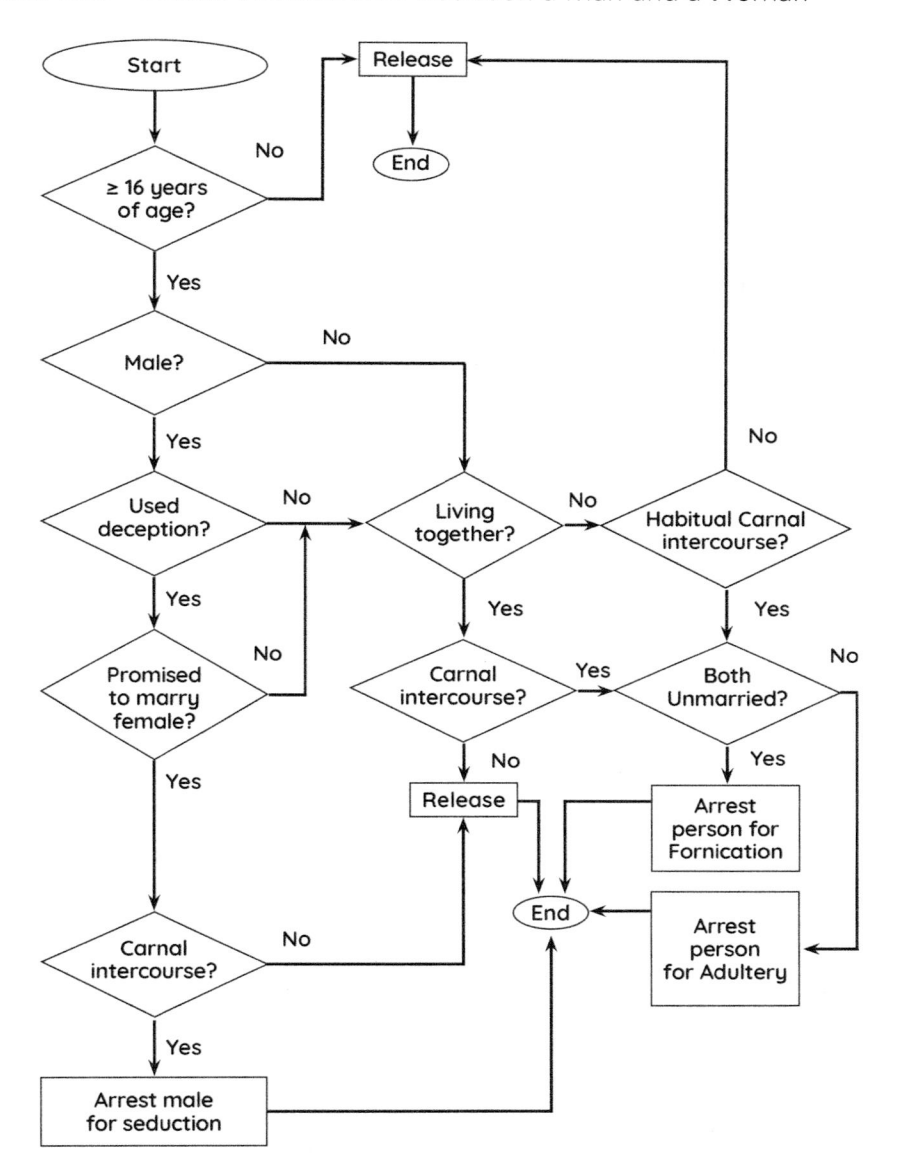

CHAPTER PROBLEMS

1. Describe the numbers that are printed in each of the algorithms below.

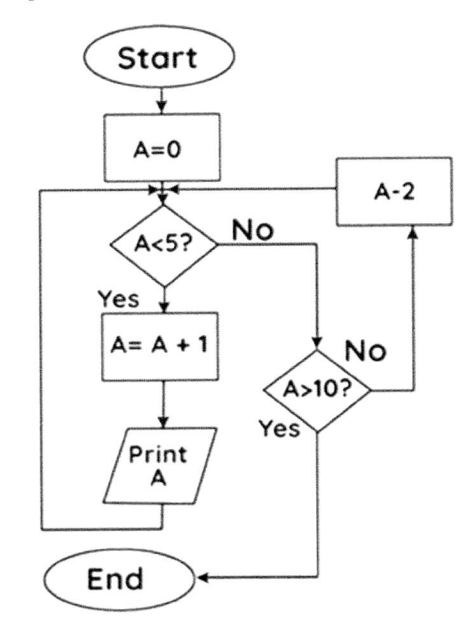

   Output: _____

2. Describe the numbers that are printed in each of the algorithms below.

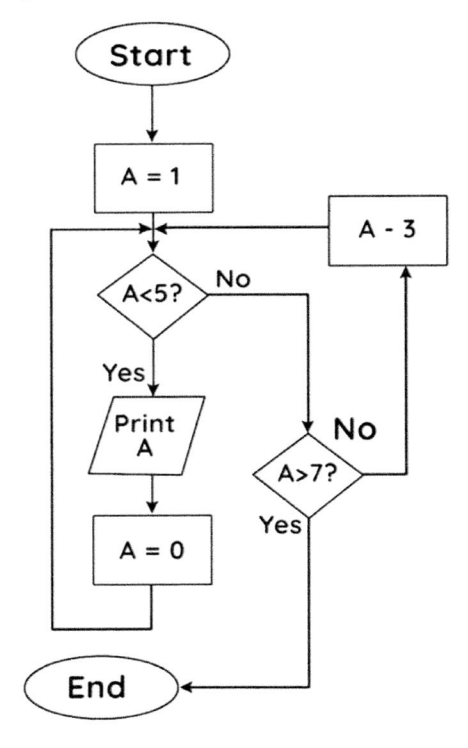

   Output: _____

3. Describe the numbers that are printed in each of the algorithms below.

```
Start
  ↓
A = 0
  ↓
Print A  ←──────────── A = A - 2
  ↓                        ↑
A = A + 1                   |
  ↓                         |
A > 4? ──Yes────────────────┘
  │
  No
  ↓
(loops back to Print A)
```

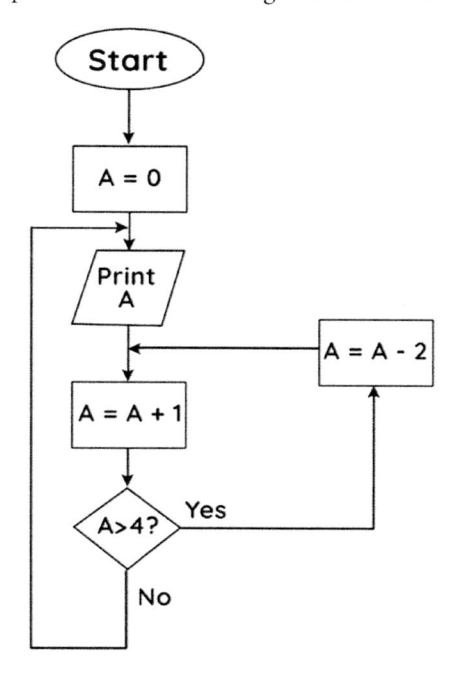

Output: _____

4. Describe the numbers that are printed in each of the algorithms below.

```
Start
  ↓
A = 0
  ↓
Print A  ←──────────── A = A - 2
  ↓                        ↑
A = A + 1                   |
  ↓                         |
A > 4? ──No─────────────────┘
  │
  Yes
  ↓
End
```

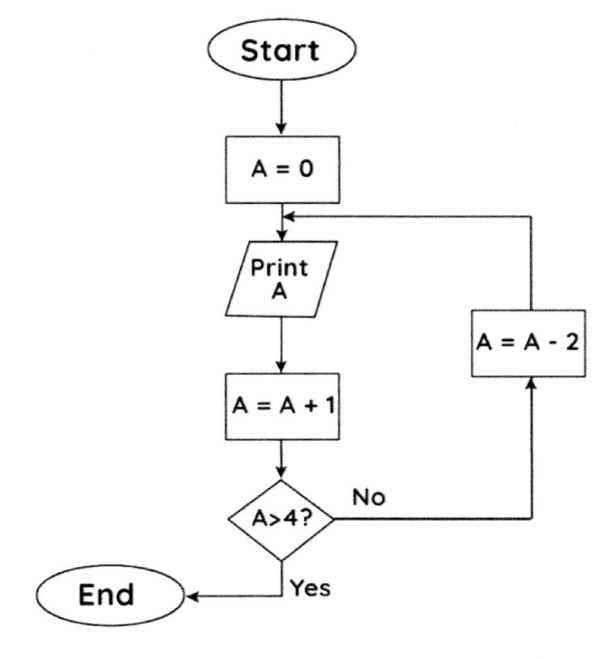

Output: _____

5. Describe the numbers that are printed in each of the algorithms below.

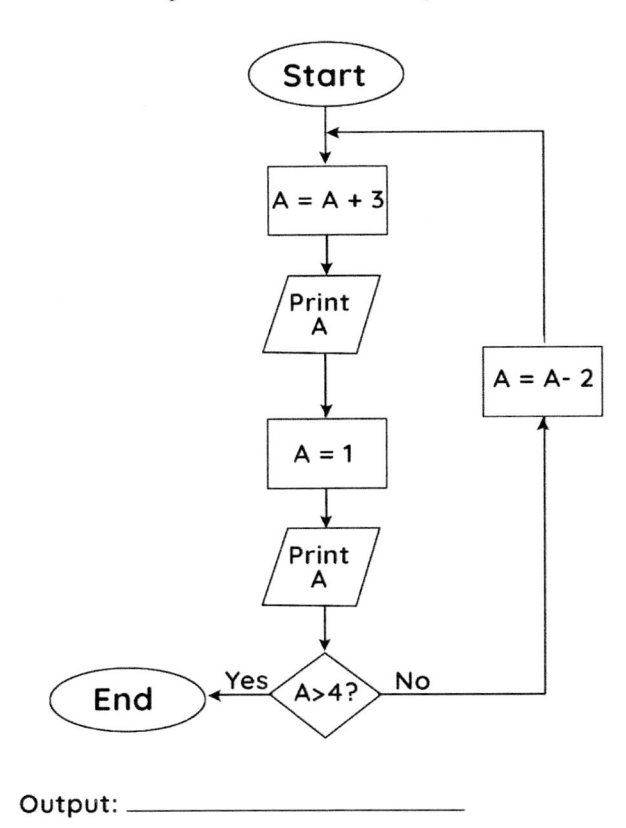

```
Start
  ↓
A = A + 3
  ↓
Print A
  ↓
A = 1
  ↓
Print A
  ↓
A > 4?  --No--> A = A - 2 --> (back to Start loop)
  |Yes
  ↓
End
```

Output: _____

6. Create a flowchart for the following law enforcement situation on a roadway with a maximum speed limit of 65 MPH and a minimum speed limit of 45 MPH.

   Make flow chart

   If car is traveling from 45-65 MPH disregard vehicle.

   If car is traveling from 66–79 MPH, write the driver a warning for speed.

   If car is traveling $\geq$ 80 MPH, write the driver a citation for speed, unless driver needs an ambulance. If driver needs an ambulance, call an ambulance and disregard enforcement action. If driver does not need an ambulance, write the driver a citation.

   If car is traveling from 40–44 MPH, write the driver a warning for speed too slow.

   If car is traveling from $\leq$ 39 MPH, write the driver a citation for speed too slow, unless the driver needs a wrecker. If driver needs a wrecker, call a wrecker and disregard enforcement action. If driver does not need a wrecker, write the driver a citation.

7. Create a flowchart for provocation.

   A person at least 16 years of age who knowingly, or intentionally engages in conduct that is likely to provoke a reasonable person to commit battery commits provocation.

8. Create a flowchart for visiting a common nuisance

   A person at least 16 years of age who knowingly or intentionally visits a structure, residence, or vehicle that is used by any person to unlawfully use a controlled substance commits visiting a common nuisance.

9. Create a flowchart for bonding out of jail

   If the crime is a felony, then the suspect will be required to see the judge. If the crime is a misdemeanor, then the suspect will call a bondsman. If the suspect is from out of state, then the bondsman will only cover 50% on the bond. If the driver is from within state, then the bondsman will cover 90% on the bond. If the suspect does not have the required balance, then the bond will be denied. If the suspect has the balance, then the suspect will be released. If the suspect is required to see the judge, bail will be refused for any crime related to a personal injury violation. Otherwise, the suspect will be released on his or her own recognizance.

10. Implement multiple intelligences to teach officers

    Discuss how you would implement two different intellectual capacities (i.e., Howard Gardner's multiple intelligences) to teach police officers how to better do their job.

KEYWORDS

Algorithm

Binary decision

Critical thinking

Flowchart

Multiple intelligences

Totality of circumstances

REFERENCES

Bell, N., Matthews, T., Lassiter, K., & Leverett, J. (2002). Validity of the Wonderlic personnel test as a measure of fluid or crystallized intelligence: Implications for career assessment, *North American Journal of Psychology, 4*(1), 113.

Brualdi, A. (November 1, 1998). Gardner's theory. *Teacher Librarian.*

Cavanaugh, J. & Blanchard-Fields, F. (2006). *Adult development and aging* (5th ed.). Belmont, CA: Thomson Wadsworth.

Flow Chart Examples (2002). http://elsmar.com/pdf_files/ Flow_Charts_for_2000.pdf

How are you smart? The multiple intelligences (n.d.). https://imgv2-2-f.scribdassets.com/img/document/255602530/original/0bd2a2b482/1547865050?v=1

Lunenburg, F.C., & Lunenburg, M.R. (2014). Applying multiple intelligences in the classroom: A fresh look at teaching writing. *International Journal of Scholarly Academic Intellectual Diversity, 16*(1), 1–14.

Paul, R. & Elder, L. (2009). *The miniature guide to critical thinking: Concepts and tools.* Dillon Beach, CA: Foundation for Critical Thinking.

Ryan, K., & Cooper, J. (2007). *Those who can, teach* (11th ed.). Boston, MA: Houghton Mifflin.

Smith, S., Eggen, M., St. Andre, R. (2006). *A transition to advanced mathematics* (6th ed.). Belmont, CA: Thomson Brooks/Cole.

Stoner, S. (1982). Age differences in crystallized and fluid intellectual abilities. *The Journal of Psychology, 110*(1), 7–10.

Whisenand, P.M. (2011). *Supervising police personnel: The fifteen responsibilities* (7th ed.). Upper Saddle River, NJ: Prentice Hall.

CHAPTER 4

The Law, Truth Tables, and Venn Diagrams

LEARNING OBJECTIVES

Turn an English logical statement (e.g., the law) into a mathematical logical statement.
Create a truth table to represent and interpret the law.
Create a Venn diagram to represent and interpret the law.

INTRODUCTION

An important objective of this chapter is to understand how to mathematical and objectively assess information via truth tables and Venn diagrams. Truth tables and Venn diagrams present the same information, but in different formats. A law that is written as an English logical statement can be converted into a mathematical logical statement and assessed via a truth table. A truth table will have one column for each input variable (e.g., each element of the law) and one final column that represents the law. A truth table will provide all possible combinations of the elements of a law and will indicate which combinations of input variables, based on whether each input variable is true or false, are violations of the law. Venn diagrams provide the same information as truth tables. However, a Venn diagram is a graphical representation of a numeric truth table. Using truth tables and Venn diagrams, the legality of a person's actions can be clearly displayed. This chapter will first discuss truth tables and then look at Venn diagrams.

BOOLEAN ALGEBRA

Boolean algebra is the branch of algebra in which the values of the variables are the truth values, which are either true or false and are usually denoted as 1 and 0, respectively (Gillie, 1965; Smith et al., 2006; Tan, 2015). Boolean algebra is used to describe logical operations. The main operators of Boolean algebra are the conjunction (AND), which is denoted as ∩, the disjunction (OR), which is denoted as U, and the negation (NOT), which is denoted as ~. Because laws are written in English logical statements using conjunctions, disjunctions, and negations, and the laws are either violated or not violated, it is easy to see how Boolean algebra can be applied to the law.

TRUTH TABLES

The work of a police officer can be objectively and mathematically assessed in the courtroom via Boolean algebra. Thus, it is important to understand Boolean algebra because the law is written in binary language (i.e., a law was either violated or not violated). Laws that are written as English logical statements (using ANDs and ORs), can be converted into mathematical logical statements and objectively assessed via truth tables. A truth table will have one column for each input variable (e.g., each element of the law) and one final column that represents the law (Smith et al., 2006; Tan, 2015). A truth table will provide all possible combinations of the elements of a law and will indicate which combinations of input variables, based on whether each input variable is true or false, are violations of the law. In short, truth tables will indicate the legality of actions for both police officers and civilians.

When a specific configuration of input variable values (e.g., A = 1, B = 0, and C = 0) is inserted directly into the law, this will match the corresponding row of the truth table with the same input variable configuration. If police officers want to be fair and consistent, and if they want to properly enforce the law, they should understand and apply truth tables (Boolean algebra) to articulate the legality of their actions. This process can also be applied to rules, regulations, policies, police reports, and other works that are written as English logical statements.

When creating truth tables, and when assessing the law, a variable, or element of the law, is either true or false (i.e., binary data representing one of two conceptually opposed values). If it is not true, then it is false. If it is not false, then it is true. For this book, a 1 will mean the variable is true, and a 0 will mean the variable is false. In addition, $\cap$ will mean AND, $\cup$ will mean OR, and ~A will mean not A. See below for a summary of the definitions.

1 = true
0 = false
~ = not (~ will never be used alone)
~1 = 0 = false
~0 = 1 = true
~A = not A
$\cap$ = AND
$\cup$ = OR.

The operators will be applied in the following order:

- NOT,
- AND, then
- OR.

In addition, just like in typical mathematics, nested parentheses will be completed inward to outward. The work inside a pair of parentheses must be completed before it is compared to anything outside the pair of parentheses. If a NOT is applied to a pair of parentheses, then, after the information inside the parentheses is worked out, it must be negated before it is compared to anything else.

For two or more sets of data, an AND logical operator represents the intersection of data or values that simultaneously exist across the data sets.

If A = {0, 1, 2, 3, 4, 5} and B = {2, 4, 7, 9},

Then

A $\cap$ B = {2, 4}

When AND logical operators are used for binary values, the resultant will be true only if all input variables are true (Smith et al., 2006). Thus, the possibility that the resultant is true will get smaller as more AND logical operators are used because it only takes one input variable to be false to make the resultant false.

1 ∩ 1 ∩ 1 ∩ 1 = 1 (true, because all input variables are true).

1 ∩ 1 ∩ 1 ∩ 0 = 0 (false, because not all input variables are true).

0 ∩ 0 ∩ 0 ∩ 0 = 0 (false, because none of the input variables is true).

For two or more sets of data, an OR logical operator represents the union of data, or values that exist in any of the data sets.

If A = {0, 1, 2, 3, 4, 5} and B = {2, 4, 7, 9},

Then

A U B = {0, 1, 2, 3, 4, 5, 7, 9}.

When OR logical operators are used for binary values, the resultant will be true if at least one input variable is true (Smith et al., 2006). Thus, the possibility that the resultant is true will get bigger as more OR logical operators are used because it only takes one input variable to be true to make the resultant true.

0 U 0 U 0 U 0 = 0 (false, because none of the input variables is true).

0 U 0 U 0 U 1 = 1 (true, because at least one input variable is true).

1 U 1 U 1 U 1 = 1 (true, because at least one input variable is true).

Examples of truth tables for one and two input variables are provided below.

A	B	A ∩ B		P	Q	P U Q		C	~C	~(~C)
0	0	0		0	0	0		0	1	0
1	0	0		1	0	1		1	0	1
0	1	0		0	1	1				
1	1	1		1	1	1				

X	Y	X ∩ Y	~(X ∩ Y)	~X	~Y	~X U ~Y	~X ∩ ~Y
0	0	0	1	1	1	1	1
1	0	0	1	0	1	1	0
0	1	0	1	1	0	1	0
1	1	1	0	0	0	0	0

For this book, always start the first row of input variables with all zeros. By doing this, you will be able to clearly see a pattern for the columns of data for the input variables. You will see that the initial setup for the input variables for a truth table is quite easy. Therefore, do not deviate from this strategy. Otherwise, the truth table will become unorganized and cumbersome to read. See the following examples for setting up the input variables. It is unimportant which letters are used to represent the input variables, as long as they distinguish one variable from another. In other words, in one example the letters A, B, and C may represent the input variables. In another example, the letters X, Y, and Z may represent the input variables. Sometimes, to save space, a single letter may be used to represent a long logical operation.

Rule: When a law, rule, or regulation is presented, the elements of the law, rule, or regulation are always defined in the positive language. For example, if an element of the law states "not intoxicated," then variable A = intoxicated (positive language) while ~ A = not intoxicated (negative language).

How many possible combinations of input variables are there?

The number of unique combinations = 2^x, where x is the number of input variables.

Therefore, if there are three input variables, then the number of unique combinations = 2^3 = 8.

If there are four input variables, then the number of unique combinations = 2^4 = 16.

If there are five input variables, then the number of unique combinations = 2^5 = 32.

When making a truth table, each unique combination of input variables will represent one row in a truth table. Thus, three input variables will have eight unique combinations, which will produce eight rows in a truth table.

Example 1: Truth Table

There are two input variables, A and B. Create a truth table. $2^X = 2^2 = 4$ rows.

Row	A	B
1	0	0
2	1	0
3	0	1
4	1	1

Notice the pattern in column A: 0-1. This pattern will continue to repeat when new input variables are added. Notice the pattern in column B: 0-0-1-1. This pattern will continue to repeat when new input variables are added. Notice that no combination of the rows is identical. Each row represents a unique combination of the input variables. Furthermore, look at the pattern from column A to B. When a new input variable is added, the number of zeros in the new column will double before the first value of one appears. Likewise, the number of ones will double to match the number of zeros.

Example 2: Truth Table

There are three input variables. Create a truth table. $2^X = 2^3 = 8$ rows.

Row	A	B	C
1	0	0	0
2	1	0	0
3	0	1	0
4	1	1	0
5	0	0	1
6	1	0	1
7	0	1	1
8	1	1	1

Notice the pattern in column A: 0-1. This pattern will continue to repeat when additional input variables are added. Notice the pattern in column B: 0-0-1-1. This pattern will continue to repeat when additional input variables are added. Notice the pattern in column C: 0-0-0-0-1-1-1-1. This pattern will continue to repeat when additional input variables are added. Notice that each row represents a unique combination of the input variables. Furthermore, look at the pattern from column A to B to C. Whenever an additional input variable is added, the number of zeros in the new column will double before the first value of one appears. Likewise, the number of ones will double to match the number of zeros.

Example 3: Truth Table

There are four input variables. Create a truth table. $2^X = 2^4 = 16$ rows.

A	B	C	D
0	0	0	0
1	0	0	0
0	1	0	0
1	1	0	0
0	0	1	0
1	0	1	0
0	1	1	0
1	1	1	0
0	0	0	1
1	0	0	1
0	1	0	1
1	1	0	1
0	0	1	1
1	0	1	1
0	1	1	1
1	1	1	1

Notice the pattern in column A: 0-1. Notice the pattern in column B: 0-0-1-1. Notice the pattern in column C: 0-0-0-0-1-1-1-1. Notice the pattern in column D: 0-0-0-0-0-0-0-0-1-1-1-1-1-1-1-1. These patterns will continue to repeat when additional input variables are added. For each new input variable that is added, the number of zeros in the new column will double before the first value of one appears. Likewise, the number of ones will double to match the number of zeros. If a fifth input variable is added, what will column E look like? See below.

Combination of input variables	A	B	C	D	E
1	0	0	0	0	0
2	1	0	0	0	0
3	0	1	0	0	0
4	1	1	0	0	0
5	0	0	1	0	0
6	1	0	1	0	0
7	0	1	1	0	0
8	1	1	1	0	0
9	0	0	0	1	0
10	1	0	0	1	0
11	0	1	0	1	0
12	1	1	0	1	0

Combination of input variables	A	B	C	D	E
13	0	0	1	1	0
14	1	0	1	1	0
15	0	1	1	1	0
16	1	1	1	1	0
17	0	0	0	0	1
18	1	0	0	0	1
19	0	1	0	0	1
20	1	1	0	0	1
21	0	0	1	0	1
22	1	0	1	0	1
23	0	1	1	0	1
24	1	1	1	0	1
25	0	0	0	1	1
26	1	0	0	1	1
27	0	1	0	1	1
28	1	1	0	1	1
29	0	0	1	1	1
30	1	0	1	1	1
31	0	1	1	1	1
32	1	1	1	1	1

Based on the patterns of zeros and ones, you should be able to quickly create a truth table for the input variables. Simply look at the pattern for the number of zeros and ones in each column. Every time a new column is added, the number of zeros in the new column will double before the first value of one appears. Likewise, the number of ones will double to match the number of zeros. Notice that none of the rows are identical, and each row represents a unique combination of input variables.

Making a Truth Table

The following exercises will demonstrate how to use truth tables to identify violations of the law. The specific laws in these exercises are not important. The goal is to create a truth table that contains a logical operation that reflects the law. Given the law, all possible combinations of the input variables can be assessed to determine which combinations of the input variables are violations of the law.

Order of Operations

1. Not
2. AND
3. OR

Note: Parentheses (nested parentheses will be completed inward to outward)

Example. Write the steps for the order of operations for the equation below.

[~ (A U ~B) U C ∩ D] U E ∩ ~F

Step 1. ~B; ~F
Step 2. (A U ~B)
Step 3. ~ (A U ~B)
Step 4. C ∩ D
Step 5. [~ (A U ~B) U (C ∩ D)]
Step 6. E ∩ ~F
Step 7. [~ (A U ~B) U (C ∩ D)] U (E ∩ ~F)

When making a truth table, you must first develop the column headings for the table with the final heading representing the law. Let us work through some examples.

Example 1. Generate the Headings for a Truth Table for the Following Violation of Law

Law violation = ~A ∩ (B U ~C).

If a violation of law is true, then we would make an arrest. In this case, there are three input variables (A, B, and C), which may be either true or false. Remember, a variable has more than one value; otherwise, it would be a constant. For example, male and female are not two variables; male and female are two values for the variable sex.

The headings in the truth table for the input variables will always be initially labeled in a positive condition (i.e., A, B, and C).

Step 1. Always start with the positive input variables. There are three input variables in this case.

| A | B | C |

Step 2. Because ~A and ~C are in the law, we will need to create them. ~A can be achieved by taking the opposite values of A.

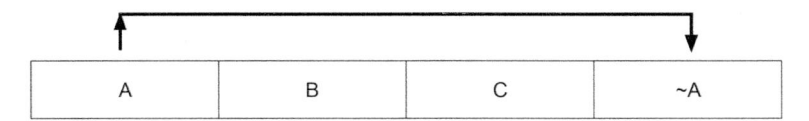

| A | B | C | ~A |

~C can be achieved by taking the opposite values of C.

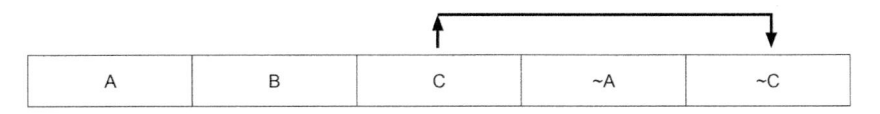

| A | B | C | ~A | ~C |

Step 4. We will next complete the operation within the parentheses. We need to create (B U ~C), which is needed for the final result. This union can be readily obtained because we already have B and ~C.

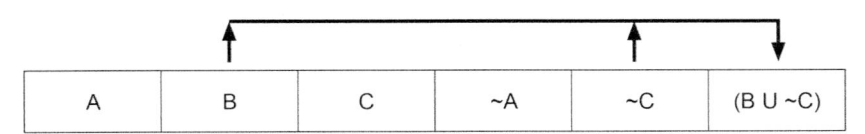

| A | B | C | ~A | ~C | (B U ~C) |

Step 5. Finally, we will create the law of interest. We have ~A and we have (B U ~C). We simply need to AND them together.

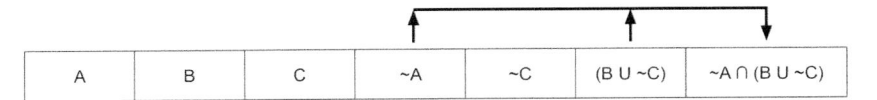

| A | B | C | ~A | ~C | (B U ~C) | ~A ∩ (B U ~C) |

In short, it does not matter how complicated the law is, the headings can be created one step at a time until the final objective is achieved. Once the desired heading for the law is obtained, you can start filling in the truth table values. Make sure you use the correct columns when using the logical operators. The most difficult thing about truth tables is staying organized. Using tables or lined paper may help keep the columns and rows neat. See the following truth table for the law of interest.

LAW

A	B	C	~A	~C	(B U ~C)	~A ∩ (B U ~C)
0	0	0	1	1	1	1
1	0	0	0	1	1	0
0	1	0	1	1	1	1
1	1	0	0	1	1	0
0	0	1	1	0	0	0
1	0	1	0	0	0	0
0	1	1	1	0	1	1
1	1	1	0	0	1	0

0 ∩ 1 = 0

Now, let us interpret the truth table.

A	B	C	~A	~C	(B U ~C)	~A ∩ (B U ~C)
0	0	0	1	1	1	1
1	0	0	0	1	1	0
0	1	0	1	1	1	1
1	1	0	0	1	1	0
0	0	1	1	0	0	0
1	0	1	0	0	0	0
0	1	1	1	0	1	1
1	1	1	0	0	1	0

When A = 1, B = 1, and C = 1, which is a specific combination of input variables, then the law violation = 0, which is false. This means that the law violation would not exist and no arrest would be made. We can confirm this statement by placing the values for the input variables directly into the law violation equation.

Let A = 1, B = 1, C = 1.   (Place these values directly into the law)

Law = ~A ∩ (B U ~C)

= ~1 ∩ (1 U ~1)

= 0 ∩ (1 U 0)

= 0 ∩ 1

= 0. Thus, an arrest would not be made, as confirmed by the truth table.

Let us look at another combination of input values. When A = 0, B = 0, and C = 0, then the law violation = 1, which is true. In other words, when A, B, and C are false, the law violation exists, and we would make an arrest.

A	B	C	~A	~C	(B U ~C)	~A ∩ (B U ~C)
0	0	0	1	1	1	1
1	0	0	0	1	1	0
0	1	0	1	1	1	1
1	1	0	0	1	1	0
0	0	1	1	0	0	0
1	0	1	0	0	0	0
0	1	1	1	0	1	1
1	1	1	0	0	1	0

We can confirm this statement by placing the values for the input variables directly into the law violation equation.

Let A = 0, B = 0, C = 0. (Place these values directly into the law)

Law = ~A ∩ (B U ~C)

= ~0 ∩ (0 U ~0)

= 1 ∩ (0 U 1)

= 1 ∩ 1

= 1. Thus, an arrest would be made, as confirmed by the truth table.

Let us look at another combination of input variable values. When A = 0, B = 1, and C = 0, then the law violation = 1, which is true. This means that the law violation exists and we would make an arrest.

A	B	C	~A	~C	(B U ~C)	~A ∩ (B U ~C)
0	0	0	1	1	1	1
1	0	0	0	1	1	0
0	1	0	1	1	1	1
1	1	0	0	1	1	0
0	0	1	1	0	0	0
1	0	1	0	0	0	0
0	1	1	1	0	1	1
1	1	1	0	0	1	0

We can confirm this statement by placing the values for the input variables directly into the law violation equation.

Let A = 0, B = 1, and C = 0. (Place these values directly into the law)

Law = ~A ∩ (B U ~C)

= ~0 ∩ (1 U ~0)

= 1 ∩ (1 U 1)

= 1 ∩ 1

= 1. Thus, an arrest would be made, as confirmed by the truth table.

Example 2. Generate the Headings for a Truth Table for the Following Law

Law = ~ (~A U B) U (B ∩ C) ∩ D

Objective: Create the headings necessary to achieve the law. See the addition of new headings at each step. Pay attention to the order of operations.

Step 1: There are four input variables

A	B	C	D

Step 2:

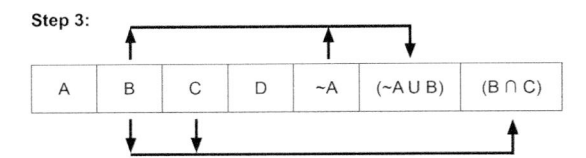

A	B	C	D	~A

Step 3:

A	B	C	D	~A	(~A U B)	(B ∩ C)

Step 4:

A	B	C	D	~A	(~A U B)	(B ∩ C)	~ (~A U B)

Step 5:

A	B	C	D	~A	(~A U B)	(B ∩ C)	~ (~A U B)	(B ∩ C) ∩ D

Step 6:

A	B	C	D	~A	(~A U B)	(B ∩ C)	~ (~A U B)	(B ∩ C) ∩ D	~(~AUB) U [(B∩C) ∩ D]

If room runs out for the headings, you may use a variable to reflect a logical operation. See example below.

The Law, Truth Tables, and Venn Diagrams   95

$$\underbrace{}_{X} \quad \underbrace{}_{Y}$$

A	B	C	D	~A	(~A U B)	(B ∩ C)	~(~A U B)	(B ∩ C) ∩ D	X U Y

Filling in the Truth Table with Values

After the headings have been created, let us create the truth table for the law. There are four input variables, which will produce 16 different combinations of input variables. These 16 different combinations are listed in the first four columns.

A	B	C	D	~A	(~A U B)	(B ∩ C)	~(~A U B)	(B ∩ C) ∩ D	~(~A U B) U [(B ∩ C) ∩ D]
0	0	0	0	1	1	0	0	0	0
1	0	0	0	0	0	0	1	0	1
0	1	0	0	1	1	0	0	0	0
1	1	0	0	0	1	0	0	0	0
0	0	1	0	1	1	0	0	0	0
1	0	1	0	0	0	0	1	0	1
0	1	1	0	1	1	1	0	0	0
1	1	1	0	0	1	1	0	0	0
0	0	0	1	1	1	0	0	0	0
1	0	0	1	0	0	0	1	0	1
0	1	0	1	1	1	0	0	0	0
1	1	0	1	0	1	0	0	0	0
0	0	1	1	1	1	0	0	0	0
1	0	1	1	0	0	0	1	0	1
0	1	1	1	1	1	1	0	1	1
1	1	1	1	0	1	1	0	1	1

Let us interpret the truth table by selecting one of the rows

A	B	C	D	~A	(~A U B)	(B ∩ C)	~(~A U B)	(B ∩ C) ∩ D	~(~A U B) U [(B ∩ C) ∩ D]
(1)	(1)	(0)	(1)	0	1	0	0	0	(0)

When A = 1, B = 1, C = 0, and D = 1, then the law violation = 0, which means there is no law violation. We would not arrest. This can be confirmed by placing the values for the input variables directly into the law.

Let A = 1, B = 1, C = 0, and D = 1 (Place these values into the law).

Law $= \sim (\sim A \cup B) \cup [(B \cap C) \cap D]$

$= \sim (\sim 1 \cup 1) \cup [(1 \cap 0) \cap 1]$

$= \sim (0 \cup 1) \cup [0 \cap 1]$

$= \sim 1 \cup 0$

$= 0 \cup 0 = 0.$

One question that might be asked is why should we complete truth tables when we could simply place the values of the input variables directly into the law? Truth tables provide complete information about the laws based on all possible combinations of the input variables. This provides the ability to compare laws to see whether they are equivalent ($\equiv$). To be equivalent, the truth values for every row must be the same.

Equivalency

Equivalence operation $\equiv$

$X \equiv Y$ when X has the same value as Y.

X	Y	$X \equiv Y$
0	0	1
1	0	0
0	1	0
1	1	1

Two laws are logically equivalent only if they have the same truth values for all possible combinations of the input variables (Smith et al., 2006). In this case, we write $X \equiv Y$ and say that X and Y are logically equivalent. If the values in any row differ, then the two laws are not equivalent. See below for examples.

In the case below, Law 1 and Law 2 are equivalent. Each row for Law 1 is the same as each row for Law 2.

Truth table row	A	B	C	Law 1	Law 2
1	0	0	0	1	1
2	1	0	0	0	0
3	0	1	0	0	0
4	1	1	0	1	1
5	0	0	1	1	1
6	1	0	1	1	1
7	0	1	1	0	0
8	1	1	1	0	0

In the case below, Law 1 and Law 2 are not equivalent. Each row for Law 1 is not the same as each row for Law 2. It only takes one row to be different for the laws not to be equivalent.

Truth table row	A	B	C	Law 1	Law 2
1	0	0	0	1	1
2	1	0	0	0	0
3	0	1	0	0	0
4	1	1	0	1	1
5	0	0	1	1	1
6	1	0	1	1	1
7	0	1	1	**0**	**1**
8	1	1	1	0	0

Determining Equivalency

Example 1. ~ A ∩ ~ B ∩ ~ C ≡ ~ (A ∩ B ∩ C)

A	B	C	~A	~B	~C	~A ∩ ~B ∩ ~C	A ∩ B ∩ C	~(A ∩ B ∩ C)
0	0	0	1	1	1	1	0	1
1	0	0	0	1	1	0	0	1
0	1	0	1	0	1	0	0	1
1	1	0	0	0	1	0	0	1
0	0	1	1	1	0	0	0	1
1	0	1	0	1	0	0	0	1
0	1	1	1	0	0	0	0	1
1	1	1	0	0	0	0	1	0

The answer is no.

~ A ∩ ~ B ∩ ~ C is not equivalent to ~ (A ∩ B ∩ C). The values are not the same in each row. Indeed, the statements are also opposite each other.

Suppose A = blue, B = glass, and C = marble. Then the following statement could be made.

It is not blue, not glass, and not marble has almost the opposite meaning as it is not blue, glass, and marble. This is extremely important because an officer may make a false arrest if the law is written as ~ A ∩ ~ B ∩ ~ C and the officer enforces the law as ~ (A ∩ B ∩ C).

There is another issue to consider. Let us consider the statement below.

Statement: It is not blue, glass, and marble.

Does this mean ~A ∩ B ∩ C or ~ (A ∩ B ∩ C)?

Because the *quantity of* is not normal language in the law book, there must be another way to clearly distinguish the statements. This is where punctuation will come into play. Punctuation in law books is used to make sentences clear and to distinguish the different logical operators. Having complete sentences is less important than clearly distinguishing the parentheses and the ANDs and ORs within the law.

Thus, the law could be written as the following.

It is not: blue, glass, and marble.

Because the word *not* is listed before the colon, the word *not* will apply to the entire text following the colon. In other words, the text following the colon will be enclosed in parentheses.

The law could also be written as the following: It is not a blue, glass, marble.

The word *a* separates the word *not* from the three input variables. In this case, the word *a* serves as the colon.

It is not: blue, glass, and marble = It is not a blue, glass, marble.

The law could also be written as the following: It is not blue; it is glass and marble.

In this case, the negated variable is in one sentence, and the positive variables are in another sentence. You can see how punctuation and grammar can significantly change the meaning of the law or a police report.

Example 2. ~ A U ~ B U ~ C ≡ ~ (A U B U C)

A	B	C	~A	~B	~C	~A U ~B U ~C	A U B U C	~(A U B U C)
0	0	0	1	1	1	1	0	1
1	0	0	0	1	1	1	1	0
0	1	0	1	0	1	1	1	0
1	1	0	0	0	1	1	1	0
0	0	1	1	1	0	1	1	0
1	0	1	0	1	0	1	1	0
0	1	1	1	0	0	1	1	0
1	1	1	0	0	0	0	1	0

The answer is no.

~ A U ~ B U ~ C is not equivalent to ~ (A U B U C).

The values are not the same in each and every row. Indeed, the statements are almost opposite each other.

Suppose A = blue, B = glass, and C = marble. Then the following statement could be made.

It is not blue, not glass, or not marble has almost the opposite meaning as it is not blue, glass, or marble. This is extremely important because the officer may make a false arrest if the law is written as ~ A U ~ B U ~ C and the officer enforces the law as ~ (A U B U C).

Let us consider the following statement: It is not blue, glass, or marble.

Does this mean ~A U B U C or ~ (A U B U C)?

Just as before, this is where punctuation will come into play. Remember, having complete sentences is less important than clearly distinguishing the parentheses and the ANDs and ORs within the law. In other words, clarity in the law trumps grammar conventions. Thus, the law could be written as the following. It is not: blue, glass, or marble, which would be ~ (A U B U C). Because the word *not* is listed before the colon, the word *not* will apply to the entire text following the colon. In other words, the text following the colon will be enclosed in parentheses. It is also possible that the law could be written as the following. It is glass or marble or not blue, which would be ~A U B U C. In this case, listing the not blue as the last variable helps clarify where the "not" is being applied. Using grammar and punctuation in this manner helps eliminate the problem with vague language.

Example 3. ~A ∩ ~ B ∩ ~C ≡ ~ (A U B U C)

A	B	C	~A	~B	~C	~A∩~B∩~C	(AUBUC)	~(AUBUC)
0	0	0	1	1	1	1	0	1
1	0	0	0	1	1	0	1	0
0	1	0	1	0	1	0	1	0
1	1	0	0	0	1	0	1	0
0	0	1	1	1	0	0	1	0
1	0	1	0	1	0	0	1	0
0	1	1	1	0	0	0	1	0
1	1	1	0	0	0	0	1	0

≡ (yes)

The answer is yes.

~A ∩ ~ B ∩ ~C is equivalent to ~ (A U B U C).

Suppose A = blue, B = glass, and C = marble. Then the following statement could be made. It is not blue, not glass, and not marble has the same meaning as it is not: blue, glass, or marble. Pay attention to the colon, the negations (NOTs), the conjunction (AND), and the disjunction (OR).

Now, let us look at several laws. The laws, *per se*, are not important. However, properly interpreting the laws is important.

Example 1. Interpret the Law
Law = It is a violation of law for a person to drink alcoholic beverages, drive a vehicle, and fail the field sobriety tests.

Let

X = drinks alcoholic beverages,

Y = drive a vehicle,

Z = fail the field sobriety tests.

Which interpretation for a violation of the law is correct?

1. X and Y and Z must be true.

2. X or Y and Z must be true.

Because we will follow the order of operations (ANDs will be assessed before ORs), the first statement is really (X and Y and Z) and the second statement is [X or (Y and Z)]. For the order of operations, the AND operation is similar to multiplication and the OR operation is similar to addition. In other words, the AND operation takes precedence over the OR operation. Furthermore, anything that is multiplied by zero is zero and using the AND operation with a zero is zero. On the other hand, adding zero to a value does not decrease the value and using the OR operation with a zero has no consequence. As in mathematics, the operation that is assessed first may change the output. In this case, the first option is correct.

The second option is incorrect because the individual items in the law are separated with commas, and the sole coordinating conjunction, which is the word *and*, has been placed before the last item. As a result, the coordinating conjunction will apply between each of the variables and will reflect an AND operation between each of the variables. Because the coordinating conjunction *or* does not appear in the sentence, it would be incorrect to simply add it. The correct interpretation of the law would be as follows: Law = It is a violation of law for a person to drink alcoholic beverages *and* to drive a vehicle *and* to fail the field sobriety tests (X and Y and Z).

Example 2. Interpret the Law
Law = It is a violation of law for a person to drink alcoholic beverages, drive a vehicle, or fail the field sobriety tests.

Let

X = drinks alcoholic beverages,

Y = drives a vehicle,

Z = fails the field sobriety tests.

Which interpretation of the law is correct for making an arrest?

1. X and Y or Z must be true.

2. X or Y or Z must be true.

Because we will follow the order of operations (ANDs will be assessed before ORs), the first equation is really [(X and Y) or Z] and the second equation is (X or Y or Z). This is significant because the operation that is assessed first may change the output, and the AND operation is quite different than an OR operation.

The second equation is correct, but the first equation is incorrect. The second equation is correct because the individual items in the law are separated with commas, and the sole coordinating conjunction, which is the word *or*, has been placed before the last item. As a result, the coordinating conjunction will apply between each of the variables and will reflect an OR operation between each of the variables. Because the coordinating conjunction *and* does not appear in the sentence, it would be incorrect to simply add it. The correct interpretation of the law would be as follows: Law = It is a violation of law for a person to drink alcoholic beverages *or* to drive a vehicle *or* to fail the field sobriety tests (X or Y or Z).

Example 3. Interpret the Law
Law = It is a violation of law for a person to drink alcoholic beverages; or to drive a vehicle and fail the field sobriety tests.

Let

X = drinks alcoholic beverages,

Y = drives a vehicle,

Z = fails the field sobriety tests.

Which interpretation of the law is correct for making an arrest?

1. [(X) U (Y ∩ Z)] must be true.

2. [(X U Y) ∩ (Z)] must be true.

In this case, the first statement is correct. The second statement is incorrect. The semicolon is used as a means to separate two sets of data. The first set of data has only X. The second set of data has Y and Z. Thus, the semicolon, in this case, is used to separate X from Y and Z. The correct interpretation of the law would be as follows: Law = It is a violation of law for a person to (1) drink alcoholic beverages or (2) drive a vehicle and fail the field sobriety tests. In short, for setting up the equation, the items on the left side of the semicolon will fall inside one pair of parentheses, and the items on the right side of the semicolon will fall inside a second pair of parentheses.

Note: Pay attention to the word that immediately follows the semicolon. In this case, it is the word *or*. Notice where the word *or* comes into play in the equation. It comes between the two sets of data.

Example 4. Interpret the Law

Breastfeeding law = A company with 50 employees or more must: provide a location where an employee can express her breast milk in privacy, and provide a refrigerator or other cold storage space for keeping milk that has been expressed; or allow the employee to provide her own portable cold storage device for keeping milk that has been expressed until the end of the workday.

To assess the law, let

A = A company with 50 employees or more

B = provide a location where an employee can express her breast milk in privacy

C = provide a refrigerator

D = provide other cold storage space

E = keeping milk that has been expressed

F = allow the employee to provide her own portable cold storage device

G = until the end of the workday

Now, write the law as a mathematical logical equation, where $\cap$ = AND and $\cup$ = OR.

If headings are used, the law may be written as follows in the law book.

A:

(i) B;

C or D; and

E; or

(ii) F,

E, and

G.

Notice that the main function of the headings, subheadings, and punctuation in the law is to bracket the law, separate variables, and distinguish the different logical operators. Having complete sentences is less important than clearly describing the law. In this case, the text prior to the colon applies to the entire law. Commas separate the variables and allow for parentheses within each section of law. Semicolons separate the subheadings within the law and allow for multiple sections of law. In addition, notice the word that immediately follows each semicolon, which will be either an AND operator or an OR operator. This operator will apply between the sections of law. Finally, as stated before, when individual items are listed in the law and are separated with commas, the coordinating conjunction listed before the last item will apply between each of the variables in that list of items.

A:
(i) B;
  C or D; and
  E; or
(ii) F,
  E, and
  G.

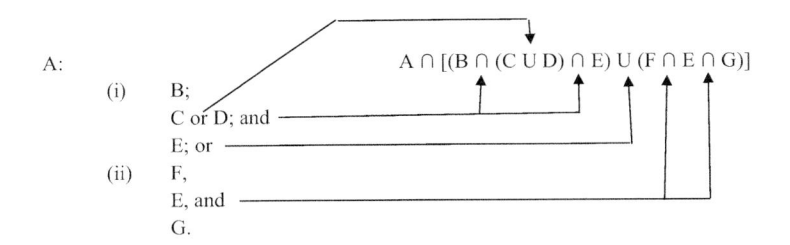

A ∩ [(B ∩ (C U D) ∩ E) U (F ∩ E ∩ G)]

Thus, the mathematical logical representation of the law is the following:

A ∩ [(B ∩ (C U D) ∩ E) U (F ∩ E ∩ G)].

Because the ANDs will be assessed before ORs, the following equation is also correct.

A ∩ [(B ∩ (C U D) ∩ E U F ∩ E ∩ G]

However, the following equation would be incorrect.

A ∩ B ∩ C U D ∩ E U F ∩ E ∩ G

Because it would be interpreted as

(A ∩ B ∩ C) U (D ∩ E) U (F ∩ E ∩ G).

The conversion process works both ways. If we are given an English logical statement, we can define the variables and generate the equation. If we are given an equation and the definitions of the variables, we can generate an English logical statement. In other words, we can convert a law into an equation, and we can convert an equation into the law. Thus, you should be able to check your responses by working through the process both ways.

Example 1. Check the Answer: Convert the Mathematical logical statement into an English logical statement (i.e., the law).

Given: A ∩ [(B ∩ (C U D) ∩ E) U (F ∩ E ∩ G)]

Let

A = A company with 50 employees or more

B = provide a location where an employee can express her breast milk in privacy

C = provide a refrigerator

D = provide other cold storage space

E = for keeping milk that has been expressed

F = allow the employee to provide her own portable cold storage device

G = until the end of the workday

I should point out that variable E, for example, could have been broken down into two smaller variables. We could have stated that (1) it must be able to keep milk and (2) the milk must have been expressed. This will simply make the equation longer, but not any more difficult. We will now write out the law by working through it.

The variable A applies to the entire rest of the law: A ∩ [...]. Thus, A must be true or else the law does not apply to the situation. This means that if the company has fewer than 50 employees, then the law does not apply.

Next, we will focus on the variables inside the parentheses, working inward to outward. Notice that there are three sets of parentheses:

(C U D),

(B ∩ (C U D) ∩ E), and

(F ∩ E ∩ G).

First, we will assess the inner most parentheses, (C U D). This indicates that the employer must either provide a refrigerator or provide other cold storage space.

Next, we will assess (B ∩ (C U D) ∩ E). This says that the employer must provide a private place to express the milk, and provide either a refrigerator or other cold storage space, and it must be able to keep milk that has been expressed.

Next, we will assess (F ∩ E ∩ G). To be true, this statement requires all three variables to be true. If the employer selects this option, then the employer must allow the employee to provide her own portable cold storage device for keeping milk, which has been expressed, until the end of the workday.

To simplify the explanation, let

(B ∩ (C U D) ∩ E) = Y and

(F ∩ E ∩ G)] = Z.

Then

A ∩ [(B ∩ (C U D) ∩ E) U (F ∩ E ∩ G)] = A ∩ [Y U Z].

For the equation A ∩ [Y U Z], A must be true and either Y or Z must be true.

Thus, A ∩ [Y U Z] = (A ∩ Y) U (A ∩ Z).

Option 1 (A ∩ Y): A company with 50 employees or more AND the company must provide a location where an employee can express her breast milk in privacy, AND (provide a refrigerator or other cold storage space) AND that can keep the milk that has been expressed.

OR

Option 2 (A ∩ Z): A company with 50 employees or more AND the company must allow the employee to provide her own portable cold storage device for keeping milk that has been expressed until the end of the workday.

Notice that option 2 does not require the company to provide a location where an employee can express her breast milk in privacy.

Example 2. Convert the mathematical logical statement into an English logical statement (i.e., the law)
Given: Law violation = (W ∩ X ∩ Y) U (Z ∩ X)

Let

W = drinks alcoholic beverage

X = drives a vehicle

Y = fails the field sobriety tests

Z = smokes marijuana

We will substitute the variables into the equation, following the order of operations.

Law violation =

(drinks alcoholic beverage, and drives a vehicle, and fails field sobriety tests)

OR

(smokes marijuana and drives a vehicle).

Putting it all together,

Law = it is a violation of law for a person to drink alcoholic beverage, drive a vehicle, and fail the field sobriety tests; or for a person to smoke marijuana and drive a car.

Notice in the law that a semicolon separates the two sections of the law and the word that immediately follows the semicolon represents the coordinating conjunction between the two sections of law.

Example 3. Convert the mathematical logical statement into an English logical statement (i.e., the rule).
Given: Rule = $(A \cap B) \cup (C \cap D)$

Let

A = officers must report to duty five minutes before the shift begins

B = work eight hours

C = officers must call in sick at least two hours in advance

D = complete an illness report the day one returns to work

Solution
Rule = $(A \cap B) \cup (C \cap D)$

$(A \cap B)$ = Officers must report to duty five minutes before the shift begins and work eight hours.

U = or

$(C \cap D)$ = Officers must call in sick at least two hours in advance and complete an illness report the day the officer returns to work.

The way the rule may be written in the rule book is described below.

An officer must: report to duty five minutes before the shift begins and work eight hours; or call in sick at least two hours in advance and complete an illness report the day the officer returns to work.

Example 4. Convert the mathematical logical statement into an English logical statement (i.e., the law).
Given: Violation of law = $(\sim A \cap B \cap C) \cup (\sim A \cap \sim C \cap D)$

Let

A = Sober

B = possessing a gun

C = private property

D = Walk

Solution
Violation of law = $(\sim A \cap B \cap C) \cup (\sim A \cap \sim C \cap D)$

It is a violation of law for a person to be intoxicated on private property while possessing a gun OR for a person to walk in public while intoxicated.

Notice that a person walking in public while intoxicated contains three variables with AND operators (walking AND intoxicated AND in public).

The way the law may be written in the law book is described below.

It is a violation of law for a person to be intoxicated: on private property with a gun; or to walk in public.

Example 5. Convert the mathematical logical statement into an English logical statement (i.e., the rule)

Given: Rule = A ∩ [(B ∩ C ∩ D) U (B ∩ E ∩ F)]

Let

A = Person who has been arrested

B = Will be Fingerprinted

C = Will be photographed

D = Will be booked into jail

E = Issued a citation

F = Released

Solution:

Rule = A ∩ [(B ∩ C ∩ D) U (B ∩ E ∩ F)]

An arrested person will be fingerprinted, photographed, and booked into jail.

OR

An arrested person will be fingerprinted, issued a citation, and released.

The way the rule may be written in the rule book is described below.

An arrested person will be fingerprinted: photographed and booked into jail; or issued a citation and released.

Exercise: Identify the Correct Combination of Input Variables

Place an X in a box in the appropriate row under each of the four persons. Each box with an X should reflect the proper combination of input variables to correctly describe each person. There should be one X under each person.

Boolean algebra is based on binary decisions. Binary decisions are made based on the variables provided. For the following table, the variables A, B, and C are defined as female, less than 21 years of age, and Canadian citizenship, respectively. In other words, the person is either a female or not female, less than 21 years of age or not less than 21 years age, and a Canadian citizen or not a Canadian citizen. Such variables may be considered for international sporting events.

Row	Combination of variables			Identify the correct combination of variables to describe each person. Place an X in the appropriate box under each person.			
	A Sex Female	B Age < 21 years of age	C Canadian citizenship	Female, age 20, U.S.	Female, age 22, Canadian	Male, age 33, Canadian	Male, age 25, U.S.
1	0	0	0				X
2	1	0	0				
3	0	1	0				
4	1	1	0	X			
5	0	0	1			X	
6	1	0	1		X		
7	0	1	1				
8	1	1	1				

VENN DIAGRAMS

Venn diagrams provide the same information as truth tables. However, a Venn diagram provides a graphical representation of a numeric truth table. A circle represents an element of the law. The area inside a circle means the input variable is true, and the element exists. The area outside a circle means the input variable is false, and the element does not exist. When circles overlap, the input variables for each circle exist simultaneously in the section that overlaps.

The universe for a Venn diagram contains all variables of interest. In the following figure, the rectangular box represents the boundary of the universe. Inside the universe, each circle represents a specific Boolean variable of interest, which will be either true or false.

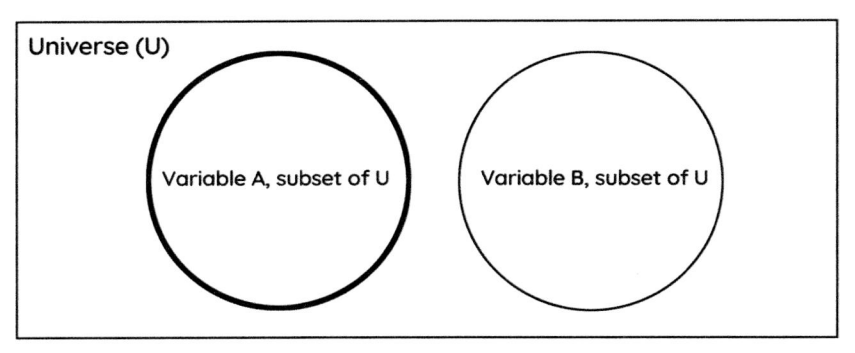

Figure 4.1 Venn diagram

There is an easy trick when working with Venn diagrams. Suppose we have been instructed to identify the section of a Venn diagram that represents the following law: A ∩ B. We know that the answer cannot be outside A. We also know that the answer cannot be outside B. The conjunction forced the answer to be inside A and inside B simultaneously. Anything outside A will be incorrect, and anything outside B will be incorrect. It is possible that variables do not intersect.

Now suppose we have been instructed to identify the section of a Venn diagram that represents the following law: A U ~ B. We know that the answer must contain the entire section inside A. We also know that the answer must contain the entire section outside B. The disjunction requires that we add the two areas together. The biggest mistake that students make is that they attempt to remove the section of A that overlaps with B because of the ~ B. Remember, when an OR is used, we never reduce the output. We will only add to the output. The section of A that overlaps with B will be included because it is part of A, and A is included.

To be clear, when two non-identical variables are assessed, when the word OR is used between the elements of the law, the resultant will be bigger than each individual variable. However, when the word AND is used between the elements of the law, the resultant will be smaller than each individual variable.

Following are examples of Venn diagrams. The letters above each box represent the law, and the law corresponds to the shaded area inside the universe.

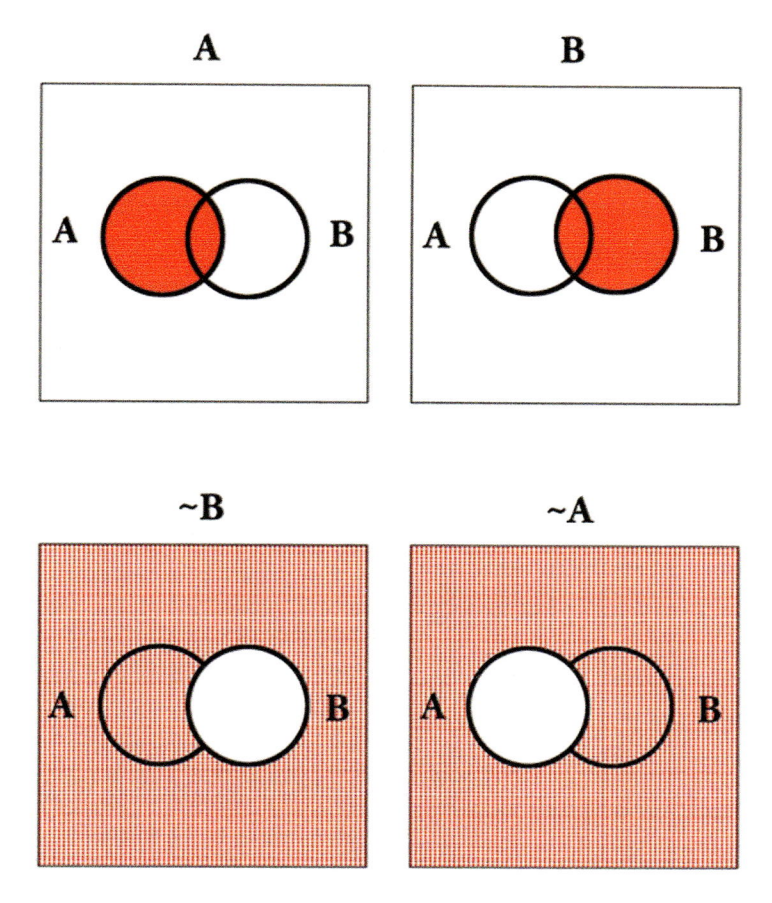

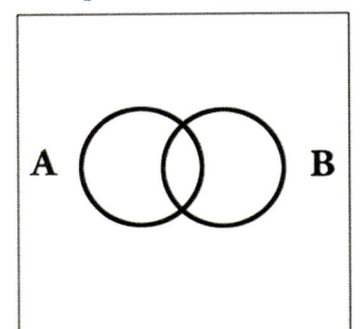

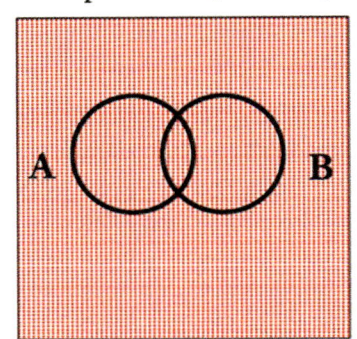

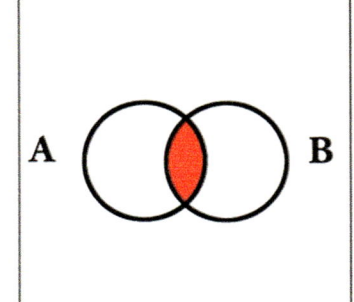

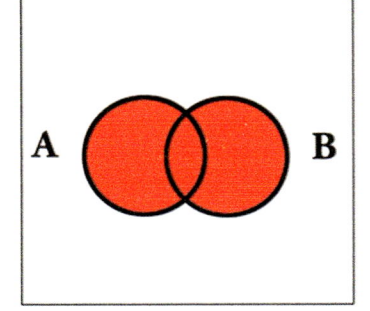

Output False (all cases)   Output True (all cases)

A∩B   A∪B

(A∪B) − (A∩B)

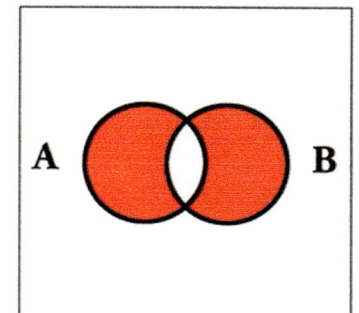

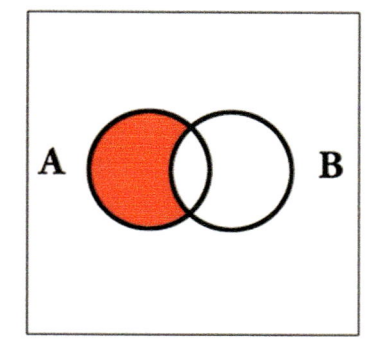

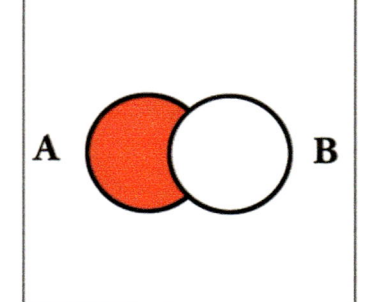

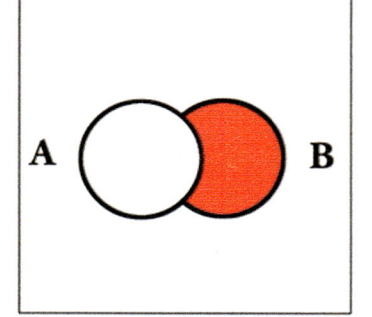

A − (A∩B)

A ∩ ~B

B ∩ ~A

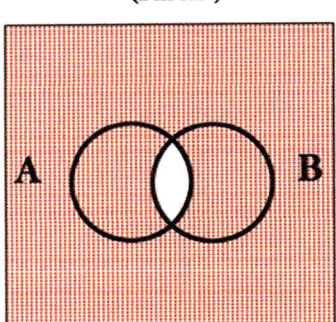

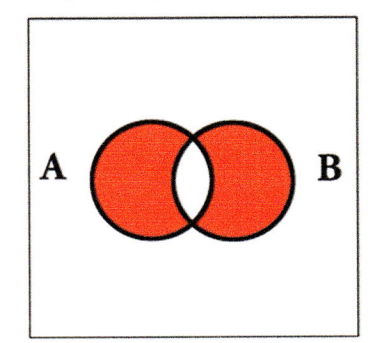

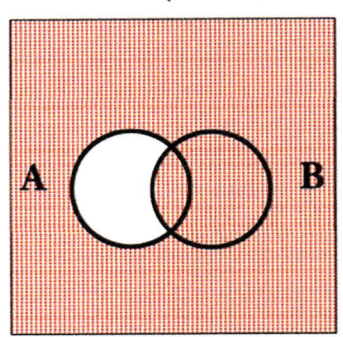

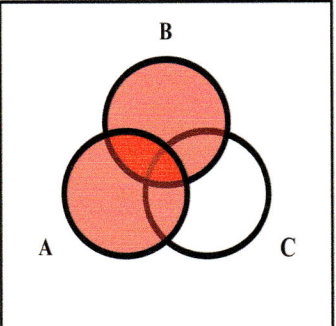

~(A∩B)

(A∪B) ∩ ~(A∩B)

~A ∪ (A∩B)

A ∪ B

A ∩ B ∩ C

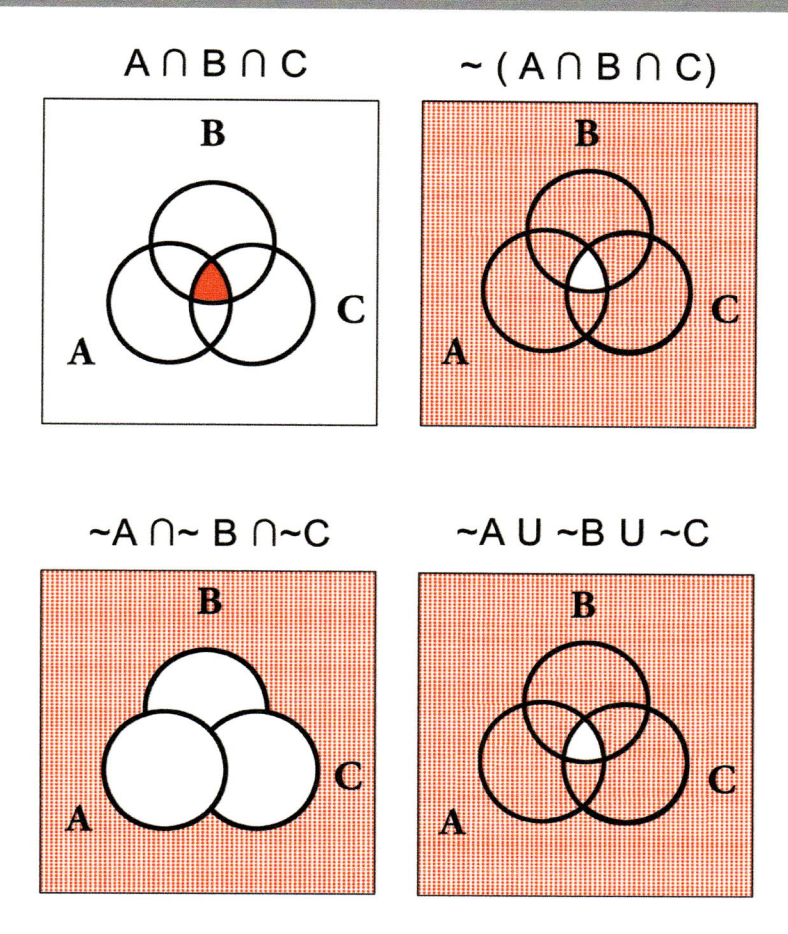

~(A ∩ B ∩ C)

~A ∩ ~B ∩ ~C

~A U ~B U ~C

Now, let us see how Venn diagrams are linked to truth tables. If there are three input variables, for example, there will be eight unique rows in a truth table and eight unique sections in a Venn diagram. Each row in a truth table represents a unique combination of the input variables, and each section in a Venn diagram represents a unique combination of the input variables. Indeed, each row in a truth table corresponds to one section in a Venn diagram. See below for the link between a truth table and Venn diagram. Each row in the truth table is labeled in the Venn diagram. For example, look at row 8 in the truth table. Row 8 states that A = 1, B = 1, and C = 1. Compare that to where 8 is located in the Venn diagram. The 8 in the Venn diagram falls within A, B, and C, which means A = 1, B = 1, and C = 1.

Row	A	B	C
1	0	0	0
2	1	0	0
3	0	1	0
4	1	1	0
5	0	0	1
6	1	0	1
7	0	1	1
8	1	1	1

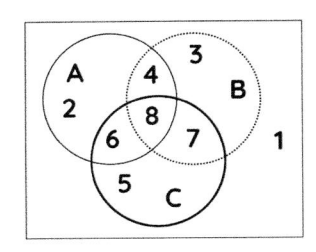

Venn Diagram Examples: Deck of Playing Cards

For examples that you can easily confirm, we will apply Venn diagrams to a regular deck of playing cards. For these examples, there are only two variables (i.e., two circles) labeled A and B in the universe. The intersection of A and B = area 3. The area outside of A and B = D. The universe will consist of 52 cards, as described below. Aces will be treated as ones. Jokers will not be considered.

Universe = total cards = 52; Red cards = 26; Black cards = 26.

Face cards = Jacks, Queens, and Kings.

Red cards: Hearts = 13 cards; Diamonds = 13 cards.

Black cards: Spades = 13 cards; Clubs = 13 cards.

A = area 1 + area 3

B = area 2 + area 3

A ∩ B = area 3

A U B = area 1 + area 2 + area 3

D = area 4 (items that are not contained in areas 1, 2, or 3).

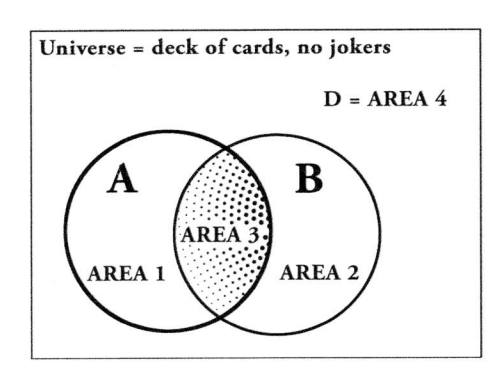

Problem 1: Use a regular deck of playing cards (no jokers)

A = RED CARDS

B = FACE CARDS

1. How many cards are in area 1?
2. How many cards are in area 2?
3. How many cards are in area 3?
4. How many cards are in area 4?

Solution:

A = Red cards = 26 (but how many of these 26 cards are also inside B?)

B = Face cards = 12. Because 6 of these face cards are red, they must be inside A (specifically, inside area 3). The 6 black face cards must be inside B but cannot be in A, which means they cannot be in area 3.

There are 52 cards total, so the summation of the cards in areas 1, 2, 3, and 4 must equal 52. D = 52 - 20 - 6 - 6 = 20.

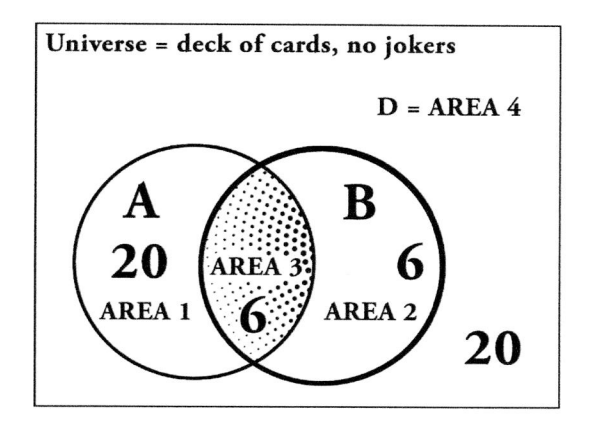

```
Universe = deck of cards, no jokers

                              D = AREA 4

       A            B
      20           6
         AREA 3
    AREA 1   6   AREA 2
                              20
```

Problem 2: Use a regular deck of playing cards (no jokers)

A = RED CARDS

B = BLACK CARDS

1. How many cards are in area 1?
2. How many cards are in area 2?
3. How many cards are in area 3?
4. How many cards are in area 4?

Solution

Twenty-six of the cards are red and must be inside A. However, because the red cards are not black, they cannot be in circle B.

Twenty-six of the cards are black and must be inside B. However, because the black cards are not red, they cannot be in circle A.

Because all of the cards are either red or black, none of them will be in area D.

D = 52 − area 1 − area 3 − area 2 = 52 − 26 − 0 − 26 = 0.

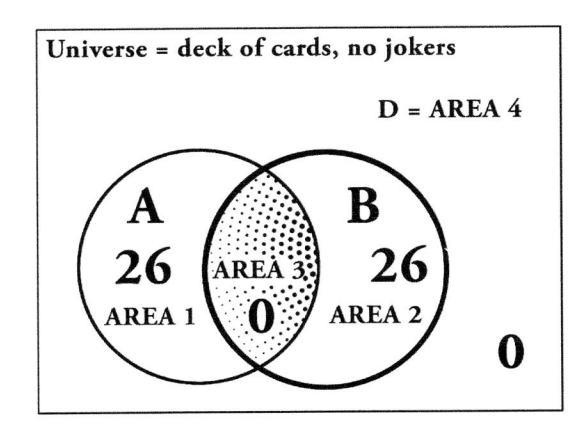

Universe = deck of cards, no jokers

```
        D = AREA 4
   ┌─────┐ ┌─────┐
   │  A  │ │  B  │
   │ 26  │ │ 26  │
   │AREA1│0│AREA2│
   └─────┘ └─────┘
              0
  (AREA 3 = 0, shaded intersection)
```

Problem 3: Use a regular deck of playing cards (no jokers)

A = DIAMONDS

B = EVEN CARDS (NO FACE CARDS)

1. How many cards are in area 1?
2. How many cards are in area 2?
3. How many cards are in area 3?
4. How many cards are in area 4?

Solution

A = There are 13 diamonds. Thus, 13 cards must be inside A.

B = There are 20 total even cards (2, 4, 6, 8, 10 for each of the four suits). Thus, 20 cards must be inside B. Of those 20 cards inside B, five are both even and diamond.

D = 52 − area 1 − area 3 − area 2 = 52 − 8 − 5 − 15 = 24.

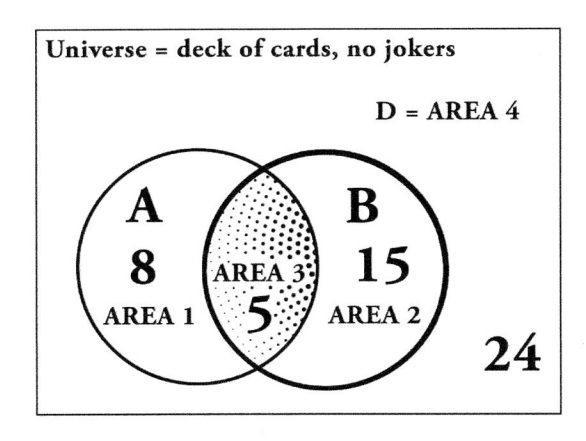

Universe = deck of cards, no jokers

```
        D = AREA 4
   ┌─────┐ ┌─────┐
   │  A  │ │  B  │
   │  8  │ │ 15  │
   │AREA1│5│AREA2│
   └─────┘ └─────┘
              24
  (AREA 3 = 5, shaded intersection)
```

Problem 4: Use a regular deck of playing cards (no jokers).

A = HEARTS

B = JACKS

1. How many cards are in area 1?
2. How many cards are in area 2?

3. How many cards are in area 3?

4. How many cards are in area 4?

Solution

A = There are 13 hearts. Thus, 13 cards must be inside A.

B = There are 4 Jacks (one for each of the four suits). Thus, four cards must be inside B. Of the four cards inside B, one is both a Jack and a heart.

D = 52 − area 1 − area 3 − area 2 = 52 − 12 − 1 − 3 = 36.

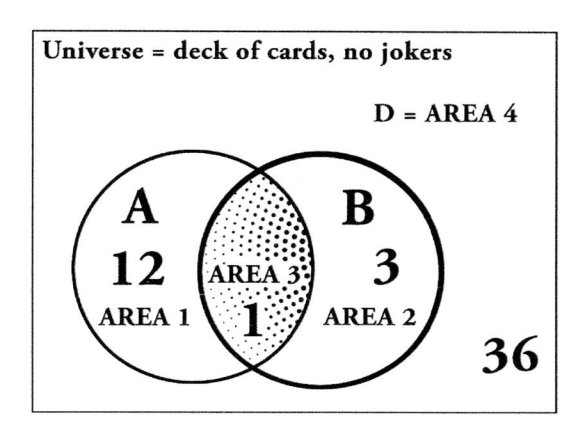

```
Universe = deck of cards, no jokers

                              D = AREA 4

      A            B
     12           3
   AREA 1       AREA 2
         AREA 3
            1
                              36
```

Venn Diagrams: Age, Sex, Hair Color

Now let us apply Venn diagrams to people. We will consider three variables. Each variable is represented by a circle. Because a variable has more than one value (otherwise, it is a constant), inside the circle will represent one value and outside the circle will represent a different value. The first circle represents age, the second circle represents males, and the final circle represents blond hair. Individuals who are inside the age circle are at least 21 years of age; if they are outside the circle, then they are younger than 21 years of age. Individuals who are inside the male circle are male; if they are outside the circle, then they are not male. Individuals who are inside the blond hair circle have blond hair; if they are outside the circle, then they do not have blond hair. Colors are labeled in the Venn diagram to represent each of the eight different combinations of the three variables. You could argue that there are hundreds of variables that could apply to people and there could be hundreds of circles within the Venn diagram. This is a correct statement; however, the other variables are irrelevant. Thus, there is no need to draw them in the Venn diagram because they have no consequence. If you did decide to draw them, they would be disregarded because they are not the variables of interest.

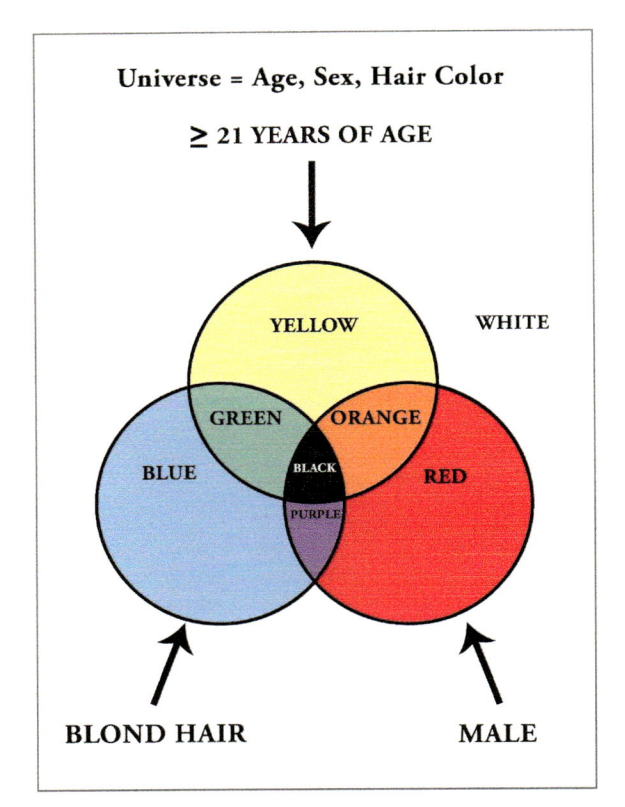

Figure 4.2 Venn diagram of age, sex, and hair color

Now, let us interpret the Venn diagram for at least 21 years of age, male, and blond hair.

Table 4.1 Interpretation of Figure 4.2 Venn diagram

Color listed in Venn diagram	Description of Individual		
Red	Male	< 21 years of age	Not blond hair
Blue	Not male	< 21 years of age	Blond hair
Yellow	Not male	≥ 21 years of age	Not blond hair
Orange	Male	≥ 21 years of age	Not blond hair
Green	Not male	≥ 21 years of age	Blond hair
Purple	Male	< 21 years of age	Blond hair
Black	Male	≥ 21 years of age	Blond hair
White	Not male	< 21 years of age	Not blond hair

There is a quick way to see whether everything balances. When looking at all possible combinations of the input variables, notice that each binary variable will be true half the time, and it will be false half the time. If each variable is not evenly balanced, you know a mistake has been made.

Now, let us create a Venn diagram for the following three variables: ≥ 0.08% Breath Alcohol Concentration (BrAC), the driver of the vehicle, and the passing of field sobriety tests (FSTs). Remember, variables are labeled in a positive language. Colors are labeled in the Venn diagram to represent each of the eight different combinations of the three variables. To be consistent with its corresponding truth table, and to ease the comparison with its corresponding truth table, the variables in the Venn diagram should be labeled in the same manner as they are listed in its corresponding truth table.

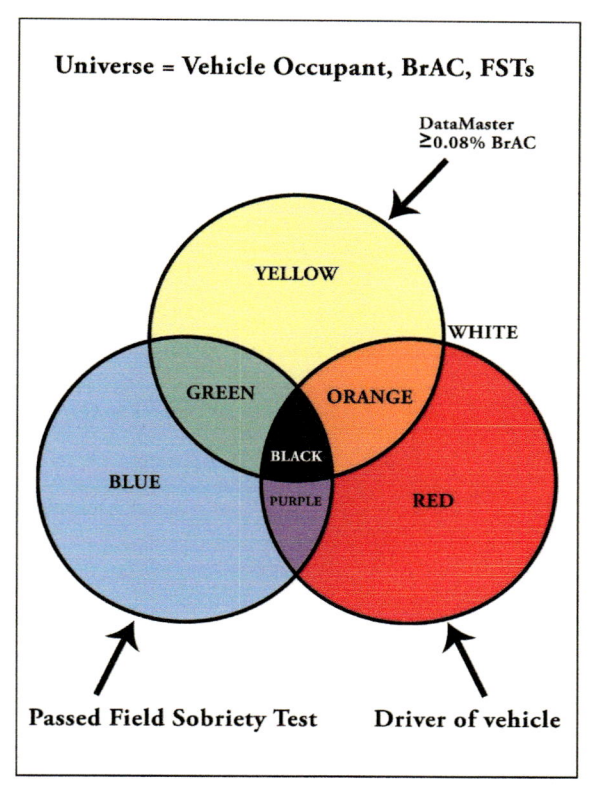

Figure 4.3 DUI Venn diagram

Table 4.2 Interpretation of Figure 4.3 DUI Venn diagram

Place YES or NO in each box based on the color in the Venn diagram. Yes = variable is true; No = variable is false.			
Color	Driver	≥0.08% BrAC	Passed FSTs
White	NO	NO	NO
Red	YES	NO	NO
Yellow	NO	YES	NO
Orange	YES	YES	NO
Blue	NO	NO	YES
Purple	YES	NO	YES
Green	NO	YES	YES
Black	YES	YES	YES

Notice that no two rows have the same combination of variables. In addition, if each variable is not evenly balanced, then you know a mistake has been made. Just like a truth table, half the time the responses will be true for each variable, and half the time the responses will be false. In this case, for each variable, there will be four boxes that have YES and four boxes that have NO. Notice what happens when a *yes* is converted into a one and a *no* is converted into a zero. It turns into a truth table. See below.

Table 4.3 Results from Venn diagram converted to truth table

Color	Driver	≥0.08% BrAC	Passed FSTs
White	0	0	0
Red	1	0	0
Yellow	0	1	0
Orange	1	1	0
Blue	0	0	1
Purple	1	0	1
Green	0	1	1
Black	1	1	1

KEYWORDS

Boolean algebra
Logic conjunction
Logic disjunction
Logic negation (NOT)
Truth table
Venn diagram

CHAPTER PROBLEMS

1. Turn the English logical statement into a mathematical logical statement and answer the questions.

    Policy: If you want to legally park your car at the school, you must:

    I. Request a parking permit in writing and:

    (a_1) Be a registered student and

    (b_1) Display a student parking sticker in the car window; or

    (c_1) Pay $5 for a daily parking pass; or

    II. Be a graduate of the school and:

    (a_2) Be a lifetime alumni member of the school; and

    (b_2) Be current in fees due; and

    (c_2) Display lifetime alumni member sticker in car window.

    Use ∩ and U to turn the above policy into a mathematical logical statement.

    Policy (equation): _____

    After the mathematical logical statement has been created, suppose the below conditions are true for Brooke:

    Let: I = 1 (true); II = 1 (true).

    $a_1, a_2, c_1 = 1$ (true)

    $b_1, b_2, c_2 = 0$ (false)

    Will Brooke be able to legally park her car at the school? Show work.

2. Turn the English logical statement into a mathematical logical statement and answer the questions.

   Consider the following statement (elements of the law):

   Law = Arrest a person who is intoxicated, has no excuse, and is not on own property, or a person who shoots a gun in public with no excuse.

   Let

   A = person is intoxicated
   B = has an excuse
   C = person is on own property
   D = person shoots gun

   Use the variables provided and use ∩ and U to write the law in a mathematical logical statement.

   Law (equation): _____

   Given:

   Suspect 1: A, D = true; B, C = false

   Will you arrest Suspect 1? Show work.

   Suspect 2: A, C = false; B, D = true

   Will you arrest Suspect 2? Show work.

3. Create the Headings for a Truth Table column by column to reach the following law. Fill in the table below. Make sure that you follow the proper order of operations.

   A U B ∩ ~ (C U D)

A	B	C	D				

4. Create the Headings for a Truth Table column by column to reach the following law. Fill in the table below. Make sure that you follow the proper order of operations.

   A U B U ~ (~C U D)

A	B	C	D				

5. Create the truth table for the law below. Start with all zeros in row 1.

   ~ (P U Q) ∩ R

6. Create the truth table for the law below. Start with all zeros in row 1.

   (P U ~Q) ∩ R

7. Create a Truth Table

   Suppose the following law is true. Make a Truth Table for the following law.

   Law. Seduction under promise of marriage.

   It is illegal for a male over 16 years of age to use deception and promise of marriage to seduce an unmarried woman.

   For simplicity, the suspect's sex and age will be fixed (i.e., male and over 16 years of age). In other words, suppose you have stopped a male over 16 years of age, and you are investigating the crime. Thus, make a truth table for the four variables that relate to the criminal act. For the four variables, let A = truthful, B = promise of marriage, C = seduces, and D = married woman. Start with all zeros in row 1 and number each row sequentially.

   1. Which row reflects a violation of the law?
   2. Which row reflects deception, promise of marriage, seduces, and married woman?

3. Which row reflects deception, promise of marriage, failed to seduce, and an unmarried woman?
4. Which row reflects deception, no promise of marriage, seduces, and an unmarried woman?

8. Assess whether a law violation has occurred

    Law Violation = ~ (P ∩ Q ∩ R) U (P U R)

    Place the values provided below into the equation and answer the question.

    Let P = 1 (true), Q = 1 (true), and R = 0 (false). State whether a law violation has occurred. Show your work.

9. Venn diagram: Deck of playing cards

    This exercise involves a deck of regular playing cards. Use the Venn diagram below. There are only two variables labeled A and B in the universe. Aces will be treated as ones. There are 52 cards total. Jokers will not be considered.

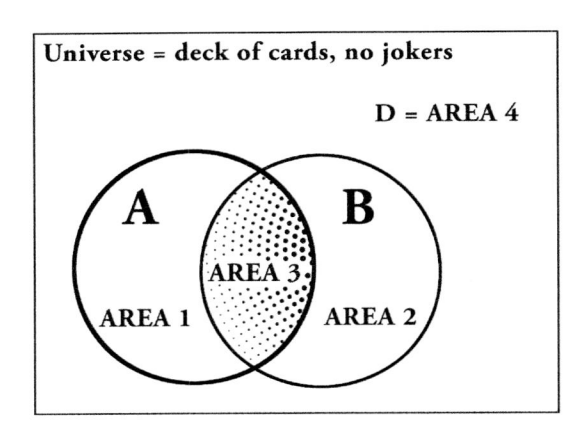

    Definitions:
    Universe = Total cards = 52; Red cards = 26; Black cards = 26.
    Face cards = Jacks, Queens, and Kings.
    Red Cards: Hearts = 13 cards; Diamonds = 13 cards.
    Black Cards: Spades = 13 cards; Clubs = 13 cards.
    A = area 1 + area 3; B = area 2 + area 3; A ∩ B = area 3; A U B = area 1 + area 2 + area 3.
    D = area 4 (items that are not contained in areas 1, 2, or 3).
    A = JACKS AND KINGS; B = FACE CARDS

    1. How many cards are in area 1?
    2. How many cards are in area 2?
    3. How many cards are in area 3?
    4. How many cards are in area 4?

10. Using the Venn diagram below, complete Table 1 and Table 2.

Universe = Ride bicycle, on sidewalk, while carrying a passenger

Ride bicycle

YELLOW

WHITE

GREEN ORANGE

BLUE BLACK RED

PURPLE

While carrying a passenger   On sidewalk

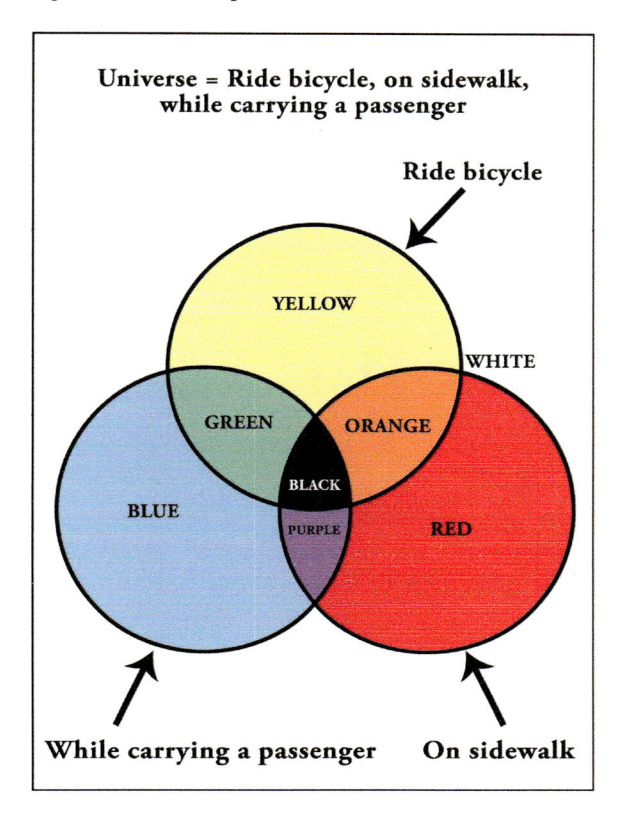

Table 1 Using the Venn diagram, indicate the color the matches the description

Description	Color
Riding bicycle, while carrying a passenger, on sidewalk.	
Riding bicycle, while carrying a passenger, on dirt bike trail.	
Riding bicycle, alone, on roadway.	
Riding bicycle, alone, on sidewalk.	
Pushing bicycle, while carrying a passenger, on grass.	
Sitting on bicycle, while carrying a passenger, on sidewalk.	
Working on bicycle, alone, on sidewalk.	
Sitting on stationary bicycle, alone, on driveway.	

Table 2 Using the Venn diagram, complete the truth table by indicating the color the matches the description (1 = true; 0 = false)

Riding bicycle	While carrying a passenger	On sidewalk	Color
0	0	0	
1	0	0	
0	1	0	
1	1	0	
0	0	1	
1	0	1	
0	1	1	
1	1	1	

REFERENCES

Gillie, A.C. (1965). *Binary arithmetic and Boolean algebra.* New York: McGraw-Hill.

Smith, D., Eggen, M., & St. Andre, R. (2006). *A transition to advanced mathematics* (6th ed.). Belmont, CA: Thomson Brooks/Cole.

Tan, S.T. (2015). *Finite mathematics: For the managerial, life, and social sciences.* Stamford, CT: Cengage.

CHAPTER 5

The Law, Logic Gates, and Logic Circuits

LEARNING OBJECTIVES

Use logic gates to create and assess laws.
Use logic circuits to create and assess laws.

INTRODUCTION

An important goal of this chapter is to understand how to assess information mathematically and objectively via logic gates and logic circuits. Logic gates and logic circuits combine aspects of truth tables, Venn diagrams, and flowcharts to arrive at the desired outcome. First, logic gates and logic circuits are like truth tables because they all utilize logical operators. Second, logic gates and logic circuits are like Venn diagrams because they all provide graphical representations of the information. Finally, logic gates and logic circuits are like flowcharts because they all follow a sequence of events to arrive at the desired outcome. Indeed, by creating the proper sequence of events, logic gates and logic circuits can be used to graphically describe rules, policies, and laws. In addition, the validity of logic gate and logic circuit designs can be tested by supplying appropriate binary data as input values. This chapter will first discuss logic gates and then examine logic circuits.

LOGIC GATES

Logic gates act as logic operators and are used to graphically represent the sequence of operations from start to finish to create the desired outcome, such as a rule, policy, or law (Ahmad, 2004; Diaz, 2012). The output for each logic gate is a logical expression. Placed in the correct sequence, logic gates can be used to create rules, policies, and laws. Furthermore, the validity of a logic gate design can easily be confirmed by inserting binary data into the logic gate design. If a certain output is expected based on the values of the input variables, and if a different output is realized, then a mistake has been made.

As with truth tables, input variables for logic gates will always initially be defined in a positive format. For example, an input variable will start as a B and not as a ~B. Although a variety of logic gates exist, any desired output can be derived from three basic logic gates: the AND, OR, and NOT gates. This means all rules, policies, and laws can be represented via the three basic logic gates.

Similar to moving from one column to the next column when we made the headings for a truth table, each logic gate is used to transform the logical expression to reach the desired rule, policy, or law. However, there are some rules to follow. A NOT gate will only have a single entry. Whatever enters a NOT gate will be negated, whether it is a single value or a sophisticated logical expression.

DOI: 10.4324/9781003252832-5

An AND gate and an OR gate will each have exactly two inputs. Each input may be a single value or a sophisticated logical expression.

BOOLEAN ALGEBRA LAWS AND THEOREMS

In Boolean algebra, variables have binary values, which have a logical significance (Ahmad, 2004; Smith et al., 2006). Boolean algebra deals with logic operations and utilizes conjunction, disjunction, and negation. Furthermore, there are many rules in Boolean algebra by which those mathematical operations are performed. In the following section, select laws and theorems for Boolean algebra will be presented. Logic gates will be used to demonstrate these laws and theorems. In some cases, truth tables will be used to verify the laws.

Laws and Theorems of Boolean Algebra (1 = True; 0 = False)

Idempotent laws: $A \cdot A = A$; $B + B = B$

$A \cdot A = A$

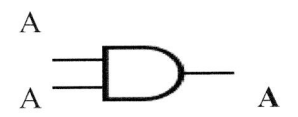

$B + B = B$

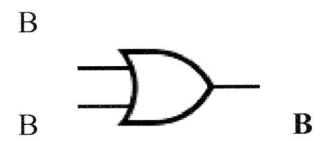

Operation AND
A AND B = A ∩ B = $A \cdot B$

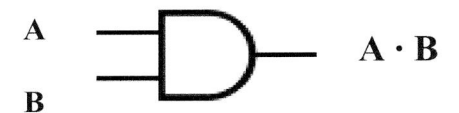

Input		Output (A AND B)
A	B	A ∩ B
0	0	0
1	0	0
0	1	0
1	1	1

Operation OR

A OR B = A U B = A + B

Input		Output (A OR B)
A	B	A U B
0	0	0
1	0	1
0	1	1
1	1	1

Operation NOT

NOT A = ~A

Input	Output (NOT A)
A	~ A
0	1
1	0

Operation NAND = NOT AND = ~ (A · B)

Input			Output
A	B	(A ∩ B)	~ (A ∩ B)
0	0	0	1
1	0	0	1
0	1	0	1
1	1	1	0

Involution law: ~ (~ C) = C

~ C   C

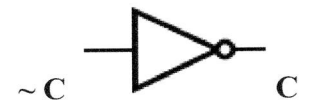

Commutative laws

A + B = B + A

A
B   A + B

B
A   B + A

A · B = B · A

A
B   A · B

B
A   B · A

Associative laws

(A + B) + C = A + B + C

A
B   A + B   C   A + B + C

$(B + C) + A = A + B + C$

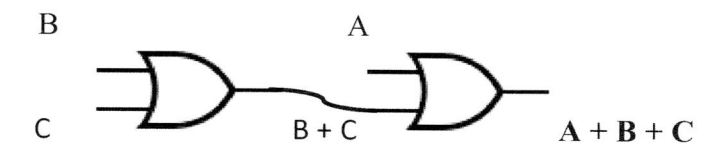

$(A \cdot B) \cdot C = A \cdot B \cdot C$

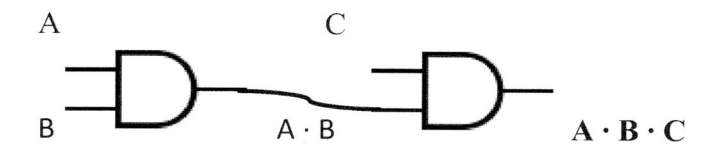

$(B \cdot C) \cdot A = A \cdot B \cdot C$

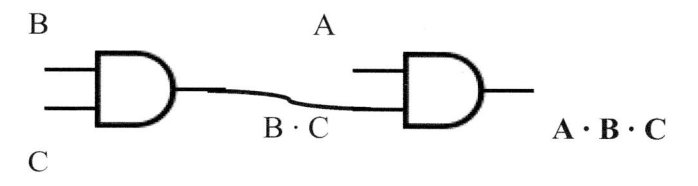

Distributive laws

$A \cdot (B + C) = (A \cdot B) + (A \cdot C)$

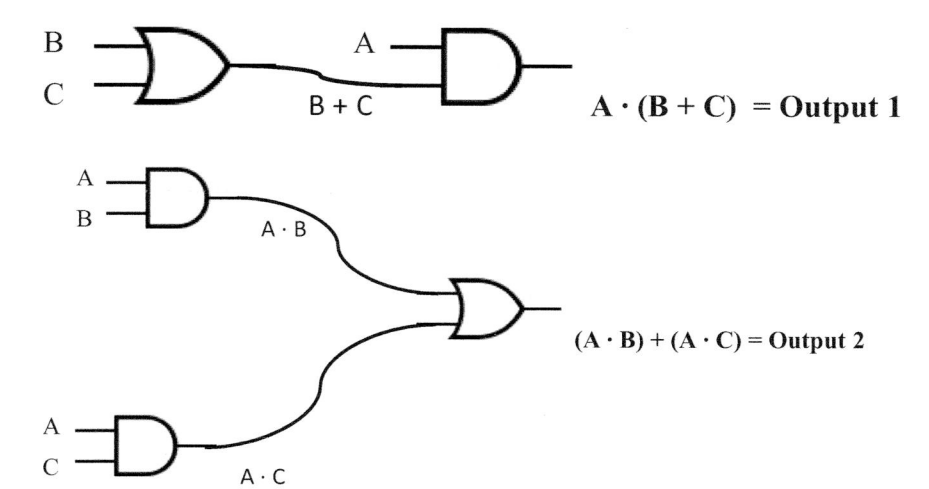

$A \cdot (B + C)$ = Output 1

$(A \cdot B) + (A \cdot C)$ = Output 2

A	B	C	B + C	Output 1 $A \cdot (B + C)$	$(A \cdot B)$	$(A \cdot C)$	Output 2 $(A \cdot B) + (A \cdot C)$
0	0	0	0	0	0	0	0
1	0	0	0	0	0	0	0
0	1	0	1	0	0	0	0
1	1	0	1	1	1	0	1
0	0	1	1	0	0	0	0
1	0	1	1	1	0	1	1
0	1	1	1	0	0	0	0
1	1	1	1	1	1	1	1

$A + (B \cdot C) = (A + B) \cdot (A + C)$

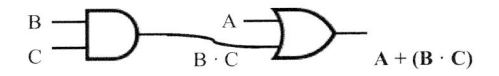

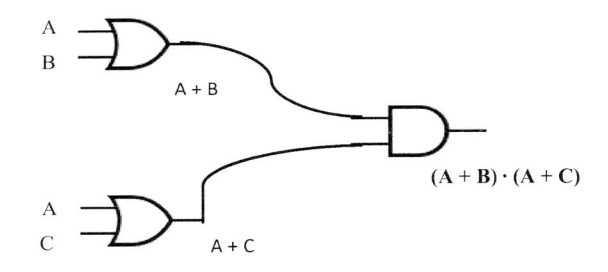

A	B	C	$(B \cdot C)$	**$A + (B \cdot C)$**	$(A + B)$	$(A + C)$	**$(A + B) \cdot (A + C)$**
0	0	0	0	**0**	0	0	**0**
1	0	0	0	**1**	1	1	**1**
0	1	0	0	**0**	1	0	**0**
1	1	0	0	**1**	1	1	**1**
0	0	1	0	**0**	0	1	**0**
1	0	1	0	**1**	1	1	**1**
0	1	1	1	**1**	1	1	**1**
1	1	1	1	**1**	1	1	**1**

Operation **NOR** = NOT OR = ~ OR

A
B ⟶ ~ (A U B)

INPUT			OUTPUT
A	B	(A U B)	~ (A U B)
0	0	0	1
1	0	1	0
0	1	1	0
1	1	1	0

Operation exclusive OR = XOR

A
B ⟶ A ⊕ B = (A + B) BUT NOT (A ∩ B)

INPUT		OUTPUT
A	B	A ⊕ B
0	0	0
1	0	1
0	1	1
1	1	0

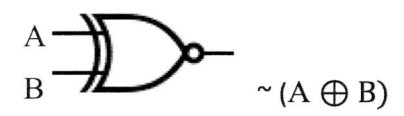

XNOR = ~ [(A + B) BUT NOT (A ∩ B)]

A
B ⟶ ~ (A ⊕ B)

Input			Output
A	B	A ⊕ B	~ (A ⊕ B)
0	0	0	1
1	0	1	0
0	1	1	0
1	1	0	1

LOGIC GATE DESIGNS

In the following section, we will use the three basic logic gates to represent various laws. The three basic logic gates are the AND gate, the OR gate, and the NOT gate. Then, given a set of input values, we will determine whether a violation occurred. If the final logical expression is true (i.e., 1), then the violation is true (i.e., it did occur). If the final logical expression is false (i.e., 0), then the violation is false (i.e., it did not occur). An arrest would be made if the final logical expression is true. An arrest would not be made if the final logical expression is false.

Example 1

Given: Law violation = $(A \cup B) \cap (\sim C \cap D)$

Create the logic gate design for the above law.

Show the output for each logic gate. See below for solution.

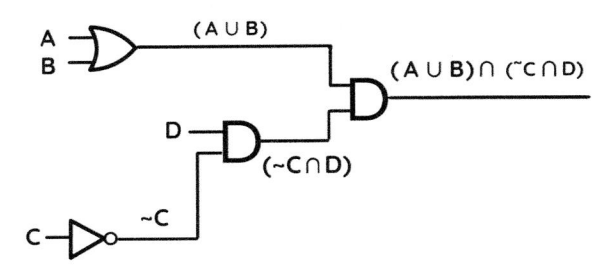

Now, given specific input values, we can check for violations of the law.

Using the logic gate design below, determine whether the law was violated.

Let A = 1, B = 1, C = 1, and D = 1. Will an arrest be made?

To answer the question, we will insert the specific input values into the logic gate design.

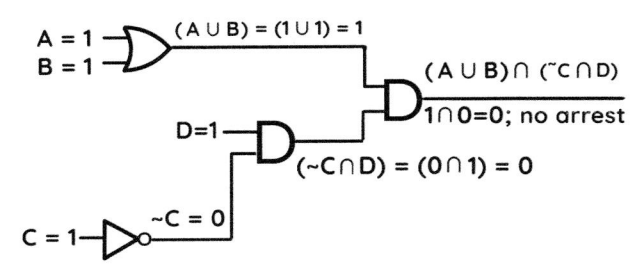

The result for the final logical expression (i.e., the law) = 0. Thus, no arrest will be made.

Example 2

Given: Law violation = ~ (A U B U C) ∩ (~C ∩ D) U E

Create the logic gate design for the above law.

Show the output for each logic gate. See below for solution.

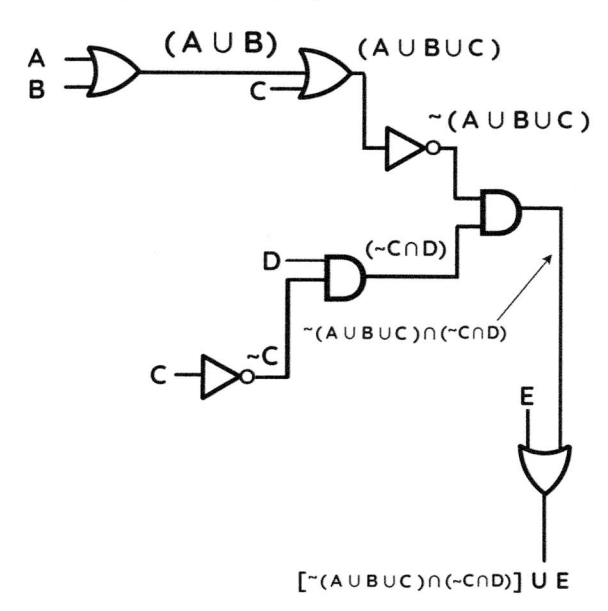

Using the logic gate design below, determine whether the law was violated.

Let A = 1, B = 0, C = 1, D = 0, and E = 1. Will an arrest be made?

To answer the question, we will insert the specific input values into the logic gate design.

The result for the final logical expression (i.e., the law) = 1. Thus, an arrest will be made.

Example 3

Given: Law violation = ~ [~ (A ∩ B) ∩ (C U D)]

Create the logic gate design for the above law.

Show the output for each logic gate. See below for solution.

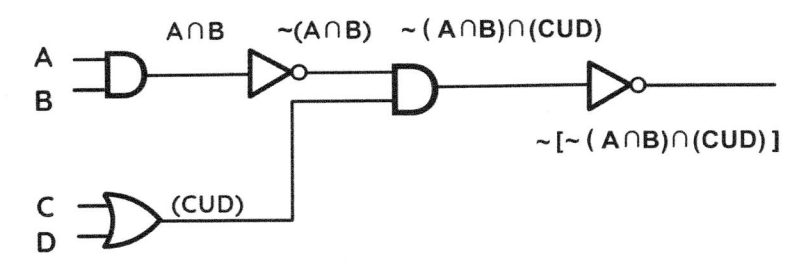

The result for the final logical expression (i.e., the law) = 0. Thus, no arrest will be made.

Using the logic gate design below, determine whether the law was violated.

Let A = 1, B = 0, C = 1, and D = 0. Will an arrest be made?

To answer the question, we will insert the specific input values into the logic gate design.

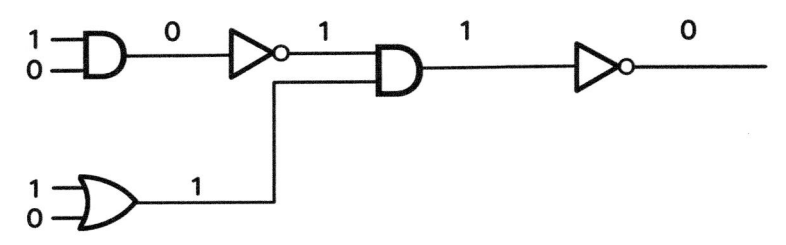

The result for the final logical expression (i.e., the law) = 0. Thus, no arrest will be made.

Example 4

Given: Law violation = ~[(A ∩ B) U (A U ~B)]

Create the logic gate design for the above law.

Show the output for each logic gate. See below for solution.

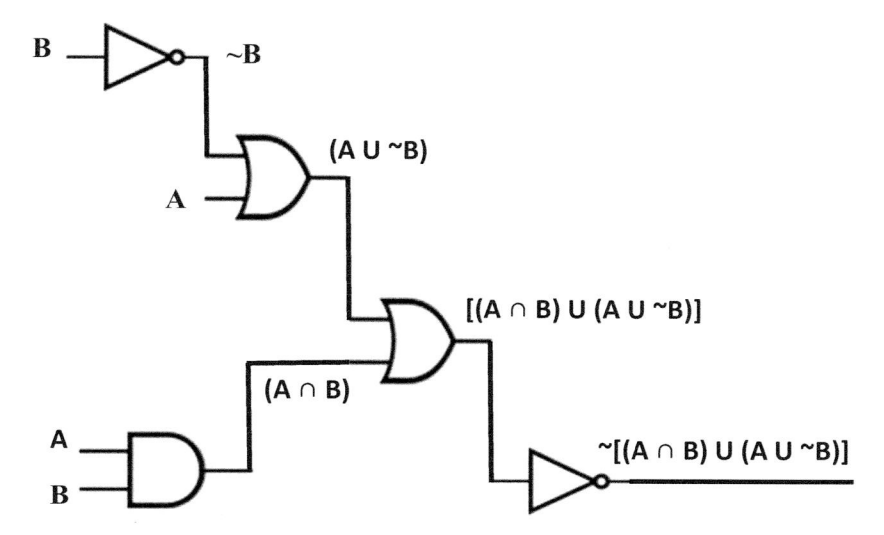

Using the logic gate design below, determine whether the law was violated.

Let A = 0, B = 0. Will an arrest be made?

To answer the question, we will insert the specific input values into the logic gate design.

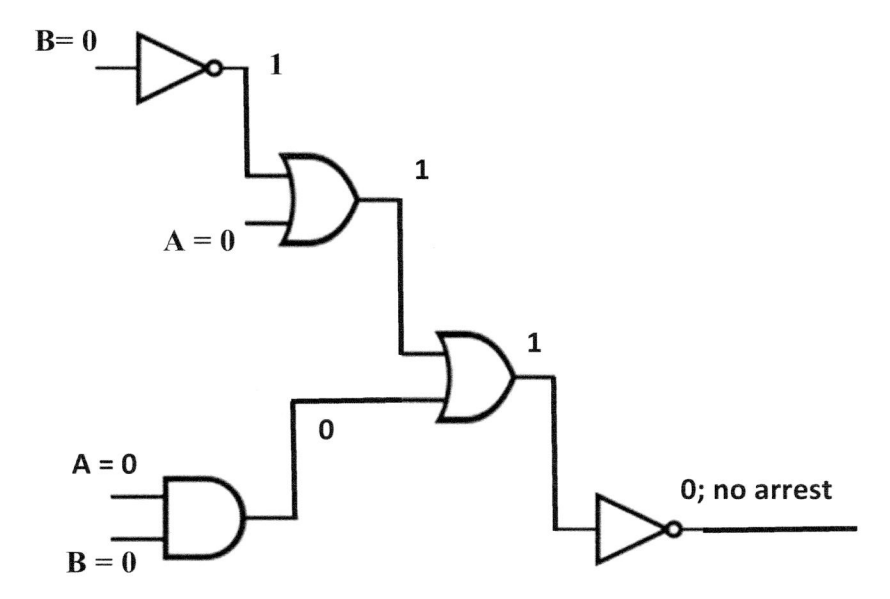

The result for the final logical expression (i.e., the law) = 0. Thus, no arrest will be made.

Example 5

Given the logic gate design below, provide the law that it represents.

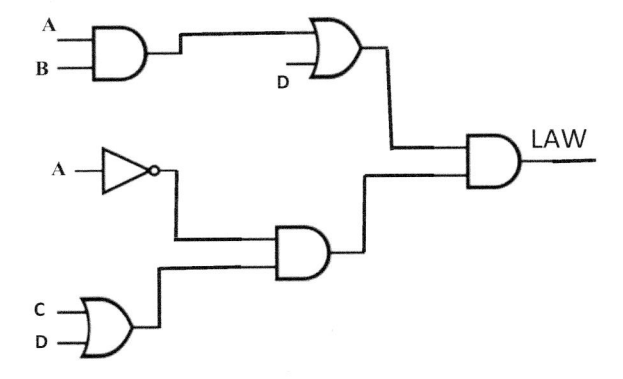

See below for the solution.

Solution: Law = $[(A \cap B) \cup D] \cap [\sim A \cap (C \cup D)]$.

See below for work. Notice the output at each gate.

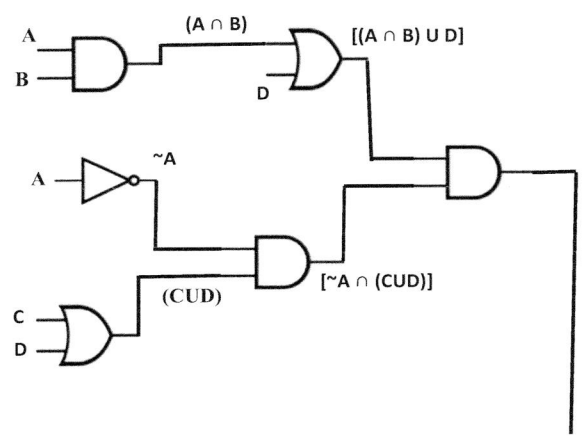

Law = $[(A \cap B) \cup D] \cap [\sim A \cap (C \cup D)]$

Example 6

Given the logic gate design below, provide the law that it represents.

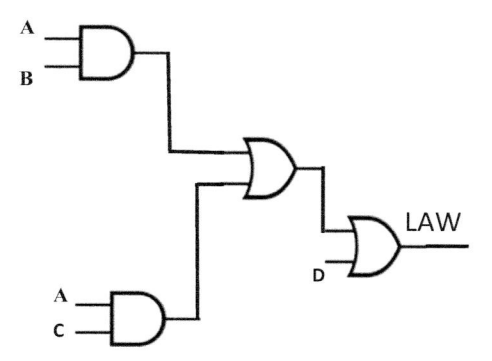

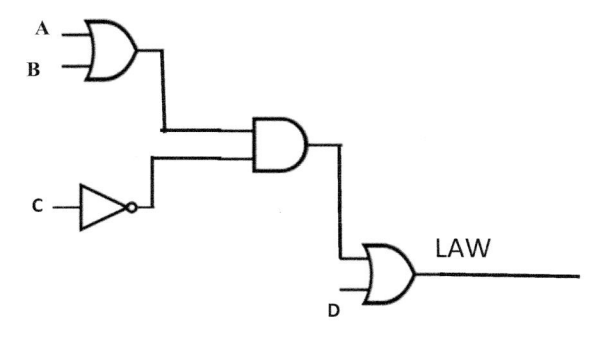

Solution: Law = [(A ∩ B) U (A ∩ C)] U D. See below for work.

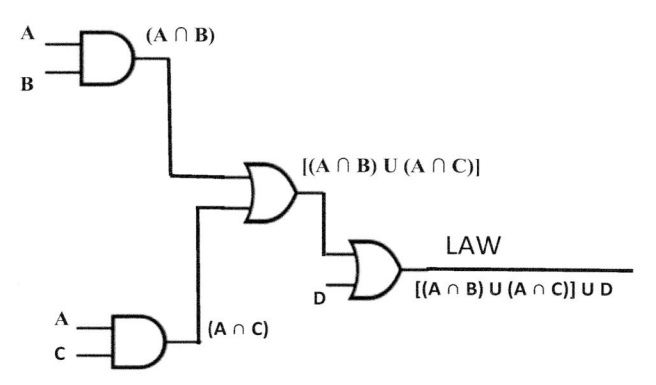

Example 7

Given the logic gate design below, provide the law that it represents.

Solution: Law = [(A U B) ∩ ~C] U D. See below for work.

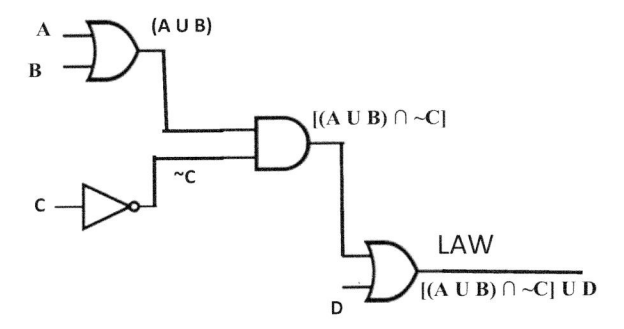

Example 8

Given the logic gate design below, provide the law that it represents.

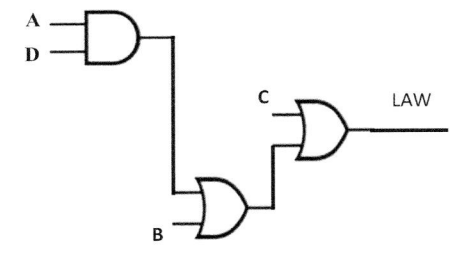

Solution: Law = C U (A ∩ D) U B. See below for work.

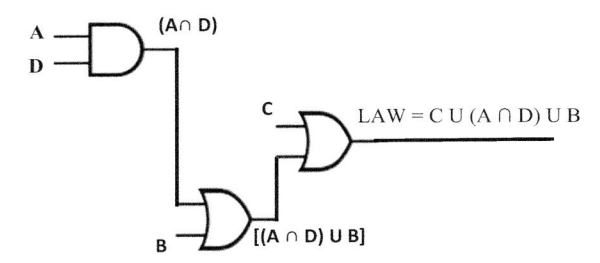

Example 9

Given a logic gate design below, provide the law that it represents.

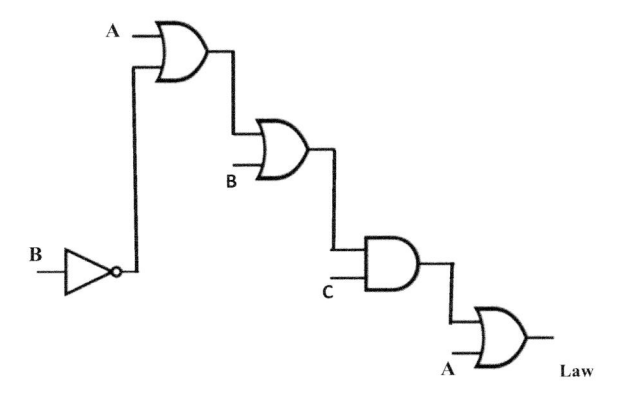

Solution: Law = [(A U ~B U D) ∩ C] U A. See below for work.

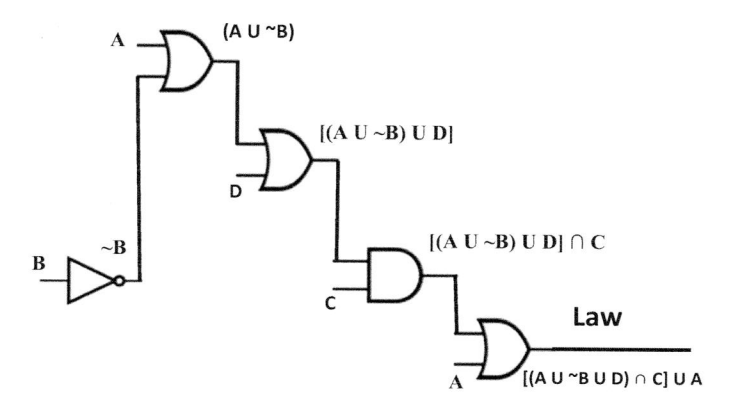

```
A ─────┐
       ├─OR── (A U ~B)
       │         └──┐
       │            ├─OR── [(A U ~B) U D]
       │         D──┘          └──┐
                                  ├─AND── [(A U ~B) U D] ∩ C
~B                             C──┘            └──┐
B──NOT──┘                                          ├─OR── Law
                                              A───┘     [(A U ~B U D) ∩ C] U A
```

LOGIC CIRCUITS

Logic circuits are used to graphically represent the sequence of operations from start to finish to create the desired outcome, such as a rule, policy, or law (Tan, 2015). Placed in the correct sequence, logic circuits can be used to create rules, policies, and laws. Furthermore, the validity of a logic circuit design can easily be confirmed by inserting binary data into the logic circuit design. If a certain output is expected based on the values of the input variables, and if a different output is realized, then a mistake has been made.

Logic circuits are like logic gates, except that they present the information in a different format. Logic circuits are like electrical circuits, and electricity either flows or it does not flow (Diaz, 2012). If a switch is closed, then electricity will flow. This represents a true statement. If a switch is open, then electricity will not flow. This represents a false statement. If two switches are sequential (i.e., in series), then this represents an AND operation (both switches must be closed for current to flow). If two switches are parallel, then this represents an OR operation (only one switch needs to be closed for current to flow). However, unlike logic gates, logic circuits do not have a NOT gate. Therefore, input variables for logic circuits may not necessarily be initially defined in a positive format.

Another way to think of logic switches is to think of drawbridges. If the switch is closed, then the drawbridge is closed and you will be able to march across the bridge. This is a true statement that you can march across the bridge. However, if the switch is open, then the drawbridge is open and you will not be able to march across the bridge. This is a false statement that you can march across the bridge. If bridges are sequential, then this means that you have no choice, and all bridges must be closed to march across them. This represents an AND statement (e.g., both A and B must be closed). If bridges are parallel, then this means that you have a choice of path to take and only one bridge must be closed to march across them. This represents an OR statement (e.g., either A or B must be closed).

See below for the logic circuit representation of an AND statement.

```
Start = Point 1                              Finish = Point 2
   ●────/  ────────────/  ──────────────●
          A                B
```

In terms of drawbridges, A and B must both be closed for you to get from point 1 to point 2. This is a series design. This represents an AND statement (A ∩ B). You do not have any alternative paths that you can take. Both switches must be closed for you to get from point 1 to point 2.

See below for the logic circuit representation of an OR statement.

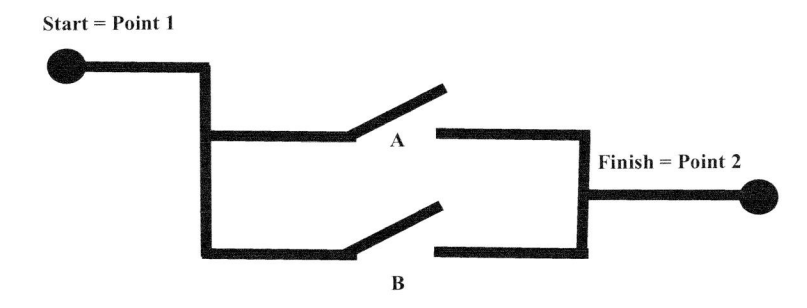

In terms of drawbridges, either A or B must be closed for you to get from point 1 to point 2. This is a parallel design. This represents an OR statement (A U B). You have a choice in terms of which path you could take. Only one switch must be closed for you to get from point 1 to point 2.

The NOT symbol has no electrical representation. A NOT B will simply be represented as ~B. See the example below.

Let us work through several examples.

Example 1: Given the following logic circuit, what is the equation for the law violation?

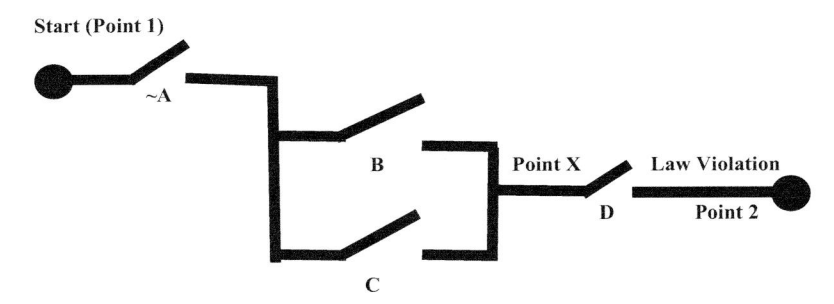

If the logic circuit switches were drawbridges, then ~A must be close. If ~A is not closed, then nothing else matters. We will never get to Point 2 if ~A is open. If ~A is closed, then we will require that either B or C be closed. If both are open, we will never get to Point X. We can, however, get to Point X if only B is closed, if only C is closed, or if both B and C are closed. We do not require that both be closed, but if both are closed, then at least one is closed. Once we get to Point X, then D must be closed or else we cannot get to Point 2. See below for the law.

Answer: Law violation = ~A ∩ (B U C) ∩ D.

For the law violation to be true (= 1), then ~A must = 1, B or C must = 1, and D must = 1.

Let us confirm the equation. Let ~A = 1, B = 0, C = 1, and D = 1.

~A ∩ (B U C) ∩ D = 1 ∩ (0 U 1) ∩ 1 = 1 ∩ 1 ∩ 1 = 1. This helps confirm the accuracy of the circuit.

If the above conditions are not satisfied, then the law violation will be false (= 0).

Let us confirm this statement. Let ~A = 1, B = 0, C = 0, and D = 1.

~A ∩ (B U C) ∩ D = 1 ∩ (0 U 0) ∩ 1 = 1 ∩ 0 ∩ 1 = 0.

This helps confirm the accuracy of the circuit.

We can confirm the equation with a truth table.

Law violation = ~A ∩ (B U C) ∩ D.

Row	A	B	C	D	~A	B U C	~A ∩ (B U C) ∩ D (Law violation)
1	0	0	0	0	1	0	0
2	1	0	0	0	0	0	0
3	0	1	0	0	1	1	0
4	1	1	0	0	0	1	0
5	0	0	1	0	1	1	0
6	1	0	1	0	0	1	0
7	0	1	1	0	1	1	0
8	1	1	1	0	0	1	0
9	0	0	0	1	1	0	0
10	1	0	0	1	0	0	0
11	0	1	0	1	1	1	1
12	1	1	0	1	0	1	0
13	0	0	1	1	1	1	1
14	1	0	1	1	0	1	0
15	0	1	1	1	1	1	1
16	1	1	1	1	0	1	0

Explanation: A law violation is true only if the truth value for the law violation is 1. There are only three rows that meet this condition: rows 11, 13, and 15. These three rows must comply with the requirements dictated earlier by the logic circuit (~A must = 1, B or C must = 1, and D must = 1).

Let us look at rows 11, 13, and 15 to confirm that the truth table matches the logic circuit.

For rows 11, 13, and 15: A = 0, therefore, ~A = 1. D = 1.

In row 11, B = 1. In row 13, C = 1. In row 15, C = 1 and D = 1.

Thus, the truth table confirms the logic circuit design.

Notice that none of the other rows in the truth table meets the requirements that ~A must = 1, B or C must = 1, and D must = 1, and this is confirmed by the zeros under the law violation in the truth table.

Example 2: Given the logic circuit, indicate the equation for the law

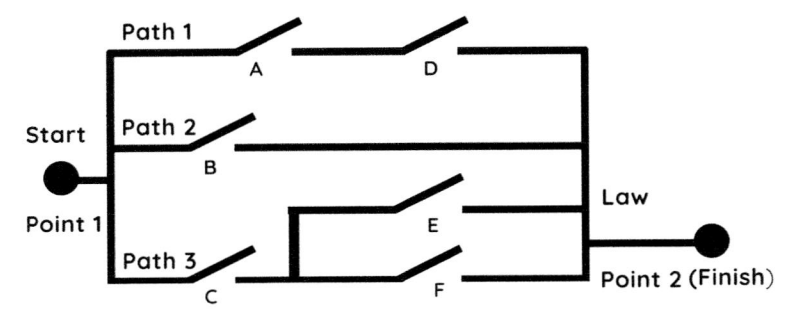

To get from Point 1 to Point 2 (from start to finish), we have three different parallel paths that we can take. We can take the top path, OR the middle path, OR the bottom path. However, if we take the top path, both A and D must be closed (A ∩ D). If we take the middle path, only B needs to be closed. If we take the bottom path, C must be closed and either E or F must be closed.

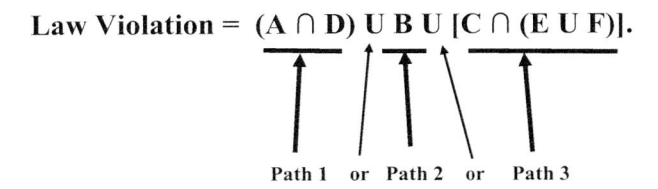

$$\text{Law Violation} = (A \cap D) \cup B \cup [C \cap (E \cup F)].$$

Path 1 or Path 2 or Path 3

Let us look at the three paths. First, let us look at the top path: A ∩ D. If A and D are closed, we will not really care about the other paths. We can make it from Point 1 to Point 2 regardless of the values in the other paths. Second, let us look at the middle path: B. If B is closed, we will not really care about the other paths. We can make it from Point 1 to Point 2 regardless of the values in the other paths. Finally, let us look at the bottom path: [C ∩ (E ∪ F)]. We will never get to the option of either E or F until after we have passed C. This means that crossing C first is mandatory. In other words, in the bottom path, C is in series with whatever follows it, which is a parallel circuit, E or F. Once C has been passed, we can get to Point 2 if E is closed, F is closed, or both E and F are closed.

Example 3: Given the logic circuit, indicate the equation for the law.

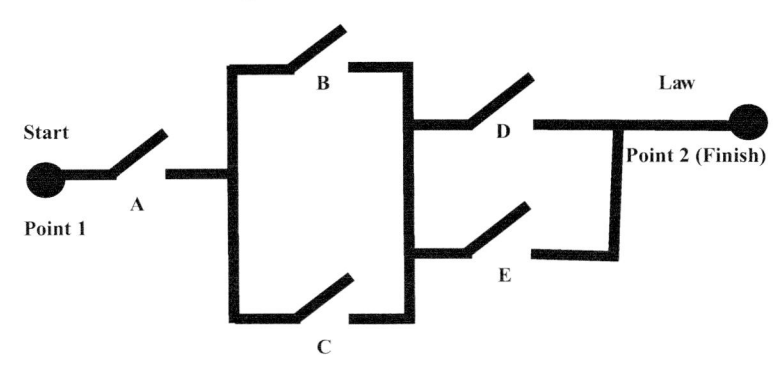

Starting at Point 1, A must be closed to move forward. There is no other way. Once A has been passed, we have a choice of either B or C. If either B or C is closed, then we can cross that section. If both B and C are closed, then that would satisfy the requirement that one of them is closed. Once we have passed B or C, we will then have another choice of D or E. If either D or E is closed, then we can cross that section. If both D and E are closed, then that would satisfy the requirement that one of them is closed. Once we have passed D or E, then we will have reached Point 2. In short, there are three sections that must be passed. Section 1 = A, Section 2 = B U C, and Section 3 = D U E. The law for the above circuit is listed below.

Answer: law = A ∩ (B U C) ∩ (D U E)

For the law to be true, the following conditions must exist:

A = 1, B or C = 1, D or E = 1.

Let us look at the truth table to confirm this.

We can check the law with a truth table.

Row	A	B	C	D	E	B U C	D U E	Law = A ∩ (B U C) ∩ (D U E)
1	0	0	0	0	0	0	0	0
2	1	0	0	0	0	0	0	0
3	0	1	0	0	0	1	0	0
4	1	1	0	0	0	1	0	0
5	0	0	1	0	0	1	0	0
6	1	0	1	0	0	1	0	0
7	0	1	1	0	0	1	0	0
8	1	1	1	0	0	1	0	0
9	0	0	0	1	0	0	1	0
10	1	0	0	1	0	0	1	0
11	0	1	0	1	0	1	1	0
12	1	1	0	1	0	1	1	1
13	0	0	1	1	0	1	1	0
14	1	0	1	1	0	1	1	1
15	0	1	1	1	0	1	1	0
16	1	1	1	1	0	1	1	1
17	0	0	0	0	1	0	1	0
18	1	0	0	0	1	0	1	0
19	0	1	0	0	1	1	1	0
20	1	1	0	0	1	1	1	1
21	0	0	1	0	1	1	1	0
22	1	0	1	0	1	1	1	1
23	0	1	1	0	1	1	1	0

Row	A	B	C	D	E	B U C	D U E	Law = A ∩ (B U C) ∩ (D U E)
24	1	1	1	0	1	1	1	1
25	0	0	0	1	1	0	1	0
26	1	0	0	1	1	0	1	0
27	0	1	0	1	1	1	1	0
28	1	1	0	1	1	1	1	1
29	0	0	1	1	1	1	1	0
30	1	0	1	1	1	1	1	1
31	0	1	1	1	1	1	1	0
32	1	1	1	1	1	1	1	1

There are nine possible combinations of input variables that produce a true value under the equation of the law: rows 12, 14, 16, 20, 22, 24, 28, 30, and 32. In every case, A is true, either B or C is true, and either D or E is true. For all of the other combinations, at least one the required conditions was not satisfied. Thus, the truth table verifies the logic circuit design.

Now, suppose we are given a rule or law and we want to create a logic circuit to represent the rule or law.

Example 1: Given the rule violation below, create a logic circuit to reflect it

Rule violation = (A ∩ B) U (A ∩ C)

Looking at the equation, there are two paths that we could take. If either path is true, then the rule violation will be true. We could either go through (A ∩ B) or we could go through (A ∩ C).

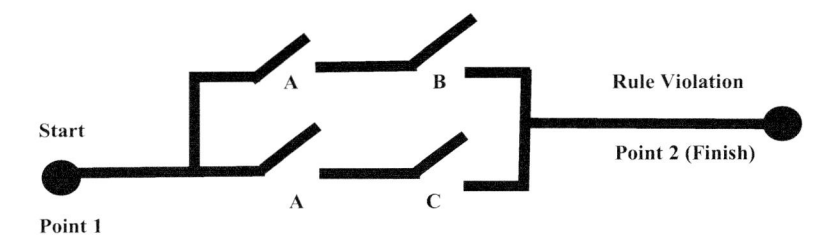

The above circuit could also be described as below. Rule = A ∩ (B U C).

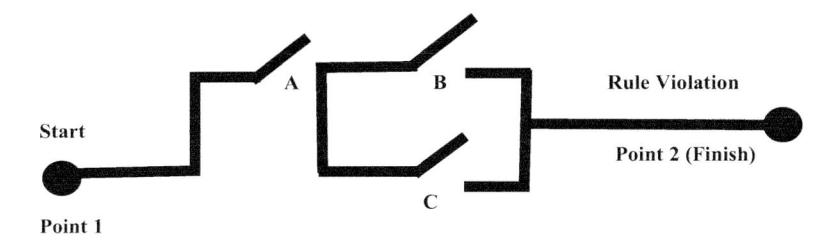

A truth table can be used to see whether the above two logic circuits are equivalent.

$(A \cap B) \cup (A \cap C) \equiv A \cap (B \cup C)$

A	B	C	$(A \cap B)$	$(A \cap C)$	$(B \cup C)$	$(A \cap B) \cup (A \cap C)$	$A \cap (B \cup C)$
0	0	0	0	0	0	0	0
1	0	0	0	0	0	0	0
0	1	0	0	0	1	0	0
1	1	0	1	0	1	1	1
0	0	1	0	0	1	0	0
1	0	1	0	1	1	1	1
0	1	1	0	0	1	0	0
1	1	1	1	1	1	1	1

Because the two columns are exactly the same for the same combinations of the three input variables, $(A \cap B) \cup (A \cap C)$ is equivalent to $A \cap (B \cup C)$. Thus, the two logic circuit designs are equivalent.

Example 2: Given the rule violation below, create a logic circuit to reflect it.

Rule violation = $A \cap B \cap (C \cup D) \cap (B \cup E)$

There will be four sections.

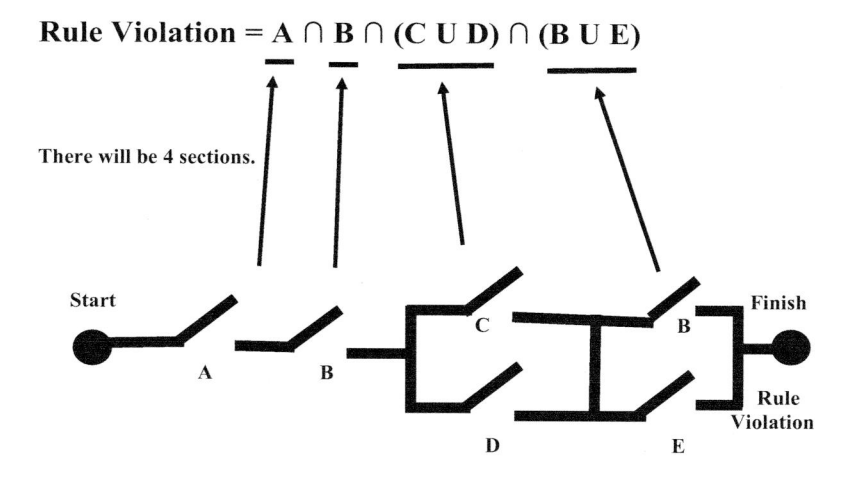

Rule Violation = $A \cap B \cap (C \cup D) \cap (B \cup E)$

There will be 4 sections.

For a violation to be true, we must be able to get to the finish point. First, to get to the finish point, it is clear that A and B must both be closed. This means that they must both be true (i.e., 1). Second, it is clear that either C or D must be closed, which means that at least one of them must be true. Finally, it is clear that either B or E must be closed, which means that at least one of them must be true. See below for a summary of the requirements for the rule violation to be true.

A = 1, B = 1, C or D = 1, B or E = 1 (however, as stated earlier, B = 1)

Notice that because B must equal 1, E becomes irrelevant. In other words, if B must be closed, then E can be bypassed in the final section. We can check the truth table to confirm that E is irrelevant.
Rule violation = $A \cap B \cap (C \cup D) \cap (B \cup E)$

A	B	C	D	E	A ∩ B	(C U D)	(B U E)	(Rule violation) A ∩ B ∩ (C U D) ∩ (B U E)
0	0	0	0	0	0	0	0	0
1	0	0	0	0	0	0	0	0
0	1	0	0	0	0	0	1	0
1	1	0	0	0	1	0	1	0
0	0	1	0	0	0	1	0	0
1	0	1	0	0	0	1	0	0
0	1	1	0	0	0	1	1	0
1	**1**	**1**	**0**	**0**	**1**	**1**	**1**	**1**
0	0	0	1	0	0	1	0	0
1	0	0	1	0	0	1	0	0
0	1	0	1	0	0	1	1	0
1	**1**	**0**	**1**	**0**	**1**	**1**	**1**	**1**
0	0	1	1	0	0	1	0	0
1	0	1	1	0	0	1	0	0
0	1	1	1	0	0	1	1	0
1	**1**	**1**	**1**	**0**	**1**	**1**	**1**	**1**
0	0	0	0	1	0	0	1	0
1	0	0	0	1	0	0	1	0
0	1	0	0	1	0	0	1	0
1	1	0	0	1	1	0	1	0
0	0	1	0	1	0	1	1	0
1	0	1	0	1	0	1	1	0
0	1	1	0	1	0	1	1	0
1	**1**	**1**	**0**	**1**	**1**	**1**	**1**	**1**
0	0	0	1	1	0	1	1	0

A	B	C	D	E	A ∩ B	(C U D)	(B U E)	(Rule violation) A ∩ B ∩ (C U D) ∩ (B U E)
1	0	0	1	1	0	1	1	0
0	1	0	1	1	0	1	1	0
1	1	0	1	1	1	1	1	1
0	0	1	1	1	0	1	1	0
1	0	1	1	1	0	1	1	0
0	1	1	1	1	0	1	1	0
1	1	1	1	1	1	1	1	1

Notice that there are six combinations of input variables that produce a rule violation. For all six combinations, A = 1, B = 1, C or D = 1, and E is irrelevant. This is in alignment with the summary of the requirements necessary for the rule violation to be true. For all of the other combinations, at least one the required conditions was not satisfied.

Now, let us check the relevancy of E by placing the two possible values of E into the logical expression for the rule violation.

Rule violation = A ∩ B ∩ (C U D) ∩ (B U E)

For the rule violation to be true, A must be true, B must be true, and (C U D) must be true. Otherwise, the rule violation will always be false. If B is true, then E is irrelevant.

This being the case, A ∩ B ∩ (C U D) ∩ (B U E) = 1 ∩ 1 ∩ (1) ∩ (1 U E).

Let E = 1.

1 ∩ 1 ∩ (1) ∩ (1 U E) = 1 ∩ 1 ∩ (1) ∩ (1 U 1) = 1 ∩ 1 ∩ 1 ∩ 1 = 1.

Let E = 0

1 ∩ 1 ∩ (1) ∩ (1 U E) = 1 ∩ 1 ∩ (1) ∩ (1 U 0) = 1 ∩ 1 ∩ (1) ∩ (1) = 1.

Thus, if B = 1, then it does not matter what E is because its union with B will always be true (i.e., always equal to one).

Logic Gate Design

Exercise 1: Create a logic gate and logic circuit design to represent the following law.

Law = (~A ∩ B) U [(C U D) ∩ E] U (F ∩ G). Show details of your work.

Logic Gate Design versus Logic Circuit Design

Logic Gate Design

$(\sim A \cap B) \cup [(C \cup D) \cap E]$

$(\sim A \cap B)$

$\sim A$

LAW

$(C \cup D)$

$[(C \cup D) \cap E]$ $(F \cap G)$

$(\sim A \cap B) \cup [(C \cup D) \cap E] \cup (F \cap G)$

Logic Circuit Design

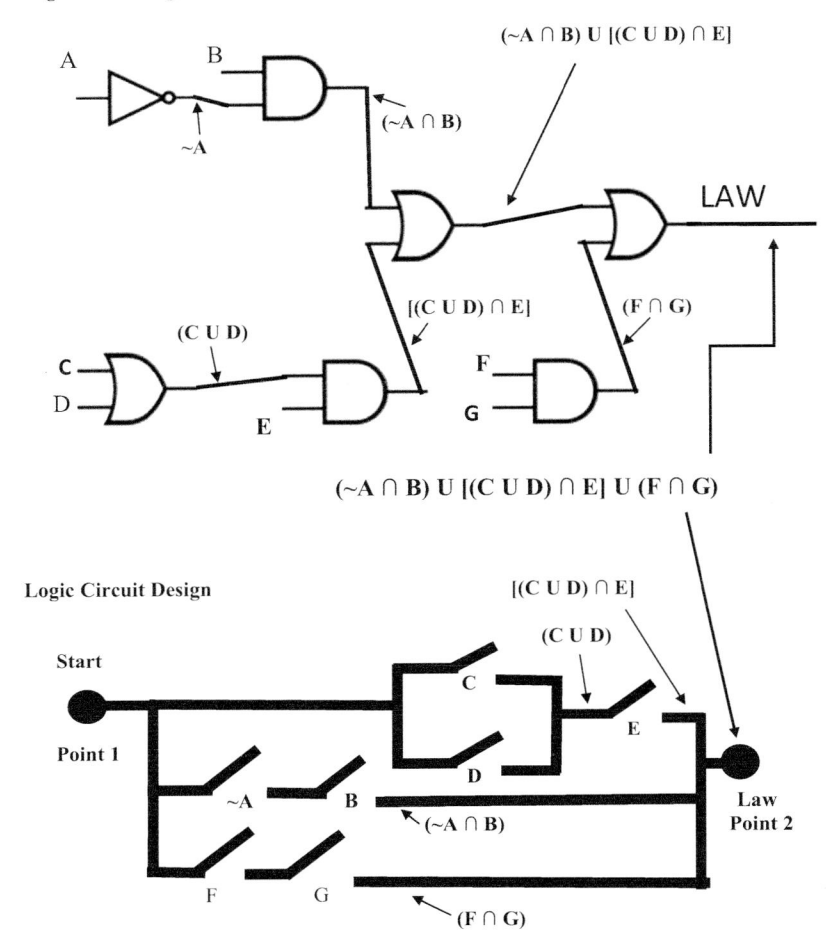

$[(C \cup D) \cap E]$

$(C \cup D)$

Start

Point 1

E

$\sim A$ B

D Law Point 2

$(\sim A \cap B)$

F G

$(F \cap G)$

Exercise 2: Create a logic gate and logic circuit design to represent the following law

Law = A U B ∩ C ∩ D U E. Show details of your work.

To make the law easier to read, the law should be rewritten using the order of operations.

Law = A U B ∩ C ∩ D U E = **A U (B ∩ C ∩ D) U E**

Logic Gate Design versus Logic Circuit Design

Logic Gate Design

B, C → (B ∩ C)
(B ∩ C), D → (B ∩ C ∩ D)
A, (B ∩ C ∩ D) → A U (B ∩ C ∩ D)
A U (B ∩ C ∩ D), E → A U (B ∩ C ∩ D) U E — LAW

Logic Circuit Design

Start — switches labeled E, E (top branch); A, A (middle branch); B, C, D (bottom branch) — Finish — Law

Bottom branch represents (B ∩ C ∩ D)

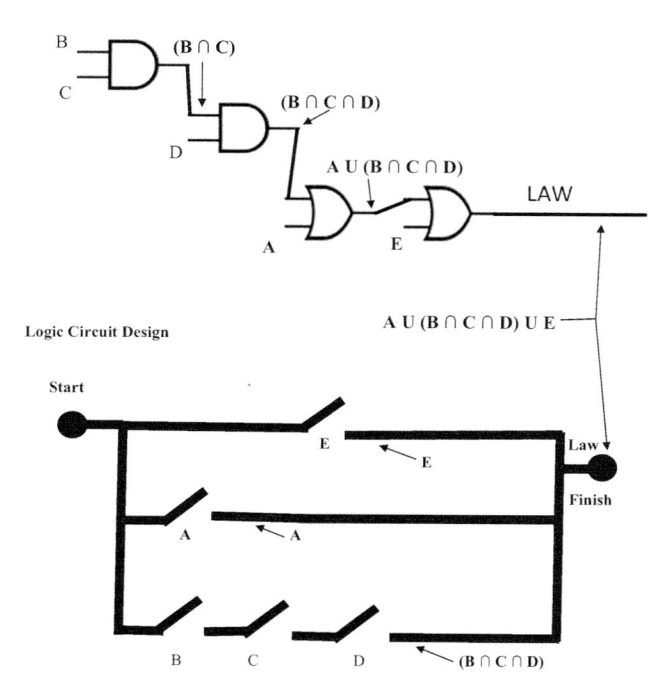

Exercise 3: Create a logic gate and logic circuit design to represent the following law.

Logic Gate Design versus Logic Circuit Design

Logic Gate Design

A, B → (A U B)
C, D → (C U D)
(A U B), (C U D) → [(A U B) ∩ (C U D)]
E, F → (E U F)
[(A U B) ∩ (C U D)], (E U F) → LAW

Law = [(A U B) ∩ (C U D)] ∩ (E U F)

Logic Circuit Design

Start — (A U B) switches A/B in parallel — [(A U B) ∩ (C U D)] switches C/D in parallel — switches E/F in parallel — LAW

[(A U B) ∩ (C U D)]

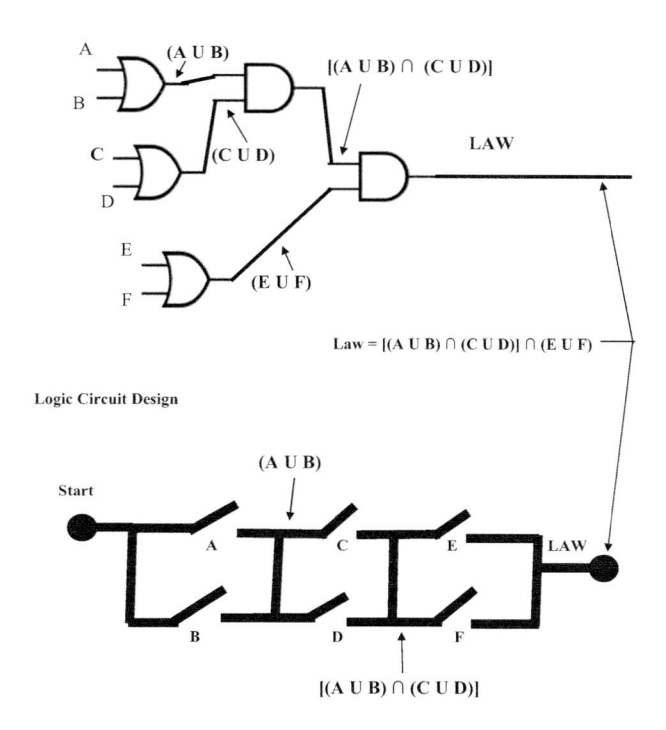

KEYWORDS

Logic circuit
Logical expression
Logic gate

CHAPTER PROBLEMS

Create a logic gate design to represent each of the following laws.

1. $(\sim A \cup B \cap C) \cap (A \cup D)$
2. $(A \cap C) \cap (A \cup D) \cup \sim C$
3. $A \cup (B \cap C) \cup D \cup (E \cap F)$

Using the logic gate design, describe the law as an equation.

4.

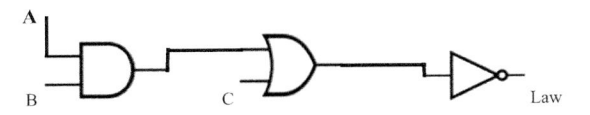

5.

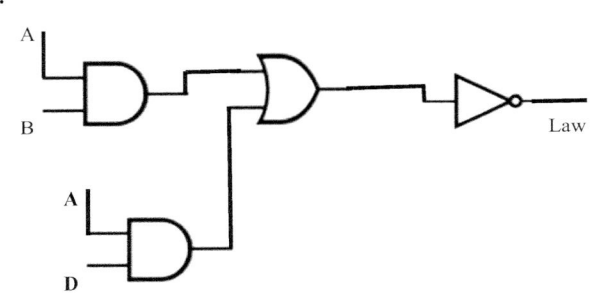

Create a logic circuit design to represent each of the following laws.

6. $(\sim A \cup B \cap C) \cap (A \cup D)$
7. $(A \cap C) \cap (A \cup D) \cup \sim C$
8. $A \cup (B \cap C) \cup D \cup (E \cap F)$

Using the circuit gate design, describe the law as an equation.

9.

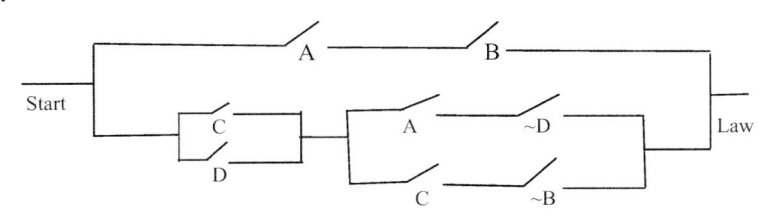

10.

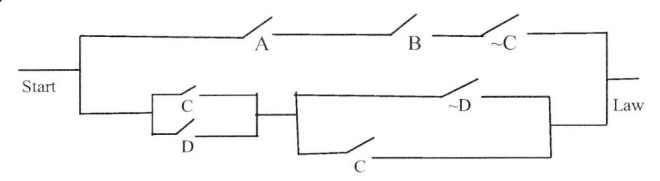

REFERENCES

Ahmad, M. (2004). *Boolean algebra*. http://imps.mcmaster.ca/courses/CAS-701-04/presentations/contributions/Ahmadi-boolean-alg.pdf

Diaz, M.O. (2012). *Boolean algebra & logic gates*. www.scribd.com/ doc/ 59329027/30/XNOR

Smith, D., Eggen, M., & St. Andre, R. (2006). *A transition to advanced mathematics* (6th ed.). Belmont, CA: Thomson Brooks/Cole.

Tan, S.T. (2015). *Finite mathematics: For the managerial, life, and social sciences*. Stamford, CT: Cengage.

CHAPTER 6

Probable Cause Affidavit, Information, Evidence, and Search Warrant

LEARNING OBJECTIVES

Understand the purpose of select police reports.

Properly record of the elements of the law on an affidavit and information.

Properly complete a driving under the influence (DUI) probable cause affidavit.

Properly complete a property record and receipt and a laboratory examination request.

INTRODUCTION

This chapter will focus on the elements of the crime as they apply to a general probable cause affidavit and an information. A probable cause affidavit and an information are required whenever an arrest is made. After an arrest, if an additional crime is discovered—such as finding illegal drugs on the suspect—additional paperwork will be required, including another probable cause affidavit and information. Each charge will require its own probable cause affidavit and information. Whenever anything is taken from a person, a property record and receipt (i.e., chain of custody) form must be completed. If the confiscated item is believed to be an illegal drug, then a laboratory examination request form will also be required. Furthermore, because safety is always the top priority and the jailer has a job to do, the jailer will need to collect intake information and medical information.

For a driving under the influence (DUI) investigation, the results of the field sobriety tests, if available, should be transferred to the DUI probable cause affidavit. The DUI probable cause affidavit will include specific details related to driving while intoxicated, which are not included on a general probable cause affidavit. If a suspect refuses to voluntarily provide incriminating evidence via a blood-alcohol test, the officer may be able to simply obtain a search warrant and forcibly collect the evidence.

COLLECTING INFORMATION

The goal for police officers is to determine and document the truth, using laws and policies as reference. However, determining and documenting the truth are insufficient if the officers cannot communicate the truth to other people. A comprehensive truth requires the officers to be culturally adroit, to be open-minded to other perspectives, and to properly complete all of the required paperwork, such as the chain-of-custody forms for evidence. Effective communication requires two-way communication, which requires listening and observing. Police officers need to encourage conversation because their job is to collect information via participation. Officers need to eliminate physical barriers because barriers conceal body language. Finally, police officers should clarify responses by asking non-compound questions one at a time in active language.

Table 6.1 *Qualities of Good Interviewers* (Swanson et al., 2009)

Qualities of good interviewers
• Adaptable
• Culturally sensitive
• Culturally informed
• Optimistic
• Role player
• Patient
• Confident
• Objective
• Sensitive to constitutional rights
• **Know the elements of the crime**

Police officers will need to communicate in different ways to different audiences. When communicating with the police dispatcher, for example, officers may use codes to keep the conversation brief because lives may be at stake if the officer ties up the radio too long. If the officer speaks with a crime victim, the officer may ask personal in-depth questions in a gentle manner to determine the extent of the crime. If the officer speaks with school children about traffic safety, the officer may use humor and will likely speak in language that the school children can understand. If the officer speaks to a suspect during a felony stop, the officer will take control of the situation and provide orders via a forceful voice.

There are several barriers to effective communication. First, officers must be self-controlled and confident when dealing with other people. Police officers must have the skills, training, and confidence necessary to complete their investigations objectively. Officers should not have an agenda, should not let their emotions affect their work, and should not attempt to manipulate the truth. Officers should let the evidence speak for itself. Second, some witnesses and suspects may be less than truthful because they are angry, jealous, or afraid, or because of personal prejudices. Some witnesses, for example, may not want to get involved with the police because they fear getting into trouble for something else. Finally, some police officers may be less than truthful in order to meet the expectations of significant other people. For example, some police officers may exaggerate the details of a crime to meet the expectations of their police department.

POLICE REPORTS

Police officers communicate with other people via many different types of police reports. Each type of police report collects a certain type of information for a specific purpose. Following is a list of several different types of law enforcement reports along with their purpose.

Report name	Purpose
Voluntary statement	Form used to document the statements of witnesses or suspects.
Miranda rights	Form used to protect the suspect's constitutional rights; form used to waive constitutional rights.
Case report	Form used to record criminal activity with probable cause; if have suspect, will include an information and probable cause affidavit.
Probable cause affidavit	Sworn statement by officer of criminal violation.
Information	Criminal charge completed by officer and filed by prosecutor's office.
Indictment	Criminal charge filed by grand jury.
Property record and receipt	Form used to document the chain of custody of the evidence.
Lab request	Form used to request tests to be performed on the evidence by lab personnel.

Report name	Purpose
Vehicle impound	Form used to remove a vehicle from the scene and to record of vehicle's damage and contents.
Intelligence report	Form used to document possible criminal activity but with no probable cause; police will record detailed information about a suspect that will be placed into the police database.
Showup report	Form used when witnesses identify possible suspects in the field.
Lineup report	Form used when witnesses identify possible suspects at the police station.
Photographic lineup	Form used when witnesses identify possible suspects via photographs in a police-controlled environment.
Jail intake form	Form used to record arrestee's administrative information.
Correctional medical survey	Form used to record arrestee's medical needs and condition.
Field interview card	Form used by police to collect information from individuals in the field.
Crash report	Form used to record vehicle damage and personal injuries related to vehicle crashes.
Salvation Army form	Form used to provide food and shelter to needy individuals free of charge.
Public speaker form	Form used to describe the information that the officer presented to the local community.
Public service form	Form used to describe the help that an officer provided to the local community (e.g., changed a flat tire for someone).
Personal illness form	Form submitted to the department and used to describe why an officer missed work due to health reasons.
Application for 72-hour medical detention	A non-criminal application for the 72-hour detention of a person who may be mentally ill and needs to be evaluated by medical personnel.
Custody order/custody hold form	Form completed by an officer and submitted to the jailer that indicates the criminal charges being filed against the suspect, which gives the jailer the authority to detain the suspect.
Temporary hold form	Form used by officers to hold suspects for 24 hours without charging them with a crime.

Figure 6.1 Law Enforcement Reports and their Purpose

Probable Cause Affidavit and Information

Any time an arrest is made, the police are required to complete and file paperwork. Two of the required forms include a probable cause affidavit and an information. A probable cause affidavit is a sworn statement that a specific person has committed a crime. An information is a criminal charge against a specific person. It is possible that the specific person is identified by DNA and not by name. A general probable cause affidavit will be filed for a criminal offense and a DUI probable cause affidavit will be filed for a DUI violation, which is a traffic offense. Both a general probable cause affidavit and information will include the recording of the elements of the crime, which come from the law book. If illegal drugs are found, then a property record and receipt form, and a laboratory request form will also be required. The property record and receipt form will describe each piece of evidence that was collected, and it will record the chain of custody for each piece of evidence. The laboratory examination request form will describe each piece of evidence and request specific tests for specific items.

Elements of the Crime: Probable Cause Affidavit and Information

Now, let us focus on the elements of the crime for the probable cause affidavit and information. As stated before, the elements of the crime come from the law book and are the variables that define the violation of law. It is important for an officer to know the elements of the crime when the officer is interviewing a person so that the officer will know if the law has been violated. For example, if the provocation law states that it is against the law for a person to reckless and knowingly engage in conduct that is likely to get someone angry enough to want to commit battery against the perpetrator, then the officer will need to ask the potential victim whether they got mad enough to want to hit the perpetrator, based on the perpetrator's behavior.

One of the biggest mistakes that students make is to change the elements of the law on the probable cause affidavit and information. Students do not have the authority to change the law. Therefore, you should not add anything to the elements of the law. See the following example for an information and a general probable cause affidavit for a fictious law. Pay particular attention to the elements of the law. Notice the consistency between the two forms. The parts that an officer would need to write onto the information and general probable cause affidavit have been bolded and underlined. The cause number will be filled in by the court at a later date. The appropriate court will need to be used.

Provocation (Code: 14-43-120a) = It is a B class misdemeanor for a person to recklessly and knowingly engage in conduct that is likely to get someone angry enough to commit battery against the perpetrator.

Use June Doe as the offender. Her identification is: SSN = 000-43-4453.

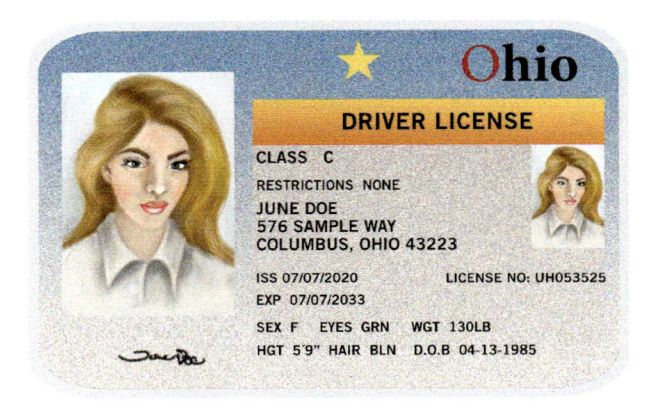

AFFIDAVIT FOR A PROBABLE CAUSE (GENERAL)

State of **Indiana**   IN THE **Superior** COURT

County of **LaGrange**   CAUSE NO. _____

STATE OF **Indiana**

VS.

June Doe

DOB: **4/13/1985**

SSN: **000-43-4453**

FOR OFFENSE (title): **Provocation** Code: **14-43-120a**

COMES NOW, **Deputy** **James Smith,** #43, who being duly sworn upon oath, says that:

1. He/she is an officer with the **Lagrange County** Police Department and believes the following to be true.

2. On or about: (date of offense) **August 1, 2021,** at the following location: **SR 9 at Michigan Ave (EB)** which is in **LaGrange** County, **IN** (State), one (defendant) **June Doe**

3. Did then and there commit the following violation (code) **14-43-120a**, by

   [describe the specific act that supports the criminal charge via **elements of the crime**]
   recklessly and knowingly engaged in conduct that was likely to get another person angry enough to commit battery against her.

4. This officer believes the above facts to be true because (check all that apply)

☐ I personally observed the activity described herein.

☐ The above was told to me by another sworn law enforcement officer, upon whom I have relied on in the past for information and found his/her information to be credible without exception.

X The above was told to me by the victim of a crime, who has no apparent motive to lie, and said statement was given in a straightforward and non-evasive manner, which indicated that the statement was credible.

☐ The above was told to me by a witness of a crime, who has no apparent motive to lie, and said statement was given in a straightforward and non-evasive manner, which indicated that the statement was credible. Further, the witness's statement was corroborated by independent evidence.

☐ The above was told to me by the defendant, which was a statement made against his/her penal interests. Further, the defendant's statement was corroborated by independent evidence.

I swear or affirm under penalty of perjury that the foregoing representations are true.

Dated on this **1st** day of **August, 2021**

Deputy James Smith, 43
Arresting Officer's Name & Badge #

Approved by: _____
Prosecutor

INFORMATION FOR VIOLATION OF LAW

State of **Indiana**   IN THE **Superior** COURT

County of **LaGrange**   CAUSE NO. _____

STATE OF **Indiana**

VS.

June Doe

DOB: **04/13/1985**

SSN: **000-43-4453**

INFORMATION FOR (OFFENSE TITLE): **Provocation**

CODE 14-43-120a CLASS B X MISDEMEANOR ☐ FELONY

COMES NOW, **James Smith, #43** (name of officer), who being duly sworn upon oath, says that on or about: (date of offense) **August 1, 2021,** at (location of offense) **SR 9 at Michigan Ave (EB)**, in **LaGrange** County, **IN** (State), one (defendant) **June Doe** of (Defendant's address) **576 Sample Way Columbus, OH 43223** did then and there RECKLESSLY, KNOWINGLY, or INTENTIONALLY: (**elements of the crime**) **recklessly and knowingly engaged in conduct that was likely to get another person angry enough to commit battery against her.**

All of which is contrary to the form of the statute in such cases made and provided, and against the peace and dignity of the State of **IN.**

I swear or affirm under penalty of perjury that the foregoing representations are true.

Dated on this **1st** day of **August, 2021**.

Deputy James Smith, 43

ARRESTING OFFICER'S NAME & BADGE #

Witness List:

Approved by: _____
                                PROSECUTOR

Suppose after the arrest, the officer finds white powder on June Doe at the LaGrange County Jail, which the officer believes to be cocaine (witness = jailer George Kelly, 2122). The officer will confiscate the evidence and will complete: (1) a property record and receipt form, which is an official government receipt for the evidence that includes a chain of custody; and (2) a laboratory examination request form, which is a formal request for laboratory technicians to examine and assess the evidence. There are three important points to make: (1) it does not matter who discovered the evidence, such as the jailer—it is the officer's case and the officer will confiscate the evidence; (2) the laboratory technicians will do exactly as requested—if you are too specific in your examination request, you may fail to identify the substance; and (3) any time a police officer takes property from someone, whether it is legal or not, the officer must provide a receipt or else it is considered theft. This is why officers do not like to confiscate beer from juveniles. If the juveniles cooperate, it is just easier to have them pour it out (if the officer pours it out, the officer could be charged with theft).

It should be pointed out in this example that although the drugs were discovered at the jail (as indicated on the chain of custody form), the field location was used on the probable cause affidavit and information forms. This is not a concern because there is probable cause to believe that she had possession of the drugs while in the field during the initial contact. Finding the drugs at the jail would be a continuation of the initial investigation. Alternatively, the jail location could have been used on the probable cause affidavit and information forms.

When completing the paperwork for confiscated evidence, it is important to note that the officer will file a possession of cocaine charge, but the officer will not describe the white powder as cocaine. Remember, the officer does not need to be correct when making an arrest. The officer only needs to be 51% confident that a crime has occurred. The official receipt, on the other hand, must be accurate beyond reasonable doubt. Thus, let the experts classify the substance. If the officer labeled the substance as cocaine on the official receipt, but the powder was confirmed to be heroin by the laboratory, this would be problematic. The defendant will show the official receipt in court, which will not match the evidence.

In the property record and receipt example that follows, the officer will store the evidence at the police post. A laboratory technician will later transport the evidence from the police post to the laboratory. There must be no gaps in the chain of custody. From the time the evidence is first collected to the time it is locked up in a storage locker, anyone who handles the evidence should be included on the chain of custody form. A common mistake that many students make is the recording of the initial point of collection. The name of the person who initially possessed the drug will be placed in the first Signature & Badge # box. The evidence started with this person. If the officer places their own name in the first Signature & Badge # box, then this means the evidence started with the officer. In other words, the officer has just confessed to possession of illegal drugs. If the drugs were found on the sidewalk, for example, then the information in the first Signature & Badge # box will indicate that the evidence was found.

As stated earlier, it is important to know that the laboratory technicians will do exactly as requested. If the officer requests the laboratory to test the substance for cocaine, that is exactly what the technicians will do. If the substance happens to be heroin, for example, then the officer will have made a huge mistake. The laboratory report will simply state that the substance tested negative for cocaine. Thus, officers should ask the laboratory technicians to test for all controlled substances.

Because there is only one charge allowed per probable cause affidavit and information, an additional probable cause affidavit and information must be completed for possession of cocaine (in addition to the probable cause affidavit and information for provocation). *Note:* The ORI is the police department's identification number, as recognized by the FBI.

Use the following fictitious code: Possession of Cocaine (Code = 44-55-111d). It is a B felony to possess cocaine in this state without a valid prescription.

AFFIDAVIT FOR PROBABLE CAUSE (GENERAL)

State of **Indiana**　　　　　　　　　　　IN THE **Superior** COURT

County of **LaGrange**　　　　　　　　　CAUSE NO. _____

STATE OF **Indiana**

VS.

June Doe

DOB: **4/13/1985**

SSN: **000-43-4453**

FOR OFFENSE (title): **Possession of Cocaine** Code: **44-55-111d**

COMES NOW, <u>Deputy</u> **James Smith, 43** who being duly sworn upon oath, says that:

5. He/she is an officer with the **Lagrange County** Police Department and believes the following to be true.

6. On or about: (date of offense) **August 1, 2021,** at the following location: **SR 9 at Michigan Ave (EB)** which is in **LaGrange** County, **IN** (State), one (defendant) **June Doe**

7. Did then and there commit the following violation (code) **44-5-111d**, by

    (describe the specific act that supports the criminal charge via **elements of the crime**)
    Possessed cocaine in this state without a valid prescription.

8. This officer believes the above facts to be true because (check all that apply)

    X   I personally observed the activity described herein.

    ☐   The above was told to me by another sworn law enforcement officer, upon whom I have relied on in the past for information and found his/her information to be credible without exception.

    ☐   The above was told to me by the victim of a crime, who has no apparent motive to lie, and said statement was given in a straightforward and non-evasive manner, which indicated that the statement was credible.

    ☐   The above was told to me by a witness of a crime, who has no apparent motive to lie, and said statement was given in a straightforward and non-evasive manner, which indicated that the statement was credible. Further, witness' statement was corroborated by independent evidence.

    ☐   The above was told to me by the defendant, which was a statement made against his/her penal interests. Further, Defendant's statement was corroborated by independent evidence.

I swear or affirm under penalty of perjury that the foregoing representations are true.

Dated on this **1st** day of **August, 2021**

Deputy James Smith, 43
Arresting Officer's Name & Badge #

Approved by: _____
Prosecutor

INFORMATION FOR VIOLATION OF LAW

State of **Indiana**　　　　　　　　　　　IN THE **Superior** COURT

County of **LaGrange**　　　　　　　　　CAUSE NO. _____

STATE OF Indiana

VS.

June Doe

DOB: **04/13/1985**

SSN: **000-43-4453**

INFORMATION FOR (OFFENSE TITLE): Possession of Cocaine

CODE 44-55-111d　　　**CLASS B**　　　☐ MISDEMEANOR　　　X FELONY

COMES NOW, **James Smith, 43** (name of officer), who being duly sworn upon oath, says that on or about: (date of offense) **August 1, 2021,** at (location of offense) **SR 9 at Michigan Ave (EB)**, in **LaGrange** County, **IN** (State), one (defendant) **June Doe** of (Defendant's address) **576 Sample Way Columbus, OH 43223** did then and there RECKLESSLY, KNOWINGLY, or INTENTIONALLY: (**elements of the crime**) possess cocaine in this state without a valid prescription.

All of which is contrary to the form of the statute in such cases made and provided, and against the peace and dignity of the State of **IN.**

I swear or affirm under penalty of perjury that the foregoing representations are true.

Dated on this **1st** day of **August, 2021**.

　　　　　　　　　　　　　　　　　　　　Deputy James Smith, 43

　　　　　　　　　　　　　　　　　　　　ARRESTING OFFICER'S NAME & BADGE #

Witness List: LaGrange County jailer George Kelly, 2122

Approved by: _____
　　　　　　　　　　　PROSECUTOR

POLICE PROPERTY RECORD AND RECEIPT FORM

$(α → ΣΔ → Ω)$ PRR # **AA-24B**

Name of Investigating Officer **Deputy James Smith**	Badge Number **43**	Report # / Citation # **2021-0801-099**
Name of officer submitting evidence to lab	Badge Number	Lab # (issued by lab)
Date of evidence collection **Aug 01, 2021**	Time of evidence collection **5:30 pm**	Who was evidence collected from **June DOE** **(OH DL # = UH053525)**

Location of recovery **LaGrange County Jail**	County LaGrange
Witnesses to recovery **Jailer George Kelly, 2122**	
Specific detail or title of offense (use law book if a crime) **Possession of Cocaine**	Offense code (only if criminal case) **44-55-111d**

Evidence Description for Lab (Quantity, Serial #, Color, etc.)

Item # 1	**One sealed plastic bag containing one plastic bag containing white powdery substance.**
Item #	

Chain of Custody

(If no subjects involved, use word "recovered" in "From" box.)

Item #	Date/Time	From: Signature & Badge #	To: Signature & Badge #	Code	Location	Remarks
1	8/31/2021 5:30 pm	**June Doe**	**Deputy James Smith, 43**	T	LaGrange County Jail	Confiscated
1	8/31/2021 6:01 pm	**Deputy James Smith, 496**	LaGrange County Police Department	S	Locker # 2	Stored

Code: T = Transferred; S = Stored; R = Released; D = Destroyed

REQUEST FOR POLICE LABORATORY EXAMINATION

X New Case ☐ Supplemental Case   Lab Assigned Report # _____

Name of investigating officer **Deputy James Smith**	Badge number **43**	Case # **2021-0801-099**	PRR # **AA-24B**
Police Agency & Address **LaGrange County Police Department 244 Justice Ln LaGrange, IN**		Phone # **260-555-2345**	ORI # **000760007600**
Date **08/01/2021**		Time **5:30 pm**	County of Occurrence **LaGrange**

Type of case investigation (most serious criminal violation) **Possession of Cocaine**	Code Violation: **44-55-111d**
Suspect Name **June DOE (OH DL# = UH053525)**	Victim name **State of IN**
Delivered to lab by / Badge #	Received in lab by / Date & time

Evidence Description for Lab (Quantity, Serial #, Color, etc.)

Item #	Description of Items being submitted to lab
1	**One sealed plastic bag containing one plastic bag containing white powdery substance.**

Lab Exam Request (Specify each item number to be tested (e.g., "Test item X for …")

Test item 1 for controlled substance.

_____

_____

Once the suspect is arrested, the suspect will be turned over to the jailer. The jailer will complete a variety of paperwork, which will include a jail intake form and a correctional medical survey. Because safety is the top priority, it is important, for example, to know about any medical concerns and about gang affiliations. It could be extremely dangerous if a gang member is placed into an area of an opposing gang. See the following two forms that that a jailer will be required to complete once the jailer takes possession of the arrestee.

JAIL INTAKE FORM

_____ Police Department Booking Record

Booking Number	Arresting agency	ORI #	State ID	MUG #	Inmate's photograph
Name	Sex	Race	Height	Weight	
Date of birth	Hair	Complexion	Build	Eyes	
SSN	Home phone	Work phone	Marital status	Resident status	
Driver's license #	State of DL	Home address		Place of birth	

Information given at time of booking: Name   DOB   SSN   Address

Gang affiliation	Tattoos	Place & address of employment

Emergency contact information: Name   Address   Home phone #

Ill or Injured __YES __NO	Type of illness or injury	Type of medication taking

Special management for inmate __Medical __Mental __Suicidal __High security __Other (describe):

Arresting officer	Arrest date/time	Arrest Location
Booking officer	Booking date/time	Booking Status (Complete/Pending)
Received by officer	Custodial search by	
Charge 1 (title)	State code	Charge level (M or F) & Class (A-F)
Charge 2 (title)	State code	Charge level (M or F) & Class (A-F)
Arresting officer's signature	Arresting Officer's Badge #	Arresting Officer's Department
Fine	Bail	Disposition
Inmate Tracking #	Intake Date	Block	Cell
Scheduled Release Date	Actual Release Date	Release Type

CORRECTIONAL MEDICAL SURVEY

Intake Screening and Triage

Date booked in: _____ NAME: _____ BOOKING #: _____ DOB: _____ SEX: ___

Statement of booking officer
Does the inmate seem to be under the influence of drugs, impaired, or injured in any way? ___yes ___no
Comments: _____
Officer's signature: dept: date:
Medical/mental questionnaire
1. Do you have any of the following problems?   __asthma   __ENT problems   __hernia   __intestinal disorders   __back injuries   __FX/sprains   __HIV/AIDS   __mental problems   __deformities   __heart trouble   __high blood pressure   __psych. Hospital   __tuberculosis   __dental problems   __std   __hepatitis: type____   __diabetes   __seizures   __pregnant/due date_____   __other_____ allergies_____

	Y	N
2. Are you taking or do you need to take any prescribed medications (including psychiatric medications and birth control pills)?		
3. Have you ever been treated for tuberculosis?		
4. Have you had a cough for more than three weeks with any of the following: fever, weight loss, fatigue, night sweats?		
5. Have you had a head injury/traffic accident or altercation in the past seven hours?		
6. Are you an alcoholic? Date of last drink: How much do you drink?		
7. Any seizures or delirium tremens?		
8. Do you use any street drugs such as heroin, cocaine, methamphetamine, marijuana or any other drugs?		
9. Are you receiving methadone? __detox or __maintenance		
10. Do you have any rashes, cuts, boils, abscesses, or other skin diseases?		
11. Do you have any artificial limbs, braces, dentures, hearing aid, contact lenses, or eyeglasses?		
12. Have you ever tried to harm yourself or take your own life? When:		
13. Are you thinking of harming yourself now?		
14. Are you currently receiving psychiatric treatment?		

15. Have you been a patient in a hospital within the last three months?	
16. Have you ever been treated at a regional center or diagnosed with developmental problems?	
17. Do you know of any medical reason why you cannot work in jail?	

Triage disposition	Work status
__acceptable for booking	__general
__medical	__kitchen
__refer to mental health	__light duty/no kitchen
__refused assessment	__no work
__ER reason:	__hold for follow-up/recheck on:

DUI INVESTIGATION

Now, let us look at a DUI investigation. A DUI probable cause affidavit has more detail than does a general probable cause affidavit. However, the same rule applies for the elements of the crime. For example, if the law states that it is illegal for a person to drive a vehicle in this state with a blood-alcohol level of 0.08% or more, then that is what must be recorded as the elements of the crime. You should not mention anything about the person's poor driving behaviors, nor should you mention the results of the field sobriety tests. Information about driving violations and field sobriety tests will be recorded in other sections of the DUI probable cause affidavit and in the case report.

A DUI probable cause affidavit will include the results of field sobriety tests, along with other incriminating evidence. The results for the field sobriety tests will be documented on field sobriety test forms and they must be properly transferred to the DUI probable cause affidavit. For example, if a driver passes the one leg stand test, then the DUI probable cause affidavit must have the box checked that indicates the driver passed the one leg stand test. See the following example of a DUI investigation. Pay particular attention to the elements of the law. The driver and vehicle registration are listed below.

South Carolina REGISTRATION

Plate: H84812; Expires: 9/5/2029; Red 2019 Ford Mustang; 2 Door

Vehicle No.: 1F2HF72K858304372

DUI Law (Code: 55-44-120c) = It is a class D felony (2nd offense) for a person to drive a vehicle in this state with a blood-alcohol level of 0.08% or more.

DUI INVESTIGATIVE NOTES

These are intended solely for practicing Field Sobriety Tests; there is no claim to the significance or validity of the tests. However, there must be some reference level to determine if a suspect has passed or failed each test.

Field Sobriety Directions

Walk-and-Turn

Have the suspect place their left foot on the line and their right foot in front of their left (heel to toe).

Have the suspect stand in this position. Demonstrate and explain the test before they begin.

Take nine steps.

Stay on line.

Count the steps out loud.

Watch your feet.

Once you start, do not stop.

Keep your hands at your side.

During the turn, swivel on your left foot and take small steps with your right foot to turn around.

After the turn, take nine steps and return to the starting point in the same fashion.

Do you understand? Begin.

One-leg Stand

Have the suspect stand with their heels together and their arms at their side.

Have the suspect stand in this position. Demonstrate and explain the test before they begin.

Lift your foot (either foot) 6 inches off of the ground.

Keep your leg straight in front of you.

Watch your foot.

Keep your arms at your side.

Count out loud up to 30.

Count 1001, 1002, 1003, 1004, …

Do you understand? Begin.

Horizontal Nystagmus

Face toward me and do not turn your head; only move your eyes.

Follow my finger with your eyes.

[Move finger from side to side; move finger so that eyes can be assessed at 45 degrees and at maximum deviation; record eye movements.]

Finger Count

Count from 1 to 4, touching the tip of your thumb to the tip of your fingers

Count from pinky to index finger, then index finger to pinky

Count 1, 2, 3, 4, 4, 3, 2, 1

Do you understand? Begin.

Backward Count

Example: Tell the suspect to count backward from 33 to 14.

Alphabet A–Z

Ask the suspect to indicate their level of education.

Ask the suspect whether they know the alphabet.

Ask the suspect to recite the alphabet (but not to sing it).

Alco-sensor test

Place the breath tube on the instrument.

Press the read button to indicate that no measurement is currently on the instrument.

Press the set button to set instrument.

Place the tube in the suspect's mouth.

Place your hand behind the tube to detect the suspect's breath.

Tell the suspect to blow into the breath tube.

Tell the suspect you want a steady breath and for them to blow until you tell them to stop.

After several seconds, press the read button to take a reading.

Determine the reading (a reading will automatically come up or you can press the read button).

Toggle the set and read buttons and swing the instrument to clear out the current reading.

HORIZONTAL NYSTAGMUS

Horizontal Nystagmus test results ◊ Passed X Failed

If the suspect exhibited four or more clues, then it is a failed test.

Six total clues of impairment—three for each eye:
1. Lack of smooth pursuit
2. Distinct nystagmus at maximum deviation
3. Onset of nystagmus prior to 45 degrees (includes nystagmus while eyes at rest)

Horizontal nystagmus test (check box only if characteristic observed)	Left	Right
X Lack of smooth pursuit	X	X
X Distinct nystagmus at maximum deviation	X	X
X Onset of nystagmus prior to 45 degrees (includes while eyes at rest)	X	X

Tests to detect head injuries (if "no" is checked, then the test is questionable)

Eyes have equal tracking   X Yes   ◊ No   ◊ Does not apply

Eyes have equal size pupils   X Yes   ◊ No   ◊ Does not apply

WALK-AND-TURN

Walk-and-Turn Test Results   ◊ Passed   X Failed

If suspect exhibited two or more clues, then it is a failed test.

Eight clues of impairment:

1. Cannot maintain balance during the instructions stage.
2. Starts too soon.
3. Stops while walking.
4. Misses heel-to-toe by one-half inch or more between steps.
5. Steps off the line.
6. Raises arms 6 inches or more.
7. Turns improperly.
8. Takes wrong number of steps.

		R9	L8	R7	L6	R5	L4	R3	L2	R1	←
L	R	L1	R2	L3	R4	L5	R6	L7	R8	L9	→

Walk-and-turn: Instructions Stage

Keeps balance   ◊ Yes   X No
Starts too soon   X Yes   ◊ No

Walking stage	**First nine steps**	**Second nine steps**
Stops walking	X	
Misses heel-to-toe		X
Steps off of line		
Raises arms > 6"	X	
Actual number of steps Taken	10	10

Improper turn (describe) _____

Cannot perform test (explain) _____

Other: _____

ONE-LEG STAND

One-leg stand test results   X Passed   ◊ Failed

If suspect exhibited two or more clues, then it is a failed test.

Four clues of impairment:

1. Sways while balancing.
2. Raises arms more than 6 inches.
3. Hops.
4. Puts foot down.

Puts foot down three times is a failed test. Foot stood on ____ L ____ R.

Check (if yes)	Performance
	Sways while balancing
X	Raises arms more than 6 inches
	Hops
	Puts foot down

Puts foot down three times (failed test) ◊ Yes X No

Type of footwear ____**Tennis shoes**_____

Cannot perform test (explain) _____

_____

Other _____

_____

BACKWARD COUNT

Backward count test results   ◊ Passed   X Failed

If suspect exhibited two or more clues, then it is a failed test.

Three clues of impairment:

◊ Hesitation

X Incomplete (Left out numbers) _____26_____

X Continued past number and counted to___ZERO_____

◊ Other _____

Asked participant to count from ___33_____ to _____18_____ .

ALPHABET A–Z

Alphabet (A–Z) test results   X Passed   ◊ Failed

If suspect exhibited two or more clues, then it is a failed test.

Four clues of impairment:

◊ Left out letters:_____

◊ Hesitated

◊ Incomplete

◊ Sang Alphabet

◊ Other (describe)_____

FINGER COUNT

Finger count test results   ◊ Passed   X Failed

If suspect exhibited two or more clues, then it is a failed test.

Four clues of impairment:

◊ Hesitation

X Misses tip of thumb to tip of finger

X Does not count 1-2-3-4-4-3-2-1

◊ Count not in alignment with appropriate finger

◊ Other _____

IMPLIED CONSENT WARNING

I have probable cause to believe that you have operated a vehicle while intoxicated. I must now offer you the opportunity to submit to a chemical test and to inform you that your refusal to submit to a chemical test will result in the suspension of your driving privileges for <u>six</u> months.

Will you now take a chemical test?

On the one hand, some departments will arrest at this point (before the official blood-alcohol test). After all, there is probable cause. On the other hand, some departments will arrest after the official blood-alcohol test. They give drivers the opportunity to demonstrate that they are not intoxicated. In either case, if a suspect refuses the official blood-alcohol test, the suspect will be arrested because there is probable cause.

It is important to note that not all states require the vehicles to be motorized. Horses may be considered vehicles. Thus, you need to pay attention to the elements of the law and to the definition of vehicles. With that being said, you may need to adjust the reports to reflect the proper type of vehicle. If you need to scratch out the make and model and write in the breed of horse and sex, then that is what you must do. Remember, the goal is to provide valid information.

DATAMASTER EVIDENCE TICKET

Below is information that is recorded on a DataMaster evidence ticket.

State of <u>South Carolina</u>

Instrument # **1A-3944**

Date: **31 August 2021**

Subject name: **DAVIES, Marie**

DOB **12/02/1984**

SSN **000-54-3578**

Operator's name **Trp. William Jones, 496**

Department **SC Highway Patrol**

Breath Analysis

Calibration/Self Tests **X** passed _____ failed

Subject's sample ___ passed **X** failed _____ refused BrAC % **0.22**

Start Observation Time **9:12 pm** Time of DataMaster Test **10:01 pm**

Operator's name: **Trp. William Jones** Signature _____ Badge # **496**

AFFIDAVIT FOR PROBABLE CAUSE: DRIVING WHILE INTOXICATED

State of **SC** in the **Superior** Court in the County of **Lexington**

State of **SC**

vs.

DAVIES, Marie

SC DL# = 257798213

I, **Trp. William Jones, 496**, a law enforcer with the **SC Highway Patrol** Police Department, swear that on the **31** day of **August 2021**, at about **8:45** ☐am X pm (Name) **Marie Davies**, the accused, a (race) **white**, (sex) ☐ male X female, (date of birth) **12/2/1984**, was observed at (location) **I-26 MP 110 EB** in **Lexington** County, **SC** (State) operating a motor vehicle (description) **2019 Red Ford Mustang; VIN = 1F2HF7258K8304372; Plate = H84812 (SC).**

The accused, having **x SC** (State) driver's license ☐ social security number ☐ other identification number

(list number) **257798213** operated a motor vehicle under the following circumstances:

Preliminary Observations

X I observed the accused operate the motor vehicle in my presence.

☐ _____ observed the accused operate a motor vehicle.

☐ I had reason to believe that the accused operated a motor vehicle because _____

X The accused committed the following traffic violations: **FOLLOWING TOO CLOSE (SC 56-5-1930)**

☐ On private property, the accused's driving was erratic and unusual because _____

Reason for the Traffic Investigation

X The accused committed the following traffic violations: **FOLLOWING TOO CLOSE (SC 56-5-1930)**

☐ The accused was already stopped when I approached.

☐ Other:_____

Crash?

Was there a crash involved?   **X** no   ☐ yes   Number of vehicles involved in crash _____

☐ I witnessed the accused's crash.

☐ _____ witnessed the crash and identified the accused as a driver involved in the crash.

☐ The accused admitted to being the driver involved in the crash.

☐ The result of the crash was ☐ property damage _____ ☐ personal injury (name) _____

Field observations

I had probable cause to believe that the accused was intoxicated because I observed (check all that apply):

X odor of alcoholic beverage	X alcohol beverage containers in view	X admitted consuming alcohol
X blood shot eyes	☐ improperly left vehicle in gear	☐ leaned against vehicle
X slurred Speech	☐ failed to shut off vehicle at crash scene	☐ soiled/disorderly clothing
X poor manual dexterity	☐ was involved in crash	☐ could not open door
X poor balance	☐ could not exit vehicle on own	☐ fell asleep at scene
☐ belligerent attitude	☐ staggered from vehicle	X excessive giggling

Field Sobriety Tests

(check all of the tests that were administered and the corresponding results)

X Horizontal Nystagmus	☐ Passed	**X** Failed
X Walk-and-turn	☐ Passed	**X** Failed
X One-leg stand	X Passed	☐ Failed
X Finger count	☐ Passed	**X** Failed
X Backward count	☐ Passed	**X** Failed 33 – 18; Response 26 - 0 (list range & describe response)
X Alphabet	X Passed	☐ Failed _____ (describe response)
☐ Rhomberg balance	☐ Passed	☐ Failed
☐ Finger-to-nose	☐ Passed	☐ Failed
☐ Other	☐ Passed	☐ Failed _____ (describe test)

X Alco-sensor <u>0.18</u> grams of alcohol per 210 liters of breath.   ☐ Passed   X Failed

Chemical Test

X I informed the accused of the state implied consent law & the accused   X submitted to
☐ refused the chemical test.

☐ The accused was unable to take the chemical test because ☐ injured ☐ unconscious
☐ too intoxicated

X **Trp. William Jones, 496**, a certified chemical test operator, performed a chemical DataMaster test on the accused at (location) **Lexington County Jail (SC).** The alcohol concentration was equivalent to **0.22** grams of alcohol per 210 liters of breath.

☐ I was informed by _____ that a blood test was conducted on accused at _____
☐ am ☐ pm and that the result was an alcohol concentration equivalent 0.____ gram of alcohol per 100 milliliters of blood.

☐ I was informed by _____ that a ☐ blood ☐ urine ☐ other test was conducted on accused at _____ ☐ am ☐ pm at (location) _____ and that the result was positive for the controlled substance _____.

I swear or affirm that under penalty of perjury that the foregoing facts are true.

_____, 496   Aug 31, 2021   William Jones, SC Highway Patrol
Signature of Affiant   Date Print   Name and Department

Previous Convictions

I, **Trp. William Jones, 496**, have examined the accused driving/criminal record and have determined that the accused has a prior Operating While Intoxicated conviction on (date) July 5, 2021 from **Superior** Court in **Wayne County,** MI (State) having cause number **760055-50643-564**. I swear or affirm that under penalty of perjury that the foregoing facts are true.

_____, 496   August 31, 2021
Signature of Affiant   Date

Receipt for Driver's License (confiscated by police)

SC Highway Patrol Police Department ORI # **00004300034000**

Charges **DUI 55-44-120c (2nd offense)**

Date of arrest **Aug 31, 2021** time **10:01** ☐ am **X** pm

Driver's license number **257798213** License state **SC**

Name **Marie DAVIES** DOB **12/2/1984**

Current address: **36 Sunset Street Rock Hill, SC 29730**

Sex **Female** Weight **160 lbs** Height **5-7** Eyes **Blue** Hair **Red**

The above motorist ☐ refused the alcohol test **X** failed the alcohol test **0.22% BrAC.**

County Lexington

Aug 31, 2021	**SC Highway Patrol**	_____	**496**
Date	Department	Signature of Officer	Badge #

CHARGING FORM FOR DRIVING WHILE INTOXICATED

State of **SC**   IN THE **Superior** COURT

County of **Lexington**   CAUSE NO. _____

State of **SC**

vs.

Marie DAVIES

DOB: **12/2/1984**

SSN: **000-54-3578**

INFORMATION FOR (OFFENSE TITLE): **Driving Under the Influence (DUI)**

CODE **55-44-120c**   CLASS **D**   ☐ MISDEMEANOR   **X** FELONY

COMES NOW, (name of officer), who being duly sworn upon oath, says that on or about: (date of offense) **Aug 31, 2021**, at (location of offense) **I-26 MP 110 EB**, in **Lexington** County, **SC** (State), one (defendant) **Marie DAVIES** of (Defendant's address) **36 Sunset Street Rock Hill, SC 29730** did then and there RECKLESSLY, KNOWINGLY, or INTENTIONALLY: (describe elements of the crime) **drive a vehicle in this state with a blood-alcohol level of 0.08% or more (2nd offense).**

All of which is contrary to the form of the statute in such cases made and provided, and against the peace and dignity of the State of **SC**.

I swear or affirm under penalty of perjury that the foregoing representations are true.

Date **Aug 31, 2021** Arresting officer's name (printed) **Trp. William Jones, 496**

Arresting Officer's Signature & Badge # _____ 496

Witness List: _____

Approved by (Prosecutor) _____

Search Warrant

Now, let us suppose that the driver had refused the official breath test and we really wanted to know the blood-alcohol content. It is not a major concern because the driver will be arrested for DUI refusal and the officer can then simply obtain a search warrant for blood. A search warrant is a written order, issued by the court, that directs a police officer to search for property connected with a violation of law and to bring it before the court (del Carmen & Hemmens, 2017). A search warrant needs to be very specific about the location to be searched and the items being sought. A search warrant expires when the information becomes stale, which means there is no longer probable cause to believe that the evidence sought is still at that location.

For a search warrant, the location is supposed to be defined in such detail that no mistake will be made in searching the correct location (del Carmen & Hemmens, 2017). In other words, anyone executing the search warrant would search the same location. In this case, the location to be searched will be the suspect's body. Specifically, the location is the body of Marie DAVIES (w/f; dob = 12/2/1984; SC DL# = 257798213). The item being concealed will be the illegal amount of alcohol concentration within the blood. See the following three forms for an example of the search warrant paperwork. The three forms are the affidavit for a search warrant, an order for a search warrant, and the search warrant. Once the paperwork has been completed and approved by a judge, the officer will need to transport the driver to the local hospital for blood withdrawal. Only approved medical personnel can draw blood. If an officer draws the blood, the officer could be charged with practicing medicine without a license. After the blood analysis has been completed, the officer will need to adjust the DUI probable cause affidavit to record the results.

AFFIDAVIT FOR SEARCH WARRANT

State of SC

County of Lexington

IN THE **Superior** COURT

CAUSE NO. _____

State of SC

VS.

Blood of Marie DAVIES (w/f; dob = 12/2/1984; SC DL# = 257798213)

COMES NOW, **William Jones, 496** (name of law enforcer), who being duly sworn upon oath, swears that he/she has good reason to believe that in the **body** described as **Marie DAVIES (w/f; dob = 12/2/1984; SC DL# = 257798213),** currently located at **Lexington County Jail**, seized in **Lexington** County, **SC** (State) there is now in or about said **person**, being concealed certain property, namely**: blood that contains an illegal amount of alcohol for a driver in the state of SC.**

Furthermore, the property:

_____	Was obtained unlawfully.
_____	Is possessed unlawfully.
_____	Is used or possessed with intent to be used as the means of committing another crime.
XXX	Is concealed to prevent a crime from being discovered.
XXX	Tends to show that a particular person committed a crime.

See record of proceedings for the facts and information tending to establish probable cause for the issuance of a search warrant.

This affidavit is made for the purpose of obtaining a search warrant from **Superior** Court, **Lexington** County, **SC** (State) to examine **blood in the body of Marie DAVIES** to search for the aforementioned evidence.

[signature] 496 Subscribed and sworn to be true before me this ____ day of _____, 20____

(Affiant)

_____   _____
Judge   Court

ORDER FOR SEARCH WARRANT

State of **SC**   IN THE **Superior** COURT

County of Lexington   CAUSE NO. _____

State of SC

VS.

Blood of Marie DAVIES (w/f; dob = 12/2/1984; SC DL# = 257798213).

Deputy William Jones, 496 (name of law enforcer), is a sworn law enforcer and has presented testimony to establish probable cause for the issuance of a search warrant. The court FINDS that the testimony presented does describe the items to be searched, and the things to be searched for then seized;

That it sets forth that such are things to be searched for are concealed;

That it alleges substantially the offense in violation thereto;

That it sets forth that such search is for evidence that may be lawfully searched for and seized;

That probable cause does exist for the issuance of the requested search warrant and that a search warrant shall be issued.

The officer who executes said search warrant shall make a return thereto directed to this court, which return shall indicate the date and time searched and the list of items seized. Said items seized shall be securely held by the law enforcement agency whose officer executed this warrant pursuant to Order of the court trying the cause.

SO ORDERED THIS _____ DAY OF _____ 20___.

JUDGE: _____

_____ COUNTY _____ COURT

SEARCH WARRANT

State of **SC**   IN THE **Superior** COURT

County of Lexington   CAUSE NO. _____

State of **SC**

VS.

Blood of Marie DAVIES (w/f; dob = 12/2/1984; SC DL# = 257798213)

To: Any Constable, Police Officer, Sheriff or Conservator of the Peace:

GREETINGS:

WHEREAS, there has presented before me testimony of **Deputy William Jones, 496**, a sworn law enforcement officer, for the purpose of establishing probable cause for the issuance of a Search Warrant. The Court, after hearing the testimony, now finds that probable cause exists for the issuance of said Search Warrant of the **location** described as follows: **Body of Marie DAVIES (w/f; dob = 12/2/1984; SC DL# = 257798213)**

YOU ARE, THEREFORE, commanded in the name of the State of **SC** with the necessary and proper assistance in the day time or night time to enter into the location aforementioned and there diligently search for **goods and chattels** described as**: blood that contains an illegal amount of alcohol for a driver in the state of SC.**

And that you are to bring the same or any part thereof found on such search forthwith before the Court and to be processed according to law.

GIVEN under my hand this _____ day of _____, 20____.

_____   _____ COUNTY _____ COURT
      JUDGE

KEYWORDS

Affidavit
Elements of the crime
Information
Property record and receipt
Request for laboratory examination

CHAPTER PROBLEMS

1. Describe the difference between a case report and an intelligence report.
2. What is a probable cause affidavit?
3. What is an information?
4. What is a search warrant?
5. Describe the instructions that an officer should write for how the evidence for a cocaine arrest should be tested in the lab. Discuss the importance of the wording.
6. Suppose an officer arrests a suspect for possession of cocaine. Describe how the officer should describe the evidence on the property record and receipt form. Discuss the importance of the wording.
7. Discuss the following statement. An officer took beer from a minor under the age to legally consume alcoholic beverages and he poured the beer on the ground. He then gave the minor a verbal warning and let the minor leave the scene.
8. Assume the following:

    Law: It is illegal to drive a motor vehicle while faculties are impaired.

    The driver, Jane Doe, was intoxicated and was in a one-vehicle crash. In addition, she had engaged in speeding and following too close. She also failed the horizontal nystagmus test and the one leg stand test.

    Complete the elements of the crime: _____
    _____
    _____

9. Describe why a jailer will ask an arrestee during the booking procedures whether the arrestee is a gang member. Should the arrestee answer truthfully?
10. Why is it important to let a person performing the one-leg stand test during field sobriety tests the option of selecting either foot to stand on? Why should the type of footwear be recorded? Discuss the importance of the ground surface where the test is conducted.

REFERENCES

Del Carmen, R.V., & Hemmens, C. (2017). *Criminal procedures: Laws & practice* (10th ed.). Boston, MA: Wadsworth.

Swanson, C.R., Chamelin, N.C., Territo, L., & Taylor, R.W. (2009). *Criminal investigation* (10th ed.). Boston, MA: McGraw Hill.

CHAPTER 7

Code Communication

LEARNING OBJECTIVES

Understand how to cipher and decipher information.
Understand different numeric bases.

INTRODUCTION

This chapter discusses police radio codes, numeric bases, and a variety of ciphering techniques. Individuals commonly communicate in code. Indeed, codes are often used by athletes, police departments, and inmates. Codes are used to control who can understand the transmitted information, especially if the information can be intercepted by a third party. For example, an officer may encounter a murderer in the field but may not know the person is a murderer until after the suspect's record is run via dispatch. Once the dispatcher has run the record and is aware that the suspect is a murderer, they will need to communicate this information to the officer without the suspect knowing what is being communicated. If the suspect understands that the officer knows they are a killer, there is a good chance the suspect may attempt to kill the officer. Likewise, inmates may attempt to communicate with one another in code. If the inmates are planning a riot or an escape, for example, corrections officers must be able to decipher the coded messages. Inmates may also attempt to communicate with different numeric bases. Thus, officers must be able to think outside the box.

POLICE CODES

Police communication on a police radio must be concise. Another officer may need to communicate an important message and someone's life may be at stake. Communicating in code allows messages to be brief. Codes also protect sensitive information.

> **RADIO COMMUNICATION**
> - Police officers must learn how to use the radio effectively and efficiently.
> - Officers will be dispatched and will make inquiries over the radio.
> - Many people listen to the police radio—media, police chief, other departments, political activists, FCC, civilians (it is important to talk professionally).
> - Practice enhances professional communications over the radio.

10 CODES AND SIGNAL CODES ("9-CODE, 10-CODE", N.D.; SLEEWEE, 2013)

- 10 codes are not consistent among departments.
- Signal codes are not consistent among departments.
- There is often a lack of interagency communication.

10 CODES (EXAMPLES OF DIFFERENCES)

	Dept. 1	Dept. 2
10-0	Person is dead	Signal weak
10-10	Fight in progress	Off duty
10-79	Coroner requested	Bomb threat

SIGNAL CODES (EXAMPLES OF DIFFERENCES)

	Dept. 1	Dept. 2
Signal 7	Extreme emergency	Dead person
Signal 40	Stolen	Alarm
Signal 60	Drugs	Hostage situation

Police departments may use secret codes to protect officers in the field. For example, suppose a driver who was involved in a crash is beside an officer as they are completing their paperwork. It is likely that the officer will request a computer check on the driver. Then suppose the police dispatcher obtains information that the driver is known to be armed and dangerous. The dispatcher may not want to provide that information to the officer until the dispatcher is sure the driver cannot overhear the information. Thus, the dispatcher may send a signal code to the officer over the radio that asks whether the driver can hear the message. In other words, the dispatcher is asking for privacy because they have important news for the officer. If the driver has been arrested before, the driver may be familiar with the signal code and may take immediate action.

Just like 10 codes and signal codes, there are many different versions of the phonetic alphabet. See the following for two commonly used phonetic alphabets in law enforcement.

PHONETIC ALPHABET 1

A = Adam	B = Boy	C = Charles	D = David	E = Edward
F = Frank	G = George	H = Henry	I = Ida	J = John
K = King	L = Lincoln	M = Mary	N = Nora	O = Ocean
P = Paul	Q = Queen	R = Robert	S = Sam	T = Tom
U = Union	V = Victor	W = William	X = X-Ray	Y = Young
Z = Zebra				

PHONETIC ALPHABET 2

A = Alpha	B = Bravo	C = Charlie	D = Delta	E = Echo
F = Foxtrot	G = Golf	H = Hotel	I = India	J = Juliet
K = Kilo	L = Lima	M = Mike	N = November	O = Oscar
P = PaPa	Q = Quebec	R = Romeo	S = Sierra	T = Tango
U = Uniform	V = Victor	W = Whiskey	X = X-Ray	Y = Yankee
Z = Zulu				

COMPUTER COMMUNICATION

- Creates a permanent record.
- Officers need to communicate professionally, or they may be fired.
- Police departments may require police officers to use computers to run checks.
- An officer must learn how to use the computer.

Numeric Bases

Below are different bases for numeric communication.

Decimal (base 10)	Binary (base 2)	Octal (base 8)	Hexadecimal (base 16)
$(10^4)(10^3)(10^2)(10^1)(10^0)$	$(2^4)(2^3)(2^2)(2^1)(2^0)$	$(8^4)(8^3)(8^2)(8^1)(8^0)$	$(16^4)(16^3)(16^2)(16^1)(16^0)$
0	0	0	0
1	1	1	1
2	10	2	2
3	11	3	3
4	100	4	4
5	101	5	5
6	110	6	6
7	111	7	7
8	1000	10	8
9	1001	11	9
10	1010	12	A
11	1011	13	B
12	1100	14	C

Decimal (base 10)	Binary (base 2)	Octal (base 8)	Hexadecimal (base 16)
13	1101	15	D
14	1110	16	F
15	1111	17	F
16	10000	20	10
20	10100	24	14
40	101000	50	28
200	11001000	310	C8

A number base is the number of digits that a system of counting uses to represent numbers (e.g., base 2 has two digits: 0–1; base 8 has eight digits: 0–7; base 10 has ten digits: 0–9).

Example: Write the value of 200 in decimal, binary, octal, and hexadecimal. Then use place values to demonstrate how the total value was calculated.

Show your work. All numbers below equal 200 in decimal.

$200_{10} = 2(10^2) + 0(10^1) + 0(10^0)$

$11001000_2 = 1(2^7) + 1(2^6) + 0(2^5) + 0(2^4) + 1(2^3) + 0(2^2) + 0(2^1) + 0(2^0)$

$310_8 = 3(8^2) + 1(8^1) + 0(8^0)$

$C8_{16} = C(16^1) + 8(16^0)$

The whole idea behind secret communications is to pass information to select persons without other persons understanding the information. One way to do this is to change the base for numeric communication. For example, base 10, which is our default base, consists of 10 digits (0, 1, 2, 3, 4, 5, 6, 7, 8, 9) before the numbers start to repeat. The ones column will increase from zero to nine and will reset when one more value is added (although the 10s column will increase by one).

However, decimal is not the only base that may be used to represent numbers. Notice that the decimal numbering system, which is base 10, does not count up to 10 before the ones column starts to repeat itself. Base 10 counts up to 9 before the ones column resets and a number is added to the 10s column. Likewise, a base 4 number will only count up to 3 before the ones column resets, and a base 8 number will count up to seven before the ones column resets. Any base may be used to communicate values, as long as the two parties use the same base. Below are a few examples of how to represent numbers with different bases.

It should be noted that $X^0 = 1$. Thus, $10^0 = 1$ and $8^0 = 1$. See below for examples of how to write numbers with different bases. The base is written as a subscript after the number.

4231_{10} is a decimal number.

1001_2 is a binary number.

7601_8 is an octal number.

$A93E_{16}$ is a hexadecimal number.

4231_4 is not a legitimate number because a base 4 number will not include the number 4. Understanding the place-value columns when using different bases will prevent this kind of mistake. Typically, students are taught the decimal system, which is based on powers-of-10. The place-value columns for base 10 numbers include ones, tens, hundreds, thousands, ten thousands, and so on. The same process will apply to other bases. For example, base 8 numbers will have place values that are based on powers-of-8. As a result, base 8 place-value columns consist of ones, eights, 64s, 512s, and so on. Following are examples of place-values using different bases.

Base-10 place-value columns						
Millions	Hundred-thousands	Ten-thousands	Thousands	Hundreds	Tens	Ones
10^6	10^5	10^4	10^3	10^2	10^1	10^0
Range for each place-value						
$1(10^6)-9(10^6)$	$1(10^5)-9(10^5)$	$1(10^4)-9(10^4)$	$1(10^3)-9(10^3)$	$1(10^2)-9(10^2)$	$1(10^1)-9(10^1)$	$0(10^0)-9(10^0)$
1,000,000–9,000,000	100,000–900,000	10,000–90,000	1,000–9,000	100–900	10–90	0–9

Base-2 place-value Columns						
Sixty-fours	Thirty-twos	Sixteens	Eights	Fours	Twos	Ones
2^6	2^5	2^4	2^3	2^2	2^1	2^0
Range for each place-value						
$1(2^6)$	$1(2^5)$	$1(2^4)$	$1(2^3)$	$1(2^2)$	$1(2^1)$	$0(2^0)-1(2^0)$
64	32	16	8	4	2	0-1

Base-4 place-value columns						
Four-thousand Ninety-sixes	One-thousand twenty-fours	Two-hundred Fifty-sixes	Sixty-fours	Sixteens	Fours	Ones
4^6	4^5	4^4	4^3	4^2	4^1	4^0
Range for each place value						
$1(4^6)-3(4^6)$	$1(4^5)-3(4^5)$	$1(4^4)-3(4^4)$	$1(4^3)-3(4^3)$	$1(4^2)-3(4^2)$	$1(4^1)-3(4^1)$	$0(4^0)-3(4^0)$
4,096–12,288	1,024–3,072	256–768	64–192	16–48	4–12	0–3

Base-8 place-value columns						
8^6	8^5	8^4	8^3	8^2	8^1	8^0
Range for each place value						
$1(8^6)-7(8^6)$	$1(8^5)-7(8^5)$	$1(8^4)-7(8^4)$	$1(8^3)-7(8^3)$	$1(8^2)-7(8^2)$	$1(8^1)-7(8^1)$	$0(8^0)-7(8^0)$
262,144–1,835,008	32,768–229,376	4,096–28,672	512–3,584	64–448	8–56	0–7

Base-13 place-value columns						
13^6	13^5	13^4	13^3	13^2	13^1	13^0
Range for each place value						
$1(13^6)$–$C(13^6)$	$1(13^5)$–$C(13^5)$	$1(13^4)$–$C(13^4)$	$1(13^3)$–$C(13^3)$	$1(13^2)$–$C(13^2)$	$1(13^1)$–$C(13^1)$	$0(13^0)$–$C(13^0)$

Base-16 place-value columns						
16^6	16^5	16^4	16^3	16^2	16^1	16^0
Range for each place value						
$1(16^6)$–$F(16^6)$	$1(16^5)$–$F(16^5)$	$1(16^4)$–$F(16^4)$	$1(16^3)$–$F(16^3)$	$1(16^2)$–$F(16^2)$	$1(16^1)$–$F(16^1)$	$0(16^0)$–$F(16^0)$

Base-24 Place-Value Columns						
24^6	24^5	24^4	24^3	24^2	24^1	24^0
Range for each place value						
$1(24^6)$–$N(24^6)$	$1(24^5)$–$N(24^5)$	$1(24^4)$–$N(24^4)$	$1(24^3)$–$N(24^3)$	$1(24^2)$–$N(24^2)$	$1(24^1)$–$N(24^1)$	$0(24^0)$–$N(24^0)$

Below is an example of how to use place-values for 4,231 as a base 10 number.

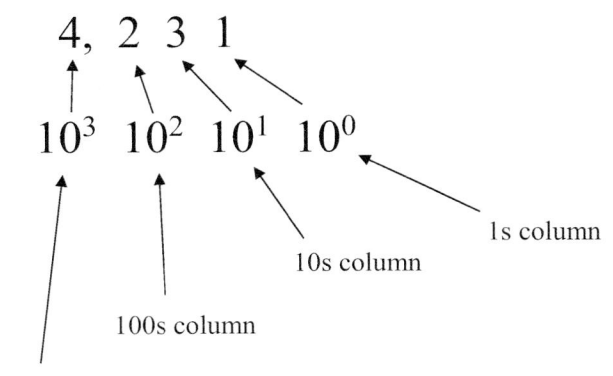

4, 2 3 1

10^3 10^2 10^1 10^0

1s column
10s column
100s column
1000s column

Base 10

$= 4,231_{10} = 4(10^3) + 2(10^2) + 3(10^1) + 1(10^0)$

$= 4(1,000) + 2(100) + 3(10) + 1(1)$

$= 4,000 + 200 + 30 + 1$

$= 4,231_{10}$

Below is an example of how to convert a base 5 number to a decimal number.

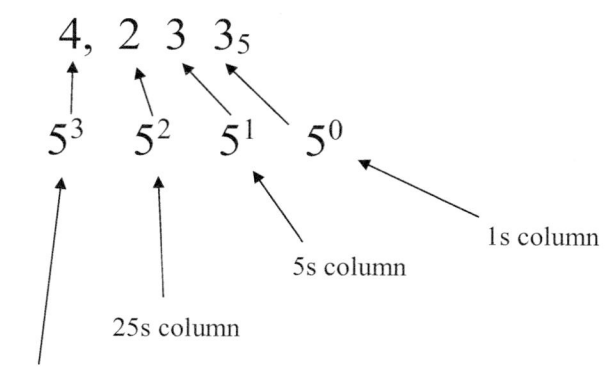

Base 5 → Base 10

$4,233_5$

$5^3 \quad 5^2 \quad 5^1 \quad 5^0$

1s column
5s column
25s column
125s column

$$\underline{\text{Base 5}}$$

$4,233_5 = 4(5^3) + 2(5^2) + 3(5^1) + 3(5^0)$

$= 4(125) + 2(25) + 3(5) + 3(1)$

$= 500 + 50 + 15 + 3$

$= 568_{10}$

Below is an example of how to convert a base 7 number to a decimal number.

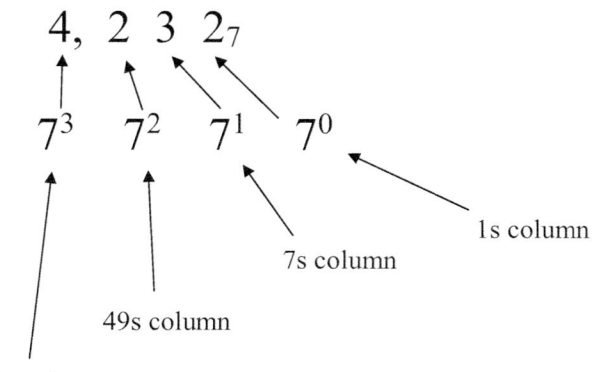

Base 7 → Base 10

$4,232_7$

$7^3 \quad 7^2 \quad 7^1 \quad 7^0$

1s column
7s column
49s column
343s column

$$4{,}232_7 = 4(7^3) + 2(7^2) + 3(7^1) + 2(7^0)$$

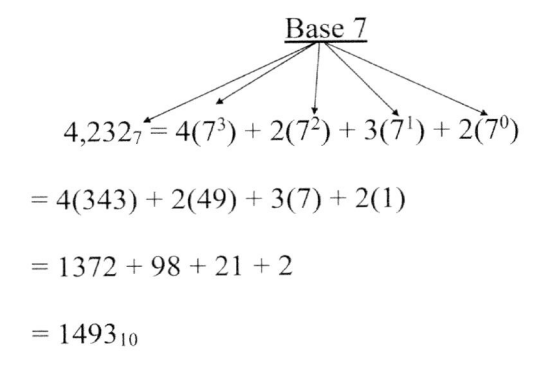

(Base 7)

$$= 4(343) + 2(49) + 3(7) + 2(1)$$

$$= 1372 + 98 + 21 + 2$$

$$= 1493_{10}$$

Below is an example of how to convert a base 10 number to a binary number using the addition/subtraction method.

Base 10 → Base 2

Convert 95_{10} to _____ $_2$.

To convert from base 10 to base 2, we will need to use enough powers-of-two to ensure that we can reach the desired value, which is 95 in this case. We will not use the place-value that exceeds the value of 95 because that will be too high. We will, however, check the place-value that is equal to 95 or that comes closest to 95 without exceeding it. See below for the place-value columns for the powers-of-two.

$$2^8 \quad 2^7 \quad 2^6 \quad 2^5 \quad 2^4 \quad 2^3 \quad 2^2 \quad 2^1 \quad 2^0$$

Below are the decimal values for the binary place-values.

256 128 64 32 16 8 4 2 1 ← Decimal values

$$2^8 \quad 2^7 \quad 2^6 \quad 2^5 \quad 2^4 \quad 2^3 \quad 2^2 \quad 2^1 \quad 2^0 \quad \leftarrow \text{Binary Place-values}$$

In short, we need to select from the numbers in the place-value columns in a manner that will allow us to obtain a sum of 95. If the place-value is needed, then we will place a 1 in that column. If the place-value is not required, then we will place a 0 in that column. The final number will start with a non-zero digit. Because 128_{10} is greater than 95_{10}, the column for the 2^7 place-value cannot be used. However, the value of 64, which is the column for the 2^6 place-value, can be used, so we will start there. Below are the binary place-values that will be required to obtain a sum of 95.

| 256 | 128 | 64 | 32 | 16 | 8 | 4 | 2 | 1 | ← Base 10 |

↑ ↑ ↑ ↑ ↑ ↑ ↑ ↑ ↑
2^8 2^7 2^6 2^5 2^4 2^3 2^2 2^1 2^0 ← Powers-of-two

| 0 | 0 | 1 | 0 | 1 | 1 | 1 | 1 | 1 |

↑ ↑ ↑ ↑ ↑ ↑ ↑ ↑ ↑
2^8 2^7 2^6 2^5 2^4 2^3 2^2 2^1 2^0

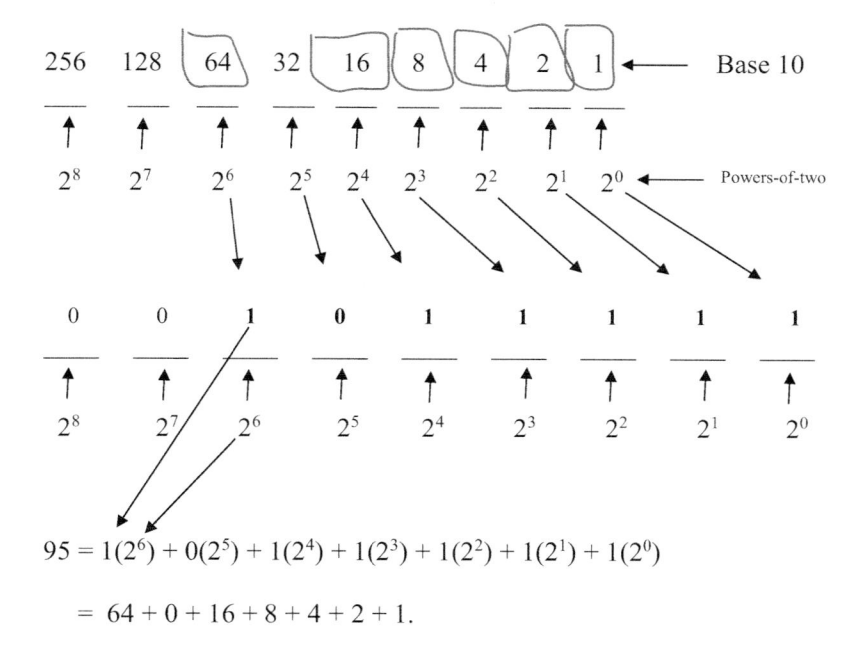

$$95 = 1(2^6) + 0(2^5) + 1(2^4) + 1(2^3) + 1(2^2) + 1(2^1) + 1(2^0)$$

$$= 64 + 0 + 16 + 8 + 4 + 2 + 1.$$

Because the final number will start with a one (i.e., non-zero digit), the answer is listed below.

$95_{10} = 1011111_2$

The zeros to the left of the first non-zero digit are irrelevant and, to be concise, should not be used. See below to assess the relevance of the zeros to the left of the first non-zero digit.

$0095_{10} = 001011111_2$

The better and more concise response is listed below.

$95_{10} = 1011111_2$

$$1 0 1 1 1 1 1_2 = 1(2^6) + 0(2^5) + 1(2^4) + 1(2^3) + 1(2^2) + 1(2^1) + 1(2^0)$$

Place-Value Columns

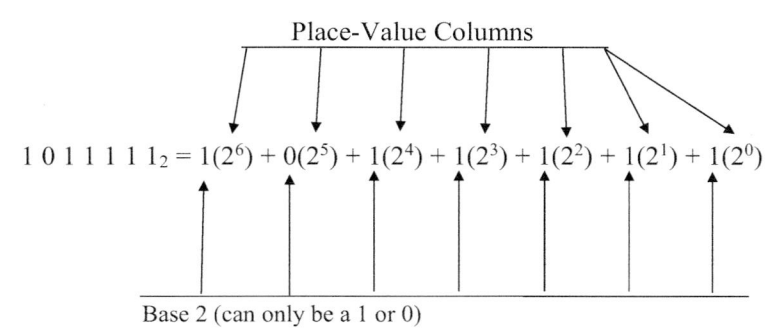

Base 2 (can only be a 1 or 0)

Whether a one or zero is in a particular place-value column, it will be multiplied by the power-of-two value for that location.

Another way to solve the problem is via successive division where the divisor is the desired base number. For this process, the quotient of the dividend is taken and used as the dividend in the next step. The division process will continue until the quotient in a division becomes zero for the first time. The remainders are recorded at each step. The solution will be then read from the most significant bit, which is the last remainder calculated, to the least significant bit, which was the first remainder calculated. An example that converts 95 base 10 to decimal follows (R = Remainder).

$95 \div 2 = 47$ R 1 (least significant bit)

$47 \div 2 = 23$ R 1

$23 \div 2 = 11$ R 1

$11 \div 2 = 5$ R 1   Read from bottom to top.

$5 \div 2 = 2$ R 1

$2 \div 2 = 1$ R 0

$1 \div 2 = 0$ R 1 (most significant bit)

Reading the remainder values from the most significant bit to the least significant bit (from bottom to top), the base-two number = 1011111. This number matches the previous example.

Let us work through another example.

Convert 57_{10} to _____ $_2$.

Because we are using binary numbers, we will need powers-of-two. Using powers-of-two, 57 = 32 + 16 + 8 + 1. These numbers are indicated below. Thus, place a value of 1 at these place-value locations.

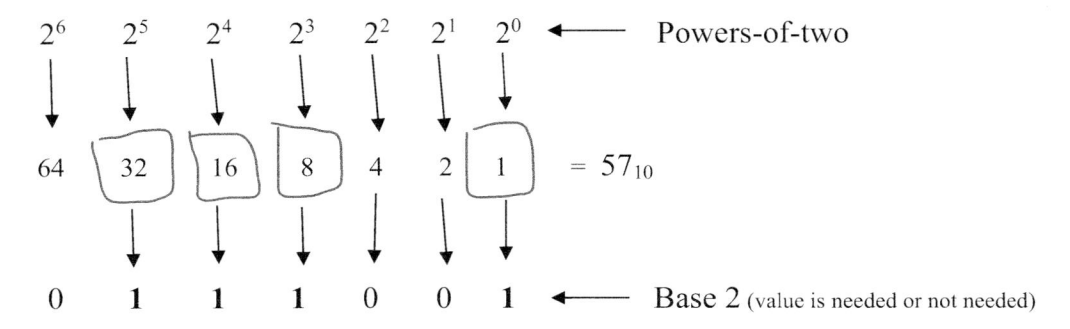

2^6	2^5	2^4	2^3	2^2	2^1	2^0	← Powers-of-two
64	32	16	8	4	2	1	= 57_{10}
0	1	1	1	0	0	1	← Base 2 (value is needed or not needed)

Zeros before the first non-zero digit simply say that there are no values before the first non-zero digit. Thus, they should be deleted. The first digit in the answer will be non-zero. However, the zeros that follow the first non-zero digit cannot be deleted because this will change the value of the number (e.g., 001010 = 1010 ≠ 11).

Thus, the final answer is the following: $57_{10} = 111001_2$.

Below is another way of looking at it. If a one or zero is located in a particular place-value location, then it will be multiplied by the power-of-two value for that location.

$1(2^5) + 1(2^4) + 1(2^3) + 0(2^2) + 0(2^1) + 1(2^0)$

$= 1(32) + 1(16) + 1(8) + 0(4) + 0(2) + 1(1)$

$= 32 + 16 + 8 + 1$

$= 57.$

Answer:

$57_{10} = 111001_2$

We can also use successive division to obtain the binary number.

Convert 57_{10} to _____ $_2$.

$57 \div 2 = 28$	R 1	(least significant bit)
$28 \div 2 = 14$	R 0	
$14 \div 2 = 7$	R 0	Read from bottom to top.
$7 \div 2 = 3$	R 1	
$3 \div 2 = 1$	R 1	
$1 \div 2 = 0$	R 1	(most significant bit)

$57_{10} = 111001_2$, which matches the prior example.

Now, let us move to hexadecimal.

Convert 196_{10} to _____ $_{16}$.

First, let us use the addition/subtraction method. Using hexadecimal, we need to figure out what place-value columns we need to obtain the decimal value of 196. Each place-value can be multiplied by a decimal value from 0 to 15 (the letter F represents 15 in hexadecimal). In this case, using 16^2 will produce a value that is too high, even if it is multiplied by one (a value of 256 is greater than 196). Thus, 16^2 cannot be used. However, 16^1 is less than decimal 196, so it can be used. The range of the 16^1 place-value column is 16 to 240 base 10 (1 times 16^1 to 15 times 16^1). See the following for the conversion.

Hexadecimal values can range from 0 to F ($C_{16} = 12_{10}$)

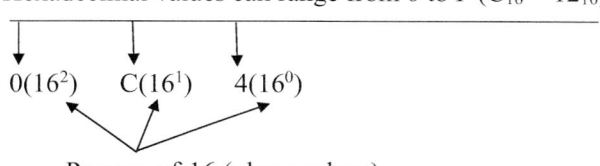

$0(16^2) \quad C(16^1) \quad 4(16^0)$

Powers-of-16 (place-values)

$196_{10} = 12(16^1) + 4(16^0) = 12(16) + 4(1) = 192 + 4 = 196_{10}$ ← Base 10

$= C4$ ← Base 16

Checking the solution: Let us use successive division to obtain the hexadecimal number for decimal 196.

$196 \div 16 = C \quad R\ 4$ ↑ (least significant bit)

$C \div 16 = 0 \quad R\ C$ (most significant bit)

Reading the remainder values from the most significant bit to the least significant bit (from bottom to top), the base-16 number = C4. This number matches the previous solution.

Now, let us convert binary directly to octal.

$1\ 0\ 1\ 1\ 0\ 1\ 0\ 1_2 =$ _____ $_8$

Because octal numbers are multiples of 2, the binary number can be broken down into groups of three digits (starting on the right most side). Each three digits of binary will equal one digit of octal.

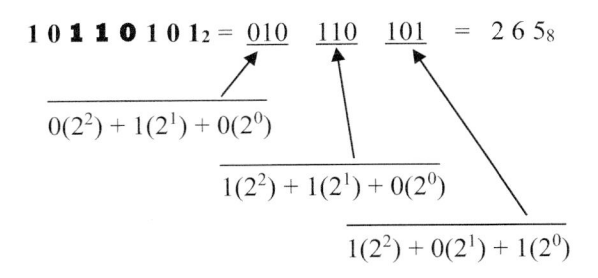

$10110101_2 = 010\ 110\ 101 = 265_8$

$0(2^2) + 1(2^1) + 0(2^0)$

$1(2^2) + 1(2^1) + 0(2^0)$

$1(2^2) + 0(2^1) + 1(2^0)$

Now let us convert octal to binary. This can be done by using the table below. Each three digits of binary will be converted into one digit of octal. Convert 265_8 into binary.

Decimal (base-10)	Binary using three digits ($2^3 = 8$)	Octal (base-8)
0	000	0
1	001	1
2	**010**	2
3	011	3
4	100	4
5	**101**	5
6	**110**	6
7	111	7

$2_8 = 010_2$

$6_8 = 110_2$

$5_8 = 101_2$

$265_8 = 010\ 110\ 101_2 = 10110101_2$

Now, let us convert binary to hexadecimal.

$10110101_2 = $ _____ $_{16}$

Because hexadecimal numbers are multiples of 2, the binary number can be broken down into groups of four digits (starting on the right most side). Each four digits of binary will equal one digit of hexadecimal.

$10110101_2 = 1011\ 0101 = B5_{16}$

$1(2^3) + 0(2^2) + 1(2^1) + 1(2^0)$ $0(2^3) + 1(2^2) + 0(2^1) + 1(2^0)$

Next, let us convert hexadecimal to binary. This can be done by using the table below. Each four digits of binary will be converted into one digit of hexadecimal. Convert $B5_{16}$ into binary.

Decimal (base-10)	Binary using four digits ($2^4 = 16$)	Hexadecimal (base-16)
0	0000	0
1	0001	1
2	0010	2
3	0011	3
4	0100	4
5	**0101**	5
6	0110	6
7	0111	7
8	1000	8
9	1001	9
10	1010	A
11	**1011**	**B**
12	1100	C
13	1101	D
14	1110	E
15	1111	F

$B_{16} = 1011_2$; $5_{16} = 0101_2$

Putting them together, $B5_{16} = 10110101_2$

Below are different codes for numeric communication.

Decimal digit	8-4-2-1 code	6-3-1-1 code
0	0000	0000
1	0001	0001
2	0010	0011
3	0011	0100
4	0100	0101
5	0101	0111
6	0110	1000
7	0111	1001
8	1000	1011
9	1001	1100

Examples

N = 7_{10} = 0111 [8-4-2-1 code] = 0(8) + 1(4) + 1(2) + 1(1)

N = 7_{10} = 1001 [6-3-1-1 code] = 1(6) + 0(3) + 0(1) + 1(1)

N = 77_{10} = 0111 0111 [8-4-2-1 code] (each digit is individually converted)

N = 77_{10} = 1001 1001 [6-3-1-1 code] (each digit is individually converted)

SPORT CODES

Baseball players, football players, and coaches use codes to communicate. In baseball, the third-base coach will give signals to the batter, indicating what the batter should do. For example, the policy may be that the first item that the coach touches after he touches his hat is the required action by the batter.

Table 7.1 Baseball secret codes

Key = Touches Hat, then touches	Required Action
Elbow	Bunt
Knee	Swing away
Shoulder	Take a pitch
Ear	Make contact with ball (man on first base is running)

FOOTBALL SECRET CODES FOR THE OFFENSE

In football, the quarterback may use an audible signal at the line of scrimmage. After the play has been called in the huddle, the quarterback will assess the defensive formation at the line of scrimmage. The quarterback may realize that the play called in the huddle will not work. Because there is no time for a re-huddle, the quarterback needs a way to change the play at the line of scrimmage. The quarterback can change the play via an audible signal. For example, the code may be to run the play immediately called after the word **BLUE**. If the play called in the huddle was "*31 dive*" and the quarterback wants to change it to "*48 sweep*", the quarterback may yell out along the line of scrimmage in each direction, "*Blue 48, Blue 48*." Thus, the play has been changed from a *31* dive (carried out by the fullback) to a *48 sweep* (carried out by the tailback). See the diagram below for an example of codes as they relate to players and holes. The first digit of the play number represents the particular back who will receive the ball, and the second digit represents the hole in which the back shall run. For example, looking at the designations listed below, a 21 is a quarterback sneak to the left of the center, and a 48 is a tailback sweep to the outside right. Notice that the even numbered holes are to the right of the center and the odd numbered holes are to the left of the center. In addition, because BLUE is the agreed upon code word for a play change, if the quarterback yells, "*RED 48*", then the original play will be carried out. To prevent the defense from figuring out what plays will be executed, the code word may be changed at any time.

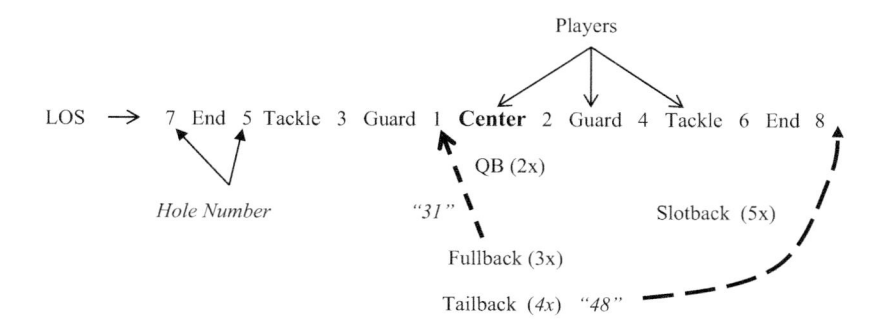

```
                                    Players
                                  ↙  ↓  ↘
       LOS →  7 End 5 Tackle 3 Guard 1 Center 2 Guard 4 Tackle 6 End 8
                  ↖                  ↑                              ⌉
                                   QB (2x)                          |
                  Hole Number     "31"                Slotback (5x) |
                                     ↑                              |
                                  Fullback (3x)                     |
                                                                    ╱
                                  Tailback (4x)  "48" ─ ─ ─ ─ ─ ─ ─
```

LOS = Line of Scrimmage; QB = Quarterback

Figure 7.1 Football codes

MARKED DECK OF PLAYING CARDS

Below is a key that may be used to read each playing card. Dots may be placed in particular boxes to indicate the card's suit and value. Of course, the box will appear on every card, but the dots' positions will vary on each card.

Diamonds	Queen	Hearts
Jack		1
10		2
9	King	3
8		4
7		5
Spades	6	Clubs

Figure 7.2 Key for marked card deck

If the dots below were indicated on the back of a playing card, what is the card?

•		
		•

The above card is the 4 of diamonds.

If the dots below were indicated on the back of a playing card, what is the card?

		•
	•	•
	•	

The above card is the ace of hearts.

SECRET CODES

Secret codes have been used since ancient times (Brook, 2014). For example, the ancient Greeks would write a message on a spy's shaven head. Once the hair grew back, the spy would deliver the message. This technique was effective because the interrogators seldom thought to shave the head of a captured spy.

Modern spies use available technology to communicate information (Brook, 2014). For example, modern computers use thousands of pixels to create images. Spies can hide secret messages within the pixels. Unless a person knows exactly where to look in an image, it will be extremely difficult to recognize the message.

Inmates may use secret codes so that they can conduct business within correctional facilities without corrections officers interfering. For example, inmates may want to import drugs into the correctional facility, they may want to plan an escape, or they may want to put a contract out to kill someone. Thus, it is important for law enforcers to recognize secret codes.

Ciphering is the process of coding information so that only select persons can understand it. For individuals who are not the intended audience, the message is unintelligible. Deciphering is the process of decoding a secret message into intelligible language.

COMPUTER TRANSLATION CODES

With modern technology, a person can write a text message and have the computer immediately alter its appearance. A computer can easily alter the language or font in such a manner that the message cannot be easily understood until the receiver deciphers it. Below are examples of a text message that has been written in English and translated to other languages and fonts. It does not matter whether the translations are grammatically accurate. It only matters that each message can be converted accurately back into the original message.

Computer language translations

English: Ciphering and deciphering codes is fun.

Greek: Η κρυπτογράφηση και η αποκρυπτογράφηση κωδικών είναι διασκεδαστική.

Russian: Шифровать и расшифровывать коды — это весело

Bookshelf Symbol 7 font:
áх √ ⚜ ⌣ ′″ x \ ∘ ∼ \ ⌒ ⌢ ⌣ ∫ x √ ⚜ ⌣ ′″ x \ ∘ ∫ ∕ ⌒ ⌣ ⋯ x ⋯ ♮ ⁂ \ ♭

Webdingsfont: 🏰ⓘ🚌🏛✗ⓘ●▇ ✓●♥ ♥🏛☐ⓘ🚌🏛✗ⓘ●▇ ☐▄♥🏛? ⓘ? 🚌🏢●▪

Code Communication 203

TECHNIQUES FOR CIPHERING AND DECIPHERING MESSAGES

The following are techniques that are used to cipher and decipher information (Brook, 2014; Janeczko, 2004; Peterson, 1966; Wrixon, 1998).

Code Stick

Wrap a strip of paper around a tube. Write the message on the paper. Remove the paper. In order to read the message, a tube with the proper diameter must be used.

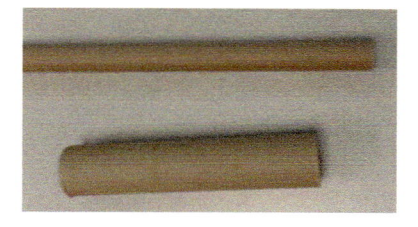

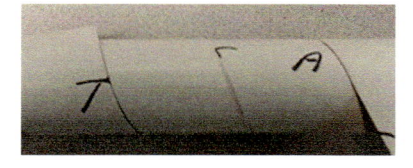

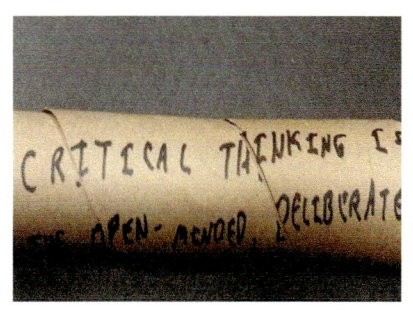

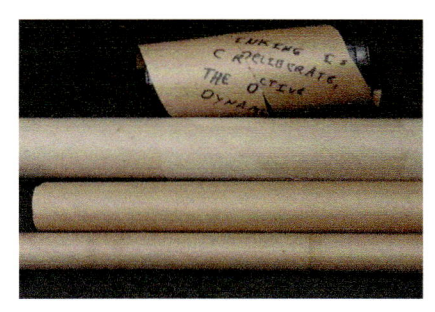

Reverse the Words

Read each word backwards. Do not change the order of the words in the message.

Example: study hard.

Code = yduts drah.

Read Every Second Letter

This is a test.

Code = TIHSIUSOIASHALTNEDSGT.

Numbers Stand for Letters

A	B	C	D	E	F	G	H	I	J	K	L	M	N	O	P	Q	R	S	T	U	V	W	X	Y	Z
1	2	3	4	5	6	7	8	9	10	11	12	13	14	15	16	17	18	19	20	21	22	23	24	25	26

Example: Help = 8 5 12 16 or 8.5.12.16

Reverse the Alphabet

A	B	C	D	E	F	G	H	I	J	K	L	M	N	O	P	Q	R	S	T	U	V	W	X	Y	Z
Z	Y	X	W	V	U	T	S	R	Q	P	O	N	M	L	K	J	I	H	G	F	E	D	C	B	A

Example:

JUSTICE = QFHGRXV

Half-Reverse Alphabet

A	B	C	D	E	F	G	H	I	J	K	L	M
N	O	P	Q	R	S	T	U	V	W	X	Y	Z

Example: JUSTICE = WHFGVPR

Pigpen

If the first letter in the pair is to be used, then no dot will be present in the symbol. If second letter is to be used, then a dot will appear in the symbol.

AB	CD	EF
GH	IJ	KL
MN	OP	QR

```
      ST
  UV  ╳  WX
      YZ
```

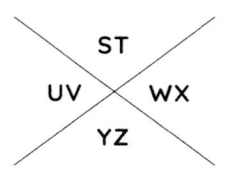

For example:

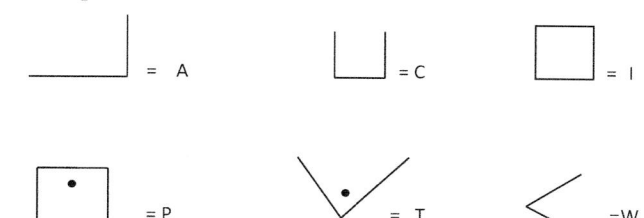

⌙ = A   ⊔ = C   □ = I

⌐• = P   ∨• = T   ⟨ = W

Rosicrucian Cipher

ABC	DEF	GHI
JKL	MNO	PQR
STU	VWX	YZ

Every letter has a dot. Align the dot with appropriate letter.

For example:

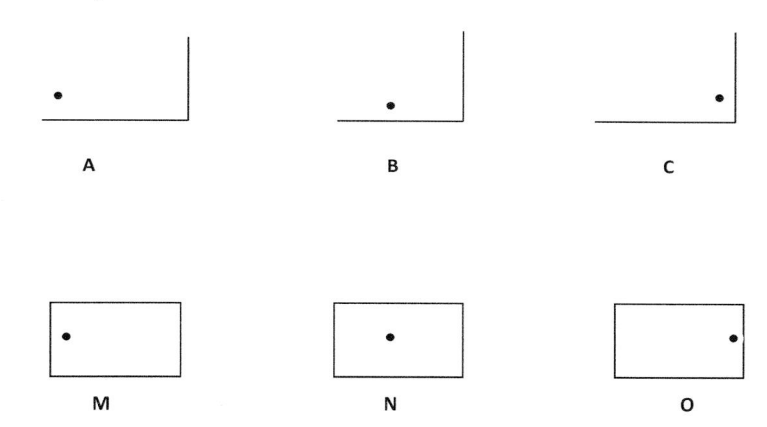

⌙• A   ⌙• B   ⌙• C

▭• M   ▭• N   ▭• O

Block Cipher

To cipher, sentences are broken down into an equal number of letters in each row. To decipher, all rows are linked. Words need to be discovered by adding spaces in appropriate places.

THIS IS VERY EASY!

THISI

SVERY

EASY!

Keyboard Cipher

Use the keyboard and shift to the left or right the predetermined number of places. When the end of the row on the keyboard is reached, the user will cycle to the far end of the same row and will continue to travel in the same direction.

Example Keyboard shift 2R (shift to the right 2 places)

QWERTYUIOP = ERTYUIOPQW

ASDFGHJKL = DFGHJKLAS

ZXCVBNM = CVBNMZX

Date Shift Cipher

Use the Date June 4, 2012

Write it as 0 6 0 4 2 0 1 2

The date will continue to repeat until the code is complete. When the end of the alphabet is reached, the alphabet will cycle around and will continue in the same direction. The direction of travel along the alphabet may be forward (+) or backward (−). To decipher the message, move in the opposite direction that was used to cipher the message.

Cipher the following message (+ direction): This is a lot of fun.

T	+	0	=	T
H	+	6	=	N
I	+	0	=	I
S	+	4	=	W
I	+	2	=	K
S	+	0	=	S
A	+	1	=	B
L	+	2	=	N
O	+	0	=	O
T	+	6	=	Z
O	+	0	=	O
F	+	4	=	J
F	+	2	=	H
U	+	0	=	U
N	+	1	=	O

Decipher the following message using the data Feb 14, 2014 (+ direction): I JNRC MZPH.
(Date = 02142014)

I	+ 0	=	I
J	+ 2	=	L
N	+ 1	=	O
R	+ 4	=	V
C	+ 2	=	E
M	+ 0	=	M
Z	+ 1	=	A
P	+ 4	=	T
H	+ 0	=	H

Answer = I LOVE MATH. Notice that the original message was ciphered using the opposite direction.

Keyboard Date Shift Cipher

This technique will combine the date shift cipher with the keyboard cipher.

Use the date August 31, 2023. Write it as 0 8 3 1 2 0 2 3. Use + 3 on the keyboard to cipher the message.

Cipher the word Affidavit.

A	+ 0	=	A
F	+ 8	=	D
F	+ 3	=	J
I	+ 1	=	O
D	+ 2	=	G
A	+ 0	=	A
V	+ 2	=	N
I	+ 3	=	Q
T	+ 0	=	T	(AFFIDAVIT = ADJOGANQT)

Dot Code Key

Cipher the word "report."

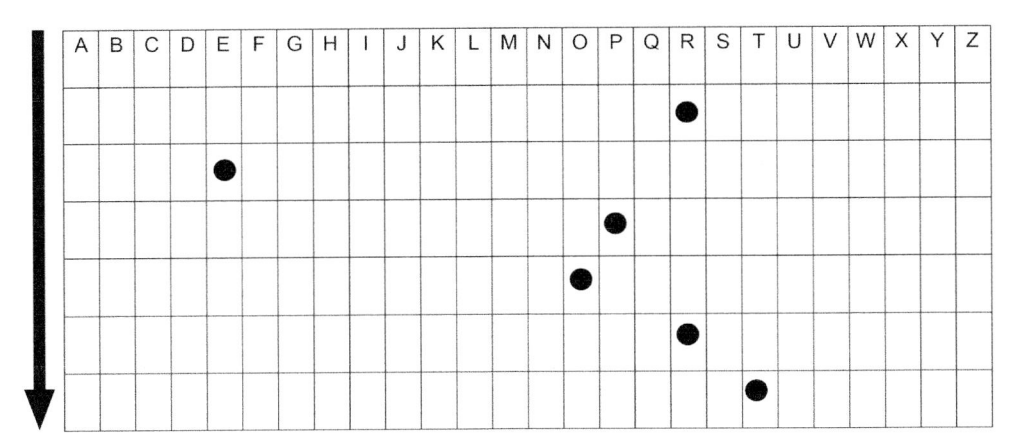

A	B	C	D	E	F	G	H	I	J	K	L	M	N	O	P	Q	R	S	T	U	V	W	X	Y	Z
																	●								
				●																					
															●										
														●											
																	●								
																			●						

Dot Code example

Line Code Key

Cipher the word Report.

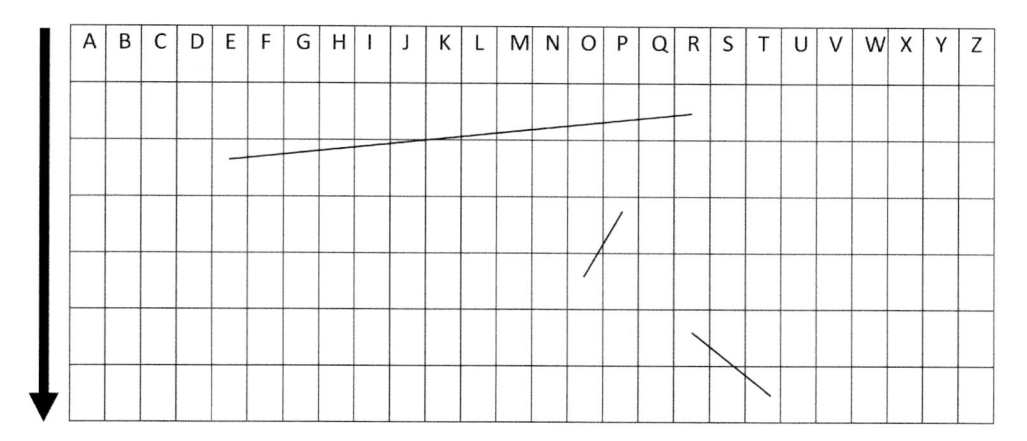

Line Code example

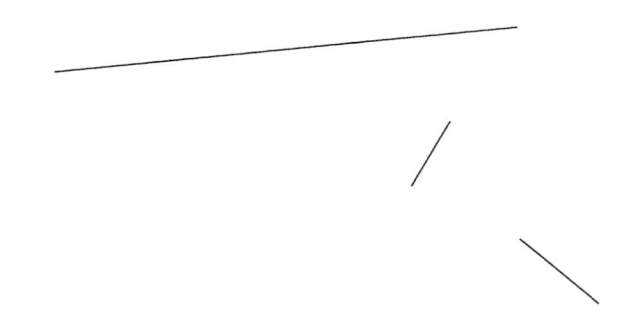

Zig Zag Key

Cipher the word Report.

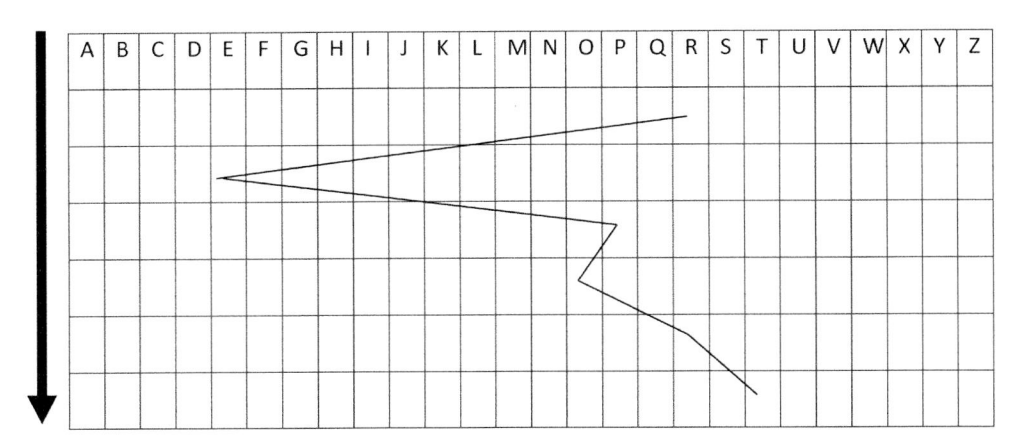

Zig Zag Code example

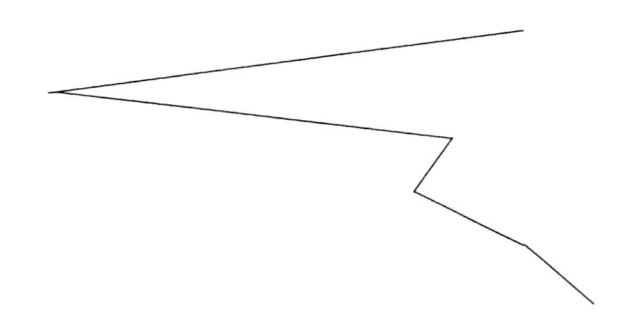

Greek Square Cipher

Cipher the text by using a row by column technique for each letter (Row, Column).

	1	2	3	4	5
1	A	B	C	D	E
2	F	G	H	IJ	K
3	L	M	N	O	P
4	Q	R	S	T	U
5	V	W	X	Y	Z

Ciphered TEXT = 32.11.44.42.24.53

Deciphered = MATRIX

Rail Fence Cipher

Remove all spaces in the text. Then make two rows of text by dropping every other letter. Moving from one letter to the next will look like a fence.

TEXT = DO NOT DELAY THIS IS NOT AN EXERCISE

D　N　T　E　A　T　I　I　N　T　N　X　R　I　E

　O　O　D　L　Y　H　S　S　O　A　E　E　C　S

Page-Paragraph-line-word-letter

7.5.11.8

Means page 7, paragraph 5, line 11, eighth word (e.g., in a book).

23.2.3.15.3

Means page 23, paragraph 2, line 3, word 15, third letter (e.g., in a book; both parties must use the same source).

Semaphore Cipher

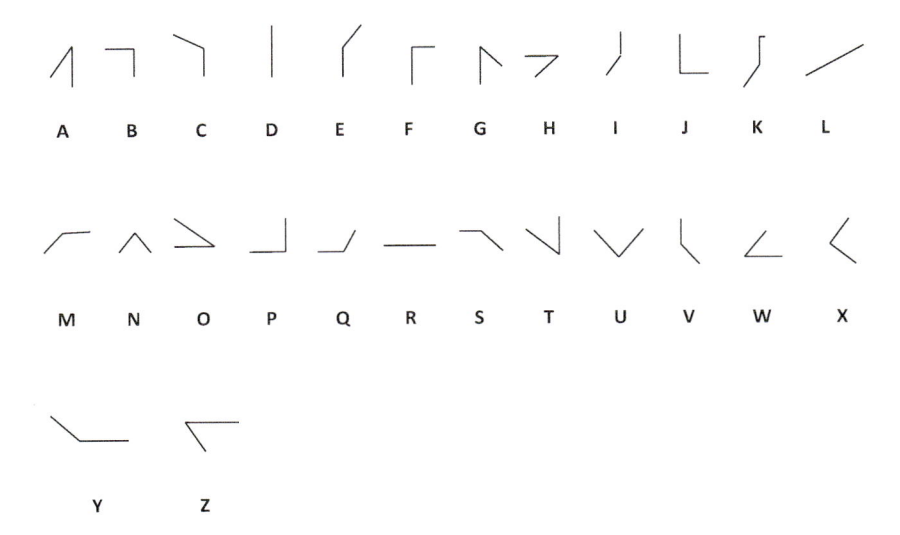

A B C D E F G H I J K L

M N O P Q R S T U V W X

Y Z

Braille

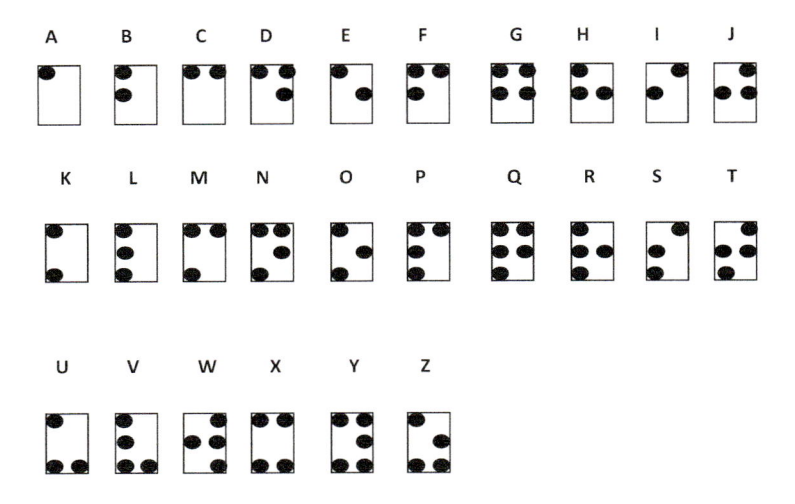

A B C D E F G H I J

K L M N O P Q R S T

U V W X Y Z

Figure 7.3 Morse code keyer

Code Communication

Morse Code
Think in terms of differential, such as short and tall)

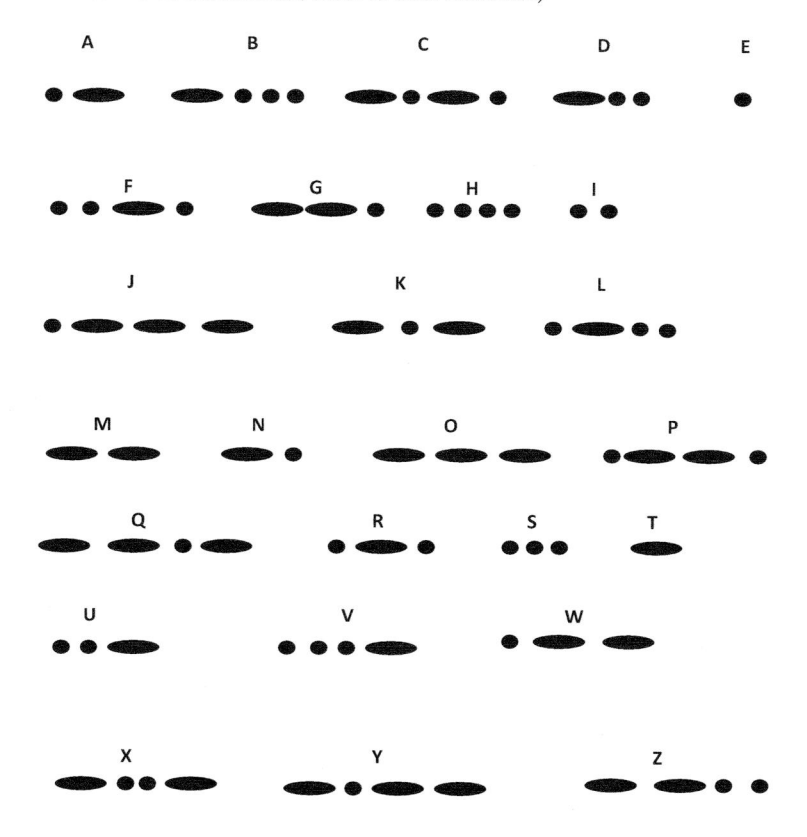

A	B	C	D	E
•—	—•••	—•—•	—••	•

F	G	H	I
••—•	——•	••••	••

J	K	L
•———	—•—	•—••

M	N	O	P
——	—•	———	•——•

Q	R	S	T
——•—	•—•	•••	—

U	V	W
••—	•••—	•——

X	Y	Z
—••—	—•——	——••

Moon's Code

A B C D E F G H I J K L M
∧ ⊔ C ⊃ ⌈ ⌊ ⌐ ⊙ I J < L ⌐

N O P Q R S T U V W X Y Z
N O ⌒ ⌒ \ / — ⌣ V ⌒ > ⌐ Z

Sebald Code

The message starts with the first word after the word **RING**, uses every 11th word until the word **RING** appears again.

I **ring** **we** do we were this test have fun store buy car **cried** a start movie hunch probable his she her yes let **much** her school **ring** alive police.

Message = We cried much.

Space Code

The words are in the correct order, but the spaces are not in the correct places. Rearrange the spaces to make the appropriate words.

Ilo vet ogotos choo land tost udyh ard.

Message = I love to go to school and to study hard.

Circle Code

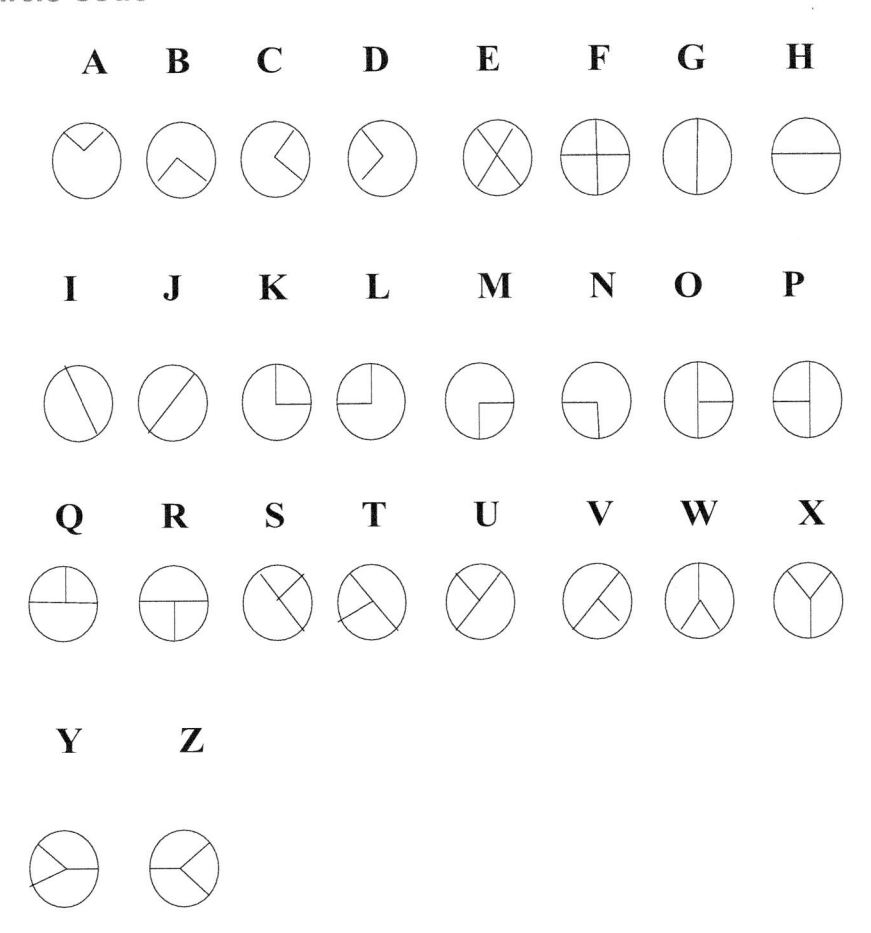

A B C D E F G H

I J K L M N O P

Q R S T U V W X

Y Z

International Code of Signal Flags

Word Grille

A grille is a cover that has holes cut out on the cover in select places. Inside the holes, words are recorded. After the final message is recorded, random words are added to the document. The message can be read if the viewer has a grille that matches the one that was used to create the message. Message = Please send assistance immediately.

PLEASE	HI		
HOW	FOOT		
KEEP	LET		
JOHN	I		
ME	100		
404	KIN		
LOOP	POOL		
ROBERT	DIAMOND		
DRUGS	MONEY		
FISH	MIRANDA		
1942	AM		
WATER	SEND		SEND
DRY	HEEP		
SUN	FOOTBALL		
AMERICAN	FLAG		
JULY	HOT		
STARS	BASEBALL		
ASSISTANCE	SUMMER	ASSISTANCE	
RAG	IMMEDIATELY		IMMEDIATELY
CAR	TRACK		

(Right side, top): PLEASE

CHAPTER PROBLEMS

Decipher the message.

1) Date Shift Cipher   04/03/2021

I POYG LQHIG AQF MCUH

2) Pigpen

V ⌐ ·⌐ ⊐ ⊏· L

3) Rosicrucian Cypher

⊐ L· ▱ ⌐· ▱· ⌐

4) Half-reverse Alphabet

ON FX R GONYY

5) Reverse the Alphabet

PLZOZH

6) Numbers Stand for Letters

19 16 15 18 20 19

7) Keyboard Cipher + 3

P X Q M Y U G Q I O

8) Morse Code

♠♠△♠ ♠ △♠♠ ♠ ♠△♠ ♠△ ♠△♠♠

9) Moon's Code

N ∧ — I O N ∧ L   ⊂ ∧ \ <

10) Braille

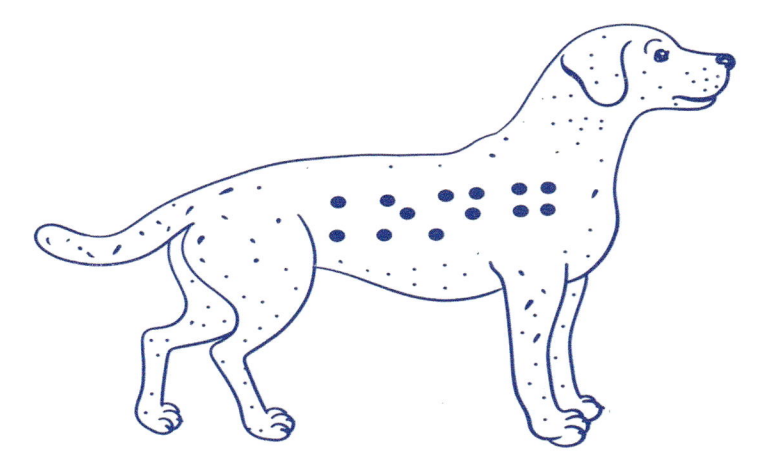

11. Convert each to binary. Show your work.
    a. 33_{10} b. 231_{10} c. 190_{10} d. 416_8 e. $AB2_{16}$
12. Convert each to decimal. Show your work.
    a. 12_3 b. 203_4 c. 123_5 d. 56_7 e. 812_{11}

KEYWORDS

Cipher
Decipher
Number base

REFERENCES

Brook, H. (2014). *Spying*. Tulsa, OK: Usborne.

Janeczko, P.B. (2004). *Top secret: A handbook of codes, ciphers, and secret writing*. Cambridge, MA: Candlewick.

9-Code, 10-Code (n.d.). *Dispatch magazine* www.911dispatch.com/info/tencode.html

Peterson, J. (1966). *How to write codes and send secret messages*. New York: Scholastic.

Sleewee (2013). *Police signal codes*. www.sleewee.com/police-signal-codes.php

Wrixon, F.B. (1998). *Codes, ciphers & other clandestine communication: Making and breaking secret messages from hieroglyphs to the Internet*. New York: Tess.

CHAPTER 8

Meaning of Truth

LEARNING OBJECTIVES

Compare and contrast deviance with criminal behavior.
Compare and contrast different lenses of truth.
Compare and contrast different ethical systems.
Compare and contrast different police department orientations.

INTRODUCTION

What is truth and what is good behavior? Is deviance good or bad? It all depends on one's point of view and the reference used to assess the behavior. Different individuals may use different lenses to assess behavior. For example, should personal experience be used to assess behaviors? Would you expect a physician to use their personal experience to interpret data? Do police officers use personal experience to help determine probable cause? Should researchers be allowed to use personal experience to interpret data? To be open and honest, any possible personal bias should be disclosed to others. In addition, individuals may have different references, or ethical systems, to judge what is considered good behavior. Finally, police departments use different orientations to judge what is considered good behavior. It could be problematic if a police officer's personal ethical system is not in alignment with the police department's orientation.

DEVIANCE

Deviance is the source of innovation that results when a person takes one measurable step away from normally accepted policies and infects the status quo. Deviance is an innovation virus that attacks traditional thinking at the core level. In other words, a person will not simply do something in a particular way because it has always been done that way. Furthermore, what is classified as deviance may be influenced by culture.

Deviance is nonconformity to the general acceptable standards. It is not necessarily criminal, and a criminal act is not necessarily deviant. Several examples are provided to demonstrate the difference. First, suppose there are male and female swimmers at the beach, and they are wearing swimsuits. If a male swimmer wears a female swimsuit, this would be considered deviant if the behavior did not conform to the general expected behaviors. Thus, a deviant act is not necessarily criminal. Second, it may be expected by many drivers on the highway that each driver will travel at least 5 miles per hour over the speed limit, which is a violation of law. Thus, a violation of law may not necessarily be deviant. Finally, if a person randomly commits battery against someone on the street, that act would be both deviant and criminal. In short, an act may be both deviant and criminal, deviant but not criminal, or criminal but not deviant.

To evaluate what is normal behavior and what is deviant behavior, some reference point is needed (Liska & Messner, 1999). Consequently, different interest groups struggle for power and the group that comes out on top—the dominant group—establishes what is considered normal behavior. Some actions are guided by what is defined as proper (acceptable) social etiquette and cultural customs, and some are defined by laws. Although many people may violate accepted cultural customs of etiquette at one point or another, this is considered normal if the behaviors are not continued for prolonged periods of time. If the behaviors are practiced over prolonged periods, then those people are labeled deviant.

Some rules are considered serious enough to write down and to enforce, punishing those who do not conform to these specific guidelines. The problem with laws is that they are not universally and evenly applied to all persons (Liska & Messner, 1999). Even though law enforcement knows that certain persons commit crimes, charges are not always filed. Even if charges are filed, there is a good chance that a prosecutor will dismiss some of the cases for one reason or another (e.g., a heavy caseload or personal acquaintance). Finally, even if a person is arrested and convicted of a crime, there is no consistency in sentencing. Outside factors, such as jail space availability, the status of the convicted person within the community, and the community's reaction to the conviction may all affect a judge's decision on a case-by-case basis.

WHAT IS TRUTH?

Before police officers can effectively serve the public, they must understand the public. However, groups of individuals may experience life's events differently from other groups, and one community member may perceive reality differently than another community member. Although not all-inclusive, the following discussion describes several different perspectives of truth. A police officer who understands that there are different interpretations of reality will be able to better serve a greater population. Indeed, a single event may be considered acceptable in one culture yet be taboo in another. In short, there are different perceptions of truth based on different references in which to interpret data. These are the different lenses of truth. If an officer believes that their truth is the only truth, then that officer will be at a disadvantage when dealing with other people.

Logical positivists argue that an objective reality exists and is independent of human mind and human behavior (Crossan, 2003). They believe that the human experience of the world reflects an objective, independent reality (Weber, 2004). It is this reality that is used as the foundation for human knowledge in the building of a reality beyond the human mind. Logic positivists argue that people are objects whose behaviors can be reliably predicted (Crossan, 2003).

Post-positivists argue that reality exists but cannot be fully understood or realized due to limited human intelligence (Hatch, 2002). Post-positivists believe that knowledge is produced through generalizations and approximations via rigorously defined qualitative studies and low-level statistics. To post-positivists, the researcher is the data-collection instrument.

Postmodernists argue that knowledge is partial, fragmented, and contingent (McLaughlin & Muncie, 2006). Indeed, reality and science are socially constructed (Holliday, 2007). In other words, everything in life that is perceived is conditioned by culture, interactions, and institutions. Life's events occur by chance and, although humans are role-makers, their roles are unstable constructions (McLaughlin & Muncie, 2006). To postmodernists, discourses are a linguistic coordinate system, and language is very influential.

Constructivists reject scientific realism and argue that there are multiple subjective realities and that absolute realities are unknowable (Glesne, 2006; Hatch, 2002). They believe that knowledge is symbolically constructed and that various realities are constructed via individual perspectives. Constructivists believe that reality is developed when individuals use their own personal beliefs, attitudes, and experiences to fit new information into what they already know. Reality is affected by the context in which an idea is taught and requires the individual to take an active role in constructing their own reality via reflection and interaction. To constructivists, investigators and participants determine truth through mutual agreement. The rules for various games are examples of individuals using social constructionism to understand unique situations.

Poststructuralists argue that there is no truth and that order is created within an individual's mind in order to give meaning to the universe (Hatch, 2002). They believe that events happen for no particular reason and that there are multiple realities, each of them equally valued. Truth is subjective, local, and changes constantly.

Pragmatists believe that truth is defined by what is effective, useful, and brings about positive consequences (Mertens, 2005). Pragmatists avoid metaphysical concepts of truth and reality because they involve useless debates and discussions. To pragmatists, truth is measured in terms of accomplishment and resolution.

Critical theorists and *feminists* argue that the world consists of historically situated structures that have a real impact on the lives of individuals based on race, social class, and gender, and that knowledge is subjective and political (Hatch, 2002). Critical theorists focus on race and social class while feminists focus on gender. Critical theorists and feminists believe that differential treatment of individuals occurs based on race, social class, and gender, and that these factors limit opportunities for certain groups of people. Specifically, the poor, minorities, and females are discriminated against in society and are generally at a disadvantage.

Feminist criminology is "a developing intellectual approach that emphasizes gender in criminology" (Schmalleger, 2007, p. G-11). According to feminists, men have dominated the field of criminal justice and have developed theories and written laws for the explanation and control of crime based on their own perspectives (Akers & Sellers, 2009). Indeed, traditional criminal justice theories make no distinction between men and women (Schmalleger, 2007). Although some theories may be applied to both men and women, such as social bonding theory and biological theory, the traditional criminology theory inadequately accounts for crimes committed by females (Akers & Sellers, 2009). Currently, there is no single well-developed theory that explains female crime.

To better understand female criminality and to address the root causes of female crime, females need to be incorporated into the development of criminal theories (Schmalleger, 2007). After all, women make up approximately 50% of the U.S. population. Thus, the failure to consider the female perspective is dismissing half of the available data, which is extremely bad in terms of academic research. In short, the female perspective is essential.

Because women obtain unique understandings of reality based upon their social and personal positions within society, their perceptions of crime may be different than men's perceptions of crime (Hammers & Brown, 2004). Thus, because the criminal justice system is predominately run by men, who use their own realities to make social policies, these policies may be ineffective for about half of the U.S. population (i.e., for women) because they may be based on flawed assumptions (i.e., they assume that there is no behavioral difference between men and women). Indeed, women's perception of truth, which is created by their personal experiences involving social class, culture, and race, may not be represented adequately in the current criminal justice system (Weber, 2004).

For females to better influence public policies, they must be equally represented within the state and federal governments. Although this may be opposed by the men in power, laws could be passed that demand 50% of all positions in the state and federal governments to be held by females. By controlling 50% of the power, females may better influence laws and public policies.

Afrocentrism involves the process of using African principles and standards as the foundation for viewing African customs and conduct (Asante, 2009). Proponents of Afrocentrism state that African cultures and contributions have been downplayed and deliberately kept hidden under the so-called *historic records*, which are controlled by Caucasians. The Afrocentrist asks what Africans would do if no Caucasians existed. Afrocentrists claim that African people are underdeveloped as a result of the lack of power and the lack of control over the global economy.

According to Hall (2000), the U.S. Supreme Court's current equal protection doctrine exploits minority groups in America's increasingly multiracial society. The Supreme Court uses the image of a mosaic America to recast Caucasians as just another group competing against other groups. By transforming Caucasians into a victim group with the same moral and legal claims as minority groups, the Court's actions fail to effectively support programs that will help minorities, such as affirmative action, while providing stronger protections for white entitlements.

According to Dotzler (2000), solutions to racial problems can be solved, but only if Caucasians face the fact that many of the current racial problems are due to the massive crime of slavery from long ago. By providing the truly disadvantaged people (i.e., African Americans) with major monetary reparations, African Americans may be able to overcome their hardships. Indeed, African Americans face social environments on a daily basis that are not experienced by Caucasians. Thus, even if a Caucasian has never owned slaves, the U.S. social environment seems to favor and reward Caucasians over African Americans. In other words, Caucasians and African Americans do not experience America in the same manner. Hence, all Caucasians in the United States have benefited from slavery and from the discrimination against African Americans.

It is difficult to solve past injustices when the injustices continue even today. Benton Harbor, Michigan is a good example of the struggle for resources and power between Caucasians and African Americans (Stevens, 2003). According to Jesse Jackson, Benton Harbor's high unemployment rate, the lack of job opportunities, and African American residents' sense of hopelessness are all believed to have been created by Caucasians. Furthermore, many individuals feel that the judicial system, the police, and the financial system, which are all under white control, continue to abuse African Americans.

Interpretivists argue that a person's perceptions and knowledge are shaped through lived experiences (Weber, 2004). Perceptions are shaped by individual experiences and are unique to each individual. Individuals constantly negotiate their perceptions with other people with whom they associate, reflecting an intersubjective reality.

Technical rationality supporters argue that scientific theory is more important than other theories because it applies theory to practice (Papell & Skolnik, 1992). Indeed, solving a complex problem depends on the general principles derived from the basic and applied sciences. However, because professional practitioners often use art and intuition to solve complex and unpredictable problems, knowledge and action are causally connected but are inadequate in describing the competencies demonstrated by professionals. Through reflection, people obtain information that allows them to adapt their behaviors continually to overcome obstacles.

Empiricists believe that knowledge comes primarily from sensory experiences (Hamlyn, n.d.). However, knowledge is tentative and subject to continual revision. Indeed, the body's five senses change over time, providing ambiguous knowledge. In addition, different individuals may perceive the same event in different manners, which may result in different learned truths.

Phenomenology focuses on lived experiences and the commonalities and shared meanings in those experiences. Phenomenology explores the essence of experience and gains a deeper understanding of an experience by uncovering hidden phenomena (Hatch, 2002). Phenomenology involves the fundamental nature of reality, and it questions what can really be known about it (Ponterotto, 2005). In other words, phenomenology is concerned with human experience, and it attempts to reveal phenomena that have been given meaning (Wimpenny & Gass, 2000). Because people are an integral part of the environment and each person has their own perspective, reality is co-created with other individuals.

Hermeneutics includes the interpretation of both verbal and nonverbal forms of communication. Practitioners of hermeneutics interpret life's events through lived experiences and language (Dowling, 2004). Supporters of hermeneutics believe that investigators have biases that play an essential part in the evidence collection, analysis, and interpretation processes (Ponterotto, 2005). These biases allow the investigator to effectively probe individuals for further information during the interview process, perhaps in the form of examples. It is believed that these biases will improve the investigator's understanding of the information provided by the individuals (Dowling, 2004). However, because everyone has different lived experiences, different investigators may develop different truths (Chessick, 1990). Indeed, two investigators who evaluate the same information may arrive at two different conclusions.

Ethnography seeks to describe a culture from the local or indigenous people's point of view (Berg, 2007). Data collection includes participant observation, participant interviewing, and artifact examination in order "to understand the cultural knowledge that group members use to make sense of the everyday experiences" (Hatch, 2002, p. 21). Artifact data analysis may include examining the writings and types of markers used in graveyards and cemeteries.

Table 8.1 Lenses of truth

Lens	Beliefs	Critiques
Logical positivists	All knowledge comes from logical reasoning and empirical evidence; if a proposition cannot be tested and verified, it is meaningless.	Admit using past personal experiences as references for the pre-understanding of the phenomenon being studied; there are assumptions about the world and the nature of knowing; hypotheses cannot be proved true (must show falsification).
Post-positivists	Reality exists but cannot be fully understood or realized due to limited human intelligence; world is not predicable due to its ambiguity, complexity, and subjectivity.	Does not offer any clear criteria for choosing among the multiple and competing explanations that it produces; may lead to intellectual incoherence.
Postmodernists	There is no single truth; truth is community-based, does not correspond to reality, and everything in life that is perceived is conditioned by culture, interactions, and institutions; life's events occur by chance and, although humans are role-makers, their roles are unstable constructions.	Postmodernism is meaningless, it deliberately restricts knowledge, and it prevents the full facts of a topic from becoming known. The truth that there is no truth is self-refuting.
Constructivists	Reject scientific realism and argue that there are multiple subjective realities; absolute realities are unknowable.	May produce negative results when individuals encounter incomplete data or misconceptions; not all people understand the same information in the same way.
Post-structuralists	There is no absolute truth; order is created within an individual's mind in order to give meaning to the universe; cultural contexts and various languages create equally valid, multiple narratives of truths; objective truth is illusionary.	Post-structuralists claim that meaning is meaningless, which is a self-refuting; incorrectly attempts to apply narratives to the physical sciences.
Pragmatists	Truth is defined by what is effective, useful, and brings about positive consequences.	One must constantly evaluate if the standards are in tune with the current times and situation; standards may be influenced by those individuals in power.
Critical theorists and feminists	World consists of historically situated structures that have a real impact on the lives of individuals based on race, social class, and gender; knowledge is subjective and political.	Critical theorists may be biased to misinterpret information from others as discriminatory; implies a priori assumptions of human nature; radical feminists assume that men and women are indistinguishable beings.

(continued)

Table 8.1 Cont.

Lens	Beliefs	Critiques
Afrocentrists	African principles and standards are used as the foundation for viewing African customs and conduct; asks what Africans would do if no Caucasians existed.	In the name of ethnic pride, exaggerated stories are taught to African American children (they are told lies, which impede their future success); most African American students are not exposed to an Afrocentric curriculum.
Interpretivists	A person's perceptions and knowledge are shaped through lived experiences; truth is unique to each individual.	Subjective; clear patterns may not emerge in data; lack of causal relationships; emotions may bias the views of an interpretivist.
Technical rationalists	Scientific theory is more important than other theories because it applies theory to practice, solving complex problems.	Does not fully consider the value of social relationships in solving problems; people resist change.
Empiricists	Knowledge comes primarily from sensory experiences; knowledge is tentative and subject to continual revision.	Sense change over time, which provides ambiguous knowledge; different individuals may perceive the same event in different ways, which may result in different learned truths.
Phenomenologists	Explore the essence of experience and gain a deeper understanding of an experience by uncovering hidden phenomena; reality is co-created with other individuals.	Small sample size prevents the data from being generalized to other populations; the knowledge is subjective; it is difficult to detect and prevent researcher-induced bias.
Hermeneutists	Interpret life's events through lived experiences and language.	Because everyone has different lived experiences, each person develops a different truth; the meanings of words change over time.
Ethnographers	Describe a culture from the local or Indigenous people's point of view.	Validity of truth is questionable because ethnography studies are difficult to replicate; truth is limited to the subjects in the study; interpretation of truth is heavily dependent on the ethnographer; to collect good data, the ethnographer must take the time to build trust with the community.

PERSONAL BIAS: POST-POSITIVISTS, PHENOMENOLOGY, AND HERMENEUTICS

Should a researcher be totally objective and interpret the data with no personal bias or should the researcher use personal experience to interpret the data? While positivists believe the investigator is an objective and neutral data analyst, supporters of hermeneutics believe that investigators have biases that play an essential part in the evidence collection, analysis, and interpretation processes (Ponterotto, 2005). Is a police officer a positivist or does a police officer use personal experience and training to interpret situations?

Post-positivists

Ontology
Ontology concerns the fundamental nature of reality, and it questions what can really be known about it (Ponterotto, 2005). Post-positivists believe there is a true reality but it is imperfect. This is because people rely upon their senses to measure and interpret information. Senses are shaped by cultural, gender, political, and other external factors.

Axiology
Axiology involves the role of the researchers' values during a research study (Ponterotto, 2005). Post-positivists believe in an objective study, free from personal values and feelings. The goal is for the researcher to identify and separate personal biases from the study. By using standardized and systematic methods, personal biases are minimized. However, the actual decision to study a particular topic may itself be biased.

Epistemology
Epistemology involves the relationship between the researcher and the participants and the study of knowledge (Ponterotto, 2005). This involves its nature, origin, methods, limits, and justifications (Hofer & Pintrich, 2002). Post-positivists believe the objectivity of researchers should be independent of the participants, although it probably is not. They acknowledge that the researcher may have some influence upon the participants; however, they do not want to get too emotionally involved with the participants.

Methodology
The process and procedures of a study make up its methodology (Ponterotto, 2005). Post-positivists use strict scientific methods to control and manipulate variables in order to be able to objectively explain relationships and to make predictions. They prefer to use mechanisms that allow for the collection of measurable quantifiable data. Post-positivism relies upon the falsification theory.

In performing research, post-positivists attempt to identify the closest possible singular truth by using multiple measures and observations, combining both quantitative and qualitative techniques (Crossan, 2003; Ponterotto, 2005). For example, by using multiple raters and performing brief interviews with the participants, the raters can reach a consensus in identifying the themes and arriving at the single proximal reality. Because post-positivists use quantitative analysis, they have the advantage of being able to identify patterns and relationships to predict future events. Furthermore, the data can be validated and generalized to a larger population. A critique of post-positivism is that it assumes that the researcher is unbiased. However, because the researcher lives life like everyone else, whose personality, attitude, and perceptions have been shaped by their environment, such as social, political, economic, and religious factors, there is no such thing as a bias-free researcher. For example, something as simple as language can affect the results of the test. To one person, the word "bad" may be interpreted as a terrible thing. To another person, the word "bad" may be interpreted as a good thing. Thus, the perception and interpretation of the word "bad" could have two different meanings and may affect the interpretation of the test results. Another example may be how physical actions are interpreted. For example, pointing a thumb upward may be perceived as a positive response or a derogatory response. The interpretation depends on culturally developed perceptions.

Phenomenology

Ontology
Phenomenology is concerned with human experience, and it attempts to reveal phenomena that have been given meaning (Wimpenny & Gass, 2000). Because people are an integral part of the environment and each person has their own perspective, reality is co-created by the researcher and the participant (Hatch, 2002).

Axiology
Phenomenology recognizes that the researcher, who has predetermined concepts, is an active part of the research process. Indeed, the researcher's personal biases are useful and an important part of a research study; this gives the researcher valuable reference by which to interpret the data (Wimpenny & Gass, 2000). However, the researcher must bracket personal preconceptions and

presuppositions in order to arrive at the participant's true reality. Phenomenology, in essence, means from the participant's point of view (Camic et al., 2003).

Epistemology

Phenomenology argues that the researchers do have prejudices because they are a part of the environment, and that they need to distance themselves from the participants by bracketing their biases so that they do not interfere with the objectivity of the study (Dowling, 2004). However, because the researcher may perform in-depth interviews, relationships are developed. As a result, the researcher and the participants may develop strong bonds (Wimpenny & Gass, 2000).

Methodology

The methodological objective is to describe what experiences mean to the people who lived them (Sadala & Adorno, 2002). Using phenomenology, the main method of data collection is through an in-depth, three-step interview process (Wimpenny & Gass, 2000). The goal is to establish the context of each participant's experience, to construct that experience, and then to find the meaning of that experience. This can be achieved by the researchers developing the skills in which to probe the participants for further information, perhaps through clarification or by referencing examples. In this manner, a more detailed and actual representation of the lived experiences will be recorded. Other ways of collecting data include examining the participants' writings, observing the participants, and studying experiential descriptions in art and literature (Hatch, 2002).

Hermeneutics

Ontology

Hermeneutics claims that the minds of people along with their values are individually developed by their unique experiences in the worldly environment. In short, each person has a unique perspective in interpreting data (Chesssick, 1990). Hence, there are multiple interpretations of reality.

Axiology

Hermeneutics claims that people are an integrated part of society in which they live and interact (Chessick, 1990). Therefore, researchers will have certain prejudices because their perceptions have already been influenced by their environments prior to the study. This is important because the understanding of information depends on the researcher using linguistic experiences for reference, and because the researcher and participant are connected by a common human consciousness (Dowling, 2004). Indeed, the researcher needs to be aware of personal biases and needs to be opened minded to the participant's meanings so that their uniqueness can be understood. Furthermore, when analyzing historic information, because meanings change over time, the data need to be evaluated in reference to its own time frame. In this way, the data will have relevance for today's applications (Chessick, 1990; Fuchs, 1993).

Epistemology

Hermeneutics claim that a researcher's prejudices are an important part of a research study. Experience and education should be used during the data collection, analysis, and interpretation processes. It is believed that experience and education are valuable tools to be used to enhance the understanding of data (Dowling, 2004).

Methodology

With hermeneutics, there are no universal principles, only many equally contingent approaches (Dowling, 2004; Fuchs, 1993). One way of collecting data is through semi-structured in-depth interviews. However, the focus is not on the collection and analysis of data, but on the process of understanding.

ETHICAL SYSTEMS

According to the Declaration of Independence, the U.S. government derives its power from the individuals it governs (Hames & Ekern, 2005). Indeed, because there are more than 400 U.S. residents for every full-time sworn police officer, law enforcement requires that people voluntarily comply with the law and assist with law enforcement efforts (U.S. Department of Justice, n.d.). Furthermore, because the Posse Comitatus Act of 1878 generally prohibits the U.S. military from engaging in domestic law enforcement, and because the U.S. Constitution protects the public against unreasonable searches and seizures (i.e., protects privacy), local police are ill-equipped to handle the crime problem alone (Brinkerhoff, 2009). Residents are stakeholders in maintaining a peaceful society and they must take an active part in promoting prosocial behaviors (Carter, 2002). However, the definition of good behaviors is relative. In short, before individuals can promote prosocial behaviors, a reference point is needed to define good behavior.

Test of Ethics

There is a test of ethics. First, the end must be justified as good (e.g., the conviction of criminals) (Pollock, 2004). Second, the means must be a plausible way to achieve the ends (e.g., police officers must articulate their actions). Third, there is no less-intrusive method to achieve the same end (e.g., instead of strip searching drug smugglers, U.S. Customs officers could x-ray the suspects). Finally, the means must not undermine some other equal or greater end (e.g., community members must not lose faith in the legal system).

Table 8.2 Canons of ethics (Christian Police & Prison Association, n.d.)

Canons of ethics
- Officers shall uphold the Constitution.
- Officers shall use ethical procedures.
- Officers shall discharge duties as a public trust.
- Officers shall conduct their private lives with integrity.
- Officers shall hold freedom as a paramount precept.
- Officers shall maintain the integrity and competence of the profession.
- Officers shall cooperate with other officials to achieve law enforcement objectives.
- Officers shall observe confidentiality.
- Officers shall not compromise their integrity by accepting gratuities.

ETHICAL DILEMMAS

Ethical dilemmas arise as a result of conflicting core ethical values and may be inherent in some situations (Perez & Moore, 2002). Situations that involve unfair advantage, conflicts between personal values and institutional goals, power differentials, abuse of power, breaches of confidentiality, hidden agendas, impropriety or boundary violations, multiple roles, and differences in perceptions may generate ethical dilemmas. Ethical dilemmas can sometimes be foreseen by noticing whether any red flags exist. These red flags may include internal conflict and doubt about the issue, violation of laws or professional standards, whether anyone can be harmed as a result of the decision, whether the decision is objective, whether there is strong opposition to the decision, whether the decision can be revealed without hesitation, and whether anyone else would be willing to make the decision. When conflict arises, professional, social, and economic pressures can make ethical decision-making difficult.

Integrity has many gray areas and is a complex subject that is not always easily defined. Generally, however, integrity is a positive, proactive system of values that is constant over time and consists of fairness, honesty, sincerity, and doing what seems to be the proper thing (Dreisbach, 2008; Harberfeld, 2006; Hess & Bennett, 2007). Several standards that may be used to evaluate the integrity of police conduct are: (1) fair access; (2) public trust; (3) safety and security versus enforcement; (4) teamwork; and (5) objectivity. Fair access relates to fair and open access of police services to all citizens. Public trust relates to the trust that the civilians give to the police officers in exchange for their right to enforce laws. Safety and security versus enforcement relates to police officers using discretion in balancing the goal of maintaining order with the goal of enforcing the law. Teamwork relates to police officers who are expected to coordinate, communicate, and cooperate with others in the law enforcement system. Objectivity relates to police officers who are expected to be impartial and a disinterested party.

ETHICAL SYSTEMS: WHAT IS GOOD BEHAVIOR?

Ethics is the study of human conduct in the light of set ideas of right and wrong (i.e., morals) (Pollock, 2004). However, there are different ideas of right and wrong in which to judge good behavior. Consequently, different ethical systems answer the question, "What is good?" in different manners.

Moral principles are set ideas of right and wrong that form the basis of ethical behaviors.

The *deontological ethical system* is concerned with goodwill, or the intent of the actor as the element of morality (Pollock, 2004). The consequence of the action is unimportant. For example, the assassination of Hitler might be unethical under a deontological system because killing is always wrong. For police officers, shooting a murderer who is about to kill again is unethical.

The *teleological ethical system* is concerned with the consequences of an action to determine goodness (Pollock, 2004). For example, the assassination of Hitler might be ethical under a teleological system because the consequence may save many lives. For police officers, shooting a murderer who is about to kill again is ethical because it may save innocent lives.

Each ethical system answers the question, "What is good?" (Pollock, 2004). In other words, good behavior is relative and depends on the reference system (i.e., morals) used to judge behavior. For example, a behavior may be considered good according to one ethical system and bad according to another ethical system. However, not all behaviors are subject to ethical judgment; only those behaviors that are performed by humans acting with free will and that impact other people are subject to ethical judgment. In addition, a particular act may be defined as bad behavior for one person but not bad behavior for another person. For example, a child under the age of reason and a person who is mentally incapacitated may lack the knowledge and intent of wrongdoing. Therefore, good behavior is relative. In addition, although personal values may influence individual moral beliefs and behaviors, not all personal values have ethical components. For example, the act of valuing one color automobile over another is ethically neutral and is based solely on personal opinion.

The deontological and teleological ethical systems are the two opposing overall ethical systems (Pollock, 2004). Branches of the deontological and teleological ethical systems use different criteria to evaluate the morality of an action. Some of these branches that shape moral and ethical principles include: (1) utilitarianism; (2) act utilitarianism; (3) rule utilitarianism; (4) ethical formalism; (5) ethical relativism; (6) cultural relativism; (7) religious ethics; (8) natural law; (9) ethics of virtue; (10) ethics of care; (11) egoism; (12) enlightened egoism; and (13) situational ethics.

Utilitarianism determines the goodness of an act by a benefit-to-cost ratio (Kraska, 2004; Pollock, 2004). The needs of the many outweigh the needs of the few. In other words, as the benefit-to-cost ratio increases, the better the act will be perceived. For example, it is okay to arrest a few innocent people by mistake if it solves a bigger problem.

Act utilitarianism determines the goodness of a particular act by measuring the utility of the specific act without regard for future acts (Pollock, 2004). For example, it is not unethical to steal food when a person is hungry and has no other way to get food.

Rule utilitarianism determines the goodness of an act by measuring the utility of the act when made into a rule for behavior (Pollock, 2004). For example, it is unethical to steal food when a person is hungry and has no other way to get food because this will result in lawlessness if people are allowed to steal food any time they are hungry and cannot afford food. Likewise, it may be unethical not to engage in high-speed chases because a no pursuit policy may encourage people to flee.

Ethical formalism states that good is defined by a person's goodwill and by doing one's duty (Pollock, 2004). Good actions are based on categorical imperatives: (1) act as if the behavior will become a universal law; (2) do not use people for your own purposes; and (3) act consistent with universal laws. For example, it may be argued that police engaging in a high-speed chase is good behavior because it is the driver's responsibility to obey the law, and it is the duty of police to enforce the law. If failing to chase cars becomes the universal law, then this may encourage additional drivers to flee. In addition, a lie is only bad if the recipient has the right to believe that they will be told the truth. For instance, the police using deception and a bait car to capture car thieves is not unethical. However, ethical formalism is problematic when there are conflicting duties (e.g., judge's order versus department policy).

Ethical relativism determines what is good or bad based on the individual or group (Pollock, 2004). For example, community members in a poor region may hunt and fish without purchasing the proper licenses. Likewise, prostitution may be encouraged and institutionalized in certain communities.

Cultural relativism defines good as that which contributes to the health and survival of society (Pollock, 2004). For example, men in certain cultures may feel that it is good to kill their wives if their wives expose their faces to strange men. This is called honor killing or shame killing. However, U.S. law enforcers may sometimes need to visually identify these females. This conflict of interest is sometimes encountered at the U.S. border.

Religious ethics determines the goodness of an act based on the concepts of good and evil, and what is good is based on God's will (Pollock, 2004). Ethics are determined by individual conscious, religious authorities, and Holy Scripture. However, problems with religious ethics are that no one may ever know exactly what the will of God is and there are current controversies within and between religions. For example, it may not be unethical or illegal for Native Americans to consume contraband mushrooms for religious practices.

An example of a controversy within religion is the use of deceit to save a life. For example, should a person lie to save an innocent child who is being sought by a gunman? Some Christian thinkers may argue for the existence of a higher ethic, namely love, and that lying to save a life is okay because it is based on good intent and love (Father F. Rogers, personal communication on 6/26/2014). If one looks at this situation as the *lesser of two evils*, then the greatest evil would be to contribute to the intended victim's death. In this case, if a lie allows the intended victim to get away safely, or if the gunman's threat can be neutralized, then a lie would be the *lesser of two evils*. The lie would have the effect of preserving life, which is a greater good and, therefore, justified.

However, from a biblical perspective, one does not have to answer the gunman's question at all (Father F. Rogers, personal communication on 6/26/2014). A person can choose to remain silent and to face the consequences. In this case, a person may choose to die rather than to sin by lying or by contributing to the harm of another person. Hence, one need not lie. In Christian ethics, self-preservation is not the ultimate good. Indeed, death is preferable to sin.

Natural law states that there is a universal set of rights and wrongs but without reference to specific supernatural beings (Pollock, 2004). What is good is determined by what is natural to humans (e.g., socialization and the right to life) and is free of passion. Indeed, the founding fathers might be described as natural law practitioners. However, identifying what is consistent and congruent with natural inclinations of humankind is a fundamental problem of this ethical system. This is evidenced by the changing of laws (e.g., marijuana use) and the development of new laws. In short, the natural law ethical system supports the golden rule: treat others as you wish to be treated.

Ethics of virtue determines the goodness of an act based on the attempt to achieve happiness, such as living a good life and achieving life goals (Pollock, 2004). Good behavior is based on the golden mean, which is the median between extreme states of character. For example, absolute police powers and civil liberties oppose one another. Effective law enforcement must compromise between the two. It is based on a person's character and includes factors such as honesty, humility, and temperance.

Ethics of care determines the goodness of an act based on meeting needs and preserving and enriching relationships (Pollock, 2004). Actions are taken based on connecting with other people, caring for the needs of other people, and being aware of other people. For example, police officers are directed to make an arrest whenever they respond to a domestic violence call when two conditions exist: (1) when a statement is made by the victim that the victim was assaulted; and (2) if there is any physical evidence of battery (e.g., a bruise). These two conditions establish probable cause, and the police will make an arrest to protect the victim.

Egoism claims that good results from pursuing self-interests (Pollock, 2004). However, every person acting in their own best interests is not logical or feasible, and this will result in great conflict. An example of egoism in law enforcement is when police officers write unnecessary tickets to meet quotas for good performance reviews.

Enlightened egoism claims that it is in one's long-term best interest to help others so that they will learn to help themselves (Pollock, 2004). For example, a police officer may refuse to change a flat tire on a car occupied with capable adults and may instead instruct them on how to change the tire themselves. Having the occupants change the tire themselves may prove valuable in the future if they get another flat tire and no assistance is available. However, community members may expect the police to provide full and immediate service, and this may result in complaints. As a way to comply with departmental policy, police officers in the field may offer full service in terms of providing a wrecker service. If drivers are dissatisfied with that response due to time and cost, this may damage police–community relations.

Situational ethics states that there are few universal truths and that different situations call for different responses (Pollock, 2004). Thus, the same action may be right in some situations and wrong in other situations. For example, it may be ethical for a person to violate the speed laws if they are racing an injured person to the hospital. However, the same action may be unethical if no such emergency exists.

Table 8.3 Ethical systems

Ethics in Law Enforcement **What is good behavior?** Ethics is the study of set ideas of right and wrong. However, there are different ideas of right and wrong in which to judge good behavior. Consequently, different ethical systems answer the question, "What is good?" in different manners.	**Moral principles** are set ideas of right and wrong that form the basis of ethical behaviors.

Table 8.3 Cont.

The **deontological ethical system** is concerned with goodwill or the intent of the actor as the element of morality. The consequence of the action is unimportant. Trying to save a life is good behavior.

The **teleological ethical system** is concerned with the consequences of an action to determine goodness. The intent of the actor (the police officer, in this case) is unimportant.

Branches of ethical systems
- Utilitarianism
- Act utilitarianism
- Rule utilitarianism
- Ethical formalism
- Ethical relativism
- Cultural relativism
- Religious
- Natural law
- Ethics of virtue
- Ethics of care
- Egoism
- Enlightened egoism
- Situational ethics

Utilitarianism
Good is based on a benefit-cost ratio. Example of good behavior: arresting an innocent person to deter crime in general.

(*continued*)

Table 8.3 Cont.

Act utilitarianism
The goodness of a particular act is measured by the utility of the specific act without regard for future acts. For example, it is not unethical to steal food when a person is hungry and has no other way to get food.

Rule utilitarianism
The goodness of an act is measured by the utility of the act when made into a rule for behavior. For example, it is unethical to steal food when a person is hungry because this will result in lawlessness if stealing is allowed to become the general rule.

Ethical formalism
Good is based on goodwill and by doing one's duty. Example of good behavior: chasing a fleeing felon, even if the violator gets hurt.

Ethical relativism
This ethical system determines what is good or bad based on the individual or group. For example, community members in a poor region may hunt and fish without purchasing the proper licenses. Also, prostitution may be encouraged and institutionalized in certain societies.

Table 8.3 Cont.

Cultural relativism
Good is based on what promotes the health and survival of society. One example of good behavior is Middle Eastern women refusing to show their faces in public.

Religious
Good is based on God's will. Example of good behavior: always providing complete and truthful information, regardless of the cost.

Natural law
Good is based on a universal set of rights (i.e., what is natural). Example of good behavior: practicing the golden rule: treat others the way you want to be treated yourself.

Ethics of virtue
Good is based on compromise. Example of good behavior: using non-intrusive x-ray machines to search for contraband.

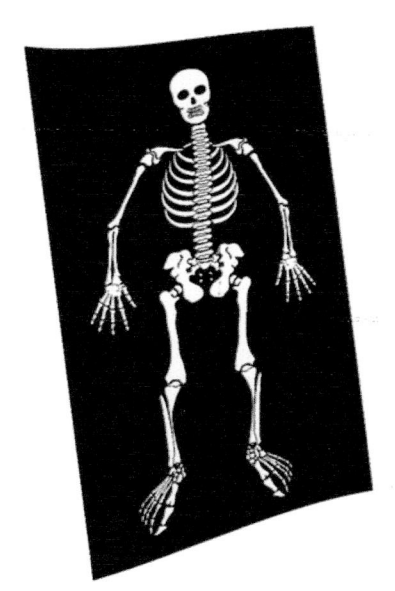

(*continued*)

Table 8.3 Cont.

Ethics of care
Good is based on the needs of those concerned. Example of good behavior: always arresting males who are involved in domestic violence to protect female victims.

Egoism
Good is based on what benefits the actor. Example of good behavior: writing a lot of tickets to meet the monthly quota for a good performance review.

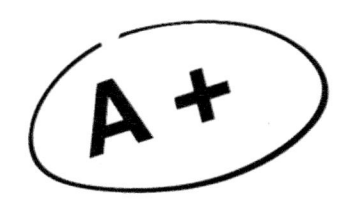

Enlightened egoism
It is in one's long-term best interest to help others so that they will learn to help themselves. For example, a police officer may refuse to change a flat tire on a car occupied with capable adults and may instead instruct them on how to change the tire themselves. Having the occupants change the tire themselves may prove valuable in the future if they get another flat tire and no assistance is available.

Situational ethics
Good is based on the particular situation at a particular time. Example of good behavior: speeding in order to get to the hospital to save a life.

DECEIVING SUSPECTS: IS IT ETHICAL FOR POLICE TO LIE?

Utilitarianism: justified, if benefits outweigh costs to society as a whole.

Act utilitarianism: justified, if necessary under the conditions to solve the case (serious crimes may be more accepting of deceit).

Rule utilitarianism: condemned, because it may undermine long-term system of laws.

Ethical formalism: justified, because a criminal does not have a right to believe they will be told the truth.

Ethical relativism: justified, because law enforcers expect other law enforcers to lie to suspects to solve cases.

Cultural relativism: justified, as long as accepted by culture.

Religious: condemned, due to lying; God is truth; possibly justified, if can argue lesser of two evils.

Natural law: justified, as long as civil rights are not violated.

Ethics of virtue: justified, if crimes are severe and if methods are moderate.

Ethics of care: justified, if it protects victims.

Egoism: justified, if profitable to police officer (e.g., good performance review).

Enlightened egoism: justified, if long-term benefits are greater than loss of trust in police.

Situational ethics: justified, if police officer can effectively articulate reasons for deception in the particular case (evaluated on a case-by-case basis).

ETHICS IN ACTION: GRATUITIES

The formal law enforcement code of ethics disapproves of a police officer accepting gratuities if they negatively influence a police officer's actions (Hess & Wrobleski, 1997). However, police officers accepting gratuities is a debatable issue because there are costs and benefits for both the police and the public when police officers accept gratuities. Furthermore, there is disagreement on what constitutes a gratuity. In any event, police officers should not use their public office for personal gain and they should not accept gratuities from people with whom they do official business.

One problem with police officers accepting gratuities is that there is no clear definition of a gratuity. According to Prenzler and Mackay (1995), a gratuity is a gift, reward, or discount that is given freely and that does not influence the police officer's performance. According to Coleman (2004), a gratuity can even be a glass of water because it has value. On the other hand, Corley (2005) states that a gratuity is something given freely in order to honor someone. Corley states that a gift given in kindness, such as a cup of coffee, is not a gratuity. He also stresses that gratuities and gifts must not be confused with one another, and that officers must use common sense to distinguish them. However, this requires proper training. If officers have doubt, and to play it safe, they must refuse all gifts and gratuities.

Cons of Police Officers Accepting Gratuities

There are several arguments against police officers accepting gratuities. Because police officers strive to improve police–community relations, it is important to consider the image that the officers portray to the public. Below are eight cons for police officers accepting gratuities.

The first con with police officers accepting gratuities is the potential that this may lead to corruption (Coleman, 2004; Prenzler & Mackay, 1995). However, while some of those who oppose gratuities equate gratuities with corruption, others disagree, stating that most gratuities are given with no strings attached. To complicate the matter, legal opinions do not clearly define what is considered acceptable behavior. For example, how much is too much? Thus, with all this confusion, the actual acceptance of gratuities is considered to be a gray area.

A second con with police officers accepting gratuities is that this actually does lead to corruption (Prenzler & Mackay, 1995). There is a chance that police officers will come to expect gratuities. When this is not realized, police officers have been known to teach business owners a lesson (Ruiz & Bono, 2004). Furthermore, because there is no clear-cut guideline between simple gratuities and huge payoffs, some officers may unknowingly cross that ill-defined line.

A third con with police officers accepting gratuities is that the public may perceive that an officer is willing to become corrupt (Coleman, 2004). If a police officer accepts gratuities, this establishes a history of the police officer accepting things without paying for them. Because the officer has not established what their limits are for accepting gratuities, the public will be doubtful about those limits.

The fourth con with police officers accepting gratuities is that it may give the impression of favoritism (Hess & Bennett, 2007; Prenzler & Mackay, 1995). If the public sees officers receiving free gifts, such as food and beverages, then the public may perceive that the provider will expect something in return. Indeed, America is a capitalistic society and people understand that nothing is free. By the officer accepting gratuities, capitalism dictates that the officer will have to return that payment in one way or another. Even though accepting gratuities is not wrong in itself, the image that it portrays may be unethical (Pozo, 2005).

The fifth con with police officers accepting gratuities is that favoritism may actually take place (Coleman, 2004). The provider may expect preferential treatment and may demand that an officer overlooks minor violations of the law, such as speeding, and the officer may feel obligated to comply (Pozo, 2005). Although most business employees offer gratuities with no strings attached, there are some who do expect favors (Corley, 2005). In fact, after not receiving special treatment, an owner billed the local police department for all of the food that had been given to the officers as gratuities (White, 2002). This business owner then went to the local media and gave them the police officers' names and the dollar amounts for the food that the officers had consumed (the officers signed receipts). The business owner did this as a means of extortion. Thus, even if police officers believe gratuities are free, they never know whether the business owners feel the same way.

A sixth con with police officers accepting gratuities is that the public is paying for services already bought (Hess & Bennett, 2007; Prenzler & Mackay, 1995; Ruiz & Bono, 2004). Police officers are paid out of a budget that has been collected from taxpayers. Because all taxpayers have contributed toward this budget, the police services for the entire community have already been purchased. By business owners providing gratuities, this is considered an additional payment in order to receive personalized police services. Thus, by accepting gratuities, police officers are double-charging the public.

A seventh con with police officers accepting gratuities is that a gratuity may be offered by a person who is unauthorized to offer gratuities, which means the police officer would be condoning theft (Coleman, 2004). For example, if only managers in a restaurant can offer gratuities, but the cashier is the one who offers the gratuity, then the cashier is giving away items that do not belong to them. By accepting the gratuity, the officer is participating in theft.

Finally, an eighth con with police officers accepting gratuities is the unfair social distribution of police services (Pozo, 2005). When police officers take their lunches at particular locations, those officers provide two services: deterrence of crime and a rapid response to emergencies. Thus, simply by being there, that location receives additional services not being offered to other locations. Other restaurant owners may not be too happy with this situation, and this may lead to complaints.

Pros of Police Officers Accepting Gratuities

There are several arguments that advocate for police officers accepting gratuities. Because police officers strive to improve police–community relations, it is important to consider the relationships that the officers build with the public. Below are seven pros for police officers accepting gratuities.

First, accepting gratuities may reduce uncomfortable public situations faced by police officers. Some business owners insist on giving gratuities out of civic friendship (Hess & Bennett, 2007; Pozo, 2005). If an officer refuses to accept the gratuity, a business owner may become upset and vocal, which may attract unwelcome attention. Arguing with the public may give the perception that the officer is unfriendly and aggressive. This may create an uncomfortable situation for the police officer and may weaken social bonds.

Second, accepting gratuities will enhance social bonds and police performance, which may promote a safer society (Coleman, 2004; Hess & Bennett, 2007). For instance, if a female rape victim offers the investigating officer a cup of coffee, failing to accept the coffee may damage the working relationship and impede the officer's job. Furthermore, because it is an American custom to leave a tip for good service, some people may feel the need to tip police officers for good service. However, as stated earlier, when a police officer provides service to the public, that service has already been purchased. Therefore, if the gratuity is offered to the officer as a tip, it must be rejected. However, if the gratuity is offered to the officer out of friendship, then accepting that gratuity may be beneficial. This is especially true if the gratuities are given after the fact, when they cannot influence any police actions. For instance, if a police officer protects a woman from being raped, she may later offer him a small gift of appreciation. Because this gift is presented after the fact, it will have no impact on the case. If, on the other hand, the officer refuses to accept the gift, the woman may come to believe that the officer never really cared about her. This may damage police–community relations.

Third, accepting gratuities improves police response time (Sewell, 2007). For example, if a restaurant owner provides a discount on food, then a police officer may be motivated to eat there. By being there, the police officer is capable of responding to emergencies quickly. If, on the other hand, the police officer is not motivated to eat at the restaurant and goes home to eat because the food is better and cheaper, then the response time may be slower. To make things worse, the response time may be significantly slower in poor weather conditions.

Fourth, accepting gratuities promotes public safety. When officers go home to eat, they are not in the public's sight. Just by being on the road, police officers deter crime. Thus, police officers have a presence when they eat their meals in the field. The police department may set a fixed dollar amount per month at each restaurant in order to discourage an officer from eating at the same restaurant too often.

Fifth, accepting gratuities prevents officers from being self-stigmatized (Coleman, 2004). If police officers are labeled as corrupt because they have already accepted a gratuity, then some may come to believe that are already deviant and corrupt. If they self-stigmatize themselves as deviant, then they may come to realize a self-fulfilling prophecy, thereby leading to additional deeds of deviance (Ryan & Cooper, 2007).

Sixth, the practice of accepting gratuities is so deeply entrenched in American culture that banning gratuities will be ineffective (White, 2002). Furthermore, most gratuities have only nominal value and are not significant enough to influence a police officer's actions. Banning gratuities will only result in unnecessary violations of department policy.

Finally, the seventh reason for allowing police officers to accept gratuities is that this will reduce the department's workload, as long as officers use discretion. If the department has a no-tolerance gratuity policy, this will increase the amount of work for the department. Every time that there is a complaint, the department will need to investigate. However, if the officers use their common sense and have some discretion, then the post commander could resolve any potential problem over the telephone. The post commander could tell the caller, for example, that officers are professionals who are well trained in ethics, and that a harsh judgment of them accepting a gratuity out of civic friendship cannot be justified within such a brief encounter (Pozo, 2005).

THEORETICAL CONCEPTS AND RESEARCH

There are several theories that may explain why police officers accept gratuities. Rational choice theory states that a police officer will perform an act when the benefits for the act outweigh the associated costs for the act (Liska & Messner, 1999). The looking-glass self theory indicates that people will react to how they perceive others judge them (Hensley, 1996). Finally, behavioral economics indicates that choices are influenced by available alternatives and environmental constraints (Tucker et al., 1999).

Rational Choice Theory

Rational choice theory states that people will perform acts when they are profitable (Barkan, 2006; Liska & Messner, 1999). There are two ways to enhance the benefit–cost ratio: by increasing the benefits so that they are greater than the costs, or by reducing the costs so that they are less than the benefits. Both cases will increase profitability.

Rational choice theory involves extrinsic and intrinsic rewards (Ryan & Cooper, 2007). The extrinsic rewards involve the actual receiving of the gratuities, which have value. Every time an officer accepts a $5.00 free meal, that is five dollars still in the officer's pocket. Intrinsic rewards, on the other hand, are the internal feelings that make an officer feel good. When an officer receives a gratuity, even if the officer does not need it, this may give the officer a feeling of superiority over the giver. This feeling of power is a reward that comes from within, which provides the officer with personal satisfaction (Ryan & Cooper, 2007).

Costs, in the form of deterrence, can be measured in three ways: (1) the severity of punishment; (2) the certainty of punishment; and (3) the celerity of punishment (Akers & Sellers, 2009). Deterrence works best when officers perceive that the severity of punishment is great, the certainty of punishment is high, and the celerity of punishment is swift. Once a policy has been established, violations of the policy must be enforced strictly and in a timely fashion. For instance, if immediate suspensions are associated with accepting gratuities, then an officer will compare the benefits of a free meal with the cost of a suspension. If the officers perceive that the policy is not enforced, they will not follow it. If disciplinary action is not guaranteed, then the policy will have minimal influence upon the officers. By posting disciplinary actions taken against officers for their indiscretions, the word will spread that the issue is serious. Thus, officers will come to realize that the punishment is severe, certain, and immediate.

The Looking-Glass Self Theory

Cooley states that people develop their self-concepts by evaluating how they believe that they appear to others, how they believe that others judge their appearance, and how they react to those judgments (Hensley, 1996). This is what Cooley calls the looking-glass self. By accepting gratuities on a regular basis, police officers may come to believe that the public expects it. Some officers may believe that gratuities are a perk that comes with the job. However, in order to redefine their self-concepts, the officers must be persuaded to change their attitudes.

Behavioral Economics Theory

Self-image is important to police departments and unethical behaviors will not be tolerated. However, the formal law enforcement code of ethics only disapproves a police officer accepting gratuities if they negatively influence a police officer's actions (Hess & Wrobleski, 1997). Thus, accepting gratuities is not always unethical (Prenzler & Mackay, 1995). As in solving any problem, the root causes of the gratuity problem must be identified. Some of the variables that are associated with the problem include: (1) officer's preference; (2) assignment location; (3) restaurant availability; and (4) social environment (Sewell, 2007). Once the issues have been identified, change must come from above and officers must be persuaded to modify their behaviors.

One possible idea is to require the officers to eat at randomly designated restaurants (Pozo, 2005). However, officers may only have few restaurants to choose from where they work. Therefore, this action may be ineffective. A second idea would be to request that the officers bring their meals from home and eat them in their police cars. However, a problem with eating meals in the police car is that is it very common to witness violations from within the vehicle. If the police officer is trying to eat lunch and does nothing, citizens will complain. If the officer chases the vehicle, then the officer will not have much of an opportunity to eat. Therefore, this suggestion may not be well received among the officers. A third idea is to have the officers bring their meals from home and ask that they eat their meals inside a squad room. The problem with that idea is that there is no incentive to eat in the squad room; officers may prefer to go home where they can watch television and spend some time with the family. If an officer does goes home for a meal, then the response time for a detail may be longer.

Conclusion

The government derives its powers with the consent of the people (Cain, 2003). Indeed, the police can only govern the people if the people agree to be governed. Thus, the police must have a good relationship with the public. It is important that the community members respect the police. When police officers accept gratuities, this makes a statement and forms an image of the officers. Although there are both pros and cons for police officers accepting gratuities, and because there is no clear-cut guideline of how much is too much, officers need to be adequately trained in this area and taught to use proper discretion. Furthermore, officers need to be persuaded to follow the department's gratuity policy. If a negative image is created by police officers accepting gratuities, then this will weaken the bond between the police and the public. Indeed, the officers must have integrity and the public must perceive that the officers have integrity. In this way, police–community relations will be enhanced, and this will promote public safety.

POLICE DEPARTMENT ORIENTATIONS

Eight theoretical orientations have been identified that describe the lenses through which police department administrators perceive crime and the criminal justice system (Kraska, 2004). The orientation that a police department follows will influence how patrol officers act toward the public. For a police officer, it may be problematic if the officer's personal ethical system conflicts with the police department's orientation. The nine police department orientations are: (1) rational, (2) system, (3) crime control, (4) due process, (5) politics, (6) growth complex, (7) social constructionist, (8) oppression, and (9) late modernity. However, each orientation is based on assumptions, which must be understood.

Rational Orientation

The rational orientation simply views law enforcement as a business. Peace and security can be achieved by controlling crime, and crime can be controlled by punishing offenders (Kraska, 2004). In other words, everyone is expected to follow the rules in order to achieve the agreed upon end result, which is peace. When, for example, someone decides not to follow the rules, they will create a tear in the fabric of peace, and this fabric must be repaired, which comes at a cost. By not following the rules, this person has encroached upon the rights of other individuals and is forcing them to pay a cost for which the offender is responsible. Because this is not fair, laws are required to balance things out. The offender must pay a cost high enough to not only repair the damage, but also deter them from disrupting social order in the future. If the penalty is not high enough to discourage future acts of deviance, then the public's confidence in public safety will be undermined. The greater the cost to the public, the greater the cost should be to the offender.

The main assumptions of the rational orientation are that everyone in society has equal value, everyone is in alignment, and everyone accepts that they must follow the agreed-upon rules. It assumes that everyone has given up a little bit of personal freedom so the government can enforce the agreed-upon rules in order to promote public safety in a fair and impartial manner (Kraska, 2004). It assumes that crime has a cost, and crime can be managed through payment.

System Orientation

The system orientation views criminal justice as an entity that consists of interacting, yet independent agencies (Kraska, 2004). The various agencies function by drawing inputs from the external environment, transforming these inputs, then sending the final product back into the environment as socially approved output. An example would be to collect convicts (input), to rehabilitate them through behavior modification programs (transform), then to release them back into society (output). The system's independent units strive to maintain balance and internal stability as they sustain each other. It is believed that crime is a rational choice and that the size and power of the system must be increased in order to accommodate increases in the crime rate.

The primary purpose of the criminal justice system, according to the system orientation, is to control crime via interagency cooperation (Kraska, 2004). It is believed that public safety can be achieved through the efficient operation of each unit of the criminal justice system, including the legislative, executive, judicial, and correctional agencies. In this way, accused persons can be processed, rehabilitated, and returned to society in an effective and efficient manner that promotes social peace.

The main assumption of the system orientation is that those who have legal authority are capable of making rational decisions, which will reduce crime in an efficient manner (Kraska, 2004). It is believed that the system can adapt itself to accommodate changes in the external environment, usually by increasing its resources. By effectively and efficiently using resources and technology, by improving laws and policies, by improving judicial processes, and by improving rehabilitation and re-entry programs, it is expected that crime can be better controlled and public safety will be enhanced.

Crime Control Orientation vs. Due Process Orientation

The main purpose of the crime control orientation is to secure peace by arresting as many law violators as possible, as fast as possible, and by using as few resources per arrest as possible (Kraska, 2004). Furthermore, because the defendants are presumed guilty (otherwise they would not have been arrested), releasing suspects due to procedural mistakes is wrong. In other words, suspects are guilty of their alleged crimes, otherwise law enforcement authorities would not spend the resources trying to prosecute the person (i.e., effective crime control does not focus on innocent people). It is believed that this quantitatively based tough-on-crime policy can be achieved by efficiently processing offenders informally and consistently through the legal system. This requires having few constitutional restraints placed upon law enforcers. However, the crime control orientation assumes that law enforcers: (1) are trustworthy and will enforce laws in a fair and legal manner; and (2) can competently reconstruct crime scenes and develop the most accurate account of the actual events in a descriptive and factual manner. In short, mistakes are tolerated up to the point where they start to interfere with the suppression of crime.

The main purpose of the due process orientation is to protect people's rights by placing constraints upon the government and by making government officials defend their investigative procedures in an adversarial courtroom (Kraska, 2004). Due process advocates believe mistakes are unacceptable, individual freedom is more valuable than absolute security, and factual guilt does not equate to legal guilt. However, unless the police are forced to present their evidence in court, it is assumed that this distinction will not be made. This qualitative based policy assumes that the defendant will be provided adequate legal representation in the courtroom and that the legal system will lead to the discovery of the truth (e.g., whether the police honored procedural safeguards, as guaranteed by law). Indeed, the due process orientation requires that an unbiased third party make an objective evaluation of legal guilt.

Due process advocates view criminal justice as a necessary means to protect social freedom by protecting all citizens from unjust acts committed by government officials (Kraska, 2004). Because the cost of being incarcerated is extremely high, the due process orientation requires that the state eliminate all doubt about whether constitutional procedural safeguards were violated. In order to control law enforcers, there must be a cost for violating the rules. Thus, in order to ensure that police officers will comply with the law, it is argued that the cost of releasing all suspects whose rights have been violated will be a high enough cost to motivate law enforcers to obey the law when they perform their duties. According to the due process orientation, corrupt police officers will cause the crime control orientation to fail.

Politics Orientation (Right Wing vs. Left Wing)

According to the politics orientation, the criminal justice system is interest-based and its primary purpose is contingent upon the political climate at the time, which constantly changes according to who may be in power (Kraska, 2004). Many interest groups fight for power and want to protect their own self-interest. Through negotiations, the different groups can protect their interests through checks and balances. This promotes an orderly offender processing system via rational policies. Politics, however, has two sides: a right wing and a left wing.

The right wing is conservative and the left wing is liberal (Kraska, 2004). On the one hand, the right wing believes that (1) the system is too lenient with offenders; (2) the system favors the rights of offenders over the rights of victims; (3) youths no longer respect authorities; (4) hard-working, law-abiding Americans are paying the high cost for crime; and (5) society is too permissive involving morality issues. The left wing, on the other hand, believes that: (1) the system inappropriately includes certain vices as crimes, which indicates a more serious crime problem than really exists; (2) authorities label people as criminals, which may stigmatize them and create a self-fulfilling prophecy; (3) correctional facilities are warehouses for criminals and they fail to rehabilitate inmates, which leads to recidivism; (4) centralized power discourages the involvement of community members in solving local problems; and (5) the criminal justice system discriminates against and segregates minorities in order to control them.

The right wing and the left wing each have their own set of assumptions (Kraska, 2004). The right wing's assumptions state that: (1) people are responsible for their own actions; (2) strong morals, based on a religious foundation, are essential for a healthy and well-functioning society; (3) people have the right to be safe and secure in the areas where they spend most of their time; (4) a healthy society requires that people obey the laws, which will be administered fairly and firmly; and (5) social order requires that major categories of persons be segregated so that they can be controlled. The left wing's assumptions state that: (1) the primary cause of crime lies in dysfunctional social conditions; (2) obsolete regulations on morality are deficient in meeting the current needs of a majority of the population; (3) there is an unequal distribution of power and resources in the country; (4) a healthy society cannot discriminate against major categories of persons; (5) official authorities stigmatize offenders by labeling them as criminals, which will lead to hardship and future crime; and (6) the crime problem is exaggerated (legal codes should be changed so that victimless crimes are not counted toward the crime problem).

Growth Complex Orientation

According to the growth complex orientation, the purpose of the criminal justice system is to build an ever-growing bureaucracy (Kraska, 2004). Administering justice and controlling crime are tools that are used to increase the agency's size and power. In an effort to meet the organizational ends in the most efficient way, scientific methods are established in order to create rules and regulations, which will get everyone to perform their duties in the same technically efficient and predictable manner. Instead of focusing on the outcome (doing the right thing), the rules and regulations become the standard for performance. Using statistics allows police departments to defend their enforcement practices. When someone challenges their apparently unfair enforcement tactics, the police can claim that individuals were arrested based on objective numeric analysis. They may also argue that without using statistics to classify and sentence people, each person's fate would be inconsistent and uncertain.

The growth complex orientation has several critiques and assumptions. Operating under the growth complex orientation, there is an incentive to lock people up. Part of the criminal justice system has become privatized and many investors hope to profit (Kraska, 2004). On the one hand, the investors create many jobs. For example, workers are needed to build prisons, supply prison food, supply prison clothes, and provide medical care. On the other hand, the investors need customers (i.e., inmates); hence, there is an incentive to confine people in prison. By locking people up in prison, the state effectively manages the surplus labor force, which is naturally generated in a capitalistic society (Kraska, 2004). Thus, politicians appear to be serving the public effectively. After all, jobs are created and there are fewer unemployed people in the marketplace. The main assumptions of the growth complex orientation are that: (1) a bureaucracy needs to survive and grow; (2) people desire to build dynasties that extend their power and create a type of immortality; (3) rational and efficient methods are the best way to measure performance; (4) capitalism and efficiency take precedence over human dignity (and, consequently, people lose sight of their morals); (5) a matrix of organizations, interests, and resources is needed for growth; (6) punishing people is good financial business and creates many jobs; and (7) profiteers are not held accountable for their faulty products and their poor-quality services.

Social Constructionist Orientation

The social constructionist orientation is based upon interpretivism, which has both subjective and objective qualities (Kraska, 2004). On the one hand, interpretivism is subjective and claims that reality and meanings are shaped via individual experiences, which are unique to each individual. On the other hand, interpretivism is objective and claims that individuals constantly negotiate their perceptions with other people with whom they associate, reflecting an intersubjective reality (Weber, 2004). Indeed, there is no one single truth; reality for each person is constructed relative to personal experiences based upon language, symbols, and the interactions with other individuals (Kraska, 2004).

According to the social constructionist orientation, the purpose of the criminal justice system is socially constructed and depends on the political climate, social sentiment, cultural values, intellectual perspective, and interests of those in power (Kraska, 2004). Using the media to manage the appearance of the system's legitimacy, the public is continually bombarded with myths until the myths become accepted as facts. The criminal justice system can provide the public with select information, which creates the perception that the status quo must be maintained. Police can effectively create their own jobs by persuading the public to support their current efforts.

The assumptions of the social constructionist orientation are that: (1) police use myths to develop problems that do not really exist, which divert public attention away from the real problems in society (e.g., unemployment and discrimination); and (2) the interests of people in power must be protected (Kraska, 2004). Using descriptive statistics and the media, who need exciting crime stories to sell their publications, the police can provide the information needed to create moral panic. For example, the police chief can increase the crime rate by ordering the officers to file multiple charges for each case report or the police chief can reduce the crime rate by ordering the officers to file a single charge for each case report. By appearing to effectively react to a problem that never really existed, the police can gain the public's support.

Late Modernity Orientation

According to the late modernity orientation, the purpose of the criminal justice system is to promote safety and security by effectively identifying and managing classes of people who are assessed to be a threat (Kraska, 2004). The "goal is not to eliminate crime but to make it tolerable through systematic coordination" (Kraska, 2004, pp. 305–307). Late modernity is not concerned with the underlying causes of crime; rather, it uses statistics to assess risk levels of particular classes of people and then tries to control populations that are identified as high-risk. By incarcerating high-risk groups of people, significant aggregate effects in crime can be realized. In other words, crime can be reduced by rearranging the type of people who are still out in the general population (i.e., it reduces the percentage of high-risk people who are roaming around in free society).

The main assumptions of the late modernity orientation are that the state cannot provide effective overall security, private persons need to invest in their own situational crime prevention programs, and people rationally choose to commit crime (Kraska, 2004). Because situational crime prevention programs require financial resources to implement, this excludes many of the poor people (who end up being labeled as outsiders). Late modernity orientation supporters claim that these misfortunate people are responsible for their own fates. By classifying these misfortunate individuals as outsiders, the dominant classes can effectively control them without the dominant classes giving up their own freedoms. Indeed, authorities can effectively control these misfortunate people because incarceration is easy to implement, it results in immediate consequence, it has few political opponents, it relies on the existing system of regulations, and it leaves the fundamental social and economic systems intact.

Oppression Orientation

The oppression orientation claims that the state protects the interests of the elite and powerful while oppressing the disadvantaged and less powerful (Kraska, 2004). In other words, the state uses the law as a tool for the political repression of those groups that threaten state power. There is a struggle for power and the groups that attain the most power are the ones who dictate the law. According to the oppression orientation, the purpose of the criminal justice system is to control people who threaten the status quo. Groups who are less powerful politically, which include minorities, women, and the poor, are used as scapegoats for America's problems. By using scapegoats, society is able to overlook the underlying factors that actually cause significant social harm (e.g., unemployment and poverty).

The assumption of oppression orientation is that the criminal justice system has built in bias against minorities, women, and the poor (Kraska, 2004). Indeed, because laws in the U.S. are based on men's perspective, the laws are inherently biased. In short, the criminal justice system abuses its power through the practice of institutional racism, sexism, and classism.

Table 8.4 Police Department orientations

Police department orientations

What is good police officer behavior?	Police department orientations	Rational
Police managers have different ideas of right and wrong in which to judge good police officer behavior. Consequently, different police department orientations answer the question, "What is good police officer behavior?" in different manners.	• Rational • Crime control • Due process • System • Politics • Growth complex • Social constructionist • Late modernity • Oppression	Law enforcement is a business. Everyone agrees to give up some freedom for peace and security. If the cost for crime is high enough, individuals will rationally choose to obey the law.
	Crime control The overall goal is to control crime by arresting as many people as possible, as fast as possible, using as few resources as possible. Mistakes are acceptable; police are trustworthy and they only arrest the guilty. 	**Due process** Personal freedom is more valuable than absolute security. People have a right to legal representation; police need to prove guilt in court. Mistakes by the police are unacceptable. 

(continued)

Table 8.4 Cont.

System
Independent agencies work together to collect deviants, to transform them, and to return them to society. Public safety can be achieved through inter-agency cooperation and efficient operation of each agency.

Growth complex
Purpose of police is to build an ever growing bureaucracy. Police rules become the standard to measure performance (quotas). Police create problems to ensure jobs. Human dignity is unimportant; punishing individuals is profitable.

Late modernity
Purpose of police is to use statistics to assess risk levels and to promote safety by controlling the classes of people who have been identified as the problem. Individuals need to take responsibility to protect themselves.

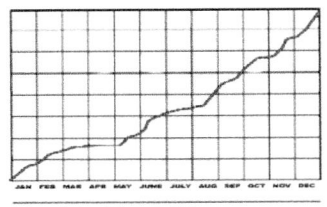

Politics
Purpose of police depends on who has political power. Right wing: system is too lenient; left wing: system is too controlling.

Social constructionist
Purpose of police is based on interpretivism. Good behavior is determined by culture, by social sentiment, and by people in power. Because there is no single truth, police use media to create myths.

Oppression
Purpose of police is to protect the elite and powerful while controlling the disadvantaged and less powerful. The police should maintain the status quo by controlling minorities.

KEYWORDS

Deviance

Ethical systems

Lenses of truth

Police department orientations

CHAPTER PROBLEMS

1. Describe the difference between deviance and criminal behavior. Provide examples of the difference.
2. What is truth?
3. Describe the difference between ethics and morals.
4. Discuss the similarities and differences between a feminist and an Afrocentrist.
5. Discuss the beliefs and critiques of pragmatists.
6. Discuss the beliefs and critiques of empiricists.
7. Compare and contrast logical positivists with postmodernists.
8. Describe how hermeneutists might explain why we have a hard time understanding old texts.

9. Discuss the following statement: "Every decision is an ethical dilemma."
10. Compare and contrast utilitarianism, act utilitarianism, and rule utilitarianism.

REFERENCES

Akers, R.L., & Sellers, C. (2009). *Criminological theories: Introduction, evaluation, and application* (5th ed.). New York: Oxford University Press.

Asante, M.K. (2009). What is Afrocentricity? www.asante.net

Barkan, S. (2006). *Criminology: A sociological understanding* (3rd ed.). Upper Saddle River, NJ: Pearson Prentice-Hall.

Berg, B. (2007). *Qualitative research methods for the social sciences* (6th ed.). Boston, MA: Pearson Education.

Brinkerhoff, J.R. (2009). Domestic operational law: The Posse Comitatus Act and homeland security. http://usacac.army.mil/cac2/call/docs/10-16/ch_12.asp

Cain, W. (2003). Declaring independence. *Society, 41*(1), 9–17.

Camic, P., Rhodes, J., & Yardley, L. (Eds.) (2003). *Qualitative research in psychology: Expanding perspectives in methodology and design*. Washington, DC: American Psychology Association.

Carter, D. (2002). *Issues in police–community relations: Taken from the police and the community* (7th ed.). Boston, MA: Pearson.

Chessick, R. (1990). Hermeneutics for psychotherapists. *American Journal of Psychotherapy, 44*(2), 256–273.

Christian Police & Prison Association (n.d.). Canons of police ethics http://cpa-usa.org/law-officers/canons-of-police-ethics

Coleman, S. (2004). When police should say "no!" to gratuities. *Criminal Justice Ethics, 23* (1), 33–44.

Corley, M. (2005). Gratuities. *FBI Law Enforcement Bulletin, 74*(10), 10–13.

Crossan, F. (2003). Research philosophy: Towards an understanding. *Nurse Researcher, 11*(1), 46–55.

Dotzler, R.J. (2000). Getting to reparations: A response to Fein. *Sociological Practice: A Journal of Clinical and Applied Sociology, 2*(3), 177–182.

Dowling, M. (2004). Hermeneutics: An exploration. *Nurse Researcher, 11*(4), 30–39.

Dreisbach, C. (2008). *Ethics in criminal justice*. Boston, MA: McGraw-Hill Irwin.

Fuchs, S. (1993). Three social epistemologies. *Social Perspectives, 36*(1), 23–44.

Glesne, C. (2006). *Becoming qualitative researchers: An introduction* (3rd ed.). Boston, MA: Pearson.

Hall, A.A. (2000). There is a lot to be repaired before we get reparations: A critique of the underlying issues of race that impact the fate of African American reparations. *St. Mary's Law Review, 1*, 22–32.

Hames, J., & Ekern, Y. (2005). *Constitutional law: Principles and practice*. Clifton Park, NY: Thomson Delmar Learning.

Hamlyn, D.W. (n.d.). *Empiricism*. http://mind.ucsd.edu/syllabi/99_00/Empiricism/Readings/Encyc_Phil/Empiricism.html

Hammers, C., & Brown, A. (2004). Towards a feminist-queer alliance: A paradigmatic shift in the research process. *Social Epistemology, 18*(1), 85–101.

Harberfeld, M.R. (2006). *Police leadership*. Upper Saddle River, NJ: Pearson Prentice-Hall.

Hatch, J. (2002). *Doing qualitative research in education settings*. Albany, NY: State University of New York Press.

Hensley, W. (1996). A theory of the valenced other: The intersection of the looking-glass self and social penetration. *Social Behavior and Personality, 24*(3), 293–308.

Hess, K.M., & Bennett, W.W. (2007). *Management and supervision in law enforcement* (5th ed.). Belmont, CA: Wadsworth Thomson.

Hess, K. & Wrobleski, H. (1997). *Police operations* (2nd ed.). St. Paul, MN: West.

Hofer, B., & Pintrich, P. (2002). *Personal epistemology: The psychology of beliefs about knowledge and knowing*. Mahwah, NJ: Lawrence Erlbaum.

Holliday, A. (2007). *Doing and writing qualitative research* (2nd ed.). Thousand Oaks, CA: Sage.

Kraska, P. (2004). *Theorizing criminal justice: Eight essential orientations*. Long Grove, IL: Waveland Press.

Liska, A. & Messner, S. (1999). *Perspectives on crime and deviance* (3rd ed.). Upper Saddle River, NJ: Prentice Hall.

McLaughlin, E., & Muncie, J. (2006). *The Sage dictionary of criminology* (2nd ed.). Thousand Oaks, CA: Sage.

Mertens, D.M. (2005). *Research and evaluation in education and psychology: Integrating diversity with quantitative, qualitative, and mixed methods* (2nd ed.). Thousand Oaks, CA: Sage.

Papell, C., & Skolnik, L. (1992). The reflective practitioner: A contemporary paradigm's relevance for social work education. *Journal of Social Work Education, 28*(1), 18–26.

Perez, D.W., & Moore, J.A. (2002). *Police ethics: A matter of character*. Incline Village, NV: Copperhouse.

Pollock, J.M. (2004). *Ethics in crime and justice: Dilemmas & decisions*. Belmont, CA: Thomas-Wadsworth.

Ponterotto, J. (2005). Qualitative research in counseling psychology: A primer on research paradigms and philosophy of science. *Journal of Counseling, 52*(2), 126–136.

Pozo, B. (2005). One dogma of police ethics: Gratuities and the "democratic ethos" of policing. *Criminal Justice Ethics, 24*(2), 25–46.

Prenzler, T., & Mackay, P. (1995). Police gratuities: What the public think. *Criminal Justice Ethics, 14*(1), 15–25.

Ruiz, J., & Bono, C. (2004). At what price a "freebie'? The real cost of police gratuities. *Criminal Justice Ethics, 23*(1), 44–54.

Ryan, K., & Cooper, J. (2007). *Those who can, teach* (11th ed.). Boston, MA: Houghton Mifflin.

Sadala, M., & Adorno, R. (2002). Phenomenology as a method to investigate the experience lived: A perspective from Husserl and Merleau Ponty's thought. *Journal of Advanced Nursing, 37*(3), 282–293.

Schmalleger, F. (2007). *Criminal justice today: An introductory text for the 21st century* (9th ed.). Upper Saddle River, NJ: Pearson Prentice Hall.

Sewell, C. (2007). Gratuities pay now or later. *FBI Law Enforcement Bulletin, 76*(4), 8–12.

Stevens, L. (2003, June 20). Jackson: All must help the city in wake of violence. *The Herald Palladium* (Benton Harbor, Michigan).

Tucker, J., Donovan, D., & Marlatt, G. (Eds.). (1999). *Changing additive behavior: Bridging clinical and public health strategies*. New York: Guilford Press.

U.S. Department of Justice, Federal Bureau of Investigation (n.d.). Crime in the United States, 2019. https://ucr.fbi.gov/crime-in-the-u.s/2019/crime-in-the-u.s.-2019/tables/table-74

Weber, R. (2004). The rhetoric of positivism versus interpretivism: A personal view. *MIS Quarterly 28*(1), iii–xii.

White, M. (2002). The problem with gratuities. *FBI Law Enforcement Bulletin, 71*(7), 20–23.

Wimpenny, P. & Gass, J. (2000). Interviewing in phenomenology and grounded theory: Is there a difference? *Journal of Advanced Nursing, 31*(6), 1485–1492.

CHAPTER 9

Interrogatory and Deposition

LEARNING OBJECTIVES

Understand the purpose of specific questions during an interrogatory.
Understand the purpose of specific questions during a deposition.

INTRODUCTION

Discovery is the formal process of exchanging information between opposing parties in a legal case. Discovery is the disclosure of the available evidence so that each party can see the strength of the other side and decide whether to move forward toward trial or to negotiate an early settlement. All parties are required to participate in the discovery process. During discovery, there are two methods that the litigants may use against the opposing party to collect information about the facts surrounding the case. These two methods are the interrogatory and the deposition. If a party refuses to cooperate with the requests made by the opposing party during discovery, the court may compel the party to comply with the request. Failure to comply with the court order may result in a contempt of court judgement against the litigant. As a result, the defiant may be fined or imprisoned. The court might even enter a default judgment for the opposing party. If information needs to be collected from a non-litigant, then a subpoena can be used to compel a person to provide the desired information.

INTERROGATORY AND DEPOSITION

What are the similarities and differences between an interrogatory and a deposition? First, an interrogatory and deposition are similar because both involve the questioning of the opposing party as part of the pretrial discovery process (Maier, 2021). Second, questions in both cases are asked under penalty of perjury. Finally, respondents in both cases can consult with their lawyers. However, there are several differences between interrogatories and depositions. First, interrogatories can be quicker, less costly, and less complicated than depositions. Second, because interrogatory questions are written and answered in private, the respondent will have much more time to think and craft answers. For example, interrogatory questions and answers may be sent via email, while depositions are recorded in front of the opposing lawyer. Finally, an interrogatory does not allow for rapid follow-up questions to gain more detailed information, as would be the case for a deposition.

An interrogatory is a list of formal questions that are sent to the opposing legal party, perhaps via email, which must be answered in writing under the penalty of perjury (Maier, 2021). The purpose of an interrogatory is to learn general information about the opposing party and to clarify matters of fact. This information will help determine in advance what facts will be presented at trial. If a person fails to answer interrogatory questions, the person may be held in contempt of court and punished.

A deposition is the sworn out-of-court testimony of a witness, usually in the opposing attorney's office, which will be transcribed into writing (Maier, 2021). It is a formal, recorded, question-and-answer session, which occurs when a witness is under oath. A deposition generally serves two purposes: it finds out what the opposing party knows, and it preserves the testimony, which may be used later at trial. Indeed, a deposition may be used to impeach the live testimony of a witness if it contradicts admissions previously made during the deposition. Deponents have a right to confer with their lawyers and may speak with their attorneys privately regarding any question and answer. Failure to tell the truth at a deposition constitutes perjury. Furthermore, a deposition may be used during trial if the witness is not available to testify.

Lawyer's Trap

At the end of a deposition, a police officer may expect the defense attorney to ask whether anything else happened. If the police officer says no, then this may be used against the officer at trial. This is a technique used by lawyers to make sure that the officer does not add anything else to the case later in court. Therefore, a better response by the officer may be to say that the officer cannot remember anything else at this time. This leaves the door open in case something else is remembered later. At a crime scene, there may be many events that actually happened. Unless a lawyer itemizes each event with a question, an officer should not universally discount all the events.

Interrogatory

Below is a two-part example of some interrogatory questions. The case is fictitious. It involves a male employee who is claiming age discrimination, gender discrimination, and a slander complaint when seeking other employment, which resulted in negative financial consequences. These are some of the questions that might be asked.

Question	Interrogatory – Part I
1	Identify each document that you intend to use as an exhibit at the trial of this matter.
2	Identify each person whom you intend to call as a trial witness in this matter. Separately state the facts and observations to which each witness is expected to testify and identify each document for which each witness is expected to testify.
3	Identify each person known or believed by you to have personal knowledge of any of the facts at issue. Separately state the facts and observations believed to be within each such person's knowledge.
4	Identify each person who has provided written, recorded, or transcribed statements, declarations, affidavits, or reports that have been secured with respect to any of the matters relating to the allegations in the complaint. For each person identified, identify each document that evidences such statements or reports.
5	Identify each person whom you intend to call as an expert witness at trial. For each person: a. State the subject matter on which the person is expected to testify. b. State the substance of the person's testimony and the summary of the basis for the testimony. c. Identify any papers, articles, treatises, or books that the person has wholly or partially authored, or to which the person has contributed. d. Identify all prior proceedings in which the person has given any testimony.
6	Identify every prospective employer to whom you have applied for a job for the last 10 years.
7	Identify any communications you have had with the defendant, employees or agents, or former employees or agents, regarding any of your claims asserted against the defendant. Include every document along with their dates.

Question	Interrogatory – Part I
8	Identify every source of income you have had for the last 10 years. For each source of income identified, state the amount you have received and the reason for the payment (e.g., wages, consultant's fee, etc.), and identify all documents that refer or relate to the source of income.
9	Identify every person or entity with whom you have been employed or to whom you have otherwise provided services during the last 10 years. Include dates of employment, positions held, compensation received, and benefits received. Describe any discipline that you have received and the reasons for the discipline, including reasons for separation. Identify and provide contact information for all immediate supervisors.
10	Identify each and every item of pecuniary or monetary expense, damage, or loss, whether alleged in your complaint or not, which you contend that you have incurred or sustained as a result of the conduct of the defendant and for which you seek to hold the defendant responsible. Describe in detail: a. a description of each type of damage claimed (for example, lost wages, medical expenses, etc.) b. the specific dollar amount of each type of damage claimed and a complete explanation of how the dollar amount was determined c. the dates upon which the claimed damage was incurred d. each person with knowledge or information related to the claimed damage, including each person, if any, whom you were required to pay for the item of expense, damage or loss, and e. each document that contains information that refers to the claimed damage.
11	Identify every statement by the defendant that you contend constitutes a statement against interest.
12	Identify all text messages, email messages, social media postings, and any other electronically stored information, which you have referenced or discussed involving the defendant, that has affected your financial opportunities.
13	Have you ever been party to any other lawsuits or administrative proceedings? If so, identify the title and court number of each lawsuit or administrative proceeding. Provide a detailed summary of the nature of each action. State the current status or ultimate disposition of each such action.
14	If any requested document or information has been or will be withheld, or if you have objected to or will object to any outstanding discovery requests on the basis of the attorney–client or any other privilege, identify each such document or item of information and the basis for the withholding. For each, provide the date, author, address, recipient, document type, and general subject matter.

Question	Interrogatory – Part II
1	Identify each person known to you to have any information or knowledge regarding the subject matter of your Petition, and for each such person, summarize what knowledge you believe they have. If, at any time after answering these interrogatories, you discover the identity and address of a person having knowledge of the facts alleged in your complaint, you must supplement your answers accordingly, pursuant to the Federal Rule of Civil Procedure.
2	Have you had any communication with an employee, agent, or representative concerning the subject matter of your claims at any time? If so: a. Identify the person with whom you have had communication. b. State the date and time of such communication, or your best approximation thereof. c. State the subject matter of the communication. d. State the manner of the communication (e.g., phone call, email, social media) and, if it is in writing, attach a copy of each writing, or state the names and addresses of the custodians of each writing.
3	Identify each physician, psychologist, psychiatrist, therapist, osteopath, dentist, chiropractor, counselor, or another member of the medical profession who has treated or examined you in the last ten (10) years, and provide the following additional information: a. the reason for said treatment or examination b. the nature, purpose, and extent of such treatment c. the dates of treatment or examination by each practitioner and, if you are still being treated, the date of your next scheduled examination or treatment

Question	Interrogatory – Part I
	d. whether you contend the treatment was necessary by the acts and omissions alleged in your Petition and, if so, the amount charged by each practitioner, indicating which charges have been paid and by who; e. a full description of the diagnosis and prognosis of each practitioner including the date on which it was made and whether it was in oral or written form; and f. whether the practitioner has prepared any written reports, letters, or memoranda relating to the treatment.
4	List all employers for whom you have worked since high school up to the present date, including any periods of self-employment or military service. Give the approximate dates of each such employment, title or position, a description of the job and what it entailed, the amount of compensation and benefits, and the reason the employment was terminated.
5	State whether you applied for employment with any other company since your hiring date with your current employer. If so, give the name, address, and contact information for each company, date of application, method of application, date of interview, if any, nature of position applied for, and disposition of the application.
6	Describe in detail each instance of gender discrimination you have suffered as alleged in your Petition. For each such instance, provide the following information: a. the adverse employment action taken b. the date of the adverse employment action c. the actor alleged to have taken the adverse employment action d. identification of all witnesses to the adverse employment action e. identification of all documents reflecting the gender discrimination f. whether you complained, formally or informally, regarding the instance of gender discrimination, and if so, the mode of the complaint, to whom the complaint was made, and the disposition of the complaint, and g. a description of the facts supporting your contention that your gender was a discriminating factor in the adverse employment action.
7	Describe the evidence you have that the employer's alleged gender discrimination was with "malice or reckless indifference" as alleged in your Petition.
8	Describe in detail each instance of age discrimination you suffered as alleged in your Petition. For each such instance, please provide the following information: a. the adverse employment action taken b. the date of the adverse employment action c. the actor alleged to have taken the adverse employment action d. identification of all witnesses to the adverse employment action e. identification of all documents reflecting the age discrimination f. whether you complained, formally or informally, regarding the instance of age discrimination, and if so, the mode of complaint, to who the complaint was made, and the disposition of the complaint, and g. a description of the facts supporting your contention that your age was a determining factor in the adverse employment action.
9	Describe the material facts and identify all material documentation showing the employer discriminates against persons 40 years of age and older.
10	Describe the evidence you have that the employer's alleged age discrimination was with "malice or reckless indifference" as alleged in your Petition.
11	State and set forth the specific dollar amount damages that you are claiming, and break down that amount to state the specific dollar amount of money damages being claimed for the following elements of damages, if any, and describe how that amount was calculated: a. emotional distress, including the emotional pain, suffering, inconvenience, mental anguish, loss of enjoyment of life, and other nonpecuniary losses alleged in your Petition b. past wages or back pay c. future wages or front pay d. punitive damages e. damages for the alleged breach of contract f. damages for the alleged defamation g. any other damages, whether special, incidental, or consequential.

Deposition

A deposition is a court proceeding used by lawyers to collect the testimony of witnesses, such as police officers, prior to trial (Nicholas, n.d.). Depositions are part of the discovery process and may be employed by either the defendant's lawyer or the plaintiff's lawyer. The deponent must answer questions truthfully under oath, which will be transcribed by a court recorder. The oral testimony locks in the officer's story, which may be used against the officer later in court. If a police officer changes their story in court, the defense lawyer will discredit the officer. Below is an outline for deposing a police officer for an operating while intoxicated investigation. The police officer should expect the defense attorney to ask about the following topics.

A. Experience
   Law enforcement experience
   Training in specific area
   Proficient with equipment
   Education
   Cultural experience

B. Location
   Direction of travel (both suspect and officer)
   Position of the officer's vehicle
   Roadway—specific location

C. Contact
   Reason for initial contact
   Whether the officer was engaging in normal police practice
   Time of day
   Hours on duty

D. Ambience
   Visibility
   Lighting
   Weather
   Road surface
   Volume of traffic

E. Witnesses
   Witnesses present with the police officer
   Witnesses present with the suspect
   Video in car
   Video at jail

F. Evidence
   Suspect's driving behavior
   Suspect's statements
   Police statements made to the suspect - coercion
   Physical evidence in suspect's vehicle (or lack thereof)
   Chain of custody

Did officer check suspect's mouth?

Any other evidence

G. Arrest

Implied consent—right to refuse DataMaster

Handcuffed—before the officer placed the suspect under arrest

DataMaster test—proper procedures

Time of arrest (e.g., before or after DataMaster test)

FICTITIOUS CASE REPORT AND RELATED DEPOSITION EXAMPLE

On 8-7-2013 at about 2:00 a.m., I (Trooper Olga Hernandez) was stationary on Telegraph Road near Lane 375 Walled Lake and I used radar and clocked a blue Chevy truck at 50 MPH headed WB in a posted 30 MPH zone. I initiated my commission's emergency lights and stopped the vehicle at Telegraph Road and Lincoln Road. The vehicle had Ohio registration OH133A. I approached the vehicle and talked with the driver, who was the only occupant in the vehicle. I noticed that his speech was slurred, and I could smell the strong odor of an alcoholic beverage on his breath. I asked the driver if he had anything to drink and he stated, "More than enough." I then asked the driver for his driver's license. The driver identified himself as John Doe having OH DL# 8234-518 (W/M DOB=4-22-68). I asked John DOE to tell me his age. He stated he was 43 (this was incorrect). I then asked him what his social security number was and he was only able to provide the first five numbers, after thinking about it for about ten seconds. I gave John DOE an also-sensor test at about 2:05 am and the result was 0.21% B.A.C. At this time, I read to him the Indiana Implied Consent Law. John Doe exited the vehicle and staggered. I double-locked handcuffed him and secured him in the front passenger seat of my commission. I then secured the Chevy truck. At about 2:17 am, I observed that nothing was in John Doe's mouth, and I transported him to the Wixom county jail. I arrived at the jail at about 2:42 am.

At the Wixom County jail, I stated to John Doe that I was going to offer him some field sobriety tests. John Doe immediately stated that he would not cooperate and would not perform any tests. I again read to John Doe the Indiana Implied Consent law, informing him of the consequences for refusing the chemical test. Mr. Doe stated that he still would not cooperate and that he would not submit to a chemical test. At that time, at about 3:13 am, John Doe was placed under arrest for operating a vehicle while intoxicated-refusal, and incarcerated.

At about 3:54 am on 8-7-2013, King Wench of Bad Axe, IN arrived at the scene and removed the vehicle as indicated on Vehicle Impound form VR3872.

Attachments:

1. Face sheet
2. Copy of UTT # W6150 and #W6151 (Uniform Traffic Tickets)
3. Copy of affidavit to establish probable cause (probable cause affidavit)
4. Copy of charging form (information)
5. Copy of Vehicle Impound form #VR3872
6. Copy of suspect's driving record

TROOPER OLGA HERNANDEZ, INDIANA STATE POLICE

Below is a fictitious deposition of Trooper Olga Hernandez for the DUI case report for John Doe. Notice that there are 19 pages in the deposition. These pages will be referenced in the problems at the end of the chapter.

STATE OF INDIANA)		IN THE WIXOM CIRCUIT COURT
COUNTY OF WIXOM)		ss.
IN THE MATTER OF:		CAUSE NO. 11C03-1212-CM-9393

STATE OF INDIANA)
               Plaintiff,)
vs.)
John Doe,)
<u>Defendant.   </u>)

               <u>The Deposition of TROOPER OLGA HERNANDEZ</u>
               <u>DATE</u>:   February 1, 2014
               <u>TIME</u>:   9:00 o'clock a.m.
               <u>PLACE</u>: The Law Office of Sue M. Good, LLP
                           111 Lane of Gold Wixom, IN

               Called as a Witness herein, in
               Accordance with the Rules of Civil Procedure.

Before Suzan Short
Certified Shorthand Reporter

                        CRYSTAL CLEAR REPORTING
                        Certified Shorthand Reporters
                                Wixom, IN
                              1-803-555-1313

APPEARANCES: 2

        Mr. Noplea
        Prosecuting Attorney
        2321 District Attorney Ave
        Wixom, IN

On behalf of the State of Indiana
Plaintiff;

        Ms. Sue M. Good
        111 Lane of Gold Wixom, IN

On behalf of John Doe,
Defendant.

INDEX   3

THE DEPOSITION OF TROOPER OLGA HERNANDEZ

DIRECT EXAMINATION By Ms. Good .... Page 4

1	TROOPER OLGA HERNANDEZ, **4**
2	Called as a Witness herein,
3	Having been first duly sworn,
4	Was examined and testified as follows:
5	
6	<u>DIRECT EXAMINATION</u>
7	BY MS. GOOD:
8	Q. Officer, would you give us your full name and business address, please?
9	A. Olga Hernandez, Indiana State Police. Address, I think,
10	is 111 Police Alley in South Bend, IN.
11	Q. Okay. And are you assigned to which district, please?
12	A. Eighty-four.
13	Q. What is your appointment date with the department?
14	A. 12-15-2007
15	Q. And has District 84 always been your assignment?
16	A. Yes.
17	Q. What is the extent of your law enforcement background, please?
18	A. About seven years law enforcement, as an auxiliary police officer in the
19	City of Wayne, Michigan and I just started with the Indiana State
20	Police in December of '07.
21	Q. What did you do in Wayne, Michigan?
22	A. Pretty much I patrolled with another officer all the time and had
23	full police powers when I was with the other officer, road patrol,
24	every now and then I did special events, parades, and watched
25	security around parks and stuff.

			5
1	Q.	Okay. In your training with the Indiana State Police,	
2		was held where, please?	
3	A.	Plainfield, Indiana.	
4	Q.	And how long were you there at the academy?	
5	A.	I believe it was 21 weeks.	
6	Q.	Twenty-one?	
7	A.	Twenty-one, maybe 22. I think it was 21.	
8	Q.	During your training at the academy or after the academy, for that	
9		matter, have you received any specialized training in any particular	
10		area of law enforcement?	
11	A.	Since then, I've gone to Breathalyzer school so I could administer	
12		breath tests.	
13	Q.	Okay. When was that?	
14	A.	I don't remember. It was about two years ago.	
15	Q.	In 2012?	
16	A.	About.	
17	Q.	And how long a school was that?	
18	A.	That was one week.	
19	Q.	And following that one week's training then, what are you authorized to	
20		do as a result of that school?	
21	A.	To use the DataMaster and Breathalyzer on individuals.	
22	Q.	DataMaster?	
23	A.	Yes.	
24	Q.	And did you say another kind of equipment?	
25	A.	For the breath tests.	

1	Q. All right. Anything other than the DataMaster?	6
2	A. There was another piece of machinery there. I don't see it	
3	very often. I don't remember what it was.	
4	Q. Is the old Breathalyzer not being used anymore?	
5	MR. Noplea: DataMaster.	
6	Intoxilyzer and DataMaster.	
7	By MS. GOOD:	
8	Q. Did you take a written exam, Trooper Hernandez, following this breath-	
9	A. I did.	
10	Q. test training?	
11	A. Yes.	
12	Q. And do you recall what grade you received on that?	
13	A. No.	
14	Q. Did you receive a grade or a numerical grade?	
15	A. I don't remember how they scored it, but I did well enough to pass.	
16	I usually do pretty well, so I don't remember doing poorly on it.	
17	Q. All right. It was more of a pass/fail sort of thing?	
18	A. I don't remember how they graded us.	
19	Q. Since your graduation from the breath test school in 2012, how many	
20	breath tests do you believe you've administered now?	
21	A. I've done about maybe 30.	
22	Q. And have these primarily been yours?	
23	A. Yes.	
24	Q. Do you run tests for other departments as well?	
25	A. I have not, to date.	

1	Q.	If I may direct your attention to the morning of August—	7
2		is that August 7	
3	A.	Yes.	
4	Q.	2013, what were your hours of employment that day?	
5	A.	I believe, since I was, it looks like I stopped him at 2:00 am, I	
6		probably started at 10:00 o'clock p.m. the day before and then	
7		6:00 am when I got off.	
8	Q.	10:00 p.m. to what please?	
9	A.	Probably 6:30 a.m. on the 7th.	
10	Q.	All right. And again, on that date you were assigned to the turnpike?	
11	A.	Yes.	
12	Q.	What section on the turnpike?	
13	A.	Zone 13, mile post 89 to the state line, Ohio State Line, 133.	
14	Q.	Okay. And your report reflects that you stopped him at 2:00 a.m.,	
15		Is that correct?	
16	A.	Yes.	
17	Q.	You stopped John Doe at 2:00 a.m.?	
18	A.	Yes.	
19	Q.	Tell me, if you would please, where you were when you first	
20		observed Mr. Doe's vehicle?	
21	A.	I was on Telegraph Road stationary, just west of Lane 375,	
22		Walled Lake.	
23	Q.	And what is it that you were doing there?	
24	A.	Using radar to clock vehicles coming westbound and eastbound.	
25	Q.	Were you with any other police officers?	

1	A.	No.
2	Q.	I apologize, but I'm confused. If I understand correctly, you
3		were assigned to the turnpike by mile post 89 to 133, but at
4		2:00 a.m. you were set up on the Telegraph Road to run radar?
5	A.	That's right.
6	Q.	What was the purpose of that? I guess I don't understand.
7	A.	I live right across the street. I stopped in front of it, clocked
8		a vehicle. Every now and then when I go home for lunch, I will clock
9		vehicles right in front of my house. That's what I was doing.
10	Q.	You had come back from lunch?
11	A.	I was going to it.
12	Q.	You were going to lunch. And do you recall what time you arrived
13		at your home?
14	A.	Approximately just prior to that.
15	Q.	Five minutes, ten minutes before.
16	A.	I don't know.
17	Q.	And when you arrived at home, you—
18	A.	This was right across from my house, is what I said.
19	Q.	All right. So, you backed in or how did you set up?
20	A.	No, across the street. I live at—well, I don't anymore, but—
21	Q.	At that time?
22	A.	Yeah. I don't know the name of the apartment complex it was.
23		It was 454 Telegraph Road.
24	Q.	Okay.
25	A.	And you have to pull into a parking lot to pull into my trailer.

8

1		I did not do that. I pulled on the other side of the street,
2		up on a hill, and I was using my lunch hour to clock traffic.
3	Q.	Okay. You were actually going home for lunch, you were just
4		using your lunch hour to clock traffic?
5	A.	Right.
6	Q.	Okay.
7	A.	I was on my lunch hour clocking traffic.
8	Q.	Okay. Did you have lunch then that morning?
9	A.	No.
10	Q.	And then after, what, did you just come off the road for an
11		hour and then return to the road, is that essentially what you did?
12	A.	Right.
13	Q.	Did you make any other arrests that morning during your lunch
14		hour other than Mr. Doe?
15	A.	No.
16	Q.	At the time you were stopped, set up with your radar unit, you
17		were facing what direction?
18	A.	I was facing eastbound.
19	Q.	And could you describe your patrol car, please?
20	A.	It's a black Indiana State Police car.
21	Q.	Fully lit?
22	A.	Yes, light bar on top.
23	Q.	Would you describe the traffic that morning on Telegraph Road?
24	A.	Very light.
25	Q.	What drew your attention to Mr. Doe's Chevy pickup truck?

1	A.	I can tell—I could see the headlights. Of course, I can	10
2		tell that it looks like it was coming pretty fast. The speed	
3		limit there is posted 30 MPH and I can tell how long it takes them	
4		to get to me and he was moving a lot faster than 30.	
5	Q.	Okay. So that was essentially what drew your attention to—	
6	A.	The speed.	
7	Q.	—Mr. Doe, was his speed?	
8	A.	Right.	
9	Q.	Did you ultimately determine what his speed was?	
10	A.	I did.	
11	Q.	What was that, please?	
12	A.	Fifty miles an hour.	
13	Q.	In a 30 zone?	
14	A.	Right.	
15	Q.	Now, would you typically write a ticket for 50 in a 30 MPH zone	
16		at 2:00 a.m. in the morning with light traffic?	
17	A.	I would.	
18	Q.	If you would, describe Mr. Doe's vehicle, please?	
19	A.	It was a blue Chevy pickup truck.	
20	Q.	Okay.	
21	A.	After I stopped it, I looked at the registration.	
22	Q.	Okay. Was Mr. Doe alone in the vehicle?	
23	A.	He was.	
24	Q.	Tell me, if you would, now you're sitting stationary, eastbound on	
25		Telegraph Road, and Mr. Doe was traveling what direction, please?	

1	A.	Westbound.
2	Q.	And how quickly after he passed you, you got your reading, did you
3		begin to follow him?
4	A.	Immediately.
5	Q.	And describe for me, if you would, what you did as soon as you
6		began the pursuit?
7	A.	I turned on—I initiated my emergency lights.
8	Q.	Right away?
9	A.	Yes.
10	Q.	And then what happened?
11	A.	And then he ended up pulling into the parking lot at Sunset Inn,
12		which is at Telegraph Road and Lincoln Road.
13	Q.	How far did you follow him before he pulled into the Sunset?
14	A.	A very short distance. Maybe several hundred yards.
15	Q.	No more than several hundred?
16	A.	Very short.
17	Q.	During the time that you've followed him during that several hundred
18		yards, could you describe for us any violations of state or—
19	A.	In addition to the speed, I saw no other violations.
20	Q.	All right. Was his vehicle otherwise in good condition?
21	A.	It looked fine.
22	Q.	Okay. Now, as you stopped the vehicle and pulled in behind Mr. Doe,
23		did it appear that he accelerated after you initiated your lights?
24	A.	No.
25	Q.	When you say he pulled on down the road and into the parking lot of the

1		Sunset Inn, you're not suggesting that he was trying to elude	12
2		you in any fashion, was he?	
3	A.	There's a stop sign there at that intersection.	
4	Q.	Okay. And he yielded to your right of way?	
5	A.	Yes.	
6	Q.	And did you flash him with your spotlight or did he respond	
7		to your—I guess you've got red and blue lights now?	
8	A.	He responded to my lights.	
9	Q.	All right. As he stopped, tell me if you would please, what next occurred?	
10	A.	I approached the vehicle and I asked him, I told him why I	
11		stopped him. I said, "I clocked you at 50 in a 30 MPH zone and that's	
12		why I'm stopping you."	
13	Q.	Okay.	
14	A.	I said, "Have you had anything to drink today?" And he said, "No."	
15		I smelled the alcoholic beverage on his breath, plus his eyes looked kind	
16		of glassy and blood shot. And then he said, "More than enough." So	
17		then I'm going to investigate further. "Let me see your driver's license."	
18	Q.	Did he produce it for you?	
19	A.	He did.	
20	Q.	Did he have any trouble getting it out?	
21	A.	Nothing special, no.	
22	Q.	Okay. What next occurred?	
23	A.	He handed it to me and I was looking at it. And I said, "I'm	
24		going to ask you some questions." Of course, I asked him what his	
25		birthday was. I said, "How old are you?" He gave me the wrong age.	

			13
1		I think he said he was 43. But that was wrong. He was 45.	
2		I'm also looking at his—	
3	Q.	Sometimes you don't feel your age when the police have you. You know,	
4		I think that's the case.	
5	A.	His driver's license had his social security number on it too.	
6	Q.	All right.	
7	A.	So, I asked him, "What's your social security number?" He	
8		sat there for a while and was thinking and couldn't come up with	
9		it after about 10 seconds. He gives me the first five numbers and	
10		he can't complete it.	
11	Q.	Okay.	
12	A.	So, I wrote that down.	
13	Q.	Did you see any open beverage containers in the vehicle?	
14	A.	No.	
15	Q.	Any empties in the vehicle?	
16	A.	No.	
17	Q.	Did you have occasion to look inside the vehicle after he was out	
18		for any kind of—	
19	A.	Yeah.	
20	Q.	— beverage containers?	
21	A.	Yes	
22	Q.	Would you describe Mr. Doe's demeanor for us, please?	
23	A.	In the vehicle, he replied that he just came from a bar, he drank—	
24	Q.	Did he tell you what bar?	
25	A.	I didn't even mark it down. I don't remember.	

1	Q.	He would have been—I'm sorry. You told me he
2		was westbound on Telegraph Road?
3	A.	Yeah. I didn't record what bar he said he—all I remember
4		was he said more than enough, so that's what I wrote down.
5	Q.	Okay.
6	A.	When I asked him to get out of the car, he staggered. I read
7		him the implied consent. I don't remember how he responded then,
8		but it wasn't that critical to me because I always give them
9		another opportunity at the jail.
10	Q.	Okay.
11	A.	And so—but he did stagger. I double-locked handcuffed,
12		he didn't resist. And once I got him in my vehicle, of course,
13		I could continue to smell the alcoholic beverage coming from him.
14		I did give him an Also-Sensor, though. Before I handcuffed him
15		and that did read .21, I believe it was, and that was more
16		probable cause indicating he's been drinking.
17	Q.	Now, did you ever give him any of these field sobriety tests,
18		the one leg stand, the walk and turn, point your finger to your
19		nose and those sort of things?
20	A.	I was going to do that at the jail, but he refused.
21	Q.	Okay. You say the Also-Sensor—
22	A.	Yes.
23	Q.	Tell me, after you got him in the vehicle, in your police vehicle,
24		did you transport him to the county jail yourself?
25	A.	I did.

1	Q.	Tell me, if you would please, what conversation, if any,	**15**
2		you had on the way to jail with Mr. Doe?	
3	A.	Nothing really of any significance. He wasn't under arrest and	
4		I wasn't planning to ask him anything at that time, anything	
5		in addition to what I already had recorded.	
6	Q.	Even though he wasn't under arrest, you had already handcuffed	
7		him though, right?	
8	A.	For officer safety, we do, when we transport. I was going to	
9		take him down and investigate further because he blew a .21 on the alco-sensor.	
10		That automatically means I'm going to take him down and investigate	
11		further. For officer safety, double-locked handcuffed him and put him	
12		in my vehicle and that's standard practice.	
13	Q.	Okay. Now, did you notice any damage to Mr. Doe's vehicle?	
14	A.	I would have recorded the damage on my impound sheet.	
15		He did have his gearshift broken, his dash was cracked,	
16		dent on the left side of the vehicle.	
17	Q.	Was that recent damage?	
18	A.	I didn't notice it. I didn't really try to put a time and date	
19		when it was damaged.	
20	Q.	Did you ask him about it or anything?	
21	A.	No.	
22	Q.	It appears to be an older vehicle of some sort, is that—	
23	A.	Yeah. I put down a '76 Chevy.	
24	Q.	Let me ask you, during your tour of duty that evening from	
25		10:00 p.m. until 2:00 a.m. when you stopped Mr. Doe,	

1		Were you in your car primarily that whole four-hour period?	**16**
2	A.	Yes.	
3	Q.	During that four-hour period, did you receive or overhear any	
4		dispatches from either local county, local city, or state police to be	
5		on the lookout for a 1976 Chevy pickup truck,	
6		reported as being intoxicated?	
7	A.	No.	
8	Q.	As you got to the county jail, tell me about that. You folks arrived,	
9		no doubt, and got Mr. Doe out of the car and got inside. I've seen	
10		your video that was taken. Tell me about what happened there, when	
11		you guys get inside.	
12	A.	I told him I was going to offer him some field sobriety tests	
13		and he immediately said he was not going to perform any tests.	
14		So, at that point, he wasn't going to give any breath tests, so he was	
15		automatically under arrest because of refusal because I had	
16		probable cause to believe that he was intoxicated.	
17	Q.	Now, when he refused the field sobriety test, did you tell him that that	
18		would be okay, he was entitled to refuse?	
19	A.	I read him the implied consent and explained to him the	
20		consequences. He still refused.	
21	Q.	And how many times did you ask him to take the test at the county jail?	
22	A.	I believe I only asked once and then he refused and I	
23		explained the consequences. He still refused and it was over at that time.	
24	Q.	So would it be fair to say, at the county jail in the presence of the	
25		DataMaster, you asked him to take the breath test one time?	

1	A.	I wasn't in the room where the DataMaster was.
2	Q.	No, but I mean the DataMaster was on station?
3	A.	Right.
4		What was the original question?
5	Q.	Do I understand correctly that at the county jail where the DataMaster
6		is located, you asked Mr. Doe to take the test one time and he refused?
7	A.	Right.
8	Q.	Did he ever make any statements to you at all explaining why
9		he wanted to refuse or where he had been or what he had been
10		drinking? Did you ever discover what it was he had been drinking?
11	A.	No, I don't know what he was drinking.
12	Q.	Okay.
13	A.	But I did run a driving history on him, so I know that he's
14		been arrested before, so he's probably experienced or knew not to
15		take it or believed that it was better for him.
16	Q.	What record did you discover?
17	A.	I have a printout or the post might have told me. When
18		I called him in, the post provided certain information. But
19		they told me it wasn't a felony, so four to five years ago.
20	Q.	That was done in Wayne County in 2007?
21	A.	I'm not sure what county. I would have to look.
22	Q.	Okay. I just noticed here on his ten-year record it shows it was
23		Wayne County.
24		Very well. Did there ever come a time after you stopped Mr. Doe
25		and talked to him at the vehicle and got him out and obtained his

17

1	license and registration and got him to the county jail, did
2	he appear to you to be able to understand your instructions?
3	A. Yes.
4	Q. Are there any other observations or is there any other information that
5	you have to indicate that Mr. Doe was intoxicated on that night?
6	A. I cannot recall any other information at this time.
7	
8	Ms. GOOD: Thank you.
9	That's all I have for this officer.
10	Mr. Noplea: That's all I have.
11	(Whereupon, the deposition was completed
12	and the Witness was excused at 9:28 a.m.)
13	
14	
15	
16	––––––––––––––––––––––––– TROOPER OLGA HERNANDEZ
17	SUBSCRIBED AND SWORN to me before
18	This _____ day of _____, A.D., 2014 –––––––––––––––––––––––––
19	Notary Public, State of: _____
20	County of Residence: _____ My commission expires: _____
21	
22	
23	
24	
25	

18

                                                                    19
                            Errata Sheet

Deponent: Trooper Olga Hernandez
Date of Deposition: February 1, 2014
Case Name: State V. Doe

PAGE	LINE	CORRECTION	REASON

I HEREBY CERTIFY under the penalties of perjury that I have read the above and foregoing deposition, and that the testimony contained therein, together with any corrections in form or substance as above set out, is a true, correct and complete record of my testimony given at said deposition on the above-shown date.

_____

TROOPER OLGA HERNANDEZ

Deponent

DATED: _____

Comments About the Deposition

There are several items to point out about the deposition. Notice the Q and A on the various lines. The Q represents a question asked by the opposing attorney and the A represents the deponent's response. Notice that when the prosecutor spoke, his name appeared in the transcript as Mr. Noplea. You may also notice incomplete sentences and interruptions throughout the deposition. The stenographer will record the information as it is spoken. Sometimes, however, the stenographer may make mistakes. The errata sheet is an attachment to the deposition that the deponent can use to make minor corrections, such as spelling, to the transcript (Abrams & Spencer, 2020). Although the errata sheet is used to make minor corrections, it is not meant to be used for major changes in the testimony. If changes are made on an errata sheet that contradict the transcript, then both versions of the testimony will be available for cross-examination.

KEYWORDS

Deposition
Discovery
Interrogatory

CHAPTER PROBLEMS

Interrogatory and deposition: In the interrogatory and deposition, describe the reasoning for the following questions. Describe the significance of the questions and what the lawyer was attempting to achieve.

1. Discuss the similarities and differences between an interrogatory and a deposition.
2. In the chapter's interrogatory, discuss the purpose of Part 1 Question 6.
3. In the chapter's interrogatory, discuss the purpose of Part 1 Question 13.
4. In the chapter's interrogatory, discuss the purpose of Part 2 Question 3.
5. In the chapter's deposition, discuss the objective of Page 4, line 17.
6. In the chapter's deposition, discuss the objective of Page 5, line 4 and lines 8–10.
7. In the chapter's deposition, discuss the objective of Page 6, lines 19–20.
8. In the chapter's deposition, discuss the objective of Page 7, line 25.
9. In the chapter's deposition, discuss the objective of Page 8, lines 2–4.
10. In the chapter's deposition, discuss the objective of Page 9, line 23 and line 25

REFERENCES

Abrams, J. D. & Spencer, D.M. (2020). Pretrial discovery strategies: Defending against a deponent's errata sheet before, during, and after a deposition. www.americanbar.org/groups/litigation/committees/commercial-business/practice/2020/deposition-errata-sheet

Maier, K. (2021). What is the difference between an interrogatory and a deposition? www.wise-geek.com/what-is-the-difference-between-an-interrogatory-and-a-deposition.htm

Nicholas, A. (n.d.). How to depose a police officer. *eHow*. www.ehow.com/print/how_8506257_depose-police-officer.html

CHAPTER 10

Interviewing and Identifying Suspects

LEARNING OBJECTIVES

Understand the different types of questions.
Understand the difference between a showup, lineup, and a photographic lineup.

INTRODUCTION

This chapter focuses on interview questions and suspect identification. Examples of open-ended and close-ended questions are presented, along with presumptive questions, probing questions, neutral questions, and leading questions. The structure of the interview is also discussed, and the relative position of the officer to the suspect during a field interview is described. An example of a volunteer statement form is presented, along with a Miranda warning form. If a witness is available, a showup, lineup, or photographic lineup may be conducted. If an officer detains a suspect in the field but has no probable cause to arrest, the officer may complete a suspect report, a field interview card, and/or an intelligence report.

POLICE–PUBLIC ENCOUNTERS (DEL CARMEN & HEMMENS, 2017)

CLASSIFICATION
- Consensual encounter
- Detention
- Arrest

CONSENSUAL ENCOUNTER
- Police officer does not need justification to initiate contact.
- Police officer does not intend to restrain.
- Officer may approach person in a public place.
- Officer does not exert any authority over person.
- Officer has no specific power to frisk or search person.
- Officer should identify self as police officer.

- Officer may ask for identification.
- Officer may shine a spotlight on the person.
- Officer may not demand person to answer questions.
- Officer may ask questions while still maintaining a consensual status.
- To make things clear, the officer should state to the suspects that they are not being detained and that they are free to leave, and then the officer should ask them whether they are willing to answer a few questions.
- Officer may ask individuals to take their hands out of their pockets.
- Notion of consensual encounter extends to the police car.
- Officer may develop probable cause to make arrest.
- Person is free to leave the scene at any time.
- Person may ignore the officer.
- Person does not have to cooperate with the officer.

DETENTION
- Police officer needs reasonable suspicion to detain a person.
- Police officer intends to restrain.
- Officer can stop a person and can ask the person questions to investigate a crime.
- Officer can frisk a person if safety is a concern.
- Officer can hold a person for a reasonable amount of time to investigate a crime (only long enough to do their job).
- Officer may ask for identification.
- Person is not free to leave the scene.
- Person may not ignore the officer.
- Person does have to cooperate with the officer.

ARREST
- Police officer needs probable cause to arrest a person.
- Officer can arrest a person if 51% confident that the person committed a crime.
- Police officer intends to arrest the person.
- Officer can search a person after an arrest.
- Person is not free to leave the scene.
- Person may not ignore the officer.
- Person does have to cooperate with the officer.

INTERVIEWS

Interviews occur frequently throughout a person's life. According to Stewart and Cash (2008), individuals are often unaware that they are voluntarily or involuntarily participating in an interview. Individuals often give or receive information, interview or recruit for a job, or are engaged in the act of persuasion. Interviews are intermingled among interpersonal interactions and conversations, and may occur in small-group environments, in public presentations, and in structured interview settings. Interviews may be structured or unstructured, sophisticated or simple, threatening or supportive, and they may take only a few minutes or last for several hours.

This chapter will focus on the essential elements of interviewing, and it will describe how interviewing is distinguished from other forms of interpersonal communication. Interviewing is a relational form of communication, and each type of interview has its pros and cons. Several types of interviews will be discussed, and several examples will be presented.

Interviews are *interactional*. There is an exchange or sharing of roles, feelings, attitudes, beliefs, values, motives, and responsibilities in the sharing of information. The relationship and roles of the interviewer and interviewee may change from time to time during the interview process. It always takes at least two people to make an interview successful. In addition, interviews frequently involve an element of risk.

Interviews are a complex and continuously changing *process*, which is a dynamic interaction of variables that usually occurs within a system or structure. No interview occurs in a vacuum, and communication and interactions are not static. While all interviews are unique, they all involve common elements of communication and interaction, which include motivation, perceptions, assumptions, expectations, verbal and non-verbal communication, levels of disclosure, listening, and feedback. Each participant brings their own unique personal history, values, beliefs, knowledge, strengths, and limitations to the interview process.

While interviews often involve more than two people, they never involve more than two *parties*: the interviewer and the interviewee. If more than two parties are participating, a group interaction is occurring, not an interview. Interviewing is a dyadic process that always involves two parties. One or both parties will bring an important goal to the interview process that will include a predetermined, serious *purpose*. The interview process includes a structured pre-planning of the selected topic, the creation of appropriate *questions*, and the collection of information. Asking questions and obtaining responses are critical to all interviews (e.g., public surveys, recruiting, employment, probing/informational/journalistic, performance assessments, counseling, and health-care applications).

Each type of interview serves a distinctly different purpose. The information-giving interviews involve orientation, instruction, training, coaching, and briefings. Information-gathering interviews include public surveys and polls, exit interviews, research and journalistic interviews, and medical and psychological interviews. Participant selection, screening, and placement are critical to the interviewing process. The interviewer must always be aware of potential interviewee problems and concerns as they relate to evaluations, appraisals, counseling, discipline, correction and reprimand, separation, and firing. The interviewer may experience difficulty in: (1) dealing with complaints and grievances; (2) receiving suggestions; and (3) discussing shared problems to achieve desirable solutions. Persuasion, therefore, is a major factor in changing the way each party thinks, acts, and feels.

Interviews are a relational form of communication between the two participating parties (the interviewer and the interviewee). Their relationship may be intimate, distant, casual, or formal, and may depend on the interview situation, which may alter the interview relationship. Stewart and Cash (2008, p. 13) describe an interview as "an interactional communication process between two parties, at least one of whom has a predetermined and serious purpose, which involves the asking and answering of questions." For an interview to be successful, one must understand the role of each party, the giving and receiving of information, the value of feedback, and the situational influence of outside factors.

The model of interpersonal communication contains many interactional variables, which include the interviewing parties, their roles, the perceptions they have of each other, the levels of communication (e.g., verbal and non-verbal, listening, and feedback), and the environment in which the interview takes place. One must develop the ability to detect empathy, to comprehend and evaluate information, to resolve problems, and to strategically utilize silence when evaluating non-verbal messages. Each party must understand the process of successful interviewing and must have an acute awareness of the interactional variables. These factors are a major determinant of the success of the interview process and whether the desired outcomes are realized.

The interviewer and interviewee need to be adaptable and flexible in deciding their interview method. The interview method may be directive (structured; the job interviewer maintains complete control), non-directive (unstructured; the job interviewer allows the interviewee a lot of latitude in answering the questions), or a combination of both (University of North Carolina—Charlotte, 2014). Each individual is unique in their approach to the particular interview scenario because each individual is a product of their own past in terms of gender, age, race, ethnic background, culture, self-concept, self-esteem, language, verbal and non-verbal communication, and territoriality. In addition, knowledge of kinesics (i.e., the study of body language) and proxemics (i.e., the study of personal space) is important because individuals in different cultures communicate and relate to one another in different ways. In short, the behaviors and personalities of individuals are strong driving forces that impact the interviewing process, and consequently individual participation.

Being able to create effective questions is the cornerstone of any good interview. A person's ability to consciously ask the specific kinds of questions needed to obtain pertinent information requires insight, awareness, and practice. Furthermore, there are multiple ways of designing questions for optimal results. Indeed, the wording and phrasing of questions will have a significant impact on the responses. If the goal of an interview is to obtain particular data, then it is crucial for the information seeker (i.e., the interviewer) to design the questions so that they generate the information sought.

Open-ended Questions

The open-ended question is one of the most frequently used questions in interviews. The primary reason for using this type of question is to gain as much information as possible. These questions are not limited by only asking for specific bits of information. These questions provide the respondents with the freedom to answer in as much detail as they desire. An open-ended question requires an essay-type response.

Examples

1. What did you find when you entered the room?
2. What thoughts came to your mind when you discovered that he had disappeared?
3. What do you know about the tenants in the room above you?
4. At what point did you decide to investigate the noises next door?

The advantage of the open-ended question is that it encourages the respondent to elaborate on their answers or observations. In addition, more in-depth answers can often give the interviewer insight into the respondent's feelings, biases, and amount of understanding of the topic being discussed. The disadvantage of the open-ended question is it can give the respondent more time to engage in rambling replies, which could contain unrelated or irrelevant information that could hinder the collection of solid factual responses.

Closed-ended Questions

Closed-ended questions are questions that are very narrow in detail. These questions limit the respondent's ability to decide how much information to provide in their answer. A closed-ended question asks respondents to choose from a distinct set of predefined responses, such as in multiple-choice questions; it does not allow for further explanation. Closed-ended questions often result in gaining only a "yes" or "no" response.

Examples

1. Were you the one driving the car?
2. Did you see someone leave the store?

3. Are you tired?
4. Are you willing to tell me the information?

Advantages of closed-ended questions include the ability to control the length of time of the interview, the ability to collect very specific information, and the ability to collect answers that are easier to record and remember. Disadvantages of closed-ended questions include less insight into the respondent's mindset and beliefs, and a lack of detailed information. Because the respondent is not able to elaborate or explain answers in detail, this could result in frustration on the respondent's part.

Exercise: Open-ended and Closed-ended Questions

Change these close-ended questions into open-ended questions:

1. Did you see another woman outside?
2. Did you leave the location?
3. Do you know people who smoke cigarettes?

Change these open-ended questions to closed-ended questions

1. How do you feel about college students binge drinking?
2. What were you thinking when the car drove away?
3. What motivated you to decide to enlist?

Presumptive Questions

Presumptive questions are questions that have a presupposition of fact that serves as a platform from which each question emerges. For example, if you are asked whether you are going to take out the trash before or after dinner, the presupposition of the question is that the trash will be taken out either way.

Examples

1. Did you take the car before or after you saw the man leave? (The presupposition is that the respondent took the car.)
2. Did you use drugs last month or this month? (The presupposition is the respondent has used drugs.)
3. Is he your friend or just someone with whom you hang around? (The presupposition is that the respondent has some relationship with the other person.)
4. Are you going to answer these questions now or after you have a drink of water? (The presupposition is that the respondent will answer the question.)

Probing Questions

Probing questions are frequently used as follow-up questions to previous answers from respondents in order to obtain more in-depth information. Reasons for asking these types of questions could be a desire to find the reason why the respondent answered a certain way previously, to look for inconsistencies in the previous response, or to assist the respondent in discussing a certain matter that they may have been hesitant to discuss.

Probing questions may also be used to rephrase the previous question so the intent of the question is easier for the respondent to comprehend. Probing questions are also effective in gaining clarification, learning the reasoning behind the respondent's actions, and summarizing the information that has been given.

Pushing Probe

This type of probing question/statement pushes the respondent to continue speaking or to supply an answer to the previous question. By pushing the respondent to continue speaking on the topic, one can gain more information and insight into the respondent's perspective.

Examples

1. Please continue.
2. And?
3. Go on.

Information-gathering Probe

Information gathering probes are used to gain additional information from respondents. Sometimes a respondent may only give partial, vague, or evasive answers when being interviewed. In order to directly get to a specific answer, it may be useful to follow up with a probing question/statement.

Examples

1. Tell me more about that situation.
2. When you say the car was dark, what color might that be?
3. When you say you were upset, how upset were you when she began yelling?
4. What else can you tell me about the fight outside the hotel?

Exercise

Provide effective probing questions/statements for the following interview interactions. Make sure the questions/statements probe into the respondent's answers without starting a new subject.

Interviewer: Are you going to discuss this issue with your attorney?
Respondent: I guess it really depends.
Interviewer:

Interviewer: Tell me about the person you saw leaving the bank.
Respondent: He was tall.
Interviewer:

Interviewer: At what point do you think she knew the answer?
Respondent: Earlier.
Interviewer:

Interviewer: What motivated you to talk to the officer?
Respondent: I noticed something.
Interviewer:

Practical exercise

Read through the following interview and write what each type of question the officer is asking, whether it is an open-ended, close-ended, presumptive, or probing question.

Officer: Hi, did you see the man who just drove off?
Respondent: Yes.
Officer: Okay. Had you seen him previously?
Respondent: No.
Officer: So, you never saw him previously?
Respondent: That's right.

Officer: How often do you come here?
Respondent: Most every day.
Officer: I see. So, you come here every day but you are saying you have never seen that person previously?
Respondent: Well, I might have seen the car.
Officer: How often have you seen the car?
Respondent: A few times.
Officer: How many times is a few?
Respondent: I guess maybe four times.
Officer: Did you ever see the car before you started coming here?
Respondent: Maybe.
Officer: Where else did you see the car?
Respondent: I can't remember.
Officer: Okay. Did you notice the car today before or after you heard the loud noise?
Respondent: I guess it was after the noise.
Officer: Did you run out into the parking lot before or after the noise?
Respondent: After.
Officer: Do you know what the man who drove the car looks like?
Respondent: No.
Officer: You have seen this car at least four times previously and you never saw the man driving it?
Respondent: I don't know.

Group exercise

1. Get into a group of three to five people. Assume there is a respondent. As a group, select a topic of interest and write down two questions for the respondent about the topic. After the group is finished, each person should take a moment and classify each question for its type. The group should then compare notes to see how many in the group agree with each person's answer.
2. Stay in the same group. This time, each group member will ask the respondent about a topic of interest using only open-ended questions.
3. Stay in the same group. This time, each group member will ask the respondent about a topic of interest using only closed-ended questions.

Neutral and Leading Questions

A neutral question is a question that permits the respondent to answer without any pressure or direction from the interviewer. When given a neutral question, the respondent will decide how much information and how much detail to give in their answer.

A leading question is a question in which the interviewer guides the respondent toward an already set answer.

Examples

1. Are you aware of the rules? (Neutral question)
2. You are aware of the rules, aren't you? (Leading question)
3. How do you feel the prosecution is treating the witness? (Neutral question)
4. Do you feel that the prosecution is treating the witness unfairly? (Leading question)
5. What do you think about the policy that was just created? (Neutral question)
6. Don't you think there are some real problems with the policy that was just created? (Leading question)
7. Have you ever stolen in the past? (Neutral question)
8. What have you stolen in the past? (Leading question)

Out-of-class exercise

1. Watch an interview program on television (news, sports, or entertainment related). Note when neutral or leading questions are asked. Pay attention to which types of questions get the best responses from the person being interviewed. Which type of question is asked most frequently on the program?

THE STRUCTURE OF THE INTERVIEW

Each interview has its own unique purpose and it is important to be aware of how the structure of an interview can facilitate or hinder the desired outcome of the interaction. It is essential to create a structure for the interview that works to the advantage of the interviewer. It is the responsibility of the interviewer to ensure that each interview's structure is appropriate to the specific setting and situation. This chapter will cover the three sections of the structure of an interview: the opening, the continuation, and the closing.

Opening of the Interview

The first minute of any interview is crucial. What the interviewer does or does not do during the opening can often influence how the respondent will judge the interviewer and the interview (Stewart & Cash, 2008). The opening of an interview usually determines how the overall interaction will play out. If the opening of an interview does not go well, it can lead to low-quality information from the respondent or can create a defensive, unpleasant interaction between the respondent and interviewer. The respondent is not obligated to speak with the interviewer and, if the respondent feels uncomfortable, they may terminate the interview at any time.

The opening of the interview is when the primary background information about the topic of discussion is obtained. In the opening, the interviewer will need to restrict their questions to pertinent aspects of the topic being discussed. One of the main goals of the opening of the interview is to set a frame of open communication between both parties. If this can be achieved, it is much more likely that the respondent will engage fully in the interview process. When the respondent feels comfortable, they may be much more willing to disclose information.

Building rapport is the most crucial part of the entire interview. As previously stated, when the respondent feels comfortable, they may be more willing to be interviewed. According to Stewart and Cash (2008, p. 77), rapport is "a process of establishing and sustaining a relationship between interviewer and interviewee by creating feelings of goodwill and trust." Rapport does not mean sweet-talking or giving false praise to the respondent. It simply means engaging in interactions with the respondents in a way that makes them feel comfortable in responding to the questions being asked. Giving the respondents polite smiles, making good eye contact, and making pleasant introductions can go a long way toward building and maintaining rapport.

Suppose you are an interviewer. To begin an interview, and to enhance rapport, you need to give an introduction (i.e., your name and title) and the reason for your presence. See the example below.

Example

"Hello sir. I'm Captain Dan Jenkins with the Sheriff's Department. I am here to talk with you about the incident that happened in your apartment complex last night."

From this point on, you explain to the respondent the purpose of your visit, how long the interview will last, how the information will be utilized, and why you decided to interview them.

Example

"As you may know, there was an assault last night in this complex and I have been directed to collect any information that may be useful in finding out what specifically happened. I only need to ask you a few questions that should take just a minute or two as I think you may be able to help me due to you living next door to where the incident happened."

Exercise

In a group of three people, each person will practice giving an opening introduction and the reason for the interview for the following scenarios:

1. You are looking for a certain car that is often in a specific neighborhood. You decide to knock on a random door to ask the person inside whether they have seen the car.
2. You are trying to find a lost child. You enter a video arcade to ask the staff whether they have seen the child.
3. You need to talk to an employee of a certain company. You are calling the manager on duty to find out whether that person is working today.

It is best to try to do these *off the cuff* to see what you need to work on in order to create an effective opening.

Continuation of the Interview

To continue the interview, use open-ended questions that are easy to understand and answer. Avoid using close-ended questions at this point because the goal of the interview is to get the respondent to open up and to divulge useful information.

Examples

"What did you notice happening last night in the apartment complex?"

"What things did you hear or see happen last night?"

Once the respondent has started talking freely, it will be easier to use closed-ended questions and probing questions to get more specific information from them. In this part of the interview, the information on the topic begins to move from a generalized view of the issue to more specific aspects of the topic.

Examples

"You are telling me that there was a loud noise?"
"So, when you said you heard a loud noise, from what direction did you hear it?"

Closing of the Interview

The closing of the interview is an important part of the interview process. If the interview ends in haste or in an abrupt manner, the rapport that had previously been established could be dissolved (Milne & Bull, 1999). The closing is not something that just happens or is hurriedly paced. The main functions of the closing are to summarize the information gained and to end the interview without ending the interaction (e.g., there may be additional interviews in the future).

Closing techniques

1. Offering to answer any questions the respondent may have about the interview.

Example

"Do you have any questions for me about what we talked about today?"

2. Expressing appreciation for the willingness to be interviewed.

Example

"I really appreciate you taking the time to discuss this matter with me today."

3. Summarizing the information gained in the interview.

Example

"Okay. You stated that you did not see anything in the complex last night, but you did hear a loud noise across the hall at close to eleven o'clock. Other than that, you were unaware of anything else happening in the complex last night. I think that about does it."

4. Making sure there is no other information that was not discussed.

Example

"Are you sure there was nothing else you noticed last night that you have not already stated? Is there anything else I may need to know?"

5. Openly state the end of the interview.

Example

"I believe that covers everything I need to know."
"Well, that's it for my questions."

Closing the interview non-verbally

Non-verbal actions can signal the end of the interview to the respondent. The following actions, along with verbal interview termination cues, can aid in closing the interview.

1. Closing your notebook and putting away the writing instrument
2. Offering to shake hands
3. Breaking eye contact
4. Standing up if you are currently seated
5. Looking at your watch

Practical Exercise

The following interview is between a police officer and a woman who lives in a neighborhood that has experienced several burglaries over the past two nights. In this interview, note where the opening section, the continuation section, and the closing section begin. In addition, name the types of questions (open-ended, close-ended, probing, etc.) that the police officer asks.

Officer: Good morning. I'm Officer Jackson with the City Police Department. I am working in the neighborhood today to find out any information I can about the burglaries that happened over the last two evenings. I would like to ask you a few questions that will only take a couple of minutes.

Woman: Okay.

Officer: Thank you. I appreciate you talking with me today. Did you see any vehicles ride through the neighborhood that were unfamiliar to you over the past week or so?

Woman: No. The only unfamiliar vehicle I saw that I can remember was a plumbing company van.

Officer: What did that van look like?

Woman: It was white and had a logo on it. I don't remember the logo or the name of the company, but I do remember seeing the word "plumbing" on it.

Officer: Do you remember when you saw the van?

Woman: Sometime last week.

Officer: How many times have you seen it over the last week?

Woman: Just once.

Officer: Okay. Did you happen to see anyone in the neighborhood who was unfamiliar to you?

Woman: I did see a new couple walking down the street the other day, but I think they just moved in three houses down.

Officer: So, the people who live three houses down are new to the neighborhood?
Woman: Yes, I think so.
Officer: Okay. Other than those people, have you seen anyone else who was unfamiliar to you?
Woman: I don't think so.
Officer: Okay. So other than the plumbing vehicle you saw only once, you have not seen any unfamiliar vehicles?
Woman: Right.
Officer: And you saw no one unfamiliar lately other than the couple you mentioned that may have moved in three houses down the street?
Woman: Correct.
Officer: I appreciate your willingness to talk with me today. If you happen to see or hear anything that you feel might be important for me to know, please feel free to contact me at the number on this card.
Woman: Okay.
Officer: Have a good day.

COMPLAINANT, WITNESS, VICTIM, SUSPECT, AND CRIMINAL INFORMANT

People are sources of intelligence (i.e., information). There are several different types of individuals who provide information that may be used during court proceedings (Swanson et al., 2009). One source of information is the *complainant*. The complainant is the person who requests that legal action be taken. A complainant may request that a police report (e.g., crash report) be completed or the complainant may file a civil action lawsuit against a person.

A *witness* is a person who saw something related to an event, such as a crime or crash. A witness may provide a written statement that provides first-hand information about the event. This may prove very valuable because a written statement may refresh the mind of a witness during court proceedings, which may be years later, or may prevent a witness from changing their story in court. For example, it is not uncommon for female victims who have suffered from spouse abuse to change their stories in court. Some female victims may feel that if their significant others are convicted and sent to jail, then their children may suffer significant hardships. If a woman is poor and has children, it may be very important to her to receive income from her spouse. If her husband is sent to jail for a year, and as a result she receives no income, then her children may suffer. The mother may feel that the benefits of food and shelter are more important than the cost of physical abuse. In some cases, victims may be hesitant to make any claim of domestic violence against their significant others. In some jurisdictions, the state may prosecute domestic violence suspects in order to protect the victims from retaliation for filing the complaints. However, victims may still suffer if their livelihoods are impacted by the arrests.

A *victim* is a person who has sustained injury as a result of a crime. It is possible for a victim to be a complainant or a witness to the crime.

A *suspect* is a person directly or indirectly involved with violating the law. For example, if a man provided a woman with a gun that she used to kill someone, the woman would be directly involved with the murder and the man would be indirectly involved with the murder. A *criminal informant*, also called a confidential informant, is a person who helps law enforcement make busts against other people accused of breaking the law. A criminal informant is not a victim, a typical witness, or a suspect.

AUDIENCE

Police officers must learn how to communicate with different audiences

- Police management/administration
- Fellow police officers
- Media
- General public (non-violators)
- School children
- Prosecutors and defense attorneys
- Violators
- Victims
- Witnesses
- Jury
- Judge
- People with intellectual disabilities

POLICE COMMUNICATIONS

- Police officers develop friendships with one another.
- Officers often share tragic experiences together.
- Police officers are required not to disclose confidential information.
- The media may view this lack of openness as a conspiracy.
- Police develop shop talk = police jargon.
- Police jargon = efficient communication in the field.
- Police officers must learn how to adjust their methods of communication for different audiences.
- Police dispatch ≠ jury ≠ media ≠ school children ≠ violators ≠ …
- Police need to speak to the jury in plain language.

COMMUNICATING WITH DEFENSE ATTORNEY: PURPOSE OF THE CROSS-EXAMINATION

- To show that the officer is in error.
- To show that the officer is forgetful.
- To show that the officer is unobservant.
- To show that the officer is opinionated.
- To show that the officer is untrustworthy.
- To show that the officer is emotional and easily angered.
- To show that the officer is discourteous.

COMMUNICATING WITH INDIVIDUALS

- To gain a quick assessment of the scene.
- To request assistance if needed.
- To assist the injured person or persons.
- To protect persons and property at the scene.
- To protect the public.
- To remove any hazardous situations.
- To contain all witnesses, drivers, and suspects.
- To document the event in a report.

POLICE–INDIVIDUAL ENCOUNTERS

When a police officer interviews a suspect in the field, the officer must maintain a safe position. The police officer should be in front of the suspect and about 45 degrees off to the side (Siddle, 2005). The police officer should be bladed in such a manner that the firearm is away from the suspect. If a police officer needs to take notes, the officer should hold the clipboard between them and the suspect so the officer can use their peripheral vision to monitor the suspect's actions. For safety reasons, the police officer should not be at the suspect's inside position or within 6 feet of the suspect. The worse place for the officer to be is directly in front of the suspect or directly behind the suspect because these are the areas where the suspect is the strongest.

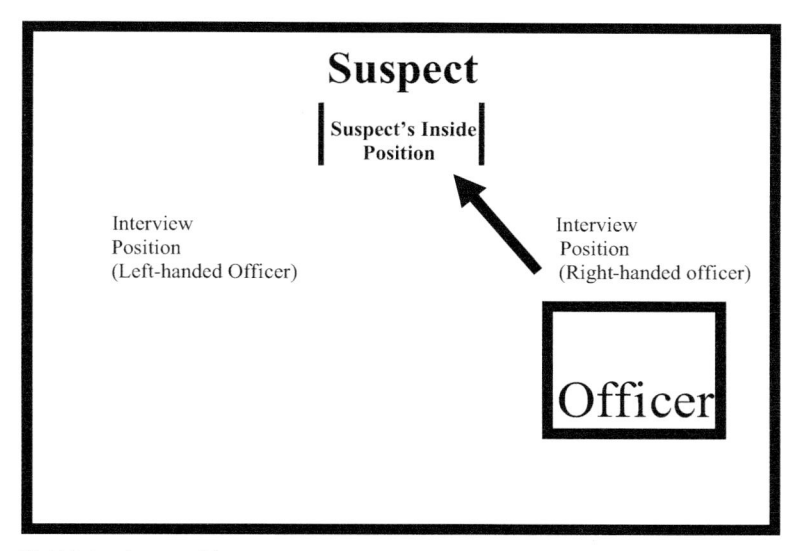

Figure 10.1 Field interview position

> **COMMUNICATING WITH WITNESSES AND SUSPECTS: VOLUNTARY STATEMENT FORMS**
> - Voluntary statements are an important part of many investigations.
> - They provide clues about what happened.
> - They dissuade persons from changing their stories.
> - They refresh memories.
> - They allow for the determination of facts.
> - Police should talk to each person privately (individuals may be reluctant to talk to police if others are listening; spectators may interrupt with their own ideas).
> - Police officers should first ask witnesses what happened.
> - If any points are not covered, officers need to ask specific questions.
> - Once all points are covered, officers should have the witnesses write their statements down on voluntary statement forms.
> - Another person (e.g., the police officer) will need to sign as a witness that the witness completed the voluntary statement.
> - If a witness refuses to sign the statement, the officer should not insist that the witness sign it (signature is not that important).

VOLUNTARY STATEMENT

Report # _____.   This is page _____ of ___.

_____ Police Department

Date_____ Place _____ time started _____

I, _____, am _____ years of age, being born on _____ have been warned by _____, with the _____ police department, that I do not have to make any statement at all, nor answer any questions. I was also warned and advised of my right to a lawyer of my own choice before or at any time during questioning, and if I am not able to hire a lawyer, I may request to have a lawyer appointed to me. I do not now want a lawyer, and I waive my right to the advice and presence of a lawyer, knowing that anything I say can and will be used against me in a court of law. I now want to make a statement.

_____

_____

_____

_____

_____

_____

_____

_____

Draw a diagonal line through all unused space. Have person place initials at end of statement.

This form was completed at (time) _____.

Signature of person providing statement _____

Witness_____ Signature_____ Badge # _____
        Print name

Witness_____ Signature_____ Badge # _____
        Print name

Page____of_____ Type of Report _____ Report #_____

INTERVIEW STATEMENT

_____
_____
_____
_____
_____
_____
_____
_____
_____
_____
_____
_____
_____
_____
_____
_____
_____
_____
_____
_____
_____
_____
_____
_____
_____

Draw a diagonal line through all unused space and initial at end of statement.

_____   _____   _____
    Print Name   Signature   Date/Time

Witness_____   Signature_____
            Print name

Witness_____   Signature_____
            Print name

MIRANDA WARNING

_____Police Department

Subject's Name: _____ SS# _____

Location of Interview: _____

Date: _____ Beginning Time of Interview _____ Ending Time of Interview _____

Miranda Rights

Before we ask you any questions, you must understand your rights. Initial each line to indicate your understanding of, and agreement with, that line.

_____ You have the right to remain silent.

_____ Anything you say can and will be used against you in a court of law.

_____ You have the right to talk to a lawyer for advice before we ask you any questions and to have them with you during questioning.

_____ If you cannot afford a lawyer, the court will appoint one to represent you without cost if you wish.

_____ If you decide to answer questions now without a lawyer present, you will still have the right to stop answering at any time. You also have the right to stop answering at any time until you talk to a lawyer.

_____ I have read this statement of my rights and I understand what my rights are.

Waiver of Rights

_____ I am willing to make a statement and answer questions. I do not want a lawyer at this time. I understand and know what I am doing. No promises or threats have been made to me and no pressure of any kind has been used against me.

_____   _____ Date: _____ Time: _____
Print Name   Signature

Witness: _____   _____
         Print Name   Signature

Witness: _____   _____
         Print Name   Signature

When interrogating a juvenile, a legal guardian's signature is also required.

Legal Guardian of Juvenile

As parent or legal guardian of _____, I have read the rights as set out above and understand them. Neither the juvenile nor I want a lawyer at this time and the juvenile is willing to answer questions.

Signed_____

Witness:_____

Witness:_____

Date_____ Time_____ ____.M.

SHOWUPS, LINEUPS, AND PHOTOGRAPHIC LINEUPS

If a witness or victim has seen the perpetrator, there are three ways to have the witness or victim identify the perpetrator: a showup, a lineup, or a photographic lineup (del Carmen & Hemmens, 2017). A *showup* is when a suspect is detained in the field and a witness is brought to the suspect for immediate identification. A *lineup* is conducted at the police station and several persons are sequentially or simultaneously presented to the witness for identification. A *photographic lineup* is similar to a regular lineup but photographs of people are used instead of actual people.

If a suspect in a showup is transported to the witness, the officer may expect the suspect to file a false arrest complaint. The officer will likely counter the argument with an exigent circumstances exception. It is the court who has the authority to make the final decision. Thus, it is safer to simply transport the witness to the suspect, if possible.

The Department of Justice has provided guidelines for identification procedures (del Carmen & Hemmens, 2017). When there are multiple suspects, a lineup should only include one suspect at a time, and the fillers should not be reused for the same witness. The fillers, who are non-suspects, should have the same general characteristics as the suspect, but they should not be too close in resemblance that it is too difficult to distinguish the individuals. Similar to students who always pick C on a multiple-choice test, some witnesses may always pick a certain number. Thus, it is important to position the suspect in random positions, unless the suspect's lawyer requests a particular position. There should be a minimum of five fillers per identification procedure and the fillers should be supplied with any unusual features that the suspect possesses (e.g., add a temporary tattoo to the fillers if the suspect has a tattoo). During a lineup, one-way mirrors are often used so that the suspect cannot see the witnesses. Police departments may also photograph the lineup as a possible defense in court if the fairness of the lineup is challenged.

A photographic lineup will be conducted similar to a typical lineup. However, a witness will view photographs instead of people (del Carmen & Hemmens, 2017). As always, due process is required. The officer should make sure that the suspect does not unduly stand out, and the officer should preserve the presentation order of the photographic lineup for court. The suspect does not have the right to a lawyer during a photographic lineup.

When a witness is in the process of identifying a suspect, it is important for the officer not to provide any signals to the witness that may lead to an identification (del Carmen & Hemmens, 2017). A good way to resolve this situation is to use an impartial administrator who does not know the identity of the suspect. This will help minimize bias and unfairness.

There is no right against self-incrimination for lineups, showups, and photographic lineups because they are not testimonial based (del Carmen & Hemmens, 2017). Furthermore, suspects do not have the right to a lawyer for a showup or a lineup until after they have been arrested. However, suspects do have the right to due process. It should be noted that eyewitness identification has been shown to be unreliable in many cases.

IN-FIELD SHOWUP REPORT

_____ Police Department

Case no._____   Priority __YES __NO

Offense	Location of Occurrence	
Victim	Date of Occurrence	County

Admonition of Victims and Witnesses:

It is requested that you look at an individual who has been temporarily detained by police. You are under no obligation to participate. This person may or may not have committed the crime. It is just as important to eliminate innocent persons from suspicion as it is to identify the perpetrator. Do not let handcuffs or police presence influence your decision. Please do not discuss the case with any other witnesses.

By signing this form, I am indicating that I fully understand the admonition presented to me by officer_____, regarding the in-field showup.

_____   _____   _____
Printed Name of Witness   Signature of Witness   Date

Identification
☐ I cannot identify this individual as the suspect.
☐ I can identify this individual as the suspect.

Additional comments of victim/witness:
_____

Signature of witness: _____ date: _____
Witnessed by officer: _____ date/time: _____
Location of in field showup _____
Date & time of in field showup _____
Name and DOB of person viewed _____

Officer's name (printed)	Officer's signature and badge #	Date	Approved by supervisor ☐ Yes ☐ No

LINEUP PROCEDURES

A lineup that is suggestive is inadmissible in court. To be sure your lineup identification will not be excluded at trial as unfair, follow these guidelines.

1. The lineup must consist of at least six individuals.

2. Everyone in the lineup should be of the same sex, race, approximate age, and general features.

3. If you have two or more witnesses, separate them before viewing the lineup, so one witness does not improperly influence another witness (the opinions need to be independent from one another).

4. If you have two or more witnesses, change the location of the suspect in the lineup.

5. Read the admonition statement to the witness and have the witness sign the admonition part of the report.

6. Display the lineup to the witness.

7. If possible, record the witness's exact words, such as, "maybe it's him", "I guarantee that's him."

LINEUP

_____ Police Department

Case no._____   Priority __YES __NO

Offense	Code	County
Location of offense	Victim	Date of occurrence

LINEUP: ON_____(Date/time),

At (Location) _____(Victim/Witness)_____

Read the following admonition, then allow victim/witness to view the lineup.

Admonition of Victims and witnesses

It is requested that you look at a group of individuals. You are under no obligation to pick out any individual. The suspect may or may not be in the lineup. It is just as important to eliminate innocent persons from suspicion as it is to identify the perpetrator. Please do not discuss the lineup with any other witnesses.

I fully understand the admonition presented to me by officer _____, regarding the lineup ☐ Yes ☐ No

_____   _____   _____
Printed name of witness   signature of witness   date

Identification: ☐ I cannot make any identification
                 ☐ I can identify individual # _____ as the suspect.

Statement of witness/victim:
_____
_____

Signature of witness: _____ date: _____

Witnessed by officer: _____

date/time:_____

Individual # _____ is that of (name): _____

Officer's name (printed)	Officer's signature and badge #	Date	Approved by supervisor ☐ Yes ☐ No

PHOTOGRAPHIC LINEUP PROCEDURES

A photographic lineup that is suggestive is inadmissible in court. To be sure your photographic lineup identification will not be excluded at trial as unfair, follow these guidelines.

1. The photographic lineup must consist of at least six photographs.

2. Use all color or all black-and-white photographs. Do not mix.

3. Everyone in the display should be of the same sex, race, approximate age, and general features.

4. Try to use photographs of the same approximate size, depicting the same approximate shots of the faces (such as all close ups or not close ups).

5. Label each photograph with a number from one (#1) through six (#6).

6. If you have two or more witnesses, separate them before viewing the photographic lineup, so one witness does not improperly influence another witness (we want independent opinions).

7. Read the admonition statement to the witness and have the witness sign the admonition part of the report.

8. Display the photographic lineup to the witness.

9. If possible, record the witness's exact words, such as, "maybe it's him", "I guarantee that's him."

PHOTOGRAPHIC LINEUP

_____ Police Department

Case no. _____   Priority __Yes __No

Offense	Code	County
Location of offense	Victim	Date of occurrence

Photographic lineup:

On_____(Date/time),

At (Location) _____(Victim/Witness)_____

Read the following admonition, then allow victim/witness to view the photograph lineup.

Admonition of victims and witnesses

It is requested that you look at a group of photographs. You are under no obligation to pick out any photographs. The suspect may or may not be in the photographic lineup. It is just as important to eliminate innocent persons from suspicion as it is to identify the perpetrator. Please do not discuss the photographs with any other witnesses.

I fully understand the admonition presented to me by officer _____, regarding the photographic lineup ☐yes ☐ no

_____   _____   _____
Printed name of witness   signature of witness   date

<u>Identification:</u>   ☐ I cannot make any identification
                ☐ I can identify photograph# _____ as the suspect.

Statement of witness/victim
_____
_____

Signature of witness: _____ date/time_____

Witnessed by officer: _____ Date/time_____

Photograph# _____is that of (name): _____

Officer's name (printed)	Officer's signature and badge #	Date	Approved by supervisor ☐ Yes ☐ No

SUSPECT REPORT, FIELD INTERVIEW CARD, AND INTELLIGENCE REPORT

Suppose a police officer believes that a crime has occurred, but the officer cannot find any evidence. For example, suppose a dog indicates that there are illegal drugs in the car. The officer can also smell the drugs and searches the car. However, suppose nothing is found. Then the driver states to the officer that the officer was one day late. What can the police officer do about it? The officer cannot make an arrest because there is no physical evidence to collect. If an arrest is made, the officer can bet that the defense attorney will demand that the officer produce the evidence in court. Although the officer cannot make an arrest, the officer can still collect intelligence about the suspect. The officer may collect information via a suspect report, a field interview card, or an intelligence report.

KEY ITEMS IN SUSPECT IDENTIFICATION
- Sex
- Height
- Weight
- Build
- Age
- Race
- Face
- Complexion
- Hair
- Forehead
- Eyebrows
- Eyes
- Nose
- Ears
- Mustache
- Mouth
- Lips
- Teeth
- Beard
- Chin
- Neck
- Distinctive marks and features (e.g., scars, tattoos)
- Peculiarities
- Clothing
- Voice
- Distinctive behaviors (e.g., walk)
- Weapon
- Jewelry

SUSPECT REPORT

_____ Police Department

Case # _____   page ___ of ___

Crime	Crime title			Code		Location		Date
Susp. Vehicle	License#	State	Year	Make	Model	Body style __2dr __4dr __convert __p/u __ straight truck __van ___rv ___m/c ___other		
	Color				Other characteristics		Disposition of vehicle	
	Registered owner							
Suspect	Suspect name		Sex	Race: __Unknown __Hisp __Native Am. __Asian __Wht __Blk __Oth				
	AKA		DOB	Age	HT	WT	Build: __Thin __Medium __Unknown __Heavy __Musclr	
	Hair: __Blk __Brn __Red __Bln __ Gray __White __N/A __ Other __Unknown				Eyes: __Blk __Grn __Gray __Unknown __Brn __Blu __Hazel __Other			
	Residence address			State	Zip	Res. phone		SSN
	Business address			State	Zip	Bus. phone		Occupation
	Clothing			Arrested ☐ Yes ☐ No	Status ☐ Driver ☐ Ped ☐ Pass	Gang affiliation How known		
	DL State & #							

Amount of hair	Hairstyle	Complexion	Tattoos/scars	Weapon(s)
__Unknown	__Unknown	__Unknown	__Unknown	__Unknown
__Thick	__Long	__Clear	__Face	__Club
__Thin	__Short	__Acne	__Teeth	__Handgun
__Receding	__Collar	__Pocked	__Neck	__Other unk gun
__Bald	__Military	__Freckled	__R/arm	__Rifle
__Other	__Crew cut	__Weathered	__L/arm	__Shotgun
	__Right part	__Albino	__R/hand	__Toy gun
	__Left part	__Other	__L/hand	__Simulated
	__Center part		__R/leg	__Pocket knife
	__Straight		__L/leg	__Butcher knife
	__Pony tail		__R/shoulder	__Hands/feet
	__Afro		__L/shoulder	__Bodily force
	__Teased		__Front torso	__Strangulation
	__Other		__Back torso	__Tire iron
			__Other	__Other

Type of hair	Facial hair	Glasses	Unique clothing	Had weapon in or about
__Unknown __Clean __Dirty __Greasy __Matted __Odor __Other	__Unknown __N/A __Cln shaven __Moustache __Full beard __Goatee __Fu Manchu __Lower lip __Side burns __Fuzz __Unshaven __Other	__Unknown __None __Yes __Reg glasses __Sunglasses __Wire frame __Plastic frame __Color __Other	__Unknown __None __Cap/hat __Gloves __Ski mask __Stocking mask __Other	__Unknown __N/A __Bag/briefcase __Newspaper __Pocket __Shoulder __Holster __Waistband __Other

R/l handed	Voice	Weapon feature
__Unknown __Right __Left	__Unknown __N/A __Lisp __Slurred __Stutter __Accent __Describe_____ __Other	__Unknown __Altered stock __Sawed off __Automatic __Bolt action __Pump __Revolver __Blue steel __Chrome/nickel __Double barrel __Single barrel __Other
Officer's name (printed)	Officer's signature and badge #	Date	Approved by supervisor ☐ Yes ☐ No

FIELD INTERVIEW CARD

_____ Police Department

County	Date	Time
Department incident number	Reason for contact	
Location of contact	Pedestrian stop ☐ Y ☐ N	Traffic stop ☐ Y ☐ N ☐ Driver ☐ Passenger
Disposition		

Name of subject				Nickname			
Address				Phone			
State ID or driver's license #			State	SSN			
Age	Sex		Race	Height	Weight	Build	Complexion
DOB	POB		Hair	Eyes	Marks/tattoos (type & location)		
Subject's parents' names							
Clothing description							
Persons with subject at scene							
Gang affiliation							
Vehicle make			Model	VIN#			
Color			Tag	State			
Owner of vehicle				Owner at scene ☐ Y ☐ N			

POLICE DEPARTMENT: INTELLIGENCE REPORT

Date:_____ time:_____ officer & badge #:_____

Subject name:_____ Alias:_____

DOB:_____ Age:_____ Race:_____ Sex:_____

SSN:_____ DL#_____ State:_____

Height:_____ Weight:_____ Hair:_____ Eyes:_____

Scars, marks, tattoos: _____

Occupation: _____

Address: _____ Phone: _____

Vehicle description: _____

Subject's associates: _____

Status of subject (circle one)   **suspect**   **wanted**   **arrested**

Information source: _____

Notes (articulate reason for suspicion):

_____

_____

_____

_____

CHAPTER PROBLEMS

1. Provide examples of 10 open-ended questions.
2. Provide examples of 10 closed-ended questions.
3. Provide examples of 10 presumptive questions.
4. Provide examples of 10 neutral questions.
5. Provide examples of 10 leading questions.
6. Discuss the importance of an interrogator developing a rapport with the suspect.
7. Discuss the proper place for the officer to stand when interviewing a suspect in the field. Discuss where the officer should not stand.
8. Discuss 10 key items that are used in suspect identification on a Suspect Report form.
9. Discuss the following statement. When there are multiple witnesses for a photographic lineup, the witnesses should meet, discuss the facts, and come to a consensus to ensure a proper identification.
10. Discuss the difference between a lineup, showup, and a photographic lineup.

KEYWORDS

Closed-ended question
Interview
Lineup
Open-ended question
Photographic lineup
Probe question
Showup

REFERENCES

Del Carmen, R.V., & Hemmens, C. (2017). *Criminal procedures: Laws & practice* (10th ed.). Boston, MA: Wadsworth.
Milne, R., & Bull, R. (1999). *Investigating interviewing: Psychology and practice*. Chichester: Wiley.
Siddle, B.K. (2005). *PPCT Defensive Tactics*. Belleville, IL: PPCT Management Systems.
Stewart, C. J., & Cash, W.B. (2008). *Interviewing: Principles and practices*. New York: McGraw-Hill.
Swanson, C.R., Chamelin, N.C., Territo, L., & Taylor, R.W. (2009). *Criminal investigation* (10th ed.). Boston: McGraw Hill.
University of North Carolina—Charlotte (2014). *Types of interviews and techniques*. http://career.uncc.edu/students/effective-interviewing/types-interviews-and-techniques

CHAPTER 11

Body Language

LEARNING OBJECTIVES

Interpret body language.

Assess the content of words.

Apply different verbal abstract techniques.

INTRODUCTION

Humans communicate both verbally and nonverbally. Body language is a type of nonverbal communication in which physical behaviors are used to express or convey information. Body language includes facial expressions, body posture, gestures, and eye movement. Indeed, humans communicate nonverbally via conscious, subconscious, and unconscious gestures, facial expressions, and body movements. Although body language may be used to replace or reinforce speech, it may also betray a person's actual mood. Kinesics is the study of body movements and gestures to interpret nonverbal communication. Verbal communication, on the other hand, is the use of words to convey a message; it includes written and oral communications. The manner in which words are spoken may alter their meanings. Voice inflection, where individuals change the volume level, tone, pace, or pitch when they speak particular words, may provide an alternate message. In addition, police officers may employ kinesics to read the meanings behind the words. This chapter will discuss how body language, choice of words, a suspect's response, and human behaviors can be used to help determine the truth.

THE HUMAN FACE

The lack of heavy facial hair distinguishes the human face from the faces of other mammals (Jackson, 2004). Humans exchange sophisticated facial expressions that are important for socialization. Thus, a lack of facial hair promotes human socialization.

Although there are about six billion human faces in the world, no two faces are exactly the same (Jackson, 2004). Even the faces of identical twins differ slightly. Although the human face can display 100,000 different expressions, only seven facial expressions are biologically based and universally recognized: happiness, sadness, anger, surprise, disgust, contempt, and fear.

The human brain processes the human face as a whole and considers overall patterns (Jackson, 2004). Patterns of light and dark and spacing among facial features allow viewers a three-dimensional view, which is necessary to distinguish among subtle facial details. Indeed, it is difficult for a human to recognize a person based solely on a two-dimensional drawing. In order to demonstrate this problem, caricaturists have learned to exaggerate distinctive facial features to help the brain recognize the subjects of the drawings.

Based on facial expressions, it has been found that police officers only have a 50/50 chance of detecting a liar (Jackson, 2004). On the other hand, Secret Service Agents, who have been trained to detect micro-expressions, consistently detect liars. Although micro-expressions are facial expressions that may last only one-fifth of a second, they reveal emotions that the suspects are trying to conceal.

Biometrics use biological or physical features to identify individuals (Jackson, 2004). By collecting information and using databases, authorities can identify people via fingerprints, eye retinas, voice patterns, and facial features. For example, although the human face has about 80 nodal points, biometric software only requires about 14 to 22 nodal points for recognition. Changes in facial expressions, hair style or color, skin tone, and lighting do not impact the software. Because the facial software focuses on the inner region of the face, growing a beard, growing older, and putting on weight have little impact on the success of the facial software. In addition, much like fingerprints, a person's ears display unique characteristics and allow for proper identification. Thus, when a police officer takes MUG photographs at the jail, the officer should include side view photographs of the suspect with a clear view of the suspect's ears.

BODY LANGUAGE AND DECEPTION

It is not uncommon for police officers to encounter individuals who are less than truthful. When police officers encounter individuals, they need to look for signs of deception. Although there are many clues that may be indicative of deception, police officers must always look at the totality of the circumstances. In other words, signs of deception are not absolute and must be considered within the context of the particular situation. Some people may be deceptive by providing false information; other people may be deceptive by only providing partial information (i.e., by leaving important information out of their story).

Police officers often engage in critical thinking, which is using the available information to make best-practice decisions. It may not be uncommon for police officers to only receive partial information during an interview. For example, if the victims, witnesses, or suspects reside far from the officer, the officer may decide to call the individuals on the telephone. As a result, the visual clues may be lacking. In addition, many individuals claim truth is relative, and the perception of reality will depend on each person's perspective (Hatch, 2002).

Individuals communicate via conscious, subconscious, and unconscious gestures, expressions, and body movements (Table 11.1). The conscious mind is logical, and individuals are aware of and respond purposefully to their surroundings. The subconscious mind regulates behaviors that are not actively in an individual's focal awareness, such as rate of breathing (Ricee, 2021). When individuals communicate unconsciously, they provide subtle and unintentional information about themselves by acting out of habit (McNichol & Nelson 1994).

Table 11.1 Body language and body movements (Lambert, 2008; Lieberman, 1998; Meyer, 2010; Pease & Pease, 2004a; Starrett & Davis, 2006).

#	Body language	Behavior interpretation
1	Little or no eye contact; glances down and moves eyes from side to side	Sign of deception; guilty; does not like to make eye contact with interrogator; those who are falsely accused tend to make eye contact and to focus on false accusation.
2	Little use of hands and arms to self-express	Sign of deception; when people try to cover the truth, they often cover their bodies with their hands and arms.

Table 11.1 Cont.

#	Body language	Behavior interpretation
3	Hands down; fists clenched.	Sign of defensiveness.
4	Palms up	Seeking information; has nothing to hide.
5	Legs and arms close to body, may be crossed	Defending self; hiding information.
6	Legs and arms stretched out	Secure, confident, comfortable.
7	Arm movement stiff and mechanical	Attempting to portray passion about a subject; artificial emotions.
8	Hand goes to mouth while speaking	Unconscious sign of deceit; trying to cover up spoken lies.
9	Suspect touches face, nose, ears while listening	Suspect does not want to listen to the officer.
10	Shoulder shrug	Suspect does not care or does not know; trying to be relaxed.

Police officers need to be aware of a suspect's inconsistent actions (Lieberman, 1998). These may include words, gestures, and emotions that seem to be contradictory in nature (Table 11.2). For example, a man may state something affirmatively as he shakes his head from side to side. However, these expressions may be brief in appearance because the suspect may quickly cover them up. Any change in behavior should be suspicious.

Table 11.2 Body language and emotions (Lambert, 2008; Lieberman, 1998; Meyer, 2010; Pease & Pease, 2004a; Starrett & Davis, 2006).

#	Body language	Behavior interpretation
1	Punctuating a point after the fact, such as expressing anger after claiming to be angry	Suspect's emotions are not authentic; suspect talks before thinking and realizes they should have shown emotions earlier.
2	Moves head on important syllables as speaks	Suspect is driving home a point; truthful.
3	Incongruence between gestures and speech	Sign of deception; for example, someone saying that they feel sorry for you when you slipped on a banana peel and is laughing as they speak.
4	Delays emotions, prolongs emotions, and truncates emotions	Sign of deception; staged emotions seem out of alignment.
5	Showing emotions while displaying movement in eyes and forehead	Sign of truthfulness; emotions displayed over wide area on face.
6	Showing emotions while not displaying movement in eyes and forehead	Sign of deceit; forced smile; emotions confined to mouth area.

Suspects who are guilty go on the defense (Lieberman, 1998). Suspects who are innocent go on the offense. Additional behaviors that an interrogator may observe are displayed in Table 11.3.

Table 11.3 Body language (Lambert, 2008; Lieberman, 1998; Meyer, 2010; Pease & Pease, 2004a; Starrett & Davis, 2006).

#	Actions	Signs
1	Movement of head away from speaker; may be slow or abrupt (not a tilt of interest)	Signs of discomfort; suspect will distance themself from the threat or source of discomfort.
2	Movement of head toward the speaker	Signs of comfort; closing the gap.
3	Erect posture; shoulders back	Confident and secure.
4	Hunched over; hands in pocket	Insecure.
5	Face to face; squared off to accuser	Truthfulness; seeks to refute false accusations.

(continued)

Table 11.3 Cont.

#	Actions	Signs
6	Shifts or turns away from speaker	Signs of deceit; does not want to confront truth.
7	Movement toward exit; body angled toward door; may place back to wall	Signs of deceit; trying to avoid ambush.
8	Suspect has little or no physical contact with interrogator	Signs of deceit; trying to minimize intimacy and psychological connection.
9	Suspect fails to use index finger to either point at interrogator or up in air	Signs of deceit; lack of conviction and authority.
10	Suspect attempts to place physical barriers and obstacles between self and interrogator (e.g., cup of coffee)	Signs of deceit; suspect trying to create a shield to protect self against interrogator.

Police officers must also consider the content of the words provided by a suspect (Table 11.4). Suspects may calculate with precision their choice of the words in order to convey a particular truth that they want the police officers to believe. In addition, suspects may throw out diversionary flares (what warplanes use to misdirect heat-tracking missiles) to see if the police take the bait. If the suspects can get the police to focus on their diversionary flares (i.e., red herrings), then perhaps the suspects can prevent the police from detecting the truth (Table 11.5).

Table 11.4 Content of words (Inbau et al., 2005; Lieberman, 1998)

#	Words	Interpretation
1	Suspect reflects/repeats the interrogator's words; repeats questions but changes a few words (e.g., Q: Did you ever …; A: I never …; Q: Was it you who …; A: It wasn't me who …, etc.).	Signs of deceit; suspect does not spend much time thinking about answer and responds out of fear; repeats interrogator's words but makes a slight modification to change the meaning 180 degrees.
2	Suspect uses bold words to immediately make their point (e.g., No!, I would never …); makes statements in absolute terms.	Signs of deceit; wants to make it crystal clear, to eliminate any doubt and to stop further questioning; suspect's statements provide shield to self.
3	Suspects make statements that are not absolute (e.g., perhaps, maybe, I cannot remember much more, etc.).	Honest suspects will make less-specific statements and will clarify statements as needed; suspect's statements provide comfort to others.
4	Suspect makes a "Freudian slip."	Police may catch a false statement; when a suspect is making a statement, the suspect will accidently change the intended sentence and say something that is on their mind.
5	Suspect introduces a fictitious belief system to support their position; offers absolute assurance of innocence.	Signs of deceit; suspect feels evidence is unfavorable, so depersonalizes and globalizes the question (e.g., suspect responds that it is a moral abomination, it is against their religious beliefs, etc.).
6	Suspect is uncomfortable with silence; suspect adds information without being probed further; speaks to fill gaps of silence; statements offered in piecemeal fashion.	Signs of deceit; suspect gets nervous if there is silence because they are not sure that their story has convinced interrogator; will speak until gets verbal confirmation to stop.
7	Suspect implies answer but does not directly answer the question (e.g., Q: Do you love me? A: I have loved no one more. Q: Did you commit a felony? A: I have never been convicted of a crime.).	Signs of deceit via omission; provides answers that attempt to satisfy interrogator without providing false information; suspect provides a diversionary flare.

Table 11.5 Interpreting a suspect's response (Inbau et al., 2005; Lieberman, 1998; Zulawski & Wicklander, 2002)

#	Suspect's response	Interpretation
1	Suspect provides a quick yes or no answer, then takes a lengthy time to provide explanation; takes longer than usually to provide response to questions about personal beliefs.	Signs of deceit; suspect needs time to come up with an explanation after quick answer; suspect wants to provide the answer that they believe the interrogator wants to hear.
2	Suspect repeats the points already made; suspect's reaction is out of proportion; suspect appears outraged; suspect tries to detach self from crime (e.g., instead of saying "my home" the suspect will say "the home").	Signs of deceit; tries to convince interrogator through emotions because they cannot through evidence; suspect fails to acknowledge personal relationships and appears to be detached from items related to the crime.
3	Suspect does not want to own their words; suspect is reluctant to use pronouns (e.g., *I*, *we*, and *us*); voice is higher; voice is flat; lack of inflection.	Signs of deceit; Q: Did you like it? Instead of saying, "Yes, I really liked it," suspect will simply state "Yes"; truth teller is comfortable with personal position and will play with words (e.g., will elongate and vary the word *really* with voice inflection); liar's voice will be flat due to a lack of voice inflection; liar under stress will have vocal cords tighten up, which leads to a higher voice.
4	Suspect mumbles and speaks very softly; words not clear; misspoken words; poor sentence structure; out of fear, suspect may speak loudly and quickly.	Signs of deceit; suspect not passionate about words; suspect may simply reply by repeating the interrogator's words; words seem forced.
5	Suspect makes statements that sound like questions (speaking style for question is different from speaking style for statement); head, voice, and eyes lift at end of statement; suspect lacks conviction.	Signs of deceit; suspect looks up at end of statement and widens their eyes, which indicates that they are unsure of their statement and are seeking confirmation from the interrogator.
6	Suspect constantly questions someone else's motives and behaviors; suspect continually states that other people are corrupt; if the suspect cannot determine the interrogator's thoughts, the suspect will continually ask whether the interrogator believes them (truthful people expect to be believed).	Signs of deceit; reflection of how the suspect sees themself; suspect projects self onto others; it takes one to know one.
7	Suspect focuses on internal factors rather than on external factors; suspect more interested in how they appear to the interrogator rather than making their point clear; suspect plays defense instead of offense (instead of focusing on winning, suspect focuses on not losing).	Signs of deceit; suspect has little self-confidence (e.g., high confidence = man focuses on how attractive a woman looks; low confidence = man focuses on how he looks to attractive woman); suspect focuses on how they sound as they make statements; suspect puts on act in order to manipulate the interrogator's perception.
8	Suspect provides information without including a third person's point of view; a third person's perspective requires the liar to be cleverer.	Signs of deceit; suspect may mention a third person but not their opinion—for example, "I came home and told my wife that I joined the military" (lie) versus "I came home and told my wife that I joined the military and she was outraged" (truth).
9	Suspect fails to include negative details in statement, unless the negatives are used as a defense; statements are one-dimensional, which focus on the positive details; only positive thoughts are primary emotions.	Signs of deceit; true events often include good and bad; a suspect making up a falsehood will focus on positive details (unless the negative details are essential to the statement).
10	Suspect willingly answers questions but fails to ask relevant questions; suspect not interested in learning anything (e.g., suspect fails to ask about the well-being of others); focused on self-interests.	Signs of deceit; suspect is only concerned about convincing interrogator that they are truthful; fails to consider other perspectives, which may be very important to everyone else.

(continued)

Table 11.5 Cont.

#	Suspect's response	Interpretation
11	Suspect appears more relaxed or happier when subject changes; suspect smiles or laughs nervously when subject changes; suspect appears less defensive when subject changes.	Signs of deceit; the truthful resent false accusations and insist that they be further explored; guilty suspects want to quickly change the subject because they feel discomfort.
12	Suspect is more concerned about how to respond to an accusation rather than about being accused; suspect is not angered that their reputation has been tarnished and that their integrity has been questioned.	Signs of deceit; truthful individuals will be caught off guard and surprised that their integrity has been questioned; the liar will remain fairly expressionless when they are accused of a crime.
13	Suspect starts sentences with "To tell the truth," or "To be perfectly honest," etc. Suspect asks, Would I lie to you?" or "I never lie."	Signs of deceit; honest people do not feel that they have to start their statements by claiming that their statements are true; criminals have good reasons to lie; unless it is part of a particular person's everyday language, stating something like "To tell the truth" means that everything before the statement was a lie and everything after the statement will be a lie; suspect has to declare their virtuous nature because they cannot prove it otherwise.
14	Suspect has an agenda; suspect may head off in own direction and provide irrelevant information; suspect's statements sound rehearsed; rehearsed statements provide information that was not asked for by the interrogator; suspects recite facts and details that should not be recalled easily.	Signs of deceit; providing too much specific information on a particular date may indicate that the suspect tried to record information on the date of the crime in order to provide an alibi.
15	Suspect tries to buy time by having the interrogator repeat the question; suspect wants to think about question and to prepare response; suspect may ask a question to buy time.	Signs of deceit; suspect delays response; suspect may ask, "What do you mean?" "Why would you ask me that?" "What do you think?"
16	Suspect says something that sounds too good to be true (e.g., I have never lied in my life).	Signs of deceit; if statement is found to be false, suspect will lose all credibility; it is better to admit an infraction and to explain it rather than to deny an infraction if it is true.
17	Suspect implies something is true by saying the opposite; suspect implies something is true without actually saying it; suspect implies something is true through denial.	Signs of deceit; suspect may say, "I do not want you to blame her for the crash because she has a problem and is an alcoholic;" suspect may say, "I do not want you to think that I dislike you, but I am too busy for the rest of my life to see you;" suspect may say, "Kris was at Alcoholics Anonymous, but she was probably just attending the meeting as a criminal justice student."
18	Suspect uses humor and sarcasm to answer a serious question; suspect wants to make interrogator look foolish about probing further; interrogator must obtain a serious answer.	Signs of deceit; interrogator may ask, "Did you cheat on you wife with your secretary?" The suspect may answer, "Yes, every time I go to work, we sleep together. In fact, we plan to have enough kids to rule the country. In fact, with hundreds of dependents for tax deductions, I am doing my wife a service."
19	Suspect may state that he does not have what the interrogator is exactly looking for but does have something similar.	Signs of deceit; before believing the suspect, interrogator needs to confirm that the suspect does not have the originally requested item.
20	Suspect provides numbers that are multiples of one another.	Signs of deceit; because a liar may have a hard time coming up with a variety of numbers quickly, a liar may provide numbers that can easily be calculated (e.g., I have two computers, four jobs, eight friends, and I make $32,000 per year).

Table 11.5 Cont.

#	Suspect's response	Interpretation
21	Suspect's face may become flushed; suspect may display signs of rapid breathing and increased perspiration; suspect may tremble; suspect's voice may crack; suspect may have a hard time swallowing; suspect's voice may increase in pitch; suspect may have a hard time focusing on the questions; suspect may whistle.	Signs of deceit; suspect may become flushed due to fear; suspect may attempt to control breathing by taking deep, audible breaths; suspect may hide hands if they are trembling; suspect's vocal cords may tighten up, causing a change in pitch; anxiety causes mucus buildup in the throat, causing suspect to clear throat; stress may cause the suspect to lose concentration; suspect may whistle to relax and to build confidence.
22	Suspect agrees with interrogator and uses the interrogator's own words to support their cause; suspect deflects the interrogator's strengths; suspect does not confront or resist the interrogator; suspect attempts to turn a negative factor into a positive factor.	Signs of deceit; the interrogator may state, "I know every road officer in the department, but I do not know you." The suspect may reply, "That's right, I am an undercover officer with top clearance, and you are not supposed to know who I am." Suppose a particular food makes people sick and gives them diarrhea. A suspect may claim that the food helps eliminate toxins from the body and helps people lose weight through a natural process.
23	Suspect attempts to eliminate the interrogator's suspicions of a crime by opposing a less significant infraction.	Signs of deceit; the suspect may claim that a wife would be a fool to keep a no-good husband who flirted with another woman, when in fact the suspect is currently cheating on his wife.
24	Suspect will try to direct attention away from real issue; suspect downplays change or extraordinary event; suspect tries to slip information in without bringing attention to it.	Signs of deceit; a change in the suspect's normal activities is suspicious; interrogator should question extraordinary events; like a magician, a suspect will attempt to direct the interrogator's attention to where the suspect wants it to go.
25	Interrogator makes a false statement and tests the suspect's truthfulness; interrogator sees if the suspect will agree with a statement that the interrogator knows is false.	Signs of deceit; if a suspect lies about one thing, the suspect will lose credibility and all of the suspect's statements will be questionable; the interrogator may state, "I know that you did not commit the crime because you were out of town that night." The suspect may reply, "That's right, I was nowhere near the crime scene." However, the interrogator has a police car video recording that places the suspect at the crime scene at the time of interest.
26	Suspect makes a story that is hard to believe and argues that it must be true because common sense indicates that a lie would not be so far-fetched.	Signs of deceit; suspect embellishes the story; suspect argues that if the story were a lie, the suspect would have made the story more believable.

Police officers can employ a variety of verbal abstract techniques (Table 11.6) to find the truth. Sometimes, it is not exactly what the interrogator says that gets a confession, but it is the manner in which it is said (Table 11.7).

Table 11.6 Verbal abstract techniques (Inbau et al., 2005; Lieberman, 1998; Zulawski & Wicklander, 2002)

#	Verbal abstract technique	Signs/interpretation/trick
1	Interrogator should allude to the suspect's deviant behavior without accusing the suspect of deviant behavior.	Signs of deceit if suspect gets defensive or inquires about the interrogator's questions; if an interrogator believes that the suspect robbed the liquor store the night before, the interrogator may ask the suspect if they went out drinking the night before.
2	Interrogator should offer the suspect a similar story with very specific behavior that involves someone else; interrogator implies that they already know the answer.	Signs of deceit if suspect gets uncomfortable and defensive by claiming that he would never do such a thing; signs of truthfulness if suspect offers good advice and is thankful for the chance to offer helpful advice; if an interrogator believes that a police officer has destroyed evidence, the interrogator will inform the officer that some police evidence has been destroyed and he will ask the officer for his advice in dealing with the destruction of evidence problem; signs of truthfulness if suspect does not ask why the interrogator brought the issue up but simply attempts to help the interrogator solve the problem.
3	Interrogator should offer the suspect a story of similar behavior but in a general manner; interrogator implies that they already know the answer.	Signs of deceit if suspect gets uncomfortable and defensive and asks about the question or if they attempt to change the subject; if an interrogator believes a police officer has destroyed evidence, the interrogator will indicate that an officer would be silly to steal evidence due to all of the video cameras in the area; if the police officer denies the claim but asks about the video evidence, this would be a sign of deceit; signs of truthfulness if suspect opens up about the surveillance cameras and discusses how to effectively use the evidence to make a prosecution.
4	Interrogator asks the suspect direct questions about the crime; technique is more effective if suspect is caught off guard and is unable to prepare for the questions; if given advanced notice, suspect may rehearse responses, may convince themselves that their actions were justified, and may practice relaxing during responses.	Interrogator should not give advance warning, reveal what they know, or interrupt the suspect when they are responding; interrogator should build a rapport (e.g., by matching the suspect's gestures, speech rate, and word choice), build a baseline to use as reference (e.g., ask questions to which the interrogator already knows the answers, and see how the suspect responds), have a relaxed posture, square off with the suspect, provide moments of silence, ask "Really?", and ask whether there is anything else.
5	Interrogator asks the suspect leading questions about the crime; interrogator confines the suspect's responses to the crime; interrogator seems disappointed with response; interrogator makes the suspect comfortable with admitting the violation via pride.	Interrogator seeks admission to crime, not confession to crime; if the interrogator believes that the suspect cheated on his wife last night with Lisa, the interrogator may ask the suspect what time he got back from Lisa's last night (if the suspect provides a time, this places the suspect with Lisa last night); interrogator may lead the suspect into confession by appearing to understand that a little deviance is expected in life.
6	Interrogator uses time (i.e., the crime is old news) as a tool to get suspect's confession; two important factors are when the crime occurred and when others became aware of the crime; interrogator makes suspect believe that the crime is no big deal; interrogator makes the suspect believe they knew about the crime all along, which gets the suspect to believe all is okay.	Suspect will perceive the crime as insignificant if it happened a long time ago; suspect will perceive the crime as insignificant if others became aware of the crime a long time ago.

Table 11.6 Cont.

#	Verbal abstract technique	Signs/interpretation/trick
7	Interrogator has no evidence but has gut feeling suspect is guilty; interrogator appears to have big concern and acts surprised or hurt about something.	Interrogator may state to the suspect that they may try to lie, but the interrogator knows the truth; interrogator may state that everyone knows about it; interrogator may state to the suspect that they both know why they are now talking together.
8	Interrogator believes the suspect is guilty but cannot prove it; interrogator provides misleading information and sets the seed of doubt.	Suspect will provide excuses to explain possible evidence; if interrogator claims that a crime occurred and fingerprints have been collected, suspect may try to explain why their prints were at the scene; if interrogator claims that there was a witness, the suspect may claim that there are many other people who look like them.
9	Interrogator maximizes the crime; interrogator gets suspect to admit to a minor infraction, which the interrogator makes the suspect believe is no big deal.	Interrogator accuses the suspect of major crimes, and many of them; interrogator claims that if it were just a minor infraction, it would be no problem (e.g., interrogator accuses the suspect of attempted murder but claims that if the suspect simply attempted to smack his wife around a little bit, which is understandable and perhaps even expected).
10	Interrogator may stare at suspect and encroach upon the suspect's personal space, causing mental claustrophobia; interrogator asks the suspect about related information in an attempt to investigate the real concern.	Signs of deceit if suspect attempts to make story fit the interrogator's facts; if a suspect claims that they were at home during a crime, the interrogator may claim that the police were at their neighbor's home for a report at the time of the crime and they noticed that the suspect's car was not there.
11	Interrogator uses a third party to plant the seed of doubt in the suspect's mind; using a third party maximizes the interrogator's credibility; innocent persons will not be interested in fixing problems that do not exist.	A third party will approach the suspect and state that they are getting tired of the suspect's misconduct; the third party will tell the suspect that the suspect's activities are common knowledge, but the third party knows how the suspect can fix the problem; the third party appears to agree with the suspect's actions but asks the suspect whether they are sure they will not get into trouble (a guilty person will hesitate and think about it).
12	Interrogator praises past crime; interrogator assumes that the suspect has already committed the crime; suspect must admit old crime in order to take advantage of new opportunities; suspect assumes the interrogator has evidence that the suspect has committed crime.	Interrogator makes suspect believe that their past crime is a valuable skill and is needed for a new job (e.g., the suspect's criminal skills may be used to make anti-crime policies); interrogator makes the suspect believe that it is an open discussion and that upper management needs the best person for the job (if the suspect hesitates, this is a sign of guilt because they are thinking about their options).
13	Interrogator provides partial information that is true; interrogator sets seed of doubt about the rest of the story, which is unknown.	Interrogator may claim that the suspect has been in jail for drugs before, which is true; the interrogator then claims that they know all about the suspect's manufacturing of drugs the night before, which is unknown; the interrogator then states that they are upset and do not want to talk about it right now (if the suspect is innocent, they will want to address the false accusation now; if the suspect is guilty, they will honor the interrogator's request and not want to escalate the hostile situation).
14	Interrogator informs the suspect but does not accuse the suspect; interrogator evaluates the suspect's response to the information; a guilty person becomes defensive and tries to not be blamed; an innocent person attempts to find out who is responsible and does not realize they are being accused.	Signs of guilt if the suspect is defensive, very focused on their response, focuses on being accused, and does not show concern about the obvious, such as being a victim; an innocent person would be concerned about all aspects of the problem, which may include being the victim.

(continued)

Table 11.6 Cont.

#	Verbal abstract technique	Signs/interpretation/trick
15	Interrogator presents the positives of telling the whole story, the negatives of failing to resolve the matter, and then forces the suspect to make a choice; the positives and negatives must be realistic and believable; interrogator tells the suspect to tell the whole story (this does not imply that the suspect is lying but it does give the suspect credit for being partially truthful).	Interrogator tells the suspect that management has big plans for the suspect, such as a promotion, a vacation home, an expense account, and a company vehicle; interrogator tells the suspect that everyone makes mistakes and that until the matter is resolved, the suspect will receive nothing; interrogator also states that if they find out that the suspect is guilty from another source, the suspect, who will be labeled a liar, will be fired and will have a hard time finding another job; interrogator then asks suspect to make a choice.
16	Interrogator gets the suspect to think emotionally; interrogator makes suspect feel that the suspect is not alone.	Interrogator admits to the suspect that they have also committed some deviant acts; interrogator asks the suspect to provide details before the interrogator will provide details; suspect will believe there is an exchange of information.
17	Interrogator focuses on the suspect's intentions, not the suspect's actions; interrogator gets suspect to admit that they committed the crime, but that it was an accident.	Interrogator tells the suspect that sometimes things get out of control and accidents are understandable; interrogator tells the suspect that if the actions were intentional, then that is not okay.
18	Interrogator praises the suspect and seeks partnership; interrogator praises suspect's behaviors as creative and innovative.	Interrogator tells the suspect that being secretive is silly and that they want a part of the action; interrogator tells suspect that being deviant is creative and wants the suspect to elaborate on their creativity.
19	Interrogator tells the suspect that they will gain nothing if they fail to cooperate; interrogator tells suspect that what the suspect has done can be overlooked, but lying about it cannot be overlooked.	If the suspect fails to cooperate with the interrogator and nothing is resolved, then both will lose (interrogator will not get confession and suspect will surely be penalized, such as by losing their job).
20	Interrogator tells the suspect that there is a deadline for talking and that the cost will go up if the deadline is not met.	Interrogator tells the suspect that once the interrogator leaves the room, nothing the suspect says will matter; interrogator tells the suspect that they want to give the suspect one last chance to tell their side of the story before the interrogator decides what to do.
21	Interrogator tells the suspect that they take full responsibility for the suspect's actions; interrogator states that they understand why the suspect committed the act; interrogator focuses on the suspect's grievances.	Interrogator tells the suspect that there were good reasons for their acts; interrogator asks the suspect what they can do for the suspect to help prevent them doing this again (interrogator assumes the suspect is guilty).
22	Interrogator tells the suspect that if they lie, there will be greater penalties; interrogator relies on the suspect's imagination to determine penalties; interrogator assesses the suspect's reaction to the possibility of a higher penalty.	Interrogator tells the suspect that they hate to do it, but based on the available information, they must do what has to be done (interrogator will not expand on what they must do).
23	Interrogator attacks the suspect's ego; this technique is very effective for those who have large egos.	Interrogator tells the suspect that they know the suspect cannot talk because the suspect is the puppet of the local drug dealer, who is pulling their strings (the suspect will confess to prove that they are no one's puppet).

Table 11.6 Cont.

#	Verbal abstract technique	Signs/interpretation/trick
24	Interrogator convinces the suspect that the interrogator is on their side; interrogator may provide an excuse for the suspect's actions and will provide a solution to eliminate any concerns.	Interrogator praises the suspect and indicates that there may be slight exaggerations. By correcting the exaggerations, the suspect will be in a better position; interrogator asks the suspect what exaggerations need to be modified.
25	Interrogator emphasizes to the suspect that the time and impact of the penalty are unknown; there is no indication of exactly when the penalty will occur; the interrogator stresses that the cost of the penalty is not isolated to this event and will impact other parts of the suspect's life.	Suspect will have a hard time enjoying life if, at any time, the penalty may be enforced; suspect will have no comfort if they believe their life will never be normal again; interrogator tells the suspect to come clean, take their slap on the hand, and move on with their life.
26	Interrogator makes the suspect believe that the suspect has no value; interrogator's apathy toward the suspect will make the suspect nervous.	If the interrogator makes the suspect believe that they do not care that the suspect is lying, then the suspect will confess just to get the interest of the interrogator.
27	Interrogator asks the suspect a direct question; question must be objective and specific; once the suspect provides an answer, the interrogator will follow up and ask additional details; interrogator relentlessly attempts to trip suspect up by comparing the many specific answers provided by the suspect.	If the suspect is truthful, they will answer right away; if the suspect takes a while to respond, they may be contriving a story; a made-up story usually lacks details and the suspect will trip up when too many specific questions are asked; a liar seeks to change the topic.
28	Interrogator asks the suspect a question, but adds false information in the question; question has to sound reasonable to be believable; suspect must have first-hand knowledge about the topic.	Sign of deceit if suspect answers the question incorrectly (e.g., suspect states that they know Jim really well and that they stayed with him last week; interrogator asks the suspect whether Jim's sister is still ill, even though the interrogator knows Jim has no sister).
29	Interrogator asks the suspect in a nonthreatening way to support their statements.	If the suspect states that they check books out of the library all the time, ask to see the suspect's library card; it is a sign of deceit if the suspect provides excuses why they cannot produce the evidence.
30	Interrogator adds presumptuous information to suspect's statement; suspect hears false information and agrees via adoptive admission.	Sign of deceit if suspect fails to correct presumptuous information (e.g., if suspect states that they failed to go to work, interrogator may state that it is understandable because the bridge was closed – even though the bridge was not closed – and the suspect does not correct statement).
31	Interrogator wants to find out about suspect's acquaintance; interrogator appeals to suspect's ego; instead of asking the suspect about what the acquaintance did wrong, the interrogator will ask the suspect what they would have done; suspect believes they are providing positive information instead of negative information.	Due to loyalty, police officer A may not want to admit that police officer B did a poor job; instead of directly asking about the poor behavior of officer B, the interrogator will ask officer A what they would have done.
32	Interrogator wants to find out the true motives from someone of power; interrogator places the suspect in a situation where the suspect feels obligated to respond truthfully.	If the suspect makes a questionable decision, the interrogator will ask the suspect to state what is required to make a different decision (which the interrogator believes is better) that achieves the same outcome; if the suspect's answer has already been shown to fail, then the suspect will feel obligated to change their position.

(continued)

Table 11.6 Cont.

#	Verbal abstract technique	Signs/interpretation/trick
33	Suspect lies to interrogator to protect the interrogator's feelings, so interrogator makes the suspect feel guilty about lying.	Interrogator tells the suspect that they have faith in the suspect and that they believe the suspect would not intentionally hurt them by being dishonest (if the suspect seeks the approval of the interrogator, the suspect will change their story).
34	Interrogator asks the suspect questions that make it clear there is an opportunity to improve the statement; interrogator makes the suspect feel comfortable in changing their statement.	Interrogator may ask the suspect whether the suspect likes their supervisor's management style. If the suspect states yes, then the interrogator will ask the suspect what it would take to love his supervisor's management style.
35	Interrogator takes proactive measures to eliminate "I don't know" responses; interrogator does not want to make the suspect feel foolish about their behavior; interrogator reduces the pressure on the suspect by seeming to ask about something else; interrogator makes the suspect believe that there was no intent involved with the suspect's actions.	Interrogator may state to the suspect that they understand that the suspect does not know the answer but they want the suspect to take their best guess; interrogator may ask the suspect to describe their feelings and how they can feel that way; interrogator may ask the suspect for any subconscious motivations (eliminates intent); interrogator may ask the suspect about past similar situations that generated the same reaction; interrogator may ask the suspect to describe just one reason for their actions (this will open the door for further probing).
36	Victim does not want to talk because they are too embarrassed; interrogator tries to minimize the embarrassment of the victim; interrogator tells the victim that they do not have to talk about it (this takes the pressure off of the victim); interrogator confides in the suspect by telling the suspect a story in which the interrogator messed up (this demonstrates that the interrogator trusts the suspect and the suspect will feel obligated to and comfortable with sharing information).	Interrogator may simply ask *yes* or *no* questions (this will not require the victim to elaborate); interrogator may tell the victim that they experienced the same thing and the interrogator may ask the victim whether they want to hear what happened; interrogator may ask the victim where they fit in on a scale of 1 to 10 (interrogator should not say *fall on the scale* because *fall* has a negative connotation and should not let 1 be nothing because this will allow the victim to select an easy out).
37	Interrogator seeks a confession when there are multiple suspects; interrogator speaks with one suspect at a time; when suspects do not feel personally responsible, they may not confess; when there are many suspects, there is a diffusion of responsibility and there is no motivation for suspects to cooperate with the interrogator.	Interrogator tells suspect that they trust the suspect and that they are not like the other suspects; interrogator tells the suspect that they can trust the interrogator; interrogator tells the suspect that what was done is not that important, but telling the truth is most important (the interrogator can count on the suspect); if this fails, the interrogator will try this tactic on the other suspects, one at a time.
38	Interrogator questions experts with advanced knowledge; interrogator does not have the expertise in the field; there is a change in personnel and the second person was supposed to carry out an order from the first person; the interrogator will ask the second person a question to see whether the second person confirms a false statement (e.g., interrogator ordered coke from person A, person B brings pop, and interrogator asks person B if the pop is root beer).	Interrogator states the opposite of what they really want, and waits to see whether the suspect agrees with it (e.g., an interrogator is looking for a drug that will make a person wired, so the interrogator asks the doctor whether the medication's side-effects will make them drowsy); if the suspect disagrees with the interrogator's statement, then the doctor is likely truthful; if the suspect agrees with the interrogator's statement, then the doctor may simply be pushing the product.
39	Interrogator is dealing with a person who has nothing to lose and who does not care to cooperate; interrogator needs to raise the stakes.	Police officer has a search warrant to take blood from a martial arts expert; martial arts expert states that they will refuse and will fight the officer; officer states that if the suspect fights the officer, the officer will file assault charges against the suspect and will also sue the suspect for any damages.

Table 11.6 Cont.

#	Verbal abstract technique	Signs/interpretation/trick
40	Interrogator attempts to get second-hand information from an individual who has talked with the suspect; interrogator makes the individual believe they already know the truth and overshadows it by showing emotions; interrogator should use the appropriate emotion (e.g., humor, concern, sympathy, surprise, etc.).	Interrogator may state that they just found out what happened and will ask the person how they are holding up or whether there is anything the interrogator can do.
41	Interrogator directs the conversation and elicits the needed information; interrogator responds first and sets the mode of information exchange (e.g., smiles, nods, etc.); interrogator sets the pace of the conversation (i.e., fast, slow, etc.); interrogator uses certain words that require the suspect to provide additional information.	After the suspect makes their statement, the interrogator will get additional information by responding with one of the following words: *meaning, and*, or *so*. Each of these words added to the end of a suspect's statement will require an explanation and additional information.
42	Interrogator turns vague responses into more direct responses; interrogator asks suspect for details.	If the suspect states that the police officer used excessive force, the interrogator will ask the suspect to articulate the facts (e.g., what exactly did the office do?); if an officer stated that the person looked suspicious, the defense attorney will ask the officer to explain what led to that conclusion (e.g., the officer needs to state that the suspect would not make eye contact, had shaking hands, was sweating, etc.).
43	Interrogator needs to stop the suspect from talking or from continually interrupting the interrogator; interrogator plays on the suspects ego and curiosity.	Interrogator may say to the suspect: "Please do not let the facts interfere with your opinion; I have some very upsetting news for you; I hate to insult your intelligence, so this is the last time I am going to say this; I am sorry that the middle of my statement ran into the beginning of your sentence," etc.
44	Interrogator assumes that their suspicions are fact; interrogator states two facts that the suspect knows are true; interrogator focuses on a reasonable request and not on a threat, which will put the suspect at ease and will open up the discussion.	**Bad technique:** Interrogator states, "Have you been smoking marijuana? Because if I find out that you have, I will lock you up and throw away the key" (focuses on the punishment). **Okay technique:** Interrogator states, "You have been smoking marijuana, haven't you?" (indicates that the interrogator may know something). **Good technique:** Interrogator states, "Let's talk about your marijuana usage" (focuses on the discussion). **Best technique**: Interrogator states, "I know that you have recently possessed and smoked marijuana, but just promise me that you use it at home and that you do not to go to work high" (has credibility because interrogator stated two facts and there is no mention of threat or punishment).
45	Suspect attempts to deceive the interrogator by telling the interrogator what the suspect believes the interrogator wants to hear; interrogator does not let the suspect know what the interrogator wants to hear, which will neutralize the suspect's deception.	**Allows suspect to know interrogator's thought:** Interrogator states, "I like Joe. Is Joe trustworthy?" **Does not allow suspect to know interrogator's thought:** Interrogator states, "What do you think about Joe?"

(continued)

Table 11.6 Cont.

#	Verbal abstract technique	Signs/interpretation/trick
46	Interrogator asks the suspect questions that are very likely true for most people; interrogator seeks to determine whether suspect is currently honest by asking about past infractions; interrogator asks a question that the suspect cannot answer in absolute terms (if the suspect does answer in absolute terms, then the interrogator knows suspect is being deceitful).	Interrogator asks the suspect whether they have ever stolen anything in their life (which is most likely "yes"); interrogator asks a kleptomaniac if they will stop stealing cold turkey (a "yes" will indicate deceit because intervention will most likely be required and a truthful suspect needs to mention it).
47	Interrogator uses embedded commands in sentences to implant suggestions in the suspect's mind; interrogator uses hand gestures during the commands to distract the conscious mind, uses short pauses before and after the commands, and changes the volume of the words during the commands; interrogator will embed commands like *tell the truth, say it, it is the right decision, clear the air now, get on with your life, tell me what happened, go straight, take care of your family*, etc.	When the human brain perceives initial information as truthful, it will perceive supplemental information as truthful; $n + p = 5$ statements, where $n = 4$ truthful statements and p = embedded command. "I know that you have never been in trouble before (true), that you are scared (true), and that you want to minimize your trouble (true). Because you want to put this behind you (true), *you need to tell the truth* (embedded command)."
48	Interrogator uses embedded commands in sentences to implant suggestions in the suspect's mind; interrogator embeds commands that illicit actions, which can be readily observed.	Interrogator may tell the suspect that they are not sure whether the suspect is lying, unless the suspect wants to admit it by blinking their eyes really fast (this may lead an untruthful suspect to blink their eyes really fast).
49	Interrogator alleviates the suspect's guilt via the process of disassociation; interrogator wears down the suspect's defenses by continually repeating phrases that distinguish the "old suspect" from the "new suspect."	Interrogator may state to the suspect, "Perhaps the old-you was capable of doing this, but I know that you would never do it today and it is only important who you are today."
50	Interrogator watches the eyes of the suspect when the suspect is thinking; interrogator evaluates whether suspect is recalling information or creating information; interrogator should start by asking questions that develop a baseline (i.e., reference).	Recalling information is a sign of truthfulness; creating information is a sign of deceit; for recalling visual memories that are true, the eyes of right-handed individuals will typically go up and to the left and the eyes of left-handed individuals will typically go up and to the right; for creating visual memories that are false, the eyes of right-handed individuals will typically go up and to the right and the eyes of left-handed individuals will typically go up and to the left.
51	Interrogator creates a conditioned response in the suspect.	Interrogator chooses a behavior and performs that behavior when asking the suspect questions that the interrogator knows will be answered truthfully; when the interrogator asks the suspect questions and wants to find the truth, the interrogator will perform the behavior, which will generate a conditioned truthful response from the suspect.
52	Interrogator develops a rapport with the suspect and then leads the suspect's thinking; interrogator explains to the suspect why having an honest conversation is important.	Interrogator may state to the suspect, "I went to your high school and I was in the same situation. I understand the pressure that friends can put on you. You talking about it is the right thing to do. Let's put this behind us so we can both move on. It is the smart thing to do."

Table 11.6 Cont.

#	Verbal abstract technique	Signs/interpretation/trick
53	Interrogator uses mild trance inducers; used to gain control of the conversation; used to gain time or to disrupt the suspect's train of thought.	Interrogator may state to the suspect, "You didn't eat yet and you're still hungry. Are you never going on vacation sometimes? If you are expecting me to give you a break, you wouldn't have asked for it." The variety of non-related subjects in the sentence disrupts the suspect's train of thought.
54	Interrogator implants an artificial suggestion in the mind of the suspect, which changes the suspect's perception of reality; interrogator plants the seed of concern in the mind of the suspect and lets it grow.	Interrogator may state to the suspect, "Everyone knows that you cheated on your wife. Have you noticed how all of your friends look at you funny?"

Table 11.7 Human behavior (Lieberman, 1998; Pease & Pease, 2004b; Pollock, 2004; Thompson & Jenkins, 2004)

Many decisions are emotionally based. An argument based solely on logic is marginally persuasive. To be effectively persuasive, arguments based on logic need to be transformed into arguments with emotions. For example, an interrogator may state to the suspect, "Your deceitfulness hurts me. If you are honest, I won't say a word to your spouse about your indiscretions."

Interrogator may dramatically increase the suspect's anxiety level by making a problem seem permanent, by making it seem more significant than it truly is, and by making it seem like it will affect other parts of the suspect's life.

Because the human mind and body are linked, changing the body will change the mind. If a suspect is in a state of denial and refuses to budge on their claim, change their physical state (for example, if they are sitting, have them stand or move around).

Suspects do not want to change their position due to ego; it is an admission of failure. However, the interrogator may introduce new information and ask the suspect to reconsider their position (this is effective if the new information is relatively recent; otherwise, the suspect may feel foolish for not knowing it).

When an interrogator cannot sway the suspect, the interrogator reverses their own direction and exaggerates the suspect's position. For example, if a suspect states that they will not leave their home because they are angry, which will cause them to miss their court date, the interrogator will tell the suspect that if they miss the court date, they will not have to worry about leaving their cell for next 20 years.

Interrogator takes control of the situation and speaks directly and softly; interrogator expects suspect to listen and does not ask for opinions. The suspect will perceive the topic to be of great importance if the interrogator makes a big deal about it. If the interrogator compliments the suspect, the suspect will be more receptive; if the interrogator criticizes the suspect, the suspect will be less receptive.

Interrogator breaks the suspect down by making them tired, hungry, and thirsty. Suspect will not think clearly under these conditions and will confess in order to end stress and achieve comfort.

Interrogator must have plans and backup plans; when the interrogator's options are limited, the suspect will have the advantage; when the interrogator has several options, they will gain leverage; for example, if the interrogator has several suspects, they do not need the first one to confess because there are other suspects who may confess, which decreases the first suspect's power.

If the interrogator wants to encourage a behavior, such as a confession, they must get the suspect to see it as something simple and as a single-task event (individuals spend time on the things they like); if the interrogator wants to discourage a behavior, they must get the suspect to see it as something difficult and as a multitask event (individuals think of the many things that bother them when they do activities they do not enjoy).

(continued)

Table 11.7 Cont.

Human behavior may be motivated via pleasure and/or pain; the suspect will act when the benefits outweigh the costs; the interrogator must get the suspect to believe that, by confessing, the topic will be behind them and that the subject will not be brought up again (benefit); if the suspect believes a lengthy interrogation will follow the confession (a high cost), they have no incentive to confess.

Individuals see what they choose to see; wishful thinking blinds individuals from seeing clues and from seeing reality; an interrogator who seeks compliments, confirmation, or confrontation will miss the true meaning of the suspect's message.

Individuals see how they have learned to see; interrogators must consider truth from different perspectives; morals determine appropriate behavior; there are many different ethical systems (e.g., cultural relativism, situational ethics, ethics of care, religious, natural law, ethical formalism, egoism, ethics of virtue, etc.).

Emotions impair judgment; the interrogator plays on emotions to manipulate behavior; for example, an interrogator may tell a feminist that their place is in the kitchen, a religious person that God expects a confession, and a vain person that no one likes them.

A suspect will attempt to deceive the interrogator by creating trust via a bond; suspect may attempt to flatter interrogator or may claim they are alike.

A suspect may offer the interrogator a gift, which may make the interrogator feel obligated to the suspect; gratuities should not be accepted by a police officer if they affect a police decision.

An individual may attempt to deceive a person by making the original offer excessively high and then by lowering the cost a little bit (the savings seem like a good deal); doubling the price and then lowering the cost by 20% seems like a good deal for the consumer; the total value must be compared with the final cost, irrelevant of any savings, when making the best-practice decision.

People resist change; people with low self-esteem resist admitting that they are wrong; people of low self-worth behave in ways that will make past actions right; people can be manipulated by getting them to commit to something small then increasing the demands over time; once individuals have developed a sense of obligation, their actions can be manipulated (e.g., this is how cults operate).

An individual may be influenced by other people's desires; a man may go a year without a date, then when one woman wants him, many women suddenly do (supply and demand); an objective person must not let other people's interests dictate their actions.

Just because someone dresses as an expert, this does not make them an expert; individuals will try to enhance their credibility via superficial means; a police officer may wear a campaign hat for image, respect, authority, and professionalism.

People want what they cannot have; rare items are often valuable (supply and demand); wise individuals must realize that just because something is rare, this does not make it valuable.

Wise individuals will always challenge the data; statistics can be manipulated and there are always limitations (variables, data collection, methodology, data analysis, interpretation, etc.); wise individuals do not accept arguments as true without confirmation.

A perpetrator will gain trust and credibility by offering some information that benefits the victim; once the perpetrator's credibility has been established, they will influence the victim to make less than optimal decisions.

A perpetrator will request a large favor from the victim, expecting the favor to be declined; once declined, the perpetrator will ask the victim for a smaller favor; the victim will feel bad for refusing the second favor because it is relatively small, compared with the original request.

A perpetrator will try to manipulate the victim by attacking their ego; the victim will act and make a poor decision in order to protect their pride. For example, a perpetrator may state to the victim, "I used to have a sweater like the one you are wearing, then my dad got a job." "Perhaps these sweaters are too expensive for you." "You should take a look at the clearance rack." This tactic may motivate a victim to purchase an expensive sweater to make a point.

ASSESSING TRUTH AND BODY LANGUAGE

(BodyLanguageCards.com, n.d.; Erskine, 2001; Inbau et al., 2005; Lambert, 2008; Lieberman, 1998; Meyer, 2010; Pease & Pease, 2004a; Starrett & Davis, 2006; Zulawski & Wicklander, 2002)

BODY LANGUAGE
- \> 7,000 different facial expressions
- \> 700,000 forms of body language
- 65% of social meanings are transmitted non-verbally
- Head (e.g., nodding)
- Face (e.g., blushing)
- Eyes (e.g., winking)
- Nose (e.g., flaring nostrils)
- Lips and mouth (e.g., smiling)
- Arms (e.g., crossing)
- Hands (e.g., thumbs up)
- Handshaking (e.g., strength of squeeze)
- Legs and feet (e.g., crossing)

TRUTH
- Same meaning for words (e.g., dinner ≠ supper)?
- Same meaning for gestures (e.g., eye contact = respect or deceit)?
- Deception (incorrect assumptions; magic trick).
- Two individuals can say exactly the same thing but have different meanings (e.g., Who's on first?).
- Officer should separate witnesses as soon as possible so that they do not contrive a common story (consensus).

DECEIT/DECEPTION
- State of being deceived or misled.
- Intrinsic part of interrogation because criminals are dishonest.
- Interrogator must be able to recognize and manage deceit.
- Interrogator must be able to recognize verbal and nonverbal signs.
- Reading a person's reactions can provide indications of deceit.

SIGNS OF DECEIT
- Verbal and nonverbal signs are incongruent.
- For example, suspect denies that they did something, then starts to sweat profusely.
- As suspect's fear of crime detection increases, so will the incongruence between their verbal and nonverbal signs (e.g., sweat more).
- Suspect is usually unaware of the incongruence.

CLUSTERED BEHAVIOR
- Truthful behaviors come in clusters.
- Deceptive behaviors come in clusters.
- Five different deceptive responses to any one question or issue are a sign of deceit; fewer than five are not enough.

TEN VERBAL WAYS TO ASSESS TRUTH
1. Suspect's verbal signs.
2. Suspect's moods.
3. Information offered by the suspect.
4. Suspect is overly polite.
5. Suspect uses delay tactics.
6. Suspect throws interrogator a bone.
7. Suspect points out truthful or cooperative behavior.
8. Suspect makes moral or honest exclamations.
9. Suspect's method of recollection.
10. Suspect gives in.

SUSPECT'S VERBAL SIGNS

How a suspect says "no" may indicate deceit. Below are signs of deceit.

1. Too friendly when saying "no."
2. Shifting body when answering.
3. Crossing legs.
4. Looking away.
5. Shutting eyes (blinking a lot).
6. Shaking head.
7. Biting lips.
8. Appearance of insincerity.
9. Hesitates before answering.
10. A breathless "no."
11. Appearing thoughtful or too casual.
12. Eyes directed somewhere else.
13. Blank stare while answering.
14. Saying "no" many times in rapid succession.

SUSPECT'S MOODS
- Moods indicate deceit when they change after a specific question is asked.
- Lying creates stress, and changes in mood may indicate an increase in stress; therefore, changes in mood may indicate deception.
- There are six states that indicate changes in mood:
  1. Anger
  2. Swearing, attacking the interrogator, victim, or case facts
  3. Depression

4. Comments about emotional problems, depression, or insomnia; any statement about personal life problems (e.g., family, health); statement about the punishment that the suspect may receive as a result of the investigation; suicidal comments
5. Denial
6. Using rationalization words ("almost, sort of, possibly"); saying that there are memory lapses (I don't remember); stalling (laughing, asking the question to be repeated); shifting blame (discussing others' culpability); irrelevant details or evading incriminating details by discussing overall issues; avoiding a question or only answering a portion of it; statements that lack emotion (refusing to discuss something hurtful or appearing to be unaffected)

INFORMATION OFFERED BY SUSPECT

- If a suspect offers additional information to support their denial, this may be a sign of deceit.
- Honest people will respond and simply say they did not do it.
- Untruthful people tend to elaborate their responses.

SUSPECT IS OVERLY POLITE

- Being overly polite or too helpful is a red flag for deceit.
- Suspect uses these tactics to get the interrogator to like them.
- Suspect trying to find out what the interrogator knows and in what direction the interrogator is headed.
- Suspect tries to direct the interrogator away from something and toward someone or something else.

SUSPECT USES DELAY TACTICS

There are several different types of delay tactics a suspect may use to buy time

- Repeats question so they can have time to think of answer.
- Answers the question with a question (does not actually answer the question).
- Says they do not understand the question.
- Says "Are you accusing me of this?" This breaks the flow of the interrogation.
- Tries to shift the blame to someone else.

SUSPECT THROWS INTERROGATOR A BONE

- It is rare that a suspect initially admits to the crime completely.
- Throwing a bone means that the suspect admits to a lesser crime.
- The suspect does this to give the impression that they are truthful.
- This is a sense of compromise and is close to a confession.

SUSPECT POINTS OUT TRUTHFUL OR COOPERATIVE BEHAVIOR
- The suspect points out how truthful or cooperative they are in order to delay answering the question.
- Often a sign of deceit.

SUSPECT MAKES MORAL OR HONEST EXCLAMATIONS
- If a suspect begins making exclamations about their morals or honesty, it may be a sign of deceit.
- "I swear to God."
- My father is a police officer/priest.
- Honestly, truthfully.

SUSPECT'S METHOD OF RECOLLECTION
- How a suspect recalls the details of the event.
- A truthful person will tell a story with only minor changes.
- An untruthful person needs to have an excellent memory to maintain a series of lies.
- The interrogator needs to get very specific about minor details.
- Have the suspect reaffirm details and ask rapid questions so the suspect has no time to think about their answers.

SUSPECT GIVES IN
- The suspect admits to the crime.
- "If I pay for the stuff, will you let me go?"
- "I'll confess if it makes you happy."
- The innocent do not generally admit guilt or offer to pay for the crime.

NONVERBAL SIGNS
- Based on the fight or flight response of humans.
- Primitive physiological response to the perception of threat (e.g., perpetrator's loss of freedom).
- Sympathetic nervous system initiates physiological changes, such as increased heart rate.

IMPORTANT NOTE
- A guilty person may perceive that the interrogator believes them, may become comfortable, and may display little stress.
- An innocent person may perceive that the interrogator does not believe them, may become uncomfortable, and may display much stress.

ALTERED BEHAVIOR
- Nonverbal clues are harder to conceal than verbal clues.
- If the interrogator points out nervous behavior, the suspect may try to alter their behavior.
- There is no single behavior that indicates absolute guilt.

FIVE FACTORS FOR NONVERBAL BEHAVIORS
1. Proxemics
2. Psychological aspects
3. Memory
4. Eye movement
5. Specific body parts

PROXEMICS
- Examination of personal space based on cultural, behavioral, and sociological aspects.
- The interrogator may manipulate the comfort space to increase or decrease the intensity of the interaction.
- The suspect may also adjust the comfort zone to manipulate the interrogator.
- For example, the suspect may move away from the interrogator in order to reduce stress.
- Nothing should be placed between the suspect and the interrogator.
- The interrogator should never get closer than 2 feet from the suspect.
- The purpose is not to threaten the suspect, but rather to control the suspect's attempt to cushion the stress level.

PSYCHOLOGICAL ASPECTS
- The automatic nervous system is primarily subconscious and is beyond the control of the conscious mind.
- It controls the heart, smooth muscles (such as blood vessels), and internal glands and organs.
- The suspect may not know that they are exhibiting signs.
- The sympathetic nervous system is of particular interest.

SYMPATHETIC NERVOUS SYSTEM
- Inhibits certain functions while preparing the body for a stressful situation.
- Peripheral blood flow is constricted, causing blood flow to the skin to decrease and overall blood flow to the heart and muscles to increase to help prepare the body for "flight or fight."
- Adrenaline is released and blood-sugar level is increased.
- Heart rate and breathing increase.

MEMORY

- Deceptive persons experience more memory lapses than persons telling the truth.
- May be due to repression, where the suspect has hidden the event from conscious thought.
- May be because the person is too emotional to discuss the event.
- Very often it is due to intentional memory loss, so suspect does not have to lie.
- If asked about a specific event, the suspect will most likely remember.
- Once the suspect remembers a specific fact, other facts will fall into place and this will make memory lapse more unbelievable.

EYE MOVEMENT (LEFT SIDE OF BRAIN = LOGIC; RIGHT SIDE OF BRAIN = CREATIVITY)

- Relates to where a person looks after being asked a question while they are thinking about the answer.
- By observing eye movements, the interrogator may tell whether the suspect is telling the truth or lying.
- A baseline is established during the baseline assessment phase of the interrogation.
- Positions are accurate about 90% of the time.
- The other 10% may be left-handed people who look in the opposite direction.
- There are exceptions to the rule; therefore, a baseline is needed.
- Ask questions to get the suspect to recall actual visual images.

From the interrogator's point of view when facing a suspect, the suspect's eyes:

- Up and to right = the person is recalling something visual that was actually experienced (truth).
- To the side and right = the person is recalling sounds actually experienced (truth).
- Down and to right = the person is getting in touch with their inner feelings or internal dialogue; talking to self.
- Up and to left = the person is creating something visually, probably not something actually experienced (lie).
- To the side and to the left = the person is creating an auditory thought (lie).
- Down and to the left = the person is thinking about their feelings.

It should be pointed out research studies have challenged the relationship between eye movement and truth/deceit (Wolchover, 2012). Research results have indicated that an interrogator cannot detect deceit via eye movement.

SPECIFIC BODY PARTS: HEAD

- Tilted = listening.
- Straight = listening, may be angry.
- Chin hits chest = depression, resignation.
- Head in hands = thinking about what was said and may be an indication of internal dialogue.
- Pyramid with hands = the suspect feels superior.
- Thinking pose (elbow on knee, fists on forehead) = the suspect is probably faking paying attention and trying to think around the topic.
- Untruthful persons will roll their head in an effort to stretch tense neck muscles = movements are quick and jerky.
- Tilt head down = submissive attitude.
- Tilt head back = arrogance; elevate self above the act in question.

SPECIFIC BODY PARTS: FACIAL EXPRESSION
- Includes mouth, eyes, nose, and complexion.
- A person who smiles and uses the whole mouth is likely truthful.
- If they show only the upper teeth, then the suspect feels they are in control of the situation.
- An overly concerned pleasant look on face is a sign that they are disguising their outward appearance to avoid revealing their fear.
- Flushing in face is an indication of fear – blood flow to large muscles due to stress response.
- Redness is a sign of anger – due to increased blood pressure.
- Eyes and lips become darker – lack of oxygen due to stress.
- Suspect freezes face – attempting to hide what is going on inside.
- Facial twitching – a quarter to half a second in duration – is a sign of stress.
- During stress, blood pressure in the nose changes, causing the nose to become irritated and itch. Thus, deceptive persons touch their noses more often.
- Muscles around mouth are controlled involuntarily by genuine emotions.
- It is hard to fake a smile that appears sincere.
- The suspect may attempt to deceive the interrogator by, for example, crying for the victim when the suspect is actually crying because they are close to getting caught.
- Quick, surprised-sounding laughs or inappropriate smirks are a sign of being insincere or deceptive.
- The carotid artery often pulsates visibly and shakes the Adam's apple when the suspect is stressed.

SPECIFIC BODY PARTS: EYE BLINKING
- A change in the amount of eye blinking is a sign of deceit—use baseline for reference.
- If the eyelids stay closed for longer than normal during an interrogation, it may be a sign of stress and that the suspect does not want to look at the interrogator.
- A decrease in the amount of blinking can be a sign of intense internal dialogue and that the suspect is considering whether to confess; it may indicate an increased interest in what the interrogator is talking about.
- Squint = nervous.
- Glance up and stare at the interrogator more than usual = nervous.
- Persons who wears glasses may push them up on the nose to hide their eyes.
- Glasses may slide down due to sweat.

SPECIFIC BODY PARTS: EYE CONTACT
- The average person maintains eye contact 40–60% of the time during conversations.
- Too much or too little eye contact may be a sign of deceit.
- May be influenced by culture or other social norms.
- Too much eye contact may be an attempt to show truthfulness or interest or to see how the interrogator is reacting.
- Too little eye contact may be an attempt to avoid looking at the interrogator so that behaviors are not identified through the eyes.

SPECIFIC BODY PARTS: MOUTH

- Yawning may indicate the need for oxygen due to the emotional demands of the interrogation.
- Yawning may be used to feign disinterest or to buy time.
- Yawning may mean the suspect is tired or bored with the interrogation.
- Keep time of day and duration of interrogation in mind when evaluating yawning.
- Breathing more rapidly = signs of deception.
- An untruthful person will breathe about 18–22 times more per minute than a truthful person.
- Breathing will be shallow, causing the suspect to gasp and sigh occasionally.
- Attempting to hide mouth may indicate trying to stop the mouth from what it is saying.
- Biting lips = sign of stress.
- Dry mouth = stress causes mouth to produce less saliva so will produce clicking sound.
- An untruthful suspect will try to wet lips and swallow more often.
- An untruthful suspect will ask for water more often.

SPECIFIC BODY PARTS: SHOULDERS AND HANDS

- Shrug shoulders = denial.
- Dropping or hunching shoulders = depression or acceptance.
- Pulling shoulders back while tightening the neck = anger.
- Protecting vital areas = stressed, threatened.
- Hugs self = self-reliance.
- Elbows and hands loose to side = relaxed.
- Excessive hand usage = nervousness (depends on culture) or poor verbal skills.
- Jerky movements = untruthful.
- Excessive rubbing = deception.
- Changes in motor skills (e.g., when writing statement) = deceptive behavior.

SPECIFIC BODY PARTS: LEGS

- Wiggling, shaking, or bouncing feet is a sign of stress.
- Slides feet under chair, especially if crossing legs while doing this = stress.
- Turns and crosses legs so that they are facing away from interrogator = rejection.
- If legs are open and facing interrogator = acceptance.
- If the suspect puts one leg out in front = maintaining distance between them and the interrogator.
- If suspect points one leg toward door = ready to leave.
- Feet flat on floor, toes pointed inward = sign of introverted person.
- Feet flat on floor, toes pointed outward = person may feel uncomfortable or superior.
- Crosses legs higher up on the knee compared with ankle = defensive posture.
- Women may cross legs according to norms of culture.
- Truthful persons may also display these signs if they become uncomfortable during the interrogation.

> **SPECIFIC BODY PARTS: SITTING POSITION**
>
> - Sitting as though ready to run, leaning to one side with feet under weight of body (may also be facing door) = stress and wants to leave.
> - Slouched back with legs kicked out, hands draped over side of chair, or hands tucked in pants = trying to appear macho or overtly bored.
> - Turning chair backwards = trying to distance self from interrogator (barrier).
> - A relaxed person will move around and change positions while sitting in a chair.
> - A deceptive person may freeze their body into one position for long periods of time, clenching fists, maintaining rigid posture, and sitting on hands.
> - A deceptive person will move the chair before sitting down and will angle it away from the interrogator; may move the chair away from the interrogator or sit in it sideways to protect abdominal area (i.e., vulnerable area).

CHAPTER PROBLEMS

1. Discuss how law enforcement utilizes biometrics.
2. Discuss how police officers interpret the movement of arms, legs, and hands.
3. How will it be interpreted if a suspect squares off to the interrogator face to face and moves their head on important syllables while speaking?
4. How will it be interpreted if a suspect makes statements that are not absolute and provides information without including a third person's point of view?
5. How will it be interpreted if a suspect constantly questions someone else's motives and starts sentences with "To tell the truth …?"
6. How will it be interpreted if a suspect asks the interrogator to repeat a question and then states that they do not have exactly what the interrogator is looking for, but they have something similar.
7. Discuss 10 verbal ways to assess the truth. Provide examples for each.
8. Discuss how eye blinking and eye contact can be used to assess the truth.
9. Discuss how the sympathetic nervous system can be used to assess the truth.
10. Discuss how an interrogator can take advantage of human behavior to reach the truth.

KEYWORDS

Biometrics
Body language
Conscious behavior
Kinesics
Red herring
Subconscious behavior
Unconscious behavior
Verbal communication
Voice inflection

REFERENCES

BodyLanguageCards.com (n.d.). www.bodylanguagecards.com

Erskine, J. (Producer/Director), & Cleese, J. (Writer). (2001). *The human face* [Motion picture]. BBC via AOL Time Warner.

Hatch, J. (2002). *Doing qualitative research in education settings.* Albany, NY: State University of New York Press.

Inbau, F.E., Reid, J.E., Buckley, J.P., & Jayne, B.C. (2005). *Essentials of the Reid technique: Criminal interrogation and confessions.* Boston: Jones and Bartlett.

Jackson, D.M. (2004). *In your face: The facts about your features.* New York: Viking.

Lambert, D. (2008). *Body language 101: The ultimate guide to knowing when people are lying, how they are feeling, what they are thinking, and more.* New York: Skyhorse.

Lieberman, D.J. (1998). *Never be lied to again: How to get the truth in 5 minutes or less in any conversation or situation.* New York: St. Martin's Press.

McNichol, A. & Nelson, J.A. (1994). *Handwriting analysis: Putting it to work for you.* New York: McGraw-Hill.

Meyer, P. (2010). *Lie spotting: Proven techniques to detect deception.* New York: St. Martin's Press.

Pease, A., & Pease B. (2004a). *The definitive book of body language.* New York: Bantam.

Pease, B., & Pease A. (2004b). *Why men don't have a clue and women always need more shoes: The ultimate guide to the opposite sex.* New York: Broadway.

Pollock, J.M. (2004). *Ethics in crime and justice: Dilemmas & decisions.* Belmont, CA: Thompson-Wadsworth.

Ricee, S. (2021). Subconscious vs unconscious: The complete comparison. *Diversity for Social Impact.* https://diversity.social/unconscious-vs-subconscious

Starrett, P., & Davis, J.N. (2006). *Interview & interrogation with eyewitness evidence* (2nd ed.) (2006). San Clemente, CA: LawTech.

Thompson, G.J., & Jenkins, J.B. (2004). *Verbal judo: The gentle art of persuasion.* New York: Harper.

Wolchover, N. (2012). *Notion that liars glance to the right debunked.* www.livescience.com/34068-eye-movements-lying.html

Zulawski, D.E., & Wicklander, D.E. (2002). *Practical aspects of interview and interrogation* (2nd ed.). New York: CRC.

CHAPTER 12

Interrogation Techniques

LEARNING OBJECTIVE

Apply different interrogation techniques.

INTRODUCTION

An interrogation is conducted in a controlled environment and is an interaction between the government and a suspect in which the government is accusing the suspect of a crime. The goal is for the police to persuade the suspect to tell the truth so incriminating evidence may be collected and used against the suspect in court. Because the goal of police is to investigate crimes and to discover the truth, and because officers commonly encounter suspects who are less than truthful during the interrogation process, the police have a variety of interrogation techniques at their disposal that they can employ to achieve their goal. During the interrogation process, the police may give the perception that they are friends with the suspect, that the violation was not that serious, and that they themselves may have wanted to act in a similar way in the past. However, the police do this as a ruse to get the suspect to confess to the crime. The police are allowed to be less than truthful and to set traps during the interrogation process. Furthermore, the interrogator may expand or shrink the proximity to the suspect in the interrogation room in an effort to manipulate the outcome. However, suspects may sometimes make false confessions. Thus, it is always important for officers to verify that each confession is valid.

INTERROGATION

Unlike an interview, which is a free-flowing, non-accusatory meeting used to collect information, an interrogation is an interaction with accusations between the government and suspect, which is conducted in a controlled environment with the goal of persuading the suspect to tell the truth (Inbau et al., 2005). The interrogator's goal is to obtain useful information that may be used against the suspect in court. Thus, to get the suspect to talk, it is important to develop a rapport or comfort level with the suspect.

Before the interrogator asks the suspect any questions directly related to the crime under investigation, the interrogator should spend a few minutes to develop a relationship of common ground with the suspect (Inbau et al., 2005). The interrogator may discuss sports, hobbies, or something else to which they can both relate. Another way to develop rapport with the suspect is to mirror the suspect's behavior. For example, if the suspect has a habit of flicking their hair back, then the interrogator may flick their own hair back (Barth, 2004). The interrogator can start the process by checking the spelling of the suspect's last name (Inbau et al., 2005). Then the interrogator may ask the suspect about their social security number, phone number, and current employment. The information may help guide the rest of the interview.

In order to become better informed and to determine whether the suspect is the likely perpetrator, the interrogator should conduct an interview with the suspect prior to conducting the interrogation (Inbau et al., 2005). The interviewer should, if possible, be thoroughly familiar with the facts of the case before beginning the interview. Because the officer needs to determine whether a crime has actually been committed, the alleged victim should be interviewed first. Following the victim, the investigator should interview the suspects who are least likely to be guilty of the crime and work toward the more likely suspect. By doing this, the officer will have more intelligence when interrogating the actual perpetrator. When interviewing a suspect, the officer should ask the suspect what they believe happened, who they believe is the perpetrator, and why they believe the person committed the crime (i.e., the motive).

Once the interrogation starts, the interrogator should generally make an introductory statement (Inbau et al., 2005). The introductory statement has three purposes: to clearly identify the crime being discussed; to establish the interrogator's objectivity; and to persuade the suspect that their lies will be detected. It has been shown that an introductory statement increases both the suspect's truthful and deceptive behavioral symptoms. Below is an example of an introductory statement.

> Victor, during the interview today, we will be discussing the allegation made against you. I want you to understand my role, which is to establish the truth. When I interview a person, it does not matter to me, one way or another, what the person did, as long as they tell the truth. Sometimes a person may be afraid to acknowledge certain statements because they may be afraid of how others may perceive it. However, if a person lies about something small, then there is a natural tendency to believe that the person might be lying about something big. Therefore, it is very important for you to tell the complete truth today.

After the introductory statement, the interrogator should begin the interrogation with an initial open-ended question (Inbau et al., 2005). The open-ended question allows the suspect to provide a narrative response. The interrogator may remain silent during the process to encourage the suspect to keep talking. Forced silence by the interrogator may create an ambience that encourages the suspect to provide a full response to the open-ended question. Following is an example of an initial open-ended question.

> Please tell me everything you know about the mascot prank at your school last Friday night.

Table 12.1 Signs of truthfulness (Inbau et al., 2005)

Similar level of detail throughout the statement	Although one individual may provide a different level of detail than another individual, each person interrogated should provide similar amounts of detail throughout their own statement.
Information out-of-sequence	People have primary and secondary memories. The primary memories, which are the most important facts, may stimulate secondary memories, which are less important facts. Secondary memories may be stimulated out of sequence.
Personal thoughts and feelings expressed	Because emotional states are psychologically linked to behaviors, a truthful statement often includes what the person felt or thought at the time of the incident.

Table 12.2 Signs of deception (Inbau et al., 2005)

Detail level varies	If a suspect is very detailed for most of the statement, then suddenly becomes quite vague, the change in behavior is suspicious.
Perfect chronological order	Although a person who has retold the account many times over may remember things in chronological order, an account that fails to make out-of-sequence statements may indicate rehearsal and the account is suspicious.

Table 12.2 Cont.

Missing personal thoughts and feelings	Individuals' emotions are intertwined with their behaviors. Thus, when a person is deceitful, they only say the facts and nothing but the facts. They fail to mention emotions that should be attached to their actions. "When I heard it, I was afraid …"
Gap-in-time statements	When a person makes a statement that skips some time, the statement is suspicious. It may be because the suspect did something during the time that they are trying to conceal. "I arrived at 3:00 pm. Before I knew it …"
Implied-action statements	Incomplete statements that require the interrogator to make assumptions are suspicious. The statement, "He started to hit me …" does not claim that the action was completed.

Interrogation questions need to be asked so that they provide the information sought. In other words, the questions need to be valid. First, the interrogator's questions should not bias the responses. Second, the questions need to elicit responses that cannot be interpreted in more than one way. Finally, the questions should be asked in a way that does not trigger defensive mechanisms, which may prevent the suspect from providing complete information.

Table 12.3 Techniques for interrogation questions (Inbau et al., 2005)

Rule	Example
Whenever practical, ask open-ended questions because they allow for more complete information without influence by the interrogator.	Closed-ended: Were you at the school on Saturday? Open-ended: Why were you at the school on Saturday?
Do not use aggressive language that triggers defensive reactions.	Incorrect: Did you steal the item? Correct: Did you take the item?
Do not use compound questions.	Incorrect: Did you see the item and did you take the item? Correct: Did you see the item? Did you take the item?
Direct questions should be short and to the point.	Did you talk to Jim on Saturday?
Do not provide memory qualifiers in the question.	Incorrect: Do you remember if Jim called you? Correct: Did Jim ever call you?
Do not ask negative questions.	Incorrect: You did not do it, did you?

Table 12.4 Handling less than complete/truthful responses (Inbau et al., 2005)

Less than complete/truthful responses	Interrogator's response
Responses that do not offer a definite answer ("I was at the school last month …").	Rephrase the same question ("Were you at the school yesterday?").
Responses that contain words that decrease the suspect's confidence or personal commitment ("To the best of my knowledge …").	Ask a hypothetical question ("Is it possible …?").
Responses that omit information ("I did commit a crime when I was 12 …").	Ask a follow-up question ("Besides that time …?").

Police officers conduct interrogations for the purpose of collecting information, which is needed in an investigation (Swanson et al., 2009). The four main objectives of an interrogation are to obtain important facts, to eliminate innocent individuals, to identify the perpetrators, and to obtain a confession. The interrogator governs the interrogation process and setting. The interrogator must ensure privacy and control the interruptions, planned or otherwise, because privacy may be the psychological tool needed to get the perpetrator to confess. Perpetrators may be more willing to talk to a single person in a private setting.

Before police officers can effectively conduct interviews or interrogations, they must familiarize themselves with the case (Swanson, et al., 2009). An officer must become familiar with the offense, the victims, and the suspect. By analyzing crime scene evidence and by theorizing about the motives, the interrogator may develop a suspect profile, which may suggest a plan of attack. See Table 12.5 for a pre-interrogation checklist.

Table 12.5 Pre-interrogation checklist (Swanson et al., 2009)

Number	Information important to interrogator
1	Law book description of the crime; elements of the crime
2	Perpetrator's motive and method of operation
3	Tools or weapons used by perpetrator
4	Time, date, and location of offense
5	Nature and value of damage
6	Physical evidence collected, including witness statements
7	Names of individuals who have information about the crime
8	Entrance and exit points of perpetrator
9	Entrance and exit routes of perpetrator
10	Weather conditions at time of crime
11	Method of perpetrator's travel to and from the crime scene
12	Details for other cases with the same modus operandi

FALSE CONFESSIONS

Although false confessions are rare, it is known that some individuals have intentionally provided false information and have claimed to have committed crimes when they did not in fact commit the crimes (Inbau et al., 2005). In some cases, after the individuals were convicted, DNA testing had identified other individuals as the perpetrators. There are five factors that appear to be consistently related to false confessions, which are: (1) the suspect is a juvenile; (2) the suspect has a mental or psychological impairment; (3) the suspect was interrogated for an inordinate amount of time; (4) the suspect was coerced with threats or promises; and (5) the suspect seeks fame and recognition.

Suspect is a Juvenile and/or has a Mental or Psychological Impairment

Juveniles and the mentally or psychologically impaired do commit serious crimes. Interrogators must use caution when interrogating juveniles or individuals who have mental or psychological impairments (Inbau, et al., 2005). If a juvenile is less than 15 years of age and has never been interrogated in the past, the officer should carefully discuss each point of the Miranda rights to ensure that the child understands them. If the child does not understand their rights, the interrogator should not conduct an interrogation.

When a juvenile or mentally or psychologically impaired person confesses, the interrogator must corroborate the information (Inbau, et al., 2005). This can be achieved when the interrogator withholds specific details about the crime from the suspect. This allows the interrogator to verify the confession's authenticity. When an interrogator corroborates a confession, the confession becomes more credible.

Suspect was Coerced or Interrogated for an Inordinate Amount of Time

A suspect's rights must be respected at all times. A police officer who uses force and/or threats (i.e., coercion) during an interrogation may be personally sanctioned. Although there is no absolute rule about the length of an interrogation, a typically interrogation usually lasts about one to two hours (Starrett & Davis, 2006). Using improper interrogation techniques and tactics may disqualify a suspect's confession from being admitted in court. Therefore, an interrogator should not make any threats or promises of leniency, and should not use physically abusive tactics to gain a confession. See Table 12.6 for examples of improper threats and/or promises.

Table 12.6 Examples of improper threats and/or promises (Inbau, et al., 2005)

Examples of improper interrogation techniques
You will face the death penalty unless you confess.
The police will hound you every day for the rest of your life if you do not confess.
If you do not confess, we will lock up all your family members.
If you confess, we will release you and you will be free to sleep in your own bed tonight.
The police do not let the suspect sleep for three days until they confess.
The police slap the suspect on their hands with a ruler until they confess.

CREDIBILITY OF CONFESSION

The interrogator should assess the credibility of a confession (Inbau, et al., 2005). If a confession is credible, it will be valid and reliable. Credibility involves the likelihood of being true. The higher the credibility, the more believable the confession will be. A high degree of credibility is important because the judge or jury will need to be convinced that the suspect is guilty of the crime beyond a reasonable doubt. If the suspect changes their story in court and the available evidence does not support the suspect's guilt, then the case may fall apart (this does not mean other charges will not be filed against the suspect). See the following table for factors that may impact the credibility of a suspect's confession.

Table 12.7 Credibility of a suspect's confession (Inbau, et al., 2005)

#	Factors that impact the credibility of a confession
1	Suspect's age (e.g., may be too young to understand what is happening)
2	Suspect's prior experience with the Miranda warning
3	Suspect's culture and understanding of the language
4	Suspect's behavior during the interrogation (e.g., body language)
5	Addressing suspect's physical needs (e.g., refusing to let suspect use the restroom)
6	Presence of witnesses during interrogation (e.g., suspect may refuse to confess if family members are present)
7	Suspect's physical, mental, and psychological condition
8	Length of interrogation (e.g., continuously questioning a suspect for two straight days)
9	The degree of detail that the suspect provides (e.g., information that only someone at the crime scene would know)
10	The interrogator's corroboration of the suspect's confession
11	The use of illegal interrogation techniques (e.g., use of pain to gain a confession)

People like to talk in order to reduce the psychological and physiological pressures that build internally (Swanson et al., 2009). It has been estimated that about 80% of all individuals will confess to a crime. Of the 80% confessions, some of these individuals are actually guilty and some are actually not guilty. Thus, convictions cannot be based on confessions alone. In other words, police officers need to corroborate each confession.

Most guilty suspects look for an opportunity to confess during an interrogation (Swanson et al., 2009). A good interrogator will provide the suspect an opportunity to confess, which will reduce the perpetrator's internal psychological and physiological pressures. In short, the interrogator's job is to make the confession easy for the perpetrator.

There are many different interrogation techniques. The following information provides an overview of various interrogation techniques (Anonymous, 1991; Inbau et al., 2005; Starrett & Davis, 2006; Zulawski & Wicklander, 2002). Multiple techniques may be combined to get the best results.

Table 12.8 Interrogation techniques

Below are 48 different interrogation techniques.

Dumb and dumber	File gimmick	Good cop, bad cop	Someone always talks
Appeal to authority	Mistake	Split pair bluff	Other guy
Everyone's doing it	Heaven and hell (hot and cold)	Can you take it back?	Compulsion to confess
Blame someone else	Appeal to intelligence	Extension	Service club or society
Appeal to intellect	Double stick (agent provocateur)	Hot confession	Conscience
Respect for position in society	Lawyer gimmick	Logical	I want you to talk
Publicity	Exaggeration	Drunk	Special needs
Face-saving	Relative	Ego deflation	Blame society
Control gimmick	Flattery	Yes or no (last chance appeal)	Technique for juveniles
Oedipus	Secretary	Conspiracy	Car thief
Suggestibility	White collar	What would you do?	Interrogation of females
Accident	Behavioral symptom	Pyramid of lies	Fetish

DUMB AND DUMBER TECHNIQUE

- There will be two interrogators.
- The first officer will provide a dumb reason for the motive of the crime.
- The second officer will disagree with the first officer and will provide a dumber motive for the crime.
- The goal is to get the suspect to agree with the first dumb motive because the second dumb motive is more ridiculous, and perhaps more embarrassing.
- It is possible that the suspect will disagree with both motives because they are both ridiculous, and the suspect may actually argue with the officers and provide the real motive.

EXAMPLE: THEFT

"I believe the suspect stole the bracelet because he was in love, it was Valentine's Day, and he was simply out of time and money. He had to provide his girlfriend with a gift or else he never would have heard the end of it. Believe me, I forgot flowers one day for my wife's birthday and my wife nagged and nagged. Stealing the bracelet was a minor cost compared to not giving her anything. Any man would understand and would have done the same in a pinch. This kind of dedication is Hollywood-type material."

"No, that is not right. He stole the bracelet because it was the patriotic thing to do. He was simply trying to create jobs. Think of some of the jobs that he has created related to this case. He has provided work for us, court personnel, jailers, food suppliers, and medical personnel, to name a few. By creating jobs, he has actually boosted the economy. In my opinion, it was the American thing to do. I am sure that the jury will probably see that his act has benefited society. He took the item because he was simply trying to help his fellow citizens when they needed it the most."

APPEAL TO AUTHORITY TECHNIQUE

- The interrogator must make an authentic statement.
- The interrogator must be flexible.
- The interrogator must be able to think of words and phrases on the spot.
- The interrogator should never use words that indicate their true feelings about the crime under investigation.
- The interrogator should avoid facial expressions that give feelings away.

EXAMPLE: RAPE

"I have heard some world-famous psychiatrists say that alpha males, such as you, are inclined to be sexually dominant. However, most of us never have the chance to be so sexually active. For one reason or another, dominant males experience a natural condition that prevents them from controlling their sex drives. There is a drive for them to spread their seed. According to Darwin, it is natural for the strong to mate and reproduce. When you think about it, this has been going on since caveman days."

EVERYBODY'S DOING IT TECHNIQUE

- The interrogator needs to play down the seriousness of the crime.
- The interrogator must assure the suspect that everyone in the world is doing it too.

EXAMPLE: SEX CRIME

"Son, do you think you are the only red-blooded male who has ever touched a girl? Guys think about it all the time. However, most of us don't have the guts to do anything about it. Girls feel the same way. Sex is just human nature; it's natural. People would think that you are strange if you didn't think about it. The way they dress and act, the broad was probably asking for it."

BLAME SOMEONE ELSE TECHNIQUE

- The interrogator needs to size up suspect (physically).
- Short and fat physique—humor them.
- Tall and slender—appeal to intellect.

EXAMPLE: THEFT

"I don't blame you for stealing a car radio from Ford Motor Company. They won't miss it with all of their millions of dollars. With how little they pay you, they owe it to you. I probably would have taken a lot more. I don't blame you at all for what you did."

APPEAL TO INTELLECT TECHNIQUE

- The interrogator needs to close the gap between the interrogator's communication level and the suspect's superior communication level.
- This technique is effective when dealing with a person with superior education or intellect and the interrogator cannot challenge the suspect in their field.
- The interrogator brings the suspect closer to their own level of education.
- The interrogator plays upon the suspect's intellect.
- The interrogator will not attach any blame to the suspect.
- The interrogator will not mention the criminal act.
- The interrogator seeks to elicit a rationalization for the act.

EXAMPLE: SEXUAL DEVIANCE

"Doctor, by community standards, you are the most respected man in society. I just can't comprehend how a man of your intellect could be involved in something like this. Please help me understand the reason for this."

RESPECT FOR POSITION IN SOCIETY TECHNIQUE

- The interrogator may be required to interrogate someone who is beyond reproach (e.g., priest).
- The interrogator must be flexible and able to ad lib.
- The interrogator must have and use a repertoire of words and phrases.
- The interrogator must keep referring to the fact that the suspect is well respected in society.

EXAMPLE: SEXUAL MISCONDUCT

"Father, most everyone respects you. I respect you. Your parishioners respect you. Since this incident happened, I have no doubt that you prayed and asked for forgiveness. Don't let us down; we respect and love you. I know in the end that this whole situation will come out right."

PUBLICITY TECHNIQUE

- The interrogator needs to refer to the amount of publicity that may result if the public ever finds out that the suspect was involved in this criminal act.
- The interrogator should never condemn the suspect.
- The interrogator should always provide the suspect with a way out.

EXAMPLE: PUBLICITY

"Sir, this matter is going to break the hearts of a lot of the people who know and love you. I just hope that there are not a lot of media in the courtroom. Maybe I can get you into court during the lunch hour, when few people will be around to see. The very last thing we want to do is to have to bring your family down to police headquarters to interview them about this situation. If we both just think really hard, maybe we can figure something out. There must be some kind of reason for what happened here. Our main goal is to keep this matter out of the press because we do not need all that attention. Can you arrange to take a vacation after this situation blows over?"

FACE-SAVING TECHNIQUE

- The interrogator supplies a justification for the incident so the suspect may save face.
- The interrogator blames someone else.
- The interrogator supplies the suspect with an excuse so that the suspect may rationalize the crime.
- The interrogator only seeks a confession and does not care about the suspect's rationalization for committing the crime.

EXAMPLE: SEXUAL MISCONDUCT

"I just don't know what gets into these kids these days. They want to try these things out and then they complain. You know those 14-year-old girls look like 20-year-old women with those short mini-skirts and makeup. I have no doubt that these girls nowadays may even ask for it. You know, nine out of 10 times these girls are to blame."

CONTROL GIMMICK TECHNIQUE

- The interrogator makes a point to let the suspect know that the interrogator is in complete control; the interrogator demonstrates authority over the suspect.
- The interrogator tells the suspect where to sit, to refrain from smoking, and so on.
- The interrogator should not use a threatening voice.
- The interrogator may let the suspect ramble.
- The interrogator may use suggestive questioning to steer the interrogation back on course.
- The interrogator must never let the suspect control the interrogation.

OEDIPUS TECHNIQUE

- The interrogator breaks down suspects who are charged with incest.
- This is a face-saving technique; blames human nature.
- Children are attracted to their opposite-sex parent and jealous of their same-sex parent.
- The interrogator should tell the story of Oedipus, who was separated from his parents, killed his father, and married his mother; once the mother realized that Oedipus was her son, she committed suicide.
- In addition, a sense of inferiority during childhood (e.g., small stature) may cause individuals to overcompensate for their disadvantage via violence; give examples such as Hitler, Napoleon, and Mussolini.
- The interrogator should research the family tree to see whether the suspect had siblings and a two-parent household, whether the father or mother was liked better, and whether the suspect felt they had to continually prove themself.

EXAMPLE: INCEST

- The interrogator will tell the suspect that the Oedipus complex exists in everyone, especially during childhood development.
- Sometimes, the repressed desire for the opposite-sex parent shows through the superego, resulting in incest – this is not the suspect's fault.
- If a male child did not have a father figure, he will learn feminine traits from his mother.
- If a female child did not have a mother figure, she will learn masculine traits from her father.
- Interrogator should go along with the suspect and suggest that larger and more powerful people are always picking on them.

SUGGESTIBILITY TECHNIQUE

- The interrogator appeals to the suspect's subconscious attitudes via direct suggestion.
- The interrogator sets the stage for a confession; this is similar to the face-saving technique but blames self-circumstances.
- The interrogator may suggest a reduced power of recall (e.g., due to intoxication) and suggest to the suspect that they may not have realized what they were doing.
- The interrogator may suggest a necessity for the crime (e.g., sickness in the family).
- The interrogator suggests possible justifications to persuade the suspect to accept a justification for committing the crime.

EXAMPLE: BREAKING AND ENTERING

The interrogator may suggest that a suspect committed a break and enter because of family financial problems (needed money to feed kids), family sickness (needed money for child's medicine), peer pressure, jealously caused by someone else's actions, or overindulgence in alcoholic beverages.

ACCIDENT TECHNIQUE

- The interrogator will blame the victim, but claim the situation was the result of an accident or misunderstanding.
- For example, the interrogator will claim that the sexual encounter was consensual up to a point, that the victim fell on the knife during the event, or that the gun fired accidentally.
- The interrogator will provide the suspect with a ready-made excuse for whatever happened during the crime; this will allow the suspect to rationalize the event.
- The goal is to get an admission; it does not matter what the excuse is.

FILE GIMMICK TECHNIQUE

- The interrogator will use a black marker to print the suspect's name in large block letters on the outside of the file so the suspect can see their name.
- The interrogator will sit in a chair, pretend to scan the contents of the file, and have an indifferent attitude.

EXAMPLE: BLANK FILE

- The interrogator will occasionally nod their head, as if confirming what was found in the file, and the interrogator will look oddly at the suspect.
- The interrogator will continue to nod and give odd looks at the suspect, which will make the suspect believe that the interrogator has conclusive evidence on file. After a while, the interrogator will ask the suspect to explain what happened.

MISTAKE TECHNIQUE

- This technique is most effective with first-time offenders or juveniles.
- The interrogator will suggest that the suspect took the item by mistake and afterwards was too afraid to return it for fear of being blamed for theft.
- The interrogator will imply that the suspect is just a victim of circumstances, which could happen to anyone.
- The interrogator will imply that the situation was created only because the suspect was trying to do the right thing.
- The interrogator will state that most people would admire such a person.

HEAVEN AND HELL TECHNIQUE (HOT AND COLD TECHNIQUE)

- This technique has been used in religion and brainwashing.
- The interrogator lets the subject see "hell" and then offers the suspect a piece of "heaven" as an alternative.
- The interrogator keeps repeating glimpses of hell and then offers some comfort.
- The interrogator will isolate the suspect and dress the suspect sloppily; the suspect will lose their dignity and identity, and will feel forsaken.
- Near the beginning of the interrogation, the interrogator will offer the suspect a reward, such as a drink; the interrogator may indicate that the suspect may be removed from isolation.
- The suspect starts to regain their identity and starts to believe that, by cooperating with those individuals in power, the damage may be minimized.

EXAMPLE: HELL THEN HEAVEN

- The interrogator will hint at loss of job, loss of children's respect, loss of wife, loss of preferred sexual activity.
- The interrogator may hint about what the suspect's young wife will do while he is in prison because she is beautiful and others will want her.
- The interrogator will ask about what the neighbors will think.
- The interrogator will imply that there will be no publicity, the neighbors will not find out, and there might be a way to save the suspect's job and social status.

APPEAL TO INTELLIGENCE OR CONSCIENCE TECHNIQUE

- The interrogator will stay away from the actual crime committed and will focus on the weapons or drugs.
- The interrogator will state that an innocent child may get hurt due to the abandoned drugs or weapons.
- The interrogator only needs the suspect to confirm that the weapons or drugs are not a danger to anyone.

EXAMPLE: CRIME WITH A GUN

"You have a child, and you know how kids have a tendency to find things in strange places. I hope you stashed that gun of yours very well. I wouldn't want your kid to accidently find that gun and to hurt or kill himself or another child. Did you hide the gun so that your kid, or any kid, won't find it?"

DOUBLE STICK (AGENT PROVOCATEUR) TECHNIQUE

- The interrogator will place agent provocateur #1 in the cell next to the suspect.
- The interrogator will place agent provocateur #2 in another cell next to the suspect so provocateur #2 can overhear the conversation between the suspect and provocateur #1.
- Only provocateur #1 will interact with the suspect.
- Provocateur #1 will pretend to show empathy for the suspect and will attempt to get the suspect to talk about the crime.

EXAMPLE: DRUG ARREST

Provocateur #1 may discuss the items below.

- People demand drugs.
- A person cannot get a job these days due to the recession.
- A father needs to feed his kids.
- No one was hurt.
- There are more important crimes for the police to enforce.

LAWYER GIMMICK TECHNIQUE

- The interrogator will imply, but will not say, that the suspect will waste money by hiring a lawyer.
- The interrogator should tell the suspect that if they are guilty, they will need to hire a very good lawyer; however, no one—including the lawyer—will be able to help the suspect.
- Only the suspect can help their own case by admitting what they have done so that they can get help; this is the first big step on the road to recovery.
- The longer the interrogator talks without interruption, the more likely it is that the suspect is guilty.

EXAMPLE: LAWYER

The interrogator will ask the suspect why they would waste good money on an expensive lawyer if they were innocent. If the suspect is guilty, however, they should hire a good lawyer because they will need it. The interrogator will tell the suspect that only they can help their situation—not their parents, their priest, their lawyer, or even their doctor will be able to help them until they tell the truth and admit that they have made a mistake. Once the suspect takes that first big step toward recovery, they will be able to receive the proper treatment.

EXAGGERATION TECHNIQUE

- The interrogator will enlarge the seriousness of the crime, increase the number of charges, or inflate the dollar value of the crime.
- The suspect may confess to one crime in order to deny the other charges.
- The interrogator should keep referring to the more serious charges when discussing the crimes.
- This creates an imbalance in the suspect's mind.
- The suspect does not know for sure whether they will be convicted; therefore, they may confess to avoid getting a harsher punishment.

EXAMPLE: SIMPLE THEFT

The objective is to get the suspect to say, "I only broke into one home, not 25."

> "So, we finally got the person who has broken into at least 25 homes. Your trademark has been found all over town. Being convicted of 25 charges will surely rack up a great many years in prison."

RELATIVE TECHNIQUE

- The interrogator will attempt to establish rapport with the suspect.
- The interrogator will keep insinuating that the suspect is a distant relative (i.e., the suspect resembles the interrogator's relative).
- The interrogator will intentionally and continually make mistakes by calling the suspect by the relative's name.
- Again, the interrogator will refer to the resemblance.
- The interrogator will state that the relative had the same concern but that they received the help required in time.
- The interrogator will suggest that their relative admitted the problem to themselves, which was the first step, before their relative was able to get professional help.
- The interrogator will state that their relative has a good job now, is married, and is doing well.
- The interrogator will state that their relative's first step was to admit the mistake.

FLATTERY TECHNIQUE

- The interrogator will inflate the suspect's ego.
- This technique works best on individuals who like flattery.
- This technique works on most people.
- This technique may not work for crimes of violence.
- This technique works well with crimes that involve employing a skill (e.g., safe-cracking).

EXAMPLE: FLATTERY

- That was a very clean job.
- I have never seen a job pulled off with such precision.
- That job required a lot of planning and complex reasoning.
- That job could only have been accomplished successfully by an expert.
- That job required a lot of guts.
- That job must have taken a very a long time to execute.
- There's no way in the world that the average guy could have done it.
- This is one for the history books.

SECRETARY TECHNIQUE

- This technique is used when there are two suspects.
- The interrogator will separate the two suspects.
- The interrogator will place Suspect 1 in an interrogation room.

- The interrogator will have Suspect 2 close by so that Suspect 2 can hear the voice of the interrogator but cannot understand what is being said.
- After a little while, the interrogator will lean out of the interrogation room door and will yell for the secretary to bring a notepad; the interrogator will yell loud enough to ensure that Suspect 2 can hear what is going on.
- The secretary will bring a notepad into the interrogation room and will remain long enough to give the perception of a confession.
- The goal is to get Suspect 2 to believe that Suspect 1 provided evidence against them; Suspect 2 may then feel compelled to provide evidence against Suspect 1.

WHITE-COLLAR TECHNIQUE

- White-collar crime may consist of employee theft or embezzlement.
- Individuals who commit white collar crime are often subjected to office management discipline.
- Individuals who commit white collar crime are not the typical criminal types police officers see in the field.
- The use of emotions is very effective against white-collar criminals.
- The interrogator may only need to pat the suspect on the shoulder or to give them a handshake to start the conversation.
- The interrogator should obtain background information on the suspect and should seek details.
- The interrogator will use sentiments against the suspect.

EXAMPLE: WHITE-COLLAR CRIME

- The interrogator should look at contents of the suspect's wallet; the suspect's photographs may prove valuable.
- The interrogator should question the suspect about individuals in the photographs (kids, spouse, etc.); the interrogator should ask the suspect about their thoughts related to their family.

BEHAVIORAL SYMPTOM TECHNIQUE

- Most individuals are nervous when being interrogated.
- A guilty suspect will display definite behavioral symptoms (i.e., body language) when asked about the crime.
- The interrogator will bring attention to the suspect's body language.
- For example, some signs include blushing, fidgeting in the chair, evading answers, sweating, movement of Adam's apple, avoiding eye contact, and dry mouth.
- The interrogator will claim that innocent individuals would not display such symptoms.
- The interrogator will imply that the suspect is falling apart, that their body is giving every indication of guilt, and that their body is killing itself because they are attempting to withhold information.
- The interrogator must train themself to look for clues, which may be subtle.

GOOD COP, BAD COP TECHNIQUE

- The interrogator must have information about the crime and background information on the suspect.
- This technique involves two officers: one bad cop and one good cop.
- During this technique, the bad cop gets the suspect mentally off-balance, which makes the suspect susceptible to the advice of the good cop.
- The bigger police officer will assume the role of bad cop.
- The bigger police officer will become impatient, start to bang on the table, yell, and make their face become flushed (to appear angry).
- The bad cop will call the suspect a liar, state that they should throw the book at the suspect, then leave the room.
- The good cop will state that the bad cop keeps getting them into trouble because of the bad cop's anger issues, that the good cop has been trying to get a new partner, that the bad cop is the boss, and that once the bad cop returns the interview is over.
- The good cop will act as though there is a conspiracy, move closer to the suspect, and lower their voice; the interrogator will state that if the suspect committed the crime, the suspect had better admit it before the bad cop comes back. The good cop will say, "Once my partner comes back, it will be too late for you because they won't let me talk to you anymore." The good cop will state that they will write the report, which is better than the bad cop writing it up.

EXAMPLE: GOOD COP, BAD COP

"This sack of crap is a lying fool. He hasn't shown a shred of honesty. I don't know why you're willing to spend so much time with him. Why don't we just lock him up? I'm not going to stand here and listen to lie after lie! We don't need to talk to him anyway. I'm done. You do as you please, but I'm out of here. I can't stand this guy!"

When the hard-nose cop leaves, the good cop will use a soft approach.

SPLIT-PAIR BLUFF TECHNIQUE

- This technique is used when there are two suspects.
- The interrogator will separate the two suspects and will place them in the same corridor with three or four cells between them so they cannot talk with one another.
- The interrogator will wait a while.
- The interrogator will then take Suspect 1 out of the cell and they will walk past the cell of Suspect 2.
- The interrogator will let Suspect 1 sit in a room for about 30 minutes.
- The interrogator will not speak to Suspect 1; the interrogator will let Suspect 1 sit alone.
- The interrogator will then take Suspect 1 back to their cell.
- As they pass Suspect 2, the interrogator will state in a loud voice, "Thanks, I think that has cleared things up, and I'll see what we can do for you."
- The interrogator will then place Suspect 1 back into their cell and the interrogator will leave the area.
- After about five or 10 minutes, the interrogator will get Suspect 2 and tell them it is their turn now.
- The goal is to get Suspect 2 to believe that Suspect 1 turned evidence on them, which may cause Suspect 2 to turn evidence on Suspect 1.

"CAN YOU TAKE IT BACK?" TECHNIQUE

- This technique is effective when there is the possibility of recovering stolen merchandise.
- The interrogator will tell the suspect that, if they return the item, or part of it, perhaps the victim may decide not to prosecute.
- The interrogator must not promise the suspect that they will not be prosecuted.
- For cases of theft from an employer, the interrogator may tell the suspect that the boss probably steals from the company on a regular basis and cheats on their taxes, but just hasn't been caught yet.
- The interrogator will tell the suspect that it is the employer's own fault by leaving money around, entrapping employees via temptation.
- The interrogator will tell the suspect that if the employer gets some of the money back, perhaps they will understand and decide not to prosecute.

EXTENSION TECHNIQUE

- The interrogator will ask the suspect questions about the suspect's background before focusing on the topic at hand.
- The interrogator will get the suspect to admit that they had thought about committing the crime in the past and how easy it would be not to get caught.
- Then, through subtle questioning, the interrogator will get the suspect to admit that at one time or another they had taken a small article from the company.
- Once the suspect admits to taking something at a particular point in time, the interrogator will extend this to a range of time, asking the suspect how much they have taken over a two-month period.
- The interrogator will keep extending the time period to the current case.
- The interrogator will tell the suspect that they have already admitted to stealing from company so the current case is no different.
- The goal is to get the suspect to admit that they thought about taking an item, then get the suspect to admit taking an item at a single point in time, and then extend the time period to the current case.

HOT CONFESSION TECHNIQUE

- This technique is effective when catching the criminal in the act because, at the time of arrest, the perpetrator will be in state of mental imbalance.
- After the suspect is placed under arrest, the officer will tell the suspect that they finally caught the perpetrator who is responsible for more than 20 similar crimes in that area.
- By increasing the number of charges against the suspect, the suspect may attempt to defend themself by confessing only to the current crime.
- The goal is to exert pressure by accusing the suspect of many crimes so the suspect will chose to minimize the damage by confessing to the current crime.

LOGICAL APPROACH TECHNIQUE
- This technique is effective with suspects who have prior criminal records.
- A perpetrator will attempt to make the best deal possible when they feel the case against them is strong.
- Because conspiracy is linked to a habitual charge, suspects with prior criminal records may be willing to make a deal to avoid a possible conspiracy charge.
- If suspects are at risk of being habitual violators, they may jump at the chance to plead guilty to lesser charges.
- If the police mention that they may file many charges against the suspect, the suspect may choose to plead guilty to fewer charges.

EXAMPLE: LOGIC
- You didn't talk last time either, and you got seven years.
- Don't talk again and see what you get—perhaps 10 years this time.
- Don't talk and maybe you'll get 10 years … maybe 12 or 14.
- I thought you were smarter than that.
- You didn't hurt anyone.
- Did the broad even see the gun?
- If she didn't see the gun, then it's simple theft.
- We'll only charge you with two counts, even though you committed more.
- Perhaps we will charge you with conspiracy, which will make you a habitual violator.

DRUNK TECHNIQUE
- A person under the influence of an intoxicant may not be afraid of authority.
- An intoxicated person may become belligerent.
- The interrogator may need to humor or flatter the suspect to get a confession.
- The interrogator should not berate an intoxicated suspect, which may only aggravate the situation.

EGO DEFLATION TECHNIQUE
- The interrogator will purposely attempt to deflate the suspect's ego.
- The interrogator must size the suspect up.
- The suspect may be insecure and clumsy or smart and prideful.

EXAMPLE: EGO DEFLATION
- Who helps you put your pants on when you get up—your mom?
- I bet your mom has to wipe your butt when you use the toilet.
- You're not smart enough to commit a crime like this.
- You should be out on the street corner asking to clean the windshields of passing cars.
- You're nothing but a worn-out record; an eight-track tape player; a has-been.
- Cut the crap. Who's your boss? What did you get for your efforts? You probably got two bucks for cleaning the guy's windshield.

YES OR NO TECHNIQUE (LAST CHANCE APPEAL TECHNIQUE)

- The interrogator will create an imbalance in the suspect's mind.
- The interrogator will tell the suspect that once the interrogator leaves the room, the suspect will not have another opportunity to talk with anyone from the police department.
- The interrogator will tell the suspect that this is the last chance to tell their side of the story, so they had better act while they still have time.

EXAMPLE: LAST CHANCE

- I got things to do. Don't waste my time.
- I don't have time to mess around with a minor-leaguer like you.
- I'm only going to give you one more chance to talk.
- Speak to me when I tell you to speak or I'll put you in your cell and let you rot.
- Lie to me and I'll leave, and that's it.
- This is your last chance.

CONSPIRACY TECHNIQUE

- The interrogator will keep their voice down while talking, acting as if there is a conspiracy.
- The interrogator will tell the suspect that the place may be bugged and that other officers may be trying to listen through the door.
- The interrogator will get close to the suspect and will tell the suspect to keep their voice down.
- The interrogator will tell the suspect that what is done is done.
- The interrogator will tell the suspect to admit to what they have done so they can put the situation behind them.
- The interrogator will tell the suspect that if it were an accident, they should just say so. Perhaps the interrogator could write up the report so that it does not sound so bad.
- The interrogator will tell the suspect that they may be able to ask for less time; maybe they can make a deal.
- The interrogator will tell the suspect to use their head, and perhaps the suspect can get off the hook.
- The interrogator will remind the suspect not to talk too loudly so no one else can hear them.

WHAT WOULD YOU DO? TECHNIQUE

- The interrogator will reverse roles with suspect; this is a very effective technique.
- The interrogator will ask the suspect what they would do if they were the police officer.
- When the suspect assumes the role of the interrogator, the suspect will often make a deal for themself.

EXAMPLE: WHAT WOULD YOU DO?

- Look, I wasn't born yesterday.
- We both know why I am here.
- What would you do if you were in my shoes?

- What do you expect me to do?
- Just give me something to work with.
- I'll work with you, but you've got to give me a break.
- You've got to give me something to work with.

PYRAMID OF LIES TECHNIQUE

- When a suspect tells a lie, they open a can of worms and must tell additional lies to support old lies; the suspect will create a pyramid of lies.
- Once the interrogator can demonstrate that the suspect has produced one lie, the pyramid of lies will collapse.
- The interrogator will provide the suspect with false information to see whether the suspect agrees with it.
- If the suspect agrees with the false statement, then the officer knows the suspect is being less than truthful.

EXAMPLE: PYRAMID OF LIES

"You say you were at Michigan Ave and Wayne Rd at about 9:00 pm last night, right? That must be true because Officer Davis stated that he saw you near that location when he was impounding a car last night. He stated that you yelled his name as you passed by."

"That's right. I did see Officer Davis last night."

"Impossible, because Officer Davis is on vacation and did not work last night."

The interrogator now knows that the suspect is lying.

SOMEONE ALWAYS TALKS TECHNIQUE

- The interrogator will tell the suspect that the first person to talk is the one the police will believe.
- The interrogator will tell the suspect that there are many people who could talk about the crime; there are witnesses and accomplices. Eventually, someone will talk about it.
- The interrogator will tell the suspect that once someone talks about it, it will be too late for the suspect and they will take the fall.
- The interrogator will tell the suspect that, if the suspect's accomplice talks first, the police will believe the accomplice; this means that the suspect will take the fall, which will cause the suspect to face an uphill legal battle.
- Therefore, the suspect needs to get their story in first.

OTHER GUY TECHNIQUE

- This technique is effective when there are two suspects.
- The interrogator will tell the suspect that it's not them they want; the interrogator wants the suspect's partner.
- The interrogator will tell the suspect that the suspect's partner carried a weapon, which makes the crime more serious; in addition, the partner has committed similar crimes in the past.

- The interrogator will continually reinforce the idea that the partner is the one who carried the weapon and is the bad apple.
- The goal is to get the suspect to admit that they did not realize their partner was carrying a weapon.

EXAMPLE: OTHER GUY

- Look, we are not concerned about you; you're not the one we're after.
- Did you know your partner was carrying a weapon?
- Your partner is the one that we want.
- Your partner pulled a similar crime last month and stabbed a guy.
- Did you know your partner was carrying a weapon when you were with them?

COMPULSION TO CONFESS APPROACH TECHNIQUE

- This technique is based on the human need to confess.
- The interrogator will tell the suspect that there are physical and psychological manifestations of guilt, which include sweating and breathing rates.
- The interrogator will tell the suspect that they know the suspect wants to tell the truth, but there is just one little thing stopping them.
- The interrogator will tell the suspect that if they can overcome this barrier, then the suspect will be able to relieve the physical and psychological pressures that have built up inside them and are displaying themselves via behavioral symptoms.
- The interrogator will tell the suspect that confession is a human compulsion.
- If the suspect is Catholic, the interrogator may use the Church's prayer of confession.

SERVICE CLUB OR SOCIETY TECHNIQUE

- This technique is effective when suspects belong to a service club or fraternity (e.g., Masons, Knights of Columbus, etc.).
- The interrogator should examine the suspect's contents (rings, pins, membership cards, photographs, etc.) to establish that they belong to a service club or fraternity/sorority.
- The interrogator should use that information against the suspect.
- The interrogator should use the ideals of the service club against the suspect's conscience.

EXAMPLE: FRATERNAL ORGANIZATION

"Hey, I see you're wearing a Masonic ring. Everyone knows that Masons support truth. Does being a Mason mean anything to you? By the standards of your club, you are required to right what is wrong. You're supposed to be truthful. Do you understand what I mean? You know what you have to do. Your wife, your kids, and the Masons will all respect you for doing the right thing. People accept that everyone is human and people make mistakes. But they will all shun you if you violate your oath to your club."

CONSCIENCE TECHNIQUE

- The interrogator must not use this technique on an individual who suffers from an antisocial personality disorder and has no conscience.
- This technique is effective on people who have sound minds and who are religious.

EXAMPLE: CONSCIENCE

"If you win this case, you will only be beating yourself. As long as you live, you will see that little girl that you killed. Her blood screams out to God for justice. You will wake up in the middle of the night and wonder when her justice will be carried out. Who knows, perhaps her justice is served by you hearing her screams in your dreams for the rest of your life. You must also wonder if you will be able to live with your own children. Perhaps the urge to kill will overcome you again and you might kill your own children. It is not too late to ask God to forgive you."

"I WANT YOU TO TALK" TECHNIQUE

- The interrogator will tell the suspect that the next question is very important and that the suspect needs to answer it very carefully, because they are going to be stuck with the first answer that they give.
- The interrogator will imply that they already know the answer to the question and that they are simply testing the suspect's truthfulness.
- This techniques implies that the interrogator expects the suspect to lie; knowing this, the suspect often tells the truth without the interrogator ever asking the question.

EXAMPLE: STUCK WITH FIRST RESPONSE

"The next question I am going to ask is very important and you need to take your time and think before you answer. You will be stuck with your first response. I am going to tell you something: I found something out recently and I have a very good reason for asking this next question. Be aware, I am not asking this question for my own health, but it may impact your health."

The goal is to get the suspect to tell the truth upon hearing this. The suspect may believe that the interrogator already knows about the crime.

SPECIAL NEEDS TECHNIQUE

- When the interrogator questions individuals with mental disabilities, the interrogator must keep it simple.
- The interrogator may have to explain each question at a fourth grade level.
- The interrogator must be sure that the suspect understands each question and that the suspect understands the answer they are providing.
- The interrogator must explain things in easy-to-understand terms.

BLAME SOCIETY TECHNIQUE

- The interrogator will blame society for the root cause of the crime.
- The interrogator will need to listen to the suspect's statements of self-pity (e.g., never got a break in life), which may provide clues of actual abuse.
- The interrogator may find something in the background that influenced the suspect to do wrong.
- The interrogator will supply the suspect with a ready-made excuse for the commission of the crime.
- The interrogator will tell the suspect that it is not their fault, but society's fault or the fault of someone who led them down the wrong path.

EXAMPLE: BLAME SOCIETY

- You have a hard life.
- Your parents are divorced and you never knew your father.
- You were bullied at school.
- Your mom kept getting evicted every few months.
- You never had the chance to attend church.
- You never had a chance to play team sports at school.
- The one time you commit a crime, you get caught.
- The cards have always been stacked against you.

TECHNIQUE FOR JUVENILES

- The interrogator must not be belligerent to juvenile suspects.
- The interrogator must try to understand the suspect's perspective.
- The interrogator must listen to the juvenile suspect.
- The interrogator may provide a ready-made excuse for the suspect's actions, which may include: (1) blaming parents, society, or school; (2) jealousy issues; (3) the need to be recognized; or (4) ignorance of the law.
- The interrogator should ask the child what they think is going to happen to them if they are found guilty.
- Most juveniles believe they will immediately go to jail if they confess.
- The interrogator should explain to them that they will not go to jail but that they will have to appear before a juvenile judge or be spoken to by a social worker.
- Knowing the process will reduce their stress.
- Provide an example of what happened to a child in a prior case (e.g., a youth was spoken to by a social worker).

CAR THIEF TECHNIQUE

- This technique is used for car thief investigations.
- The officer should ask the suspect what the mileage is on the odometer, who the suspect purchased the vehicle from, what is in the glove box and trunk, the last time and place of service, what type of oil is in the vehicle, and other questions that only the owner would know.
- The interrogator must be calm, which has a settling effect on the suspect and may get the suspect to talk.
- The interrogator may use rapid-fire questions, which provide little time for suspects to think about their answers before they respond.
- The interrogator should not ask the suspect to confess; the interrogator should simply ask the suspect to tell the truth.

INTERROGATION OF FEMALES TECHNIQUE

- A male interrogator must use caution when interrogating a female suspect, who may file a sexual complaint against the officer.
- An interrogator should video record an interrogation whenever possible or have a police officer of the same sex as the suspect to witness the interrogation.
- Because female suspects may be emotional, the interrogator may use their emotions against them.
- The interrogator will appeal to the suspect's love for her children and will stress how she will not be a part of her children's lives while she is in jail.
- The interrogator will appeal to her jealousy of her husband or boyfriend, stressing that they will enjoy life while she rots in jail.
- The interrogator will appeal to her self-worth, telling her she will just be a number and no longer an individual; she will be owned by the state.
- The interrogator should find out whether the female suspect has children; if she does have children, the interrogator needs to praise her children, telling her how good-looking her children are.
- The interrogator will stress the value of family relationships and her love for her family.

FETISH TECHNIQUE

- This technique is effective for sex crimes that involve fetishes.
- Odd trademarks (e.g., bite marks, removal of underclothing, etc.) that are discovered at crime scenes may be used to questions suspects.
- In order to determine a particular fetish, the interrogator must investigate the background of the suspect.
- The interrogator may ask the suspect about their childhood, the best and worst things that have happened to them, the ways in which they were disciplined by parents or teachers, the ways in which they were treated by other children, and their relationships with parents, siblings, and other people in society.
- The interrogator will attempt to link the fetish at the crime scene to a fetish displayed by the suspect.
- The suspect may mention something about the crime scene that no one outside of law enforcement knows.

SETTING THE ATMOSPHERE

Before an interrogation can take place, the suspect must waive their rights to remain silent and to have a lawyer present (Inbau et al., 2005). The interrogation should be conducted in a controlled area, free from distractions. A suspect is more likely to reveal secrets to an interrogator in the privacy of a room than in the presence of additional people. Because a suspect may lie in order to avoid the consequences of their crime, the interrogator should not mention the consequences of the crime if conviction is realized. A suspect may decide not to talk if they believe that not talking to the interrogator will prevent a conviction and minimize the consequences. In other words, clues must be eliminated that may remind the suspect that, if they do talk, they will be prosecuted. Thus, the police department should not have police emblems on the wall, the interrogator should be in plain clothes, and the interrogator should not display handcuffs or a badge. In addition, the interrogator should not be armed for safety reasons.

AMERICANS AND PERSONAL SPACE

Americans do not like their personal space encroached upon. Proximity is the nearness in space during an interrogation or interview. For a white American middle-class male, 27 inches is about the right proximity for an interrogation. Closer than 27 inches makes the suspect uncomfortable and more than 27 inches makes the suspect's facial signals hard to read (Swanson et al., 2009). Because individuals do not want interrogators to get too close to them, officers may use this proximity factor to their advantage during an interrogation. There should be no barriers between the interrogator and suspect, including the table. Indeed, some experts believe that interrogators should be knee to knee with the suspects, with the capability of expanding and shrinking the proximity as needed.

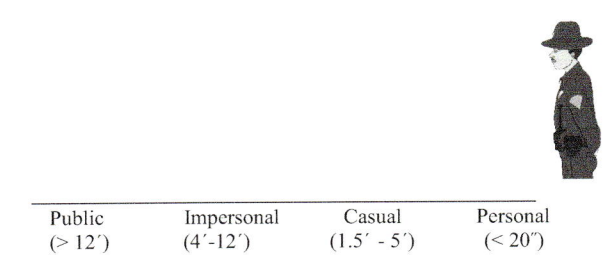

Public	Impersonal	Casual	Personal
(> 12′)	(4′-12′)	(1.5′ - 5′)	(< 20″)

Figure 12.1 Personal space (Starrett & Davis, 2006)

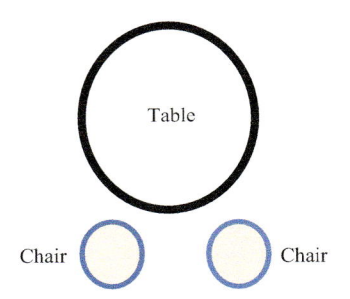

Figure 12.2 Interrogation proximity (Swanson et al., 2009)

Generally, the interrogator should be seated about 4 feet directly in front of the suspect (Inbau et al., 2005). If the chairs are offset, this may negatively impact the direction of the suspect's gaze. The chairs in the room should be straight-backed chairs and should place the interrogator and suspect at eye level. A straight-backed chair will help prevent the suspect from becoming too relaxed and from slouching, which may prevent the suspect from giving the interrogator their full attention. Chairs should place the interrogator and suspect at eye level because the suspect may be less cooperative if they are made to feel inferior by being required to look upward toward the interrogator.

There are several requirements inside an interrogation room. First, there should be ample lighting so the interrogator can clearly see the suspect's face (Inbau et al., 2005). Second, there should be a table, a microphone, and a video recording device inside the room. Third, if the suspect is of the opposite sex to the interrogator, then department policy may dictate that an observer who is of the same sex as the suspect be in the room whenever the interrogator is inside the room. Finally, if the suspect and the interrogator cannot communicate due to a language barrier, an interpreter may need to be in the room. Figure 12.3 shows a room layout of an interrogation room. Eliminate the chairs for the observer and/or interpreter if they are not needed. Nothing should be between the interrogator and the suspect.

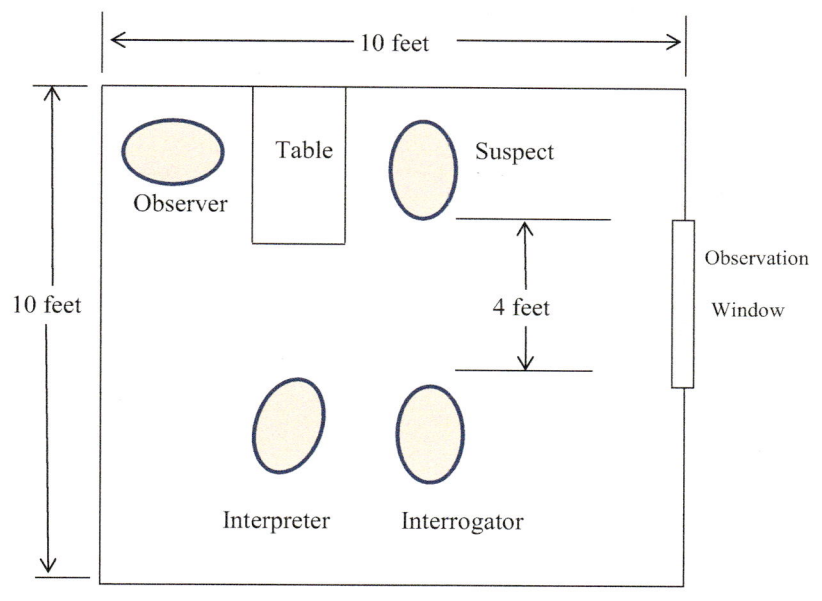

Figure 12.3 Interrogation room (Inbau et al., 2005)

CHAPTER PROBLEMS

1. Discuss the personal space of different cultures. How close do individuals from different cultures like to be when they speak to one another?
2. Discuss false confessions. Why would a person intentionally make a false confession?
3. Provide some examples of improper threats and/or promises during an interrogation. What will be the consequence of using threats?
4. Describe factors that may affect the credibility of a suspect's statement.
5. Select an offense and write the scripts for the two officers under the "dumb and dumber" interrogation technique.
6. Select an offense and provide a script that the officer may present under the "blame someone else" interrogation technique.
7. Select an offense and provide a script that the officer may present under the "hot and cold" interrogation technique.
8. Select an offense and provide a script that the officer may present under the "exaggeration" interrogation technique.
9. Select an offense and provide a script that the officer may present under the "flattery" interrogation technique.
10. Select an offense and provide a script that the officer may present under the "extension" interrogation technique.

KEYWORDS

Credibility
Coercion
False confession
Proximity

REFERENCES

Anonymous. (1991). *Interrogation: Techniques and tricks to secure evidence.* Boulder, CO: Paladin.

Barth, J. (2004). *International spy museum: Handbook of practical spying.* Washington, DC: National Geographic.

Inbau, F.E., Reid, J.E., Buckley, J.P., & Jayne, B.C. (2005). *Essentials of the Reid technique: Criminal interrogations and confessions.* Boston: Jones and Bartlett.

Starrett, P., & Davis, J.N. (2006). *Interview & interrogation with eyewitness evidence* (2nd ed.). San Clemente, CA: LawTech.

Swanson, C.R., Chamelin, N.C., Territo, L., & Taylor, R.W. (2009). *Criminal investigation* (10th ed.). Boston: McGraw Hill.

Zulawski, D.E., & Wicklander, D.E. (2002). *Practical aspects of interview and interrogation* (2nd ed.). Boca Raton, FL: CRC Press.

CHAPTER 13

Individuals with Disabilities

LEARNING OBJECTIVES

Recognize different disabilities.

Effectively communicate with persons who have disabilities.

INTRODUCTION

This chapter provides some practices to use when interviewing individuals with disabilities. A disability is a physical or mental condition that makes it more difficult for individuals with the condition to do certain activities and to interact with the world around them. First, there are general tips for a police officer who interviews a person with a disability. Then, there are specific tips for a police officer who interviews a person with a specific disability. Some individuals with a certain disability may not understand the function of the police officer or the seriousness of their actions. Some individuals may provide answers that they feel will please the officer. Some individuals may have seizures if they see the flashing lights on the police car. Some individuals have trouble balancing. Some individuals startle easily. Some individuals may interpret language in a literal manner (e.g., give me a second = exactly 1 second). Some individuals do not want to be touched. Finally, some individuals may make use of service animals. When speaking with an individual who has a disability, the officer should place emphasis on the person and not the disability. For example, the individual is a person with a visual impairment, not a blind person. In other words, the person should be listed first, not the disability.

GENERAL PRACTICES FOR INTERVIEWING PEOPLE WITH DISABILITIES

When a police officer interviews a person with has a disability, it is important to talk directly to the individual without appearing to be uncomfortable (Indiana Protection and Advocacy Services, 2008). If the person appears to be confused and agitated, it might be wise to discontinue the use of sirens and emergency lights if possible. An officer should identify themself and explain why they are present. Use a steady, calm voice. Ask simple, direct questions. Be prepared to repeat any of the questions if necessary.

If the person has a caregiver, the officer should seek to gain the caregiver's assistance to help ensure that the person with the disability understands the requests (Indiana Protection and Advocacy Services, 2008). It is important not to jump to conclusions when working with someone with a disability. For example, a person who has a physical disability may be mistaken for someone who is under the influence of alcohol. Agitation due to the inability to understand, or from being understood, could be misinterpreted as aggressive behavior. It is important to look and ask for any identification and medical alert bracelets, which could provide emergency contact information. Do not assume a person with a physical disability has an intellectual disability.

Before assisting a person with a disability, the officer should first find out, in a direct manner, how the person can be assisted (Indiana Protection and Advocacy Services, 2008). This is important because different disabilities have different needs. Do not assume that a person needs help solely on the basis that they have a disability.

Interviewing People with Intellectual Disabilities

Individuals with intellectual disabilities may not be able to understand the importance of the police officer's role in a particular situation (Indiana Protection and Advocacy Services, 2008). They may not understand the seriousness of their actions and they may appear to be nonsensical in how they discuss the situation. They may not understand what they have agreed to in the interview, and they may say anything in order to gain the approval of the officer involved in the interview.

Individuals who have intellectual disabilities may be unsure of what they remember, and they may give confusing answers (Indiana Protection and Advocacy Services, 2008). It is important to allow enough time for them to think through what they are being asked. The officer may have to use illustrations or to point to objects to ensure that the individuals are able to follow the questions. In order to maintain rapport and cooperation, it is crucial to avoid using "baby talk" when talking with a person who has an intellectual disability. Use simple, direct sentences, speak at a moderate pace, and ask one question at a time.

Interviewing Individuals with Autism Disorders

Autism is a disorder in which social and communication skills are impaired (Indiana Protection and Advocacy Services, 2008). The ability of the person to communicate is often limited; the person may demonstrate no verbal ability. Instead, the person may rely on gestures or repeated phrases. The person may make limited eye contact and could interpret any colloquial phrases in a literal manner. Individuals with autism may show signs of distress or erratic behavior for no observable reason and they can be very sensitive to touch and excess lighting. Individuals with autism may not comprehend the consequences of their actions or understand their legal rights. They may have trouble remembering details of situations and may not understand the questions being asked of them.

In order to best assist individuals with autism, the officer should speak clearly and slowly, and should ask direct and simple questions (Indiana Protection and Advocacy Services, 2008). In some cases, it may be best to remove them from situations in which there is a high level of visual and auditory stimulation. In addition, unless it is dangerous behavior, the officer should not stop them from performing repetitive motions. If the officer does, this may escalate their erratic behaviors.

Interviewing Individuals with Mental Illness

If an individual begins to act strangely and show odd behaviors, it is best to ask the person whether they have any mental health issues (Indiana Protection and Advocacy Services, 2008). Ask the question in the most respectful manner possible but be prepared for them to avoid giving an answer or deny any problem. The stigma of mental illness is quite severe in U.S. culture and most people will want to avoid that particular label.

If the person acknowledges having a mental illness, it is important not to overwhelm the person with questions (Indiana Protection and Advocacy Services, 2008). Keeping questions clear and short may produce optimal results. Give the person ample physical space in order to keep them from feeling cornered or trapped.

Interviewing Individuals with Visual Impairment

When dealing with individuals with a visual impairment, it is best for officers to announce their presence before entering the area (Indiana Protection and Advocacy Services, 2008). If another person enters the room, the officers should tell the person with the visual impairment the identity of the person who has just entered the room and the reason for the arrival. Avoid speaking more loudly to visually impaired individuals—they are likely not hearing impaired. Any written information will need to be orally communicated to the visually impaired person.

If assistance is offered to a visually impaired person, the officer should avoid grabbing the person by the arm to guide them (Indiana Protection and Advocacy Services, 2008). The officer should ask the person to describe the assistance needed. The officer should allow the person to hold their arm for guidance and should let the person know when they are approaching areas such as stairs, narrow hallways, and other challenging areas. When guiding the person to a place to sit, the officer should place the person's hand on the back of the chair.

Interviewing Individuals with Hearing Impairments

Interviewing individuals with hearing impairments can create a series of challenges, particularly when a sign language interpreter is not available (Indiana Protection and Advocacy Services, 2008). Some people with hearing impairments are not deaf; they may simply be hard of hearing. A hearing aid is not a sign that the person can fully hear and understand what is being said. Some individuals can read lips.

If someone is deaf, written communications can be very useful, as long as the officer and person with the hearing problem understand the same language (Indiana Protection and Advocacy Services, 2008). When an officer interviews a person with a hearing impairment, the officer should face the person directly and should speak in a clear voice with a normal tone. Do not shout at the person. Attempt to reduce any noise in the background that could inhibit communications. Utilize writing if possible. Write clearly and give the person enough time to read and process the questions.

A person with hearing problems may appear to be extremely confused or disoriented; this should not automatically be taken as aggressive and oppositional behavior (Indiana Protection and Advocacy Services, 2008). If a person with a severe hearing impairment is the focus of an investigation, it is important to remember that only a certified sign language interpreter should be utilized when the Miranda warning is given.

Following is a summary of how police officers should respond to individuals with disabilities (Indiana Protection and Advocacy Services, 2008). Individuals with disabilities may be suspects, victims, or witnesses. Some disabilities are easily recognizable, while other disabilities are not so easy to detect. Most people with disabilities react in the same way to law enforcement situations as the general public. Some will need special accommodations specific to their disabilities.

POLICE OFFICERS ENCOUNTERING INDIVIDUALS WITH DISABILITIES
- General tips for all people with disabilities
- Intellectual disabilities
- Autism/autism spectrum disorder
- Epilepsy
- Cerebral palsy
- Mobile impairments
- Mental illness
- Visual impairment/blind
- Hearing impairment/deaf
- Other disabilities/conditions
- People with service animals

GENERAL TIPS

- Refer to the individual before the disability. For example:
  Correct: I am speaking to a person who is blind.
  Incorrect: I am speaking to a blind person.
- Check for hearing aid; check whether it is working.
- Ask simple questions; wait for a response.
- Give one direction at a time; too many directions may confuse the person.
- Provide simple choices; some individuals may only respond to the last choice.
- Explain written documents in easy-to-understand terms (this includes the Miranda warning).
- Before seeking assistance from a caregiver, the officer should find out from the person what help is needed.
- Every person is unique; each disability is unique.
- Respect the individual's independence as much as possible; allow them to move on their own if possible.
- Ask the individual whether they need help before help is provided.
- If possible, gather all of a person's medications before the person is moved from a location.
- Collect needed communication devices (speech synthesizers, alphabet board, head pointer, etc.).
- The police department should provide contact information for support personnel who can assist with a variety of disabilities.

INTERPRETING BEHAVIOR

- Be cautious about interpreting behaviors because different conditions may exhibit similar characteristics. For example, a person with cerebral palsy may appear to be intoxicated.
- Non-compliant behavior may be due to a lack of understanding or due to fear.
- Some individuals may require extra time to process what is happening and to respond.
- The person may have an ID bracelet, emergency medical card, or a medical alert bracelet.
- The officer should seek assistance from the person's caregiver (if there is one), who may understand the person's needs and preferred method of communicating.

	Police response
If the individual	**Police officer should**
Does not seem to understand	Reword question using different and easier words; use direct and concrete phrases; if no improvement, check for hearing loss.
Seems preoccupied	Get the attention of person before asking questions.
Cannot seem to concentrate	Be brief and repeat directions.
Is agitated or over-stimulated	Be calm, remove distractions, and give firm and clear directions.
Is displaying poor judgment	Not expect to engage in rational conversation.
Is having trouble with reality	Be simple, direct, and truthful.

Is delusional	Ignore delusions and do not argue. Redirect thoughts to current situation.
Is disoriented/confused	Check for hearing loss; If no hearing loss, redirect thoughts to current situation. Give one direction at a time and use direct and clear phrases.
Is fearful	Reassure the person that they are safe.
Seems to be changing their emotions	Remain calm and ignore changes in emotions.

INTELLECTUAL DISABILITIES
- Individuals with intellectual disabilities strongly object to the term "mental retardation."
- Officers should use the term "intellectual disability."
- Individuals may not understand the seriousness of their actions.
- Individuals may not understand their Constitutional rights.
- They may be persuaded easily by others.
- They may eagerly confess in order to please the officer.
- Allow extra time for the person to process information and to respond.
- Treat the person with dignity and respect (do not use baby talk).
- Use short sentences and simple words.
- Point at pictures and objects to illustrate words.
- Make eye contact with the person; use the person's name often.
- Look for an identification card, which may provide contact information.
- Give one direction or ask one question at a time.
- Ask the person to repeat the direction/question in their own words to assess the person's understanding.
- Tell the person how long the encounter is expected to last and when things will return to normal (if known).
- Using a watch to indicate time may be meaningless to the person. Tie time to common everyday events, such as breakfast or lunch.
- Clearly indicate when the person may contact other people (family members, case managers, etc.).

AUTISM/AUTISM SPECTRUM DISORDER
- Communication and social skills may be impaired.
- Disorder may not initially be obvious.
- The individual may be non-verbal or have limited verbal skills.
- The individual may have difficulty expressing needs.
- The individual may gesture or point instead of speaking.
- The individual may repeat phrases instead of communicating conventionally.
- The individual may appear deaf; may not respond to verbal cues.
- The individual may make little, if any, eye contact.
- The individual may interpret language in literal manner. For example, if asked whether they want to waive their Miranda warning, they may wave their hand.
- Officers should avoid using words that have multiple meanings.
- In a criminal justice scenario, a person may not understand the consequence of their actions.
- The individual may have a hard time remembering facts and details.
- The individual may not understand what they are agreeing to.

- The individual may not provide credible responses.
- An individual with autism does feel pain.
- The individual may display extreme distress for no apparent reason.
- The individual may show no fear of danger.
- The individual may exhibit inappropriate giggling.
- The individual may engage in self-stimulating behavior (e.g., body rocking, repeating phrases, and so on).
- The individual may be extremely sensitive to sound, light, or touch.

INTERACTING WITH A PERSON WHO HAS AUTISM/AUTISM SPECTRUM DISORDER

- Speak slowly and clearly.
- Use simple language; rephrase as necessary.
- Explain what is going to happen before it happens, at every step.
- People with autism have difficulty with change; they prefer routine.
- The person may have trouble concentrating in highly stimulating area.
- The officer may have to lead the person to a quiet area.
- Approach individuals from the front because they may startle easily.
- Do not shout or touch the person; talk in a calm voice.
- Do not encroach upon the individual's personal space.
- Allow repetitive movements (biting self, body rocking, flickering an object) unless it is a safety concern to self or others; intervention can escalate behaviors.

INDIVIDUALS WITH EPILEPSY

- Epilepsy is an episodic medical condition in which individuals have no control; seizure activity occurs in the brain.
- A seizure may cause person to act strangely; may cause disturbance.
- May affect speech, consciousness, and movement.
- The person may not be able to respond or interact normally during a seizure or for quite a while afterward.
- The person may be confused and disoriented, and may not be able to understand the officer.

SEIZURE SYMPTOMS

- Spitting
- Running
- Biting
- Shouting/screaming
- Flailing movements
- Abusive language

PARTIAL SEIZURE SYMPTOMS
- Eyes may flutter
- Blank stare
- Person acts dazed

INTERACTING WITH A PERSON WHO HAS EPILEPSY
- Check for medical identification bracelet.
- Note length of seizure; a seizure of more than five minutes could be a medical emergency.
- If a seizure lasts for more than five minutes, have the person transported to hospital.
- If it is known that the person has epilepsy, assume observed behaviors are seizure related.
- Some individuals have a Vagus Nerve Stimulator (VNS) to help control seizures; it is an implant just under the skin in the upper chest.
- The person may have a Patient Emergency Medical Card and Cyberonics Magnet; follow the instructions on the card.
- Do not forcibly restrain a person during a seizure or just after the seizure.
- Restraints may injure the person.
- The person may perceive such actions as an attack.
- The person may try to protect themselves by forcibly resisting.
- If a person has a seizure while in custody, provide medical attention.
- If a person has convulsive seizure, place them on their side to prevent choking.
- Do not place anything in person's mouth to hold the tongue down.
- Hog-tying, placing a person face down, or using a choke hold on a person who is having a seizure or who has just had a seizure can obstruct breathing and cause death.
- Failure to provide medication in a timely manner to a person with epilepsy could produce fatal rebound seizures.

PERSON WITH CEREBRAL PALSY
- Disorder caused by damage to brain.
- Affects ability to control movements and posture.
- May vary from mild to extreme.
- Mild cerebral palsy impacts balance and may make the person appear to be intoxicated or under the influence of drugs.
- Severe cerebral palsy will alter major motor activities.

CEREBRAL PALSY
- Sometimes associated with other problems, such as epilepsy, hearing problems, vision problems, or intellectual problems.
- Do not assume a person with cerebral palsy has an intellectual disability.
- Do not assume the person is intoxicated.
- If you have difficulty understanding the person's speech, slow down and ask one question at a time.

- Give the person time to respond; ask them to repeat their response if necessary
- If person is using a communication board or other communication device, allow them time to communicate.
- If a person has a mobility or intellectual problem, deal with those issues too.

INTERACTING WITH INDIVIDUALS WITH MOBILITY IMPAIRMENT

- Do not make assumptions about mobility limitations.
- Communicate with person about their ability to move about.
- Two individuals may be using a mobility device for different reasons (one may use it to alleviate pain while moving about and one may need it to move about).
- If conversation will take several minutes, sit down and speak with the individual at eye level.
- If the officer needs to move the individual out of a wheelchair, the officer should ask the individual about the most effective way to accomplish this task.
- Placing the individual in a police car may not be safe.
- Consider using a van suitable for transporting an individual in a wheelchair.
- Individuals who use wheelchairs are trained to move about.
- The officer should offer assistance but should provide only what the individual requests.
- If the individual is placed in a paddy wagon, the officer should ensure that the individual knows how to hold onto the railing when handcuffed.
- The officer should not assume that an individual who has a mobility impairment has an intellectual impairment.
- The officer should speak to the individual normally.
- Only move the individual when required, and inform the individual what needs to be done.
- Use care when removing individuals from their mobility devices because it may cause harm.

INTERACTING WITH INDIVIDUALS WITH MENTAL ILLNESS

- An individual with a mental illness may become confused.
- The individual may exhibit bizarre behaviors.
- The officer should ask the person about mental health issues.
- The individual may refuse to discuss personal health concerns.
- The officer should use simple, clear, and brief language.
- The officer should address one issue at a time.
- If the individual becomes agitated, move them to a quiet area.
- The officer should speak calmly and give the individual plenty of space.
- The officer should remain focused on the purpose of the assignment.
- If removing individuals from site, let them bring along their prescription medications.

INTERACTING WITH INDIVIDUALS WITH VISUAL IMPAIRMENTS/BLINDNESS

- Some individuals are legally blind but still have some sight; others are totally sightless.
- The officer should speak out and announce their presence before entering the area.
- The officer should announce when people enter and leave the area.
- The officer should announce when bystanders are around.
- Visual impairment does not equate to hearing impairment; speak normally and do not avoid words like "see" and "look."
- Do not touch the person unless assistance is needed.
- The officer may need to let the individual grasp their arm for guidance.
- The individual may walk slightly behind the officer to gauge the officer's reactions to obstacles.
- The officer should announce the presence of doors, steps, and other obstacles.
- When about to sit down, officer should place the individual's hand on back of the chair.
- The officer will have to read written information out loud.

INTERACTING WITH INDIVIDUALS WITH HEARING IMPAIRMENTS/DEAFNESS

- There are varying degrees of hearing impairment; some people are totally deaf.
- Hearing aids may increase volume, which includes background noise, and may not necessarily enhance clarity.
- Individuals may not understand what is being said.
- The officer may have to communicate by written means; some people may not understand English.
- Some individuals may read lips, others may require a sign language interpreter.
- When entering a room, officer should toggle lights to get the individual's attention.
- The officer should get the individual's attention before speaking.
- The officer should face the individual when speaking and should not obstruct their mouth.
- The officer should reduce background noise, and speak slowly and normally.
- If an interpreter is present, the officer should make eye contact with the individual and not the interpreter.
- The officer may be able to write down information.
- One officer should communicate at a time.
- The officer may use hand gestures as visual cues.
- The individual may appear confused as a result of miscommunication.
- The Miranda warning should be provided by a certified sign language interpreter.

INDIVIDUALS WITH COMMUNICATION IMPAIRMENTS

- Individuals may stutter or may have had a stroke.
- The officer should slow down and ask one question at a time.
- Individuals may use an electronic communication board.
- The officer should provide the individual with enough time to use the board and answer the questions.

BEHAVIORAL DISTURBANCE
- An individual who displays a medical or psychiatric problem and is a safety concern should be evaluated by medical personnel.

INDIVIDUALS WITH TOURETTE'S SYNDROME
- The individual may display frequent and repetitive movements of the face, arms, and limbs.
- The individual may have vocal tics.
- The individual may swear involuntarily.

INDIVIDUALS WITH TRAUMATIC BRAIN INJURY
- Individuals with traumatic brain injury may perceive information differently than the officer.
- The individual may be argumentative or belligerent.
- The officer needs to keep the individual focused on the issue at hand.
- The officer should slow down, ask one question at a time, and allow enough time for a response.

INDIVIDUALS WITH SERVICE ANIMALS
- Many different kinds of animals are used to assist individuals with disabilities.
- A service animal is a dog or other common domestic animal specifically trained to assist a person with a disability.
- Animals may help with psychiatric, cognitive, and mental disabilities.
- Service animals are not wild animals, farm animals, rabbits, reptiles, ferrets, rodents, or amphibians.
- Individuals who have disabilities have the right to train their service dogs themselves and are not required to use a professional service dog-training program.
- The Americans with Disabilities Act does not require documentation for service animals.
- Service animals provide services that include guiding individuals who are visually impaired, alerting individuals who are hearing impaired, pulling wheelchairs, fetching items, warning individuals who are about to have a seizure, retrieving the phone or medications, and assisting individuals with navigation.
- Animals that provide comfort, emotional support, therapeutic benefits, and emotional support are companion animals and not service animals.
- Service animals should be moved with the owner.
- The owner must have control over the service animal.
- The service animal can be removed if it is a threat.
- Seek the owner's permission before touching the animal or speaking to the animal.
- Use a leash if required to move the animal.
- An individual who employs a service animal is not required to show an officer proof that a service animal is required.
- An officer may ask about the service that the animal provides to the individual.
- If you have doubt about the legitimacy of the service animal, investigate with a supervisor later.

72-HOUR MEDICAL DETENTION

If a person engages in behavior that is dangerous and unsafe, then the officer may consider a 72-hour medical detention. This is the court-ordered holding of a person against their wishes in a medical facility so that licensed medical personnel can examine the person to determine whether the person is a danger to themself or others. The person can be held for 72 hours.

Before a judge will issue a court order, the judge will want the recommendation of a licensed medical doctor. Therefore, the police officer will need to take the individual to a physician, who will initially assess the situation. If the doctor believes the person is a danger to themself or others, the doctor will need to find a bed for the individual at a proper medical facility so that the individual may be detained for a 72-hour observation. Once the doctor finds a bed and provides a commitment order, the officer will need to take the order with the application for a 72-hour medical detention to a judge for final approval.

It is important to note that a 72-hour medical detention is designed to promote safety. Thus, if an individual's actions do not pose the likelihood of serious harm, then the person should not be detained for a 72-hour medical evaluation. In addition, a police officer does not have the authority to practice medicine without a license. This means that the officer cannot commit the person to the hospital. A licensed medical doctor will provide the order that the individual should be detained, which must be approved by the court. The police officer, however, may be required to transport the individual to the proper facility if necessary.

APPLICATION FOR 72-HOUR MEDICAL DETENTION

State of _____ Incident # _____ Date _____

To: _____ Court of _____ County, _____ (state)
In the matter of _____, patient DOB: _____ Sex ___ male ___ female

The officer herein states to the court the following:

1. That the patient _____ age _____ DOB _____, resides at _____

   And is now at _____.

2. That this officer has reason to believe that the respondent is mentally disordered as defined by law and presents the likelihood of serious harm to self or others, and thus is in need of detention, evaluation, and treatment.

3. The facts that support the officer's belief that the respondent is mentally disordered are:

4. The facts that support the officer's belief that the respondent presents a likelihood of serious harm are:

5. This officer requests the court to order that the patient be held in custody and transferred to _____ for detention, evaluation, and treatment for a period not to exceed 72 hours pursuant to law.

This officer verifies and affirms that the facts stated in this application are true.

Attachment: doctor's order

Officer's name & badge #	Department address
Officer's signature	Department telephone
Judge's name	Judge's signature	Phone #

CHAPTER PROBLEMS

1. Discuss the following statement: "Any animal may be used as a service animal."
2. Discuss the following statement: "A service animal should never be removed from its owner."
3. Discuss the following statement: "If a person lies to the police about the legitimacy of a service animal, there is nothing the officer can do about it."
4. Discuss the following statement. "If a person is acting dangerous to self, a police officer should commit the person for a 72-hour medical evaluation."
5. Discuss the following statement when speaking to a person who is visually impaired. "I am speaking to a blind person."
6. Discuss what medical conditions outlined in the chapter may be problematic for individuals when they are in the presence of flashing lights or sirens.
7. Compare and contrast how an officer should respond when working with a person with mental illness and a person with intellectual disabilities.
8. Compare and contrast how an officer should respond when working with a person with epilepsy and a person with cerebral palsy.
9. Compare and contrast how an officer should respond when working with a person with visual impairment and a person with hearing impairment.
10. Compare and contrast how an officer should respond when working with a person with autism and a person with mobile impairments.

KEYWORDS

Disability

Service animal

72-hour medical detention

REFERENCE

Indiana Protection and Advocacy Services (2008). *Tips for law enforcement and corrections personnel: Encounters involving people with disabilities.* Indianapolis, IN: Indiana Protection and Advocacy Services.

CHAPTER 14

Science and Truth

LEARNING OBJECTIVES

Assess writing characteristics to compare handwriting samples.

Examine writing characteristics to infer a person's character.

INTRODUCTION

Science and technology can be used to assess truth. Polygraph tests, voice stress analyses, brain scans, brain fingerprinting, DNA, and handwriting characteristics can be used to identify individuals, match evidence to suspects, and assess truth. Because the Miranda warning only applies to information that is testimonial or communicative in nature, it does not apply to self-incriminating evidence that is nontestimonial. In other words, the Miranda warning will apply to questions that seek a person to confess to a crime, but it will not apply to evidence that simply identifies a person and links the person to a crime scene. Thus, because fingerprints, DNA, and handwriting samples are not actual confessions to a crime, the Miranda warning will not apply. However, the defendant can challenge any test in court because the test results depend on the skills and interpretation of the laboratory technicians. In addition, it is important that the technicians follow standardized procedures to ensure that the results are valid. Although the Employee Polygraph Protection Act of 1988 prohibits most private employers and companies from using the polygraph test for pre-employment screening, this does not apply to law enforcement agencies, which may require applicants to submit to a polygraph examination.

POLYGRAPH TESTS

Polygraph tests are not generally accepted in court as evidence for either criminal or civil proceedings because they have shown to be unreliable (del Carmen & Hemmens, 2017). In federal courts, the trial court judge has discretion over whether to admit the results of a polygraph test. Even if a polygraph test supports the defendant, a judge may not allow the evidence at trial. However, if a person is forced to take a polygraph test, the person may object based on self-incrimination.

A polygraph test (i.e., lie detector test) is given to a suspect to ascertain whether statements made by the suspect are deceptive (Frith, 2007; Harrelson, 1998; Lykken, 1998). During a polygraph test, the suspect is monitored by a polygraph machine while being interviewed and interrogated. The polygraph machine measures any changes that occur in the subject's breathing, blood pressure, heart rate, and amount of sweat.

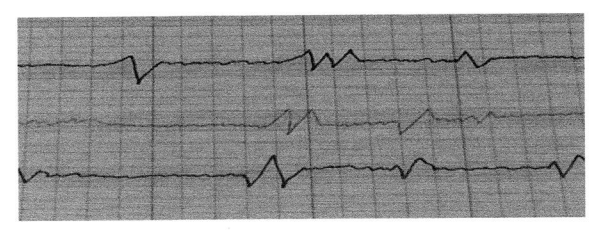

Figure 14.1 Polygraph test output

Polygraph machines have three main components (Frith, 2007). Each component has the separate ability to record the physiological responses of the subject while they are being questioned. The first part of the polygraph is the pneumograph, which records the subject's breathing rate. The second part is the galvanograph, which records electrodermal responses. The third part is the cardiograph, which records changes in the subject's blood pressure and pulse rate. The cardiograph is often considered to be more reliable in detecting deception. The typical findings of a polygraph test are: (1) no deception indicated; (2) deception indicated; and (3) inconclusive.

There is debate over polygraph test results. Proponents of the polygraph test believe that a subject who is being deceptive will often exhibit involuntary physiological responses that can be scientifically recorded by the polygraph machine (Hess & Orthmann, 2010). Indeed, the correlation between positive test results and guilt is very high, with some claiming 95% accuracy. Opponents of the polygraph test argue that the results are unreliable, as confirmed by the U.S. Supreme Court (del Carmen & Hemmens, 2017). First, the Office of Technology Assessment has indicated that correct detections range from 35% to 100%. Second, sometimes people who are simply nervous show signs of strong reaction that resemble signs of deception (Frith, 2007). Third, respiration is susceptible to voluntary control and, once triggered, the galvanic skin response is slow to recover (Jones, 2008). Fourth, individuals may be able to think of a lie after each question in order to manipulate the results. Finally, a person cannot cross-examine the machine to detect any problems (Hess & Orthmann, 2010).

The polygraph test should supplement a field investigation and not be a stand-alone method of investigation. The success of the polygraph test will largely depend on the thoroughness of the investigation that happens long before the suspect ever takes the test. Having the investigator and polygraph examiner work together is the optimal way to maximize the effectiveness of the test.

In order to prevent employers from forcing employees to submit to polygraph tests, the Federal Polygraph Protection Act was passed in 1988 (American Polygraph Association, 2010). This law protects private sector employees; however, it does not protect employees of government agencies, which can include school officials, correctional facility staff, public agencies, and businesses that are under contract to the federal government.

VOICE STRESS ANALYSIS

Proponents of the voice stress analysis (VSA) believe they are able to detect deception by performing an analysis of the levels of stress in a subject's voice using a computer stress analysis device (Hopkins et al., n.d.). The stress is detected by examining traces made by micro-tremors in the larynx, which proponents believe are associated with stress and may be a signal that the subject is attempting to lie (Hess & Orthmann, 2010). However, a study by the National Institute of Justice indicates that detecting deception via voice analysis is no better than flipping a coin.

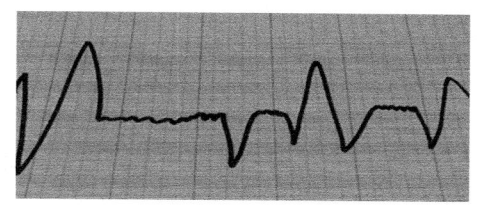

Figure 14.2 Electronic voice output

The National Institute of Justice's study was corroborated by Damphousse (2008), who studied over 300 arrestees. The arrestees' statements were confirmed by comparing their statements with their corresponding urine drug test results. The voice stress analysis system correctly identified 15% of the arrestees who told a lie; however, the voice stress analysis system incorrectly labeled 8.5% of the arrestees as liars, even though they were truthful. In short, the current ability of voice stress analysis system to accurately detect deception is less than effective.

BRAIN SCAN

Positron emission tomography (PET) and magnetic resonance imaging (MRI) may be used to detect changes in the brain and to make predictions about future criminal behavior. PET has indicated that decreased blood flow and hypo-metabolism in the frontal and temporal lobes of the brain may be linked to aggressive behaviors (Wacker Foundation, 2007). MRI has been used to determine whether individuals have pedophilic tendencies (Braconnier, 2011). A person who has been convicted as a pedophile and who has been treated for the problem (e.g., via civil commitment) can be shown photographs of naked children. If the person has not been treated successfully, the regions of the brain related to sexual impulses will be aroused when the naked children are viewed. The Court has ruled that a person may be held in confinement until treated successfully (Seiter, 2011). As technology improves, perhaps these brain scans will one day be able to detect when people lie.

BRAIN FINGERPRINTING

Brain fingerprinting is a real-time psycho-physiological assessment of a suspect's response to words or pictures presented on a computer monitor (del Carmen & Hemmens, 2017). The test can assess the suspect's knowledge about a crime. For example, if the suspect is shown a picture of the crime scene, the suspect's brain will respond in a certain way if the crime scene image has been stored in the brain. In other words, if the crime scene is recognized by the suspect, the brain will respond in a way that can be recorded. If the suspect does not recognize the crime scene, the brain will not respond to the stimuli. Because brain fingerprinting is fairly new, its admissibility in court will continue to be tested.

DNA

Deoxyribonucleic acid (DNA) contains the complex genetic blueprint that distinguishes each person with more than 99% accuracy (James, 2009). Forensic testing can determine whether distinctive patterns in the genetic material found at a crime scene match the DNA in a suspect. If the DNA at the crime scene matches the DNA of the suspect, this means there is a very strong possibility that the suspect was at the crime scene. However, DNA testing does not indicate when the suspect was at the crime scene, which means the DNA could have been left at the crime scene before or after the crime occurred. Furthermore, it is possible that a person's DNA was transferred to the crime scene by a third party.

Although DNA test result are based on strong scientific evidence, a defendant does not have the right to DNA testing after conviction (del Carmen & Hemmens, 2017). The U.S. Supreme Court ruled that defendants have the right to DNA evidence prior to and during trial, but not after a conviction. This may be problematic because there have been at least 329 post-conviction DNA exonerations since 1989. Of these exonerations, 17 have been on death row.

Habeas corpus is ineffective when individuals are legally convicted (del Carmen & Hemmens, 2017). Habeas corpus only applies when a person's constitutional rights have been violated. New information that becomes available after the appeal process has expired is irrelevant because new information that becomes available has nothing to do with the violation of someone's rights. Thus, when the appeal process has expired, a wrongfully convicted person may have little recourse. Remember, the court is not there to be nice; it is there to enforce the rules. However, there are advocacy groups that help the wrongfully convicted. They use evidence to help pressure the government to do the right thing and to release the innocent.

Listed below are sources of DNA and common places where law enforcers should look to find DNA evidence (del Carmen & Hemmens, 2017).

Table 14.1 Sources of DNA

Source of DNA	Places to find DNA evidence
Sweat	Handle of weapon; hat; eyeglasses; pillow; blanket; sheet; fingernail; tape
Blood	Handle of weapon; cotton swab; dirty laundry; bullet; fingernail
Mucus	Cotton swab; facial tissue
Earwax	Cotton swab; facial tissue
Semen	Pillow; blanket; sheet; used condom; dirty laundry; facial tissue
Saliva	Toothpick; used cigarette; stamp; envelope; bottle; can; glass; bite mark
Skin	Handle of weapon; eyeglasses; tape
Dandruff	Hat; bandanna; mask
Hair	Hat; bandanna; mask; used comb; pillow; blanket; sheet
Tissue	Handle of weapon; fingernail
Urine	Pillow; blanket; sheet

HANDWRITING ANALYSIS

Handwriting analysis is the documentation and classification of the characteristics of a specific writing. There are three different types of forgery: traced forgery, simulated forgery, and freehand forgery (Swanson et al., 2009). A traced forgery is created when the perpetrator traces over the original signature. A simulated forgery is created after the perpetrator learns to mimic a genuine signature. Finally, a freehand forgery is created when the perpetrator simply signs the victim's signature without making any attempt to mimic the victim's signature.

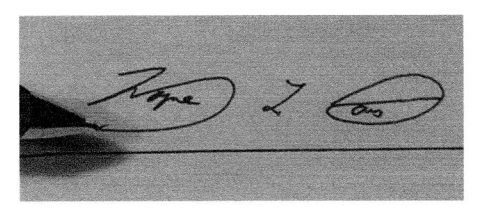

Figure 14.3 Handwriting analysis

Experts who examine documents claim that no two individuals write exactly the same (Frith, 2007; Saferstein, 2011). Although children may make a conscious effort to copy standard letter forms when they first learn to write, writing skills that are associated with nerve and motor responses become subconscious over time. Consequently, each person develops habits that result in unique shapes and patterns, which distinguishes that person's writing from that of other individuals. Some of the variables that distinguish one person's handwriting from that of another person include slope, angularity, letter and words spacing, margins, pen movement, connections, relative dimensions of letters, and pressure.

Table 14.2 Handwriting characteristics (Wiese & Melton, 2003)

Characteristic	Description
Flying start	This is where and how the person starts the first letter of each word (e.g., upward stroke or downward stroke).
Retrace	During the retrace, does the person follow the original line exactly?
Loops	Does the person form rounded or narrow loops? Are the loops open or closed?
Upstrokes	Are letters that extend upward tall or short?
Lifts	When a letter requires a second stroke or mark (e.g., i or t), is the second stroke or mark high or low relative to the rest of the letter?
Connectors	Are the connectors level or do they dip? Does the person connect letters or are there breaks between certain letters?
Flying stop	Does the last letter stop abruptly or does it have a tail?
Spacing	Does the person space the letters out in words or are they close together?

A person's handwriting changes slightly each time the person writes (Wiese & Melton, 2003). Factors that may impact a person's handwriting include whether the person is tired, excited, hurried, nervous, and so on. However, the shape of the letters and the way they are formed are mostly consistent. Below are some characteristics that may help police officers identify forgeries.

Example of flying start

Example of exact retrace and loose retrace

Example of narrow and wide loop

Example of closed loops and open loops

Example of short T and high T (upstrokes)

Example of high and low dot and high and low bar (lifts)

Example of level connector and dip connector following the "o"

Example of connected and disconnected letters

Example of quick stop and flying stop

Example of letters close together and letters spaced apart

Handwriting where the authenticity of the source is questionable is called a questioned document (Saferstein, 2009). In other words, the questioned document is the document that is being investigated and the author of the document is unknown. When suspects provide writings to law enforcement, these are the known sources. The goal is to match a known source to a questioned document. Ideally, the writings of the known source should contain the same letters and words as the questioned document.

Table 14.3 Handwriting comparison guidelines (Swanson et al., 2009)

#	Guidelines
1	The officer should provide the suspect with same type of paper and writing tool as used for the questioned document.
2	The officer should direct the suspect to use the same writing style (e.g., print or cursive) as in the questioned document.
3	The officer should remove each completed page from the suspect's view.
4	The officer should not provide the suspect with information on the format or grammar.
5	For very short forgeries (e.g., a name), have the suspect write the information about 20 times; for longer documents, the officer should dictate the information to the suspect and have the suspect write the complete message three times.
6	For reference, the officer should obtain at least 10 signatures from the victim.
7	If the suspect appears to be writing strangely, the officer should have the suspect speed up, slow down, or switch hands.
8	The officer should obtain non-dictated writings from the suspect from other sources (e.g., employment records).
9	The officer and the suspect should initial each page of the suspect's writing sample.

Following is a table that may be used to assess the totality of circumstances in order to determine whether a questioned document has the same author as a known source. Record the characteristics for the known source and for each questioned document. For these exercises, let us say that the author of the questioned document will be the same as that of the known document if six characteristics match between the writings.

Table 14.4 Handwriting assessment form

	1	2	3	4	5	6	7	8	
	Flying start	Retrace	Loops	Upstrokes	Lifts	Connector breaks	Flying stop	Spacing	
	Upward or downward	Yes or No	Round or narrow	Tall or short	High or low	Yes: letters _____ or no	Quickly or flows on	Close or apart	Number of clues that match the known document
K									-
QD 1									
QD 2									
QD 3									
QD 4									
QD 5									

K = known source; QD = questioned document

GRAPHOLOGY

A person's physical, emotional, and intellectual states combine to produce the person's handwriting style (McNichol & Nelson 1994). The science of graphology, which is based on empirical research, is the study of graphic movement, which includes written and printed symbols to infer a person's character. Although individuals may consciously alter their writing style, once individuals have learned a system of writing, they perform many of their graphic movements unconsciously and via habit.

Handwriting can reveal a person's physical, mental, and emotional aspects (McNichol & Nelson, 1994). Because handwriting is partly physiological, the writing of an individual will reflect the person's physical state of health. For example, handwriting samples can be used to determine whether the writer was intoxicated at the time of the writing or whether the writer has a long-term problem, such as a neurological disease. For the mental aspects, a handwriting sample can be used to determine: (1) whether the writer is an introvert or extrovert; (2) the amount of concentration exhibited by the writer; and (3) the writer's aptitude as it applies to career choice. Finally, handwriting can reveal a writer's emotional aspects, such as how the writer feels, thinks, and behaves.

The following discussion involves the Palmer method of handwriting for adults (McNichol & Nelson, 1994). Because most individuals are right-handed, the development of the ink pen motivated countries across the world to write from left to right. This avoided the smearing of the ink for most individuals. When writing from left to right, children are taught to lean in the direction of movement. Although children are taught to slant to the right when writing, about 25 to 30 percent of writers do not slant their letters to the right. However, this has nothing to do with being left-handed or right-handed. Indeed, it is a fallacy to think that a greater percentage of left-handers slant their letters to the left. In terms of graphology, there is no difference between left-handed and right-handed writers. There are just fewer left-handed writers in the world.

The direction that individuals choose to slant their letters is caused by their emotions (McNichol & Nelson, 1994). The amount of slant can be used to assess a person's mental health. Table 14.5 describes the direction of the slanting letters and their meanings.

Table 14.5 The slanting of letters

Direction of the slanting letters	Degree to which the writer is expressing real emotions to others	Example of slanted letters
To the right	Expressing real feelings to others	*Graphology is exciting.*
Vertical	Suppressing real feelings to others	*Graphology is exciting.*
To the left	Repressing real feelings to others	*Graphology is exciting.*

Certain writing characteristics can be used to assess truthfulness and a person's demeanor (McNichol & Nelson, 1994). The felon's claw, for example, has been shown to appear in the writings of over 80% of convicted felons. Graphology has become sophisticated enough to distinguish between violent and nonviolent criminals and between persons who engage in impulsive crimes and premediated crimes. Table 14.6 describes several writing characteristics and their meanings.

Table 14.6 Writing characteristics and their meanings

Writing characteristic	Meaning	Example
Slowly	Unless required to be neat (e.g., wedding invitation), it is a sign of dishonesty.	
Double or triple looped ovals—loops are on top	Secretiveness; many triple loops reflect deceit.	
Stabs in the ovals—line crosses through oval-shaped letter from side or bottom	Lying, especially in the sentence that contains the stabs.	
Wedging—looks like teeth of saw blade or little sailboats	Dishonest.	
Felon's claw—looks like a claw	Subconscious guilt; bitterness; bad instincts.	
Omitted letters	Devious; partial truth.	
Continual mistakes	The person is lying.	
Retouching – going back to touch up letters	If there is a great deal of retouching, then it is a sign of deception.	
Signature quite different than writing	Putting on a show; pretending.	
Exaggerated writing	Con artist.	
Ovals made upside down—clockwise circle	Sign of deception.	
Retracing—staying on the same line when backtracking on the letter	If about a third of letters that are excessively taller than other letters are retraced, this is a sign of deception.	

Another writing characteristic is the baseline. A baseline is the imaginary line upon which individuals write on a blank piece of paper (McNichol & Nelson, 1994). Baselines can be used to determine general moods, attitudes towards reaching goals, and attitudes toward life. Table 14.7 describes various types of baselines and their meanings.

Table 14.7 Baselines and their meanings

Type of baseline	Meaning	Example
Naturally straight baseline: words end wherever they end on each line.	Person is stable; exerts control over self.	*This is an example of a naturally straight baseline. Unlike an overly rigid straight baseline, the margins on the right side of this baseline will not be in alignment.*
Overly rigid straight Baseline: words on each line start and end in alignment	One step away from losing control over self.	*This is an example of an overly rigid straight baseline. Unlike the naturally straight baseline, margins on the right side for this baseline will be in alignment.*
True ascending baseline	Healthy mental energy; likes to stay busy.	*The true ascending baseline will angle upward and to the right.*
False ascending: initially ascends but descends at the end	A quitter; quits at the last moment.	*I study math and logic. I study five hours per day.*
Convex baseline	A quitter; quits halfway through the process.	*I study math and logic.*
Partial ascending: a word ascends in the text	Emotional high or elevated feeling about the words that go up.	*I went for a walk in the park.*
Descending baseline	Fatalists; pessimist.	*The descending baseline will angle downward and to the right.*

Table 14.7 Cont.

Type of baseline	Meaning	Example
Suicidal baseline: word descends at the end of a line	Suicidal feelings; accident prone; unhappy.	I went for a walk in the park yesterday. However, it started to rain and I got wet. Next time, I will bring an umbrella.
Partial descending baseline: a word descends in the text	A sudden sinking feeling about the words that go down.	I went for a walk in the park yesterday. However, it started to rain and I got wet. Next time, I will bring an umbrella.
Concave baseline	A person who starts with enthusiasm, loses enthusiasm during the process, then regains enthusiasm before the end.	I study math and logic.
Erratic baseline: the lines are bouncy	Moody; temperamental.	Graphology is very exciting to study. This is an interesting field to study in college.
Incoherent baseline	Sociopath.	I was born in Panama and I work in Michigan. I'm the boss at the factory.

Another writing characteristic involves the margins. A margin is the amount of space to the left and right of the text and to the top and bottom of the text. Although the left margin can easily be controlled, the writer does not always know where the last word on the line will finish. Table 14.8 describes various types of margins and their meanings (McNichol & Nelson, 1994).

Table 14.8 Margins and their meanings

Type of margin	Meaning	Example
Even margins all around	Appearance-conscious; seeks order and balance.	

(continued)

Table 14.8 Cont.

Type of margin	Meaning	Example
Overly wide left margin	Placing barrier between self and past; indicates a terrible past experience.	
Overly wide right margin	Indicates the limiting of one's own success in life.	
Margins too wide all around	Cannot make it on own; a person who is socially maladjusted.	
Left margin widens as writing descends	Haste in making a point or reaching a goal.	
Left margin narrows as writing descends	Fearful and apprehensive; loses spontaneity.	
Narrow margins on left and right side	Indicates a person who does not consider other people's point of view; may violate the rights of others.	
Uneven left margin	Indicates waywardness, hostility, and one who gets out of line.	

Table 14.8 Cont.

Type of margin	Meaning	Example
No margins at all	Compulsively busy.	
Wide upper margin	Shows formal and respectful feelings to the person reading the message.	
Narrow upper margin	Feeling more familiar than formal; refuses to show respect to others.	
Wide lower margin	Fear of future; avoids moving forward.	
Narrow lower margin	Someone who delays the inevitable; procrastinator.	
Crushed right margin	Dangerous impulsiveness; does not learn from mistakes.	

Connecting strokes are the little lines that connect one letter to the next letter in a word that is written in cursive. There are four basic types of connecting strokes: garlands, arcades, angles, and threads (McNichol & Nelson, 1994). Table 14.9 describes the types of connecting strokes and their meanings.

Table 14.9 Connecting strokes and their meanings

Connecting strokes	Observation	Meaning	Example
Garlands	Connector takes a dip between each letter.	Friendly, sociable, flexible, communicates easily.	
Clothesline garlands	Straight across connecting line between the letters.	A person who likes to advertise their goodness to others.	
Droopy garlands	Line that excessively hangs down – may be between letters or at end of word.	Person feels oppressed, burdened, overloaded weighted down.	
Sham garlands	Letters that are supposed to be made overhanded are made underhanded and vice versa (an m will look like a w and an n will look like a u).	Person who is pretending to be nice; shyster.	
Arcades	Fancy writing.	Hypocrite who has something to hide; a self-protective gesture.	
Big arcades	Excessively fancy writing.	Likes to show off; pretentious.	
Arcades with angular twists	Sharp angles in fancy writing.	Twisted mind; psychosis; potentially dangerous.	
Angles	Many sharp angles in the writing.	Aggressive; competitive; serious; determined; not easily influenced by others.	
Overly angular	A great many sharp angles in the writing.	Uptight; tense.	
Threads	Squiggly line that cannot be read.	Threading only at the end of words is a sign of deception.	

Spacing refers to the distance between the letters, the words, and the various lines of the text. Spacing is used to assess the writer's feelings about other people, the writer's social behaviors, and the writer's functional intelligence, which is how intelligently the person is behaving (McNichol & Nelson, 1994). Table 14.6 describes the types of spacing and their meanings.

Table 14.10 Spacing and its meaning

Spacing	Meaning
Overly wide spacing between words	Paranoia; apprehensive; suspicious of the motives of others.
Overly wide spacing between letters	Socially isolated.
Overly narrow spacing between letters	Narrow-minded; uptight.
Closely spaced letters with overly wide separations between words	Uptight; paranoid; socially maladjusted.
Cramped letters and cramped spacing between words	Narrow mindedness; uptight; invades the personal space of others.
Tangled lines	Confusion.
Uneven spacing	Inferior functioning intelligence.
Generally large spacing between letters, words, and lines	Generosity of spirit; openness of attitude.

Pressure is the amount of force a writer exerts while writing, and it reveals the amount of mental energy the writer is currently using (McNichol & Nelson, 1994). Downstrokes require the muscles of the hand to contract, while upstrokes require muscles to relax. As a result, downstrokes are naturally stronger and produce heavier marks on paper. The amount of pressure that a writer uses can change frequently, depending on the current mood. Pressure can reveal the strength and intensity of the writer's appetites and desires.

Handwriting may be used to detect truthfulness (McNichol & Nelson, 1994; Meyer, 2010). Research has been conducted using wireless electronic pens with pressure-sensitive tips. Participants were asked to write two paragraphs, one true and one false. The researchers measured how hard the participants pressed the pens. The findings indicated that subjects pressed harder when they lied. It has been suggested that cognitive stress causes liars to press harder. Thus, lie-writing, a lie detector that analyzes handwriting, may be better than a polygraph test because it does not depend on human interpretation. Table 14.11 describes the type of pressure and their meanings.

Table 14.11 Pressure and its meaning

Pressure	Meaning
Change of pressure as writing.	Indicates deceit.
Heavy pressure.	Assertive; energetic; alert; forceful; intense; dynamic; pugnacious.
Pressure that is too heavy.	Frustration; violence.
Light pressure.	A follower; passive; spiritual.
Pressure that is too light.	Overly timid; submissive; lacks willpower.
Uneven pressure.	Worrier; nervous.
Very heavy pressure on the downstroke.	Self-determinization to an exaggerated degree.
Very light pressure on the upstroke.	Weakness of inner strength; lack of conviction.
Clubbed strokes—excessive ink at the beginning or end of writing stroke	Potential for cruelty.

There are four categories of a t-bar crossing, which is the horizontal line that crosses the letter t (McNichol & Nelson, 1994). The t-bar line that crosses the letter t may be high or low, it may be long or short, it may involve heavy pressure or light pressure, and it may travel up, down, or straight across. The t-bar crossing has been associated with weak, average, and strong ambition, work drive, and willpower. Table 14.12 describes various types of t-bar crossings as they relate to ambition, work drive, and willpower.

Table 14.12 T-bar crossings and personal behavior

Ambition, work drive, and willpower		
Weak	Average	Strong
Low crossing; short length; light pressure; Downward-angled crossing.	Middle crossing; medium length; medium pressure; straight line cross.	High crossing; long length; heavy pressure; upward-angled crossing.

CHAPTER PROBLEMS

1. Discuss the accuracy of the polygraph test. Discuss court rulings on the polygraph test.
2. Discuss brain scans and brain fingerprinting and how they might be used in law enforcement.
3. Discuss the following statement. "Because the courts seek truth, courts are required to allow DNA testing to prove a defendant's innocence anytime the evidence becomes available."
4. Discuss the following statement. "When new evidence becomes available after a conviction, and after the appeal process has expired, the convicted person is entitled to a new trial by filing a habeas corpus petition in order to get the new evidence in court."
5. Describe 10 different sources of DNA and where the evidence is likely to be discovered.
6. Discuss how the letter t can be used in handwriting analysis.
7. Describe the eight different handwriting characteristics mentioned in the chapter. Provide an example of each characteristic.
8. Discuss other ways that can be used to match two writing samples, such as the slant of letters, writing pressure, where the pen has been lifted off of the paper, and the type of ink used.
9. Complete the following handwriting assessment form to assess you own handwriting. Write the following sentence in cursive and assess it.

Because I plan to be a criminal investigator later in life, I study math and logic in my criminal justice college courses.

Handwriting Assessment Form

1	2	3	4	5	6	7	8
Flying start	Retrace	Loops	Upstrokes	Lifts	Connector breaks	Flying stop	Spacing
Upward or downward	Yes or no	Round or narrow	Tall or short	High or low	Yes: letters _____ or No	Quickly or flows on	Close or apart

10. Review the writings on the following pages. Use the handwriting assessment form to match the numbered sentences with the lettered sentences. Each numbered sentence will match only one lettered sentence. The more characteristics that match, the more likely the two writings are the same. The assessment form follows the sample writings.

1. I study math and logic in criminal justice

2. I study math and logic in Criminal Justice.

3. I study math and logic in criminal justice

4. I study math and logic in criminal justice

5. I study math and logic in criminal justice.

6. I study math and logic in criminal justice

7. I study math and logic in criminal justice

A. I plan to be a criminal investigator later in his life.

B. I plan to be a criminal investigator later in life.

C. I plan to be a criminal investigator later in life

D. I plan to be a criminal investigator later in life

E. I plan to be a criminal investigator later in life

F. I plan to be a criminal investigator later in life

G. i plan to be a criminal investiguar later in life

Handwriting Assessment Form

	1	2	3	4	5	6	7	8	
	Flying start	Retrace	Loops	Upstrokes	Lifts	Connector breaks	Flying stop	Spacing	
	Upward or downward	Yes or no	Round or narrow	Tall or short	High or low	Yes: letters _____ or no	Quickly or flows on	Close or apart	List the pair that match. For example: A-2
1									
2									
3									
4									
5									
6									
7									
A									
B									
C									
D									
E									
F									
G									

KEYWORDS

Polygraph test
Voice stress analysis
Graphology
Handwriting analysis
Known source
Questioned document

REFERENCES

American Polygraph Association (2010). *Employee Polygraph Protection Act (EPPA)*. www.polygraph.org/section/resources/employee-polygraph-protection-act-eppa

Braconnier, D. (2011). Can brain scans be used to detect pedophiles? *Medical Xpress*. https://medicalxpress.com/news/2011-10-brain-scans-pedophiles.html

Damphousse, K. R. (2008). *Voice stress analysis: Only 15 percent of lies about drug use detected in field test.* www.nij.gov/journals/259/Pages/voice-stress-analysis.aspx

Del Carmen, R.V., & Hemmens, C. (2017). *Criminal procedures: Laws & practice* (10th ed.). Boston, MA: Wadsworth.

Frith, A. (2007). *Forensic science.* Tulsa, OK: Usborne.

Harrelson, L. (1998). *Lietest: Deception, truth and the polygraph.* Ft. Wayne, IN: Jonas.

Hess, K.M., & Orthmann, C.H. (2010). *Criminal investigation* (9th ed.). Clifton Park, NY: Cengage.

Hopkins, C.S., Ratley, R.J., Benincasa, D.S., & Grieco, J.J. (n.d.). *Evaluation of voice stress analysis technology.* www.nemesysco.com/press/AFRL_REPORT2.pdf

James, R. (2009, June 19). A brief history of DNA testing. *Time USA.* http://content.time.com/time/nation/article/0,8599,1905706,00.html

Jones, D. (Ed.). (2008). *The CIA document of human manipulation: KUBARK counterintelligence manual* (1963). New York: Mind Control.

Lykken, D.T. (1998). *A tremor in the blood: Uses and abuses of the lie detector.* Reading, MA: Perseus Books.

McNichol, A. & Nelson, J.A. (1994). *Handwriting analysis: Putting it to work for you.* New York: McGraw-Hill.

Meyer, P. (2010). *Lie spotting: Proven techniques to detect deception.* New York: St. Martin's.

Saferstein, R. (2009). *Forensic Science: From the crime scene to the crime lab.* Upper Saddle River, NJ: Prentice-Hall.

Saferstein, R. (2011). *Criminalistics: An introduction to forensic science* (10th ed.). Boston: Prentice Hall.

Seiter, R.P. (2011). *Corrections: An introduction* (3rd ed.). Upper Saddle River, NJ: Pearson.

Swanson, C.R., Chamelin, N.C., Territo, L., & Taylor, R.W. (2009). *Criminal investigation* (10th ed.). Boston, MA: McGraw Hill.

Wacker Foundation (2007). [Review of the book hardwired behavior: What neuroscience reveals about morality]. *Crime Times.* www.crimetimes.org/06a/ w06ap9.htm

Wiese, J., & Melton, H.K. (2003). *The spy's guide to security.* New York: Scholastic.

CHAPTER 15

Media, Cybercrime, Technology, and Special Situations

LEARNING OBJECTIVES

Understand the importance of the media.

Understand types of hostage-takers.

Understand the steps needed to control a hostage situation.

Understand how to protect children against cybercrime.

Understand how to investigate crimes against children.

Understand the information that should be collected during a bomb threat.

INTRODUCTION

This chapter will discuss several special topics. The police and the media have a common goal: to serve the public. The media are the agencies that use communication channels to disseminate news, promotional messages, education, and other data to the general public. Some of the channels used by the media include television, radio, newspapers, magazines, and the internet. Because the media can influence public support, the police should have a good working relationship with the media. However, some people argue that the major media agencies, which are controlled by powerful elites, may present less than accurate information. To counter this problem, individuals in the general public may use a variety of other media sources to spread their own information. However, as the use of technology and the internet increases, people will be at a greater risk of experiencing cyberspace crimes. Several ways are discussed to protect children from internet dangers. For optimal performance, police departments must consider using all available resources, including advanced technology. When technology is required by a police department, the department must take steps to ensure its successful implementation. Finally, this chapter discusses hostage negotiations, the collection of bomb threat intelligence, death notices, abused children, sudden infant death syndrome (SIDS), domestic violence, and a felony stop. In all of these special situations, police officers may collect, assess, and/or present information (i.e., intelligence).

MASS MEDIA AND POLICE

The police and the media have a common goal: to serve the public. The relationship between the police and the media is symbiotic (Miller, Hess, & Orthmann, 2011). For example, the police and the media may work together to put out a crime alert or to advertise unsafe neighborhood practices. However, because the media are guided by the 1st Amendment (the public's right to know) and the police by the 4th Amendment (the right to privacy), there may be conflict between the agencies (del Carmen & Hemmens, 2017).

There are several consequences when police have poor media relations (Whisenand, 2011). For example, the police may lose their professional reputation and public support. The police are accountable to the public and the media are the community watchdogs. Thus, when a crisis event occurs, the police must have a trained officer readily available to communicate with the media. Subsequently, the police need to monitor the messages the media deliver to the public because police departments are hypersensitive to criticism and will take defensive countermeasures. For example, the department may take away a valuable tool used by officers because one officer was portrayed by the media as using the tool improperly. Finally, the police should use the media as a conduit to obtain third-party support. The public often want to help the police in crisis situations and the media can assist.

If the police are required to lie to the media, then the police should offer an explanation or apology at the appropriate time (Miller, Hess, & Orthmann, 2011). For example, public safety may require the police to be less than truthful. However, once the threat has passed, the police should clear things up.

Developing a partnership with the media is essential for effective police–community relations (Miller, Hess, & Orthmann, 2011). The media are powerful, and they can influence local residents to support their local police. On the other hand, the media can also influence residents not to support the local police.

Police departments may learn how to use the media for their personal agendas. Bureaucratic police departments have a vested interest in justifying their existence via statistics (Kappeler & Potter, 2005). Advertising high crime rates will give the public the perception that the police are needed. In other words, it is good police business when the media create myths that crime rates are high, especially when the crime rates are not actually high. If the media continue to repeat this information, it soon becomes a truism.

MASS MEDIA AND THE PUBLIC

Mass communication is a formal system of conveying much information to large groups of people in a short amount of time (Kappeler & Potter, 2005). Consequently, the media can spread fear over a great distance very quickly. By advertising particular crimes, the media may create an epidemic where none really exists. Media frenzies spread quickly, which give false impressions about the magnitudes of criminal events. Once a theme has been established, similar stories are accepted as newsworthy. In addition, stories that do not match the theme may be modified to match the theme. Thus, the misperception of a crime wave may continue to grow out of control.

A small number of people control most of the information (Kappeler & Potter, 2005). Although about 80% of all crime does not attract an audience, the media select the crime problems they want to publicize, which are often the most gruesome criminal acts that are uncovered. The choice of crime coverage is driven by the competitive market and by the demands of consumers.

In addition, television media use graphics to get attention (Kappeler & Potter, 2005). Because television media are under time constraints, they are unable to provide the context that gives the information true meaning. Thus, the viewers only hear part of the story and they generate truth based on limited intelligence. Because some repugnant crimes do occur, partial truths that exaggerate such crimes only make the problem seem worse.

MASS MEDIA: THE ELITE CONTROLLING MINORITIES

The media supply the public with what it demands (the public will only pay for what it wants to hear). Over time, the media's distorted coverage of crime helps to shape crime as a social problem

(Kappeler & Potter, 2005). Instead of focusing on the root causes of crime, such as poverty and unemployment, the media coverage gives the perception that the only way to control crime is by hiring more police officers, passing more laws, building more prisons, and handing down longer prison sentences.

The media are for-profit businesses, and they like readily available and exciting information (Kraska, 2004). Indeed, the job of the media is to sell information, but their goal is to make money. This is the reason why marijuana became illegal in the United States in the first place: it was due to greed rather than health issues.

During the 1920s, New Orleans was the largest party city in America (Yaroschuk, 2000). The city consisted of many different cultures, including American, European, French Cajun, Spanish, African American, and Chinese. Jazz music was quite popular in that environment and was directly related to the pleasures of marijuana consumption. Furthermore, marijuana was the only legal drug available in New Orleans, since alcohol was banned. Marijuana cigarettes were commonplace, relatively cheap, and socially acceptable. However, the media were about to get involved.

Hemp, collected from the cannabis plant, makes a higher quality paper at a lower cost than does wood pulp (Gahlinger, 2004). Hence, up until the 1880s, hemp was commonly grown. However, because William Hearst, a huge newspaper publisher at the time, owned millions of acres of woodland, he lobbied to outlaw marijuana. By criminalizing marijuana, there would be a bigger demand for paper made from wood. This would result in bigger profits for him. During the 1920s, Hearst linked the marijuana consumption in New Orleans to murder, rape, poverty, and disease (Yaroschuk, 2000). This served two purposes: (1) to make money by selling newspapers; and (2) to persuade lawmakers in Congress to pass laws outlawing the growing of hemp. Although this did not result in the passage of federal laws outlawing the cultivation of hemp, Louisiana jumped on the opportunity to restrict the use of marijuana, hoping that it would be a means to control the black population.

Then the Great Depression hit in 1929. Prior to that time, Mexicans in the southwest were considered a welcome labor force (Gahlinger, 2004; Yaroschuk, 2000). However, once the Great Depression hit, the Mexican labor force was no longer needed. To reduce the number of Mexican residents working within the United States, the *San Antonio Gazette* published newspaper articles that stigmatized Mexicans, stating that they commonly used marijuana, which turned them into frenzied and dangerous criminals. The goal of the media was to turn people against marijuana by scapegoating Mexicans.

In the early 1930s, there was no federal law that prohibited marijuana use (Gahlinger, 2004; Yaroschuk, 2000). After the Prohibition Act was repealed, Harry Anslinger, who was a lead enforcer of Prohibition laws, became the head of the newly formed Federal Bureau of Narcotics. Although Anslinger saw no dangers in the use of marijuana, Texas, California, Arizona, and Colorado pressured Congress to pass marijuana laws in order to reduce the number of Mexicans in their states. Anslinger then visited Hearst and they became allies in the campaign against marijuana. Together, they used the media—in the form of newspaper articles, radio announcements, and films—to stigmatize the use of marijuana. By exaggerating the effects of marijuana, labeling marijuana as Mexico's "devil's weed" (a foreign product), and linking marijuana with violent predatory crimes committed by Mexicans toward Americans, this helped feed the fear that already existed due to the Great Depression (Yaroschuk, 2000). This pressured Congress to pass the Marihuana Tax Act of 1937. Although this Act did not directly outlaw marijuana possession, it did indirectly outlaw it. It accomplished this because, in order to legally possess marijuana, a person had to purchase a marijuana stamp. However, the federal government refused to issue any marijuana stamps. Furthermore, the law stated that in order to get a marijuana stamp, one must have the marijuana in hand; however, to have it in hand without the stamp was illegal.

On the one hand, the news media have stigmatized marijuana and have linked it to predatory and violent crimes (Yaroschuk, 2000). In this case, the media advertised that marijuana is harmful via posters, brochures, radio announcements, and television commercials. With the 1986 drug overdose death of the Boston Celtics' number one draft choice, Len Bias, the media took advantage of this opportunity as a means to generate support for the Partnership for a Drug Free America (Leonard, 1993).

On the other hand, some media promote marijuana consumption. There are many songs, websites, and several magazines, such as *High Times*, *Weed World*, *The Cannabis Grow Bible*, and *Cannabis Culture*, which all endorse marijuana use. They distrust the government and the formal news media. For example, in 1936, *Reefer Madness* was used by the formal media as a scare tactic to describe the dangers of smoking marijuana (Leonard, 1993; Roleff, 2005). However, because the film overly exaggerated the effects of marijuana use, the formal media lost their credibility, which is still in question today. Consequently, marijuana advocates now transmit their own information using other types of media, such as bumper stickers, t-shirts, music, and magazines.

MEDIA OF THE LESS POWERFUL

Various forms of media can be used by the less powerful to spread their messages. For example, minorities and the poor, who have been labeled as social deviants by the elite and powerful, may use music and magazines to communicate with society. Rappers may speak about police corruption; others may challenge questionable laws. *High Times*, *Cannabis Culture*, *Cloud Magazine*, and *SKUNK* are the voice of the marijuana community. If the police are effectively going to serve the public, then the police need to listen to what the public is saying. Some of the words may be harsh, but they may be the truth as perceived by those who speak them.

SMALL-TOWN MEDIA

Sometimes in small towns, the media may depend heavily on the police to get their stories. If the media upset the police, there is a chance that the police may no longer cooperate with the media and provide them with needed information. Because the media may need the information to survive, particularly in small towns where not much activity is taking place, the media may hesitate to publish negative information about the police department. The media may publish negative information about an officer that the department wants to discipline, but the media will only target that particular officer and not the department.

FREEDOM OF INFORMATION ACT

The Freedom of Information Act makes the records of government agencies accessible to the public (Miller, Hess, & Orthmann, 2011). The act supports the idea that the people have a right to know. However, police departments may withhold certain information that involves national security, an active case, or the privacy rights of an individual. In addition, the timeframe for providing the requested information is vague.

TERRORISM

Terrorists use the media to arouse passion for their ideals and to generate anger toward a common enemy: America (Sookhdeo, 2005). Anti-Western propaganda is televised around the world where information is carefully manipulated. Persistent broadcasts of biased information may create the desired response of community hatred. In short, terrorists need the media as a way to advertise their violence and to generate support for their cause.

CYBERSPACE CRIME: INTERNET DANGERS

Cyberspace is the internet environment and involves communication via interconnected computers and computer networks. Although there are internet safety laws to protect children, such as the Children's Online Privacy Protection Act, which is designed to keep anyone from obtaining a child's personal information, these laws may not be particularly effective because internet predators may not voluntarily follow them (Dowshen, 2015; U.S. Department of Justice, Federal Bureau of Investigation, n.d.). Furthermore, because no one knows the number of chat room predators who are actually out there, children may commonly be targeted. Indeed, there are pedophiles on the internet who aggressively seek to exploit children.

The internet can expose users to many different people and different cultures (U.S. Department of Justice, Federal Bureau of Investigation, n.d.). Furthermore, some people use the internet to target children for sexual exploitation. Although some predators immediately engage in sexually explicit conversation with children, others seduce their targets by grooming them, providing attention, kindness, affection, and gifts, then slowly introducing sexual content. Because adolescents are at the age where they are moving away from the control of their parents and are becoming curious about their sexuality, they are prime targets for sexual predators on the internet.

There are several ways in which parents can protect their children from internet predators, including observing the warning signs and taking appropriate action (U.S. Department of Justice, Federal Bureau of Investigation, n.d.). The warning signs that indicate a child may be in the process of being seduced by an online predator include the following: (1) the child spends a large amount of time online, especially at night; (2) there is pornography on the child's computer; (3) the child receives telephone calls from strangers; (4) the child receives gifts in the mail from strangers; (5) the child turns the computer off when a parent walks into the room; (6) the child becomes withdrawn from the family; and (7) the child uses another person's online account.

To minimize the chances that children will be exploited by online predators, there are several things parents can do. First, parents need to openly communicate with their children and explain the potential dangers that exist online. Second, parents can spend time with their children online and have their children demonstrate their favorite online activities. Third, parents need to keep computers in common areas so that they can monitor their children's communications. Fourth, parents can utilize parental controls and blocking software to create barricades that prevent their children from accessing highly suspect areas. Fifth, parents should randomly check their children's email information to see whether predators are in the process of attacking their children (however, the U.S. postal service may also be used). Sixth, parents need to teach their children how to use the many legitimate and appropriate websites that are available online. Seventh, parents should investigate the computer safeguards that are on other computers that their children may commonly use, which include the computers at school, the computers at the local library, and computers at friends' homes. Eighth, the parents must realize that if their children are targeted by predators, their children are the victims and are not responsible for being attacked. Ninth, parents need to instruct their children never to meet face to face with people who they have only met online; never to upload photographs of themselves or provide any personal information; and never respond to bulletin board postings that are sexually suggestive. It should be stressed that internet information is often deceitful. Finally, in order to find out more about internet safety, parents can investigate the many different websites that are available (Inhope—Internet hotline providers, 2008).

Table 15.1 Protecting children from internet predators

	Ways to protect children from internet predators
1	Parents should observe the warning signs and take appropriate action.
2	Parents can spend time with their children online and have their children demonstrate their favorite online activities.
3	Parents should keep computers in common areas so that they can monitor their children's communications.
4	Parents can utilize parental controls and blocking software to create barricades that prevent their children from accessing highly suspect areas.

Table 15.1 Cont.

	Ways to protect children from internet predators
5	Parents should randomly check their children's email information to see whether predators are in the process of attacking their children.
6	Parents need to teach their children how to use the many legitimate and appropriate websites that are available online.
7	Parents should investigate the computer safeguards that are on other computers that their children may commonly use, which include the computers at school, the computers at the local library, and computers at friends' homes.
8	Parents must realize that if their children are targeted by predators, their children are the victims and are not responsible for being attacked.
9	Parents need to instruct their children never to meet face to face with people they have only met online, never to upload photographs of themselves or provide any personal information, and never respond to bulletin board postings that are sexually suggestive. Parents need to inform their children that internet information is often deceitful.
10	To find out more about internet safety, parents can investigate the many different websites that are available.

In 2011, the Office of Community Oriented Policing Services provided $12 million in funding to state and local governments to help combat child sexual predators (U.S. Department of Justice, n.d.). However, local law enforcement is designed to keep peace in the local community here and now. Internet crimes cross many jurisdictions, the perpetrators have anonymity, and solving such problems can consume a lot of resources (if they can be solved). Local law enforcement departments, whose officers may be evaluated by quotas, do not have the right structure to handle internet crimes. The federal government, on the other hand, can cross state lines and spend more resources to focus on these specific problems. Thus, federal law enforcement agencies, such as the Federal Bureau of Investigation (FBI), can do a much better job at investigating domestic internet crimes.

CYBERSPACE AND ELECTRONIC INFORMATION

Cyberspace and electronic information are essential parts of American culture (Purpura, 2007). Businesses, governments, the economy, and society all depend on information technology. Spyware, malware, phishing, spam, viruses, worms, and identity theft are all part of the electronic communication system. Indeed, criminals engage in cyberterrorism by exploiting and attacking cyberspace as a method to achieve their goals. Furthermore, because identity theft is a major problem today, many Americans are personally at risk of being attacked. Consequently, personal credits may be ruined and much financial damage may be realized. Because computers are all around us, cyberterrorism is a potential threat for many people.

Police officers need to enhance their job performance by using modern technology. Because a central mission of the police community is to continuously improve public service, attention must be given to all available resources. When officers attempt a job, best practice dictates that officers make use of all available resources if practical. Otherwise, the officers' performance will be less than optimal, which will be a disservice to the public. Therefore, administrators must support the implementation of technology in order to help officers best serve local residents. Indeed, society is becoming more sophisticated as technology continues to improve. In order to be successful in today's community, officers must learn to effectively use the tools that are currently available.

Incorporating technology in law enforcement is beneficial to officers. By using electronic bulletin boards, newsletters, and emails, for example, officers will be able to share information with one another in order to improve the learning process. Indeed, officers will be able to guide one another to continually improve the way that they work.

TECHNOLOGY AND PUBLIC SERVICE

Law and order largely depend on local residents. Thus, police departments must utilize the public as a resource. This means the police must engage community members in crime-prevention strategies. This can only happen if the police work with community members.

Police officers need to combine technology with project-based activities to draw local residents into the subject matter. This will encourage cooperation and foster the residents' ability to internalize new concepts. Indeed, residents are eager to work with computers and they are more receptive to information when it is presented via technology. Furthermore, technology-based activities will allow the residents to have some control over projects, which will allow them to learn through trial and error. Thus, using technology to perform project-based activities will create a more active and engaging environment that will foster the local residents' ability to think critically and solve problems; it will also help local residents to better communicate with the global community.

BARRIERS TO TECHNOLOGY

There are several barriers to implementing technology in the field. Some of the major barriers may include a lack of adequate training, a lack of hardware, a lack of software, and a lack of input concerning choice of software. Although there is a great amount of technological information available, overwhelming officers with this information is an ineffective way to promote the use of technology in the field. Instead, administrators need to focus on sound educational principles and create the conditions, as well as the motivation and competencies, for officers to implement technology in the field. In short, learning is a team effort and administrators must provide officers with the necessary support so that they can achieve their goals. As in football, without proper training, equipment, and direction, it is unreasonable to expect success.

OVERCOMING BARRIERS

There are several ways to overcome the barriers that impede the use of technology in the field. First, because officers will respond to technology that is directed at helping them achieve their goals, training should be curriculum rich and should focus on properly applying technology. Second, administrators need to provide professional development plans and mentors to ensure that adequate support is provided. Finally, before officers will be able to effectively use available technology, they must know that the tools exist. Hence, officers must be exposed to the existence of available resources via training and mentoring.

FACTORS FOR SUCCESS

Several factors will help the successful implementation of technology in the field. First, a detailed plan that provides a clear vision of the goals and steps necessary for the effective implementation and management of the technology will need to be developed. This will include funding, which may be obtained from the government, and the installation of the technology. Second, officers will need to know how to integrate the technology into the field, which will require ongoing training. Third, administrators will need to support the process by providing funding and other support, such as by restructuring the officers' schedules. Finally, administrators will need to reflect on the process so any corrective adjustments can be made. As stated earlier, any system without feedback is unstable.

Table 15.2 Successful implementation of technology

Factors for the successful implementation of technology in the field
Provide a detailed plan that provides a clear vision of the goals and steps necessary for the effective implementation and management of the technology.
Provide ongoing training.
Provide funding and other support.
Provide feedback; any system without feedback is unstable.

INTERVIEWING A SEX-ABUSED CHILD

The only witness to a child sexual assault may be the young child who was abused. It is possible that the whole investigation will ride on the child's ability to recall what happened. It is crucial to obtain good solid facts from the child in order to confirm warranted suspicions and to avoid misleading accusations.

An interview protocol devised by the Eunice Kennedy Shriver National Institute of Child and Health Development (NICHD) has shown promise in working with children in these kinds of cases (Harris, 2010). This interview procedure is broken into three sections: introduction, rapport building, and free recall. The interview will begin with the officer discussing what will be covered in the interview. The officer will then proceed to talk with the child about topics that are not related to the abuse. This will create a more relaxed interaction between the child and officer and will create a deeper level of rapport between the two.

In the latter part of the interview, the officer will discuss with the child any recollection that the child may have of the incident and will encourage the child to talk in as much detail as possible about the incident. The officer's goal is to get the child to talk without much prodding by only asking open-ended questions. This procedure may elicit more information from the child than asking closed-ended questions.

SEX OFFENDER REGISTRIES

There is evidence that sex offender registries, which provide local law enforcement with information on the whereabouts of sexual predators, and community notification, which notifies community residents of the home addresses of the predators, reduce the frequency of sex offenses, but only those involving local victims (Prescott & Rockoff, 2008). However, there is little evidence that these measures reduce sexual crimes against strangers. The problem with the registry system is that it requires lawbreakers to comply with the law and to register with authorities (Graham, 2006). Many times, the information provided by the offenders is less than accurate. Because many offenders believe the burden of registering is too much, they simply take their chances of being caught and prosecuted. Therefore, the state registry system needs to include the physical verification of all the information provided by the sexual offenders. Without this, sex offender programs may not be very effective and may not be an adequate warning system for parents. However, because the internet crosses vast distances, and because true identities can be hidden, the registering of sexual offenders in local communities may still be inconsequential in preventing internet crimes.

CRIMES AGAINST CHILDREN (HESS & ORTHMANN, 2010)

CRIMES AGAINST CHILDREN
- Maltreatment (neglect and abuse)
- Sexual exploitation (pornography and prostitution)
- Trafficking and abduction

COMMON TYPES OF MALTREATMENT
- Neglect (most commonly linked to fatalities)
- Physical abuse
- Emotional abuse
- Sexual abuse

CHILDREN AS VICTIMS
- Twenty-five percent of violent crime victims are juveniles; most are female.
- More than one-third of juvenile victims of violent crime are less than 12 years of age.
- Around two-thirds of violent crimes involving juveniles occur within the home.
- Most statutory rapes involve adult men and girls under 14 years of age.
- African American youths are twice as likely to be murdered than Caucasian youths.

CHILD ABUSE
- The biggest single cause of death of young children.
- Can result in serious permanent physical, mental, and emotional damage.
- May lead to future criminal behavior.

CAUSES OF CHILD ABUSE
- Poverty.
- Violence between parents.

THREE COMPONENTS OF CHILD ABUSE LAW
- Criminal definitions and penalties.
- Mandate to report suspected cases.
- Civil process for removing abused children from home.

CHILD PROTECTIVE SERVICES
- Act on behalf of children.
- Require professionals who come into contact with children to report abuse.

CHALLENGES IN INVESTIGATING CHILD ABUSE
- Need to protect child.
- Possibility of parental involvement.
- Need to collaborate with other agencies.
- Difficulty of interviewing children.
- Credibility of children.

PROTECT THE CHILD
If the possibility of present danger to a child exists, the child must be removed into protective custody.

INTERVIEWING A CHILD
- Consider the age of the child.
- Consider the ability of child to describe what happened.
- Be aware of potential for retaliation by the suspect.
- In most child abuse cases, children tell the truth to the best of their ability.
- Most reports of child abuse are made by a third party, such as a teacher, doctor, or sibling.
- It is essential to establish a comfortable rapport when interviewing a child.
- Use anatomical dolls.

EVIDENCE OF ABUSE
- Surroundings.
- Home conditions.
- Clothing.
- Bruises.
- Medical reports.
- Behaviors.

CHILD ABUSE
- Often by people the child knows.
- Most perpetrators are women who are younger than 40 years of age.
- Sexual abuse in the family is the most common sexual abuse problem, but it is often not reported.

SUDDEN INFANT DEATH SYNDROME (SIDS)
- Most frequently determined cause of sudden unexplained infant death (3,000–4,000 each year).
- The police officer must observe the infant's position (oftentimes moved).
- The police officer must observe the crib and surrounding area.
- The police officer must observe the presence of objects in the crib.
- The police officer must observe dangerous items in the room.
- The police officer must observe any medications given to the infant.
- The police officer must observe the temperature of room.
- The police officer must observe the air quality.

PEDOPHILES' REACTIONS TO BEING DISCOVERED
- Deny completely.
- Minimize the act.
- Justify the act.
- Blame the victim.
- Claim to be sick.

CHILDREN AS WITNESSES IN COURT
- Courtroom testimony may not be the best way to elicit information from children.
- Some courts have attempted to help children testify in court (e.g., by removing the accused from the courtroom).
- Some courts allow child interviews to be videotaped to avoid multiple interviews.
- Being challenged under 6th Amendment to confront witnesses.

PREVENTING CRIMES AGAINST CHILDREN
- Educate children about potential dangers.
- Maintain open communications.
- Guidebook, *Personal Safety for Children* (www.missingkids.com).
- Digital technology (fingerprints, personal information) can be dispatched within minutes.

DOMESTIC VIOLENCE
- Physical, sexual, economic, and emotional abuse, alone or in combination, often by an intimate partner to establish and maintain power over the other partner.
- Three phases: honeymoon, tension-building, acute battering episode.

POLICE RESPONSE
- Many departments have a mandatory arrest policy for domestic abuse if two conditions exist: a statement of being victimized and some sort of physical evidence (e.g., a bruise).
- Arrest with probable cause even without a signed complaint from the victim.
- Research suggests that arresting the suspect may be a deterrent.
- However, other research suggests that arresting the suspect may intensify the problem.
- Victims may be afraid to call the police.
- Some couples like to argue and fight.
- Separate victim, witnesses, and suspects as soon as practical before interviewing them.
- Use persuasion during interrogation.
- Cannot give the suspect the third degree—physical force is illegal.
- Deception is allowed— select morals and ethical systems are used to determine good behavior.

RESTRAINING ORDERS
- Court ordered.
- Enforceable nationwide.
- Usually take several weeks to obtain.
- Can obtain emergency restraining order within 24 hours.

ELDERLY ABUSE
- Physical and emotional abuse, financial exploitation, and general neglect of the elderly.
- Current level of elderly abuse is unknown.

SIGNS OF PHYSICAL ELDERLY ABUSE
- Injury incompatible with explanation given.
- Burns.
- Cuts, pinch marks, scratches.
- Bruises.
- Dehydration.
- Sunken eyes.
- Soiled clothing.
- Hidden injuries.
- Frequent visits to emergency room.

DOCTORS ASK

- Has anyone at home hurt you?
- Has anyone scolded or threatened you?
- Have you ever signed documents that you do not understand?
- Are you often alone?
- Are you afraid of anyone at home?
- Has anyone touched you without your consent?
- Has anyone made you do things that you did not want to do?

SIGNS OF FINANCIAL ABUSE

- Recent acquaintance expresses interest in finances.
- A relative who has no visible means of support is overtly interested in an elder's financial affairs.
- A relative expresses concern over spending an elder's money for medical care.
- Utility and other bills not being paid.
- The elder's placement is not consistent with estate.
- A relative isolates elder and provides excuses.
- A relative gives implausible explanations for finances.
- Bank information is sent to a relative and is unavailable to the elder.
- A relative attends the bank with an elder and refuses to let the elder talk for themself.
- The elder is confused about missing money.
- Suspicious signatures appear on the elder's checks.
- The elder has signed blank checks.
- There is an unusual amount of bank activity.
- A will or power of attorney is drafted but the elder does not understand it.

ABUSE AT CARE FACILITY

- Physical condition/quality of care, untreated injuries, undocumented injuries.
- Characteristics of facility (odors, urine).
- Inconsistencies (medical records, statements).
- Staff behaviors (follow investigator too closely, lack of knowledge about client).

HOSTAGE NEGOTIATIONS

A hostage is a person taken by force to secure the taker's demands. Negotiating with individuals who have taken innocent bystanders hostage as a bargaining tool requires specialized communication training. According to Wallace and Roberson (2013), hostage negotiation is one of the most highly publicized procedures in which law enforcement officers engage. The process of negotiating with a criminal or mentally unstable person in a hostage situation can be the supreme test of a law enforcement officer's communication skills.

The ability to totally control the hostage situation is usually very limited. However, the officer needs to take as much control as possible because lives may depend on the officer's actions. The officer who is on scene will need to do their best to contain the situation until someone who is specifically trained in hostage negotiations is able to take charge. Until that time, the officer will need to utilize exceptional communication skills to engage the suspect in dialogue.

Hostage situations may be placed into five different categories: criminal, ideological, domestic, frustration-driven, and thought-disordered (Harmening, 2014). The good news for the law enforcement officer is that the techniques for each scenario will be the same (Fuselier & Noesner, 1990). A solid understanding of hostage negotiation procedures is crucial for all law enforcement professionals as they may be involved with such scenarios during their tenure in public service.

Table 15.3 Types of hostage-taker (Harmening, 2014)

Type of Hostage-taker	Description
Criminal	Purposeful, if hostage-taker uses hostages as a means to a criminal act.
	Defensive, if hostage-taker did not intend to take hostages but did so as events developed (may use them as a bargaining chip).
Ideological	Passive, if hostage-taker does not intend to harm hostages but plans to live on in order to protest cause in future (e.g., animal activists). Often ends peacefully.
	Violent, if hostage-taker is willing to kill hostages to make a political, social, or religious statement.
Domestic	Custody: when parent takes child in violation of court order.
	Relationship: when, after a breakup, a person holds spouse or significant other at gunpoint for revenge.
	Defensive: when a person attacks approaching police and barricades self in home with family members (there is no intent to harm family members).
Frustration-driven	Final statement: when a hostage-taker believes they are out of options and plans to kill the hostages, self, or both to make frustrations heard via dramatic event.
	Passive: when a person is frustrated with a personal situation and takes hostages to remedy a personal problem. Often ends peacefully.
Thought-disordered	Paranoid: when a hostage-taker is mentally ill and suffers from delusional beliefs. Hostage-taker believes they are in danger and may believe hostages are involved (may harm hostages); may use hostages as a bargaining chip to get out of imagined danger.
	Mission-oriented: when delusional hostage-taker takes hostages because some imaginary force "directed" them to do so.

Steps for Controlling the Situation

1. Secure a perimeter and contain the situation (Harmening, 2014). Cut off all potential escape routes. Do not let any unauthorized persons enter the scene. Once negotiations have started, do not let bystanders or the media disrupt the negotiations.

2. Establish a communication link (Harmening, 2014). Engage the hostage-takers immediately to distract them from responding violently when additional police arrive at the scene. Make contact by any available means. Telephones and cell phones may be used, a throw phone may be used, or, as a last resort, a bullhorn may be used.

3. Establish a rapport with the hostage-takers (Harmening, 2014). The negotiator should convey honesty, credibility, and a sense of confidence that the situation can be resolved peacefully. The negotiator's voice should remain calm, and the negotiator should allow the hostage-takers to vent. The negotiator should keep the discussion focused on the hostage-takers and not on the hostages, should downplay the event, and should complement the hostage-takers for any positive actions taken.

4. Never give the hostage-takers anything without getting something back in return (Harmening, 2014). Get concessions without agitating the hostage-takers. Hostage-takers expect a give-and-take relationship. Never solicit a demand, never give more than agreed to, and avoid saying "no" to a demand. Every time the hostage-takers give concessions, the negotiator increases their own power over the situation.

5. If possible, the negotiator should strive to offer the hostage-takers a win–win solution so both parties feel they are getting what they desire (Fuselier & Noesner, 1990). However, the reality

of each situation is different and there is no guarantee that such a solution is available. Often, negotiators will work toward moving the hostage-takers from pursuing demands that are not realistic to objectives that are more achievable. If hostage-takers desire to surrender, the negotiator will need to communicate the process for surrender directly to the hostage-takers to ensure a smooth resolution to the situation.

Table 15.4 Signs of hostage-taker negotiations (Harmening, 2014)

Signs of success	Signs of danger
When hostage-takers talk about personal needs and concerns.	When the hostage-takers deny suicidal thoughts (not being honest).
When the hostage-takers talk for extended periods of time.	When the hostage-takers refuse to establish rapport.
If no hostage has been harmed, that may indicate there is no intention to harm hostages.	When the hostage-takers insist on face-to-face negotiations (violent intentions).
When the hostage-takers refer to hostages by their first names.	When the hostage-takers set a deadline for their own deaths.
When the hostage-takers let a deadline pass without consequence.	When the hostage-takers start discussing the final disposition of their property (i.e., their will).
When the hostage-takers release a hostage.	When the hostage-takers refuse to negotiate.
When the hostage-takers routinely exchange material goods for hostages.	When the hostage-takers insist that a particular person be brought to the scene (gain audience for own deaths).
When the hostage-takers shift from offensive threats to defensive threats.	When the hostage-takers isolate or dehumanize the hostages (hostages are viewed as objects).
When the hostage-takers reduce their expectations.	When the hostage-takers tie weapons to their hands (no intention of giving up weapons).
When the hostage-takers decrease their threatening behavior.	When the hostage-takers make outrageous demands, continually change their demands, or make ambiguous demands (they may be stalling for time; hostage-taker may be enjoying the attention or building up courage for final stand).

BOMBS

Bombs come in all sizes (Marks, 2003). Some have been found in books, luggage, envelopes, and belts. Military munitions include grenades, anti-personnel mines, and anti-tank mines. Bombs can be made of common materials and are relatively low tech. An explosion occurs when the material burns at or greater than the speed of sound. Shockwaves travel at 29,000 feet per second. The thermal wave can reach 4,500°F. Heavy fragments can break through barricades. For example, a 1.5-ton anchor had enough force to be hurled 2 miles.

After the initial explosion, there are lingering hazards (Marks, 2003). There may be: (1) secondary explosions; (2) smoke, dust and toxins; and (3) damaged structures. For the secondary explosions, terrorists may plant bombs in likely staging areas. For smoke, dust, and toxins, the World Trade Center attack put high concentrations of asbestos, lead, and mercury into the air. For damaged structures, buildings may result in total collapse, they may be standing with substantial damage and hanging debris, or they may have a compromised support system.

If a building collapses, the building may fall straight down or it may topple and fall like a tree (Marks, 2003). If a building topples, the structure may impact an area 150% its height. This area is known as the deadly arc. This distance may increase if the building falls down a slope.

There are three primary components of a bomb: trigger, detonator, and explosive charge (Marks, 2003). There are many types of triggers. They include remote switches (e.g., cell phones or garage door openers), spring switches, mercury switches, trembler switches, and motion sensor toys. If a remote signal is used to detonate a bomb, the signal may be required to initiate the explosion or to prevent the explosion. Detonators may include Detcords, dust initiators, blasting caps, timers, and fuses. The explosive charge may include plastic explosives, binary explosives, dynamite, nitroglycerine, and gunpowder.

Dirty Bomb

A dirty bomb uses a traditional bomb to spread radioactive material over a target area (Cornish, 2007). The required materials are available and can be distributed easily. Some of the radiological materials that may be used include americium-241, caesium-137, californium-252, cobalt-60, iridium-192, plutonium-238, radium-226, strontium-90, and yttrium-90.

Bomb Threat Procedures

If a bomb threat is received, the established procedures must be followed. Because safety is always the top priority, all bomb threats must be taken seriously. If a bomb threat is not taken seriously, someone may die.

- Get as much information as possible.
- Keep the caller on the line and record everything.
- Notify building management.
- Do not touch any suspicious packages.
- Clear the area around the package.
- Do not assume that there is only one device planted in the area.
- Avoid standing in front of windows or other hazardous areas.
- Do not block sidewalks or access areas.
- Officers should not use radios, pagers, or cell phones because they may trigger an explosive device.

Below is a summary of information that should be documented in response to a bomb threat call.

BOMB THREAT CALL CHECKLIST FOR DISPATCHER (INDIANA UNIVERSITY, 2021)

☐ Caller's name and address _____

☐ Caller ID number _____

☐ Time of call _____

☐ Length of call _____

☐ Caller's age _____

☐ Caller's gender _____

☐ When will the bomb explode? _____

☐ Where is the bomb? _____

☐ What does it look like? _____

☐ What will cause it to explode? _____

☐ What building is it in? _____

☐ What floor is it on? _____

☐ Did you place the bomb? Why? _____

Background Sounds (Indiana University, 2021).

☐ None   ☐ Traffic   ☐ Music   ☐ Loudspeaker

☐ Animals   ☐ Conversations   ☐ Trains/Subways Trains   ☐ Restaurant Noise

☐ Weather   ☐ Factory Machines   ☐ Sporting Event   ☐ River

☐ Other _____

Characteristics of the Caller's Voice (Indiana University, 2021).

Nationality of accent _____

☐ Familiar (sounds like who?) _____

☐ Distinct words that were used _____

☐ Deep   ☐ Loud   ☐ Soft   ☐ Lisp   ☐ Raspy

☐ Nasal Voice   ☐ Spoke slowly   ☐ Stuttered   ☐ Angry   ☐ Laughed

☐ Spoke Quickly   ☐ Calm   ☐ Excited   ☐ Coughed   ☐ Cried

☐ Cracking Voice   ☐ Disguised Voice   ☐ Ragged   ☐ Other _____

Language of the Caller During the Threat (Indiana University, 2021).

☐ Well-spoken   ☐ Incoherent   ☐ Taped Message   ☐ Profane

☐ Irrational   ☐ Read Scripted Message   ☐ Other _____

Incident Command and Control Zones

If the police do encounter a HazMat situation as the result of an explosion, the area of concern must be isolated and secured (Levy, 2000). A HazMat team must set up control zones, which must consider environmental variables. For example, the HazMat team will set up the area of operations upwind in order to minimize possible exposure to dangerous chemicals. There are three control areas around the HazMat scene: hot (exclusion); warm (contamination reduction); and cold (support). The hot zone is the most dangerous zone and it is closest to the HazMat incident. The hot zone surrounds the incident and needs to extend far enough so individuals outside the hot zone are not adversely affected by any released chemicals in the hot zone. In addition, only properly trained persons with the proper personal protective equipment should be allowed to enter the hot zone. The warm zone is the area where decontamination procedures take place. Once individuals and equipment leave the hot zone, they must be decontaminated in the warm zone before they are allowed to enter the green zone. The green zone is a clean area outside of the contamination control line. The green zone is where command and support functions take place. Although personal protective equipment is not required in the cold zone, and this area is safe for the media and the public, civilians should not be allowed to enter the green zone because they may interfere with command and support functions. Therefore, authorities should establish a well-marked perimeter that encompasses the green zone. The area that extends beyond the green zone should be designated for the public and the media.

Specific access control points should be established to control movement between the zones (Levy, 2000). However, an alternate exit route should be established for personnel working in these zones in case the primary escape route becomes blocked or there is a change in circumstances that creates an emergency, such as a change in the wind direction.

Control Zones

Hot = area immediately surrounding the dangerous materials; red zone; restricted.

Warm = area between hot and cold zones where personnel and equipment are decontaminated and hot zone support takes place; yellow zone; limited access.

Cold = area where command post and support functions are necessary to control the incident; green zone.

Safety

The general rule of emergency response is to protect life, environment, and property (Callan, 2001). Distance from a HazMat scene is the best safety precaution. If a person stretches their arm out and points the thumb upward, if the incident can be seen around the thumb, then the person is too close. However, first responders cannot always remain at a safe distance. Therefore, when first responders are required to enter a HazMat zone, they need to use their personal protective equipment. This may include protective suits, foot covers, gloves, self-contained breathing apparatus, eye protection, and so on.

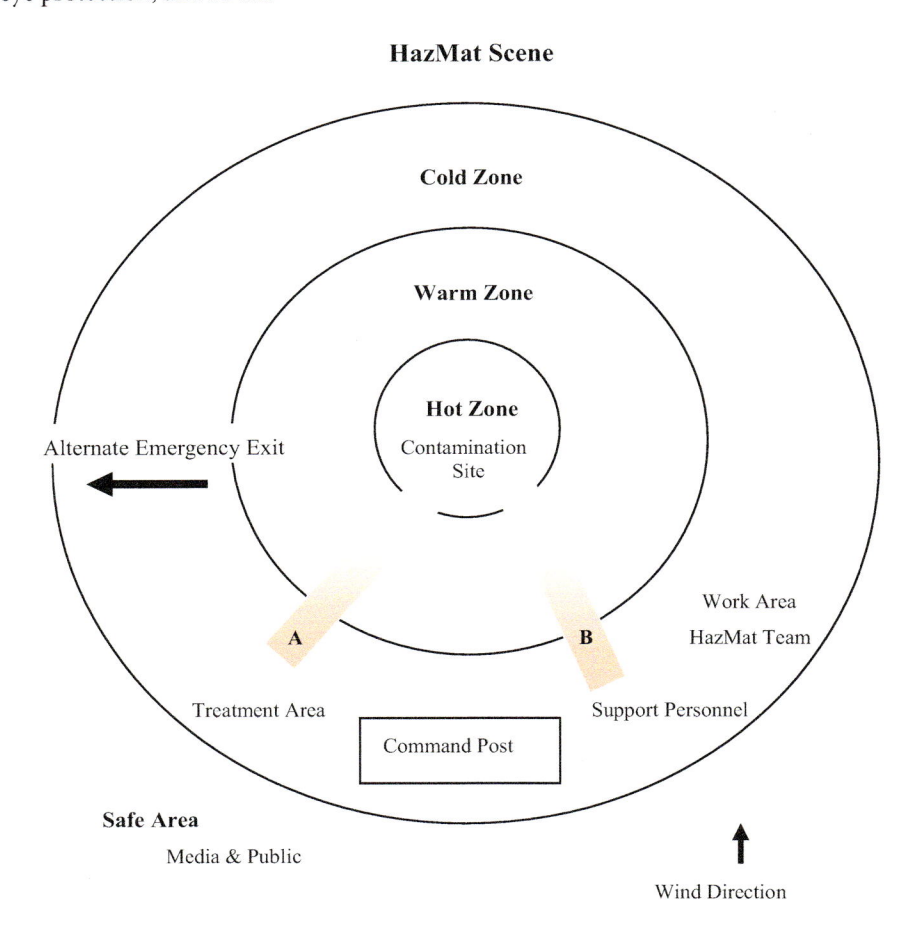

HazMat Scene

A = Decontamination Corridor
B = Access Control Points

Figure 15.1 Incident command and control zones at HatMat scene

Perception

Where a person stands will directly impact the person's perception of the emergency (Callan, 2001). The three areas in which a person may stand are safe, unsafe, and dangerous. In the safe area, the first responder will experience no harmful effects from the chemicals. However, wind is a variable and the situation may change. In other words, a safe area may not always be a safe area. In the unsafe area, the first responders are exposed to the hazardous materials but not enough to cause immediate harm. However, prolonged exposure may cause permanent damage. In the dangerous area, responders are exposed to the hazardous materials, which will cause immediate harm. First responders should not rush into a HazMat scene; they need to take the time to figure out what they are up against.

If first responders do nothing else, they should control the scene (Callan, 2001). First responders should set the perimeter, close off the scene, and call for help. People will not get hurt if they are prevented from getting close enough to get hurt. Simply controlling the scene may be the best-practice decision at the time. In other words, non-intervention is a plausible response action. If officers do not recognize what they are up against, it may be smarter not to enter the area.

There are several clues listed below that can help a first responder to identify hazardous material.

- Type of manufacturing in which the chemicals are used.
- Where a chemical is located.
- The shape and size of the containers (round-ended cylinders = gas; 55 gallon drums = liquid).
- Colors of containers (blue = health hazard; red = flammable; yellow = reactive; white = special).
- Marking on containers (0 = no hazard; 1 = slight; 2 = moderate; 3 = serious; 4 = severe).

Table 15.5 Risk level for HazMat identifiers (Callan, 2001)

High risk → Low risk	
High risk	Personal senses (touch, taste, smell, feel)
	Shipping papers
	Placards
	Markings and colors
	Container shape and size
	Type of manufacturing in which the chemicals are used and where the chemicals are located
Low risk	

The U.S. Department of Transportation requires placards and labels on containers that are used to store and transport hazardous materials (Callan, 2001). In addition, there are Material Safety Data Sheets, Shipping Papers (used during transportation), and Chemical Abstract Service numbers (identifies each chemical by formula). First responders should use this information to help identify the chemicals at a HazMat scene. First responders should never touch, taste, smell, or examine hazardous materials under any circumstances.

There are limitations when first responders rely on using placards and documented information. First, the placards may not be visible from a safe distance (Callan, 2001). Fog, smoke, and the vehicle being overturned may all impact the visibility of the placard. The shipping papers may not be in the vehicle (especially during a serious crash), individuals may not have listed the chemicals correctly, or chemical residue from a previous shipment may interact with the current shipment (the same container may be used to ship different materials at different times).

Gathering information is important, but effectively using the information is the key to survival (Callan, 2001). The value of the information depends on its quality, the time it took to acquire the information, and the ability to use the information. Poor information will result in poor decisions and may cost people their lives. For example, if explosives are present but the information is not transmitted because the quality of the information is poor, then people may die. Also, responding fast to a problem will help to minimize the problem. This can best be achieved through preparedness, training, and emergency planning. Finally, effectively using the information in a timely manner is essential. The information is valueless if it is not used by the appropriate people at the appropriate time.

Table 15.6 Level of training for HazMat response (Callan, 2001)

Level of training and associated HazMat response

Training	Response
First responder awareness level	Observe and initiate emergency response system.
First responder operations level	Defensive response: protect people, environment, and property.
HazMat technician	Aggressive role: plug or stop chemical release.
HazMat specialist	Aggressive role: support technician with advanced knowledge and skills.
On-scene incident commander	In charge of operations above awareness level.

Table 15.7 Decision-making at HazMat scene (DECIDE) (Callan, 2001)

Detect the problem.
Estimate likely harm with and without intervention.
Choose response objectives.
Identify action options.
Do the best option.
Evaluate progress.

Table 15.8 Eight-step HazMat process (Callan, 2001)

Process	Description
Site control and management.	Manage physical layout of scene.
Identify materials.	Determine the kinds of uncontrolled materials.
Evaluate hazards and risks.	Assess dangers to personnel; help commander make right tactical decisions.
Select proper protective equipment and clothing.	Structural firefighting clothing; chemical splash protective clothing; chemical vapor protective clothing; high-temperature protective clothing.
Coordinate resources; develop plan of operation.	Establish a clearly identifiable post command (close enough to see scene, but not too close to become contaminated and not too close to staging area); make difficult decisions; all responding agencies need to have quick access to incident commander.
Implement response objectives.	Method of implementing successful actions.
Implement decontamination and clean-up activities.	Make people and equipment safe by eliminating harmful substances.
Implement termination activities.	Document the incident for legal, medical, and training purposes; critique the emergency and response.

Table 15.9 HazMat team member job descriptions (Callan, 2001)

HazMat team members	Job description
Team leader	Forward and functional extension of incident commander; responsible for all operations inside warm and hot zones.
Equipment/resource officer	Responsible for supplying all logistics.
Medical officer	Responsible for the health of all response personnel.
Safety officer	Responsible for the overall safety of the operation.
Risk assessment officer	Responsible for gathering and analyzing data about the chemicals.
Information officer	Responsible for gathering information for risk assessment.
Decontamination officer	Responsible for cleaning, removing, or neutralizing contaminants from response personnel and equipment.

There is a general rule when it comes to clouds at a HazMat scene (Callan, 2001). A cloud is bad and a colored cloud is worse. When flammables are present, first responders should anticipate that ignition will occur. Furthermore, chemicals may become more reactive when they are introduced to heat, pressure, or oxygen. Flammable liquids are always toxic, and they become more flammable as the concentration increases (less diluted).

There are two different types of danger: matter and energy (Callan, 2001). Danger from matter comes from gases, vapors, liquids, and solids. Danger from energy comes from pressure, explosives, reactives, and radioactives.

Police officers may be the first responders to arrive at a HazMat incident. Police officers must not rush into a dangerous scene before assessing the risk. Instead, they need to identify and assess information. If an officer rushes into a hazardous scene without taking the proper precautions, then the officer becomes part of the problem. Not only will the officer fail to be a rescuer, they will become a victim, which will require another rescuer.

DEATH NOTIFICATIONS

Sometimes law enforcement officers may have to inform family members of the death of their loved one. This can be one of the most devastating moments of any family member's life. This moment can be made worse if it is not conducted in a sensitive, professional manner. When giving a death notification, it is important to have as much information about the specifics of the death as possible. Death notifications should be made in person and not over the telephone. When arriving to give notification, officers should ask to enter the home of the family by stating they have information about the family member that they would rather discuss inside the home. After entering the home, officers will need to make sure the appropriate family members are available. Once the family members are present, the officers will need to tell the family members in a clear, straightforward, and sensitive manner that their relative has died.

It is not uncommon for family members to sob, faint, become angry, or become despondent. The officers will need to focus on helping the family members with their needs. The officers should provide the family members with all available information. This is one of the toughest parts of law enforcement work, but it is a necessary duty.

TRAFFIC STOPS (MILLER, SCHULTZ, & HUNT, 2011)

OFFICER–VIOLATOR CONTACT
- Explain in a polite but confident manner the reason for the traffic stop.
- During routine traffic stops only, have the driver remain seated in the vehicle.
- Never stand between the vehicles.
- After completing the citation, present it to the offender.
- May have the offender sign it, promising to appear (not an admission of guilt).
- During the final period of contact, remain polite and control the conversation.
- Do not enter into a debate or argument with the driver.
- Tell the driver they are free to leave and to drive safely.

SUMMARY OF TRAFFIC STOP
- Do stop your car out of the traffic lane, behind the violator's car.
- Do record the license plate before approaching the car (write it inside vehicle and call it in to the post for a radio check—which will document the license plate.
- Do decide what you are going to do and say.
- Do make a direct and active statement regarding alleged violation.
- Do assess information on the driver's license and establish identity.
- Do write a citation/warning as rapidly as possible, while monitoring the vehicle and its occupants.
- Do explain the citation and how to handle it.
- Do retain the driver's license until the citation is completed and signed.
- Let the driver know when they are free to leave.
- Do not consider the traffic violation as a personal affront.
- Do not argue with, berate, or threaten the violator.
- Do not expose yourself to personal hazards—be alert.
- Do not open the conversation in a sarcastic or derogatory manner.
- Do not accept anything the violator offers you except the documents requested.
- Do not detain the violator any longer than is absolutely necessary to do your job.
- Do not follow the violator's vehicle immediately after termination of enforcement action (unless the driver commits another violation when leaving the scene).
- Do not quote fines (if the quote is wrong, the officer will attract a complaint).

FELONY STOP (MILLER, SCHULTZ, & HUNT, 2011)

REMOVING VEHICLE OCCUPANTS (IN CHRONOLOGICAL ORDER)
1. Driver.
2. Front-seat passengers.
3. Rear-seat passengers.

FELONY STOP PROCEDURE

- Assume all suspects are experts in weapons and hand fighting, and have a criminal record.
- Once the suspect's vehicle is stopped, immediately exit the police car and draw your weapon.
- Take cover behind the police car's open door.
- Always leave passenger side unlocked prior to stop for access by support officers.
- Depending on the situation, the backup officer may use a shotgun as the primary weapon.
- Give commands in a loud and clear voice.
- May use public address system.
- Order the driver to shut off the engine and to place their palms flat against the windshield.
- Order the front-seat passengers to place their palms flat against the windshield.
- Order the rear-seat passengers to place their hands on top of their heads and in plain view.

POLICE OFFICER'S DIRECTIONS TO DRIVER

- Driver, use left hand only, carefully remove the ignition keys.
- Driver, with left hand, drop keys out of the window.
- Driver, place both hands out of open window.
- Driver, open the driver's side door from the outside.
- Driver, exit the vehicle, raise hands, face away from me, take several steps to the left.
- Driver, raise your arms as high as you can (if shirt is tucked in, have the driver grip the back shirt neck and lift up to expose waist).
- Have suspect turn slowly around while in a standing position so officers can view all sides of the driver's waist and body for possible weapons.
- Driver, walk backwards toward me (guide suspect to proper location).
- Place the suspect in kneeling or prone position close to the police car or order the suspect to walk backwards to a designated team of arresting officers.
- Handcuff/secure driver.
- Repeat the process for passengers (modify process as necessary).
- After all known occupants are secured, order any other passengers out of the vehicle (they may be hiding); do not approach the vehicle yet.
- If no one responds, with weapons drawn, approach the vehicle and secure it.

FRONT-SEAT PASSENGERS

- Order passengers to slide across the seat and exit via the driver's door with hands up and in plain sight.
- Give orders similar to those for the driver.

REAR-SEAT PASSENGERS TWO-DOOR VEHICLES

- Order passengers, one at a time, to crawl over the front seat and exit the driver's side door.
- Give orders similar to those for the driver.

> **REAR-SEAT PASSENGERS FOUR-DOOR VEHICLES**
>
> - Order the rear seat passenger on the left-hand side to open the left rear door from outside with their left hand.
> - Tell them to exit the vehicle from the left side.
> - Any other passengers should slide over and exit from same door with hands always in plain view above their heads.
> - Give orders similar to those for the driver.

CHAPTER PROBLEMS

1. Discuss an issue where the message in a major news media agency differed from the message in the media from the less powerful.
2. Compare and contrast two different magazines that non-major news media use to communicate with the public.
3. Describe the Freedom of Information Act and the time requirement for the government to respond.
4. Describe ways to protect children from cyber dangers.
5. Discuss whether the police should be allowed to go undercover and to deceive child predators in order to make an undercover bust.
6. Describe the problem of enforcing internet crimes.
7. Discuss the difference between a typical traffic stop and a felony stop.
8. Describe some barriers to implementing technology.
9. Describe signs of physical abuse against the elderly.
10. Describe signs of financial abuse against the elderly.

KEYWORDS

Media

Freedom of Information Act

Hostage

Cyberspace

REFERENCES

Callan, M. (2001). *Street Smart HazMat* [DVD]. Red Hat.

Cornish, P. (2007). *The CBRN system: Assessing the threat of terrorist use of chemical, biological, radiological and nuclear weapons in the United Kingdom*. www.nuclearfiles.org/menu/key-issues/nuclear-weapons/issues/policy/british-nuclear-policy/PDFs/3401_cbrn0207%5B1%5D.pdf

Del Carmen, R.V., & Hemmens, C. (2017). *Criminal procedures: Laws & practice* (10th ed.). Boston: Wadsworth.

Dowshen, S. (2015). *Internet safety*. The Nemours Foundation/KidsHealth. www.rchsd.org/health-articles/internet-safety

Fuselier, G.D. & Noesner, G.W. (1990). Confronting the terrorist hostage taker. *Law Enforcement Bulletin*, 59(7), 6–11.

Gahlinger, P. (2004). *Illegal drugs: A complete guide to their history, chemistry, use, and abuse*. New York: Plume.

Graham, C. (2006, June 19). Virginia beefs up sex-offender registry: Are enhancements enough to make registry an effective tool? *Augusta Free Press*. http://augustafreepress.com/index.php?s=enhancements+enough+registry+effective+tool

Harmening, W.M. (2014). *Crisis intervention: The criminal justice response to chaos, mayhem, and disorder.* Boston: Pearson.

Harris, S. (2010). *Toward a better way to interview child victims of sexual abuse.* www.nij.gov/journals/267/Pages/child-victim-interview.aspx

Hess, K.M., & Orthmann, C.H. (2010). *Criminal investigation* (9th ed.). Clifton Park, NY: Delmar Cengage.

Indiana University (2021). Bomb threats. https://protect.iu.edu/emergency-planning/procedures/bomb-threats.html

Inhope—Internet hotline providers (2008). *DMOZ: Open directory project.* www.dmoz.org/Computers/Internet/Child_Safety

Kappeler, V.E., & Potter, G.W. (2005). *The mythology of crime and criminal justice* (4th ed.). Long Grove, IL: Waveland Press.

Kraska, P. (2004). *Theorizing criminal justice: Eight essential orientations.* Long Grove, IL: Waveland Press.

Leonard, M. (Director). (1993). *Altered states: A history of drug use in America.* [Motion Picture]. Films Media Group.

Levy, J.M. (2000*). The first responder's pocket guide to hazardous materials emergency response* (2nd ed.). Campbell, CA: Firebelle.

Marks, M.E. (2003). *Emergency responder's guide to terrorism* [DVD]. USA: Red Hat.

Miller, L.S., Hess, K.M., & Orthmann, C.H. (2011). *Community policing: Partnerships for problem solving* (6th ed.). Clifton Park, NY: Delmar Cengage.

Miller, M.R., Schultz, D.O., & Hunt, D.D. (2011). *Police patrol.* Mason, OH: Cengage.

Prescott, J., and Rockoff, J. (2008). Are sex offender registries effective? *Sentencing Law and Policy*. http://sentencing.typepad.com/sentencing_law_and_policy/2008/03/are-sex-offende.html

Purpura, P. (2007). *Terrorism and homeland security: An introduction with applications.* Boston: Pearson.

Roleff, T. (2005). *Drug Abuse: Opposing viewpoints.* Farmington Hills, MI: Thomson Gale.

Sookhdeo, P. (2005). Television influences suicide bombers. In L.S. Friedman (Ed.) *What motivates suicide bombers?* (pp. 64–71). Farmington Hills, MI: Thomson Gale.

U.S. Department of Justice (n.d.). *Community Oriented Policing Services* (COPS). www.justice.gov/sites/default/files/jmd/legacy/2014/07/13/fy11-cops-bud-summary.pdf

U.S. Department of Justice, Federal Bureau of Investigation (n.d.). *A parent's guide to internet safety.* www2.fbi.gov/publications/pguide/pguidee.htm

Wallace, H. & Roberson, C. (2013). *Written and interpersonal communication: Methods for law enforcement.* (5th Ed). Boston: Pearson.

Whisenand, P.M. (2011). *Supervising police personnel: The fifteen responsibilities* (7th ed.). Upper Saddle River, NJ: Prentice Hall.

Yaroschuk, T. (Producer & Writer). (2000). *Hooked: Illegal drugs and how they got that way* (Vol. 1) [Motion Picture]. The History Channel: A&E.

CHAPTER 16

Qualitative Information

LEARNING OBJECTIVES

Understand information from different perspectives.

Understand proper research practices for qualitative studies.

Practice theme analysis via music lyrics.

Practice ethnography data collection and analysis.

Practice artifact data collection and analysis.

Practice focus group data collection and analysis.

INTRODUCTION

Qualitative research studies are subjective in nature and are not designed to make numeric predictions. Qualitative studies attempt to find out why people feel in certain ways, and they involve feelings, opinions, and beliefs. The appropriate qualitative research design will depend on the study's purpose, focus, data collection, and data analysis. Police officers cannot serve the community effectively if the officers do not understand the community. Therefore, police officers need to understand the qualitative information that is being transmitted by community members. Police officers need only to look around to see how people communicate. There is much information everywhere. This chapter involves some qualitative research examples. Because the collection and analysis of qualitative research data differ from study to study, several different studies are presented to demonstrate the differences. One example involves themes analysis using music lyrics; one involves an ethnography study in a natural setting; one involves artifact analysis using tombstones; and one involves a focus group that investigates how community members feel about the local police department. The four examples are only cursory, but they make the point.

ASSESSING QUALITATIVE INFORMATION

Relative Value of Information

The value of information is relative. What is considered important information to some individuals may be considered less important to others. Police officers need to understand that certain individuals will seek out particular information. They will be more effective if they understand what information certain people value.

Read the following paragraph and highlight important information.

A man entered a home. There were surveillance cameras all about the home. Inside the home, there was a strong odor of mold in the air. There was a big flat-screen TV and a laptop in the living room. In the kitchen was a backed-up sink and the pipe was leaking. Near the sink were a woman's diamond ring and a gold watch. There was a desk in a study in which there was a wad of cash; there was also a safe in one of the closets. In one of the bedrooms was the sound of someone snoring; there was also some water dripping from the bedroom's ceiling. A car then pulled into the driveway.

Now read the following paragraph and highlight important information from a thief's point of view. Assume the man who entered the home was the thief.

A man entered a home. There were **surveillance cameras** all about the home. Inside the home, there was a strong odor of mold in the air. There was a **big flat-screen TV** and a **laptop** in the living room. In the kitchen was a backed-up sink and the pipe was leaking. Near the sink were a woman's **diamond ring** and a **gold watch**. There was a desk in a study in which there was a wad of **cash**; there was also a **safe** in one of the closets. In one of the bedrooms was the sound of **someone snoring**; there was also some water dripping from the bedroom's ceiling. A **car then pulled into the driveway**.

Now, read the following paragraph and highlight important information from a potential home buyer's point of view. Assume the man who entered the home was the potential home buyer.

A man entered a home. There were surveillance cameras all about the home. Inside the home, there was a strong **odor of mold** in the air. There was a big flat-screen TV and a laptop in the living room. In the kitchen was a **backed-up sink** and the **pipe was leaking**. Near the sink were a woman's diamond ring and a gold watch. There was a desk in a study in which there was a wad of cash; there was also a safe in one of the closets. In one of the bedrooms was the sound of someone snoring; there was also some **water dripping** from the bedroom's ceiling. A car then pulled into the driveway.

Conclusion

A thief and potential home buyer will value the same information differently. What is important to the thief may not be important to the potential home buyer. Likewise, what is important to the potential home buyer may not be important to the thief.

VOICE INFLECTION

One sentence may have many meanings, depending on which words are emphasized. Individuals may change the volume level, tone, pace, or pitch when they speak particular words. Suspects may try to emphasize a particular word in a sentence, which may provide an alternate message. For example, let us look at the following sentence.

Olga received a $500 fine for cutting down a state-owned tree.

If the word "Olga" is emphasized, then the sentence focuses on the importance of who cut down the tree (e.g., I never expected Olga to cut down a state-owned tree). If the word "received" is emphasized, then the sentence focuses on the fact that the punishment already happened (e.g., I expected the police to issue a warning for a first-time offense). If the words "a $500 fine" are emphasized, then the sentence focuses on the importance of the cost of the crime (e.g., I expected a $20 fine for the violation). If the words "for cutting down" are emphasized, then the importance of the sentence is how the tree was destroyed (e.g., burning down the tree may be okay, perhaps due to insect control). If the words "state-owned" are emphasized, then the importance of the sentence focuses on ownership of the trees (e.g., there may be no fine for cutting down county-owned trees). If the word "tree" is emphasized, then the importance of the sentence focuses on the object of the crime (e.g., there may be no fine for cutting down state-owned bushes). When the words of a suspect are written down in a police report, any emphasis and the actual meaning of the sentence may be lost. In short, it is not just the words that are spoken that matter; it is also how the words are spoken.

ACADEMIC RESEARCH: NOMOTHETIC AND IDIOGRAPHIC CAUSAL RELATIONSHIPS

For both quantitative and qualitative academic research studies, police departments may want to manipulate one variable to control another variable. For example, police departments may want to know if there is a negative relationship between the *number of hours that officers are trained* (the independent variable) and the *number of public complaints* (the dependent variable). The police department may be able to manipulate the number of hours trained to reduce the number of complaints. In other words, a quantitative research question will attempt to assess the *nomothetic* causal relationship between the independent and dependent variable (Schutt, 2022). On the other hand, the department may want to know whether a community member *believes that more police training* (the independent variable) may improve *how the person feels toward police officers* (the dependent variable). In this case, there are no numeric predictions. A qualitative research question searches for an *idiographic* causal relationship between the two variables (Schutt, 2022). At least for the person interviewed, the person is indicating that a change may be needed in their beliefs about police training to modify how they feel toward the police. In both quantitative and qualitative scenarios, the police department is trying to change the outcome (the number of complaints for the quantitative study and the person's feelings about the police for the qualitative study) by manipulating an input variable.

QUALITATIVE INFORMATION

Police officers cannot serve the community effectively if the officers do not understand the community. Therefore, police officers need to understand the information that is transmitted by community members. Qualitative data, which cannot be objectively measured or counted and is subjective in nature, describes the reasons why people feel in certain ways. When people get angry, they may lash out and engage in disorderly conduct. If the police want to maintain peace, they need to understand the motives of residents. The police will need to obtain information about the feelings, attitudes, and beliefs of residents. Indeed, people are emotional beings. The police can look at music lyrics and artifact data, they can observe others in their natural settings, and they can ask groups of individuals about their feelings involving certain issues.

When investigating a topic that cannot be quantitatively predicted, such as human nature, qualitative investigations are most effective. Indeed, qualitative investigations are preferred for describing and interpreting experiences in context-specific settings because each person's reality is construed in their own mind; qualitative research attempts to reveal the meanings that participants have given to various phenomena (Adams, 1999; Ponterotto, 2005). This kind of information cannot be attained through quantitative analysis and requires probing the participants for greater detail through in-depth interviews using open-ended questions. In law enforcement terms, quantitative studies seek to understand the modus operandi while qualitative studies seek to understand the motive.

QUALITATIVE STUDY RESEARCH DESIGNS

Table 16.1 Qualitative research (Berg, 2007; Hatch, 2002; Leedy & Ormrod, 2005)

Qualitative study research design	Purpose	Focus	Data collection	Data analysis
Phenomenological	To understand truth and reality from the participants' point of view	A specific event as perceived by an individual	Purposive sampling consisting of 5–25 individuals for in-depth and unstructured interviews	Identify common themes and synthesize them into an overall concept
Ethnography	To understand how the participants' behaviors reflect the culture of a group in a natural setting	A specific location where a group of people share a common culture	Artifact collection, participation observation, and structured and unstructured interviews	Identify underlying beliefs and phenomena and synthesize them into a general behavior
Focus group study	To understand truth and reality from the participants' point of view	Specific events as perceived by a small group of individuals	Interviews and any other relevant data sources	Identify common themes and synthesize them into an overall concept
Case study	To understand one person or event in great detail because the situation is poorly understood	One case in its natural environment or a few cases in their natural environment.	Interviews, observation, written documents, and audio visual information.	Identify common themes and synthesize them into an overall concept.
Grounded theory	To derive a theory by collecting and interpreting data in a natural setting in multiple stages	The process of human actions and interactions and how they impact each other	Interviews and any other relevant data sources	Prescribed and systematic way of coding the data to identify interrelationships in the data in order to construct a theory
Content analysis	To identify themes and patterns in a body of material through a systematic examination of the data	Any communication displayed in verbal, visual, or behavioral fashion	Sampling the specific material to be analyzed and coding the material in a precisely defined manner	Tabulation of the frequency of each coded theme for descriptive and inferential statistical analysis

General Practices for Qualitative Research

1. In order to protect participants, all university researchers must obtain the approval of the Institutional Review Board (IRB) prior to gathering participant data (Berg, 2007).
2. The researcher must describe the topic of the qualitative research in an interesting manner. For example, the study's aim and purpose must be clear and important to gain the attention of potential participants. Otherwise, many individuals may ignore the study.
3. The researcher must consider the availability of the data before the researcher commits to a study. If the data are controlled by the government, for example, and the information is sensitive, then the data might not be available for analysis. Individuals may simply refuse to participate in the study.

4. The researcher must establish the need for a qualitative study (Seale et al., 2004). Qualitative studies provide thorough investigations of individuals in specific social settings and include detailed behavioral and psychological descriptions of persons in those settings (Champion, 2006). These findings may not be generalized to other populations (Creswell, 2009). If predictions are needed and generalizations to larger populations are required, then quantitative techniques should be investigated.

5. The researcher must select the proper kind of qualitative research to be performed (Hatch, 2002). Each qualitative research method is designed to obtain information in a different way. Thus, a research question may be better answered by a particular kind of qualitative research method. For example, a longitudinal case study may be better in assessing incremental changes over time than a focus group interview. Align the method of research with the research question.

6. A researcher must have an open mind and must be willing to interpret data that are unexpected and contrary to personal beliefs (Seale et al., 2004). The participants are being studied, not the researcher.

7. The researcher must present authentic findings (Creswell, 2009). The researcher must not fudge the data; otherwise, the researcher will have no credibility and the study will be questionable. Indeed, perhaps the significance of the study will indicate that the study's question was not the right question for solving the problem.

8. The researcher must make a clear distinction between the evidence and the interpretation of the evidence (Seale et al., 2004). This is important because mixing the two is misleading and less than ethical. The goal is to provide legitimate information; it is not to try to trick someone.

9. The researcher needs to select the appropriate participants for the study. For example, if police officers are the subject of study, then the researcher should investigate police officers. A purposive sampling is appropriate for a difficult to reach, specialized population (Neuman, 2006).

Below are specific practices for qualitative research. These are important in carrying out a qualitative study.

Specific Practices for Qualitative Research

1. The researcher needs to record the evidence as accurately as possible. Video record the data (i.e., interviews) if possible because this will provide a more complete visual and audio account. Always supplement the data-collection process with note-taking, just in case a problem develops with the audio-visual equipment.

2. For a qualitative one-on-one interview, the researcher needs to develop a question that is open-ended and allows for in-depth answers (Creswell, 2009). Qualitative studies seek to understand the meanings, concepts, symbols, and characteristics of things. This requires narrative-style answers. In addition, develop probe questions for further elaboration.

3. The researcher needs to protect the participants (Berg, 2007). The researcher needs to follow ethical guidelines and to protect the privacy and confidentiality of the participants by explaining the research process to them and by obtaining their permission to proceed.

4. The researcher needs to perform a literature review (Balian, 1988). The goal is to add to the body of knowledge. Gaps in the knowledge will not be known unless prior studies are examined. Otherwise, the study may be meaningless, especially if the topic has already been exhausted.

5. The researcher needs to use triangulation (Creswell, 2009). This will help to validate the data and may provide additional insights or generate additional questions. There are several ways to use triangulation in research (Berg, 2007). These include data triangulation, investigator triangulation, theory triangulation, and methodological triangulation. All help to enhance the validity of the study.

6. The researcher needs to obtain the proper software for content (data) analysis and needs to practice using it for identifying themes (Berg, 2007). The software is only useful if it is used in the right manner. Free qualitative software packages are available online, and the researchers should familiarize themselves with what is available.
7. During interviews, the researcher needs to keep the participants focused on the topic. The data sought should seek to answer the research question. Because the amount of raw data can be overwhelming, the researcher should continually evaluate whether the data are related to the question. This will allow the researcher to manage the huge amount of data. Do not get sidetracked.
8. The researcher needs to interview the participants in a comfortable and secure place (Berg, 2007). If the participants are afraid that someone may overhear their responses, especially if those responses are sensitive and may get them into trouble, then they may withhold valuable information.
9. The researcher needs to be flexible (Berg, 2007). The researcher may need to adjust personal schedules to meet with the participants. After all, the participants are going out of their way to provide data, so personal schedules may need to be adjusted to meet the participants when they are available.
10. The researcher needs to dress appropriately (Berg, 2007). If the researcher fails to dress professionally, then the participants may doubt the quality of the study and the confidentiality of the data. The image of the researcher may reflect the quality of the study.
11. For focus group interviews, use a round table so all participants can be observed. Otherwise, valuable information may be missed.

QUALITATIVE THEME ANALYSIS

Qualitative content analysis research studies attempt to understand why events happen by discovering themes in the data. There are many different techniques for identifying themes in qualitative data. Some work better for short, open-ended responses while others work better for rich, complex narratives. There is no single technique that is optimal for all situations. See Table 16.2 for several techniques that are used to identify themes in qualitative data.

Table 16.2 Several techniques used in qualitative research for identifying themes (Ryan & Bernard, n.d.)

General technique	Specific technique	Description
Analysis of words	Word repetitions	Informal: Note unique words (and their synonyms) that are used often because they determine important ideas.
		Formal: count the number of times unique words are used to create a list of important ideas.
	Indigenous categories	Experience and expertise often use specialized vocabulary. Create categories by seeking terms that sound unfamiliar or are used in unfamiliar ways.
	Keywords in context	Look at how concepts are used. Identify keywords and search the text to find all instances of how the words are used. Assess the immediate context. Themes are identified by sorting examples into piles of similar meaning.
Analysis of blocks of text	Compare and contrast	Conduct a line-by-line analysis to identify the idea in the current line and how the idea is similar or different from the previous line.
	Social science queries	Search for specific topics that may generate major social and cultural themes (e.g., managing interpersonal social relationships, informal methods of social control, achieving social status, etc.).

Table 16.2 Cont.

General technique	Specific technique	Description
Intentional analysis of linguistic features	Searching for missing information	Search for themes that are absent from the text. Silence may indicate a topic that the person is unwilling or afraid to discuss.
	Metaphors and analogies	Look for metaphors that produce patterns of underlying principles.
	Transitions	Look for naturally occurring shifts in thematic content (new paragraphs in written text and pauses in oral speech).
	Connectors	Look for phrases that indicate relationships among topics (e.g., causal relationships, conditional relationships, time-oriented relationships, and spatial orientations).
Physical manipulation of text	Unmarked texts	Read the text several times, highlight different salient themes, and group similar themes. Then, in the remaining text, look for less obtrusive themes.
	Pawing	Read the text several times, separate the key phrases, and look for patterns in the data via the interocular percussion test.
	Cutting and sorting	Look for quotes that seem important; group similar quotes to identify themes. Good for identifying subthemes

EXAMPLE 1: THE MESSAGE OF MUSIC

Local residents use music to communicate. Therefore, officers need to pay attention to the music of minorities because their songs may be transmitting qualitative messages about how they perceive society. For example, there must be a reason why minorities sing songs about excessive police force. Perhaps they have experienced such events. Even if the officers do not believe these messages, the minorities may believe them. Hence, it is important for the police to listen to what community members are saying and to understand their meanings.

Example 1. Assessing Information in Love Songs

The lyrics for 10 love songs, which have all been ranked number one on the charts, have been collected and examined (About.com: Country music, n.d.; AlaskaJim.com, 2007; Songfacts, n.d.; Songlyrics.com, n.d.). Five of the songs are performed by men and five are performed by women. The five songs performed by men are: (1) "Pretty Woman" by Roy Orbison; (2) "Daydream Believer" by The Monkees; (3) "El Paso" by Marty Robbins; (4) "Running Bear" by Johnny Preston; and (5) "Hello, I Love You" by The Doors. The five songs performed by women are: (1) "I Will Always Love You" by Dolly Parton; (2) "To Sir With Love" by Lulu; (3) "Love Child" by The Supremes; (4) "Will You Love Me Tomorrow?" by The Shirelles; and (5) "Respect" by Aretha Franklin. The themes of the lyrics in the songs performed by men will be compared with those in the songs performed by women. All the lyrics performed for each sex will be combined and an overall comparison will be made.

The unit of analysis, which "is the amount of text that is assigned a code" (Neuman, 2006, p. 327), will be the stanza. Furthermore, because the words "I love you" may actually mean "I am infatuated with you and want sexual intercourse even though I do not know you," the theme of each stanza will be evaluated by using latent coding. Indeed, latent coding may be more valid than manifest coding, which simply counts the number of times that the words appear. This means that the entire song must be read prior to any evaluations so that the overtone can be assessed. In addition, a stanza may include more than one theme. However, before a content analysis can commence, a list of variable categories needs to be developed (Sproull, 1995).

The variable (love) categories are:

1. Long-term love—a long term commitment, perhaps as in marriage.
2. Infatuation—lust; sexual gratification; short-term love.
3. Puppy love—nonsexual and superficial.
4. Gain love—want other person to submit/provide love.
5. Give love—willing to submit/sacrifice oneself for love.

Table 16.3 provides the overall themes in the songs.

Table 16.3 Summary of the five variable categories for the lyrics of 10 love songs

Variable	No. of times variable appeared (men)	No. of times variable appeared (women)
1	9	17
2	17	1
3	1	0
4	5	2
5	9	4

Relatively speaking, men seemed to focus more on immediate sexual gratification than women, while women focused more on marriage. In addition, although men more often wanted women to submit themselves than women did with men, men were also more willing to die for sex. Of course, content analysis depends on the researcher recognizing terms that reflect love.

Content analysis is a useful way to assess information in everyday life. Being a police officer, it is important to analyze what is being said through both verbal and nonverbal means. For example, if a police officer stops a pickup truck and is suspicious that there might be drugs in the vehicle, if the suspects clench their fists, they may be preparing to fight; if they take off their hats and sunglasses, they do not want to damage them; if they start whispering to one another, they may be making a plan of attack; if they try to keep certain parts of their bodies shielded, they may be trying to conceal weapons; if they start looking around, they may be looking for witnesses, weapons, or escape routes; and if they try to position the officer between them, this may indicate that violence is about to occur. Indeed, being able to recognize such themes may save an officer's life.

EXAMPLE 2: ETHNOGRAPHY—ASSESSING INFORMATION IN A NATURAL SETTING

Date: Monday, November 9, 2020

Location: Wana Cup Restaurant in Shipshewana, Indiana

Time: 11:00–11:30 am

An ethnography study seeks to describe a culture from the local or Indigenous people's point of view (Berg, 2007). Data collection includes participant observation, participant interviewing, and artifact examination in order "to understand the cultural knowledge that group members use to make sense of the everyday experiences" (Hatch, 2002, p. 21). Thus, I entered a local restaurant to observe customers.

Sense of Vision

As I pulled up to the restaurant, I observed one car parked in front of the restaurant and four horse-and-buggies parked on the side of the restaurant. All the horses were either brown or black and all the buggies were black. The car, on the other hand, was red. All the lights on the outside of the restaurant were gas lanterns. The entire building was gray, even the roof-top. Furthermore, there was a white wooden fence in front of the building. In short, there were no extravagant colors advertising this restaurant.

Once inside the building, I observed eight customers: four men and four women. All the customers seemed to be between 50 and 60 years of age. The customers sat at two tables, two men and two women at each table. The men sat across from the women.

The men had some particular characteristics. First, all four men had full beards but none had mustaches. Second, none wore belts; instead, they all wore suspenders. Third, all four men wore dark-blue pants, which appeared rugged, like work pants (they were not blue jeans). Fourth, all four men wore black coats, black boots, and black hats. Fifth, all four men wore eye glasses (versus contact lenses). Sixth, none of the men wore any jewelry.

The four women seemed to match the men they accompanied. First, all four women wore black coats and white bonnets. Second, all the women wore either black or blue dresses. In other words, the colors were conservative and they were not blue jeans. Third, all four women wore black boots and black stockings. Fourth, all these women wore eye glasses (versus contact lenses). Fifth, all the women had black purses. Sixth, none of the women wore any jewelry.

As far as the environment was concerned, I noticed that there was a wooden sign on the wall with the Lord's Prayer on it. This seemed to be significant; indeed, the men and women closed their eyes and seemed to pray before they ate. Furthermore, I noticed that the advertisement signs above the cash register were made of cardboard, although they did have professional-looking drawings on them. For example, a banana split sign had a very good drawing of a banana split on it. In addition, the colors in the building were simple. The walls had wood paneling halfway up them. Above that, the walls were white. Finally, the unisex bathroom utilized a single cloth roller towel (i.e., a single towel that everyone uses). Thus, all the clues indicated that this restaurant was low tech.

Finally, I noticed that there was some money (an unknown amount of dollar bills) resting on a tray on top of the garbage can. No one seemed to care that it sat there. This indicates that the people probably trusted one another not to take it. The waitress finally picked the money up about 10 minutes later.

Sense of Smell

Sitting next to the group, I was overwhelmed by their body odor. It seemed as though the individuals may not bathe daily. However, this odor did not seem to bother them.

Sense of Hearing

Except for the talking among the individuals, the inside of the restaurant was quiet. There was no music playing and there were no cell phones. In addition, the entire group appeared to speak a combination of German and English. However, when a man dressed in a suit approached them, they started speaking English to him.

Summary

In short, this culture is quite different than my culture. They do not desire modern technology and do not fancy materialistic products. Indeed, they do not even drive motor vehicles. However, they do seem to have strong social bonds within their community. Furthermore, they do not seem to be concerned about what outsiders think (as evidenced by the Lord's Prayer on the wall).

EXAMPLE 3: ARTIFACT DATA—ASSESSING INFORMATION IN CEMETERIES

Artifact

An artifact is a human made object that provides information about an earlier time and culture. Tombstones are artifacts. Much unobtrusive actuarial data can be obtained from tombstones in cemeteries (Berg, 2007).

Greenwood Cemetery (Lagrange, Indiana)

Greenwood Cemetery in Lagrange, Indiana is a public cemetery with thousands of grave sites. This cemetery does not have a policy requiring that flat stones be used. Consequently, there are many different types of headstones used in this cemetery. All the headstones face east, a Christian tradition, and there is an overall Christian theme at the site (other religious denominations are not obvious) ("Graves," 2006).

Headstones from 200 years ago

Greenwood Cemetery, a municipality cemetery, contains headstones with dates ranging from persons who fought in the American Revolutionary War until the present day. Most of the headstones for military personnel are similar to one another. They are about 3 feet high, white, and contain a cross at the top. A military headstone contains the name of the deceased, the state identifying where the person came from, the rank of the person during the war, the name of the war fought in, and the dates of birth and death. In many cases, the commanding officer's name is also included on the headstone. For example, one headstone reads as follows, "Abel Mattoon, Massachusetts, PVT, Capt. T. Williams Co, Revolutionary War, 1759–1837." Next to each of these headstones for military personnel is a metal rod, about 2 feet high, with a five-point star on top with the word, "Comrade" on it.

Analysis

It appears that individuals in this era wanted to advertise great accomplishments. By listing the commanders' names on the headstones, it appears that these historic headstones allow for confirmation of the facts. In addition, by having crosses near the top of the headstones, the headstones appear to indicate loyalty to God and country.

Headstones from 100 years ago

Another section of the cemetery contains family plots. In one example, there are six headstones for one family. The one on the farthest right is a 10 foot-high megalith, which looks like the Washington Monument (Butterfield, 2003). Near the top are decorative images of diamonds. The front of this headstone reads, "In memory, father and mother." The back side states a name, the date of death, and the age in years, months, and days; no date of birth is listed. The other five family members' headstones are to the left of the monument and are about 2 feet high and attached to one another via a concrete slab. For these, only names and dates are provided (e.g., Jacob Brown, 1829–1906). Of these five headstones, a male's name appears to be on both the farthest right and on the farthest left with three female names between them. Due to their relative positions to one another, it seems as though the females are being protected by the males. Many headstones in this era seem to describe men as independent human beings, but women are depicted as attached to men.

Analysis

Headstones in this era describe women by their social relationships to men. Often, a woman's headstone lists her name, that she is the wife of [man's name], and dates of birth and death. However, the headstones of men do not describe the men's social relationships to women. Although most of these headstones have symbols on them, such as crosses, a hand holding the Bible, doves, and a variety of flowers (e.g., roses or Easter lilies), the text on them is brief.

Headstones from about 30 years ago
More recent headstones appear to be custom designed by making use of laser and digital technologies (Heller, 2008). Indeed, recent headstones in Greenwood Cemetery contain photographs, images, and text statements. For example, one young female who passed away in 1990 has her photograph in the center of the headstone, a sorority emblem on the left side, an image of a swimmer on the right side, a Southwest Allen County Fire Department emblem at the bottom, and four statements from loved ones on the back. These statements include, "My darling Allison, God gave me the most precious gift in the world, it was you. You will always be with me in my heart, love always, Mom," and "To Allison, though lovers be lost, love shall not. Death shall have no dominion, Mike." In this section of the cemetery, headstones often have marriage dates on them with symbolic pictures (e.g., wedding rings interlocked or two hands holding one another), the name of the spouse, children's names, etches of recreational activities (e.g., fishing), occupations (e.g., a tractor-trailer), and they are surrounded by urns, flowers, solar lights (which represent the eternal flame), and statues of pets, such as dogs.

Analysis
These headstones seem to describe family unity, social memberships, personal accomplishments, recreational activities, occupations, and pets. Furthermore, many of them contain colored photographs of the deceased, which can provide valuable physical characteristics. At the same time, crosses, angels, and doves indicate a Christian atmosphere.

Headstones from about 20 years ago
There is a baby section of headstones that date about the year 2000. On these headstones are words like, "our little angel," and "forever in our hearts." Moreover, surrounding these headstones are an abundance of angels, Easter bunnies, bears in the form of angels, toys, crosses, and flowers.

Analysis
The atmosphere seems to suggest a spiritual connotation where parents are trying to assure that their children are protected and cared for. In other words, the babies are not alone. Indeed, this area is heavily visited.

Eastbaren Cemetery (Shipshewana, Indiana)
Because there are many Amish in Lagrange County, Indiana, Eastbaren Cemetery, a private Amish cemetery with about 200 grave sites, was also examined. Every headstone in this cemetery is less than 2 feet high and all but four are white. The older headstones (in the 1800 era), simply state names and dates of birth and death. If marriages were involved, the spouse's name with the words "wife of" or "husband of" may be included on the headstones. More recent headstones (dated in the 1970s) may include the names of surviving family members (e.g., loving mother of James and Sara) along with Bible verses on the back. For example, the back of one headstone reads, "Fear not little flock; for it is your Father's good pleasure to give you the kingdom. Luke 12:32." Several headstones dated in the 1990s have both male and female names on them along with marriage dates.

About 10% of the grave markers in this cemetery simply state a name and date. In one case, there is a wooden cross made of weathered barn siding with a date of 2008. On this cross is a handwritten message made with a black marker that states, "What a great sacrifice so others can live," and "we miss you."

Analysis
This cemetery seeks simplicity and uniformity. There are no flowers, urns, photographs, solar lights, or statues. There are just headstones and crosses. Although some social statuses are indicated

(e.g., wife of), significant others are listed (e.g., surviving family members' names), and significant events recorded (e.g., wedding dates), the atmosphere seems to focus on the afterlife and not on personal accomplishments in life. This is in sharp contrast to the Greenwood Cemetery.

EXAMPLE 4: FOCUS GROUP STUDY

Focus group interviews, where individuals who share common traits and experiences interact and provide data beyond what any single participant can provide, are most appropriate for studies that are explanatory in nature (Hatch, 2002). Focus groups are nice because the themes can be validated in real time at the end of the session. A quotation from one of the participants will be used to reflect the group's answer for each question. However, a weakness in this technique is that the group consensus may overshadow a particular individual's perspective (Berg, 2007; Hatch, 2002). Following is a cursory example of a focus group study on police profiling.

Focus Group Instrument

The purpose of this study is to discover how people feel about their local police department. If residents are upset with the police department, changes may need to be made.

Following is a statement of the basic rules (Berg, 2007). The discussion will be conducted in a polite and professional manner. Indeed, different points of view and experiences will provide an overall understanding of the issue. Therefore, all opinions are valued. A question will be asked, each participant will be asked to provide a short response, then the question will be open for group discussion. Everyone is encouraged to respond.

Research Question: What is your perception of police officers and your respect for police?

The open-ended research question will be the first question asked during the interview. In addition, five probing questions will be asked to provide a more comprehensive understanding of the situation.

Additional probing questions

- Why do you perceive that the police, through their behaviors, have not earned your respect?
- What is your perception of the relationship between the police and minorities?
- What is your perception of the relationship between minorities and whites?
- What is your experience with police profiling or racial discrimination?
- What do you feel is the goal of the police department and why?

In order to gather a general feeling of civilians' perceptions of the local police, a focus group interview was conducted involving seven participants. The interview was conducted in a room at a local university. The ground rules were described to the participants as: (1) a question will be asked; (2) each participant will be asked to provide a short response; and (3) the question will then be open for group discussion. The seven participants are: (1) O. Zing, a 32-year-old Asian American female who was born in China; (2) L. Cloud, a 50-year-old Native American female; (3) P. Cheddar, a 50 year white male, retired from the U.S. Army; (4) O. Twinkles, a 50-year-old white female with nine years of business experience; (5) T. Witne, a 50-year-old white female with five years of manufacturing experience; (6) P. Proud, a 50-year-old white female and homemaker; and (7) L. Rodriguez, a 41-year-old Hispanic female born in Panama. It should be noted that all the participants who have stated that they are 50 years of age are probably not actually 50. Three of the females did not want to provide their actual ages. They simply stated "50 plus or minus." In short, the focus group participants are from different backgrounds and are able to provide different perspectives about the topic. Below is the essence of what the focus group participants stated.

Research Question: What is your perception of police officers and your respect for police?

"I respect the police out of fear" (O. Zing, personal communication, September 22, 2011). The overall consensus is that those who respect the police do it because of the officers' position, not because of the officers' behaviors. Overall, it appears that all the participants believe there are police–community concerns.

Probe Question: Why you perceive that the police, through their behaviors, have not earned your respect?

"In general, the community does not respect the local police because the police are idiots. In fact, one police officer was forced to resign because he is a thief" (P. Cheddar, personal communication, September 22, 2011). Because this event was advertised in the local media, the case being described was common knowledge among the group. Thus, all participants agreed with this statement. The group consensus was that the police were respected only because of their position of authority and not because of their behaviors.

Probe Question: What is your perception of the relationship between the police and minorities?

"The police do profile. Anyone who is dark they profile. My son was walking with two blond-hair boys. A cop pulled up next to them and questioned them about smoking. The cop let the two blond-hair boys go but made my son empty out his pockets to prove that he did not have any cigarettes" (L. Cloud, personal communication, September 22, 2011). Although all the Caucasians in this group stated that they had had no personal experiences with the police, the Native American, the Chinese American, and the Hispanic American stated that they were aware of police discrimination against minorities. Only one female Caucasian stated that she believed discrimination occurred against minorities, but only because of what she had seen in the movies.

Probe Question: What is your perception of the relationship between minorities and whites?

"Some minorities exaggerate ethnic problems. Some Chinese do not like to talk to whites because they do not think that whites like them. I say, how would they know until they talk with them? People feel comfortable talking to those who look similar" (O. Zing, personal communication, September 22, 2011). Zing also stated that several years ago, at Indiana University, a Chinese American mom had a sick 12-year-old son. She let her son sleep with her so she could take care of him. Zing stated that this is common practice in China. However, social workers came, charged the mom with sexual abuse and took her son away; subsequently, her son died soon afterwards. Zing stated that whites need to learn about different cultural practices. The general consensus of the group was that whites do not communicate well with other cultures. The rest of the group backed this up with another example. They stated that, just a little while ago, there was an accident nearby and a Hispanic was killed. No one in the area knew how to speak Spanish and so no one could communicate with the victim's family. Thus, the entire group claimed that there is definitely a communication problem between cultures.

Probe Question: What is your experience with police profiling or racial discrimination?

"I only know what I have seen on TV and in the movies. White police officers pick on minorities" (P. Proud, personal communication, September 22, 2011). The overall consensus is that the participants have had no personal experience with police profiling or racial discrimination, and that they have learned their perceptions through second-hand information. Only the Hispanic female may actually have experienced a profiling incident. In her case, she stated that she had pulled into a grocery store and that a white male city police officer was staring her down

(L. Rodriguez, personal communication, September 22, 2011). She stated that after she left the store, about 20 minutes later, the officer followed her for about 4 miles out of the city. He then pulled her over and gave her a bogus excuse.

Probe Question: What do you feel is the goal of the local police department and why?

"The goal is to write tickets and make money" (P. Cheddar, personal communication, September 22, 2011). The overall consensus is that the police officers focus on meeting their monthly quotas and do not focus on serving residents. T. White stated that she was issued four tickets in one traffic stop. She felt that the officer was nitpicky with her in order to meet his monthly quota. Other participants pointed out that state police officers only issue one ticket per car because that delivers the message without overdoing it.

CHAPTER PROBLEMS

1. Describe the purpose of the Institutional Review Board (IRB).
2. What is a qualitative content analysis study?
3. What is an ethnography study?
4. What is artifact analysis?
5. Discuss some specific practices that are required for qualitative studies.
6. Read the following paragraph and highlight the important information that may affect the track runner's performance during the race.

    The athlete is a junior in college and is the team's captain. The track is a dirt track and requires long spikes for optimal traction. The day of the events will be on Saturday, which is expected to be windy. Any false starts will result in an immediate disqualification. The event will be recorded by the school's mascot, who has served as the school's mascot for five years. The winner of each event will be forwarded to the national competition. The cost of admissions will be $10 for visitors.

7. Complete a theme analysis investigation. Select a variable with three to five categories. Then select five songs related to the variable that are sung by women and five songs that are sung by men. Define the unit of analysis. Create a table that summarizes the variable counts and interpret the results.
8. Complete an ethnography investigation. Go to a location that contains a culture different from your own. Use your five senses and describe the information that you collect using each sense. Provide a summary of the results.
9. Complete an artifact analysis. Go to a cemetery or other location where information has been recorded over many years. Then provide examples of information in each period and an analysis of what information was deemed important in each period.
10. Complete a focus group investigation. Select a variable of interest, such as camera use for traffic enforcement. Ask five to eight people to meet together to answer some questions about the variable of interest. Create a main research question (e.g., Why do you feel that the use of traffic enforcement cameras affects police-community relations?) and three-five probing questions (e.g., Have you ever received a camera traffic ticket that you felt was unjustified?). Generate the ground rules for how the questions will be asked and answered. For each question, provide a quotation to reflect how a majority of the group feels, summarize the group consensus, and mention any opposing viewpoints. Ask the group whether your interpretation of their responses is correct before the group members leave.

KEYWORDS

Artifact

Content analysis

Ethnography

Focus group

REFERENCES

About.com: Country music (n.d.). *Dolly Parton—Jolene.* http://countrymusic.about.com/od/cdreviewsmz/fr/Jolene.htm

Adams, W. (1999). The interpretation of self and world: Empirical research, existential phenomenology, and transpersonal psychology. *Journal of Phenomenological Psychology, 30*(2), 39–65.

AlaskaJim.com (2007). Top songs of the 1960s. www.alaskajim.com/polls/2002topsongs1960s_results.htm

Balian, E.S. (1988). *How to design, analyze, and write doctoral or master's research* (2nd ed.). New York: University Press of America.

Berg, B. (2007). *Qualitative research methods for the social sciences* (6th ed.). Boston: Pearson.

Butterfield, A. (2003). Monuments and memorials. *New Republic, 228*(4), 27–32.

Champion, D. (2006). *Research methods for criminal justice and criminology* (3rd ed.). Upper Saddle River, NJ: Pearson Merrill Prentice-Hall.

Creswell, J. (2009). *Research design: Qualitative, quantitative, and mixed methods approaches* (3rd ed.). Thousand Oaks, CA: Sage.

Graves 'will be allowed to face east' (2006, September 26). *Europe Intelligence Wire.*

Hatch, J. (2002). *Doing qualitative research in education settings.* Albany, NY: State University of New York Press.

Heller, S. (2008). Death, be not staid. *Print, 62*(4), 90–95.

Leedy, P., and Ormrod, J. (2005). *Practical research: Planning and design* (8th ed.). Upper Saddle River, NJ: Pearson Merrill Prentice-Hall.

Neuman, W. (2006). *Social research methods: Qualitative and quantitative approaches* (6th ed.). Boston: Pearson.

Ponterotto, J. (2005). Qualitative research in counseling psychology: A primer on research paradigms and philosophy of science. *Journal of Counseling, 52*(2), 126–136.

Ryan, G.W., & Bernard, H.R. (n.d.). Techniques to identify themes in qualitative data. www.analytictech.com/mb870/readings/ryan-bernard_techniques_to_identify_themes_in.htm

Schutt, R.K. (2022). *Investigating the social world: The process and practice of research* (10th ed.). Thousand Oaks, CA: Sage.

Seale, C., Gobo, G., Gubrium, J., & Silverman, D. (2004). Introduction: Inside qualitative research. In C. Seale, G. Gobo, J. Gubrium, & D. Silverman (Eds.), *Qualitative research practice* (pp. 1–12). Thousand Oaks, CA: Sage.

Songfacts (n.d.). *To sir with love.* www.songfacts.com/detail.php?id=2780

Songlyrics.com (n.d.). www.songlyrics.com/

Sproull, N. (1995). *Handbook of research methods: A guide for practitioners and students in the social sciences* (2nd ed.). Lanham, MD: Scarecrow Press.

CHAPTER 17

Résumé, Job Interview, and Oral Presentations

LEARNING OBJECTIVES

Understand the reverse chronological résumé.

Understand the functional résumé.

Understand the different types of interview questions and the expected answers.

Describe the different types of evidence to support a speech.

Practice impromptu speeches.

INTRODUCTION

First, law enforcement typically requires a résumé, which provides a person's background information. You can expect that a police department will perform a background check on all job applicants before they are offered jobs. Therefore, you should keep track of all employment, skills, and accomplishments, which should include dates, titles, contact information, and other relevant information. Second, the law enforcement job interview is a meeting where the employer will ask the applicant a variety of questions to determine whether the applicant is a good fit for both the job and the department. Interviewers will ask applicants open-ended questions to gain insight about their personality, common sense, drive, and dedication. Therefore, be prepared to explain how you have prepared yourself for the job and the reasons for you wanting the job. Although law enforcement has three main categories (public service, traffic investigations, and criminal investigations), the one you mention first may indicate to the department which one you emphasize the most. Expect to explain your strengths and weaknesses. Finally, along with officers in the field, applicants may be expected to provide oral presentations that are not planned, organized, or rehearsed. Impromptu speeches will test the presenter's ability to calmly react to the issue at hand while addressing the problem.

RÉSUMÉ

A résumé, sometimes spelled "resume," is a document created and used by individuals to present their background, skills, and accomplishments. Résumés are often required by police departments when applicants apply for employment. In order to best prepare a résumé for maximum success, it is best to begin thinking from the potential employer's perspective about what qualities they are looking for in a future employee. The résumé is the information that the potential employer will use to decide who has the skills and qualities that are best suited for the job description. If the résumé is less than stellar, the likelihood of being asked in for an interview is very low. A good résumé is the first step in obtaining an interview.

There are two major types of résumés. The first type of résumé is the reverse chronological résumé. This lists employment from the most recent to the least recent (i.e., from newest to oldest). Employers are looking for large gaps in employment and short lengths of employment. If there are large gaps of unemployment, or you do not work long enough at various jobs, these will give the appearance of laziness and instability. Thus, be prepared to explain these issues if they exist. Although the reverse chronological résumé presents a good timeline of employment and shows advancement, it does not focus on accumulated job skills. The functional résumé, however, is organized by categories based on the person's skills or qualifications. However, because functional résumés appear to cover up large gaps of unemployment, this type of résumé may not be accepted by police departments. To resolve this problem, the job application process for law enforcement is designed to specially walk the applicants through a reverse chronological résumé.

The following two steps are a simplified method of putting together a résumé that is professional and attention getting (Kursmark, 2003).

Step 1

Identify the kind of job you desire. The more specific you are about the type of job you are seeking, the more you will be able to write a résumé that fits that particular job description. If your résumé is too generic, it might not catch the attention of the employer, who will be going through many different résumés.

Start by describing the specific type of work that you are interested in performing. Using non-specific words such as "law enforcement" is not going to give your résumé a clear-cut edge over other non-specific résumés that the employer will have to read. Instead of simply stating "law enforcement," one could write "crash scene reconstructionist" or "computer crime investigations" to get a more specific goal in mind.

Step 2

Identity the main qualifications and duties of the position desired. Make sure you thoroughly investigate what the job you want entails in terms of work expectations and the level of experience required. The job description may carry much of this information. If not, then an internet search of similar jobs may give you some good ideas about what will be expected from you as an employee.

Begin to target the specific skills set, experience, and education that you have, which will make you a good candidate for the job. Then write out the qualities that you have that will make you a good candidate for the position (e.g., communication skills, critical thinking skills, interpersonal skills). Depending on the job, these qualities are sometimes more important than your employment history or education.

You will want to give quality information for the following sections:

- *Education:* List any degrees or certifications that you have earned. When listing these, make sure to list the title of the degree or certification, where it was obtained, and the date you obtained it. You could also list your grade point average and any awards or honors that you have earned.
- *Skills section:* The skills section of the résumé will include any relevant skills that you possess pertaining to the job you are seeking (e.g., proficient in statistical analysis software, accident reconstruction software, Excel, and PowerPoint). Make sure you describe the level of your ability. There is a big difference between someone who is "proficient" and someone who is merely "familiar with" a certain skill-set.
- *Other qualities:* In this section, you can include anything that you believe will show you have more to offer than just the minimum requirements (e.g., bilingual, good public speaker, effective multi-tasker).

- *Experience:* The experience section of the résumé will include your work history and any other experiences related to work in the field you are seeking (e.g., law enforcement internships). It is important to include all relevant information about your previous experience. This will include the title of your job, your personal title or position, the name of the company for which you worked, the dates of your employment, your job responsibilities, and any awards or significant accomplishments that you obtained while working at the company.

Following are examples of two types of résumés: the reverse chronological résumé and the functional résumé. Generally, the reverse chronological résumé is preferred. See the following table for the pros and cons of the reverse chronological and functional résumés.

Table 17.1 Pros and cons of reverse chronological and functional résumés

Résumé type	Pros	Cons
Reverse chronological résumé	Preferred by hiring professionals. Good if no large gaps in employment. Focuses on dates of employment. Indicates seamless employment. Highlights well-respected employers. Shows consistent growth and advancement. Easy to review and to obtain particular information.	Highlights employers who have bad reputations. Advertises large gaps in employment, too many changes in jobs, or too little experience.
Functional résumé	Focuses on jobs skills accumulated. Groups job skills by type of experience. May be able to conceal large gaps in employment, too many changes in jobs, and too little experience.	Difficult to review. May be discarded because it takes too much effort to review. Suspicious because may be trying to cover up large gaps in employment, too many changes in jobs, or too little experience.

REVERSE CHRONOLOGICAL RÉSUMÉ

Olga E. Hernandez, Ph.D.

ph: 313-555-0472; email: ohernandez@anywebaddress.com

Work experience

Wayne Technical College – Department Chair for Criminal Justice: 2010–present

My responsibilities have included changing a philosophy-based criminal justice program into an application-based criminal justice program that employs critical thinking. I have: (a) designed a new curriculum; (b) developed program objectives, goals, syllabi, and addendums; (c) collaborated with local law enforcement departments to ensure that the program is in alignment with community needs; (d) developed the content for each course ensuring that the content adheres to state standards; (e) developed student learning outcomes and program assessment standards; (f) determined needed resources for the program and completed purchase orders in order to obtain the resources; (g) participated in the development of divisional and departmental strategic plans; (h) created and developed a new capstone course in the state approved curriculum; (i) selected textbooks; (j) taught a variety of law enforcement courses; (k) developed the college's first online courses in criminal justice; (l) chaired advisory committee meetings; (m) recruited adjunct professors; (n) advised students; and (o) managed the criminal justice program budget.

U.S. Dept. of Homeland Security—U.S. Customs & Border Protection: 2000–2007

I was responsible for protecting the American public against terrorists and instruments of terror while facilitating the timely movement of legitimate cargo and travelers. This required enforcing laws related to revenue and trade, seizing contraband, examining agricultural items for pests and diseases, and inspecting persons in determining their admissibility into the United States. Responsibilities also included enforcing the laws of numerous federal agencies, checking criminal records, conducting searches, writing reports, making arrests, collecting duties, and resolving radioactive anomalies. This included using a variety of tools, including numerous computer databases and many non-intrusive detection devices.

Indiana State Police—Master Trooper: 1990–2000

My job responsibilities included public service, traffic enforcement, and criminal investigations. Some of my responsibilities included collecting, preserving and documenting evidence, writing reports, administering field sobriety tests, investigating and protecting crash scenes, administering emergency first-aid to crash victims, enforcing traffic laws, making criminal arrests, testifying in court, providing assistance to the general public, speaking to school children about drug concerns and traffic safety issues, and training new police officers. Some major cases that I have investigated and resolved include attempted murder, forgery, counterfeiting, intimidation, battery, theft, criminal recklessness, and a variety of drug violations. I was post commander for the district and incident commander at many hazardous scenes. I was the lead investigator, and usually the sole investigator, of any case that I initiated.

Ford Motor Company—Program Manager/ Design Engineer: 1985–1990

I was a product design engineer and program manager. I was responsible for a variety of programs. I was the engineer to first implement the electronic control module into the pleasure boat industry. This included meeting design requirements, writing product specifications, performing test-to-failure statistical research, negotiating the sales and warranty agreements, and working with the manufacturing plant to ensure production quality. Other programs for which I was responsible include audio systems, powertrain systems, passive restraint systems, warranty claims analysis, and cost analysis forecasting.

Education

Wayne State University, Detroit, MI—Doctorate: Criminal Justice

Eastern Michigan University, Ypsilanti, MI—Master's Degree: Accounting

University of Michigan, Ann Arbor, MI—Bachelor's Degree: Electrical Engineering

Federal Law Enforcement Training Center, Glynco, GA—U.S. Department of Homeland Security/ U.S. Customs & Border Protection

Indiana Law Enforcement Academy, Plainfield, IN—Trooper, Indiana State Police

Additional Training/Certifications

FAA: Helicopter Pilot License

PADI: Advanced Open Water Scuba Diver

FCC: Technician Plus Amateur Radio License

State of Michigan: Basic Emergency Medical Technician

Technical Skills

Excel, Lotus, Word, Word Perfect, PowerPoint, SPSS

Important Writings

1. Terrorism and Homeland Security (ABC Publishing)
2. Police-Community Relations (ABC Publishing)
3. Emotional Intelligence and Criminal Justice (XYZ Publishing)
4. Cybercrime and Hacker Techniques (XYZ Publishing)
5. Criminology and Crime Prevention (LoGiudice Publishing)

Awards/Honors

1. U.S. Department of Homeland Security Commissioner's Award
2. U.S. Department of Homeland Security Scholastic Award
3. Ford Motor Company's Worldwide Leadership Excellence Award
4. University of Michigan Upperclassman Engineering Departmental Award
5. President of the National Electrical Engineering Honor Society
6. Graduated with Distinction (University of Michigan-D)

FUNCTIONAL RÉSUMÉ

Estenia O. Hernandez

ph: 734-555-8432; email: ehernandez@anywebaddress.com

Summary of Qualifications

An experienced leader with a management style that empowers and motivates others to achieve a common set of goals. Demonstrated ability to recruit, hire, coach, and develop staff in the areas of customer service, sales, operations, and accounting.

Skills and Accomplishments

Management

- Streamlined six customer service departments to one central location.
- Streamlined accounting procedures, which eliminated the need for second shift and second location.
- Implemented company-wide cross-training, which saved the company $120,000 annually.
- Reduced overtime by 90%, which saved the company over $75,000 annually.
- Established company policies and procedures for Customer Service, Sales, Distribution, and Accounting Departments in multiple locations.
- Responsible and accountable for departmental budget.

Sales

- Managed and trained outside sales staff of 300.
- Started up a Merchandising Department, which increased sales by 50%.
- Coordinated with national suppliers, introduced new products, and marketed plans and strategies.
- Managed entire Nestlé blue box freezer program for the state of Ohio.
- Achieved gold level status with St. Johns Pharmaceuticals for sales accomplishments.

- Visited customers and accounts to check sales, service levels, and product placement.
- Directed all business-to-business sales activities on a daily basis for key accounts.

Customer Service/Call Center

- Managed 450 customer service representatives in a local call center.
- Introduced and implemented new marketing programs to call centers.
- Monitored agents on phones and provided feedback for quality control.
- Researched and proposed solutions to improve email performance, to reduce cost, and to streamline processes for improved overall efficiency operation.
- Created scripting and rebuttals for customer service representatives on various procedures.
- Analyzed reports to determine and gage metrics, conversion rates, trends, potential issues, and forecasts.

Human Resources

- Conducted two-week interval training classes for new hires in two national locations.
- Updated training manual and classroom exercises for training classes.
- Created and updated job descriptions.
- Participated in company-sponsored job fairs.
- Recruited, interviewed, and tested new applicants.
- Trained and coached new supervisors and managers in all aspects of management and operations.
- Trained hourly employees in accounting, customer service, and sales.
- Implemented and initiated various employee motivational events.
- Received certificates of recognition for high school co-op programs.

Accounting and Finance

- Monitored, balanced, and analyzed an $83 million advertising budget for 54 brands.
- Saved $3 million annually by ensuring discounts were taken on payments to vendors.
- Reduced late payments to vendors by 72%.

Technical Skills

- Excel, Lotus, Word, Word Perfect, PowerPoint, SPSS
- Licensed Realtor since 1985

Employment History February 2002–Present

Mayflower Corporation, Atlanta, Michigan
Customer Service Manager

Blue Bird Real Estate Services, Romulus, Michigan
Managing Partner / Realtor

Hawkeye Publications, Belleville, Michigan
Customer Service Program Manager

Otrompke Farms, LLC, Mackinac, Michigan

Three positions based on promotions:

- Department Head of Customer Service, Sales and Merchandising
- Business Operations Manager
- Route Accounting Supervisor

LoGiudice Brewery Corporate Headquarters, Wayne, Michigan

Three positions based on promotions:

- Direct Marketing Expense Coordinator
- Accounts Receivable/Credit
- Accounts Payable

Education

Wayne State University, Detroit, MI 2002
Master's Degree: Marketing

Ferris State University, Big Rapids, MI 1998
Bachelor's Degree: Accounting

JOB INTERVIEW

Many law enforcement agencies require an oral interview as part of the hiring process. These interviews provide law enforcement agencies with first-hand observation of whether or not the applicants meet specific criteria and whether they are in alignment with the particular department's philosophy. The purpose of the oral board interview is to assess skills that cannot be assessed by written examinations alone, such as motivation, attitudes, oral communication skills, problem-solving skills, and an understanding of police work (Denton, 2009).

Typically, a law enforcement interview will be conducted by a board panel, which often comprises three board members who are trained to assess the responses to the questions at the oral interview (Denton, 2009). The questions themselves are created by experts in the subject matter. This allows the panel to ask questions that are relevant to the job. To standardize the oral interview, and to reduce complaints (and lawsuits) about being unfair, the same set of predetermined questions are asked of all applicants. In addition, the applicants are only allowed a predetermined amount of time to complete the entire interview. For example, the board may indicate to the applicant that they have 25 minutes to answer 13 questions. The applicant may spend as much time as necessary on each particular response. However, once 25 minutes have passed, the interview is complete. Questions may be repeated, but the questions will not be rephrased or paraphrased.

A very important point to make is that the oral board will only assess the information that the applicant provides. Therefore, the applicants need to articulate their responses and to provide the best possible answers. Even if a particular response does not directly apply to the question, the applicant must provide some information that can be assessed. For example, if the oral board asks if you were in the military, and if you were never in the military, you would not simply respond by saying, "No." This provides little information to assess and will result in a failing score. The applicant should respond by mentioning any experiences related to teamwork, discipline, obtaining constructive objectives, physical fitness, following orders, giving orders, meeting timelines, training, and any other information similar to what the military provides. For example, if the applicant played sports, this can be used to describe some of the factors that military experience can provide. The applicant should respond by saying that although they have no military experience, they have played sports, which promotes teamwork, discipline, physical fitness, and so on.

When applying for police work, applicants must understand that law enforcement can be broken down into three general categories: criminal investigation, public service, and traffic enforcement. Each response should be directed toward one or more of these categories. For example, an applicant with a college degree may indicate that they can properly process a crime scene, can effectively serve the public because they understand the community, and can effectively budget time and resources.

Prior to the Job Interview

An applicant should prepare for a law enforcement interview. An applicant will appear to be less than serious if the oral board asks the applicant general questions about the department and the applicant cannot respond. An applicant should review information about the department, the essential job functions, the salary, the department's philosophy, and the local community before the date of the interview.

At the Job Interview

Applicants need to be professional. They need to dress and speak professionally. In addition, they should sit up straight, make eye contact with the board members, and show body language that indicates interest. This means applicants should not continually look at their watches during the interview, which may indicate that the applicant is worried about wasting valuable time at the interview. The oral board will observe body language, just as interrogators evaluate body language during an interrogation. Near the conclusion of the interview, the board members may ask the applicant for any final comments. The applicant should take this opportunity to thank the oral board for their time and consideration. In addition, the applicant should use this time to provide an overview of personal qualifications, to indicate excitement about the position, and to indicate that they will do what it takes to be successful.

Commonly Asked Questions at Police Job Interviews

1. What have you done to prepare yourself for police work?
2. What was a major problem that you experienced and what did you do to resolve it?
3. Why do you want to be a police officer?
4. Where do you plan to be in 10 years?
5. Explain what police officers do.
6. If a traffic violator screams in your face, what will you do about it?
7. If your partner does something that is inappropriate, what will you do about it?
8. If you stop an officer and the officer is intoxicated, what will you do about it?
9. Provide three words that best describe you.
10. If you are the first officer who arrives at a house that is on fire and a person near the home suddenly flees as you approach, what will you do?
11. What is your biggest weakness?
12. What do you do to relieve stress?

Appropriate Answers for Job Interview Questions

1. What have you done to prepare yourself for police work? Discuss the following.
    - Education and training. Address what you know about criminal investigation, public service, and traffic enforcement.
    - Sport participation, teamwork, discipline, physically fit.
    - Leadership roles.
    - Work experience and responsibilities.

- Military.
- Deal with people on continual basis; resolve customer concerns.
- Understand community concerns.

2. What was a major problem that you experienced and what did you do to resolve it?
   - Articulate the use of critical thinking (making best-practice decision based on available information).
   - Discuss the variables, who were impacted, and why it was a tough issue.
   - Discuss something that had a positive outcome based on your decision.

3. Why do you want to be a police officer?
   - To serve the community
   - Provides a significant purpose in life, which is to help other people.
   - Exciting and challenging work; always something different.
   - It is a way of life, not just a job.
   - Enjoy that type of work; if you enjoy the work, you will be good at it; if you are good, you will get promoted.

4. Where do you plan to be in 10 years?
   - Indicate that you plan to be with the same department; otherwise, they will not be interested in expending the resources to train you for another department.
   - Indicate that because you like law enforcement, you will be good at your job; because you are good at your job, you will be promoted; when promoted, you will be at a position where you can help other police officers to better serve the public.

5. If a traffic violator screams in your face, what will you do about it?
   - As long at the violator obeys your lawful orders, continue to do your job.
   - Let the violator vent their anger, as long as there are no safety concerns.
   - The violator has a right to protest the government.

6. Explain what police officers do.
   - Criminal investigation:
     - Set perimeters.
     - Search crime scenes.
     - Sketch crime scenes.
     - Collect evidence and complete property record and receipt forms.
     - Collect latent fingerprints.
     - Roll fingerprints.
     - Radio communications.
     - Case reports, intelligence reports, firearms reports, probable cause affidavits, charging forms, use of force reports, search warrants, fingerprint cards, etc.
   - Public service:
     - Create and present anti-crime brochures.
     - Change car tires; provide transportation to persons in distress.
     - Conduct safety and anti-drug presentations at the local schools.
   - Traffic enforcement:
     - Complete DUI investigations, including probable cause affidavits and charging forms.
     - Use RADAR, VASCAR, and LASER.

- Write citations and warnings for traffic violations to enhance public safety.
- Complete crash investigations, use drag sleds for speed calculations, use software to draw crash diagrams, and photograph crash scenes.

7. If your partner does something that is inappropriate, what will you do about it?
    - You must distinguish between minor policy violations and law violations.
    - For a minor policy violation, you should approach the officer and discuss the rule violation. If the officer corrects their behavior, then it was handled.
    - For a minor policy violation where the officer fails to correct their behavior, you should proceed up the chain of command and immediately report it to the supervisor.
    - For a major policy violation, you should inform the officer that their actions were inappropriate then proceed up the chain of command and report it to the supervisor.
    - For a law violation, you must make the scene safe and protect any possible victims at the scene. Once the scene is safe, you should inform the officer that their actions were inappropriate, and you must immediately report it to a supervisor.

8. If you stop an officer who is driving and the officer seems intoxicated, what will you do about it?
    - Because public safety is a concern, the investigating officer should call a supervisor to the scene and investigate the case like any other case.

9. State three words that describe you. Try to select three words that create a complete composite of you as a good police officer. You may want to align your words with the department's motto.

Ambitious	Assertive	Brave
Charismatic	Cheerful	Compassionate
Educated	Fidelity	Friendly
Funny	Generous	Hard-working
Honest	Honorable	Industrious
Integrity	Law-abiding	Listener
Logical	Loyal	Moral
Fair	Objective	Persistent
Punctual	Reliable	Responsible
Smart	Strong	Thorough
Truthful	Wise	Upstanding

10. If you are the first public safety officer who arrives at a house that is on fire and a person near the home suddenly flees as you approach, what do you do?
    - Safety is always the most important law enforcement function.
    - Call out the suspect information over the police radio; let them flee.
    - Try to rescue individuals in the home if possible.
    - Protect the scene; prevent individuals from entering the scene and from getting hurt.

11. What is your biggest weakness? Be honest, but do not give a weakness that may disqualify you.
    - *Example:* I do not speak Spanish. I understand its importance in law enforcement, and I plan to study it when I get a chance. I have been focusing my resources on developing other skills.
    - *Example:* I am objectively driven and I have high expectations. Sometimes other individuals do not feel the same way that I feel and they believe my expectations are too high.

- Stating that you do not have a weakness is unlikely to be true and will not be believed.
- Stating that your biggest weakness is that you work too hard or too long will be perceived as refusing to answer the question truthfully.

12. What do you do to relieve stress?
    - I enjoy exercising, competing with friends in a variety of games, which include both physical games and games of strategy, and just going for walks.

ORAL PRESENTATIONS

Police officers may be required to present public speeches. Some officers may speak to students, some to community residents, some to the media, and some to police administrators. Some officers may speak to inform, some to persuade, and some to commemorate (Lucas, 2007). The speaker is the individual who is presenting the oral message, the channel is the mechanism by which the information is transmitted, the listener is the individual who receives the message, the message is the information that is transmitted from one person to another, and the feedback is the information that is sent from the listener to the speaker. Public speaking is more formal than daily conversation. Therefore, a police officer must organize their thoughts in advance, tailor the message to the audience, convey the information with maximum impact, and adapt the information to listener feedback. Many speeches contain two to five major points.

Research studies indicate that clear organization is important for an effective speech (Lucas, 2007). Individuals who listen to speeches demand coherence. Therefore, police officers need to employ critical thinking when making speeches. Critical thinking is the "focused, organized thinking about such things as the logical relationships among ideas, the soundness of evidence, and the difference between fact and opinion" (Lucas, 2007, p. 16). In short, an effective speech needs to have a specific purpose, a thesis (central idea), an introduction, a body (main points), and a conclusion. In addition, there should be a transition from the introduction to the body, from one main point to another main point, and from the body to the conclusion.

There are different ways in which to support the information within a speech. The different types of evidence include testimony, statistics, illustration, analogy, comparison and contrast, and explanation (BleedingEdge.net, 2012; Lucas, 2007). See Table 17.2.

Table 17.2 Different types of evidence to support a speech

Evidence	Description
Testimony	Using quotations or paraphrases to support information in speech.
Statistics	Using numerical data and figures to support information in speech.
Illustration	Using real-life situations to demonstrate information in speech.
Analogy	Comparing two similar cases and inferring that what is true for the first case is also true for the second case.
Comparison and contrast	Comparing the similarities and differences between two cases; one case may be better than the other case.
Explanation	Using facts to clarify a topic or process in a speech.

Following are several examples of outlines for speeches.

Example 1: Outline for Speech—Fireworks Speech

Specific purpose: To convince the audience that the U.S. Consumer Product Safety Commission should ban all consumer fireworks within the United States.

Thesis: The U.S. Consumer Product Safety Commission should ban all consumer fireworks within the United States.

Introduction:

Testimony	I. The Declaration, n.d.: U.S. democratic principles and citizens' expectations.
	II. Overview of my credentials.
	III. Why I have interest in consumer fireworks.
	IV. Center, 2000: Reasons for the audience to have interest in consumer fireworks.
	V. Preview of thesis and main points.

Transition: To effectively protect the public, the U.S. Consumer Product Safety Commission should ban all consumer fireworks. Main point number 1.

Body:

Testimony	I. Consumer fireworks pose a significant threat.
	A. Consumer fireworks pose a significant threat and kill and injure many people each year.
Testimony	1. Graves, 2006; Greene, 2007; Hall, 2007; HealthGrades, 2007: Experts agree that consumer fireworks are weapons that kill and injure many people each year.
Statistics	2. Greene, 2007; Hall, 2007: ongoing danger—statistics
Illustration	a. Coloian, 2004: Stacy Miller in PA, nurse severely injured
Analogy	b. U.S., 2006: Sparklers are like power outlets
Analogy	c. Areddy, 2007: Russian roulette - recalls
Explanation	3. Safra, 2002: fireworks are weapons
Comparison/analogy	a. handguns: fireworks
Analogy	b. do not swim with sharks, swim with piranhas

Transition: In addition to injuring people, fireworks also damage property.

	B. Consumer fireworks pose a significant threat and damage much property each year.
Testimony	1. Hall, 2007: fireworks result in much property damage.
Explanation	a. fires
Illustration	1) Braswell, 2007: wildfires
Illustration	2) Hall, 2007: structural fires
Statistics	b. cost

Transition: In addition to injuring people and property, fireworks also terrorize animals.

    C. Consumer fireworks pose a significant threat and terrorize many animals each year.

Explanation	1.	Consumer fireworks cause distress to animals.
Testimony		a. Equine, 2000: horses
Testimony		b. Crosby, 2007; Hahn, 2007; King, 2007: dogs, cats
Illustration		1) Wilkes, 1997: Sammy

    Transition: Consumer fireworks are dangerous to person, property, and animals. Main point number 2.

II. Current federal consumer fireworks laws and regulations are ineffective.

    A. Federal laws and regulations are ineffective.

Testimony	1.	National, 2007; U.S., 2001: Current laws – U.S. Consumer Product Safety Commission, U.S. Department of Transportation
Explanation	2.	Inadequacies of current law
Testimony		a. American, 2008; Areddy, 2007; Higgins, 2006: capitalism and patriotism – supply and demand
Statistics		b. Hall, 2007: 95% injuries with approved fireworks
Analogy		c. pass the buck to the states

    B. State and local laws are ineffective.

Testimony	1.	American, 2008; Center, 2000; National, 2007: states' laws are a nightmare
Testimony		a. American, 2008: Only 5 states have banned consumer fireworks
Analogy		1. fireworks are like ants: they're everywhere
Testimony/ Analogy		b. Indiana, 2007; Morris, 2006: Indiana passes the buck
Explanation		c. general police response
Testimony		1. Clarke, 2007; Downs, 2007: low priority for police
Testimony/ Analogy		2. Editorial, 2007: the straw that's breaking the camel's back
Testimony	2.	National, 2007; U.S., 2006: states do not follow national safety guidelines

    Transition: The dangers of fireworks will not go away by themselves. Something must be done. Main point number 3.

III. The U.S. Consumer Product Safety Commission should ban all consumer fireworks within the United States.

   A. This proposal is workable.

Testimony	1. U.S., 2004; U.S., 2001: regulating agency is in place—U.S. Consumer Product Safety Commission
Explanation	a. define all consumer fireworks as display fireworks, requiring permit
Explanation	b. enforce in third year: inform, warn, enforce
Explanation	c. penalties would fall under current Forest Service fire laws
Testimony	1) Forest, 2007: $5,000 individual or $10,000 corp. and/or 6 months in jail
Explanation	2. Enforcement agency is in place – Alcohol Tobacco Firearms Explosives

   B. Consumer fireworks problems will be solved because consumer fireworks will not be available to the public.

Testimony	1. Greene, 2007: protect people
Testimony	2. Hall, 2007: protect property
Testimony	3. Hahn, 2007: protect animals

Conclusion:

   I. In conclusion, consumer fireworks are dangerous and, in order to protect life and property, they must be banned.

   II. Restate thesis and main points.

   [Cap:] As stated earlier, U.S. citizens expect to be protected by their government and United States democratic principles demand that *all* citizens have equal protection of their rights under the law. Consumer fireworks threaten both of these ideas. Patriotism, therefore, demands that consumer fireworks be banned within the United States. Be patriotic! Be American! Ban backyard fireworks!

   III. Invite questions from the audience.

Example 2: Outline for Subpoint Speech

This outline is based on a main subpoint that might fit in support of the following thesis:

> Effective laws that control the importation, possession, and use of dangerous fireworks need to be passed and enforced.

Main subpoint: Backyard do-it-yourself fireworks are dangerous and, in order to protect society, their use must be controlled.

1. Graves, 2006; Greene, 2007; Hall, 2007: experts agree that federally approved backyard fireworks are weapons that kill and injure many people each year.
   a. Graves, 2006; Greene, 2007; Hall, 2007: on-going danger – figures
   Coloian, 2004: Stacy Miller in PA, nurse severely injured
2. Safra, 2002: by definition, fireworks are dangerous weapons.
   a) fireworks are like handguns—both can kill and need to be controlled
   b) sharks or piranhas, giant tarantulas or black widows, polar bears or black bears, giant anacondas or rattle snakes
3. The government's job is like that of the spur-winged plover to the Nile crocodile—promoting the health and well-being of its host.
   a. Areddy, 2007: patriotism and capitalism – the use of fireworks increase
   b. society is a child in a great sea of danger without a life jacket

Example 3. Outline for Persuasion Speech

Purpose: To persuade the audience to act.

I. Attention step
   A. A young man is sitting in class. A beautiful young lady with long brown hair, brilliant green eyes, and luscious lips sits next to him. She has little white flowers at her neckline on her silky pink dress. Their eyes meet; they lock together. Her pupils dilate. She leans toward him, and he is pulled to her like a magnet. Achoo! Her little white flowers are now green lily pads.

II. Need step
   - You are congested, you feel like you're being smothered, you have sinus headaches—but do not like using nasal sprays nor antibiotics
   - Bromley, 2000; Harvard, 2004: You have trouble smelling things—10,000 different odors—health consequences
   - Bromley, 2000; Harvard, 2004: You're unable to taste foods—health consequences
   - Waldrop, 1993: You have a job and cannot afford to call in sick—Americans miss 3.5 million workdays each year.
   - Waldrop, 1993: You have children and value their education—129 million schooldays missed each year.
   - You want fun and romance with your partner without nasal drip.
   - Indoor, 1995: 100,000 dust mites per one sq yard of carpet.
   - Waldrop, 1993: Twenty-two million people in the United States have hay fever.
   - Why suffer?
   - The answer: wash away the problem by spring cleaning your nose.

III. Satisfaction step
   - MoldenSnozle: Developed by sinus expert Robert MoldenSnozle in 1997, the MoldenSnozle is clinically proven to provide instant relief from hay fever problems by washing away contaminants within the nasal passage.
   - MoldenSnozle is an all-natural saline solution nasal washing system, which uses no drugs or harmful additives.
   - MoldenSnozle is a Neti Pot; it is safe, easy to use, and ergonomically shaped for a comfortable irrigating procedure.
   - MoldenSnozle is not made of ceramic like competitor brands but is made with an unbreakable, antibacterial plastic, which is dishwasher safe.
   - By cleansing out the nasal passages of dust, pollen, and other irritants, you will be able to breathe deeply without obstruction or burning sensation.
   - You will be able to smell and taste again—potentially saving the lives of you and your family.
   - You will be able to again smell hot, oven-baked cinnamon buns and smell that special arousing fragrance that your honey wears.
   - You will be able to savor the taste of that scrumptious raspberry cream pie, enjoying the simple pleasures in life.
   - You will be healthy and able to enjoy your work.

- Your kids will be healthy and able to get that education.
- You will be able to again enjoy that long sought-after social intercourse with your partner.
- So let you and your family be hay fever free by using MoldenSnozle.

IV. Visualization step
    A. Picture yourself taking a walk with your sweetheart out in the country during spring. You are swimming through the pollen like a fish, and you love it. Life is great. You look at your sweetheart and your eyes lock. You lean forward and your sweetheart is drawn to you like a magnet. You close your eyes. Achoo! Your face is drenched. Your sweetheart should have used MoldenSnozle.

V. Action step
- So, hurry up and buy yours today.
- Hay fever season is upon us, and supplies are limited.
- $12.99.
- Available at local pharmacies.
- So act now. Don't be left in the dust … mites.

Example 4: Outline for Courtroom Testimony Speech

Purpose: To inform the audience that a police officer's verbal and nonverbal communication in the courtroom influences the jury's decision.

Thesis: A police officer's verbal and nonverbal communications in the courtroom impact the police officer's credibility as a witness.

Introduction:

I. Woods, 2007: Demonstrate the need for testifying well—statistics.
II. Overview of my credentials.
III. Why I have interest in effective courtroom testimony.
IV. Bank, 2001; Kingsbury, 2006: Reasons for the audience to have interest in courtroom testimony.
V. Preview of thesis and main points.

Transition: To effectively serve the public, a police officer must be a credible witness in the courtroom during a jury trial.

Body:

I. A police officer's verbal communications in the courtroom impact the police officer's credibility as a witness.
    A. A police officer's written reports impact the police officer's credibility as a witness.
        1. Have good content
            a. Stewart, 2007: if not written, cannot use
                1) no pulling rabbit out of magic hat
            b. Be objective and complete—perform pre-flight helicopter check.
            c. Lucas, 2007: Be accurate and clear
                Undefeated does not mean won all games
            d. be relevant—focus on what was seen, not on what was not seen
        2. Navarro, 2004: Be organized, structured
            Do not keep changing channels
        3. Grammar = competence
            a. Who is the bigger fool, the fool or the one who follows the fool?
        4. Lewis, 2001: Weaknesses in a police officer's written report will be exposed and this impacts the police officer's credibility as a witness.
    B. A police officer's oral testimony impacts the police officer's credibility as a witness.
        1. Stewart, 2007: Be truthful.
            a. Lewis, 2001: If you do not know, admit it—do not weave a web of deceit.
            b. Being, 2001: Never start sentence with, "To be honest …"
            c. Lewis, 2001: If you make a mistake, admit it as soon as it is realized.

2. Lewis, 2001; Navarro, 2004; Stewart, 2007: Use plain language
      a. Do not use slang or police lingo—examples
   3. Navarro, 2004: Testifying is an art and the police officer is a performer.
      a. Picture the jury in an amusement park.
         1) Boccaccini, 2002: Do not memorize; seems rehearsed
            a) Merry-go-round
         2) Boccaccini, 2002; Navarro, 2004: Beware of vocal pauses
            a) Ferris wheel
         3) Boccaccini, 2002: Speak moderately fast with variations in pitch/loudness
            a) Roller coaster
   4. Lewis, 2001: Weaknesses in a police officer's oral testimony will be exposed and this impacts the police officer's credibility as a witness.

   Transition: However, verbal communication is only part of the story. Police officers also communicate nonverbally.

II. A police officer's nonverbal communications in the courtroom also impact the police officer's credibility as a witness.
   A. A police officer's appearance impacts the police officer's credibility as a witness.
      1. Navarro, 2004; Stewart, 2007: Maintain outward appearance.
         a. Dirty yard = dirty house
   B. A police officer's conduct impacts the police officer's credibility as a witness.
      1. Navarro, 2004: Project information with confidence
      2. Boccaccini, 2002; Navarro, 2004: Have a posture that shows interest.
         a. Like boy kissing girl
      3. Navarro, 2004; Tower, 2007: Avoid negative body language.
         a. Examples of fidgeting by demonstration.
         b. LaGrange, IN attempted murder trial, lost case—June 2001.

Conclusion

   I. In conclusion, a police officer's effectiveness in courtroom is determined by the jury's assessment of the police officer's credibility as a witness.
   II. Restate thesis and main points.

   [Cap:] Bank, 2001: As stated earlier, United States democratic principles rely on discovering the truth through courtroom testimony. Communicate well and be credible. Be democratic! Be American!
   III. Invite questions from the audience.

IMPROMPTU SPEECH

Sometimes police officers are required to give impromptu speeches. The media may want to interview the officer for an ongoing event, the officer may be assigned to provide a presentation to high school students, or the officer may have to control a large-scale scene with many individuals. The following table contains words and phrases that are commonly seen in law enforcement and/or criminal justice. Students are to randomly select 12 boxes. Select 12 rows and roll a die for each row. Once the student has selected the 12 boxes, the student will take a minute and will be required to tell a story that uses all 12 words/phrases.

Table 17.3 Words for impromptu storytelling

#	1	2	3	4	5	6
1	Police car	Helicopter	Horse	Off-road vehicle	Snowmobile	Motorcycle
2	Juvenile	Students	Residents	Adult	Infant	Minor
3	Victim	Media	Suspect	Accused	Perpetrator	Individual
4	CPR	Badge	Identification	Radar	Resistance	Idiographic
5	Baton	Firearm	Pepper spray	Handcuffs	Taser	Bean bags
6	Hunch	Reasonable suspicion	Probable cause	Preponderance of the evidence	Clear and convincing evidence	Beyond a reasonable doubt
7	Incident report	Intelligence report	Case report	Use of force report	Probable cause affidavit	Charging form
8	Radio	Flares	Fire extinguisher	Evidence kit	Verbal commands	Non-compliant
9	Falsification	Witnesses	Explosives	Hazmat	Radiation leak	Vehicle search
10	Interstate	County road	Ditch	Median	Berm	Rumble strip
11	Fog line	Center line	DataMaster	Jail	Book	Law
12	Witness statement	Lineup	Showup	Compass	Canine	Method of operation
13	Miranda warning	Perimeter	Direct traffic	Stop light	Spill	Field sobriety tests
14	Latent fingerprints	Rolled fingerprints	Property record and receipt form	Citation	Warning	Hot pursuit
15	Training	Factory	Registration	Nomothetic	Complaint	Police–community relations
16	Airplane	Chemicals	Water	Shyster	Lake	Speed zone
17	Ice	Sunny	Snow	Foggy	Storm	Hail
18	Lawyer	Judge	Jury	Police officer	Maintenance workers	Restaurant employee
19	Crash	Bank robber	Flat tire	Hostage	Tractor	Work zone
20	Black eye	Question	Warrant	45 mph	70 mph	120 mph

Table 17.3 Cont.

#	1	2	3	4	5	6
21	Happy	Sad	Mad	Creeping	Love	Married
22	Sweating	Hands shaking	Shifty eyes	Hesitant to answer	Pulsating artery	Cried
23	Blamed	Motive	Interrogate	Lost	Found	Interview
24	Infraction	Civil matter	Contract	Hired	Private investigator	Active shooter
25	Passport	Driver's license	Home	Farm	Theory	Report
26	Booby trap	Fishing	Diversionary flare	Computer	Policy	Politician
27	Mystery	End of shift	Adoptive admission	Double jeopardy	Confession	Admission
28	Inspection	Parole	Probation	Field training officer	Probationary officer	Target
29	Scene	Watch	Observed	Incline	Brakes	Fire
30	Siren	Alarm	Evacuation	Riot	Cell	Bar
31	Undocumented foreign nationals	Mental	Social worker	Child abuse	Elderly abuse	Homeless
32	Culture	Perspective	Profile	Quota	Department	Tree
33	Obstacle	Race	Reasoning	Entrapment	Glasses	Deer
34	Power	Privileged	Justice	Persuade	Calculations	Deposition
35	Disposition	Alibi	Crime scene	Documents	File	Lead
36	Canvass	Doughnut	Speed	Counterfeit	Money	Contraband
37	Fair	Prison	Coroner	Prosecutor	Emergency lights	Fire truck
38	Ambulance	Hospital	Doctor	Medicine	Best-practice decision	Collect
39	Evaluated	Weapon	Information	Hands	Foot patrol	Road closed
40	Jurisdiction	Privacy	Secret	Vice	Detective	Forensic lab
41	Coffee	Break	On duty	Off duty	Mob	Emergency
42	Conditional statement	Casting	Passport	Bounty hunter	Fool	State line
43	Parking lot	Plea bargain	Bail	Tape measure	Hydroplane	Guardrail
44	Quarantine	Metal detector	Radiation detector	Chance	Alco-sensor	Light
45	Vest	Megaphone	Laser	Lightning	Bridge	Voluntary statement

(*continued*)

Table 17.3 Cont.

#	1	2	3	4	5	6
46	Magic	Moon	Time	Letter	Eye	Castle
47	World	Flashlight	Plain view	Ladder	Building	Flower
48	Lock	Key	Decipher	Fish	Parachute	Arrow
49	Statement	Sleep	Star	Magnetic	Dragnet	Footprint
50	Sting operation	Food	Feds	Wanted	Missing	Dead
51	Convict	Cop	Indicted	Nude	Cipher	Defend
52	Correlation	Crazy	Brave	Save	Sue	Lost
53	Civil	Revealed	Mayor	Blames	Lawyer	Shoot
54	Stun	Cruel	Mourns	Psychic	Tycoon	Scam
55	Actor	Loyal	Smash	Strike	Snub	DNA
56	Rare	Tricks	Blast	Industrious	Discombobulated	Angel
57	Romantic	Bored	Hit	Thug	Secret	Crooked
58	Angry	350 lb	Slay	Hero	Attack	Bizarre
59	Weep	Rehab	Child protection	Priest	Stab	Movie
60	Lover	Steal	Drugs	White-collar crime	Tourist	Killer
61	Bite	Spouse	Limitation	Game	Partner	Animal
62	Sign language	Odor	Burn	Hot	Cold	Body language
63	Lie	Polygraph	Voice analysis	Handwriting analysis	Communicate	Hill
64	Mountain	Tax	Beer	Fear	Integrity	Dedicated
65	Bike	Interrogatory	First aid	Command post	Music	Ordinance
66	Magazine	Double-lock	Escape	Committed	Service	Exacerbated
67	Business	Causation	Totality of circumstances	Singing	Riot	Gear
68	Skid mark	Friction	Stop sticks	Stop	Ram	Mirror
69	X-ray	Knock	Liability	Plaintiff	Status quo	Error
70	Clothes	Travel	Base	Position	Known source	Shoes
71	Disaster	Recovery	Impound	Inventory	Mask	Excise police
72	Conceal	Code	Logic	Conservation officer	Statistics	Intent
73	Wilful	Reasonable	Roadblock	Announcement	Open field	Seizure
74	Map	Directions	Transport	Waiver	File	Myth

Table 17.3 Cont.

#	1	2	3	4	5	6
75	Due process	Crime control	Drag sled	Serial	Organized	Promotion
76	Merge	Resume	Protect	Shy	Spirit	Exigent circumstances
77	Parallel	Hatchet	Errata	Good faith	Habeas corpus	Jump
78	Puzzle	Village	Crime scene search pattern	Pressure	Heavy	Drop
79	Snake	Trooper	Curtilage	Rock	Boat	Box
80	Piracy	Photo	Drink	Heart	Stolen	Monkey wrench
81	Public service	Traffic enforcement	Gang	Identity theft	Blood	Mug number
82	Assumption	Flowchart	Subset	Quantifier	Equivalency	Ethics
83	Fake	Forgery	Illusion	Lens of truth	Truth value	Venn diagram
84	Bribe	Song lyrics	Regulation	Grammar	Hearsay	Detain

CHAPTER PROBLEMS

1. Write a chronological résumé.
2. Write a functional résumé.
3. If you were the chief of police, which résumé would you prefer and why?
4. What have you done to prepare yourself for police work?
5. What was a major problem that you experienced and what did you do to resolve it?
6. Why do you want to be a police officer?
7. Explain what police officers do.
8. If your partner handcuffs a suspect and places the suspect in the back of their patrol car, then punches the suspect in the face, what will you do about it?
9. If you have stopped your spouse for speeding, what will you do about it?
10. Provide three words that best describe you. Describe the three words that the FBI uses as its motto. Find another agency that uses words for its motto and describe the words.

KEYWORDS

Analogy evidence
Compare and contrast evidence
Explanation evidence
Functional résumé
Illustration evidence

Résumé

Reverse chronological résumé

Statistics evidence

Testimony evidence

REFERENCES

American Pyrotechnics Association (2008). Fireworks related injuries; Frequently asked questions about fireworks; Glossary of pyrotechnic terms; and 2007 state fireworks control laws. www.americanpyro.com

Areddy, J.T. (2007, June 29). Behind the boom in Chinese fireworks. *Wall Street Journal*, 29. http://online.wsj.com/article/SB118306391850951969.html

Bank, S. (2001, Fall). From mental health professional to expert witness: Testifying in court. *New Directions for Mental Health Services*, 57–66.

Being an Effective Witness (2001). *A Bureau of Business Practice Newsletter: Labor Relations Bulletin, 726*, 1, 2, 6.

BleedingEdge.net (2012). *Public Speaking Tips*. www.speaking-tips.com/Glossary.aspx#I

Boccaccini, M. (2002). What do we really know about witness preparation? *Behavioral Sciences Law, 20*, 161–189.

Braswell, G. (2007, July 5). Four wildfires set: Police seek persons who witnesses saw using fireworks on Highway 92. *Sierra Vista Herald*. www.svherald.com/articles/2007/07/05/news/doc468c9adecc8be076576986.txt

Bromley, S. (2000). Smell and taste disorders: A primary care approach. *American Family Physician, 61*(2), 427–436.

Center for Disease Control and Prevention (2000). Notice to readers: Injuries from fireworks in the United States. *Morbidity and Mortality Weekly Report, 49*(24), 545–546.

Clarke, C. (2007). Fireworks complaints slip down list of priorities. *York Daily Record*. 2007. www.ydr.com/doverwestyork/ci_6325328

Coloian, M. (2004, Sept/Oct). Fireworks: A story about fireworks in untrained hands. *NFPA Journal*. www.nfpa.org/itemDetail.asp?categoryID=297&itemID=28463&URL=Research%20&%20Reports/Fact%20sheets/Seasonal%20safety/Fireworks

Crosby, J. (2007). Fireworks safety and loud noises. *Pets and Fireworks*. http://vetmedicine.about.com/cs/diseasesall/a/petsworks.htm

The Declaration of Independence (n.d.). www.ushistory.org/declaration/document/index.htm

Denton, M. (2009). *Police oral board: The ultimate guide to a successful oral board interview*. Charleston, SC: Createspace.

Downs, M. (2007). Fireworks complaints flood police phone lines. *Florida Today*. www.floridatoday.com

Editorial: Stay safe from those rockets' red glare (2007, July 2). *Detroit Free Press*.

Equine Research Center (2000). Safety around horses: A basic guide for beginning horse people. www.petcaretips.net/ horse_safety.html

Forest Service (2007). Frequently asked questions and answers for stage I fire restrictions. www.fs.fed.us/r4/caribou-targhee/eiifc/restrictions/faq_stage_ 1%20.pdf

Graves, C., Perkins, S., & Powell, T. (2006, September). Fireworks-related injuries. *Indiana Epidemiology Newsletter, 9*(9). www.in.gov/isdh/programs/injury /pdf/FireworksInjuryReport2006.pdf

Greene, M. (2007). Fireworks-related deaths, emergency department-treated injuries, and enforcement activities during 2006. *2006 Fireworks Annual Report*.

Hahn, J. (2007). Some pets petrified when it's raining cats and dogs. Office of Public Engagement. www.cvm.uiuc.edu/petcolumns/show article_pf.cfm?id=176

Hall, J. R. (2007). Fireworks. National Fire Protection Association. www.nfpa.org/categoryList.asp?categoryID=297

Harvard Medical School (2004). Taste and smell: Your sensitive senses. *Harvard Men's Health Watch, 8*(9), 1–4.

HealthGrades (2007). Physician's snapshot: Dr. Charlene Graves, MD. www.healthgrades.com

Higgins, W. (2006, June 29). Will new law help spark sales? *Indianapolis Star*.

Indiana (2007). *Indiana Legislative Bills: IC 22-11-14-10.5*. www.in.gov/legislative/bills/2007/PDF/SE/SE0009.1.pdf

Indoor allergy alert: Contractors should take charge now (1995). *Air Conditioning Heating & Refrigeration News, 196*(14), 35.

King County Animal Services (2007). Fear of loud noises. www.kingcounty.gov/safety/AnimalService/pettips/dogtips/loudnoises.aspx

Kingsbury, K. (2006). The next crime wave. *Time, 168*(24), 70–77.

Kursmark, L.M. (2003). *Best resumes for college students and new grads*. Indianapolis, IN: JIST Works.

Lewis, D. (2001). *The police officer in the courtroom*. Springfield, IL: Charles C. Thomas.

Lucas, S.E. (2007). *The art of public speaking* (9th ed.). Boston: McGraw Hill.

Morris, L. (2006, July 18). Editorial: A welcome local boost: The fury over fireworks is growing, and the state is starting to pay attention. *News-Sentinel (Fort Wayne, IN)*.

National Council of Fireworks (2007). The classification of fireworks. www.fireworksafety.com/home.htm

Navarro, J. (2004). Testifying in the theater of the courtroom. *FBI Law Enforcement Bulletin, 73*(9), 26–30.

Safra, J. (2002). Fireworks. *The New Encyclopedia Britannica, 15*(4).

Stewart, S. (2007). Effective courtroom performance by Indiana law enforcement. *Clark County Prosecuting Attorney for Police Officers*. www.clarkprosecutor.org/html/police/police2.htm

Tower, W. (2007). Courtroom demeanor. *Kidjacked*. http://kidjacked.com/defense/courtroom_demeanor.asp

U.S. Consumer Product Safety Commission (2001). Office of compliance summary of fireworks regulations, 16 C.F.R. Part 1500 & 1507. www.cpsc.gov/businfo/regsumfirework.pdf

U.S. Consumer Product Safety Commission (2004, June 30). Federal government working to keep Americans safe on 4th of July. www.cpsc.gov/cpscpub/prerel/prhtm104/04172.html

U.S. Consumer Product Safety Commission (2006). CPSC warns consumers that using professional fireworks often has deadly results. www.cpsc.gov/cpscpub/prerel/prhtm106/06197.html

Waldrop, J. (1993). Spring sneezes. *American Demographics, 15*(5), 4.

Wilkes, G. (1997). The boom box – Sammy in a kennel. www.clickandtreat.com/webart107.htm

Woods, S. (2007). By the numbers. *Dttp: A Quarterly Journal of Government Information Practice & Perspective, 35*(1), 10–12.

CHAPTER 18

Crime Scene Investigations

LEARNING OBJECTIVES

Understand the different crime scene search patterns.

Complete a crime scene entry log sheet.

Complete a photograph log sheet.

Understand the steps for investigating a crime scene.

Understand how to collect crime scene evidence.

Understand the information that should be recorded on an evidence bag.

Understand ways to identify fakes, forgeries, and counterfeits.

INTRODUCTION

At a crime scene, it is the job of the police officer to find and collect evidence. This can be accomplished by searching the scene. There are several different types of crime scene search patterns, and the lead crime scene investigator should select the appropriate pattern. If blood is collected as evidence, it is important not to seal the blood in a plastic bag because it will putrefy and be ruined. Officers should have basic crime scene supplies to ensure that they can properly collect any type of evidence that they encounter. Officers should maintain a crime scene entry log to document all persons who enter the crime scene. Because persons who enter the crime scene may contaminate the crime scene, anyone who enters the crime scene should expect to be subpoenaed for a court appearance. They will need to explain the reason that they needed to enter the crime scene. In addition, a photography log should be maintained for all photographs of evidence. Steps are provided for searching different types of locations, including a vehicle and person. Finally, this chapter discusses ways to identify fakes, forgeries, and counterfeits.

CRIME SCENE INVESTIGATION

Criminal investigations are an important part of police work. People's lives may depend on the consequences of an investigation. In order to effectively determine the method of operation, and who may be responsible for the crime, police officers must properly investigate a variety of crime scene locations. Above all else, safety at the crime scene is most important. After all safety issues have been resolved, and all injured individuals have been handled, evidence needs to be collected. Failure to properly collect evidence may result in disciplinary action.

CRIME SCENE SUPPLIES

Police officers must be prepared to encounter a crime scene whenever they are working. Above all else, police officers must practice safe techniques. This means police officers must use the right equipment and tools, and employ proper police practices (e.g., using latex gloves). See Table 18.1 for a short list of some basic crime scene supplies.

Table 18.1 Basic crime scene supplies (Swanson et al., 2009)

Crime scene barrier tape
Stakes/poles
Evidence markers
Spray paints/chalk
Privacy screen/blanket
Magnifying glass
Magnetic compass/global positioning system
Area map
Rain-repellent tarps
Small mirror
Metal detector
Ladders
Rope
Video recorder/audio recorder/camera
Disinfectant wipes
Gloves/booties
Biohazard bags
Evidence containers/tape/markers
Casting material—substance that is poured into an impression, hardened, then removed to create a three-dimensional image of the impression.
Fingerprint powders
Crime scene entry log sheet
Photography log sheet

TECHNIQUES FOR SEARCHING THE CRIME SCENE

The purpose of a crime scene search is to locate physical evidence, which may be used to help solve a crime (Swanson et al., 2009). Evidence may help determine: (1) whether a crime was committed; (2) the motive; (3) the method of operation; (4) the suspect; and (5) those individuals who are not suspects. Police officers commonly search crime scenes. It is important to search the crime scene correctly and thoroughly because any evidence found at the scene may make or break a case. Not only may evidence indicate a person's guilt, it may also indicate a person's innocence. However, before crime scene evidence can be used in court, it must first be discovered by police officers in the field. Eight different crime scene search patterns will be discussed, which are the specific paths that the officers will take to look for evidence. The particular crime scene search pattern that an officer should use will depend on several variables, including available resources, the surrounding environment, and how the crime scene and evidence present themselves.

Table 18.2 Crime scene search patterns (Saferstein, 2009)

Crime scene search pattern	Pros	Cons
Line	Can find small items in known area.	May take many officers and resources; should have well-established boundaries.
Strip	May be employed by one officer.	Not as detailed as grid search, thus, may overlook evidence; should have well-established boundaries.
Grid	Two sequential strip searches perpendicular to one another; very detailed search; search same area twice in different directions.	May take much time and resources; should have well established boundaries.
Lane	Concurrent strip search by two officers; their paths never cross; two sets of eyes are better than one.	Needs two officers; not as detailed as grid search, thus may overlook evidence.
Circle	May be employed with no visibility and without the capability of maintaining position (e.g., underwater in current).	Not very practical at many crime scene locations.
Spiral	May be employed by one officer; allows overview of crime scene while minimizing crime scene contamination	May not be a perfect spiral, thus, may miss evidence.
Quadrant or zone	Good for large area; can use a different search pattern in each zone.	May take many officers and resources.
Ray or Wheel	Good for large area; if known starting point, can search in all directions; can find items when have no idea of which direction to look.	As searchers spread out, the distance between the individual searchers increases and evidence may be overlooked.

Line Search Pattern

The line search pattern involves one or more officers who start on a line and proceed in the same direction. This technique is effective if the officers want to cover a large area in a particular direction or if they want to cover a small area in great detail. If the search of the area is not performed correctly, evidence may be missed (Saferstein, 2009).

Strip Search Pattern

The strip search pattern involves an officer who weaves back and forth through the crime scene. The officer starts at the boundary on one side of the crime scene and moves toward the other side. Once near the other side, the officer makes a U-turn and continues back toward the original side. The officer continues this pattern while moving across the crime scene. This search pattern allows a police department to cover a reasonable amount of area with limited human resources and time. This technique is effective if the crime scene has clear boundaries (Saferstein, 2009). If the boundaries are not clearly defined, then valuable evidence may be overlooked.

Grid Search Pattern

The grid search pattern involves an officer who performs two overlapping strip searches, which form a grid (Saferstein, 2009). A grid search pattern is basically two strip search patterns that are perpendicular to each other. Although this technique is thorough, it consumes more time and human resources than a single strip search pattern. This technique is good if the crime scene has clear boundaries. If the boundaries are not clearly defined, then valuable evidence may be overlooked.

Lane Search Pattern

The lane search pattern involves two officers who weave back and forth through the crime scene but do not cross each other's path. The officers start at the boundary on one side of the crime scene and move toward the other side (Saferstein, 2009). Once near the other side, the officers make a U-turn and continue back toward the original side. The officers continue this pattern as they move across the crime scene. This technique is good if the crime scene has clear boundaries. If the boundaries are not clearly defined, then valuable evidence may be overlooked.

Circle Search Pattern

The circle search pattern involves an officer searching the scene via concentric circles. The officer will have a rope with knots tied in it about every 5 feet (arm span of the officer) and the officer will tie the rope to a stake. The officer will set the stake at a fixed point. The officer will start from the knot closest to the stake and will search a circular area around the stake. Once cleared, the officer will move outward toward the next knot and continue the process. This technique is very good when searching areas that have no visibility and where the officer cannot verify or maintain their exact position. For example, an officer who is scuba driving in dark waters with strong currents may use this technique effectively. The officer will feel for evidence in the black and unstable environment. However, the fixed point (i.e., the stake) must be near the evidence or the evidence will not be discovered using this search pattern.

Spiral Search Pattern

The spiral search pattern is usually performed outdoors and involves only one officer (Saferstein, 2009; Swanson et al., 2009). The inward spiral is useful because an officer will move from an area with little evidence toward an area that is more heavily concentrated with evidence. The outward spiral pattern may be useful if an officer happens to come upon the main piece of evidence before the officer realizes they are in a crime scene. In general, either spiral technique is effective for locating footprints entering and exiting the crime scene. However, because the spiral search pattern may not be a true spiral, important evidence may be missed.

Quadrant or Zone Search Pattern

The quadrant or zone search pattern involves breaking down a large crime scene into smaller and more manageable sections. The proper search pattern employed in each section will be independent of the other sections. Different officers can search different zones.

Ray or Wheel Search Pattern

The ray or wheel search pattern will be used when the officers have a known starting point but do not know the direction in which the evidence will be found. Officers proceed in every direction and may cover a large area (e.g., a technique used by warships to look for enemy ships at sea). This technique may be good if a child is lost in the woods and the searching officers only know where the child started. However, as the officers move outward, this search pattern fails to cover much area between the rays (i.e., between the searching officers).

Line:

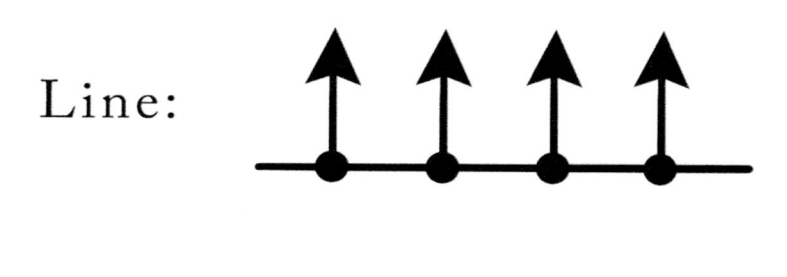

Strip:

Grid:

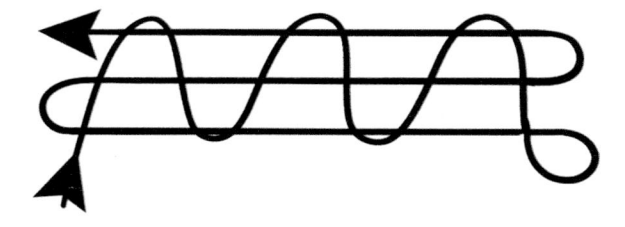

Lane:

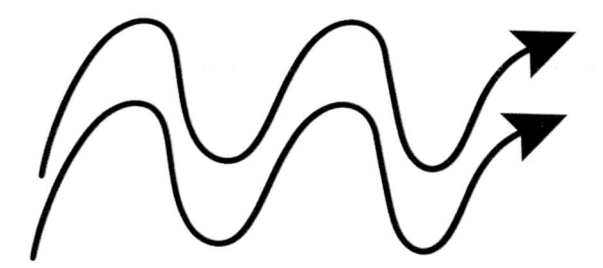

Figure 18.1 Crime scene search patterns

Circle:

Spiral:

Quadrant or Zone:

Ray or Wheel:

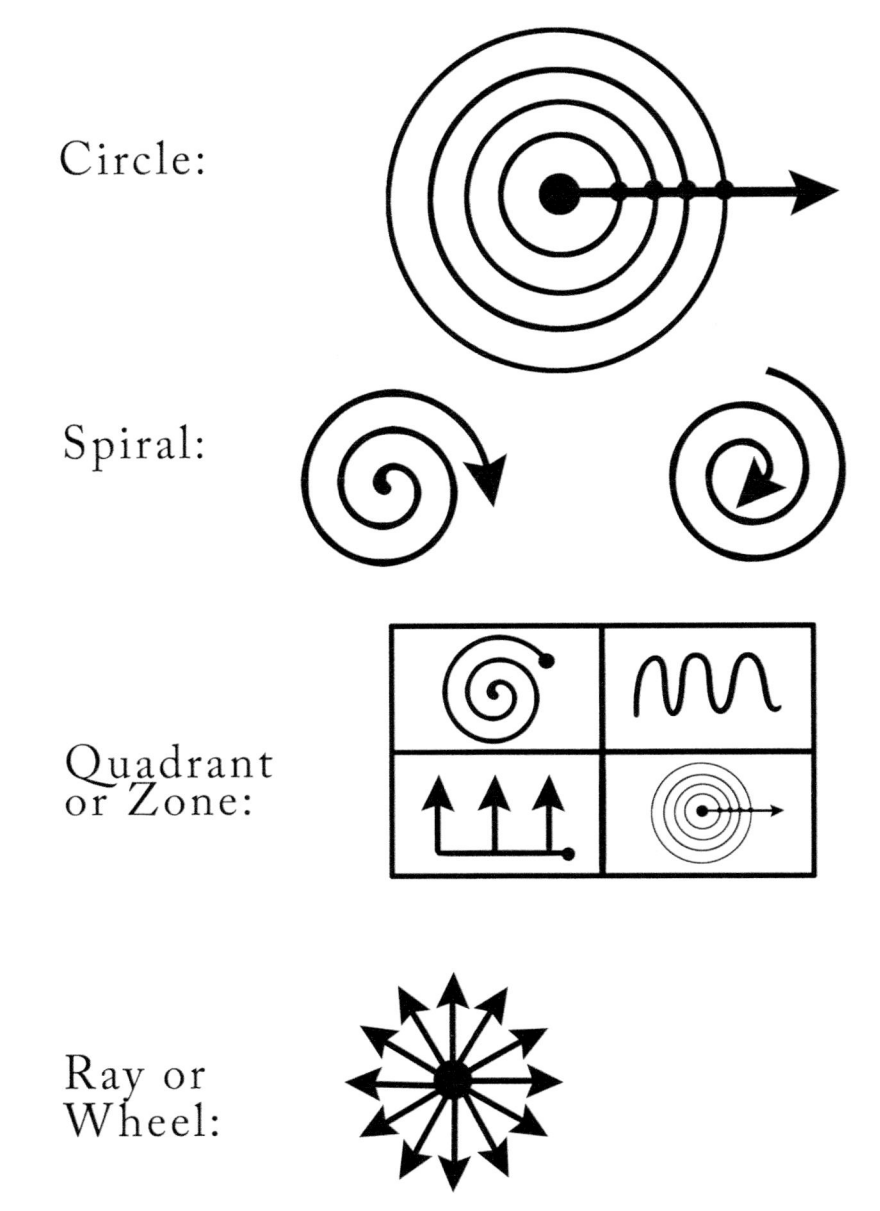

Figure 18.1 (Continued)

Line Search Pattern. If there is more than one officer, the lines may be conducted concurrently. Follow the sequence for the search pattern. Assume in this case that there are barriers along each row and at the end of each row such that you can only enter each row from the start line. Searching the rows in a movie theater is a good example.

1 → . . . .

2 → . . . .

3 → . . . .

4 → . . . .

5 → . . . .

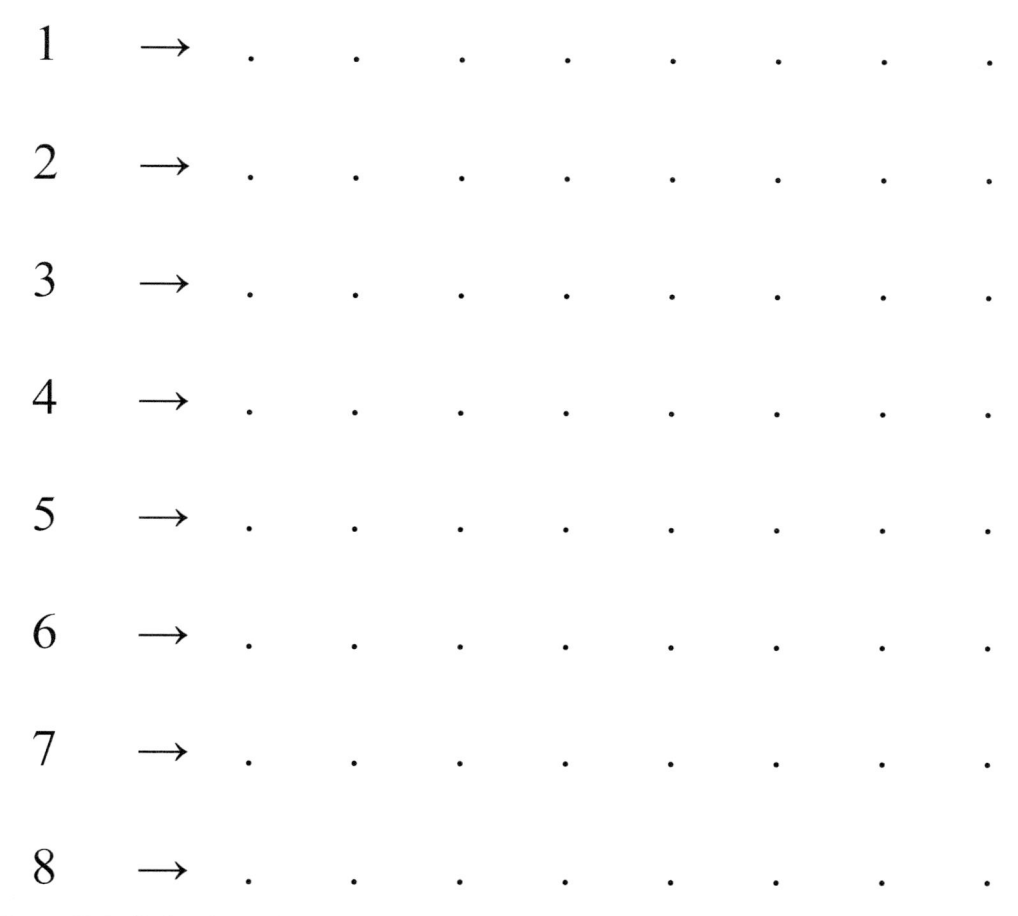

6 → . . . .

7 → . . . .

8 → . . . .

Figure 18.2 Performing a crime scene search pattern

Strip Search Pattern. In the most effective and efficient way possible, we are seeking an item that is four spaces wide that is not diagonal. Follow the sequence for the search pattern shown (make sure that you go from end to end). Continue and complete the last six rows.

.   .   .   1   .   .   .   2   .   .

.   .   4   .   .   .   3   .   .   .

.   5   .   .   .   6   .   .   .   7

10 .   .   .   9   .   .   .   8   .

.   .   .   11 .   .   .   12 .   .

.   .   14 .   .   .   13 .   .   .

.   .   .   .

.   .   .   .

.   .   .   .

.   .   .   .

.   .   .   .

.   .   .   .

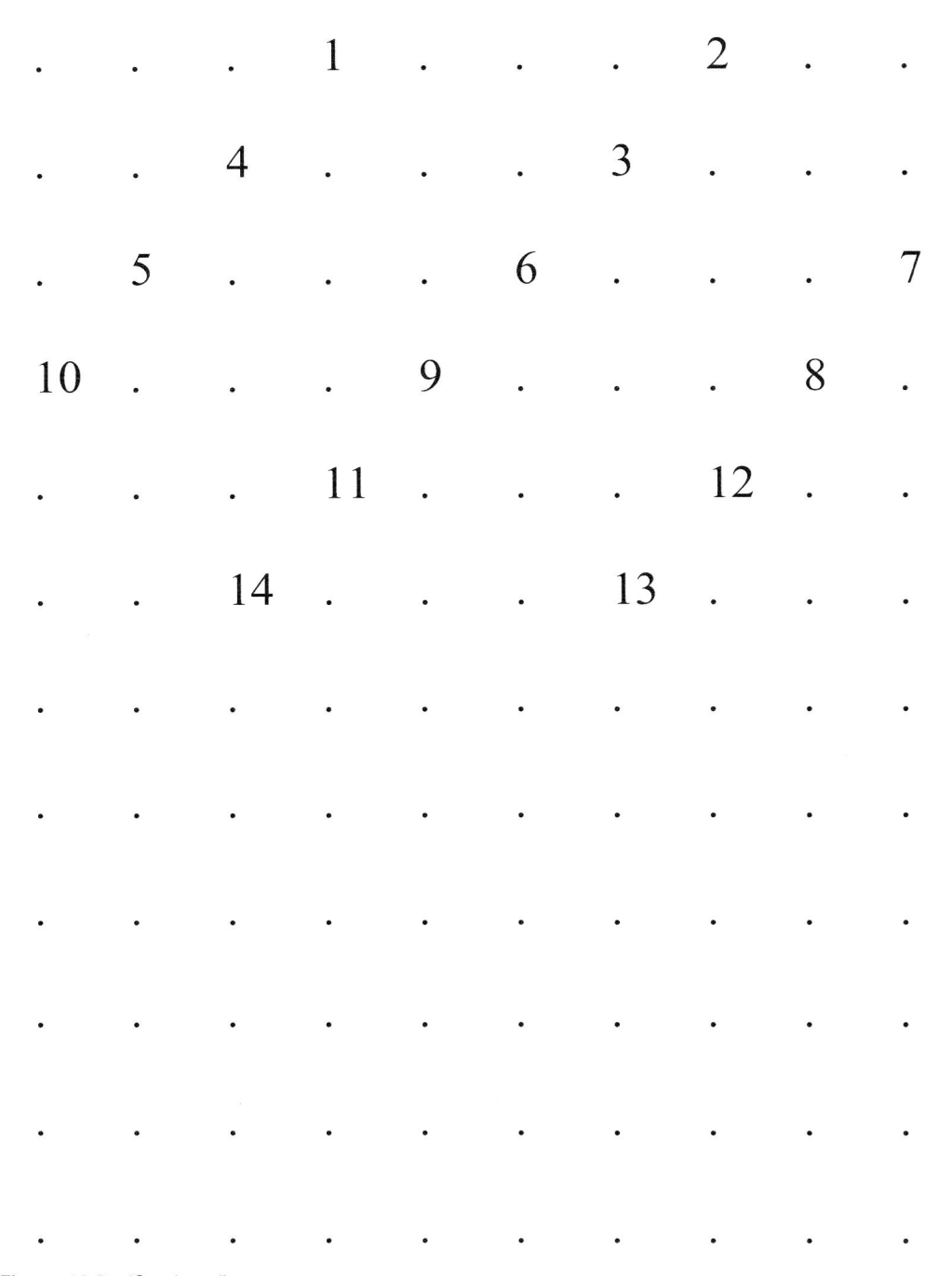

Figure 18.2 (Continued)

Quadrant Search Pattern. Follow the sequence of steps for the search pattern. Notice that the area has been broken down into four smaller sections.

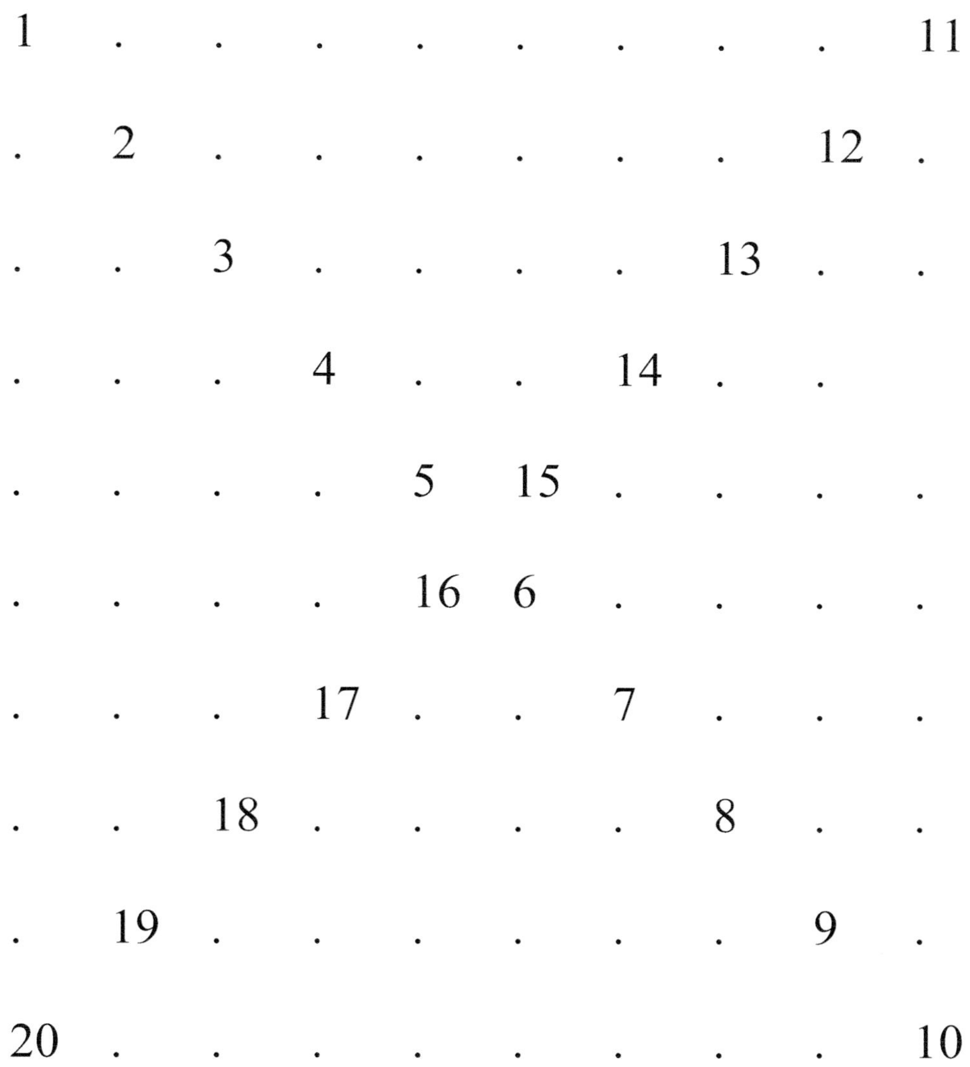

```
1   .   .   .   .   .   .   .   .   .   11
    .   2   .   .   .   .   .   .   12  .
    .   .   3   .   .   .   .   13  .   .
    .   .   .   4   .   .   14  .   .   .
    .   .   .   .   5   15  .   .   .   .
    .   .   .   .   16  6   .   .   .   .
    .   .   .   17  .   .   7   .   .   .
    .   .   18  .   .   .   .   8   .   .
    .   19  .   .   .   .   .   .   9   .
20  .   .   .   .   .   .   .   .   .   10
```

Figure 18.2 (Continued)

Perform an outward spiral search pattern. Write the numbers on the chart in sequence, and draw a line connecting the numbers so that the reader can follow your path.

Figure 18.2 (Continued)

CRIME SCENE INVESTIGATIONS

Crime scenes can be hazardous for police officers in a variety of ways (Swanson et al., 2009). First, officers may be stung by bees, bitten by ticks carrying Lyme disease, bitten by mosquitoes carrying West Nile Virus, and bitten by dogs. Second, officers may be exposed to poisonous plants, such as poison ivy and poison oak. Third, police officers may breathe in deadly fumes, dust, or other contaminants. Fourth, contaminants may be absorbed through the skin. Finally, perpetrators may set up booby traps. Health consequences that may be experienced by police officers include blindness, breathing problems, and death.

Police officers search crime scenes to locate and collect evidence, which may be used to identify perpetrators and to eliminate innocent individuals as suspects (Swanson et al., 2009). In addition, the evidence may be used to identify a perpetrator's method of operation, which may be a distinguishing trademark. However, the first priority for an officer at a crime scene is safety, which includes personal safety. Medical attention must be provided to all persons who need it.

A police officer should maintain a crime scene entry log to document all persons who enter and leave the crime scene. Because persons who enter the crime scene may contaminate the crime scene, any persons who enter the crime scene should expect to be subpoenaed for a court appearance to explain why they needed to enter the crime scene. All individuals who enter the crime scene will document the time when they entered the scene, the time they left the scene, and the reason for their entry. If an individual refuses to sign the crime scene entry log sheet, such as a superior officer pulling rank, then the log officer should print the superior officer's name onto the log sheet. The threat of being subpoenaed by a defense attorney may discourage a superior officer from inappropriately disturbing the crime scene.

For the photography log sheet on the following page, look at the column for the Evidence Marker #. Whether the evidence marker is in the photograph or not, record the evidence marker number that is linked to each piece of evidence. This is necessary because the reader will want to be able to link each photograph to a specific evidence marker number. Your job is to be clear and to link each photograph to a specific evidence marker number (even if the marker is not in the photograph). Except for the overall crime scene photographs, which do not use evidence markers, the evidence marker box should never be blank.

CRIME SCENE ENTRY LOG SHEET

All persons entering the crime scene must sign this sheet

Agency: _____ Case #: _____

Scene location: _____

Note: Officers assigned to maintain scene security must also log in and out on this sheet and should state their reason as "Log Officers."

Name and title	Signature	Agency	In Date/time	Out Date/time	Reason for entering scene
			/	/	
			/	/	
			/	/	
			/	/	
			/	/	
			/	/	
			/	/	
			/	/	

Page _____ of _____

It is possible for medical personnel to respond to the scene and to leave the scene before the police officers arrive. In this case, the responding police officers should interview anyone at the scene to find out what happened. Moreover, an officer will have to go to the hospital and interview all medical personnel who worked at the scene. This is important because the medical personnel may have changed the crime scene (e.g., may have moved something).

The first officer arriving at the crime scene is charged with preserving and protecting the area (Saferstein, 2009). The lead investigator is charged with developing the most effective strategy for systematically searching and documenting the entire crime scene. The investigating officer should perform an initial walk-through to determine the perpetrator's path of entry and exit. The investigating officer may follow the path established by medical personnel, if medical personnel responded to the scene, to avoid any additional disturbance of the crime scene. If no path has been established by medical personnel, the officer should follow an indirect path toward the center of the crime scene. Following the perpetrator's path may cause the officer to destroy important evidence by accident.

During the initial walk-through, the investigating officer should develop an overall plan to mark and photograph the evidence (photographing the overall crime scene from the four corners of the crime scene is a minimum). The goal is to mark and photograph the evidence without damaging any of it. Thus, the investigating officer must have an organized plan of action. The lead investigator is responsible for both determining the crime scene search pattern and determining what evidence will be marked for photographing.

The crime scene photographer should maintain a photography log for all photographs of evidence. Before any evidence is collected, the overall crime scene must be photographed. This means that the entire crime scene will be photographed from all four corners. After that, each piece of evidence will be photographed at mid-range and close-up, with and without a crime scene marker. In other words, each piece of evidence will be photographed at least four separate times.

For the photography log sheet on the following page, look at the column for the Evidence Marker #. Whether the evidence marker is in the photograph or not, record the evidence marker number that is linked to each piece of evidence. This is necessary because the reader will want to be able to link each photograph to a specific evidence marker number. Except for the overall crime scene photographs, which do not use evidence markers, every Evidence Marker # box should contain an evidence marker number.

PHOTOGRAPHY LOG SHEET

Pg _____ of _____

Agency: _____ Case #: _____

Scene location: _____

Photo #	Evidence Marker #	Description of Evidence Photographed

_____   _____   _____   _____
Name & Title   Badge   # Signature   Agency

After the crime scene is photographed (photographing the overall crime scene from the four corners of the crime scene is a minimum), the crime scene will then be sketched. The officer should take measurements and may draw a rough sketch in the field. Once back at the police post, the officer may use a computer program to create a more professional-looking crime scene drawing.

After the scene has been sketched, the evidence will then be collected. The officer must bag the evidence and record certain information on a property record and receipt form. The information required on the evidence bag includes the case number, date, suspect's name, property record and receipt number, item number, a description of the evidence, officer's name, officer's identification number, and the name of the officer's police department.

Table 18.3 Information recorded on the evidence bag

1	Case number
2	Date
3	Suspect's name
4	Property record and receipt number
5	Item number
6	Description of the evidence
7	Officer's name
8	Officer's identification number
9	Name of the officer's police department

A crime may occur in many different types of locations. Officers who search the various scenes need to take the proper steps to promote safety and to ensure that the scene is processed correctly. Following are the steps to be taken at different types of crime scene locations.

STEPS FOR GRASSY AREA: ABANDONED VEHICLE SEARCH

1. Call for backup.
2. Interview everyone already at the scene. If there is a person at the crime scene before the officer arrives, the officer will need to interview the potential witness. If the victims are gone, the officer will need to find out where they went. If paramedics took victims to the hospital, send an officer to the hospital to interview paramedics and victims. Find out exactly what they did at the scene. The victims may provide additional information.
3. With backup, approach the abandoned vehicle in a direct manner; check for victim/suspect.
4. Set the perimeter.
5. Create a crime scene entry log.
6. Use latex gloves.
7. Photographer will photograph entire scene from outside the perimeter.
8. The lead investigator decides the crime scene search pattern.
9. The lead investigator determines the evidence and marks evidence.
10. The photographer photographs all evidence with and without marker (medium range and close up). All evidence needs to be recorded before any evidence is disturbed and before the crime scene changes (e.g., due to weather).
11. The backup officer sketches the scene.
12. After photographs and the sketch, if there is a body at the scene, the body will need to be rolled halfway over to see whether there is any evidence under the body. The body will be returned to its original position.
13. A single officer should collect all evidence to make the chain of custody cleaner.

STEPS FOR OUTDOOR CRIME SCENE: NO SUSPECTS AT SCENE

1. Call for backup.
2. Interview everyone already at the scene. If there is a person at the crime scene before the officer arrives, the officer will need to interview the potential witness. If the victims are gone, the officer will need to find out where they went. If paramedics took victims to the hospital, send an officer to the hospital to interview paramedics and victims. Find out exactly what they did at the scene. The victims may provide additional information.
3. Set the perimeter.
4. Create a crime scene entry log.
5. Use latex gloves.
6. The photographer will photograph entire scene from outside the perimeter.
7. The lead investigator decides the crime scene search pattern.
8. The lead investigator determines the evidence and marks the evidence.
9. The photographer photographs all evidence with and without marker (medium range and close up). All evidence needs to be recorded before any evidence is disturbed and before the crime scene changes (e.g., due to weather).
10. The backup officer sketches the scene.
11. After photographs and sketch, if there is a body at the scene, the body will need to be rolled halfway over to see whether there is any evidence under the body. The body will be returned to its original position.
12. A single officer should collect all evidence to make the chain of custody cleaner.

STEPS FOR CRIME SCENE: INSIDE A ROOM

1. Call for backup.
2. Interview everyone already at the scene. If there is a person at the crime scene before the officer arrives, the officer will need to interview the potential witness. If the victims are gone, the officer will need to find out where they went. If paramedics took victims to the hospital, send an officer to the hospital to interview the paramedics and victims. Find out exactly what they did at the scene. The victims may provide additional information.
3. Set the perimeter.
4. Create a crime scene entry log.
5. Use latex gloves.
6. The lead investigator will walk through the area without disturbing evidence and observe items of evidence (approach the four corners of the room).
7. The photographer will photograph overview of crime scene from all four corners of the room.
8. The lead investigator will decide the crime scene search pattern.
9. The lead investigator determines the evidence and marks the evidence.
10. The photographer will photograph all evidence with and without marker (medium range and close up). All evidence needs to be recorded before any evidence is disturbed and before the crime scene changes (e.g., due to rodents).
11. The backup officer will sketch the scene.
12. After photographs and the sketch, if there is a body at the scene, the body will need to be rolled halfway over to see whether there is any evidence under the body. The body will be returned to its original position.
13. A single officer should collect all evidence to make the chain of custody cleaner.

STEPS FOR VEHICLE SEARCH: TRAFFIC STOP

1. Use leather gloves.
2. Decide on search pattern (front seat then back seat, driver side then passenger side, and so on).
3. Be consistent in search pattern from car to car.

For this example, the officer searches the front seat, the back seat, and then the trunk.

4. Search driver side front seat first, start from top and work downward.
5. Search passenger side front seat, start from top and work downward.
6. Search driver side back seat, start from top and work downward.
7. Search passenger side back seat, start from top and work downward.
8. Search trunk.

Common places to find contraband: ashtrays, glove box, center console, under seats, visor, door tray, and in back pouch of each front seat.

STEPS FOR SEARCH OF PERSON

1. Use leather gloves.
2. Same-sex searches (to minimize liability).
3. Double-lock handcuff suspect.
4. Start at top and work downward (head to feet).
5. Decide on search pattern (front then back, left side then right side, and so on).
6. Be consistent from person to person.
7. Grab and twist areas across torso.
8. Safely pull pockets out (do not reach into pockets).
9. Remove belt and inspect belt.
10. Sit suspect down and remove shoes.
11. Inspect socks and inside of shoes.

Common places to find contraband: waistline, pockets, shoes, hair, groin area, and bra.

If blood is collected as evidence, it is important not to seal the blood in a plastic bag because it will putrefy and be ruined. Blood evidence should be sealed in a box or paper bag, which will breathe. Using a box or paper bag to collect evidence will apply to all bodily fluids. Boxes and paper bags promote air permeability, which is beneficial with this type of evidence.

STEPS FOR COLLECTING BLOOD EVIDENCE

Dry Blood

1. Put on latex gloves.
2. Use distilled water to moisten a cotton swab.
3. Rub or tap the cotton swab onto blood-covered surface (do not cover entire swab in blood).
4. Let blood on swab air dry.
5. Place swab into box or paper bag.
6. Mark evidence bag/box.

7. Place biohazard sticker on evidence bag/box.
8. Place latex gloves in biohazard container.

Wet Blood

1. Put on latex gloves.
2. Rub or tap a cotton swab onto blood-covered surface (do not cover entire swab in blood).
3. Let blood on swab air dry.
4. Place swab into box or paper bag.
5. Mark evidence bag/box.
6. Place biohazard sticker on evidence bag/box.
7. Place latex gloves in biohazard container.

STEPS FOR CASTINGS: OVERVIEW

Footprint casting

1. Put latex gloves on.
2. Set a metal ring around the footprint.
3. Use tweezers to remove grass/debris from inside footprint.
4. Spray hardening material into footprint.
5. Mix casting material so it is not lumpy.
6. Pour casting material next to print and let it initially run into the print.
7. After the casting layer is inside the print, pour the rest of the casting directly inside the print.
8. Let set until dry.

Forensic casting – chisel mark

1. Put latex gloves on.
2. Obtain the correct amount of casting (e.g., Mikrosil) and hardening material.
3. Properly mix the casting and hardening materials.
4. Use a tool (e.g., flat stick) to spread casting material over chisel mark.
5. Allow to dry.
6. Peel dried casting off of mark.

COMMUNICATING WITH NATURE

Clues from crime may come from nature (Frith, 2007). For example, entomologists are experts who study insects to find clues that may reveal when and where a person died. When samples are collected from insects, the growth stage of the insect may indicate the length of time of death, and the type of insect may indicate the time of day of death (e.g., some insects are only active at certain times of the day).

Leaves, soil, seeds, dust, fungus, and pollen may attach themselves to people in the area (Frith, 2007). If, for example, a certain type of pollen only exists in a particular area, and if the same pollen is discovered on a suspect, then that may indicate that the suspect was in the area. Crime scene investigators may search for pollen in a corpse's nose to determine whether the victim was in the same area as the suspect. Such information has led to convictions in court.

Although fires, if hot enough, may reduce nearly everything to soot and ash, fires will eventually go out and will allow for the examination of evidence (Frith, 2007). As a general rule, fires travel up and out, creating a V shape of soot and burned areas. The bottom of the V indicates the origin of the fire. Thus, fire scene investigators may work back through the trail of burned-out debris to locate the origin of the fire. It is not uncommon for arsonists to want to destroy something near the origin of the fire.

Once a fire starts, it will keep burning as long as it has enough fuel and oxygen (Frith, 2007). If a suspect wants to start a fire quickly, they may use an accelerant, such as gasoline or alcohol. If there is a heavily burned trail on the floor, this may indicate a spilled accelerant. Crime scene investigators will look for evidence of accelerants to determine whether the fire was intentionally set. Police may use canines to detect accelerants.

FORGERIES AND FAKES

All articles can be faked. Users of fraudulent documents include terrorists, fugitives, drug traffickers, and undocumented foreign nationals. A counterfeit document is a copy or imitation of an authentic document without legal authority with the intent to pass off the document as genuine. An altered document is a genuine document that has been modified in one or more of its elements without destroying the identity of the original document. Art and antique forgery, although criminal, can be quite profitable in a capitalistic society (Dickens, 2008). Therefore, police officers need to be aware of what to look for when investigating articles for fakes.

Table 18.4 Ways to identify fakes, forgeries, and counterfeits (Dickens, 2008; U.S. Department of the Treasury, n.d.)

	Clues	Description/example
1	Odor	Antique paintings should smell old; the odor of succinic acid indicates an inappropriate amber varnish.
2	Discounted price	To attract bargain hunters, forgers often price forgeries at about half of the actual painting's worth.
3	Catalog description	The catalog and label description may not match the description on the receipt; terms in the catalog may be used to mislead the buyer (e.g., in the style of …).
4	Pattern of wear	Wear should be uneven and consistent with everyday use (e.g., a chair's feet may be uneven).
5	Signs of aging	Items may be artificially aged and advertised as high quality; a chair, for example, may be examined with a magnifying glass to exam low quality stress cracks at holes; used and worn items should not be rough—therefore, look underneath items (e.g., chairs) for smoothness; if painted, look in nooks and crannies for cover-ups.
6	Overpainting	Forgers may paint over an old painting. Shine a bright light through the painting to see if images from a prior painting show through.
7	Labels	Frayed edges on the item's label suggests that the labels are not original or that the item is fake; tea is used to age labels.
8	Printed transfers	Colored items that are produced on a copy machine will reveal tiny dots of color.
9	Fixings	Look at the nails, screws, and hooks to see whether they are old.
10	Opaquing marks	Missing details, such as part of a line or box is missing, as if covered up before it was photocopied.
11	Trash marks	Small remnants of original data that the forger failed to remove from the original document and are still visible on the document.
12	Embossing	A relief impression stamped into the document that can assessed using side-lighting.
13	Hologram	This creates a three-dimension appearance on the document that is difficult to reproduce.
14	Titled laser image	A laser engraved image on the document that appears to be a lenticular printing.

(continued)

Table 18.4 Cont.

	Clues	Description/example
15	Security thread	A thin thread or ribbon running through the bank note.
16	Microprinting	Print appears as a line to the naked eye but can be read under magnification; difficult to photocopy.
17	Watermark	Varying paper density that appears darker or lighter when held up to a light source; does not copy on color copiers.
18	Color-shifting inks	Color of ink changes when image viewed at different angles.
19	Special inks	Fluorescent ink, photochromic ink, fugitive ink, and magnetic ink. Fluorescent ink becomes visible under ultraviolet light. Photochromic ink will darken and stay dark for several minutes after exposure to ultraviolet light. Fugitive ink easily dissolves in solvents and protects against chemical tampering. Magnetic ink can be read by computers.
20	Intaglio	This is raised printing on the document that can be felt.
21	Planchettes	Small dots randomly added to the document that may be iridescent.
22	Scrambled indicia	Must use a transparent cover, which will overlay the document, to make the image visible.
23	See-through register	Images on the front and back of the document create a completed image. When the document is held up to the light, the parts of the design printed on the back will fit exactly within the unprinted areas on the front to produce the completed design.

CHAPTER PROBLEMS

1. You are a log officer. Complete a crime scene entry log as your supervisor would expect to see it. Ray Johnson is the lead investigator. Steve Phipps is the photographer. Kyle Thompson is the sketch artist. For the case number, use today's date with the following format: year, month, day, and report number for the day (e.g., 2022-0317-011 = the 11th report on March 17, 2022). Assume that it is the 11th report today and that you know your own badge number. Assume that you know agency names, scene location, and other information required to complete the form.

2. Complete a photography log sheet as your supervisor would expect to see it. Select a piece of evidence from a crime scene. You have discretion for the location and piece of evidence. Take the proper number and type of photographs. You work for the Richland County Sheriff's Department. For the case number, use today's date and the following format: year, month, day, and report number for the day (e.g., 2022-0317-011 = the 11th report on March 17, 2022). Assume that it is the 44th report today. Assume that you know your own badge number.

3. Complete the information that will be recorded on the evidence bag as your supervisor would expect to see it. Suppose you collect some brown powdery substance that you believe is heroin. For the case number, use today's date and the following format: year, month, day, and daily report number (e.g., 2022-0317-011 = the 11th report on March 17, 2022). Assume that it is the 109th report today. Assume that you know your agency name, badge number, and other information required to complete the information.

4. Suppose you are on a 10x10 grid and there is an object that consumes five spaces, which are either horizontal or vertical, but not diagonal. If you use a strip crime scene search pattern, what is the minimum number of points would you need to choose to guarantee that you land on the item?

5. Use a 10x10 grid. Suppose you a looking for something that consumes five spaces, which are either horizontal or vertical, but not diagonal. Place numbers in the proper sequence and location to represent the most efficient and effective strip crime scene search pattern. In other words, use the minimum number of points to ensure that you find the item. Draw a line that connects the sequential numbers to show the path taken.

6. How will the lead investigator decide the proper search pattern for the crime scene?
7. Who decides what gets photographed as evidence? Describe how the crime scene and evidence are photographed.
8. You collect a knife as evidence that appears to have wet blood on it. You are interested in the blood itself. How should you collect the blood? How would you collect the blood if the blood is dry?
9. What is the proper sequence for searching a car? For example, will an officer search the left side of the car then the right side, or the front seats then the back seats?
10. Describe some of the ways that are used to make the counterfeiting of U.S. currency more difficult. Select a foreign currency and describe some of the ways that are used to make the counterfeiting of the foreign currency more difficult.

KEYWORDS

Casting material

Counterfeit

Crime scene search patterns

REFERENCES

Dickens, E. (2008). *Fakes & forgeries*. Sywell: Igloo.

Frith, A. (2007). *Forensic science*. Tulsa, OK: Usborne.

Saferstein, R. (2009). *Forensic science: From the crime scene to the crime lab*. Upper Saddle River, NJ: Pearson Prentice-Hall.

Swanson, C.R., Chamelin, N.C., Territo, L., & Taylor, R.W. (2009). *Criminal investigation* (10th ed.). Boston: McGraw Hill.

U.S. Department of the Treasury, Bureau of Engraving and Printing (n.d.). Security features. www.moneyfactory.gov/anticounterfeiting/securityfeatures.html

Glossary

admission The suspect admits to something related to an act but does not claim they committed the act; contains some information concerning the elements of a crime, but falls short of a full confession.

adoptive admission After being provided with incriminating evidence, a person does not deny allegations made against them when given the opportunity.

affidavit A written statement of facts provided under oath by a law enforcement officer.

algorithm A process or set of rules to be followed for problem-solving operations.

analogy evidence Comparing two similar cases and inferring that what is true for the first case is also true for the second case.

arrest The taking of a person into custody against the person's will for the purpose of criminal prosecution or interrogation.

artifact Anything human-made, such as a tool or a work of art; an object remaining from a particular period.

assumption Something believed to be true without proof.

binary decision A choice with only two options.

biometrics Unique physical characteristics, such as fingerprints, that can be used for automated recognition.

body language Nonverbal communication in which physical behaviors are used to express or convey the information.

Boolean algebra Branch of mathematics that assesses logical operations with binary variables.

Boolean algebra theorems Statements that have been proved true, which are used to change the form of Boolean expressions.

casting material A substance that is poured into an impression, hardened, then removed to create a three-dimensional image of the impression.

causal relationship Refers to the relationship of cause and effect between the independent variable and the dependent variable.

cipher A secret or disguised way of writing or communicating; a code.

close-ended question A question that can be answered without elaboration (e.g., yes or no).

codes, police Ciphered information to represent common police activities and needs.

coercion Compelling a party to act in an involuntary manner by using threats and/or force.

comparison and contrast evidence Comparing the similarities and differences between two cases; one case may be better than the other case.

conditional statement If p, then q; an if–then statement in which p is the antecedent and q is the consequence.

confession Someone states that they committed the act.

conscious The conscious mind is logical, and individuals are aware of and respond purposefully to their surroundings.

content analysis Attempts to understand why events happen by discovering themes in the data.

correlation relationship A statistical association and degree to which a pair of variables are linearly related.

counterfeit An imitation of something that is used to deceive or defraud.

credibility The quality of being trusted.

crime scene entry log sheet A police form that is used to record all individuals who enter and leave the crime scene.

crime scene investigations Defining and securing areas that may contain evidence; examining and documenting the crime scene; collecting, preserving, packaging, and storing physical evidence that will eventually be submitted to the laboratory for analysis.

crime scene search pattern Technique used to examine a crime scene for evidence in the most effective and efficient manner; the path taken to look for evidence.

crimes against children Violations of law that target those individuals who are too young to be considered adults.

critical thinking Using a totality of circumstances to make the best-practice decision.

curtilage The location where a person engages in daily intimate activities linked to the sanctity of a person's home.

cyberspace Communications via computers over the internet.

death notification Informing family members of the death of a relative.

decipher To decode a secret message into intelligible language.

deposition The sworn out-of-court testimony of a witness, usually in the opposing attorney's office, which will be transcribed into writing.

detention The restraining of a person by police for some official purpose.

deviance Nonconformity to the general acceptable standards.

disability A physical or mental condition that limits the person's movements, senses, or activities.

discovery A pretrial procedure by which one party gains information held by the opposing party.

disposition The final outcome of the case.

DNA, sources Locations where residual evidence from a person's body may be discovered.

DUI investigation paperwork Typically, at a minimum, a DUI arrest will include a traffic citation, case report, field sobriety test results, results for a blood test (refused, voluntarily provided, or forcibly obtained), a search warrant if blood was forcibly obtained, a probable cause affidavit, an information, a MUG photograph, and a fingerprint card.

elderly abuse An act or lack of appropriate action that causes distress to an older person where there is an expectation of trust in the relationship.

elements of the crime/elements of the law Components of the law that define the conditions for its violation; the variables contained within the text of the law with their corresponding logical operators.

equivalency Two laws are logically equivalent only if they have the same truth values for all possible combinations of the input variables.

errata sheet An attachment to the deposition that the deponent can use to make minor corrections, such as spelling, to the transcript.

ethical system References for which to judge what is considered good behavior.

ethics, canons Prescribed standards of ethical conduct or code of professional responsibility.

ethnography Seeks to describe a culture from the local or Indigenous people's point of view.

evidence bag information Data documented on the outside of the evidence bag; information must match data on corresponding reports.

exclusionary rule Evidence collected by police in violation of the 4th Amendment will be excluded from court during the criminal prosecution to prove guilt.

existential quantifier The condition is true if it exists at least one time.

explanation evidence Using facts to clarify a topic or process in a speech.

false confession A lie that a person tells about having committed a crime when the person did not in fact commit the crime.

falsification Instead of showing that something is true, showing that it is not false.

felony stop A serious traffic stop where the occupants are brought back to the officers.

field interview card Form used by police to collect information from individuals in the field.

flowchart Type of diagram that represents a workflow or process.

focus group Where individuals who share common traits and experiences interact and provide data beyond what any single participant could provide; most appropriate for studies that are explanatory in nature.

forgery/fake Something that is not genuine; counterfeit.
Freedom of Information Act Makes the records of government agencies accessible to the public.
graphology The study of graphic movement, which includes written and printed symbols to infer a person's character.
habeas corpus A writ requiring a person under arrest to be brought before a judge to secure the person's release unless lawful grounds can be shown for the person's detention.
handwriting analysis The examination of someone's writing as a way of learning something about the person.
hearsay information The report of another person's words by a witness.
hostage A person taken by force to secure the taker's demands.
hostage-taker A person who captures an individual and holds the individual prisoner, and who may injure or kill the prisoner if others do not do what the person is asking.
illustration evidence Using real-life situations to demonstrate information in speech.
information A criminal charge filed by the prosecutor.
input variables Factors that can change values, which can affect the output of the system; the components of the law.
integrity The quality of being honest and having strong moral principles.
intelligence Knowledge gained through study, communication, research, instruction, and so on; totality of circumstances.
intelligence report Form used to document possible criminal activity but with no probable cause; police will record detailed information about a suspect that will be placed into the police database.
intelligences, multiple Different techniques for learning material.
interrogate To ask an arrestee questions about a crime for which the person has been charged.
interrogation techniques Different ways to obtain a confession from an arrestee; eliciting useful information related to a crime.
interrogatory A list of formal questions that are sent to the opposing legal party, perhaps via email, which must be answered in writing under the penalty of perjury.
interview Asking a person, who is not under arrest, about an incident.
job interview A meeting where the employer will ask the applicants a variety of questions to determine whether they are a good fit for both the job and the department.
kinesics The study of body movements and gestures as a form of nonverbal communication.
known source A writing with an identified author.
lenses of truth References that are used to assess reality and truth.
levels of certainty The amount of knowledge that must exist before certain actions can be taken.
limitation A restriction of the application.
lineup Possible suspects presented to a witness at the police station for identification.
logical expression A statement that can either be true or false.
logic circuit Used to graphically represent the sequence of operations from start to finish to create the desired outcome, such as a rule, policy, or law; does not have a NOT gate; similar to electrical circuit and the flow of electricity.
logic conjunction The AND logical operator; a truth-functional operator; true if and only if all of its operands are true.
logic disjunction The OR logical operator; a truth-functional operator; true if at least one of its operands is true.
logic gates Used to graphically represent the sequence of operations from start to finish to create the desired outcome, such as a rule, policy, or law; NOT gate will have exactly one input; all other gates will have exactly two inputs.
logic negation The NOT operator in Boolean algebra.
media Agencies that use communication channels to disseminate information.
Miranda warning The warning the police will provide to a person in custody that they may remain silent and have the right to a lawyer.

modifier A word that changes, clarifies, qualifies, or limits a particular word in a sentence to make its meaning more specific.

number base The number of digits that a system of counting uses to represent numbers (e.g., base 2 has two digits: 0–1; base 8 has eight digits: 0–7; base 10 has ten digits: 0–9).

open-ended question A question that requires an essay or narrative response.

open field Area outside of curtilage.

oral presentations By word of mouth; spoken; a speech to an audience.

persuasion The act of influencing people to do something or to change their mind.

persuasion theories Different tactics to change the mind of jurors.

photographic lineup Showing a set of photographs to a witness for suspect identification.

photography log sheet Form used to document all photographs taken at a crime scene.

police department orientations Lenses through which police department administrators perceive crime and the criminal justice system; used to judge police officer behaviors.

polygraph test Lie detector test.

probable cause More likely than not that a crime has occurred or is occurring; 51% certainty for practical purposes.

probing question A follow-up question for a previous answer in order to obtain more in-depth information.

property record and receipt Form used to document the chain of custody.

proxemics The study of personal space.

proximity Nearness in space during an interrogation or interview.

qualitative study In law enforcement terms, investigating the motive or why people do things.

quantifiers A logic expression (e.g., it exists at least once or it always exists) that indicates the scope of a term to which it is attached.

quantitative study In law enforcement terms, investigating the modus operandi or how people do things.

questioned document A piece of writing with an unidentified author.

reasonable suspicion An amount of knowledge that is necessary to convince a police officer, based on their training and experience, that criminal activity is at hand.

reasoning Thinking about something in a logical, sensible way.

red herring A diversionary flare; information that intentionally misleads or distracts from the truth.

reliable Consistent.

reports, police Paperwork that documents something; each type of report focuses on a different activity.

request for laboratory examination A form that formally asks lab technicians to perform a specific test on the submitted evidence.

résumé Document created and used by a person to present the person's background, skills, and accomplishments.

résumé, functional Organized by categories based on the person's skills or qualifications.

résumé, reverse chronological Organized by dates of employment; lists employment from most recent to least recent.

search To explore and examine a specific location, which is not public, for contraband that will be used against a suspect in a court of law.

search warrant A written order, issued by a judge, directing a police officer to search for property connected to a crime and to bring the evidence before the court.

seizure When the police, based on a totality of circumstances, create a situation for which a reasonable person would not feel free to leave.

service animal Common domestic animal specifically trained to assist a person with a disability.

72-hour medical detention A court-ordered holding of a person against their wishes in a medical facility so licensed medical personnel can examine the person to determine whether they are a danger to themself or others.

showup A police supervised one-on-one confrontation in the field between the suspect of a crime and a witness.
speech A formal address or discourse delivered to an audience.
statistics evidence Using numerical data and figures to support information in speech.
stop and frisk Detaining a person briefly so the officer can ask questions (the stop) and patting-down the detainee for weapons when safety is a concern (the frisk).
subconscious The subconscious mind regulates behaviors that are not actively in an individual's focal awareness, such as rate of breathing.
subset A part of a larger group of related things.
suspect report A police form that is used in the field to collect information about a suspect.
sympathetic nervous system System that primarily works unconsciously in the human body to regulate the body's many functions.
testimony evidence Using quotations or paraphrases to support information in a speech.
theme analysis Applied to a set of texts to identify common topics, ideas, and patterns of meaning that come up repeatedly.
theory Logical explanation for why something happens. Every theory has a limitation.
totality of circumstances The cumulative evidence; all the available evidence.
truth The interpretation of reality.
truth tables A mathematical table based on Boolean algebra that is used to determine whether a compound statement is true or false.
unconscious The part of the mind that allows the body to act out of habit.
universal quantifier The condition is true if and only if it is always true.
U.S. Constitutional law Laws that control police officer behaviors; laws that protect people against the government; provides minimal protection.
valid True and accurate information.
Venn diagrams A diagram representing logical sets pictorially as circles within an enclosing rectangle that represents the universe; common elements of the sets are represented by the areas of overlap among the circles.
verbal communications The use of words to convey a message; written and oral communications.
voice inflection A rise or fall in the sound of a person's voice for certain words.
voice stress analysis Using a computer stress analysis device to analyze the levels of stress in a subject's voice generated by micro-tremors in the larynx.
voluntary statement Occurs when a suspect provides a statement without coercion and of their own free will.
volunteered statement Occurs when a person provides a statement freely without being interrogated.

Index

A

Accelerants, 477
Accident interrogation technique, 340
Act utilitarianism, 230, 234, 236
Admission, 6, 481
Adoptive admission, 6, 481
Affidavit, 48, 151, 152, 153–154, 481
    cocaine possession example, 158–160
        DUI investigation, 166, 177–180, 182–183
        provocation law example, 155–156
Afrocentrism 223–224, 226
Age-graded theory, 43
Agent provocateur interrogation technique, 342
Algorithms, 69–72, 481
Alimentary canal smugglers, detention, 22
Analogy evidence, 443, 444, 445, 481
AND logic gate, 123, 124, 130–137, 146–147
AND operation, 124, 137
Appeal to authority interrogation technique, 337
Appeal to conscience interrogation technique, 341
Appeal to intellect interrogation technique, 338
Appeal to intelligence interrogation technique, 341
Arrest, 3, 18, 23–24, 276, 481
    vs. stop and frisk, 18
Artifacts, 225, 426–428, 481
Associative laws, 126–127
Assumptions, 38, 40–42, 50, 52, 64–65, 241–245, 481
Attribution theory, 55, 56
Autism disorders, people with, 358, 361–362
Automatic nervous system, 325
Axiology, 227–228

B

Balance theory, 54–55, 56
Baseball codes, 200
Baselines, graphology, 380–381
Base numbers, *see* Number base
Behavioral disturbance, people with, 366
Behavioral economics theory, 240
Behavioral symptom interrogation technique, 344
Behavior theory, 43
Bias, personal, 226–228
    witness identification of suspect, 292
Binary data
    Boolean algebra, 85, 86
    logic circuits, 137
    logic gates, 123
    truth tables, 85–87
Binary decisions, 69, 481
    Boolean algebra, 105
Binary numbers, 189–190, 191, 194–195, 196–199
Binary variables, 35
    Venn diagrams, 116
Biological theory, 42, 43, 223
Biometrics, 306, 481
Blame society interrogation technique, 352
Blame someone else interrogation technique, 337
Blindness and visual impairment, people with, 359, 365
Block cipher, 205
Blood-alcohol test 73, 175–176, 180
    search warrant, 182
Blood evidence, collecting, 475–476
Bodily-kinesthetic learners, 62, 63
Body language, 54, 152, 305, 481
    behavioral symptom interrogation technique, 344
    deception, 306–329
    and emotions, 307
    interpretation, 306–307
    interviews, 278
    job interviews, 440
    truth assessment, 321–329
Bombs, 405–407
Booking after arrest, 24
Boolean algebra, 85, 481
    theorems, 124–129, 481
    truth tables, 85–86, 105
Border search, 21–22
Braille, 212
Brain fingerprinting, 373
Brain injury, people with, 366
Brain scans, 373
Breastfeeding law, truth table, 101–103
Breathing patterns, and truth assessment, 328
Broken window theory, 45

C

"Can you take it back?" interrogation technique, 346
Cardiographs, 372
Caregivers for people with disabilities, 357, 360
Car thief interrogation technique, 352
Case reports, 152
Case studies, 420
Casting material, 460, 476, 481
Causal relationship, 38, 481
    flawed assumptions, 38, 42
    idiographic, 419
    nomothetic, 419
Cerebral palsy, people with, 360, 363–364
Certainty, levels of, 5, 39–40, 483
Chain of custody; *see also* Property record and receipt
    cocaine possession example, 158, 162
Charging form, *see* Information: for violation of law
Chemicals, HazMat incidents, 407, 409–411

Children
  abused, 399–400
  as courtroom witnesses, 401
  crimes against, 399–401, 482
  cyberspace, 394–395
  false confessions, 334
  interrogation technique, 352
  interviewing, 398, 400
  protective services, 400
  sudden infant death syndrome (SIDS), 401
Children's Online Privacy Protection Act, 395
Chisel mark, 476
Cipher, 202, 203–216, 481
Circle code, 214
Circle search pattern, 461, 462, 464
Circuit courts, 4
Closed-ended questions, 278–279, 283, 481
  exercises, 279, 280–281
  interrogations, 333
  interviewing sex-abused children, 398
Clustered behavior, 322
Cocaine possession, 158–163
Codes
  computer translation, 202
  playing cards, 201–202
  police, 187–189, 481
  secret, 202
  signal, 188
  sport, 200–201, 10, 188
Code sticks, 203
Coercion, 334–335, 481
Cognitive dissonance theory, 55–56
Communication, 52; *see also* Body language; Interrogation; Interrogatory; Interviews
  audiences, 286
  codes, 187–202
  computer, 189
  death notifications, 411
  with defense attorney, 286
  effective and efficient 47–48, 151–152
  hostage negotiations, 403–405
  with individuals, 286
  with other police officers, 286
  persuasion, 52–54
  speech outline, 448–449
  radio, 187
  theories, 52–56
  verbal abstract techniques, 311–319
Communication impairments, people with, 365
Commutative laws, 126
Comparison and contrast evidence, 443, 444, 481
Complainants, 285
Compulsion to confess interrogation technique, 350
Computer communication, 189
Computer translation codes, 202
Conditional statements, 31–33, 481
Confession, 6, 481
  compulsion to confess interrogation technique, 350
  credibility, 335
  false, 331, 334–335, 482
  hot confession interrogation technique, 346

  truth assessment, 323–324
Confidential informants, 285
Congruity principle theory, 55, 56
Conjunction, *see* Logic conjunction (AND)
Connecting strokes, graphology, 383–384
Conscience interrogation technique, 351
Conscious, 306, 481
Consensual encounter, 275–276
  with police car, 14
Conspiracy interrogation technique, 348
Constructivism, 222–223, 225
Containment theory, 44
Content analysis, 420, 422–424, 481
Control gimmick interrogation technique, 339
Control zones, HazMat incidents, 407–408
Convict criminology, 45
Cooperation, suspect's pointing out of, 324
Correctional medical survey, 153, 163, 165–166
Correlation relationship, 38, 481
  flawed assumptions, 42
Corruption
  crime control orientation vs. due process orientation, 242
  gratuities, 237–238, 239
Counter-attitudinal advocacy theory, 56
Counterfeits, 477–478, 481
Courtroom testimony speech outline, 450–451
Crash report, 153
Credibility, 481
  of confession, 335
  of qualitative information, 421
Crime control orientation, police department, 242, 245
Crimes against children, 399–401, 482
Crime scene
  entry log sheet, 469, 470, 481
  investigations, 459, 469–478, 482
  search patterns, 460–468, 482
  supplies, 460
Criminal hostage-takers, 404
Criminal informants, 285
Critical social theory, 46
Critical theory, 223, 225
Critical thinking, 52, 61, 65, 306, 482
  oral presentations, 443
Cross-examination, 286
Crystallized intelligence, 63
Cultural conflict theory, 44
Cultural relativism, 231, 235, 237
Curtilage, 4, 482
Customs and Border Protection, 47
Custody, chain of; *see also* Property record and receipt
  cocaine possession example, 158, 162
Custody order/custody hold form, 153
Cyberspace, 394–396, 482
Cyberterrorism, 396

D
DataMaster test, *see* Blood-alcohol test
Date shift cipher, 206–207
Deadly arc, 405

Deafness and hearing impairments, people with, 359, 360, 365
Death notification, 411, 482
Deception
    body language, 306–329
    graphology, 379, 385
    interrogations, 332–333
    by police officers, 236–237
    polygraph tests, 371–372
    pyramid of lies interrogation technique, 349
    voice stress analysis, 372–373
Decimal numbers, 189–191, 192–197, 198, 199
Decipher, 202, 203–216, 482
Deductive reasoning, 65
Delay tactics of suspect, 323
Delinquent development theory, 46
Deontological ethical system, 230, 233
Deposition, 249, 250, 253, 482
    example, 254–273
    outline, 253–254
Descriptive statistics, 48–51
    totality of circumstances, 66–67
Detention, 15, 276, 482
    alimentary canal smugglers, 22
    field, 15
    foreign nationals, 21
    length, 24
    stationhouse, 20–21
Deterrence theory, 43
    Megan's Law, 42
Developmental pathways, 46
Deviance, 221–222, 482
    gratuities, 237–238
Dichotomous variables, *see* Binary variables
Differential association theory, 44
Dirty bombs, 406
Disabilities, people with, 357–366, 482
Discovery, 249, 482
Disjunction, *see* Logic disjunction (OR)
Disposition, 24, 25, 482
Distraction, 41
Distributive laws, 127–128
DNA, sources, 373–374, 482
Dog sniffs, 4
Domestic hostage-takers, 404
Domestic violence, 285, 401–402
Dot code key, 208
Double stick interrogation technique, 342
Driving under the influence (DUI)
    investigations, 73–75
    deposition example, 254–273
    paperwork, 153, 166–185, 482
    probable cause affidavit, 151
    law
    truth tables, 99–101, 103–104, 117–118
    Venn diagram, 116–118
Drunk interrogation technique, 347
Dual taxonomic theory, 45
Due process, 11
Due process orientation, police department, 242, 245

DUI, *see* Driving under the influence (DUI)
Dumb and dumber interrogation technique, 336

E
Ecological theory, 44
Ego deflation interrogation technique, 347
Egoism, 232, 236, 237
Elderly abuse, 402–403, 482
Electronic information, 396
Elements of the crime/law, 151, 153–161, 482
    DUI investigation, 166, 181
Emotions, and body language, 307
Empiricism, 224, 226
Employee Polygraph Protection Act, 371, 372
Enlightened egoism, 232, 236, 237
Entomology, 476
Entrapment, 36–37
Environmental design, crime prevention through, 46
Epilepsy, people with, 362–363
Epistemology, 227, 228
Equivalency, 96–99, 482
Errata sheet, 272, 273, 482
Ethical dilemmas, 229–230
Ethical formalism, 231, 234, 237
Ethical relativism, 231, 234, 237
Ethical systems, 229, 230–236, 482
Ethics, 230, 232
    canons, 229, 482
    gratuities, 237–239, 240
    lying by police officers, 236–237
    religious, 231, 235, 237
    research practices, 421
    situational, 232, 236, 237
    test of, 229
Ethics of care, 232, 236, 237
Ethics of virtue, 232, 235, 237
Ethnography, 420, 424–425, 482
    truth, 225, 226
Ethos, 51
Everybody's doing it interrogation technique, 337
Evidence
    admission, 6, 481
    erroneously admitted, 11
    illegally obtained, 13
    mistakes during collection, 2
Evidence bag information, 473, 482
Exaggeration interrogation technique, 342–343
Exclusionary rule, 10–11, 482
    exceptions, 2, 11–13
Existential intelligence, 62, 63
Existential quantifier, 34–35, 482
Explanation evidence, 443, 444, 445, 446, 482
Extension interrogation technique, 346
Eye blinking, and truth assessment, 327
Eye contact, and truth assessment, 327
Eye movements, and truth assessment, 326

F
Faces, 305–306
Face-saving interrogation technique, 339

Facial expressions, 305
    truth assessment, 306, 327
Fakes and forgeries, 374–377, 477–478, 483
False confessions, 331, 334–335, 482
Falsification, 39–40, 482
    post-positivism, 227
Favoritism, 238
Federal vs. state jurisdiction, 2
Felony stops, 412–414, 482
Female suspects, interrogation, 353
Feminism, 223, 225
Feminist criminology, 46
Fetish interrogation technique, 353
Field detention, 15
Field interview card, 153, 298, 301, 482
Field interviews, positioning during, 287
Field sobriety tests, 73, 166–174, 178
File gimmick interrogation technique, 340
Financial abuse, 403
Fingerprinting
    of brain, 373
        field detention, 15
        stationhouse detention, 20
Fire scene investigation, 477
First-person reports, 47
Flags, international code of, 215
Flattery interrogation technique, 343
Flight, unprovoked, 3, 18
Flowcharts, 69–73, 482
    DUI investigation, 73–75
    sexual violation law between a man and a woman, 77–79
    stop and frisk, 76
    symbols, 70–71
    vehicle search, 77
Fluid intelligence, 63–64
Focus groups, 420, 422, 428–430, 482
Football codes, 200–201
Footprint casting, 476
Force, appropriate amount of, 2–3
Foreign nationals
    detention, 21
    factory surveys, 22
    passport law, 33
Forensic casting, 476
Forgeries and fakes, 374–377, 477–478, 483
Fraternity interrogation technique, 350
Freedom of Information Act, 394, 483
Freehand forgery, 374
Frisk, *see* Stop and frisk
Frustration-driven hostage-takers, 404
Functional resumés, 434, 435, 437–439, 484
Functional theory, 56

G

Galvanographs, 372
Gender, 223, 225, 226
Gifts, *see* Gratuities and gifts
    ethics, 237–239, 240
    theoretical concepts and research, 239–241
Good behavior, 230–236

Good cop, bad cop interrogation technique, 345
Grammar
    importance, 29–30, 35, 97, 98
    mistakes, 30–31, 53
Graphology, 378–386, 483
Grassy areas, crime scene investigation, 473
Gratuities and gifts
    ethics, 237–239, 240
    theoretical concepts and research, 239–241
Greek square cipher, 211
Grid search pattern, 461, 463
Grounded theory, 420
Growth complex orientation, police department, 243–244, 246

H

Habeas corpus, 11, 483
    wrongful convictions, 374
Half-reversing the alphabet ciphering/deciphering technique, 204
Hand movements, and truth assessment, 328
Handwriting analysis, 374–377, 483
    graphology, 378–386, 483
HazMat incidents, 407–411
Head posture, and truth assessment, 326
Hearing impairments, people with, 359, 360, 365
Hearsay information, 19, 48, 483
Heaven and hell interrogation technique, 341
Hermeneutics
    personal bias, 226, 228
    truth, 225, 226
Hexadecimal numbers, 189–190, 192, 197, 198–199
Honest exclamations by suspect, 324
Hostages, 403–405, 483
Hostage-takers, 403–405, 483
Hot and cold interrogation technique, 341
Hot confession interrogation technique, 346

I

Idempotent laws, 124
Identity theft, 396
Ideological hostage-takers, 404
Idiographic causal relationships, 419
Illustration evidence, 443, 444, 445, 483
Impromptu speeches, 452–455
Indictment, 152
Individual–police encounters, 287–291
Indoor crime scene investigation, 474
Inductive reasoning, 65, 66
Inferential statistics, 48–49, 50–51
    totality of circumstances, 66, 67
Information
    collection, 151–152
    HazMat incidents, 409–410
    hearsay, 19, 48, 483
    offered by suspect, truth assessment, 323
    relative value of, 417–418
    for violation of law, 48, 151, 152, 153–154, 483
        cocaine possession example, 158, 161
        DUI example, 181
        provocation law example, 157

Information-gathering probes, 280
Inoculation theory, 56
Input variables, 85, 483
 truth tables, 86–97, 105–106, 111
 Venn diagrams, 106, 111, 116
Integrity, 229–230, 241, 483
Intellectual disabilities, people with, 358, 361
Intellectual standards, 64
Intelligence, 63–64, 483
 crystallized, 63
 existential, 62, 63
 fluid, 63–64
 naturalist, 62, 63
Intelligence reports, 153, 298, 302, 483
Intelligences, multiple, 61–63, 483
Interactional theory, 45
International code of signal flags, 215
Internet dangers, 394–396
Interpersonal learners, 62, 63
Interpretivism
 social constructionist orientation, 244, 246
 truth, 224, 226
Interrogation, 5–6, 483
 stationhouse detention, 21
 techniques, 331–353, 483
 proximity, 354–355
 setting the atmosphere, 353
Interrogation of females technique, 353
Interrogation rooms, 354–355
Interrogatory, 249–250, 483
 example, 250–252
Interviews, 5–6, 276–278, 483
 children, 400
 sex-abuse victims, 398
 disabilities, people with, 357–366
 good interviewers, qualities of, 152
 job, 439–443
 pre-interrogation, 332
 qualitative research, 419, 421, 422
 focus groups, 428–430
 question types, 278–282
 structure, 282–285
Interview statements, 289
Intrapersonal learners, 62, 63
Introductory statement, in interrogation, 332
Involution law, 126
"I want you to talk" interrogation technique, 351

J
Jail intake form, 153, 163–164
Job interviews, 439–443, 483
Jury trials, 25
 communication and persuasion, 47, 52–56
 totality of circumstances, 66
 Type I and Type II errors, 40
Juveniles, *see* Children

K
Keyboard cipher, 205–206
Keyboard date shift cipher, 207

Kinesics, 278, 305, 483
Known source, 376–377, 483

L
Labeling theory, 45
 Megan's Law, 42
Laboratory examination request, 151, 152, 153, 484
 cocaine possession example, 158, 163
Lane search pattern, 461, 462, 463
Last chance appeal interrogation technique, 348
Late modernity orientation, police department, 244, 246
Law book, 47–48
 elements of the crime, 153
Laws, 69
 flowchart, 77–79
Lawyer gimmick interrogation technique, 342
Leading questions, 281–282
Learning theory, 56
Left-wing orientation, police department, 242–243, 246
Leg movements/posture, and truth assessment, 328
Lenses of truth, 222–226, 483
Levels of certainty, 5, 39–40, 483
Life course theory, 45
Limitations, 483
 of criminal theories 42–46
Line code key, 209
Line search pattern, 461, 463, 465
Lineups, 292, 483
 form, 295
 procedures, 294
 reports, 153
Linguistic learners 62, 63
Lip reading, 359, 365
Literature reviews, 421
Logical approach interrogation technique, 347
Logical expressions, 483
 logic circuits, 145
 logic gates, 123–124, 130, 131, 132, 133
Logical-mathematical learners, 62, 63
Logical positivism, 222, 225
Logic circuits, 137–147, 483
 logic gates comparison, 137, 145–147
Logic conjunction (AND), 85, 86–87, 90, 106, 107, 483; *see also* AND logic gate; AND operation; Truth tables; Venn diagrams
Logic disjunction (OR), 85, 86, 87, 90, 106–107, 483; *see also* OR logic gate; OR operation; Truth tables; Venn diagrams
Logic gates, 123–124, 483
 Boolean algebra laws and theorems, 124–129
 designs, 130–137
 logic circuits comparison, 137, 145–147
Logic negation (NOT), 85, 86, 90, 106–107, 483; *see also* NOT logic gate; NOT operation; Truth tables; Venn diagrams
Logos, 51–52
Looking-glass self theory, 239, 240
Lying
 body language, 306–329

brain scans, 373
graphology, 385
interrogations, 332–333
by police officers, 236–237
polygraph tests, 371–372
pyramid of lies interrogation technique, 349
voice stress analysis, 372–373

M
Magnetic resonance imaging (MRI), 373
Maltreatment of children, 399
Margins, graphology, 381–383
Marijuana law, 393–394
Media, 391–394, 483
Megan's Law, 42
Memory, and truth assessment, 324, 326
Mental illness, people with, 358, 364
Mental impairment, and false confessions, 334
Methodology, 227, 228
Micro-expressions, 306
Miranda warning, 3, 6–8, 290–291, 483
    children, 334
    disabilities, people with, 359, 360
    hearing impairments, people with, 359, 365
    and nontestimonial evidence, 371
    report, 152
Misdirection, 41
Mistake interrogation technique, 341
Mobility impairment, people with, 364
Modeling theory, 43
Modifiers, 484
    existential and universal quantifiers, 34–35
    misplaced and dangling 29–31, 35, 37–38
Moods, suspect's, 322–323
Moon's code, 213
Moral exclamations by suspect, 324
Moral principles, 230, 232
Morse code, 212–213
Mouth, and truth assessment, 328
Multiple intelligences, 61–63, 483
Musical learners, 62, 63

N
NAND operation, 125
Naturalist intelligence, 62, 63
Natural law, 231, 235, 237
Nature, and crime scene investigation, 476–477
Negation, *see* Logic negation (NOT)
Neoclassical theory, 43
Neutral questions, 281–282
Nomothetic causal relationships, 419
Nonparametric statistics, 50
Nonverbal communication; *see also* Body language
    persuasion, 53–54
Normative sponsorship theory, 45
NOR operation, 129
NOT logic gate, 123, 130–137, 146
NOT operation, 125
    logic circuits, 137, 138

Number base, 189–200, 484
Numbers standing for letters ciphering/deciphering technique, 204

O
Octal numbers, 189–191, 197–198
Oedipus interrogation technique, 339
Ontology, 226, 227, 228
Open-ended questions, 278, 283, 484
    exercises, 279, 280–281
    interrogations, 332, 333
    interviewing sex-abused children, 398
    qualitative research, 419, 421
    focus groups, 428
Open field, 4, 484
Oppression orientation, police department, 245, 246
Oral persuasion, 52–53
    speech outline, 448–449
Oral presentations, 443–451, 484
OR logic gate, 123, 124, 130–137, 146–147
OR operation, 125
    logic circuits, 137, 138
Other guy interrogation technique, 349–350
Outdoor crime scene investigation, 474

P
Page-paragraph-line-word-letter ciphering/deciphering technique, 211
Parametric statistics, 50
Parolees, stop of, 19
Passport law, 33
Pathos, 51
Peacemaking criminology, 46
Pedophiles
    brain scans, 373
    reactions to being discovered, 401
Performance review, 66–69
Perjury, 249, 250
Personal bias, 226–228
    witness identification of suspect, 292
Personal illness form, 153
Personal protective equipment, 407, 408
Personal space, 354
Persuasion, 52, 484
    modes, 51–52
    nonverbal, 53–54
    theories, 51, 54–56, 484
    verbal, 52–53
    speech outline, 448–449
Phenomenological research, 420
Phenomenology
    personal bias, 227–228
    truth, 224, 226
Phonetic alphabets, 188–189
Photographic lineups, 292, 484
    form, 297
    procedures, 296
    reports, 153
Photography log sheet, 469, 471, 472, 484
Pigpen ciphering/deciphering technique, 204–205

Plain view, 4
Playing cards, marked deck, 201–202
Plea bargain, 25
Pneumographs, 372
Police car, consensual encounter with, 14
Police codes, 187–189, 481
Police department orientations, 241–246, 484
Police–individual encounters, 286–291
Police officer performance review, 66–69
Police–public encounters, classification of, 275
Police reports, 152–166, 484
Polite suspect, 323
Politics orientation, police department, 242–243, 246
Polygraph tests, 371–372, 484
Positivism, 226
Positron emission tomography (PET), 373
Postmodern criminology, 45
Postmodernism, 222, 225
Post-positivism
    personal bias, 226–227
    truth, 222, 225
Poststructuralism, 223, 225
Pragmatism, 223, 225
Pre-interrogation checklist, 334
Presentations, oral, 443–451
Pressure, graphology, 385
Presumptive questions, 279
    exercise, 280–281
Privacy
    in interrogations, 333
    qualitative research participants, 421
    right to, 4
Probable cause, 3, 8–9, 484
    affidavit, *see* Affidavit
Probing questions, 279–280, 283, 484
    exercise, 280–281
    focus groups, 428, 429–430
    pushing probes, 280–281
Procedures, 69
    flowcharts, 69
    DUI investigation, 73–75
    stop and frisk, 76
    vehicle search, 77
Property record and receipt, 151, 152, 153, 484
    cocaine possession example, 158, 162
Provocation law, 153–157
Proxemics, 484
    interviews, 278
    truth assessment, 325
Proximity, 484
    interrogation techniques, 354–355
Psychoanalytic perspective theory, 43
Psychological impairment, and false confessions, 334
Publicity interrogation technique, 338
Public–police encounters, classification of, 275–276
Public service
    form, 153
    technology, 397

Public speaking
    form, 153
    impromptu, 452–455
    oral presentations, 443–451
Pushing probes, 280–281
p-value, 49
Pyramid of lies interrogation technique, 349

Q
Quadrant search pattern, 461, 462, 464, 467
Qualitative studies, 39, 417, 419, 484
    artifact data, 426–428
    assessing, 417–418
    ethnography, 424–425
    focus groups, 428–430
    nomothetic and idiographic causal relationships, 419
    research designs, 420
    research practices, 420–422
    theme analysis, 422–424
    voice inflection, 418–419
Quantifiers, 34–35, 38, 484
    existential, 34–35, 482
    universal, 34–35, 485
Quantitative studies, 39, 419, 484
    nomothetic and idiographic causal relationships, 419
    research practices, 421
Questioned document, 376–377, 484
Question types, interviews, 278–282
Quotas, 66–67

R
Race, 223–224, 226
Radio communication, 187
Rail fence cipher, 211
Rapport
    disabilities, people with, 358
    hostage negotiations, 404
    interrogations, 331–332
    interviews, 282, 283
    sex-abused children, 398
Rational choice theory, 43
    gratuities, 239, 240
    Megan's Law, 42
Rational orientation, police department, 241, 245
Ray search pattern, 461, 462, 464
Reading every second letter ciphering/deciphering technique, 204
Reasonable suspicion, 2, 8, 484
Reasoning, 64, 65, 484
    deductive, 65
    inductive, 65, 66
Red herrings, 35, 308, 484
Regulations, 69
Relative interrogation technique, 343
Reliability, 38, 484
    confessions, 335
Religious ethics, 231, 235, 237

Reports, police, 152–166, 484
Request for laboratory examination, 151, 152, 153, 484
   cocaine possession example, 158, 163
Research; *see also* Qualitative studies; Quantitative studies
   nomothetic and idiographic causal relationships, 419
   personal bias, 226–228
Respect for position in society interrogation technique, 338
Restraining orders, 402
Résumés, 433–435, 484
   functional, 434, 435, 437–439, 484
   reverse chronological, 434, 435–437, 484
Reversing the alphabet ciphering/deciphering technique, 204
Reversing the words ciphering/deciphering technique, 204
Right-wing politics orientation, police department, 242–243, 246
Rosicrucian cipher, 205
Routine activities theory, 43
Rules, 73
Rule utilitarianism, 230–231, 234, 237

S
Safety
   bomb threat procedures, 406
   crime scene investigations, 459, 469
   gratuities, 238
   HazMat incidents, 408
   internet, 394–396
   jailers' responsibilities, 151, 163
   media, 392
   promote, 4
   risk, 3
Salvation Army form, 153
Searches, 484
   authority to allow, 4, 10
   border, 21–22
   crime scene search patterns, 460–468
   curtilage, 4
   grassy areas, 473
   indoors, 474
   outdoors, 473–474
   probable cause, 3
   suspects, 475
   vehicle, 77, 475
      abandoned, 473
   warrantless, 2
Search warrants, 484
   affidavit, 182–183
   DUI investigation, 182–185
   order, 184
Sebald code, 213
Secretary interrogation technique, 343–344
Secret codes, 202
Seizure, 14–16, 23, 484
   probable cause, 3

   reasonable suspicion, 2
Seizure symptoms, 362
Self-control theory, 44
Semaphore cipher, 212
Service animals, 366, 484
Service club interrogation technique, 350
Sets, 33
72-hour medical detention, 367–368, 484
   application form, 153, 368
Sex abuse
   child, 398, 400
Sex offenders
   Megan's Law, 42
   registries, 398
Shoulder movements/posture, and truth assessment, 328
Showups, 292, 485
   reports, 153, 293
Signal codes, 188
Signal flags, international code of, 215
Sign language interpreters, 359, 365
Simulated forgery, 374
Sitting position, and truth assessment, 329
Situational crime prevention, 46
Situational ethics, 232, 236, 237
Sobriety tests, 73, 166–174, 178
Social bond theory, 44, 223
Social conflict theory, 45
Social constructionist orientation, police department, 244, 246
Social control theory, 44
Social learning theory, 44
Society interrogation technique, 350
Sociobiology theory, 43
Someone always talks interrogation technique, 349
Space code, 214
Spacing, graphology, 385
Special needs interrogation technique, 351
Speeches, 485
   impromptu, 452–455
   oral presentations, 443–451
Spiral search pattern, 461, 462, 464, 468
Split-pair bluff interrogation technique, 345
Sport codes, 200–201
State law book, 47–48
   elements of the crime, 153
State vs. federal jurisdiction, 2
Stationhouse detention, 20–21
Statistics
   descriptive, *see* Descriptive statistics
   evidence, 443, 444, 445, 485
   inferential, *see* Inferential statistics
Stop and frisk, 3, 16–20, 485
   airport, 21
   flowchart, 76
Strain theory, 44
Strip search pattern, 461, 463, 466
Subconscious, 306, 485; *see also* Body language
Subsets, 33–34, 485
Sudden infant death syndrome (SIDS), 401

Suggestibility interrogation technique, 340
Suspect report, 298–300, 485
Suspects, 285
   field interview position, 287
   interviews, 332
   moods, 322–323
   profiles, 334
   search, 475
   voluntary statement forms, 287
Suspicion, 8
   reasonable, 2, 8, 484
Sympathetic nervous system, 325, 485
System orientation, police department, 241–242, 246

T
t-bar crossings, graphology, 386
Technical rationality, 224, 226
Technique for interrogating juveniles, 352
Technology 396–398
Teleological ethical system, 230, 233
Temporary hold form, 153
10 codes, 188
Terrorism, 394
   bombs, 405
   cyberterrorism, 396
Terry v. Ohio (1968), 16–17
Testimony evidence, 443, 444, 445, 446, 485
Testimony speech outline, 450–451
Theme analysis, 422–424, 485
Theories, 485
   criminal, 39, 42–46
Third-person reports, 47
Thought-disordered hostage-takers, 404
Throwing a bone by suspect, 323
Totality of circumstances, 5, 66, 485
   handwriting analysis, 377
   police officer performance review, 66–69
Tourette's syndrome, people with, 366
Traced forgery, 374
Traffic, *see* Vehicles
Traumatic brain injury, people with, 366
Trespassing, state vs. federal jurisdiction, 2
Triangulation, 421
Trichotomous variables, 35–38
Truth, 222, 485
   body language, 321–329
   interrogations, 332
   lenses of, 222–226, 483
   scientific assessment, 371
   graphology, 378, 385
   suspect's pointing out of, 324
Truth tables, 85–106, 485
   Boolean algebra laws and theorems, 124–129
   conditional statement, 31–33
   and logic circuits, 139, 141–143, 144–145
   and Venn diagrams, 106, 111, 116–118
Type I and Type II errors, 40

U
Unconscious, 306, 485; *see also* Body language
Universal quantifier, 34–35, 485
Unprovoked flight, 3, 18
U.S. Constitutional law, 1–25, 485
U.S. Customs and Border Protection, 47
U.S. visa, 33
Utilitarianism 230, 233, 236

V
Validity, 38, 485
   confessions, 335
   interrogation questions, 333
Vehicles
   arrest of passengers, 24
   impound form, 153
   searches, 475
   abandoned vehicles, 473
   flowchart, 77
   stop, 3, 18, 412
   border, 22
   dog sniffs, 4
   searches, 475
Venn diagrams, 106–118, 485
   and truth tables, 106, 111, 116–118
Verbal abstract techniques, 311–319
Verbal communications, 305, 485; *see also* Communication
Verbal persuasion, 52–53
   speech outline, 448–449
Victim precipitation theory, 45
Victims, 285
   children, 399
   sex abuse, 398
   interviews, 332
Visa, U.S., 33
Visual impairment, people with, 359, 365
Visual spatial learners, 62, 63
Voice inflection, 305, 418–419, 485
Voice stress analysis (VSA), 372–373, 485
Voluntary statements, 3, 152, 287–289, 485
Volunteered statements, 3, 485

W
Warrantless searches, 2
Warrants; *see also* Search warrants
   probable cause, 3
What would you do? interrogation technique, 348–349
Wheel search pattern, 461, 462, 464
White-collar interrogation technique, 344
Witnesses, 285
   children's courtroom testimony, 401
   voluntary statement forms, 287
Word grille, 216
Words
   content of, 308

interpretation, 309–311
Wrongful convictions, 39–40
   habeas corpus, 374

X
XNOR operation, 129
XOR operation, 129

Y
Yawning, and truth assessment 328
Yes or no interrogation technique, 348

Z
Zig zag key, 210
Zone (quadrant) search pattern, 461, 462, 464, 467